Cursing with God

Cursing
WITH God

The Imprecatory Psalms
and the Ethics of Christian Prayer

Trevor Laurence

BAYLOR UNIVERSITY PRESS

Cover and book design by Kasey McBeath
Cover image: *The Great Day of His Wrath*, c. 18. Martin, John (1789–1854). Credit: Laing Art Gallery, Newcastle-upon-Tyne, UK Tyne & Wear, Archives & Museums/Bridgeman Images.

A version of the material in the section "The Imprecator Petitions from Love" (p. 160) appears in "Violent Prayers of Love: An Ethical (Re)Assessment of the Imprecatory Psalms," in *Violent Biblical Texts: New Approaches*, ed. Trevor Laurence and Helen Paynter (Sheffield: Sheffield Phoenix Press, 2022). A version of the material in the sections "The Enemy Is the Serpent Seed" (p. 135) and "The Imprecator Is the Royal-Priestly Son of God" (p. 171) appears in "Serpent Seed and Son of God: The Enemy and the Imprecator in the Psalms of Vengeance," *Criswell Theological Review* 17, no. 2 (Spring 2020): 93–121.

The Library of Congress has cataloged this book under hardcover ISBN 978-1-4813-1636-1.
Library of Congress Control Number: 2022940709

Paperback format first issued in 2023 under ISBN 978-1-4813-1647-7

To Sylvia

Perhaps this is what we're supposed to do

Contents

Foreword

Trevor Laurence has written *the* book on imprecatory psalms. Others have defended the "mean psalms," but no one has exposed their deep biblical roots so skillfully or thoroughly. Read, learn, mark, and inwardly digest it.

Imprecations echo Yahweh's Edenic promise of a deliverer who will crush the serpent's head (Gen 3:15). Throughout the Psalter, the Psalmists plead with God to do what he's promised. David's enemies are predatory beasts (35:17; 58:6), often serpents. The unjust "gods" of Psalm 58 are children of vipers who attack "sons of Adam." Like Eden's serpent, they're liars. David asks Yahweh to break their teeth, so they can't poison anyone else. At the end of the psalm, David imagines himself as the promised seed of the woman, trampling serpents; his heel shatters their heads and he bathes his feet in their blood. Psalm 83 follows a similar logic. As Laurence puts it, Asaph "begs that God will crush the heads of the crafty serpent nations in the same way he shattered serpent skulls in former days."

Imprecations express fundamental biblical convictions about God and the world. When we pray for justice, we ask God to be what he truly is— Judge of all the earth. Yahweh promised to curse those who curse Abraham (Gen 12:3). When David asks God to deflect curses back onto the cursers, he's asking him to be faithful to the Abrahamic covenant. Imprecations are rooted in Torah's principle of just retribution, the *lex talionis*, "eye for eye, tooth for tooth." The wicked of Psalm 109 open a "deceitful mouth" to speak with a "lying tongue," accusing David; David asks Yahweh to surround them with accusers. David's enemies refuse mercy, so

David asks that they receive no mercy. They persecute the weak, so David asks that they be persecuted. They clothe themselves with curses, so David asks Yahweh to wrap them in dishonor and shame. Psalm 109 is a plea to the Judge to do justice.

Imprecation needs theological defense because these Psalms are commonly dismissed as primitive, vindictive, and hateful. They need defense too because imprecations are pervasive in the Psalter. Take a moment to peruse the first ten psalms and you'll notice that more than half include warnings about God's judgment, prayers for judgment, or promises of judgment (Pss 2:10–12; 3:7–8; 5:8–10; 6:10; 7:6–16; 9:19–20; 10:2, 15). It doesn't stop with Psalm 10. Excising imprecations would leave the Psalter as tattered as Jefferson's edition of the Gospels. Defending the imprecatory psalms is nothing less than defending the Psalter itself.

Defense isn't sufficient. If we approve these psalms, as we should, we should pray and sing them, without embarrassment. This is the pastoral and political fruit of Laurence's brilliant exegesis: By singing of the Seed's victory over the serpent, we participate in that victory. Singing psalms, *we* break predators' teeth, blunt arrows, disable unjust hands, silence lying tongues. These psalms arouse a hunger and thirst for justice, as we take up the cries of orphans, widows, abused immigrants, trafficked children, and the helpless unborn as our own (Ps 94).

Imprecatory psalms plant us in the real world with all its horrors and dangers. They rebuke our craving to retreat into safe, spiritualized, anodyne, Pollyannaish piety. They're a form of church discipline, as we ask Jesus to uproot liars and predators from his field, the church. Through these prayers, we defend the house and kingdom of God, and participate in the Lord's work of establishing justice, vindicating the innocent, rescuing the defenseless. We do good and leave room for the wrath of God, and ask God to take just vengeance. As we sing the "mean" psalms, Satan is trampled under *our* feet (Rom 16:20).

We may not be under threat, but the psalms keep the daily dangers of persecuted brothers and sisters before us and before God. We live in a world where gunmen open fire on Nigerian Catholics during their Pentecost Mass, where Indian pastors are beaten by Hindu mobs, where Chinese Christians languish in prison on trumped-up charges. We need an earthquake, and we should pray for one: "How long, holy and true, will you refrain from judging and avenging their blood? How long before you do some judging to *prove* you are Judge?"

The ultimate answer to the imprecatory psalms is Jesus, the Seed and Last Adam, who succeeds where Adam failed. The ultimate message of the psalms is Jesus' post-Easter message: Fear not. Fear not: There is a God who judges. Fear not: God takes up the cause of the oppressed. Fear not: God casts down the proud and raises the dead.

Peter J. Leithart
July 2022

Abbreviations

(in alpha order by abbreviation)

AB	Anchor Bible
ACNT	Augsburg Commentary on the New Testament
AGJU	Arbeiten zur Geschichte des Antiken Judentums und Des Urchristentums
AJET	*Africa Journal of Evangelical Theology*
ANF	*Ante-Nicene Fathers*
ANTC	Abingdon New Testament Commentaries
AOAT	Alter Orient und Altes Testament
AOTC	Abingdon Old Testament Commentaries
AUSS	*Andrews University Seminary Studies*
AYB	Anchor Yale Bible
BBC	Blackwell Bible Commentaries
BBR	*Bulletin for Biblical Research*
BBRSup	Bulletin for Biblical Research Supplement
BC	Belgic Confession
BCOTWP	Baker Commentary on the Old Testament Wisdom and Psalms
BDAG	Frederick W. Danker, Walter Bauer, William F. Arndt, and F. Wilbur Gingrich, *Greek-English Lexicon of the New Testament and Other Early Christian Literature*, 3rd ed. (Chicago: University of Chicago Press, 2000)

BECNT	Baker Exegetical Commentary on the New Testament
BETL	Bibliotheca Ephemeridum Theologicarum Lovaniensium
BibInt	*Biblical Interpretation*
BIS	Biblical Interpretation Series
BNTC	Black's New Testament Commentaries
BR	*Biblical Research*
BSac	*Bibliotheca Sacra*
BTCB	Brazos Theological Commentary on the Bible
CBQ	*Catholic Biblical Quarterly*
CBR	*Currents in Biblical Research*
Chu	*Churchman*
CJP	*Canadian Journal of Philosophy*
CNTOT	G. K. Beale and D. A. Carson, eds., *Commentary on the New Testament Use of the Old Testament* (Grand Rapids: Baker Academic, 2007)
ConJ	*Concordia Journal*
Cross Curr.	*CrossCurrents*
CSIR	Cambridge Studies in Ideology and Religion
CTJ	*Calvin Theological Journal*
DSE	Joel B. Green, ed., *Dictionary of Scripture and Ethics* (Grand Rapids: Baker Academic, 2011)
DTIB	Kevin J. Vanhoozer, ed., *Dictionary for Theological Interpretation of the Bible* (Grand Rapids: Baker Academic, 2005)
EBC	Expositor's Bible Commentary
EBTC	Evangelical Biblical Theological Commentary
ECC	Eerdmans Critical Commentary
EDT	Walter A. Elwell, ed., *Evangelical Dictionary of Theology*, 2nd ed., Baker Reference Library (Grand Rapids: Baker Academic, 2001)
Eur. Judaism	*European Judaism*
EUSLR	Emory University Studies in Law and Religion
ExpTim	*Expository Times*

FAT	Forschungen zum Alten Testament
FH	*Fides et Historia*
FOTL	The Forms of Old Testament Literature
HALOT	Ludwig Köhler, Walter Baumgartner, and Johann Jakob Stamm, eds., *The Hebrew and Aramaic Lexicon of the Old Testament*, trans. M. E. J. Richardson, 5 vols. (Leiden: Brill, 1994–2000)
HBT	*Horizons in Biblical Theology*
HTR	*Harvard Theological Review*
Hermeneia	Hermeneia: A Critical and Historical Commentary on the Bible
HNTC	Harper's New Testament Commentaries
HTKNT	Herders Theologischer Kommentar zum Neuen Testament
ICC	International Critical Commentary
Int	*Interpretation: A Journal of Bible and Theology*
ITC	International Theological Commentary
IVPNTC	IVP New Testament Commentary
JAAR	*Journal of the American Academy of Religion*
JBL	*Journal of Biblical Literature*
J. Consult. Clin. Psychol.	*Journal of Consulting and Clinical Psychology*
JETS	*Journal of the Evangelical Theological Society*
JHS	*Journal of Hebrew Scriptures*
JLRS	*Journal of Law, Religion and State*
J. Med. Philos.	*Journal of Medicine and Philosophy*
JNSL	*Journal of Northwest Semitic Languages*
JPT	*Journal of Psychology and Theology*
JRE	*Journal of Religious Ethics*
JRT	*Journal of Reformed Theology*
JSCE	*Journal of the Society of Christian Ethics*
JSNT	*Journal for the Study of the New Testament*
JSNTSup	Journal for the Study of the New Testament Supplement

JSOT	*Journal for the Study of the Old Testament*
JSOTSup	Journal for the Study of the Old Testament Supplement
JTI	*Journal of Theological Interpretation*
J. Trauma. Stress	*Journal of Traumatic Stress*
JTS	*Journal of Theological Studies*
KEL	Kregel Exegetical Library
Law & Contemp. Probs.	*Law and Contemporary Problems*
LNTS	Library of New Testament Studies
LTP	*Laval Théologique et Philosophique*
MNTC	Moffatt New Testament Commentary
NA27	Eberhard Nestle, Erwin Nestle, Barbara Aland, Kurt Aland, Johannes Karavidopoulos, Carlo M. Martini, and Bruce M. Metzger, eds. *Novum Testamentum Graece*. 27th ed. Stuttgart: Deutsche Bibelgesellschaft, 1993.
NAC	New American Commentary
NCB	New Century Bible
NCBC	New Cambridge Bible Commentary
NDBT	T. Desmond Alexander, Brian S. Rosner, D. A. Carson, and Graeme Goldsworthy, eds., *New Dictionary of Biblical Theology* (Downers Grove, Ill.: InterVarsity Press, 2000)
NDT	Sinclair B. Ferguson, David F. Wright, and J. I. Packer, eds., *New Dictionary of Theology* (Downers Grove, Ill.: InterVarsity Press, 1988)
Neot	*Neotestamentica*
NGTT	*Nederduitse Gereformeerde Teologiese Tydskrif*
NIB	*New Interpreter's Bible*
NICNT	New International Commentary on the New Testament
NICOT	New International Commentary on the Old Testament
NIGTC	New International Greek Testament Commentary
NIVAC	The NIV Application Commentary
NovT	*Novum Testamentum*

NPNF	*Nicene and Post-Nicene Fathers*
NSBT	New Studies in Biblical Theology
NTC	New Testament Commentary
NTL	New Testament Library
NTM	New Testament Message: A Biblical-Theological Commentary
NTS	*New Testament Studies*
OBO	Orbis Biblicus et Orientalis
OTL	Old Testament Library
OtSt	Oudtestamentische Studiën
PBM	Paternoster Biblical Monographs
Philos Soc Critic	*Philosophy and Social Criticism*
PNTC	Pillar New Testament Commentary
PTR	*Princeton Theological Review*
RBL	*Review of Biblical Literature*
ResQ	*Restoration Quarterly*
RevExp	*Review & Expositor*
RTR	*Reformed Theological Review*
SAN	Studia Aarhusiana Neotestamentica
SBJT	*Southern Baptist Journal of Theology*
SBLDS	Society of Biblical Literature Dissertation Series
SBLSymS	Society of Biblical Literature Symposium Series
SBT	Studies in Biblical Theology
SJT	*Scottish Journal of Theology*
SNTSMS	Society for New Testament Studies Monograph Series
SP	Sacra Pagina
StIKGCh	Studien zur interkulturellen Geschichte des Christentums
TBC	Torch Bible Commentaries
TDNT	Gerhard Kittel and Gerhard Friedrich, eds., *Theological Dictionary of the New Testament*, trans. and ed. Geoffrey W. Bromiley, 10 vols. (Grand Rapids: Eerdmans, 1964–1976)

TDOT	G. Johannes Botterweck, Helmer Ringgren, and Heinz-Josef Fabry, eds., *Theological Dictionary of the Old Testament*, 15 vols. (Grand Rapids: Eerdmans, 1974–2006)
Them	*Themelios*
THOTC	Two Horizons Old Testament Commentary
ThTo	*Theology Today*
TOTC	Tyndale Old Testament Commentaries
TSF Bulletin	*Theological Students Fellowship Bulletin*
TynBul	*Tyndale Bulletin*
VT	*Vetus Testamentum*
VTSupp	Supplements to Vetus Testamentum
WBBC	Wiley Blackwell Biblical Commentaries
WBC	Word Biblical Commentary
WCF	Westminster Confession of Faith
WLC	Westminster Larger Catechism
WSC	Westminster Shorter Catechism
WTJ	*Westminster Theological Journal*
WUNT	Wissenschaftliche Untersuchungen zum Neuen Testament
WW	*Word and World*
ZECNT	Zondervan Exegetical Commentary on the New Testament

Acknowledgments

For six years now I have poured myself into the imprecatory psalms—the questions they raise, the world they unfold, the God they petition, the violence they expose, the pain they express, the witness they bear, the comfort they offer, the hope they exhibit and catalyze. And by God's grace, as I have poured myself into the psalms and into these pages, others have poured themselves into me. Obedience to the scriptural command to pay "honor to whom honor is owed" (Rom 13:7) involves far more than a few sentences of gratitude, but these sentences are a beginning.

To Esther Reed and Louise Lawrence, thank you for guiding me through the process of research, writing, and revision. You have taught me how to be a scholar of virtue—how to seek out answers and listen to others and formulate arguments with circumspection, humility, diligence, and charity. Your investments have made this work better than it could otherwise have been, and they have formed me, too, into a better thinker, interpreter, writer, person than I could otherwise have been.

To my mother and father, thank you for your encouragement, your enthusiasm, your support, and your love. You were the first to model for me what it looks like to take the words of God with the utmost seriousness. I hope this book returns that blessing to you.

To Derek Radney, thank you for many years of friendship, many conversations about the inexhaustible riches of Scripture, many hidden moments where you shepherded me with wisdom and grace. A fair number of the ideas in this book were hypothesized, explored, and sharpened in illuminating dialogue with you. Your presence in my life has been a gift, a blessing to me. First Samuel 18:1 makes the remarkable statement that "the soul of Jonathan was knit to the soul of David, and Jonathan loved him as his own soul." You are a David to me, dear friend.

To the anonymous benefactor who helped financially sustain my family during the research process, you were God's kindness and provision to us. This book is a fruit of your generosity, and I pray the Lord sees fit to use it to prompt prayer and worship and holiness in his temple-kingdom in ways you never imagined.

To Tiernan, Jack, and Alasdair, my precious children, thank you for bearing with your daddy when reading and writing demanded my time and when my preoccupation with this work seeped into our home and distracted me from giving myself to you fully. I love you, little ones, and I look forward to growing up in Jesus together as we pray and sing the psalms God has given us.

And finally, to Sylvia, thank you for your strength, your perseverance, your sacrifice, your consistent exhortations to keep pressing on, your confident belief that there is something in this work worth saying. More than any other, you have borne the weight of this time, stepping with me into an uncertain future, not knowing where we might be swept off to. It was your question that started this long journey, and this long answer is dedicated to you. You have captivated my heart, my sister, my bride—best of wives and best of women.

Introduction

Ethics, Biblical Theology, and the Imprecatory Psalms

> Arise, O Lord, in your anger;
>   lift yourself up against the fury of my enemies;
>   awake for me; you have appointed a judgment. (Ps 7:6)[1]

"Well, what are we supposed to do with that?"

The open Bible lay on my lap as my wife's question settled over us. Just a week earlier, we had begun praying a psalm together each night before bed, allowing the Psalter's poetry of prayer and praise to direct us in communion with God. Now, my wife's face wore the troubled confusion that both of us were experiencing as she awaited a response from a husband who spent his days studying Scripture and shepherding a church. Internal pressure rising and thoughts racing, I performed theological somersaults in my head working out how to neatly resolve the tension between the psalmist's angry prayer for God's fury against his enemies and our obligations as followers of the Christ who commanded and embodied enemy love all the way to the cross. I muttered something neither memorable nor helpful, hoping that, if I talked long enough, I might stumble over some solution.

I didn't. That was the last psalm we read together.

The apparent incongruity of the imprecatory psalms and Christian ethics was, for us, shocking and disconcerting enough to bring our journey

---

[1]   All subsequent Scripture citations are from the ESV unless otherwise noted.

through the Psalter to an abrupt halt. Certainly, the psalmic prayers for vengeance—the so-called "cursing psalms"—are not the only difficult, upsetting, tough-to-justify texts in the Bible, but even at an intuitive level, my wife and I understood that the psalms make certain claims upon us. They pull us in, exert an unmistakable force upon us, demand a response. Historical narratives of brutal injustice, bloodshed, and rape, gut-wrenching as they are to read, may be explained as nonprescriptive descriptions of events. Divine commands of conquest may be theologically situated in a manner that plausibly delegitimizes the same practices today.[2] But the psalms are *sui generis* to the extent that they put words in our mouths, calling for our tacit affirmation and implicating us in their prayers. With their liturgical indicators and first-person pronouns, the psalms reach from the past into the present and invite us to make their petitions our own. Demanding to be taken up and prayed, the psalms implicate us in their affirmations and denials, their loves and longings, and these implicatory imprecatory prayers thus pose distinct challenges for any Christian who dares wander into the Psalter.

Three years after personally "shutting the book" on the imprecatory psalms, the pastoral decision to preach through the Psalter raised the problem of the psalms of judgment afresh: as my fellow elders and I lead this local church in exploring the Psalter, will we even acknowledge these cries for vengeance as a community by reading them aloud? In recent decades, various liturgical traditions have opted to edit and, in many cases, excise from their worship books entirely these most severe biblical prayers.[3]

---

[2] See, e.g., Paul Copan, *Is God a Moral Monster? Making Sense of the Old Testament God* (Grand Rapids: Baker Books, 2011), 158–97; John H. Walton and J. Harvey Walton, *The Lost World of the Israelite Conquest: Covenant, Retribution, and the Fate of the Canaanites* (Downers Grove, Ill.: IVP Academic, 2017); Arie Versluis, *The Command to Exterminate the Canaanites: Deuteronomy 7*, OtSt 71 (Leiden: Brill, 2017).

[3] The Roman Catholic *Liturgy of the Hours* omits Psalms 58; 83; 109 in their entirety and imprecatory verses from numerous additional psalms. See Gabriel Torretta, "Rediscovering the Imprecatory Psalms: A Thomistic Approach," *The Thomist: A Speculative Quarterly Review* 80, no. 1 (2016): 24n6, for a complete list of verses excluded. The *General Instruction on the Liturgy of the Hours*, §131, explains the omissions thus: "Three psalms are omitted from the current Psalter because of their imprecatory character. These are Ps 57 [58], Ps 82 [83] and Ps 108 [109]. For similar reasons verses from several psalms are passed over; these verses are noted at the beginning of the psalm. Such omissions are made because of certain psychological difficulties, even though the

Overt omission of the imprecations, appealing as that prospect may have been for this preacher, would introduce as many theological questions for our evangelical, Reformed community as it would avoid. Are these psalms the word of God? Are they trustworthy in their claims, imitation-worthy in their example of piety? Gladly bound by the Westminster Confession of Faith's declaration that Scripture's authority, "for which it ought to be believed, and obeyed, dependeth not upon the testimony of any man, or church; but wholly upon God (who is truth itself) the author thereof,"[4] I felt a pastoral obligation—and sensed a pastoral opportunity—to publicly embrace this problematic portion of the Psalter in the confidence that even these violent petitions for justice address the believing community as the gracious words of a covenant God.

The decision to open up the imprecatory psalms with the local church only multiplied my questions, each query leading naturally to another. Biblically and theologically, how do the imprecatory psalms fit into the scriptural story of God's works in the world, and how do they bear witness to the Christ who, "beginning with Moses and all the Prophets . . . interpreted to them in all the Scriptures the things concerning himself" (Luke 24:27)? Ethically, may Christians pray the Psalter's vengeance petitions while remaining faithful to their identity as citizens of the kingdom of the crucified Lord? Existentially, what posture—what orientation of heart—would such faithful Christian performance of the imprecations require? Affectively, how might prayerful enactment of the imprecations act upon the petitioner—immersing the pray-er in a theologically charged world, generating internal associations, cultivating new affections in the very practice of prayer? Liturgically, ought the church to include such psalms not only in her preaching but also in her public reading, praying, and singing? And if so, what might an ethically faithful, pastorally sensitive liturgy of imprecation look like for this particular community?

In the spring of 2015, I preached a sermon on Psalm 35, the product of the preacher's six days of prayer, study, and writing in preparation for the ever-approaching Lord's Day. But the questions remained, simmering

---

imprecatory psalms themselves may be found quoted in the New Testament, e.g., Rev 6:10, and in no way are intended to be used as curses." See Daniel Michael Nehrbass, "The Therapeutic and Preaching Value of the Imprecatory Psalms" (PhD diss., Fuller Theological Seminary, 2012), 171–72, for helpful charts detailing the omissions from the *Revised Common Lectionary*, *United Methodist Hymnal*, and *Episcopal Sunday Lectionary*.

4 WCF 1.4.

right under the surface of my consciousness, seeping into my communion with God, growing in intensity, vying for attention. Pressing diligently into those questions over the ensuing years since that first homiletical foray into the imprecatory psalms, I have become convinced that the psalms of wrath are not merely a permissible but indeed a necessary element in the church's communion with God, prayers that carry an irreplaceable capacity to shape the body of Christ for healing, virtue, and witness in a world gone wrong.

Violent Words for a Violent World

Ours is an age of violence. Over the past several years, the presence of ISIS destabilized an entire region, the threat of ISIS fostered deep anxieties everywhere else, and, though this particular iteration may have been weakened,[5] there is always another ISIS—another ideologically driven group zealous to violently recreate the world—on the horizon. Blood-stained, full-color photographs of genocide, civil war, and dislocated refugees are a mainstay of newspaper front pages. Rape is regularly deployed as a weapon of war. Horrific accounts of suicide bombings and mass shootings emerge afresh on a weekly—and more often, daily—basis. Political regimes persecute dissidents, massacre their own citizens, and shuttle ethnic and religious others away for "reeducation." The specter of nuclear conflict casts its long shadow over embattled international relations. Christian ministers are imprisoned by repressive governments, and precious brothers and sisters in the Lord are abducted, shot, beheaded for the testimony of Jesus and for the word of God. Individual and systemic racism terrorize minority communities as emboldened white nationalists march through American streets. The proliferation of public misinformation and outright lies creates epistemic chaos and stretches the social fabric to its breaking point. Women and girls raise their oft-ignored voices against objectification, harassment, and assault to say, "Me too." The innocent blood of unborn children is shed under the euphemistic guise of reproductive health. Places of worship are bombed and burned to the ground. And lest the church believe that all of the world's problems lie outside her borders, the exposure of pastoral abuse, racism, sexual predation, domestic violence, ethnic nationalism, and a ready willingness to conceal ugly truths when victims of the church's bad acts come

---

5   Though see Department of Defense Office of Inspector General, "Lead Inspector General for Operation Inherent Resolve Quarterly Report to the United States Congress | January 1, 2021–March 21, 2021," accessed June 10, 2021, https:// www.dodig.mil/Reports/Lead-Inspector-General-Reports/Article/2594393/lead -inspector-general-for-operation-inherent-resolve-quarterly-report-to-the-u.

forward has revealed Christians' complicity in the injustices of the world. Of course, every age may lay claim to the mantle of being an age of violence. But in this age, new technologies have maximized humanity's destructive potential and multiplied the victims of violence as instantaneous digital communication has generated a context in which violence and its victims are ever before our eyes. Our inability to escape humanity's inhumanity is itself inhumane.

How are the citizens of God's kingdom to pray, to sing, to worship when "the dark places of the land are full of the habitations of violence" (Ps 74:20)? The sanitized liturgies of many modern churches fail to accurately reflect the realities of life in this kind of world. One could hardly gather from a typical Sunday service, particularly of the American evangelical variety, that violence abounds and that image-bearers everywhere, including in the pews, suffer its harms. When the church's preaching and songs and prayers neglect the horrors of oppression and injustice—captured most poignantly and protested most vividly in the imprecatory psalms—the vision of the world constructed inside the sanctuary's walls differs markedly, incommensurably even, from the world that truly exists outside, and her disciples emerge ill-equipped for the challenges of faithful witness in a violent context.

Catechized by liturgies of glory, triumph, positivity, and prosperity, too many Christians find themselves bereft of meaningful, biblical language to name the terrors that saturate the world, to proclaim God's commitment to righting violent wrongs, to cry out for God's justice against the slaughter of so many innocents, to channel and express the pain-filled fury of personal victimization. Absent psalmic discipleship in praying for justice, the Father's hurting children are left to wonder if their desires that God would act in accord with his promises to deal rightly with sin are themselves sinful, compounding the agony of experienced violence with the guilt of longing for violence to end. The imprecatory psalms resource the body of Christ to tell the truth about the world and God and to respond in faith and beauty to the tragedy of violent wickedness that corrupts God's good creation. But the community that does not learn together through Scripture's psalmic script how to bring its wounds and the wounds of the world before God, cultivate a rightly ordered anger, and plead in prayer for the justice of divine judgment will be uncertain whether their longings for justice belong in the presence of God at all and will risk inadvertently shaping its members to nurse wounds, vent anger, and pursue justice after the pattern of the world—contributing to, rather than confronting and challenging, the seemingly perpetual cycles of violence.

If the church is to experience a liturgical recovery of the imprecatory psalms and the fruitful formation that results from having our conceptions of and desires for justice discipled and directed by God, we will have to address the ethical questions that have instigated their liturgical elision in the first place and develop a positive vision for their place in the prayerful life of faith. How ought the church to interpret and perform the imprecatory psalms? And how ought the psalms of vengeance act upon her as she enacts them? This book is a humble attempt at a faithful answer.

Starting Points

The possibility of purely objective, presuppositionless interpretation of Scripture is a chimera that has been exposed and rightly dismissed.[6] Theological assumptions inevitably influence the interpreter's hermeneutical approach to the text and convictions regarding what constitutes permissible and responsible readings of Scripture, and this is as evident in ethical treatments of the imprecatory psalms as anywhere else. Rather than leaving the reader to divine my theological commitments, here I explicitly identify the doctrinal presuppositions that color my engagement with the text and shape my hermeneutical posture and principles, presuppositions that may be broadly characterized as Reformed and evangelical.

My approach begins with the *ontological primacy of the Trinity*, by which I mean the reality of the triune God as the self-existing and self-communicating author of all that is, the fundamental source of all being and meaning. The Westminster Confession of Faith 2.2 declares, "God hath all life, glory, goodness, blessedness in and of himself; and is alone in and unto himself all-sufficient. . . . He is the alone fountain of all being, of whom, through whom, and to whom are all things; and hath most sovereign dominion over them, to do by them, for them, or upon them whatsoever himself pleaseth." This sovereign, self-sufficient, aseitous God is Father, Son, and Spirit—one God in three persons.[7] The triune God communicates himself to his creatures by his word inscripturate and his Word incarnate,[8] and he

---

[6]   See, e.g., Rudolf Bultmann, "Is Exegesis without Presuppositions Possible? (1957)," in *New Testament and Mythology and Other Basic Writings*, ed. and trans. Schubert M. Ogden (Philadelphia: Fortress, 1984), 145–52.

[7]   WCF 2.3; BC 8–9.

[8]   WCF 1.1, 8.1; BC 2, 10. Kevin J. Vanhoozer, *Is There a Meaning in This Text? The Bible, the Reader, and the Morality of Literary Knowledge* (Grand Rapids: Zondervan, 1998), 161: "*Christian orthodoxy believes that God is essentially*

created human beings in the *imago Dei* to receive his communication and to live in covenant with him.[9] Confidence in the communicative efficacy and comprehensibility of language is grounded in the interrelated convictions that language is a gift for the sake of covenantal communion,[10] that the God who speaks is able to make himself known, and that human image-bearers have the necessary faculties to receive and respond to the divine address as covenant partners.

As the word of the self-revealing triune God, Scripture is both *inspired and authoritative*. Following the Bible's testimony about itself, not least 2 Tim 3:16, I affirm that the word of God is not only a word about God, but that it is a word from God—*God's* word.[11] I understand this to mean that the Holy Spirit was involved in the composition of Scripture such that, while Scripture was written by human authors whose historical, cultural, and literary particularities must be taken into account, the Bible's ultimate author is God himself, and the words of Scripture are the words of God.[12] As a hermeneutical corollary to this doctrine of inspiration, I consider the biblical text to be both human and divine discourse.[13] Authorial intentions

---

the one who communicates himself to others in trinitarian fashion. A trinitarian theology of the Word of God conceives God as author, as message, and as power of reception: 'In the beginning was the communicative act.'" Emphasis original.

[9] WCF 4.2; BC 14; John Calvin, *Institutes of the Christian Religion*, ed. John T. McNeill, trans. Ford Lewis Battles (Louisville: Westminster John Knox, 1960), 1.15.3–4. Cf. Vanhoozer, *Is There a Meaning in This Text?* 457; Graeme Goldsworthy, *Gospel-Centered Hermeneutics: Foundations and Principles of Evangelical Biblical Interpretation* (Downers Grove, Ill.: InterVarsity Press, 2006), 56; Michael Horton, *The Christian Faith: A Systematic Theology for Pilgrims on the Way* (Grand Rapids: Zondervan, 2011), 379–406.

[10] See Craig G. Bartholomew, *Introducing Biblical Hermeneutics: A Comprehensive Framework for Hearing God in Scripture* (Grand Rapids: Baker Academic, 2015), 327–28; Vanhoozer, *Is There a Meaning in This Text?* 205.

[11] WCF 1.2.

[12] See Herman Bavinck, *Reformed Dogmatics*, ed. John Bolt, trans. John Vriend (Grand Rapids: Baker Academic, 2003), 1:426. Cf. John Webster, *Holy Scripture: A Dogmatic Sketch*, Current Issues in Theology (Cambridge: Cambridge University Press, 2003), 17–39.

[13] Nicholas Wolterstorff's concept of double-agency discourse, wherein a communicative agent may perform an illocution by means of a different communicative agent's locution or illocution, offers a helpful framework for respecting the scriptural text as simultaneously human and divine discourse. See Wolterstorff, "The Promise of Speech-act Theory for Biblical Interpretation," in *After Pentecost: Language and Biblical Interpretation*, ed. Craig Bartholomew, Colin Greene, and Karl Möller. Scripture and Hermeneutics Series 2 (Grand Rapids: Zondervan, 2001), 82–90; *Divine Discourse: Philosophical Reflections*

(whether human or divine) as psychological phenomena are not observable for the interpreter, but developments in speech-act theory provide resources for exploring what authors as communicative agents are *doing* with their words—what illocutions they are performing.[14] By attending carefully to the illocutionary force of the author's words, biblical interpretation becomes a practice in honoring the author as a true other, an actor whose presence is mediated by meaningful speech. Because Scripture is the inspired word of the triune God, it confronts us with all the authority of the covenant Lord and is therefore to be received as the trustworthy and binding address of God.[15] Such a posture toward the text, in addition to necessitating a hermeneutical humility,[16] will consciously limit the possible theological and ethical conclusions available to the biblical interpreter.[17]

---

on the Claim That God Speaks (New York: Cambridge University Press, 1995), 38–54, 183–222. Such a distinction is particularly constructive for interpretation of the psalms, which, as canonical prayers, may be understood as both the words of God's people to God and the words of God to God's people.

[14] Speech-act theory as presented by J. L. Austin and John Searle distinguishes between the locution (what is said), illocution (what is done by what is said), and perlocution (the effect of what is said) of speech acts. On speech-act theory as a resource in biblical interpretation, see, e.g., Vanhoozer, *Is There a Meaning in This Text?* 208–10, 221–32; "From Speech Acts to Scripture Acts: The Covenant of Discourse and the Discourse of Covenant," in Bartholomew, Greene, and Möller, *After Pentecost*, 1–49; Wolterstorff, "Promise of Speech-act Theory," 73–90; *Divine Discourse*, esp. 13; Anthony C. Thiselton, *New Horizons in Hermeneutics: The Theory and Practice of Transforming Biblical Reading* (Grand Rapids: Zondervan, 1992), 283–307; Eckhard J. Schnabel, "Scripture," in *NDBT*, 39–40. Kit Barker, *Imprecation as Divine Discourse: Speech Act Theory, Dual Authorship, and Theological Interpretation* (Winona Lake, Ind.: Eisenbrauns, 2016), foregrounds speech-act theory as a lens for interpreting the imprecatory psalms specifically.

[15] WCF 1.4; cf. Calvin, *Institutes*, 1.7.1; Bavinck, *Reformed Dogmatics*, 1:465. Cf. also Peter Jensen, *The Revelation of God*, Contours of Christian Theology (Downers Grove, Ill.: InterVarsity Press, 2002), 145–78; Meredith G. Kline, *The Structure of Biblical Authority*, 2nd ed. (Eugene, Ore.: Wipf & Stock, 1997), 21–110.

[16] WLC Q. 157 commends reading the Scriptures "with a firm persuasion that they are the very Word of God, and that he only can enable us to understand them," and "with meditation, application, self-denial, and prayer." See Vanhoozer, *Is There a Meaning in This Text?* 377, 463–66, who describes a hermeneutics of humility and conviction—cognizant of epistemological fallibility, yet confident in the possibility of adequate knowledge—and argues that the gospel itself is the premier catalyst of interpretive humility. Faith in the gospel thus bears the fruit of hermeneutic humility necessary for responsible interpretation.

[17] E.g., readings that attempt to explain a text in purely immanent historical or anthropological terms as well as readings that quickly evaluate a text's

As a consequence of the divine authorship of Scripture, the Bible exhibits *unity amid diversity*. Due attention must be given to the "discrete witness of the testaments"[18] and to the various theological emphases and generic conventions of the biblical literature, but reception of Scripture as the word of God will also involve attending to the unity of the testaments. I understand the Old and New Testaments to be unified in that they tell the story of God's redemptive activity in his world, which centers on the person and work of Jesus Christ.[19] In agreement with Jesus' own testimony in, for example, Luke 24:27, 44, Scripture is therefore *Christocentric*: every biblical text contributes to the overarching narrative of God's redeeming work in Christ and subsequently must be interpreted in light of the Christ event, which serves as the climax of the narrative of which the text is a part.[20] My adoption of a narratival, biblical-theological approach in my engagement with Scripture

---

theological message as erroneous—while of a certain limited utility—will not be wholly accepted by the interpreter who affirms the inspiration and authority of Scripture. When interpretive issues arise, as they do with the imprecatory psalms, the reader who receives the words of Scripture as the words of God will neither blithely paper over difficulties nor reactively assume that apparent inconsistencies constitute evidence of intractable contradictions but will rather permit such issues to stimulate further critical reflection on both the scriptural text and her interpretive presuppositions.

[18]   Bartholomew, *Biblical Hermeneutics*, 9–12, quote 9. Cf. Calvin, *Institutes*, 2.11.

[19]   This approach to Scripture as the unified narrative of redemptive history has significant roots in the Reformed tradition. Cf. WCF 7; Calvin, *Institutes*, 2.10; Jonathan Edwards, *A History of the Work of Redemption*, in *The Works of Jonathan Edwards* (Peabody, Mass.: Hendrickson, 2007), 1:532–619. J. I. Packer, foreword to *Biblical Theology: The History of Theology from Adam to Christ*, by John Owen (Morgan, Pa.: Soli Deo Gloria Publications, 1994), xi, points to Geerhardus Vos (1862–1949) as a landmark figure in the development of Reformed redemptive-historical biblical theology but maintains that Owen "produced a treatise on the progress of theology in this world, and the proper way for Christians to study it, which covers in a pioneering way and from a consistently believing standpoint the whole field of Biblical Theology as Vos later came to define it." Packer, *Biblical Theology*, xii. Cf. also Craig G. Bartholomew and Michael W. Goheen, *The Drama of Scripture: Finding Our Place in the Biblical Story*, 2nd ed. (Grand Rapids: Baker Academic, 2014), 20; Richard B. Hays, "Can Narrative Criticism Recover the Theological Unity of Scripture?" *JTI* 2, no. 2 (2008): 201–2.

[20]   "As de Lubac declares, Christ is 'Master both of the first Testament and of the second. He made them both for one another. He separates them, and he also unites them in himself.' . . . Christ is both the exegesis of Scripture and its exegete. He explains it to us by his Spirit, and in explaining it he is himself

is consonant with my assumptions about its unified, Christocentric character and will permit me to interpret the imprecatory psalms in relation to the
larger, story-shaped witness of Scripture.

I assume that the *canon* of Scripture comprises the sixty-six books that
are affirmed by the Westminster Confession of Faith 1.2 and that appear
in most Protestant Bibles.[21] My biblical-theological consideration of the
redemptive-historical narrative of Scripture will thus focus on the unfolding canonical story, though extracanonical sources will be consulted
where appropriate to aid in illuminating this canonical narrative.[22]

The Story and the Psalms

An imprecatory psalm is any psalm that contains an imprecation, a speech
act that calls for, demands, requests, or expresses a wish for divine judgment and vengeance to befall an enemy, whether an individual or corporate entity. In some psalms, the imprecatory element is foregrounded as
a distinguishing characteristic of the psalm, including Psalms 7; 10; 12;
35; 58; 59; 69; 70; 74; 79; 83; 94; 109; 129; 137; 140.[23] In other psalms, the
invocation of divine judgment upon enemies is a more secondary, periph-
eral concern, sometimes occupying only a single verse.[24] Throughout, I

---

explained." Bartholomew, *Biblical Hermeneutics*, 54, quoting H. de Lubac, *Scripture in the Tradition*, trans. L. O'Neill (New York: Crossroad, 2000), 103.

[21]   Cf. BC 4 and the helpful treatment of Roger T. Beckwith, "The Canon of
Scripture," in *NDBT*, 27–34.

[22]   Cf. Edward W. Klink III and Darian R. Lockett, *Understanding Biblical Theology: A Comparison of Theory and Practice* (Grand Rapids: Zondervan,
2012), 64.

[23]   Nancy L. deClaissé-Walford, "The Theology of the Imprecatory Psalms,"
in *Soundings in the Theology of the Psalms: Perspectives and Methods in Contemporary Scholarship*, ed. Rolf A. Jacobson (Minneapolis: Fortress, 2011), 77,
refers to Psalms 12; 58; 69; 83; 94; 109; 129; 137 as imprecatory psalms. Johannes
G. Vos, "The Ethical Problem of the Imprecatory Psalms," *WTJ* 4 (1942): 123,
includes Psalms 55; 59; 69; 79; 109; 137. John N. Day, "The Imprecatory Psalms
and Christian Ethics" (PhD diss., Dallas Theological Seminary, 2001), 14, gives
the designation to fourteen psalms: 7; 35; 55; 58; 59; 69; 79; 83; 94; 109; 129;
137; 139; 140. Even this brief survey indicates the variation among scholarly
attempts to identify which psalms may be classified as imprecatory.

[24]   The following is a list (with standard English versification) of every imprecation in the Psalter: 3:7; 5:10; 7:6, 9; 9:19–20; 10:2, 12, 15; 11:6; 12:3–4; 17:13–14;
28:4; 31:17–18; 35:1–6, 8, 19, 23–26; 40:14–15; 41:10; 54:5; 55:9, 15; 56:7; 58:6–9;
59:5, 11–13; 68:30; 69:22–25, 27–28; 70:2–3; 71:13; 72:4, 9; 74:11, 22–23; 79:6, 10, 12;
80:16; 82:8; 83:9–18; 86:7; 94:1–2; 104:35; 109:6–15, 19–20, 29; 119:78; 125:5; 129:5–
8; 137:7–9; 139:19; 140:8–11; 141:10; 143:12; 144:6. Cf. Roy Ben Zuck, "The Problem

refer to both classes of psalm as imprecatory psalms, though additional form-critical designations may also accurately describe many psalms containing imprecations.[25]

This study of these imprecatory psalms is an exercise in what I am calling redemptive-historical ethics. I bring together the resources of redemptive-historical biblical theology and narrative ethics to investigate the relationship of the imprecatory psalms to Scripture's Christocentric narrative of the world and to discern the shape of ethically faithful Christian performance of the imprecatory psalms within the morally determinative narrative that Scripture unfolds. Though several different, and at points competing, approaches toward biblical theology are currently operative in theological scholarship,[26] I practice biblical theology as the discipline that characteristically focuses on the interrelatedness and unity of the Christian Scriptures, describing the development of biblical themes, situating individual texts, and synthesizing scriptural teachings in light of the canon's Christocentric narrative of redemptive history, utilizing the conceptual categories that arise from the biblical text itself.[27] By *redemptive history*, I mean the unfolding, historical sequence of events in God's revealing, restoring, reconciling, and

---

of the Imprecatory Psalms" (ThM thesis, Dallas Theological Seminary, 1957), 10–18. In addition to these, simple imperfects expressing confidence in future judgment on enemies exhibit an implicit imprecatory quality, and perfect statements of God's past judgments celebrate the reality and precedent of divine vengeance in a manner that shares features with imprecatory petition. Such instances, however, are not explicit requests and thus do not fall within the scope of this study.

[25]   Many imprecatory psalms are typically categorized as individual laments (e.g., 35; 109) or communal laments (e.g., 83; 137). Psalms 68; 104; 139 are hymns. Psalm 144 is a royal psalm. Psalm 119 has characteristics of wisdom, hymnic, and lament psalms. The various form-critical designations are clearly not mutually exclusive, and an imprecatory element may appear in a wide range of psalmic genres.

[26]   For a helpful survey of several prominent approaches to biblical theology, cf. Klink and Lockett, *Understanding Biblical Theology*. They organize the field of biblical theology into five types: biblical theology as historical description, history of redemption, worldview story, canonical approach, and theological construction. This fivefold division should be considered a heuristic device for coming to terms with the major characteristics of what in reality are the carefully nuanced, frequently overlapping, and often idiosyncratic positions of individual scholars.

[27]   Cf. Brian Rosner, "Biblical Theology," in *NDBT*, 10; Bartholomew, *Biblical Hermeneutics*, 52; Graeme Goldsworthy, *Christ-Centered Biblical Theology: Hermeneutical Foundations and Principles* (Downers Grove, Ill.: InterVarsity Press, 2012), 80.

redeeming work in his creation as narrated and theologically interpreted by the Christian Scriptures.[28] The very concept of redemptive history presupposes that God is, that he acts within human history, and that he has faithfully recorded and interpreted these acts in the Bible. A redemptive-historical biblical-theological perspective utilizes redemptive history as the organizing principle that organically emerges from within the canon, consequently reading both narrative and non-narrative portions of Scripture in terms of how they relate to the biblical superstructure of God's progressive, redeeming acts—how they emerge from, contribute to, and are developed by the unfolding narrative of Scripture.[29]

Valuable in developing a biblical-theological reading of any text is interpretive sensitivity to the phenomenon of intertextuality. I utilize this term to describe the process by which a scriptural text refers to a prior text, importing the structures, figures, and/or themes of the referred text onto the interpretive horizon of the referring text in a manner that enriches the communicative potency of the referring text.[30] Such intra-canonical reference may take the form of quotations or citations that explicitly reproduce the language of a prior text, as well as allusions or echoes that more subtly and with varying degrees of verbal correspondence and probability refer to the linguistic or conceptual contours of a prior text.[31] Intertextual echo is a regular feature of both

---

[28]   Tracing its broadest contours, redemptive history moves from creation and the fall of humanity into sin through God's dealings with Israel to the climactic incarnation, crucifixion, and resurrection of Jesus Christ, before reaching its consummation in the new creation of God's realized eschatological kingdom.

[29]   See D. A. Carson, "Systematic Theology and Biblical Theology," in *NDBT*, 89–104, for an exploration of the relationship between biblical theology, exegesis, historical theology, and systematic theology.

[30]   On the variety of textual phenomena to which the term "intertextuality" may refer in scholarly discourse on the Bible, see Steve Moyise, "Intertextuality and the Study of the Old Testament in the New Testament," in *The Old Testament in the New Testament: Essays in Honor of J. L. North*, ed. Steve Moyise, JSNTSup 189 (Sheffield: Sheffield Academic Press, 2000), 14–41. I use the term in a manner similar to Richard B. Hays, *Echoes of Scripture in the Letters of Paul* (New Haven: Yale University Press, 1989), 15, who is concerned with intertextuality "in a more limited sense, focusing on [Paul's] actual citations of and allusions to specific texts." Cf. G. K. Beale, *Handbook on the New Testament Use of the Old Testament: Exegesis and Interpretation* (Grand Rapids: Baker Academic, 2012), 40; Bartholomew, *Biblical Hermeneutics*, 121–26.

[31]   Margaret Daly-Denton, *David in the Fourth Gospel: The Johannine Reception of the Psalms*, AGJU 47 (Leiden: Brill, 2000), 9, explains, "These three

the Old and New Testaments, permitting the biblical authors to evoke an entire matrix of thematic and theological associations with a phrase, image, or even a peculiarly resonant word. Earlier scriptural texts supply the primary grammar that later scriptural authors employ to communicate the ways and works of God, and awareness of the intertextual richness of the biblical text enables the interpreter to recognize how the text itself establishes potentially salient connections with other eras, episodes, events, and entities in the redemptive-historical narrative such that biblical-theological conclusions emerge organically from the intertextual relationships signaled by the author. Though the presence of a given allusion or echo is by its very nature less certain than a quotation, several criteria may aid in the identification of these types of intertextual reference, including the availability of the alluded text, the volume of linguistic similarity, the recurrence of references to the same alluded text, the thematic coherence of the alluded and alluding texts, the historical plausibility of the reference, the recognition of the reference by others in the history of interpretation, and the satisfaction of the resultant reading.[32]

Biblical theology so defined serves as a fitting partner for ethical inquiry into the psalms and the church's performance of them. The Bible presents a diverse yet unified narrative of God's kingdom-restoring work in his world, which finds its ultimate meaning and fulfillment in the person and work of Jesus Christ, a story that supplies the narrative basis and teleological structure necessary for ethical reflection in God's reality. At the risk of oversimplification, we might say that biblical theology asks, *What is God's story of*

---

modes of reference to an existing text—quotation, allusion and echo—function on a 'sliding scale' of diminishing intentionality on the part of the author and decreasing visibility on the surface of the text, requiring a correspondingly increasing competence on the part of the reader. Authors quote intentionally, their allusions may plausibly be presumed to be intentional, but they can echo an earlier work quite inadvertently." Beale, *Handbook*, 32n11, likewise affirms that echoes may involve "an author's unconscious reference to the OT, though such references are more subtle and more difficult to validate." Cf. Steve Moyise, "Quotations," in *As It Is Written: Studying Paul's Use of Scripture*, SBLSymS 50, ed. Stanley E. Porter and Christopher D. Stanley (Atlanta: SBL Press, 2008), 15–28; Stanley E. Porter, "Allusions and Echoes," in Porter and Stanley, *As It Is Written*, 29–40; Richard B. Hays, *Echoes of Scripture in the Gospels* (Waco, Tex.: Baylor University Press, 2016), 10.

[32] See Hays, *Echoes of Scripture in the Letters of Paul*, 21–33; cf. Beale, *Handbook*, 31–35.

reality? while ethics considers, *How ought we to live faithfully in this story?*[33] A biblical-theological perspective is thus able to situate both the imprecatory psalms and the church in God's unfolding narrative of redemptive history, a narrative that determines whether and how the church may ethically appropriate the prayers of vengeance as her own.

The fundamental thesis of this work is that prayerful performance of the imprecatory psalms is an ethically permissible—even obligatory—means by which the Christian church faithfully enacts her God-given calling as a royal priesthood in the world. More specifically, I aim to articulate a vision of ethically faithful Christian enactment of the judgment psalms that is both redemptive-historically informed and Christologically nuanced. In turn I explore how performance of the imprecatory psalms that is sensitive to their polyvalent Christological witness has the capacity to generate the very affections of faith, hope, and love that are necessary for ethical imprecatory prayer and integral to the life of Christian virtue. What follows is a roadmap of sorts—charting a course through the ensuing chapters, surveying the terrain through which I will journey as I work toward developing an ethical proposal for Christian imprecation that coheres with the church's place and part in God's story of reality.

Chapter 1 ("From Israelite Psalms to Christian Prayer: Paths Old and New") begins with a detailed survey of four influential proposals for Christian appropriation of the imprecatory psalms, focusing on post–World War II scholarship that continues to figure prominently in shaping contemporary ecclesial attitudes toward the imprecations. This examination of the major views on offer describes each approach to the imprecations and their performance by Christians, identifies the determinative theological issues that shape interaction with the psalms of vengeance, and poses questions to each proposal in an attempt to expose weaknesses, tensions, and lacunae in the available research that require further examination. With this analysis of the current landscape in view, I turn toward outlining the method of the present study, a method I believe is more capable of satisfactorily addressing the ethics of Christian performance of the imprecatory psalms. I articulate the contours of and rationale for my exercise in redemptive-historical ethics, reflecting on the ineluctably narrative character of ethical deliberation, demonstrating the conceptual compatibility

---

[33]   Alasdair MacIntyre, *After Virtue: A Study in Moral Theory*, 3rd ed. (Notre Dame: University of Notre Dame Press, 2007), 216; Stanley Hauerwas, *The Peaceable Kingdom: A Primer in Christian Ethics* (Notre Dame: University of Notre Dame Press, 1983), 24.

of redemptive-historical biblical theology with narrative-oriented ethical inquiry, and examining the capacity of redemptive-historical approaches to Scripture to supply a substantive narrative framework for Christian ethical investigation.

Chapter 2 ("Cursing in the Psalms: The Imprecatory Psalms in Redemptive-Historical Perspective") begins in earnest the constructive work described in chapter 1 with a sustained examination of the imprecatory psalms themselves. Here, I inquire, "What kind of world do these psalms assume, project, operate within?" I map the theological architecture of the narrative universe of the imprecatory psalms—the world of the text, the storied vision of reality constructed by the prayers of vengeance—by examining the three principal actors within the psalms: the enemy against whom imprecation is offered, the petitioner who submits imprecatory prayers, and the divine judge who receives the petitioner's imprecations. I investigate the identities, characteristics, and futures of these figures, attending in particular to the ways that the imprecatory psalms frame these actors by means of intertextual reference to other Old Testament texts and their record of prior events in redemptive history. The result is a redemptive-historical reading that situates the imprecatory psalms within the scriptural narrative to which they allude, a narrative that renders the imprecations' pleas and expectations ethically intelligible.

The New Testament continues the Old Testament's story of God's advancing purposes in the world by narrating and reflecting upon God's action in Jesus in a manner that intertextually draws upon the text, players, and themes of the imprecatory psalms. Chapter 3 ("Cursing and Christ: The Imprecatory Psalms and the New Testament") explores these diverse ways that the New Testament authors invoke and transform features of the judgment psalms to tell their story about God, his Son, his people, his enemies, and his holy dwelling place. The New Testament authors refer to the judgment psalms with a perhaps surprising frequency, evoking and developing the various figures and structures of the imprecatory psalms to theologically characterize the players in the Christian-era act of redemptive history and to articulate the story of God's work in Christ as the extension and culmination of the narrative universe of the imprecatory psalms. With this chapter, I interrogate a wide collection of underexamined echoes of the imprecations, considering how the New Testament's intertextual appeals to the psalmic imprecator, enemy, and divine judge function to depict a variety of characters—not least Jesus himself—with reference to the inhabitants of the imprecations' storied world and the roles they play therein. Beyond appealing to and thematically developing the narrative world of the imprecatory psalms, the New Testament also engages in its own imprecatory speech acts, and attention to the presence and discernment of the logic of these petitions for divine judgment is necessary for any examination of the ethical propriety of Christian imprecation. The chapter thus concludes with a theological and ethical reading of Luke 18:1–8; Gal 1:8–9; 5:12; 1 Cor 16:22; Rev 6:10. When the redemptive-historical narrative lens generated by the New Testament's interaction with the imprecations is utilized as an interpretive lens, the New Testament's imprecatory speech acts come into focus as morally comprehensible prayers within God's ethically determinative narrative of the world.

The scriptural narrative of history purports to be the narrative within which the Christian church lives and acts, and ethical Christian performance of the imprecatory psalms must therefore align with the *telos* of God's story and the church's vocation and location within it. Chapter 4 ("Cursing in Christ: Ethically Faithful Christian Performance of the Imprecatory Psalms") articulates a proposal for ethical ecclesial imprecation that accounts for the New Testament's intertextual deployment of the imprecatory psalms and that coheres with the church's time and calling in the continuing narrative of God's redemptive work in the world. Situating ethical reflection within the redemptive-historical story developed across the preceding chapters, I identify the appropriate agents, objects, and content of Christian performance of the imprecatory psalms and articulate how such prayer might be an exercise of love—including love for the enemy—that fulfills the New Testament's moral commands. This chapter closes with an exploration of the affective dynamics of Christian performance of the Christologically polyvalent imprecatory psalms—what happens at the level of the affections to a petitioner when one prays the psalms of vengeance in a manner that follows their Christological witness to the foot of the cross and the horizon of the age to come. As the church prays the vengeance psalms in union with the Christ to whom they point, the dynamic rehearsal of God's psalm-fulfilling works in Jesus has the capacity to generate the virtues of faith, hope, and love. In such Christically rich performance of the imprecatory psalms, the church enacts the prayers as the prayers simultaneously act upon the church, cultivating the very affections required for ethical ecclesial imprecation and for faithful witness more broadly in the world as the people of God. The story that ethically governs the church's practice of imprecation is the same story into which the church is immersed through the practice of imprecation. Christians' cries for God's justice may thus serve as a powerful resource for forming disciples to both pray and live virtuously in a world where "the wicked prowl, as vileness is exalted among the children of man" (Ps 12:8).

After a brief conclusion, an appendix offers a sample liturgy of imprecation that illustrates how churches might corporately practice the imprecatory psalms in a manner consistent with the proposal for ethical Christian performance advanced in this book.

The Prayers of the People

This study has the potential to contribute to several ongoing scholarly discussions. The proposed redemptive-historical reading of the imprecatory psalms aims to further illuminate how the psalms of vengeance cohere with the unfolding narrative of Scripture, devoting unprecedented attention to the intracanonical, intertextual appeals by which the imprecations construct a storied world within which their pleas for divine judgment make moral sense. The ensuing consideration of the New Testament's intertextual reference to and thematic development of the imprecatory psalms has the capacity to clarify not only how the judgment psalms bear polyvalent witness to the polyvalent Christ but also how the church fits into the redemptive-historical narrative within which the imprecations arise and from which they derive their theological and ethical rationale.

Because ethical reflection on the church's performance of the imprecatory psalms de facto involves (at least implicitly) a form of synthetic, biblical-theological reasoning,[34] any developments in a biblical-theological understanding of the redemptive-historical relationship between the church and the psalmic imprecations will introduce morally relevant considerations that promise to enrich ethical accounts of Christian imprecatory prayer. Indeed, the ethical examination that emerges from this sustained biblical-theological exploration exhibits a theological coherence and ethical specificity that has heretofore been lacking in treatments of the imprecations, which have given less attention to the morally determinative narrative that frames both the imprecatory psalms and the church's performance of them. More generally, a method that integrates

---

[34] E.g., ethical deliberation on Christian performance of the imprecatory psalms, by the very nature of the question, will proceed from some understanding of the relationship between the Old and New Testaments and, more specifically, between Jesus' moral teachings and the ethic exhibited in the imprecatory psalms. See chap. 1 for a detailed consideration of this point.

biblical-theological reflection on the story of Scripture with ethical reflection on faithful Christian conduct within Scripture's story of reality charts a fruitful path forward for ethical investigation of theologically and morally problematic biblical texts. In addition, the specific redemptive-historical structures foregrounded in this study may prove generative for further biblical-theological research into the narrative unity of Scripture and the intelligibility of judgment and divinely sanctioned violence in the storied world that Scripture unfolds.

Additionally, by including a focus on the affective dynamics of Christically sensitive Christian performance of the imprecatory psalms, this work contributes (to considerations of the psalms' ethical Christian enactment) an exploration of their potential to act in ethically salient ways upon the Christian petitioner. That is, this project takes up not only how the church ought to pray the imprecations but also how these Christologically rich psalms might subjectively immerse the imprecating church in God's narrative in a manner that stimulates the affective conditions of ethical prayer. While advocates of what I refer to as relinquishment readings of the imprecatory psalms have attended to some of the existential dynamics of imprecatory enactment, helpfully positing that the vengeance psalms may serve as a prayerful means of handing over vengeance to God, the treatment offered herein explores the affective kinetics of Christian imprecation in a manner that presses beyond the relinquishment of vengeance and into the capacity of imprecatory performance to cultivate the faith, hope, and love that are foundational not only to ethical prayer but to the entire moral life.

If this study only contributes to scholarly research and discussions within the academic guild, however, it will have fallen short of this author's intentions. Should the conclusions proffered prove credible and persuasive, this research has the potential to spark a recovery of the imprecatory psalms in the liturgical worship of the Christian church and the private piety of individual Christians. In so doing, this work equips Christ's *ekklesia* with the prayerful resources to voice the agony of violence, commune with God in Christ, exercise her divinely commissioned vocation, and experience the immersive and ethically formative re-narration of reality in the midst of even the most profound forms of suffering.

In that regard, this book is submitted as a small gift to the church, an offering for her life of faithfulness to her Lord in a violent world where life is often painful, and faithfulness is never easy.

1

From Israelite Psalms to Christian Prayer

Paths Old and New

They say, "A deadly thing is poured out on him;
    he will not rise again from where he lies."
Even my close friend in whom I trusted,
    who ate my bread, has lifted his heel against me.
But you, O Lord, be gracious to me,
    and raise me up, that I may repay them!
By this I know that you delight in me:
    my enemy will not shout in triumph over me. (Ps 41:8–11)

Raise me up, that I may repay them. The existence of such a prayer in the pages of sacred Scripture is, for many Bible readers, an affront to their most basic theological commitments, ethical sensibilities, and expectations for what ought to be included in the word of God. We may at some level find conceivable how the depths of physical, emotional, relational, psychological, and spiritual distress expressed in Psalm 41 could elicit this sort of apparently violent response, but that it should be inscribed in the Psalter—extending to us an implicit invitation to *mimesis* through inclusion in the Bible's songbook—is far less immediately comprehensible. The Davidic psalmist does not merely petition in the abstract for God to intervene with justice against oppressors; he specifically requests that God manifest his grace by raising up the psalmist for the purpose that the psalmist might act as the mediator of God's just recompense upon the petitioner's foes. What is more, the psalmist assumes the acceptability of his prayer and confidently declares that the Lord will indeed grant what he has asked: victory over his assailants. Beyond generic queries concerning the licitness of pleas for judgment, Psalm 41 confronts us with a host of other questions. Is the psalmist's prayer to repay his enemies a spontaneous outburst of vindictiveness, or does this expectation of human agency in the exercise of divine justice have roots in the wider theology of the Old Testament? Are the psalmists' theological convictions and explicit assertions about God determinative for Christian readers as we navigate the Psalter, or is it possible that their theological vision and concomitant ethical claims are skewed, incomplete, or even offensive to God? Should Christ's own Christological reading of v. 9 in John 13:18 influence our ethical evaluation of the subsequent petition in v. 10? Could Jesus' claim that the imprecator's experience will somehow be fulfilled in the unfolding events of his impending passion open new possibilities for the church's reading and performance of this and other imprecatory psalms? Is the psalmist morally right to pray this way? And can Christians under the new covenant follow after his example?

With such substantive and involved questions evoked by just a few verses of one imprecatory psalm, it is no wonder that strategies for interpreting and practicing the imprecations have been both abundant and diverse. The task of ethically employing Israelite psalms as Christian prayers is one fraught with difficulty, and before attempting an answer ourselves, we will be well-served to understand and appreciate those already-ventured answers that have gained a measure of scholarly acceptance. In so doing, we not only will be able to apprehend the characteristic concerns and moves of each proposal but will have an opportunity to interrogate the reasoning and claims of existing treatments of the imprecations in a manner that isolates and illuminates the weaknesses, tensions, and lacunae that require further examination and merit reappraisal if we are to arrive at a more suitable and coherent position. Along the way, we may also begin to locate the controlling theological and hermeneutical loci—the tectonic issues—that undergird and shape how psalmic interpreters engage the psalmic prayers for judgment, identifying the foundational concepts that inform the interpretive decisions readers make and the conclusions at which they arrive.

Devilish and Diabolical:
The Imprecatory Psalms as Aberrant Human Sentiment

C. S. Lewis begins his exploration of the psalms with a disclaimer: "This is not a work of scholarship. I am no Hebraist, no higher critic, no ancient historian, no archaeologist. I write for the unlearned about things in which

I am unlearned myself."[1] Lewis' *Reflections on the Psalms* is neither biblical commentary nor carefully defended theological argument. Rather, Lewis offers in his work the ruminations of a self-professed amateur on a variety of issues one encounters when engaging the psalms—a "comparing [of] notes" intended to intrigue and aid other inexpert readers in their interactions with the Psalter.[2] Yet, far from rendering Lewis' work unworthy of scholarly consideration, the consciously unlearned quality of Lewis' approach is precisely why it must be taken seriously. Lewis gives eloquent voice to the initial discomfort, even the visceral disgust, that many Christians instinctively experience when confronted by the Psalter's justice songs. Given the overt pastoral impulse of this work—my concern with the place of the imprecatory psalms in the Christian's piety and the church's worship—his position thus merits careful attention and provides a reasonable starting point for reflection on the influential ethical proposals for Christian performance of the imprecatory psalms currently on offer to the church. Lewis' reading of the imprecatory psalms, unencumbered by more technical exegetical, historical, and critical concerns, is attractive for my purposes because—not in spite—of its intuitiveness and simplicity. In his commentary on Psalms 1–50, Peter Craigie reiterates and commends the basic structure of Lewis' interpretation,[3] demonstrating that Lewis' argument—intended as it is for an audience of nonspecialists—is nevertheless able to withstand scholarly scrutiny. Simplicity in this case does not entail a lack of sophistication.

Lewis claims without equivocation that the imprecatory psalms are the impious, immoral, petty, vulgar voicings of hate-filled vindictiveness.[4] The vengeful petitions are "devilish"[5] and "diabolical,"[6] "terrible or (dare we

---

[1]   C. S. Lewis, *Reflections on the Psalms* (San Diego: Harcourt Brace Jovanovich, 1958), 1.

[2]   Lewis, *Reflections on the Psalms*, 1–2, quote 2.

[3]   Peter C. Craigie and Marvin E. Tate, *Psalms 1–50*, WBC 19, 2nd ed. (Grand Rapids: Zondervan, 2004), 41–42. Craigie's explicit consideration of the imprecatory psalms is brief and focuses primarily on summarizing the contours of Lewis' reading. Craigie articulates the view that the imprecations are instances of aberrant human emotion for an academic audience, but he does not make any significant original contribution to the proposal.

[4]   Lewis, *Reflections on the Psalms*, 20–22.

[5]   Lewis, *Reflections on the Psalms*, 20.

[6]   Lewis, *Reflections on the Psalms*, 21. Cf. Roland E. Murphy, *The Psalms, Job*, Proclamation Commentaries: The Old Testament Witnesses for Preaching (Philadelphia: Fortress, 1977), 46, who declares that the imprecations "exemplify the demonic in every human heart."

say?) contemptible."[7] Lewis describes the psalmists who penned the imprecations as "ferocious, self-pitying, barbaric men,"[8] laboring to emphasize the
moral bankruptcy of both the prayers and the pray-ers. In Lewis' view, these
vengeful petitions resound as the vile, odious, repugnant expressions of an
aberrant and abhorrent ethic, prayers that are irreconcilable with both the
Old Testament commands of enemy love and the New Testament teachings of
Jesus.[9] With the assertion that the utilization of the imprecations as a model for
Christian prayer would serve as nothing more than a wicked justification of
the worst dimensions of the human heart, Lewis concludes that these psalms,
as petitions against human enemies, have no place on a Christian's lips.[10]

The renowned apologist's unapologetic distaste for and vehement
opposition to the imprecatory psalms does not mean, however, that Lewis
finds nothing of pedagogical value within them. His convictions that all
the Scriptures were written for instruction, that the historical use of the
Psalter by the church could not have been entirely misguided, and that
Jesus' thoughts and speech were saturated with the psalms drive him to
find some beneficial way to make use of the psalmic curses as a Christian.[11] Lewis submits four such potential uses for consideration.

First, the morally detestable imprecatory psalms may be used to expose
similar detestable sentiments in oneself. Lewis suggests that "we live . . . in
a milder age" than the world of bloody violence inhabited by the psalmists

---

[7] Lewis, *Reflections on the Psalms*, 21–22.

[8] Lewis, *Reflections on the Psalms*, 24.

[9] *Contra* advocates of covenantal inferiority readings such as Artur
Weiser, *The Psalms: A Commentary*, trans. Herbert Hartwell, OTL (Philadelphia: Westminster, 1962); William L. Holladay, *Long Ago God Spoke: How Christians May Hear the Old Testament Today* (Minneapolis: Fortress, 1995), 302–18;
Roy Ben Zuck, "The Problem of the Imprecatory Psalms" (ThM thesis, Dallas
Theological Seminary, 1957); W. Graham Scroggie, *A Guide to the Psalms: A
Comprehensive Analysis of the Psalms* (1978; repr., Grand Rapids: Kregel, 1995),
32. Lewis bases his moral rejection of the imprecatory psalms not on the claim
that the ethic of Jesus in the New Testament is superior to a deficient Old Testament morality but on the assertion that both testaments contain ethical commands that indict the hatred of the imprecatory psalms. Lewis maintains that
Jesus' teaching is fundamentally consistent with, and not a novel reinterpretation of or divergence from, Old Testament morality. Lewis, *Reflections on the
Psalms*, 26–27. Cf. Craigie, *Psalms 1–50*, 41; James Limburg, *Psalms*, Westminster Bible Companion, ed. Patrick D. Miller and David L. Bartlett (Louisville:
Westminster John Knox, 2000), 467.

[10] Lewis, *Reflections on the Psalms*, 22.

[11] Lewis, *Reflections on the Psalms*, 22.

but argues that this only means that the manifestations of vindictiveness will have become less apparent, harder to detect, taking more nuanced and subtle forms that remain culturally acceptable in polite modern society.[12] "We are, after all, blood-brothers to these ferocious, self-pitying, barbaric men."[13] For Lewis, the maledictory psalms offer a much-needed mirror, forcing us to take note of the family resemblance and recognize ourselves in the petty vulgarities and hateful bitterness to which they give expression.[14]

Second, Lewis maintains that these vengeful psalms reveal the devastating transformation that takes place when humans suffer terrible injustice.[15] The deep resentment that naturally festers in one who has been severely wronged is in the imprecatory psalms put on display with forceful clarity. Though the psalmists' responses may be ethically unjustifiable, they are nevertheless true to life—truthful portrayals of the wounded human soul. With this insight, Lewis intends to put the imprecations in perspective, demonstrating that the psalmists did not curse in a vacuum; they were made by the kind of people who breathe out invectives by others who deprived them of justice and showered them with cruel abuses. By giving uncensored access to the recesses of the injured heart, the psalms in Lewis' reading demand that the Christian consider how his or her unjust actions toward others may in fact push their victims down the road of resentment and conform them to the psalmists' unseemly image.[16]

---

[12]   Lewis, *Reflections on the Psalms*, 23–24, quote 23. Lewis' characterization of his own age as milder than the age of the psalmists may align with the modern ideology of progress, but it does not fit the evidence. In just the half century preceding the 1958 publication of *Reflections on the Psalms*, the world faced the carnage of two world wars, Nazism, Stalinism, mass killings by the Japanese government, and nuclear strikes on Hiroshima and Nagasaki. Lewis insightfully notes that there is a form of relational violence in the modern age that is in many ways quite subtle, but there is undoubtedly also an overt form of violence in the modern age that operates on a greater scale and with more devastating consequences than in previous eras.

[13]   Lewis, *Reflections on the Psalms*, 24. Intriguingly, Lewis' statement here is simultaneously one of self-critical solidarity with the psalmists and self-assured condemnation of their character and ethic.

[14]   Cf. Murphy, *Psalms, Job*, 46; Dominick D. Hankle, "The Therapeutic Implications of the Imprecatory Psalms in the Christian Counseling Setting," *JPT* 38, no. 4 (2010): 279.

[15]   Lewis, *Reflections on the Psalms*, 24; cf. Craigie, *Psalms 1–50*, 41; Limburg, *Psalms*, 376–78.

[16]   Lewis, *Reflections on the Psalms*, 24–26.

Third, Lewis suggests that the imprecatory psalms teach about both the world and God. The unremitting anger of the imprecations reminds Christians that there is in fact something in the world worthy of anger.[17] Though stopping short of condoning the psalmists' fury, Lewis maintains that the writers of the imprecations were yet near to God in their recognition of evil as evil—certainly nearer to God than the apathetic moral malaise he discerns in his own context.[18] The world is a violent place, and through their responses to such violence, the violent psalms call us to confront this reality. And in Lewis' estimation, the "implacable hostility"[19] the psalmists direct at their enemies is, in a certain sense, a revelation of God. "Though hideously distorted by the human instrument, something of the Divine voice can be heard in these passages."[20] Citing Ezekiel's assertion that God does not desire the death of the sinner (cf. Ezek 18:23, 32; 33:11), Lewis argues that, whereas God does not share the psalmists' vitriolic perspective of their enemies, he undoubtedly experiences an equally fierce hatred toward their enemies' sin.[21] While he emphasizes that the despicable ventings of the imprecatory psalms are dangerously ripe for misuse,

---

[17] Lewis, *Reflections on the Psalms*, 33. Lewis claims that "the absence of anger, especially that sort of anger which we call *indignation*, can, in my opinion, be a most alarming symptom." Lewis, *Reflections on the Psalms*, 30, emphasis original.

[18] Lewis, *Reflections on the Psalms*, 27–32. Lewis offers an extended reflection in defense of the paradoxical notion that certain heinous temptations only present themselves to those with greater virtue, or as he summarizes, "The higher, the more in danger." Lewis, *Reflections on the Psalms*, 28. "If the Jews cursed more bitterly than the Pagans this was, I think, at least in part because they took right and wrong more seriously. For if we look at their railings we find they are usually angry not simply because these things have been done to them but because these things are manifestly wrong, are hateful to God as well as to the victim. . . . The Jews sinned in this matter worse than the Pagans not because they were further from God but because they were nearer to him." Lewis, *Reflections on the Psalms*, 30–31. For Lewis then, the condemnable curses of the psalmists emerge from a praiseworthy indignation over evil that is itself rooted in a commendable moral seriousness.

[19] Lewis, *Reflections on the Psalms*, 32.

[20] Lewis, *Reflections on the Psalms*, 32.

[21] Lewis, *Reflections on the Psalms*. Cf. Craigie, *Psalms 1–50*, 41. *Contra* the claim that God hates the sin and not the sinner, the psalmist declares to God in Ps 5:5–6, "The boastful shall not stand before your eyes; you hate all evildoers. You destroy those who speak lies; the LORD abhors the bloodthirsty and deceitful man." Cf. Ps 11:5.

Lewis maintains that God's word can still be heard through the raging, speaking the truth about a ruthless world and a God who despises sin.[22]

In his first three uses of the judgment psalms, Lewis proposes that they are usable as profound sources of knowledge—knowledge of one's own desires for vengeance, of one's contributions to others' desires for vengeance, of the violence in the world, and the God who hates it. But is there any sense in which the imprecations may be prayed (and not merely reflected upon) by the Christian?

Perhaps surprisingly, Lewis' answer is a qualified *yes*, and his fourth use of the imprecatory psalms focuses on this devotional potential for Christians. Lewis has already clearly contended that no Christian may pray the psalmists' petitions against their human enemies, but through the process of moral and spiritual allegorization—where the objects of imprecation are not people but vices internal to oneself that require repentance and mortification—Lewis suggests that the imprecations may become valuable resources for Christian prayer.[23] Legitimate Christian appropriation requires for Lewis an inward turn such that one's judgment pleas are directed exclusively at oneself. "From this point of view I can use even the horrible passage in [Psalm] 137 about dashing Babylonian babies against the stones."[24] By allegorizing the Babylonian babies into seedlike desires that can easily grow into destructive patterns of thought and behavior, Lewis permits himself to embrace the psalmists' rage and direct it toward what he deems a more fitting end.[25]

In his pursuit of a Christian reading of the imprecatory psalms, Lewis endeavors to bring the violent petitions of the Psalter into dialogue with the teachings of Jesus and the ethics of his kingdom, assessing whether or not the Christian's primary allegiance to Christ permits vocalization of

---

[22] Lewis, *Reflections on the Psalms*, 33.

[23] Lewis, *Reflections on the Psalms*, 136.

[24] Lewis, *Reflections on the Psalms*, 136.

[25] His conclusion concerning Psalm 137 is characteristically provocative: "Against all such infants . . . the advice of the Psalm is best. Knock the little bastards' brains out." Lewis, *Reflections on the Psalms*, 136. In his allegorization, Lewis' reading follows Augustine: "What are the little ones of Babylon? Evil desires at their birth." Augustin [sic], *Saint Augustin: Expositions on the Book of Psalms*, ed. A. Cleveland Coxe, vol. 8 of *NPNF*, ed. Philip Schaff, trans. J. E. Tweed, T. Scratton, H. M. Wilkins, C. Marriott, and H. Walford (New York: Christian Literature Company, 1888), 137.12. Cf. Gregory A. Boyd, *The Crucifixion of the Warrior God: Interpreting the Old Testament's Violent Portraits of God in Light of the Cross* (Minneapolis: Fortress, 2017), 2:1095–97.

such pleas.[26] Lewis' conclusion that Jesus' teaching "allows no quarter"[27] for the passions that fill the imprecatory psalms is an attempt to take seriously the apparent dissonance between the psalmists' requests concerning their enemies and the Lord's explicit commands of enemy love and enemy blessing. But while the tone, style, and accessibility of Lewis' work are well served by his avoidance of cumbersome citations and technical asides, his case would be strengthened by engagement with the biblical evidence that seems to press against his position. Lewis neglects to mention Jesus' parabolic commendation of the practice of petitioning for divine justice (Luke 18:1–8) and the various imprecations that the New Testament places in the mouths of Paul and the heavenly saints.[28] If the cries of these psalms are as reprehensible to Christian ethics as Lewis supposes, why then are prayers for justice endorsed by the Lord Jesus himself? And why are similar petitions found in the canonical writings of an apostle and the postmortem petitions of slain disciples? Lewis makes no attempt at an answer.

In his consideration of the imprecatory psalms as the anatomy of the scorched soul, Lewis makes an insightful turn toward hearing in these prayers the voices of the victims of violence. In his haste, however, to warn against turning into (or making others into) the type of people who cry like the psalmists, Lewis misses a potentially fruitful avenue for inquiry. Perhaps these psalms are not opprobrious expressions of reified hate in response to atrocity—the prayers of people whom we must strive never to become—but exceedingly faithful expressions of hope on the long journey through tribulation toward virtue and healing. In an age of ethnic conflict, terrorism, nuclear proliferation, and the pervasive anxiety to which all of these contribute, could the imprecatory psalms be the very God-ordained petitions we must take on our own bloodied lips if the natural course of resentment is to be interrupted? How the imprecations might address us as God's good gift for sufferers and cultivate ethical affections is a question worthy of further pursuit.

Despite his conviction that the imprecatory psalms exhibit an indefensible morality, Lewis seeks to retain some sense of the pedagogical value of these psalms for Christians, arguing that the vengeance psalms might serve as a resource for knowledge of self, world, and God as well as the basis for allegorized devotional prayers. This perspective, however,

---

26 Lewis, *Reflections on the Psalms*, 19.
27 Lewis, *Reflections on the Psalms*, 19.
28 See, e.g., Gal 1:8–9; 5:12; 1 Cor 16:22; Rev 6:10.

passes over a potentially significant pedagogical function of the Psalter. In their canonical form, the psalms of judgment are presented as neither the rash and raw ravings of barbarians[29] nor the historical record of pain-filled emotion, passed down through generations primarily for the sake of scholarly curiosity, aloof reflection, or objective study. A developing scholarly consensus, especially in the wake of Gerald Henry Wilson's *The Editing of the Hebrew Psalter*,[30] indicates rather that the canonical psalms are intentionally selected units in the carefully edited, organized, and pre-served worship book of Israel. Further, this purposefully crafted Psalter has been persuasively shown to exercise an instructional function, direct-ing the Israelite community in the path of faith and life.[31] Within Israel's liturgical life, then, the psalms that Lewis so confidently rejects served as key elements in a communal pedagogy of prayer—model prayers that not only taught the Israelite faithful how to commune with their God but that also explicitly formed their speech with God as the congregation performed the psalms together.[32] And the New Testament suggests that

---

[29] Though his language is more reserved than Lewis', Craigie, *Psalms 1–50*, 41, nevertheless characterizes the imprecations as "often natural and sponta-neous, not always pure and good," drawing attention to the impromptu, extem-poraneous, reactionary quality of the prayers. However, Chalmers Martin, "The Imprecations in the Psalms," *PTR* 1, no. 4 (1903): 540, argues that the psalms in their canonical form are not the immediate products of raw moments of severe provocation but are highly artistic pieces of literature, lyric poems intended for utilization in Israel's corporate worship.

[30] Gerald Henry Wilson, *The Editing of the Hebrew Psalter*, SBLDS 76 (Chico, Calif.: Scholars Press, 1985).

[31] See David G. Firth, "The Teaching of the Psalms," in *Interpreting the Psalms: Issues and Approaches*, ed. Philip S. Johnston and David G. Firth (Downers Grove, Ill.: InterVarsity Press, 2005), 159–74; Kit Barker, *Imprecation as Divine Discourse: Speech Act Theory, Dual Authorship, and Theological Inter-pretation* (Winona Lake, Ind.: Eisenbrauns, 2016), 109–12, 133–34; Gordon J. Wenham, *Psalms as Torah: Reading Biblical Songs Ethically*, Studies in Theo-logical Interpretation (Grand Rapids: Baker Academic, 2012), 57–76; Sigmund Mowinckel, *The Psalms in Israel's Worship*, trans. D. R. Ap-Thomas (Oxford: Basil Blackwell, 1962), 2:205; J. Clinton McCann, Jr., *A Theological Introduction to the Book of Psalms: The Psalms as Torah* (Nashville: Abingdon, 1993), 25–40; Wilson, *Editing of the Hebrew Psalter*, 143, 172–3; Martin, "Imprecations in the Psalms," 540; Samuel Onchonga Asuma, "Speech Ethics in the Hebrew Psalter" (PhD diss., Southern Baptist Theological Seminary, 2012), 104–15.

[32] Gordon Wenham, "Prayer and Practice in the Psalms," in *Psalms and Prayers: Papers Read at the Joint Meeting of the Society of Old Testament Study and Het Oudtestamentisch Werkgezelchap in Nederland en België, Apeldoorn*

this liturgical, pedagogical function of the Psalter carried over from Israel into the apostolic church, where psalm singing was recognized as a means of internalization of the word of Christ and beneficial mutual teaching within the community.[33] Lewis' dismissal of the imprecations as immoral individual prayers indicts not only the psalmists who penned them but also the entire Israelite community who received and practiced them, and his proposal disregards the ostensibly prescriptive character of the psalms within Israel and the Christian church.

Foundational to Lewis' moral rejection and proposed uses of the imprecatory psalms are his doctrine of Scripture and corresponding hermeneutic. Lewis plainly states his understanding of the inspiration of Scripture: "all Holy Scripture is *in some sense*—though not all parts of it in the same sense—the word of God."[34] "Something of the Divine voice"[35] can be discerned through the white noise of contemptible human animosity.[36] But the distance Lewis introduces between the word of God and the word of Scripture raises significant hermeneutical issues. In which biblical passages is God's word identifiable with the text itself? And who decides? A doctrine of Scripture that separates God's word from Scripture's word may potentially be used to legitimize all sorts of hermeneutical

---

August 2006, OtSt 55, ed. Bob Becking and Eric Peels (Leiden: Brill, 2007), 290; cf. Catherine Petrany, *Pedagogy, Prayer and Praise: The Wisdom of the Psalms and Psalter*, FAT 2, Reihe 83 (Mohr Siebeck: Tübingen, 2015), 95–96. In his analysis of the historical psalms, Walter Brueggemann, *Abiding Astonishment: Psalms, Modernity, and the Making of History*, Literary Currents in Biblical Interpretation, ed. Danna Nolan Fewell and David M. Gunn (Louisville: Westminster John Knox, 1991), 21, suggests that the psalms of historical recital functioned constructively for Israel, encouraging them to understand and inhabit God's world in a particular way. It could be argued that all the psalms, including the imprecatory psalms, exhibit a similar world-making potential.

[33] See Col 3:16, where singing the Psalter is connected with wise teaching and admonition, and Eph 5:19, where the psalms are a means of Spirit-filled address within the Christian community.

[34] Lewis, *Reflections on the Psalms*, 19, emphasis added. But concerning the psalms specifically, Mark 12:36 records Jesus' statement that David spoke in the Holy Spirit, and in Acts 1:16 Peter attributes the words of David in Psalms 69; 109—imprecatory psalms—to the Holy Spirit (cf. also Acts 4:25). Indeed, according to 2 Sam 23:2, David's self-understanding was as one through whom the Spirit of the Lord spoke. Cf. John N. Day, "The Imprecatory Psalms and Christian Ethics" (PhD diss., Dallas Theological Seminary, 2001), 29–30.

[35] Lewis, *Reflections on the Psalms*, 32.

[36] Cf. Craigie, *Psalms 1–50*, 41; Limburg, *Psalms*, 473; Boyd, *Crucifixion of the Warrior God*, 2:1096–97.

moves that do little more than reflect and impose the previously held theological and ethical convictions of the interpreter. Consequently, the clarity with which an interpreter believes God's voice rings through the imprecatory psalms may be directly related to the psalms' alignment with his or her personal biases or prevailing cultural assumptions. Lewis' doctrine of inspiration permits him to receive prophetic affirmations of God's loving mercy (e.g., "He 'desireth not the death of a sinner'"[37]) as straightforward revelations of God's character while relegating psalmic petitions to a God of vengeance to the status of theologically mistaken and morally diabolical cruelty through which the Christian must strain to hear God's address to his people. The inherent danger of Lewis' approach to Scripture is that it may inadvertently sanction a hermeneutic that opens the door for an all-too-easy escape from the imprecatory psalms and the unexpected, uncomfortable ways in which they might stake their claim on the church as the word of God.

The Prayers of Christ: Christological Readings of the Imprecatory Psalms

For Dietrich Bonhoeffer and James Adams, the fundamental issue upon which the proper interpretation and performance of the imprecatory psalms hinges is the identity of the imprecator: "Who is praying for God to destroy His enemies?"[38] By identifying the righteous, guiltless, innocent Christ as the chief petitioner of the Psalter's most violent prayers, their Christological readings aim to resolve the ethical tensions introduced by the imprecations, envisioning Christian vocalization of the imprecatory psalms not as vindictive and personal requests for vengeance but as prayer with Jesus, alongside the Messiah, echoing the Christ who alone is worthy to pray against his enemies. Pointing to a manner in which Christians may faithfully engage the imprecations, Bonhoeffer and Adams thus open the way for homiletical interaction with and prayerful appropriation of the imprecatory psalms in local churches.[39]

---

[37] Lewis, *Reflections on the Psalms*, 32.
[38] James E. Adams, *War Psalms of the Prince of Peace: Lessons from the Imprecatory Psalms* (Phillipsburg, N.J.: Presbyterian and Reformed, 1991), 21.
[39] Adams intersperses his work with exhortations to recover the imprecatory psalms in Christian preaching and piety. See, e.g., Adams, *War Psalms*, 3. Dietrich Bonhoeffer, *Prayerbook of the Bible: An Introduction to the Psalms*, ed. Geffrey B. Kelly, trans. James H. Burtness, vol. 5 of *Dietrich Bonhoeffer Works* (Minneapolis: Fortress, 1996), 162, demonstrates a similar concern: "Whenever the Psalter is abandoned, an incomparable treasure is lost to the Christian church."

Dietrich Bonhoeffer offers a Christological reading of the imprecatory psalms in his pastoral writings on communal piety and the life of prayer dating from 1937 to 1940, during which Bonhoeffer experienced the closing of Finkenwalde by the Gestapo and the increasingly intense scrutiny of the Third Reich.[40] Sensitive to Christians' ethical objection to taking up the petitions for vengeance as their own, Bonhoeffer maintains that this instinctive hesitation is a clue that there is in fact another supplicant in these psalms calling for God's wrath upon his enemies, and this supplicant is Jesus Christ.[41] Bonhoeffer argues that Scripture presents David, the anointed king over God's covenant people and paradigmatic psalmist in whose voice the entire Psalter is written,[42] as a prototypical forerunner *of* Jesus whose words are attributed in the New Testament directly *to* Jesus.[43] "The same words that David spoke, therefore, the future Messiah spoke in him. Christ prayed along with the prayers of David or, more accurately, it is none other than Christ who prayed them in Christ's own forerunner, David."[44] According to Bonhoeffer, it is the voice of Christ that thunders through the mouth of David as Jesus imprecates through the imprecating psalmist.

[40]   Dietrich Bonhoeffer preached his "Sermon on a Psalm of Vengeance—Psalm 58," in *Meditating on the Word*, trans. and ed. David M. Gracie, 84–96 (Cambridge, Mass.: Cowley, 1986), on July 11, 1937, a mere two months before the Gestapo closed Finkenwalde. Gracie notes that the sermon "can be seen as an attempt to pronounce the judgment of God on the Nazi regime, while still holding Christians back from any direct role as agents of that judgment." Bonhoeffer, "Sermon on a Psalm of Vengeance," 86. Geffrey B. Kelly, introduction to *Life Together*, by Dietrich Bonhoeffer, ed. Geffrey B. Kelly, trans. Daniel W. Bloesch, vol. 5 of *Dietrich Bonhoeffer Works* (Minneapolis: Fortress, 1996), 3, argues, "In an ironical way we are indebted to the Gestapo for this remarkable book." The clarity and accessibility of Bonhoeffer's articulation makes his work a helpful introduction to the Christological reading. However, given the occasional nature of his "Sermon on a Psalm of Vengeance" and the brief and unsystematic treatments in *Life Together* and *Prayerbook of the Bible*, Bonhoeffer's writings offer neither the most detailed explication nor the most comprehensive defense of this proposal.

[41]   Bonhoeffer, *Life Together* (1954), 45.

[42]   Bonhoeffer, *Prayerbook of the Bible*, 158–59; cf. Bruce K. Waltke, "A Canonical Process Approach to the Psalms," in *Tradition and Testament: Essays in Honor of Charles Lee Feinberg*, ed. John S. Feinberg and Paul D. Feinberg (Chicago: Moody, 1981), 13.

[43]   Bonhoeffer, *Prayerbook of the Bible*, 158–59, citing Heb 2:12; 10:5.

[44]   Bonhoeffer, *Prayerbook of the Bible*, 159. Bonhoeffer continues: "It is important for us that even David prayed not only out of the personal raptures of his heart, but from the Christ dwelling in him. To be sure, the one who prays these psalms, David, remains himself; but Christ dwells in him and with him." Cf. Waltke, "Canonical Process Approach to the Psalms," 16.

In Bonhoeffer's view, the Christological reading that ultimately locates the imprecations on the lips of Jesus not only makes sense of the exegetical evidence in the New Testament but also solves a significant ethical conundrum associated with the psalms of vengeance. A fundamental reason, Bonhoeffer suggests, why imprecatory prayer is inappropriate for human beings is that human beings, without exception, are themselves already guilty of sin and deserving of the very judgment they would call upon their enemies.[45] Concerning Psalm 58, Bonhoeffer reasons,

> Only one who is without guilt can pray in this way. This psalm of vengeance is the prayer of the innocent. David is the one who prays this psalm, although David himself is not innocent. . . . David could never have prayed against his enemies in this way on his own behalf. . . . But in David is Christ, and thereby also the church of God. So his enemies are the enemies of Jesus Christ and his holy church. . . . Thus it is the innocence of Christ himself that prays this psalm of David—and with Christ the whole church of God. No, we sinners do not pray this song of vengeance, innocence alone prays this psalm. The innocence of Christ steps before the world and accuses it. And when Christ accuses the world of sin, are we not ourselves also among the accused?[46]

Turning upside down a common objection to the imprecatory psalms, Bonhoeffer argues not that humans are too good to pray these wicked prayers but that humans are too wicked to pray these righteous prayers.[47] Consequently, human beings—fallen in sin—have no standing to bring

---

[45]   Bonhoeffer, "Sermon on a Psalm of Vengeance," 86.

[46]   Bonhoeffer, "Sermon on a Psalm of Vengeance," 87. Cf. Adams, *War Psalms*, 102–3, where Adams clearly follows the line of logic Bonhoeffer employs: "Only one who is just can rightfully accuse others of injustice; only someone who is guiltless can pray this way. This psalm is the prayer of the innocent man. According to its title, David is the author of this psalm. So David prays this psalm; but *he* is not innocent. . . . David could never have prayed against his enemies this way on his own behalf or merely to preserve his own life. . . . But Christ was in David, so David's enemies are the enemies of Jesus Christ. Truly the innocent Christ was praying this psalm with David. God himself is here accusing the wicked of their guilt." Emphasis original.

[47]   Bonhoeffer, "Sermon on a Psalm of Vengeance," 87. Cf. Adams, *War Psalms*, 102.

charges against others in the divine courtroom.[48] Imprecatory prayer on the lips of sinful humans is therefore self-defeating, an invocation of wrath upon oneself, who stands accused together with the enemy in the tribunal of God. Maledictions of the sort found in the imprecatory psalms can only be legitimately offered by one upon whom God's wrath may stake no claim—the perfect innocent.[49] The assertion that the flawlessly righteous Christ is the psalmic speaker in, with, and through David allows Bonhoeffer to conclude that the psalms are in fact ethically appropriate prayers, justly presented to God the Father by God the Son.[50]

Consciously expanding on Bonhoeffer's Christological reading,[51] James Adams offers the most extensive contemporary articulation of this perspective. With a pastoral eye—reflective of his experience as a Reformed Baptist minister—toward both preachers and Christian laypeople who find themselves unsettled by the vehement cries for vengeance that exist alongside the Psalter's soothing poetry, Adams explicates and defends his interpretation of the imprecatory psalms as the prayers of Christ and considers how the church might gladly recover these oft-neglected psalms in her proclamation and prayer.

Adams presents the apparent problem of the imprecatory psalms and his Christological solution with a poignant contrast: "If *you* were to ask God to destroy your personal enemy, that would be in essence cursing the enemy and, therefore, sinful. But if the King of Peace asks God to destroy *His* enemies, that is another matter!"[52] Adams maintains with Bonhoeffer that the New Testament authors demonstrate a willingness to place the psalmic prayers directly in the mouth of Christ,[53] but he focuses additional attention on the words of Jesus as recorded in the Gospels. Referencing Jesus' frequent identification with the experience and petitions of the psalmists, Adams maintains not only that the New Testament presents

[48] Bonhoeffer's foregrounding of a distinct awareness of human sin—even in Christians—is consistent with Luther's *simul iustus et pecattor*.

[49] Cf. Holladay, *Long Ago God Spoke*, 316.

[50] For a helpful analysis of Bonhoeffer's "Sermon on a Psalm of Vengeance," see Brad Pribbenow, "Prayerbook of Christ, Prayerbook of the Church: Dietrich Bonhoeffer's Christological Interpretation of the Psalms" (PhD diss., Concordia Seminary, 2017), 79–87.

[51] Despite theological differences, Adams quotes frequently and approvingly from Bonhoeffer's works. See Adams, *War Psalms*, xii.

[52] Adams, *War Psalms*, 21, emphasis original.

[53] Adams, *War Psalms*, 24–25. Adams specifically cites Heb 10:5 (cf. Ps 40:6–8); Heb 2:11–12 (cf. Ps 22:22). Cf. Bonhoeffer, *Prayerbook of the Bible*, 159.

Jesus as the true supplicant of the imprecatory psalms but that Jesus presents *himself* as the voice of the Psalter.[54] "The Spirit of Christ was in the psalmists, speaking through them centuries before He came to earth as the long-awaited Messiah."[55] Adams contends that David is thus able to pray in a manner otherwise impossible as the ultimate Davidic Messiah offers his prayers through his royal progenitor.[56]

If Jesus is the imprecator par excellence—the only one permitted to pray for vengeance upon his enemies—what role might the imprecatory psalms serve in Christian piety? May Christians take up the prayers of Christ in the Psalter as their own? Both Bonhoeffer and Adams unequivocally maintain that Christians must never merely pray the psalms of vengeance from personal vindictiveness.[57] However, advocates of the Christological reading suggest that when the imprecatory psalms are understood first as the prayers of Jesus, these violent petitions may then be approached and appropriated in renewed ways.

Adams describes faithful Christian performance of the imprecatory psalms as prayer *in Christ*.[58] For Adams, praying in Christ means petitioning against Jesus' enemies for the sake of Jesus' kingdom such

---

[54]   Adams, *War Psalms*, 23–24.

[55]   Adams, *War Psalms*, 25.

[56]   Adams, *War Psalms*, 27: "David, by the Spirit of Christ in him, speaks far beyond his own understanding and experience. He anticipates the coming, suffering, deliverance, and exaltation of his Son and Lord—Jesus, the Christ." In Adams' view, Jesus' agency as the true petitioner of the imprecations introduces new elements into the psalmic prayers that could not have emerged merely from David's theology or role. Adams appears to suggest that David "anticipates" Jesus not passively, as a type may unconsciously prefigure the antitype, but actively, as one consciously looking to the horizon for the appearance of another. Adams, *War Psalms*, 26, follows Bonhoeffer in asserting that his Christological reading does not depend on the strict Davidic authorship of the entire Psalter, suggesting that while a variety of authors contributed to the Psalter, "the whole of the Psalms are written 'in the ink' of the Lord's Anointed—the Christ."

[57]   Bonhoeffer, "Sermon on a Psalm of Vengeance," 86, begins his sermon on Psalm 58 thus: "Is this fearful psalm of vengeance to be our prayer? May we pray in this way? Certainly not!" In reference to the song of Deborah and Barak in Judg 5:25–27, Adams, *War Psalms*, 56, states, "So, do we say: 'Do it again, Lord! Do that to my own enemy!'? *Never!* Never may God's people pray so out of a spirit of personal vengeance against their enemies." Both Bonhoeffer and Adams are clearly concerned to guard against the potential abuses associated with simplistic appropriations of the imprecatory psalms.

[58]   Adams, *War Psalms*, 56.

that one relinquishes the right to exact vengeance to God alone.[59] This vision of Christian imprecation involves the Christian praying the prayers of Christ after him, joining voices with the innocent Messiah as he makes his prayers for justice to God, offering an "Amen" to Jesus' supplications.[60] Adams envisions the God of the Bible as simultaneously merciful and just, and at the same time gracious and righteous—a God who invites his enemies to share in the blessings of salvation by faith in the justice-satisfying work of Christ in the gospel even as he promises to pour out his wrath upon those unwaveringly committed to their rebellion.[61] Consequently, Adams argues that the primary goal—the first petition, as it were—of Christians' imprecatory prayer must be for God's justice to be manifested through the conversion and reconciliation of the enemies of God's kingdom through the propitiation of Christ.[62] But in the event that Jesus' enemies remain resolute in their unrepentance, Christians must desire and pray for the manifestation of God's justice in final judgment.[63]

Bonhoeffer likewise calls for Christians to plead for the enemies of the gospel to be brought to repentance and faith and for the imminent consummation of Christ's kingdom, wherein God will judge the impenitent

---

[59] Adams, *War Psalms*, 56–57. Bonhoeffer, "Sermon on a Psalm of Vengeance," 91, similarly maintains that "whoever calls for the vengeance of God renounces thereby any vengeance of his own. Whoever wants to avenge himself still does not know with whom he is dealing; he still wants to take things into his own hands." The necessity of the relinquishment of vengeance in imprecatory prayer receives much fuller treatment from, e.g, Erich Zenger, *A God of Vengeance? Understanding the Psalms of Divine Wrath*, trans. Linda M. Maloney (Louisville: Westminster John Knox, 1996) and the numerous works of Walter Brueggemann (see below).

[60] *Contra* Daniel Michael Nehrbass, "The Therapeutic and Preaching Value of the Imprecatory Psalms" (PhD diss., Fuller Theological Seminary, 2012), 61–62, who understands Adams to be advocating the perspective that Christians may not pray the imprecations. Cf. Waltke, "Canonical Process Approach to the Psalms," 16.

[61] See, e.g., Adams, *War Psalms*, 62, 106.

[62] Adams, *War Psalms*, 59–60. Adams offers Ps 83:16 as evidence of such a desire within the Psalter.

[63] Adams, *War Psalms*, 62. Adams offers his own prayer as a model for how Christians might pray for both conversion and final judgment: "Let this be the prayer of our hearts: 'O Christ, come in power and show forth the glory of God. Bring judgment to the wicked that they may seek you . . . and if not, O God, destroy all who won't bow to you. Let them know that only you, whose name is the Lord, are the Most High over all the earth.'" Adams, *War Psalms*, 63.

with flawless justice.[64] Quite interestingly, however, while Adams commends praying in Christ with language that evokes the theological concept of union with Christ, it is Bonhoeffer who specifically addresses how the Christian's union with Christ impacts the existential dimensions of prayer—the disposition of heart from which one petitions God. Bonhoeffer asserts that the imprecatory psalms must be prayed from a posture of humility and thanksgiving,[65] emphasizing that Jesus, the godly and innocent, took the place of the godless and guilty in his death on the cross, satisfying the demands of God's righteousness and the petitions of the imprecatory psalms.[66] Jesus is therefore the answer to Jesus' prayers, and Christians may only echo these prayers in the awareness that the judgment of the cross rescues them from the judgment they request. In Bonhoeffer's conception, whenever Christians imprecate against God's enemies for their conversion and, only secondarily, their final condemnation, they do so as recipients of the deliverance secured by the Christ who bore God's vengeance and prayed for their forgiveness,[67] and Bonhoeffer suggests

[64] Bonhoeffer, "Sermon on a Psalm of Vengeance," 96. Day, "Imprecatory Psalms," 57–58, argues that Bonhoeffer understands the prayers for divine vengeance to have been fully and exhaustively fulfilled in the cross of Christ such that no further acts of vengeance are expected or required. But while Bonhoeffer certainly emphasizes the cross as the locus of God's judgment in history, he explicitly states that those enemies who remain opposed to Christ will incur divine judgment at the *parousia*. See Bonhoeffer, "Sermon on a Psalm of Vengeance," 95.

[65] Bonhoeffer, "Sermon on a Psalm of Vengeance," 96.

[66] Bonhoeffer, "Sermon on a Psalm of Vengeance," 94. James W. Sire, *Praying the Psalms of Jesus* (Downers Grove, Ill.: InterVarsity Press, 2007), 122, likewise suggests that Jesus bears the guilt of the unrighteous on the cross such that reading the imprecatory psalms leads the Christian to reencounter God's grace in Christ. Sire, however, emphasizes that Jesus receives "the guilt of our guilty anger and vindictiveness," which he presumably sees reflected in the vindictive requests of the imprecations. In a sample prayer responding to Ps 69:22–28, Sire states, "Lord, these are awful words to say, awful thoughts to contemplate. Yet in my anguish, this attitude is mine too. . . . I can easily imagine them as the words of David, for his fallen humanity is mine. But I cannot imagine Jesus praying these verses. I rejoice, however, that he took into himself all the guilt of David's and my sinful character and misguided moral indignation." Sire, *Praying the Psalms of Jesus*, 127. For Sire then, the imprecations are the prayers of fallen humanity that point to Christ in that Jesus bears God's wrath for such vindictiveness.

[67] Bonhoeffer, "Sermon on a Psalm of Vengeance," 94. Marti J. Steussy, "The Enemy in the Psalms," *WW* 28, no. 1 (2008): 12, suggests that Bonhoeffer's reading enables Christians to inhabit the place of both victim and enemy, identifying with each.

that conscious recognition of that gift will exercise a dynamic force in the heart, prompting a posture of repentant meekness and joyful gratitude.

Underneath these specific proposals for Christian engagement with the imprecatory psalms lie certain foundational and interrelated conceptions of divine justice, salvation, and the kingdom of God. For Bonhoeffer and Adams, God's righteousness and justice require that human sin be judged, whether in Christ's cross in the middle of history or in eternal death at the conclusion of history.[68] Consequently, the good news of the gospel is that Jesus vicariously received God's just wrath at the cross,[69] making possible the salvific transformation of the enemies of God into kingdom citizens by faith in Christ's propitiatory work. The cross that satisfies God's justice does not, however, exhaust divine justice, and those enemies who remain opposed to God's reign must bear for themselves the death which Jesus bore for the world.[70] In this conception, God's justice is revealed both at Golgotha against Christ on behalf of the repentant and in the *parousia* by Christ against the unrepentant. Christ's death is sufficient for the inclusion of every repentant enemy even as God will righteously judge the impenitent at the consummation of his visible kingdom. Related to these perspectives on divine justice and salvation, the kingdom of God in this view includes the contrite, welcomes the enemy currently on the outside, and ultimately excludes those hardened in rebellion, withholding

[68]   Bonhoeffer, "Sermon on a Psalm of Vengeance," 93–95; Adams, *War Psalms*, 62, 106–7. Bonhoeffer, *Sanctorum Communio: A Theological Study of the Sociology of the Church*, ed. Clifford J. Green, trans. Reinhard Krauss and Nancy Lukens, vol. 1 of *Dietrich Bonhoeffer Works* (Minneapolis: Fortress, 1998), 286–87, introduces the hopeful notion of apocatastasis (universal salvation) as he discusses the necessary "dual outcome" of salvation and judgment. Bonhoeffer here seems content to let the concepts of apocatastasis and the dual outcome of divine judgment rest in tension, albeit unevenly. Even so, his explicit statement in "Sermon on a Psalm of Vengeance," 95, that "whoever will not come, whoever will not cast himself down before the cross of Christ, whoever despises the cross, will suffer God's wrathful judgment, the vengeance of God . . . unto eternal death" is presented as an unequivocal affirmation of ultimate divine judgment against the impenitent in the context of his discussion of the imprecatory psalms, despite his apocatastatic hope expressed elsewhere.

[69]   See esp. Bonhoeffer, "Sermon on a Psalm of Vengeance," 94; Adams, *War Psalms*, 106. Cf. A. James Reimer, "Jesus Christ, the Man for Others: The Suffering God in the Thought of Paul Tillich and Dietrich Bonhoeffer," *LTP* 62, no. 3 (2006): 502–6.

[70]   Bonhoeffer, "Sermon on a Psalm of Vengeance," 95; Adams, *War Psalms*, 106–7.

totalizing judgment in the present while guaranteeing it in the future. Christian imprecatory prayer for the manifestation of God's justice and kingdom is for Bonhoeffer and Adams accordingly a dual prayer that hopes for enemies' submission to God's reign through conversion to the propitiating Christ and yet clings to the possibility that the justice of God's reign may only be manifest in final judgment.[71] Bonhoeffer and Adams' vision of faithful imprecation thus follows the contours of their theologies of divine justice, salvation, and the nature of God's kingdom. Stated differently, these interconnected theological positions are largely determinative of what permissible Christian imprecation may include.

Both Adams and Bonhoeffer seek to take seriously the theological claim that the imprecatory psalms are the words of God, which merit the church's attention. Operating from the theological conviction that the psalms of vengeance are inspired by God such that their words are God's words,[72] Adams expresses wariness toward the modern tendency to permit personal disposition or cultural acceptability to dictate Christians' reactions to the psalms.[73] Adams' doctrine of Scripture pushes him away from facile evasions and into the biblical text with the confidence that the seemingly disparate voices within Scripture do in fact merge into a comprehensible and even delightful harmony, provided

[71]   Adams, *War Psalms*, 62, quotes the instruction of Martin Luther, *What Luther Says: An Anthology*, ed. Ewald M. Plass (St. Louis: Concordia, 1959), 1100, in defense of his proposal: "We should pray that our enemies be converted and become our friends, and if not, that their doing and designing be bound to fail and have no success and that their persons perish rather than the Gospel and the kingdom of Christ. . . . So we, too, pray for our angry enemies, not that God protect and strengthen them in their ways, as we pray for Christians, or that He help them, but that they be converted, if they can be; or, if they refuse, that God oppose them, stop them and end the game to their harm and misfortune."

[72]   Adams, *War Psalms*, 7–18.

[73]   Adams, *War Psalms*, 7–8. Adams, *War Psalms*, 8, cites a quote from J. I. Packer, "Introductory Essay," in *The Doctrine of Justification*, by James Buchanan (London: Banner of Truth, 1961), 5, that effectively communicates what he too believes is at stake with the question of inspiration: "This modern view expressly allows for the possibility that sometimes the biblical writers, being children of their age, had their minds so narrowed by conditioning factors in their environment that, albeit unwillingly, they twisted and misstated God's truth. And when any particular biblical idea cuts across what men today like to think, modern Protestants are fatally prone to conclude that this is a case in point, where the Bible saw things crooked, but we today, differently conditioned, can see them straight."

the interpreter's ears are humble enough to hear.[74] Though Bonhoeffer does not share Adams' precise doctrine of inspiration,[75] he nevertheless calls for a similar reverence, maintaining that the Psalter is commended to Christians as an inestimable gift by the early church, whose piety was permeated by the psalms, and by Jesus, who prayed from the Psalter in his crucifixion.[76] To neglect any part of the Psalter is, according to Bonhoeffer, an act of disrespect toward Scripture's prayerbook and a presumptuous exercise in spiritual arrogance, which audaciously claims to know how to pray more faithfully than God himself.[77] This posture toward Scripture prohibits rejection of the imprecatory psalms or their attribution to faulty, incomplete, or sub-Christian theology. The conviction that these most violent psalmic prayers must be received as the authoritative and valuable words from God to his people informs Adams and Bonhoeffer in their attempts to carefully integrate the imprecations into a consistent biblical ethic that recovers their applicability to the Christian church.

Additionally, this Christological proposal depends upon a conscientious effort to consider the extensive intertextual resonances from the psalms embedded in the New Testament. Adams in particular not only identifies texts where Jesus and the New Testament authors quote and allude to the psalms;[78] he theologically interrogates this intertextuality, asking *what it means* about Jesus' self-understanding, the apostles' understanding of Jesus, and Christians' subsequent reading of the psalms that the New Testament readily presents Jesus as the Davidic antitype and

---

[74]   See Adams, *War Psalms*, 13–16.

[75]   See his critique of the doctrine of the verbal inspiration of Scripture in, e.g., *Act and Being: Transcendental Philosophy and Ontology in Systematic Theology*, ed. Wayne Whitson Floyd, Jr., trans. H. Martin Rumscheidt, vol. 2 of *Dietrich Bonhoeffer Works* (Minneapolis: Fortress, 1996), 104, 108; *Creation and Fall: A Theological Exposition of Genesis 1–3*, ed. John W. de Gruchy, trans. Douglas Stephen Bax, vol. 3 of *Dietrich Bonhoeffer Works* (Minneapolis: Fortress, 1997), 51. Cf. Richard Weikart, "Scripture and Myth in Dietrich Bonhoeffer," *FH* 25, no. 1 (1993): 12–25.

[76]   Bonhoeffer, *Prayerbook of the Bible*, 162.

[77]   Bonhoeffer, *Prayerbook of the Bible*, 162: "We also ought not to select psalms at our own discretion, exhibiting disrespect to the prayerbook of the Bible and thinking that we know better than even God does what we should pray."

[78]   See esp. Adams, *War Psalms*, 23–25. See also Adams, *War Psalms*, 117–21; Adams compiles an extensive and helpful chart of New Testament references to the psalms.

speaker of the psalms.[79] The conclusion that the imprecatory psalms are the prayers of Christ emerges from an attempt at biblical-theological synthesis that listens to the witness of both the psalms and the New Testament and explores how these texts cohere and mutually inform one another in the polyphonic, yet unified, testimony of Scripture.

The Christological treatment of the imprecatory psalms, however, raises a number of questions. By identifying Jesus as the primary petitioner of the psalmic prayers, this reading risks eclipsing the original theological and historical context of the psalms. For Bonhoeffer and Adams, Jesus is not the typological fulfillment of legitimate Davidic imprecations, but the ultimate original imprecator whose prayers could never have appropriately arisen from David alone (or any other psalmists).[80] The nature of this perceived relationship between Jesus and the psalms permits the interpreter to overlook significant lines of inquiry: How do the imprecations fit into the theology of the Psalter and the Old Testament?[81] How does David's role as king, son of God, and the Lord's anointed illuminate the pleas of the imprecations? How might the cursing psalms reflect a specific redemptive-historical milieu and exhibit faithful prayer within such a matrix? And how might these observations in turn open up themes for further Christological and biblical-theological consideration? When the Christological turn is made too quickly—when the imprecatory psalms

---

[79] This theological interrogation is on display in Adams, *War Psalms*, 21–36. Cf. Bonhoeffer, *Prayerbook of the Bible*, 158–60.

[80] See Adams, *War Psalms*, 27, 102, for Adams' distancing of the imprecations from David's experience and agency. Cf. Bonhoeffer, *Prayerbook of the Bible*, 159; "Sermon on a Psalm of Vengeance," 87. It should be noted that the centrality of the Old Testament Psalter in Bonhoeffer's vision of Christian piety was itself a prophetic rebuke of anti-Semitic Nazi ideology. Cf. Kelly, editor's introduction to *Prayerbook of the Bible*, 143–44. Still, Bonhoeffer's reading of the psalms opens him up to the charge of a form of hermeneutical supersessionism.

[81] Adams, *War Psalms*, 57–59, does attempt to situate the psalmic curses in the context of the curses of the Mosaic covenant, arguing that God's intention to curse covenant breakers forms "an earlier scriptural principle and precedent that guided *even the psalmist's attitude*." Quote 57, emphasis added; cf. Adams, *War Psalms*, 68–73. But while Adams maintains that this covenantal context may have informed the psalmists' attitudes in some manner, he clearly does not believe that this context legitimizes the practice of imprecation in the psalms. Adams' explicit assertion is that the psalmic imprecations are valid and faithful only if they originate from Jesus, who prays the curses through the psalmists. Despite the encompassing covenantal matrix of the Mosaic code, the imprecatory psalms remain for Adams a Christological interruption in Israelite piety.

are located immediately in the mouth of Jesus to the exclusion of their place on the lips of the psalmists—the character of the psalms as Israelite prayers is in danger of being subsumed by their messianic import.[82] But historico-theological awareness and Christological sensitivity need not compete as mutually exclusive adversaries in a zero-sum game. A reading that, alternatively, considers the imprecatory psalms from a redemptive-historical perspective—as godly, pious prayers reflective of a particular moment in God's Christocentric story of the world—has the potential to give due attention to the Christological significance of the psalms in addition to and in light of their historical and theological context.

While the Christological reading appears in one sense too expansive—eclipsing the historical and theological context of the imprecations—this reading seems simultaneously too narrow. Focusing primarily on the identification of Jesus as the supreme petitioner of the psalms, Bonhoeffer and Adams depend upon what may in fact be an overly reductionistic messianic perspective that overlooks the polyvalent Christological and ecclesiological significance of the Psalter. Is Jesus *only* the praying imprecator? Or might the New Testament present him as the typological fulfillment of a variety of the patterns, roles, and hopes that together give the imprecatory psalms their distinctive shape?[83] Is Jesus the *only* praying imprecator? Or might the New Testament depict the church as well through appeal to the imprecator in the psalms?[84] A more flexible, multidimensional intertextual reading holds out the possibility of further clarifying the imprecations'

[82]   This messianic eclipse of historical context is on display in Adams' treatment of Psalm 137. In his interpretation of the rock in v. 9, Adams quickly weaves together rock/stone imagery from Matt 21:42–44; Dan 2:34–35; Num 20:8ff; Ps 114:8; 1 Cor 10:4 to assert that "the 'Daughter of Babylon' and her 'infants' have rejected Christ, the Rock." Adams, *War Psalms*, 111–12, quote 112. This reading too rapidly bypasses the (post)exilic context of Psalm 137, potential historical referents within the prayer, and the web of symbolic and intertextual associations conjured by such imagery in its literary context with its immediate insertion of Jesus into the psalm.

[83]   Adams briefly acknowledges that "there are varying ways in which the Psalms speak of the Christ," noting that Ps 2:7, echoed at Jesus' baptism (e.g., Matt 3:17) and transfiguration (e.g., Matt 17:5), is spoken by the Father about the Son. Adams, *War Psalms*, 25. But Adams' hermeneutical insistence that the psalms be read as prayers of Christ offers little guidance on how to determine when they might in fact be prayers *about* Christ, and he nowhere considers how the imprecatory psalms in particular might speak of the Christ in such varying ways.

[84]   See, e.g., Rev 6:9–10, where the heavenly martyrs are presented as taking up the imprecatory speech of Ps 79:10 in their own Godward prayers for justice.

use in the New Testament, their place in the redemptive narrative of God, their performance in the life of the church, and the existential dynamics of faithful Christian imprecation.[85] Instead, this strict reading of the Psalter as the prayers of Christ may inadvertently flatten out the diversity of the New Testament witness concerning Jesus' and his church's relationship to the psalms and introduce new interpretive challenges to replace those resolved by this proposal.[86]

Undergirding both Bonhoeffer's and Adams' argument that Jesus alone can truly pray the imprecations is a distinct moral logic, an ethical line of reasoning that, if accepted, further justifies their Christological reading of the psalms: "Only one who is just can rightfully accuse others of injustice; only someone who is guiltless can pray this way."[87] But why should this be the case? This perhaps initially intuitive principle does not hold up under closer scrutiny. The function of the Psalter as the worship book of Israel suggests that these psalms were intended to be enacted by the entire covenant community, and prayers for divine vengeance arise in a number of places in the Old Testament, offered by non-Davidic figures to whom specific messianic identification—rooted as it is in Davidic typology—does not strictly apply.[88] Jesus' parable of

---

[85]   Bonhoeffer, "Sermon on a Psalm of Vengeance," 94–96, explores how Christian prayer of the imprecations with Jesus involves recognition of one's own deliverance from judgment in Christ and consequently prompts a posture of humility and thanksgiving. If the imprecatory psalms, however, point to Jesus in multiple ways, then Christian performance of the imprecations that takes such polyvalent Christological significance into account may prompt and cultivate a variety of attitudinal postures within petitioners.

[86]   E.g., whereas the Christological reading brings a certain resolution to an ethical tension of the imprecatory psalms, the assertion that Jesus is the petitioner of the Psalter raises new questions about the penitential psalms. How is Jesus—the innocent one—the primary speaker in the psalmic confessions of guilt? Adams, War Psalms, 27–31, addresses this objection, claiming that Jesus prays such psalms in his capacity as the sinless substitute who bears the guilt of others in order to make atonement. The rigidity and immediacy of Adams' placement of the whole Psalter in the mouth of Christ requires such theological justifications for those aspects of the psalmic prayers that are not transparently reconcilable with Jesus' status and experience.

[87]   Adams, War Psalms, 102. Cf. Bonhoeffer, "Sermon on a Psalm of Vengeance," 86–87.

[88]   Adams, War Psalms, 2, acknowledges the existence of imprecations throughout the Old Testament but does not consider how the non-Davidic character of the imprecators might challenge his view. Cf. Day, "Imprecatory Psalms," 59:

the persistent widow in Luke 18:1–8 also calls into question the insistence that only the perfectly innocent may accuse, for the widow who ceaselessly calls for justice against her adversary is held up as a model for believers' prayers to the God who will give justice with no suggestion that flawless personal righteousness is a prerequisite for such a petition. Such evidence potentially indicates that ethically appropriate petitions for justice may originate in sinful human beings who are themselves at some level guilty of injustice, that individuals other than Jesus may indeed offer faithful imprecatory pleas to God. A broader consideration of Scripture's examples and endorsements of human prayers for divine justice—and the non-messianic identities of the petitioners from whom those prayers originate—invites us to reconsider the moral logic that grounds the Christological interpretation of the imprecatory psalms as the exclusive prayers of Jesus and to reevaluate the corresponding proposal for Christian performance that envisions faithful imprecation primarily as joining with Jesus in his perfectly innocent petitions.[89]

The Christological reading represents an attempt to theologically synthesize a range of biblical material in a manner that both commends the imprecatory psalms and offers practical guidance for their performance in the church. While such a synthesis helpfully permits various portions of Scripture to inform how the psalms are received and practiced, the questions raised by this reading suggest that the details of the Christological proposal require further revision.

Prayers of the Covenant: Covenantal Readings of the Imprecatory Psalms

Several approaches to the imprecatory psalms are united by their foregrounding of the biblical category of covenant. Covenantal readings

---

"If imprecations against one's enemies and the enemies of God are deemed morally legitimate in other parts of Scripture—and these are not rendered legitimate by placing them on the lips of Christ, then this proposal offers no genuine solution to the issue of imprecation in the Psalms, nor to the issue of imprecation in general."

[89]   The pressing ethical question for the imprecatory psalms appears to be not, "How can guilty humans accuse others of injustice?" but rather, "How can humans call for divine justice against others in a manner that is consistent with Jesus' command to love enemies and bless those who curse?" Adams, *War Psalms*, 39–49, devotes an entire chapter to arguing that the prayers of Christ in the imprecatory psalms are consistent with Jesus' prayer for forgiveness of his enemies from the cross, but neither he nor Bonhoeffer attempts to reconcile Christian performance of the imprecatory psalms with Christ's command for enemy love. This leaves Christians in a predicament: How does one pray Jesus' prayers while simultaneously obeying Jesus' commands?

interpret the judgment psalms within the theological context and ethical framework established by God's revelation to and relationship with Israel while simultaneously situating the church—God's new covenant community—in relation to the old covenant prayers for vengeance in a manner that illuminates how Christians should appropriate the imprecations in their own practice. Despite their utilization of the same organizing concept, covenantal readings are distinguishable on the basis of their formulation of the relationship between the various scriptural covenants. *How do God's covenantal arrangements with Israel and the church fit together?* is a question each covenantal reading must answer, and the diverse answers offered introduce significant differences between their evaluations of the ethical appropriateness of the imprecatory psalms and their proposals for Christian performance. Covenant proves to be a flexible controlling category, allowing for a variety of positions regarding the connection between the testaments, and is thus utilized by scholars from a range of theological traditions who operate from sometimes disparate doctrinal presuppositions.

Covenantal Inferiority: The Imprecations as Sub-Christian Prayers

One explication of the covenantal reading understands the imprecatory psalms as born from and expressive of a lower morality, endemic to God's covenant with Israel, relative to the ethics of the new covenant community articulated by Jesus. This reading interprets the psalmic prayers for vengeance as emerging from a sub-Christian covenantal arrangement and concomitant ethical paradigm that is not merely different from the moral vision of the New Testament but is fundamentally substandard—inferior—by comparison.[90] The scriptural

---

[90] Questions surrounding the alleged inferiority of the old covenant to the new covenant are related to broader scholarly debates concerning the relationship between Judaism and Christianity. E. P. Sanders, *Paul and Palestinian Judaism: A Comparison of Patterns of Religion* (Philadelphia: Fortress, 1977), 33–59, offers an academic genealogy that traces the proliferation of negative evaluations of Judaism among Christian (especially New Testament) scholars. Sanders follows the rise of this perspective from Ferdinand Weber (1836–1879) through Wilhelm Bousset (1865–1920) to Paul Billerbeck (1853–1932) and Rudolf Bultmann (1884–1976). Sanders argues that for Weber, "Judaism is the antithesis of Christianity," a religion in which grace is rendered fundamentally inoperative. Sanders, *Paul and Palestinian Judaism*, 38. According to Sanders' analysis, however, it is Bultmann, for whom "Judaism is the foil over against which the superiority of Jesus is presented," who truly popularizes the negative appraisal of Judaism as essentially legalistic and lacking in the grace so present

progression from old covenant to new covenant is depicted as a shift from a problematic Jewish ethic that permits hateful enemy cursing to a higher and more acceptable Christian ethic that adjures enemy love and prohibits imprecation.

Artur Weiser forcefully articulates this perspective in his commentary on Ps 58:10–11, in which the psalmist declares that the righteous will celebrate when the divine vengeance requested in vv. 6–9 is finally revealed:

> Though ultimately the cause of God is at stake in that judgment, the psalm's conclusion, speaking of the effect of the judgment on the righteous, shows on the other hand the undisguised gloating and the cruel vindictiveness of an intolerant religious fanaticism (cf. Ps 68:23); it is one of those dangerous poisonous blossoms which are liable to grow even on the tree of religious knowledge and clearly show the limits set to the Old Testament religion.[91]

In his discussions of the imprecatory language of Psalms 41 and 54, Weiser argues that Old Testament thought is bound by all-too-human emotions of indignation and vindictiveness, which detrimentally influence the psalmists' conceptions of and relationship to God. He also argues that such prayers, when rightly subjected to the critical judgment of the New Testament perspective, fail to attain the heights of Christian morality.[92] The psalmists' cries for justice are thus evaluated by the standards of New Testament ethics and found lacking.[93]

William L. Holladay approaches the imprecations similarly. Pointing to the instructions of both Jesus and Paul to lovingly bless one's oppressors, Holladay asserts that the spirit of the New Testament diverges markedly from the spirit of hatred evident in the psalmists' petitions for vengeance against their enemies.[94] Sympathizing with those who declare,

---

in Christianity. Sanders, *Paul and Palestinian Judaism*, 44. Much of Sanders' work is aimed at challenging such conceptions of Judaism, particularly second temple Judaism, and its relationship to Christianity. Cf. also Sanders, *Jesus and Judaism* (Philadelphia: Fortress, 1985).

[91]   Weiser, *Psalms*, 432.

[92]   Weiser, *Psalms*, 345, 416–17.

[93]   Cf. Weiser's comments on Psalms 15; 91; 139; Weiser, *Psalms*, 170, 613, 807. Zenger, *God of Vengeance?* 14–15, extensively quotes Weiser in his critique of this interpretive approach to the imprecatory psalms.

[94]   Holladay, *Long Ago God Spoke*, 302.

"The Psalms are sub-Christian,"[95] and who pine for a less objectionable Christian Psalter, Holladay argues that the imprecations are the product of mistaken Old Testament theological assumptions, particularly concerning the nature of the self. The psalmists' desires for judgment emerge, Holladay maintains, from a vision of a unified self—undivided by conflicting passions and motivations—that justifies the misguided conviction that the psalmists themselves are entirely pure, wholly innocent, free of any participation in the wickedness against which they lob their curses.[96] "When [the psalmist] refers to the evil in the world . . . then he locates that evil entirely *out there*, external to himself. He is, in short, self-righteous."[97] From Holladay's perspective, erroneous theological assumptions introduce inappropriate modes of communion into the psalmists' covenantal life with God. The imprecatory psalms are therefore the ethically inferior and "psychologically naïve" fruit of an Old Testament anthropology much in need of New Testament correction.[98] Despite this evaluation of the Psalter's judgment petitions, Holladay asserts that Christians may benefit from the imprecatory psalms—not by utilizing them to call for vengeance but by finding in them resources for empathetically identifying with

[95]   Holladay, *Long Ago God Spoke*, 302. Holladay recounts that he knew a spiritual director who expressed such a sentiment and continues, "If this is so, then on the face of it we cannot dependably hear God's will for our worship in the Psalms. What resources can we marshal in these difficulties?" Holladay never explicitly refers to the imprecatory psalms as sub-Christian in his own words, but in his sympathetic citation of the spiritual director's perspective, he assumes the legitimacy of the covenantal inferiority reading as a starting point for his investigation.

[96]   Holladay, *Long Ago God Spoke*, 302–5. Holladay's characterization of the vision of the self that is operative in the psalms is unconvincing, however. Even a cursory reading of those psalms often categorized as penitential (e.g., Psalm 51) reveals the psalmists' acute awareness of their penchant for unfaithfulness in the midst of competing desires for faithfulness. Such prayers of repentance are, after all, the prayers of the faithful regarding their acknowledged unfaithfulness. In addition, the back-and-forth internal dialogue of the laments in Psalms 42–43 evidences the self-understanding of one who simultaneously hopes and fails to hope in God, who recognizes his dividedness and intentionally seeks to address his conflicting affections. Considered as a whole, the psalms do not present the overly simplistic and undernuanced vision of the self that Holladay suggests.

[97]   Holladay, *Long Ago God Spoke*, 304, emphasis original.

[98]   Holladay, *Long Ago God Spoke*, 304, 310, quote 310.

victims of violence,[99] introspectively discerning the destructive dimensions of one's personality,[100] and hearing the Godward prayers of the innocent Christ.[101] With these strategies for interacting with the imprecations, Holladay seeks to recover some usefulness from prayers which, because of their inadequate morality, cannot be recited in their plain sense.

For Weiser and Holladay, the imprecatory psalms grow out of and evince a covenantal framework and corresponding ethic that is tainted by Israel's incorrect conceptions of God, herself in relation to God, and the moral obligations of life with God. That is, the inferiority of the Old Testament ethics exhibited in the imprecatory psalms is a product of confused human deliberation concerning the nature and obligations of the covenant relationship. It is not the covenant as a God-given structure that is deficient, but Israel's understanding of the covenant.

Whereas Weiser and Holladay argue that Israel's perceptions of the covenant permit imprecation because of the contamination of human emotion and improper theological convictions, Roy Zuck conceives of the covenant as a divinely instituted relationship that accurately reflects God's will for Israel as his covenant nation.[102] Approaching the imprecatory psalms from a dispensational evangelical perspective,[103] Zuck main-

---

[99] Holladay, *Long Ago God Spoke*, 308–9.

[100] Holladay, *Long Ago God Spoke*, 309–16. Holladay makes a series of creative moves in defense of this approach. First, he spiritualizes the enemies of the psalms such that the target of Christian imprecatory prayer becomes "Jesus' enemies, namely Satan and the demons, whom God wishes to defeat." Holladay, *Long Ago God Spoke*, 309. Second, sensitive to modern skepticism regarding the existence of such demonic spiritual forces, Holladay *despiritualizes* his spiritualization, connecting the biblical testimony regarding demons to the experience of "the demonic forces in our personalities" such as low self-esteem, ethnocentrism, and addiction. Holladay, *Long Ago God Spoke*, 313. Holladay thus alleviates the ethical attention associated with cursing human beings with a spiritualization that coheres with modern naturalistic proclivities.

[101] Holladay, *Long Ago God Spoke*, 316–17. Though Holladay's proposal here bears similarities to the Christological readings of Bonhoeffer and Adams, he neither identifies Jesus as the true petitioner of the imprecations (with and through the original psalmists) nor advocates Christian participation with Christ in his prayers. Rather, Holladay's brief articulation presents Jesus as one who may legitimately take up the imprecations as his own as Christians "watch and listen as Jesus Christ prays the psalms." Holladay, *Long Ago God Spoke*, 316.

[102] See Zuck, "Problem of the Imprecatory Psalms," 19.

[103] Dispensationalism is a hermeneutical framework that became popular among evangelicals in the early twentieth century, due in large part to the

tains that the covenantal ethics demonstrated in the imprecatory psalms express, from the privileged vantage of the New Testament, a lower stage of morality that arises from God's decision to reveal less to and require less from Israel.[104] Crucial to Zuck's argument is a particular notion of progressive revelation, wherein the progression of God's self-revelation toward greater clarity correlates with an analogous progression of God's moral demands from lower to higher stages.[105] As Zuck maintains:

> The imprecatory psalms, then, find their place in the progress of the unfolding of morality which coincides with the unfolding of revelational content. It is true that David lived in a dispensation when the higher moral precepts of the New Testament were not in existence; he lived during the time of the Law, a dispensation which was preparatory to the Gospel.[106]

The members of the old covenant community who had neither heard the teachings of Christ, nor witnessed the example of Christ, nor received the permanent indwelling of the Spirit of Christ were not obligated to conduct themselves according to the more advanced ethics of Christ.[107] This interpretation allows Zuck to simultaneously affirm the God-givenness and inspiration of the imprecatory psalms while relegating them to a lower ethical plane.

In defense of his lower-higher distinction between the Old and New Testaments, Zuck argues, "There exists in the two testaments an obvious

---

publication of the Scofield Reference Bible. See C. Blaising, "Dispensation, Dispensationalism," in *EDT*, 343–44. Dispensationalism understands Israel and the church to be distinct institutions under distinct covenantal arrangements that give rise to distinct promises and reflect distinct purposes in God's plan.

[104] Zuck, "Problem of the Imprecatory Psalms," 56–57. Cf. Zuck, "Problem of the Imprecatory Psalms," 63, 70, 73.

[105] Zuck, "Problem of the Imprecatory Psalms," 56–58. Zuck is careful to emphasize that this ethical progression is not from the immoral to the moral but only from the lower to the higher. It is not immediately apparent, however, precisely how a lower ethic (which permits conduct a higher ethic would prohibit) manages to totally avoid the charge of immorality.

[106] Zuck, "Problem of the Imprecatory Psalms," 58; cf. Zuck, "Problem of the Imprecatory Psalms," 73. See also Scroggie, *Guide to the Psalms*, 32.

[107] Zuck, "Problem of the Imprecatory Psalms," 57: "We know that in Old Testament times God did not require as much of those who were not permanently indwelt by the Holy Spirit as he does of us today whose bodies are the temple of the Holy Spirit." Cf. Zuck, "Problem of the Imprecatory Psalms," 63.

distinction in regard to one's attitude toward enemies."[108] By his reading, the Old Testament conspicuously lacks any command to forgive or love the obstinate opponents of God,[109] while the New Testament is replete with explicit injunctions and imitable examples of love and forgiveness toward enemies, most notably in Jesus' Sermon on the Mount.[110] The imprecatory psalms may be devoid of enemy love, Zuck reasons, but that is because the inferior covenantal ethics of the Old Testament enjoin no such duty. Though Zuck asserts that the New Testament manifests a higher morality, he nevertheless concedes that numerous imprecations arise from its pages.[111] These invocations of divine judgment are, however, only directed against those enemies Zuck identifies as "avowed adversaries of the Lord,"[112] those "inexorably opposed and relentlessly antagonistic to the gospel of Jesus Christ,"[113] and Zuck understands this to be a sufficient explanation for the apparent deviation from the New Testament's overall posture toward enemies. The practical conclusion of Zuck's argument is that Christians must demonstrate love by praying for the salvation and conversion of their enemies but may also—following Paul's apostolic example—offer imprecatory petitions for the judgment of God against hardened, obdurate enemies of Christ's kingdom.[114]

---

[108] Zuck, "Problem of the Imprecatory Psalms," 63.

[109] Zuck, "Problem of the Imprecatory Psalms," 60.

[110] Zuck, "Problem of the Imprecatory Psalms," 63–64.

[111] Zuck, "Problem of the Imprecatory Psalms," 64–66. Zuck examines 1 Cor 16:22; Gal 1:8–9; 5:12; 2 Tim 4:14; Rev 6:9–10. Zuck's dispensational paradigm is evident in his interpretation of the prayer in Rev 6:9–10, which he understands to be the Jewish prayer of a Jewish remnant that will be prayed during the period of the great tribulation. Cf. Blaising, "Dispensation, Dispensationalism," in *EDT*, 344: "Dispensationalism is a form of premillennialism and is especially known for its doctrine of the pretribulational rapture as separate from the post-tribulational second advent of Christ."

[112] Zuck, "Problem of the Imprecatory Psalms," 64.

[113] Zuck, "Problem of the Imprecatory Psalms," 66.

[114] Zuck, "Problem of the Imprecatory Psalms," 77–79. Zuck approvingly quotes Franz Delitzsch, *Biblical Commentary on the Psalms*, trans. Francis Bolton (Grand Rapids: Eerdmans, 1952), 1:74: "The desire for their [enemies'] removal is certainly outweighed by the desire for their conversion; but, assuming, that they will not be converted and will not anticipate their punishment by penitence, the transition from a feeling of love to that of wrath is warranted in the New Testament (e.g., Gal 5:12), and assuming their absolute Satanic hardness of heart the Christian even may not shrink from praying for their final overthrow." Zuck, "Problem of the Imprecatory Psalms," 78. Zuck,

Zuck's articulation of the covenantal inferiority reading of the imprecatory psalms raises several significant questions for his specific proposal
and the covenantal inferiority approach in general. The first concerns
Zuck's evaluation of Old Testament ethics. Is his claim that the Old Testament lacks any mandate of enemy love indeed accurate? This is a pivotal
component of Zuck's contention regarding the inferiority of old covenant
ethics, but texts such as Exod 23:4–5 and Prov 25:21 enjoin members of
the covenant community to perform concrete acts of mercy for the benefit
of their enemies, and Lev 19:17–18 prohibits harboring hatred, bearing
a grudge, or exercising vengeance against a neighbor who has presumably committed an offense.[115] In addition, Zuck neglects to consider how
a narrative might mold moral imagination with regard to the other (e.g.,
Josh 2; 6:22–25), how accounts of exemplary figures practicing the nonviolent eschewal of retribution might implicitly present such actions as
ethically admirable and worthy of imitation (e.g., 1 Sam 24–25), or how
problematic episodes might encourage moral reflection or warn against
similar behaviors (e.g., 2 Sam 21:1–14).[116] Zuck may be right that the
Old Testament never commands forgiveness and love toward enemies in
those precise terms, but to then conclude that the Old Testament lacks
prescriptions of enemy love entirely—or that Old Testament commands

---

however, makes no mention of how one might distinguish an enemy as sufficiently unrepentant to warrant imprecation. Every enemy appears hardened
and obdurate in the moment. How long must such opposition continue, how
many overtures for reconciliation must be rebuffed, before an enemy may
be deemed an "inveterate, confirmed transgressor"? Zuck, "Problem of the
Imprecatory Psalms," 78.

[115]   Cf. Jace Broadhurst, "Should Cursing Continue? An Argument for
Imprecatory Psalms in Biblical Theology," *AJET* 23, no. 1 (2004): 72; Day,
"Imprecatory Psalms," 151–53; Nomeriano C. Bernardino, "A Reconsideration
of 'Imprecations' in the Psalms," (ThM thesis, Calvin Theological Seminary,
1986), 22–23; John Shepherd, "The Place of the Imprecatory Psalms in the
Canon of Scripture," *Chu* 111, no. 2 (1997): 111; Allen P. Ross, *A Commentary on the Psalms: Volume 1 (1–41)*, KEL (Grand Rapids: Kregel Publications,
2011), 115–16; J. Carl Laney, "A Fresh Look at the Imprecatory Psalms," *BSac*
138 (1981): 39. Lewis, *Reflections on the Psalms*, 26, suggests that such texts
demonstrate the consistency of Old Testament ethics with the New Testament,
though he maintains that the imprecations flout both.

[116]   On the paradigmatic potential of Old Testament narrative, see Christo-
pher J. H. Wright, *Old Testament Ethics for the People of God* (Downers Grove,
Ill.: InterVarsity Press, 2004), 70. Cf. John Barton, *Understanding Old Testament
Ethics: Approaches and Explorations* (Louisville: Westminster John Knox, 2003), 4.

of love necessarily exclude enemies[117]—seems to involve an impoverished understanding of the way Scripture may communicate ethical instruction and make moral claims on the people of God.[118] Perhaps the disjunction between the ethics of the Old Testament and New Testament is not as substantial as Zuck supposes.

A second question focuses on the presence of imprecatory language in the New Testament. Zuck readily acknowledges that the New Testament contains numerous instances of imprecation that parallel the petitions of the Psalter.[119] Seeking to ameliorate the apparent inconsistency of the New Testament's vengeful petitions with its calls to enemy love, Zuck suggests that New Testament imprecation is solely directed against recalcitrant enemies of God,[120] but it is not immediately clear how he envisions such prayers harmonizing with—rather than contravening—Christ's commands,[121] and these same recalcitrant enemies of God are indeed the very people whom

---

[117] Zuck, "Problem of the Imprecatory Psalms," 60–63, surveys a variety of Old Testament texts (e.g., Exod 23:9; Lev 19:18, 34; Deut 10:19), concluding that such commands concern fellow Israelites and resident aliens, not enemies. This of course neglects the possibility that these categories may overlap considerably, as in Ps 55:9–15, where the enemy against whom the psalmist petitions is a (presumably Israelite) companion who participated in the temple assembly with the psalmist.

[118] William Klassen, *Love of Enemies: The Way to Peace* (Eugene, Ore.: Wipf and Stock, 2002), 28: "The commandment, 'love your enemy,' occurs nowhere in the Old Testament. The concept, however, cannot be confined to the words themselves. When enemies are fed and cared for, rather than killed or mistreated, then in effect love for the enemy is being practiced." Cf. Day, "Imprecatory Psalms," 151–52.

[119] Zuck, "Problem of the Imprecatory Psalms," 64–66. Cf. Hans-Joachim Kraus, *Theology of the Psalms*, trans. Keith Crim (Minneapolis: Augsburg, 1986), 67: "It is expected that Yahweh will manifest his power in the world of the nations. Not alone in the Old Testament, but in the New Testament as well there is a certainty that this will not take place in an invisible, ideal realm of retribution, but in the reality of this world. Therefore there rings out a cry for revenge and for God's judgment in the face of the unbearable suffering and torment of God's people, on down to the Revelation of John (6:10)."

[120] Zuck, "Problem of the Imprecatory Psalms," 64–66.

[121] Zuck states that "though some valid imprecations do occur in the New Testament—the testament of love, tenderness, and grace toward enemies—they are all instances of denunciations upon those who are inexorably opposed and relentlessly antagonistic to the gospel of Jesus Christ." Zuck, "Problem of the Imprecatory Psalms," 66. However, he offers no explanation as to how identifying the objects of New Testament imprecation as enemies of the gospel

he argues the psalmic petitions target.[122] By Zuck's own admission, the two testaments contain similar imprecatory language aimed at similar groups of people. On what basis, then, can the inferiority-superiority distinction between the covenants and their ethics be maintained?[123]

Taken together, these questions introduce significant concerns regarding the adequacy of the covenantal structure appealed to by the proponents of covenantal inferiority readings. If the Old Testament advocates enemy love in a manner consistent with the New, and if the New Testament permits imprecation against God's opponents in a manner consistent with the Old, then the viability of this proposed relationship between the old and new covenants—as one of inferiority and superiority, the lesser and the greater, the lower and the higher—sustains a serious challenge and therefore may not provide the most suitable framework for discerning proper Christian engagement with the imprecatory psalms.

Covenantal Discontinuity: The Imprecations as Faithful Old Covenant Prayers

A second iteration of the covenantal reading also interprets the imprecatory psalms as a product of God's revelatory relationship with Israel and Israel's corresponding ethical responsibilities. Unlike covenantal inferiority readings, however, which evaluate the psalmic prayers for vengeance as indicative of a lower morality, covenantal discontinuity readings conceive of the imprecatory psalms as faithful expressions of piety—ethically appropriate forms of communion with God—in the framework of God's dealings with the Israelite nation. Whereas inferiority proposals portray the shift from old covenant to new covenant as a progression from lower to higher, discontinuity proposals abstain from such evaluative appraisals, instead emphasizing the presence of *difference* between the covenant arrangements governing Israel and the Christian church and the corresponding difference regarding the ethical fittingness of imprecation for both communities. As will become evident, covenantal discontinuity proposals are by no means monolithic; the specific points of discontinuity

---

alleviates the tension between such prayers and his characterization of the New Testament as the testament of love toward enemies.

[122] Zuck, "Problem of the Imprecatory Psalms," 69.

[123] Neither Weiser nor Holladay makes mention of the presence of New Testament imprecations in their treatments of the imprecatory psalms. This omission prevents them from offering a justification for the lower-higher distinction between the covenants, which takes into account the parallel language of the New Testament.

highlighted vary, as do the visions of ethical Christian imprecation. Yet they are united in positing disjunction between Israelite and Christian ethics on the basis of distinctiveness in God's action and revelation before and after the coming of Christ.

American evangelical J. Carl Laney argues that the Abrahamic covenant of Gen 12:1–3 establishes the fundamental theological justification for imprecation in Israel.[124] Because God promises to curse those who dishonor Abraham and his descendants, Laney reasons that the psalmists have moral warrant to petition God to act in keeping with his covenantal word.[125] God's commitment to exact judgment upon those who oppose Abraham's family therefore legitimizes the Israelite practice of imprecatory prayer against their enemies. John Shepherd—an evangelical Anglican scholar—similarly connects the ethical propriety of the imprecatory psalms with the divine guarantees of the Abrahamic covenant,[126] but Shepherd also suggests that the curses of Deuteronomy 27–28, which outline the judgments that will befall Israelite rebellion against God's law, are relevant to the covenantal matrix from which the psalms of vengeance emerge.[127] In Shepherd's view, the Pentateuch establishes God's intention to curse both antagonists external to the covenant community and opponents internal to the assembly of God's people, thereby providing a covenantal rationale for the permissibility of imprecation, irrespective of the enemy's identity and origin.[128]

While the psalmists were morally right to request divine justice against their foes within the parameters of God's revelation to and purposes for Israel, advocates of covenantal discontinuity readings stress that the Christian church relates to God through a novel covenant arrangement that renders imprecation—at least in the form exhibited in the psalms—ethically inappropriate. Arguing from a characteristically dispensational perspective that envisions the Abrahamic covenant as applying solely to the physical descendants of Abraham,[129] Laney maintains that Christians lack the

---

[124] Carl Laney, "A Fresh Look at the Imprecatory Psalms," *BSac* 138 (1981): 41–42.

[125] Laney, "Fresh Look," 42.

[126] Shepherd, "Place of the Imprecatory Psalms," 115.

[127] Shepherd, "Place of the Imprecatory Psalms," 115–17; cf. Adams, *War Psalms*, 57–59.

[128] Shepherd, "Place of the Imprecatory Psalms," 117.

[129] H. H. Rowdon, "Dispensational Theology," in *NDT*, 201, notes that the fundamental hermeneutical commitment of dispensationalism is to literal interpretation. Dispensationalism asserts that "the promises of an earthly kingdom given to Israel as a nation must be fulfilled literally in a future, millennial kingdom," and "the

covenantal basis for petitioning divine judgment against their enemies.[130] Drawing an analogy to Old Testament dietary regulations, Laney asserts that the imprecations are similarly obsolescent, no longer germane to the structure and dynamics of the church's covenantal life with God.[131]

Shepherd, by contrast, more readily identifies a place for the imprecatory psalms in Christian piety. While arguing that Christians are prohibited from utilizing these psalms as prayers against specific human opponents, Shepherd nevertheless suggests that Christians may be instructed by the imprecations in various aspects of doctrine and devotion and may direct the imprecatory psalms against demonic forces.[132] Shepherd spiritualizes the targets of the church's imprecatory prayer, claiming that the New Testament teaches that the Christian's true foes are Satan and other spiritual forces, not human beings, and that prayer for human enemies' conversion is the chief means of waging war against such principalities and powers.[133] Faithful Christian prayer in Shepherd's view may include petitions for Christ's return and justice for the victims of hostility, and he acknowledges that such requests implicitly call for judgment on the impenitent as the corollary of God's exercise of justice, but for Shepherd these implicit calls for judgment on humans must remain implicit—that is, nonspecific, contingent ramifications of Christians' explicit prayers for Satan's defeat, human conversion, deliverance for the oppressed, and the coming of Christ.[134]

---

promises made to the natural seed of Abraham await the premillennial return of Christ with his church for their fulfilment." Dispensationalism's principle of literal interpretation thus requires that the promises made to Abraham and his offspring come to literal fruition in two related senses: in the literal terms of the promises, and for the literal nation of Israel as physical descendants of Abraham.

[130]   Laney, "Fresh Look," 44. Laney does not clarify what his position might mean for a church-age believer who is a physical descendant of Abraham—that is, a Jewish Christian.

[131]   Laney, "Fresh Look," 44.

[132]   Shepherd, "Place of the Imprecatory Psalms," 125. Shepherd states that the imprecatory psalms teach Christians concerning the necessity of theocentricity, God's hatred and judgment of sin, the importance of trusting God instead of exacting vengeance, God's vindication of the righteous, and the appropriateness of indignation at everything that opposes God.

[133]   Shepherd, "Place of the Imprecatory Psalms," 125.

[134]   Shepherd, "Place of the Imprecatory Psalms," 125; cf. Tremper Longman III, *How to Read the Psalms* (Downers Grove, Ill.: InterVarsity Press, 1988), 140. J. W. Wenham, *The Goodness of God* (London: InterVarsity Press, 1974), 164–68, alternatively argues that the implicit calls for judgment latent in many

Sharing many affinities with this perspective, Tremper Longman III maintains that the New Testament signals a shift in the covenant community's posture toward outsiders such that judgment prayers may only be offered against spiritual beings and forces, and he too names petitions for human opponents' conversion as the Christian's principal form of antagonistic prayer in opposition to Satan.[135] For H. G. L. Peels, the eschatological character of God's kingdom during the era of the church as both already here and not yet consummated—wherein God's judgment has been revealed at the cross and will be fully revealed at the eschaton—reduces the urgency and frequency of imprecatory petitions.[136] Peels thus calls for an "eschatologizing and partially spiritualizing transformation of the imprecatory prayer,"[137] arguing that the church's redemptive-historical moment is one qualified by grace and patience such that Christians ought to pray for their particular enemies' repentance as they direct performance of the vengeance psalms against the powers of darkness and plead generally for the consummation of the kingdom.[138]

Derek Kidner likewise deems the imprecatory psalms unfit for Christian practice against human enemies. The gospel, Kidner contends, reshapes Christians' attitudes toward their oppressors and experiences of oppression not only by conferring upon them a new identity as messengers of reconciliation for the world,[139] but also by opening up the

---

Christian prayers reveal that the typical unwillingness to explicitly pray for such judgment is both inconsistent and unrealistic.

[135]   Longman, *How to Read the Psalms*, 138–40.

[136]   H. G. L. Peels, *The Vengeance of God: The Meaning of the Root NQM and the Function of the NQM-texts in the Context of Divine Revelation in the Old Testament*, OtSt 31 (Leiden: Brill, 1995), 245–46; Eric Peels, *Shadow Sides: The Revelation of God in the Old Testament* (Carlisle, UK: Paternoster, 2003), 102–4.

[137]   Peels, *Vengeance of God*, 246.

[138]   Peels, *Vengeance of God*, 246: "The Christian imprecatory prayer, in the post-Biblical period, could take the form of a general anathema against all opposing powers. The Christian prays for deliverance from the Evil One, the total breaking of the darkness and the coming of God's kingdom." Christians may thus pray nonspecifically for the consummation of the kingdom, which will mean the judgment of human enemies, and may imprecate against spiritual powers, but Peels prohibits petitions for judgment against specific human enemies, for whom the Christian must pray for conversion. Cf. Peels, *Shadow Sides*, 104; Eric Peels, "'I Hate Them with Perfect Hatred' (Psalm 139:21–22)," *TynBul* 59, no. 1 (2008): 50–51.

[139]   Cf. the claim of Francis Watson, *Text and Truth: Redefining Biblical Theology* (Grand Rapids: Eerdmans, 1997), 119–22, that Psalm 137 "is not

eschatological horizon and assuring them of the certainty of an ultimate judgment and restoration in the age to come.[140] From Kidner's perspective, the Old Testament's focus on temporal justice in the present world and relative lack of clarity regarding the eschatological vindication of God's people in a life that transcends death renders the psalmists' petitions for vengeance understandable.[141] But the New Testament's revelation of a life to come—most notably through the resurrection of Jesus—guarantees justice at the end of history, making pleas for vengeance in the middle of history both unnecessary and inappropriate.[142] Kidner concludes that while the church may affirm God's justice and condemn spiritual enemies, the cross that divides Christians' experience from the psalmists' requires that they pray for their human foes' conversion, not their cursing.[143] James L. Mays and Claus Westermann advance related arguments, linking the Psalter's imprecatory pleas to a limited eschatological perspective that is expanded by the New Testament.[144] Westermann consequently maintains that all prayer against enemies is prohibited for the Christian and recommends that psalms dominated by vengeful rhetoric against enemies not be granted a prominent position in the church's performance and piety,[145] and Mays suggests that Christian ethics as determined by Jesus and Paul disallows any literal appropriation of the imprecatory psalms as prayers against human enemies in Christian worship or prayer.[146]

---

permitted to enact its total communicative intention" for Christians because of the life and teachings of Christ, which make up the center of Christian Scripture. Quote, 121.

[140]   Derek Kidner, *Psalms 1–72: An Introduction and Commentary*, TOTC 15 (Downers Grove, Ill.: InterVarsity Press, 1973), 40.

[141]   Cf. Peels, *Vengeance of God*, 214; "'I Hate Them with Perfect Hatred,'" 50.

[142]   Kidner, *Psalms 1–72*, 40. Cf. Bernhard W. Anderson and Steven Bishop, *Out of the Depths: The Psalms Speak for Us Today*, 3rd ed. (Louisville: Westminster John Knox, 2000), 74–75; John Shepherd, "The Place of the Imprecatory Psalms in the Canon of Scripture," *Chu* 111, no. 1 (1997): 44–45.

[143]   Kidner, *Psalms 1–72*, 46–47.

[144]   James L. Mays, *The Lord Reigns: A Theological Handbook to the Psalms* (Louisville: Westminster John Knox, 1994), 38–39. Claus Westermann, *The Psalms: Structure, Content, and Message*, trans. Ralph D. Gehrke (Minneapolis: Augsburg, 1980), 68–69.

[145]   Westermann, *Psalms*, 69: "Petitions for enemies' destruction (in fact every petition against enemies in general) have once and for all been taken away from Christ's congregation." Cf. Watson, *Text and Truth*, 121.

[146]   Mays, *Lord Reigns*, 38: "Jesus (Matt 5:43–48; Luke 9:51–56) and Paul (Rom 12:14–21) instruct Christians to love, bless, and pray for their enemies.

Reformed evangelical scholars Meredith Kline, Harry Mennega, and Allan Harman utilize the innovative concept of *intrusion* to disconnect the imprecatory psalms from the performance of the church under God's new covenant regime.[147] On this view, since the fall of humanity and the introduction of sin, God has compassionately delayed totalizing judgment and patiently upheld his world by common grace in order that God's special, redeeming grace might be revealed in history and reconcile at least some of his creatures to himself prior to the consummation.[148] During this period of common grace, love of neighbor—even if that neighbor happens to be a hostile enemy—is the normative ethic.[149] With the consummation, however, the unrepentant enemy will become the object of God's unrestrained wrath and therefore the rightful target of the holy

---

That instruction forbids prayer against our human enemies. The use of the imprecations in liturgy in any plain or literal sense is rejected. We remember, however, that the early church established a tradition of opposing sin, death, and the devil with such psalms." Mays appears cautiously open to Christian performance of the imprecations so long as they are directed toward spiritualized referents.

[147] Harry Mennega, "The Ethical Problem of the Imprecatory Psalms" (ThM thesis, Westminster Theological Seminary, 1959), 80–81, and Allan M. Harman, "The Continuity of the Covenant Curses in the Imprecations of the Psalter," *RTR* 54, no. 2 (1995): 71–72, explicitly cite Kline's work and build from his proposals. Cf. Broadhurst, "Should Cursing Continue?" 83–84; G. K. Beale, *The Morality of God in the Old Testament*, Christian Answers to Hard Questions (Philadelphia: Westminster Seminary Press; Phillipsburg, N.J.: P&R Publishing, 2013), 17–27.

[148] Meredith G. Kline, *The Structure of Biblical Authority*, 2nd ed. (Eugene, Ore.: Wipf & Stock, 1997), 155, states that common grace "provides the field of operation for redemptive grace."

[149] Mennega, "Ethical Problem," 83. Cf. Michael Horton, *The Christian Faith: A Systematic Theology for Pilgrims on the Way* (Grand Rapids: Zondervan, 2011), 961. Kline ties this ethic of love to the commingling of elect and reprobate during the era of common grace. Prior to the consummation, God's people are unable to know with certainty whom God has secretly chosen, and "we may not seek to destroy those for whom, perchance, Christ has died." Kline, *Structure of Biblical Authority*, 161; cf. Johannes G. Vos, "The Ethical Problem of the Imprecatory Psalms," *WTJ* 4 (1942): 137–38. Johannes Vos' reading of the imprecatory psalms posits that ethical imprecation against specific persons requires supernaturally revealed knowledge of the enemies' status in the eternal decrees of God, a knowledge that the inspired psalmists possessed but that Christians lack. For an extended summary and critique of his approach to the imprecations, see my "Cursing with God: The Imprecatory Psalms and the Ethics of Christian Prayer" (PhD diss., University of Exeter, 2020), 70–81.

hatred of the righteous.[150] Kline argues that at various points in the Old Testament, the ethics of consummation intrudes into the era of common grace, temporarily interrupting this age of common grace and abrogating its concomitant moral obligations as an anticipatory revelation of God's judgment. Such intrusions are moments of realized eschatology when God's consummation-era activity breaks into the normal flow of human history, and the imprecatory psalms are one dimension of this intrusion.[151] The psalmic petitions for divine vengeance thus operate in accordance with the intruding ethics of consummation, pleading for immediate manifestations of judgment in the present.[152] Since this reading understands intrusion as a unique feature of the Old Testament, "the [Christian] believer's attitudes toward the unbeliever are conditioned by the principle of common grace."[153] The church, therefore, may not take up the imprecatory psalms as her own prayers against her human enemies because the intruding ethics of consummation that justified their calls for judgment do not apply to the people of the new covenant.[154]

The intrusion proposal provides an intriguing lens for reading the imprecatory psalms, utilizing the explanatory concept of eschatology in addition to the category of covenant to interpret the imprecations and discern their connection to Christians. For Kline, Mennega, and Harman, the psalms of vengeance must be read from a biblical-theological perspective that considers the eschatological character of the kingdom of God as manifested in Israel and the typological significance of this kingdom

[150]   Kline, *Structure of Biblical Authority*, 159–60.

[151]   Kline, *Structure of Biblical Authority*, 158–62. Kline contends, "The Intrusion has realized eschatology as its core," maintaining that many dimensions of Israel's life and governance serve as an anticipatory instantiation of the completed eschatological kingdom of God, embodying its principles in history in a manner that points forward to the consummation. Kline, *Structure of Biblical Authority*, 158. Cf. Mennega, "Ethical Problem," 84.

[152]   Kline, *Structure of Biblical Authority*, 161–62. Cf. Mennega, "Ethical Problem," 83–84; Harman, "Continuity of the Covenant Curses," 72.

[153]   Kline, *Structure of Biblical Authority*, 161.

[154]   Mennega, "Ethical Problem," 89–92, maintains that, on the basis of Eph 6:12, the church's enemies are spiritual forces in opposition to God, concluding that Christians should practice the imprecations in reference to the spiritual kingdom of Satan. Horton, *Christian Faith*, 961–62: "The imprecatory Psalms, invoking God's judgment on enemies, are appropriate on the lips of David and the martyrs in heaven. However, they are entirely out of place on the lips of Christians today, guided as we are not by the ethics of intrusion but by the ethics of common grace."

structure in the progression of redemptive history.[155] The claim that God's administration over his covenant people in the Old Testament is best understood in terms of an anticipatory realized eschatology creatively clarifies the immediacy of the psalmic prayers for judgment and opens further avenues for inquiry into the relationship between the eschatological character of God's kingdom at different stages of redemptive history and the ethical propriety of imprecation for his kingdom citizens at any given moment. Intrusion proponents prioritize the concept of common grace when considering the Christian's moral obligations,[156] but is common grace in fact the most appropriate theological category in which to ground the ethics of the new covenant community and our reflection upon them? How might the distinct eschatological features of Christ's inaugurated kingdom in the age between his resurrection and *parousia* shed light on proper Christian performance of the imprecatory psalms?[157] Such a specific exploration of the relationship between eschatology and ethics may yield fruitful contributions to research on the moral fitness of Christian practice of the imprecations.

The overall framework of the discontinuity approach—with its principal emphasis on the difference between the arrangement and concomitant ethics of the old and new covenants—neither requires nor precludes any one specific doctrine of Scripture or judgment but may be utilized by scholars working from a variety of theological presuppositions.[158] Intriguingly, this

[155] Kline, *Structure of Biblical Authority*, 162.

[156] Kline, *Structure of Biblical Authority*, 161–62. Kline associates the moral obligations of the new covenant with the "ethical requirements normally in force during the course of common grace" into which the ethics of consummation intrudes. Kline, *Structure of Biblical Authority*, 162. Cf. Harman, "Continuity of the Covenant Curses," 72; Mennega, "Ethical Problem," 83. Kline unpacks his understanding of common grace further in his *Kingdom Prologue: Genesis Foundations for a Covenantal Worldview* (Eugene, Ore.: Wipf and Stock, 2006), 153–60, 244–62.

[157] Peels, *Vengeance of God*, 245–46; and *Shadow Sides*, 102–4, considers the eschatological character of Christ's already-not-yet kingdom, concluding that Christian imprecation is most appropriately directed at spiritual forces or modified into general calls for the consummation of the kingdom during this era of patience and grace. But does Peels' conclusion adequately account for the specific imprecations in the New Testament? The presence of imprecatory language in the New Testament that is aimed at particular human beings suggests that there may be significant features of the postresurrection, pre-*parousia* kingdom of God that Peels has not considered.

[158] Cf., e.g., Westermann, *Psalms*, 10; Laney, "Fresh Look," 38.

perspective on the relationship between the covenants allows evangelical interpreters in particular the freedom to unequivocally affirm the inspiration of the imprecatory psalms as God-given Scripture and the ethical faithfulness of imprecation in the context of the old covenant while simultaneously denying the performance of the psalmic curses as a valid Christian practice—at least without substantial modification.[159] With frameworks for synthesizing the Bible that, in spite of their idiosyncrasies, similarly underscore the distinction between the covenantal configurations governing the ethics of the psalmists and the church, many advocates of discontinuity readings are able to articulate a vision of Christian appropriation of the imprecatory psalms that either spiritualizes their referents or prohibits their utilization altogether and yet still receive these prayers as God's word in a manner consistent with standard evangelical understandings of Scripture.

A structuring of the biblical covenants that foregrounds discontinuity between the administration and ethics of the old and new covenants also permits evangelical interpreters to hold convictions regarding retributive eschatological divine justice and simultaneously endorse a functional distancing of the imprecations from the life of the church. Evangelical proponents of this discontinuity approach do not prohibit or significantly adapt Christian appropriation of the imprecatory psalms primarily because of a vision of judgment that is inconsistent with eschatological retribution. To the contrary, such proponents frequently demonstrate the viable coexistence of the discontinuity framework with evangelical visions of divine justice through explicit affirmations that God in Christ will indeed exact vengeance on his impenitent enemies.[160] The proposed relationship of discontinuity between the old and new covenants, however, enables interpreters to recommend that Christian petitioners zealously hope in God's eschatological vengeance while abstaining from active petition for the realization of such vengeance against specific persons.[161] For the discontinuity reading, the chief factor in determining the impropriety of Christian performance of the imprecatory psalms is not the incompatibility of such

---

[159] See Longman, *How to Read the Psalms*, 138–39; Horton, *Christian Faith*, 962.

[160] See, e.g., Laney, "Fresh Look," 44; Kidner, *Psalms 1–72*, 40; Kline, *Structure of Biblical Authority*, 161–62; Mennega, "Ethical Problem," 67–70; Shepherd, "Place of the Imprecatory Psalms," 123.

[161] In the case of Kidner, *Psalms 1–72*, 40, this hope of retributive justice—expanded and clarified in the New Testament—facilitates and empowers abstention from prayer for retributive justice.

prayers with God's ultimate intentions regarding judgment but rather the alleged incompatibility of such prayers with the current covenant arrangement that organizes the ethical life of Christ's church. On this view, the new covenant—without abrogating perforce the expectation of God's retributive justice—requires a novel response to this retributive justice that proscribes the invocation of divine judgment against human enemies in prayer. Discontinuity readings therefore relieve the tension between the imprecatory psalms and Christ's command of enemy love by removing imprecation (at least in its most straightforward forms) from Christian practice without necessarily compromising standard evangelical convictions concerning Scripture and judgment.

The various discontinuity readings, however, raise issues that warrant critical examination. Laney's evangelical dispensationalism undergirds his argument that the Abrahamic covenant, which provides the covenantal basis for Israel's practice of imprecation, applies exclusively to the physical descendants of Abraham. But does this understanding of the Abrahamic covenant comport with the Pauline contention that by faith in Jesus, Gentiles are made members of Abraham's family and blessed with Abraham in accordance with God's promises to the patriarch?[162] The New Testament claim that people of any ethnic background may be made Abraham's offspring and heirs through faith in the gospel suggests that Laney's structuring of the covenants, which provides the foundation for his eschewal of Christian imprecation, merits reconsideration.

Further, the diverse iterations of the covenantal discontinuity reading, with their focus on the distinctions between God's revelation to and action with Israel and the church, ultimately face the same obstacle that challenges every other proposal that removes the imprecatory psalms from Christians' lips—namely, the instances of imprecation in the New Testament. Can discontinuity readings satisfactorily account for all the biblical data? Shepherd, Peels, and Mennega acknowledge the presence of New Testament imprecatory language,[163] but none considers how such petitions for vengeance against specific human opponents might conflict with their proposed stipulations about the appropriate referents of Christian imprecatory prayer. Kidner addresses what he refers

---

[162] See, e.g., Gal 3:7–29; Rom 2:29; 4:11–16. Cf. Day, "Imprecatory Psalms," 46.

[163] Shepherd, "Place of the Imprecatory Psalms," 120–22; Peels, *Shadow Sides*, 101–2; Mennega, "Ethical Problem," 39–40. Each considers 1 Cor 16:22; Gal 1:9; 5:12; Rev 6:10. Longman, *How to Read the Psalms*, 138–40, does not address the existence of New Testament imprecation.

to as "the occasional equivalent of cursing in the New Testament,"[164] yet he rather conspicuously omits the clearest New Testament examples of prayer for divine judgment that push against his contention that the New Testament's expanded eschatological horizon invalidates the Christian practice of imprecation against human foes. Kline, on the other hand, makes no mention of New Testament imprecation whatsoever, neglecting a significant opportunity to clarify how his understandings of intrusion and the ethics of common grace harmonize with this ostensibly incompatible scriptural evidence. If the New Testament writings neither shun imprecation nor exclusively spiritualize their calls for justice by directing them against demonic forces—if, stated positively, they actively imprecate against God's human enemies—then the proposals for Christian engagement with the imprecatory psalms advanced by proponents of the covenantal discontinuity approach problematically diverge from the practice of the New Testament authors. Might there exist a greater continuity between the old and new covenants than discontinuity readings detect?

Covenantal Continuity:
The Imprecations as Faithful Old and New Covenant Prayers

Covenantal continuity readings of the imprecatory psalms, like all covenantal readings, interpret the psalmic curses as arising from the theo-ethical matrix of Israel's relationship with God. Contrary to the inferiority and discontinuity approaches, however, continuity readings maintain that there exists a fundamental unity and connectedness between the old covenant that governed life in Israel and the new covenant that dictates faithful piety in the Christian church.

In his doctoral dissertation on the imprecatory psalms, John N. Day offers the most detailed and extensive articulation of the continuity reading. Day argues that the psalmists' practice of cursing is theologically rooted in the Abrahamic covenant (Gen 12:1–3), the Song of Moses (Deut 32), and the principle of divine justice contained in the *lex talionis*.[165] According to Day, God's vow to curse those who curse Abraham and his family provides the covenantal foundation for imprecation such that petitions for divine vengeance are valid and faithful pleas for God

---

[164] Kidner, *Psalms 1–72*, 46. Among these alleged equivalents Kidner includes Mark 11:14; 12:9; Rev 2ff.; 1 Cor 5:5; 2 Tim 4:14.

[165] Day, "Imprecatory Psalms," 3; cf. Day, "Imprecatory Psalms," 98.

to act on the basis of his binding promises.[166] The Song of Moses, with its God-given promises of vengeance on enemies and vindication of the covenant community, serves a similar function—justifying the practice of imprecation—and Day detects allusions to Deuteronomy 32 in a number of psalms.[167] Day additionally maintains that the "law of just recompense"[168] as summarized in the *lex talionis*, which mandates that retributive judicial action be proportionate to the offense, provides a divine standard of justice that both legitimizes and limits imprecation. This *lex talionis* legitimizes requests for proportionate divine retribution in reaction to injustice while simultaneously limiting requests to commensurate responses and disallowing prayers for excessive punishment.[169] In Day's reading, the covenantal structures of the Abrahamic covenant, the Song of Moses, and the *lex talionis* thus provide a theological and ethical framework within which the practice of imprecation is not only understandable but wholly appropriate—a commendable act of faith.

Crucial to Day's argument is his contention that these covenantal structures are not restricted to the Old Testament but extend into the New Testament. Day finds evidence in Galatians 3 that the Abrahamic covenant remains in effect for Christians,[170] and he observes that Deuteronomy 32 is cited in Rom 12:19; Heb 10:30 as a guarantee of divine vengeance and that the song of the glorified saints in Rev 15:2–4, proclaimed in response to God's acts of judgment, is explicitly referred to as the Song of Moses.[171] The *lex talionis* as a principle of divine justice likewise persists

---

[166]   Day, "Imprecatory Psalms," 84; cf. Day, "Imprecatory Psalms," 140. Day detects multiple echoes of Gen 12:3 in the imprecations of Psalm 109. Day, "Imprecatory Psalms," 138–42.

[167]   See, e.g., Psalms 58; 79; 94. Day, "Imprecatory Psalms," 98–106.

[168]   Day, "Imprecatory Psalms," 118.

[169]   Day, "Imprecatory Psalms," 117–24. Day sees the principle of *lex talionis* as the theological foundation for the petitions of Ps 137:7–9 and the extended imprecations of Psalm 109. Day, "Imprecatory Psalms," 121–24, 126–27. Cf. David G. Firth, *Surrendering Retribution in the Psalms: Responses to Violence in Individual Complaints*, PBM (Eugene, Ore.: Wipf & Stock, 2005), 42; Barker, *Imprecation as Divine Discourse*, 170–71. Wenham, *Psalms as Torah*, 170, argues that the imprecations of Psalm 35 are shaped by the principle of *lex talionis*.

[170]   Day, "Imprecatory Psalms," 45–47, 142. Cf. Reed Lessing, "Broken Teeth, Bloody Baths, and Baby Bashing: Is There Any Place in the Church for Imprecatory Psalms?" *ConJ* 32, no. 4 (2006): 369.

[171]   Day, "Imprecatory Psalms," 107–9. Day also identifies an allusion to Deut 32:43 in Rev 18:20.

in the New Testament, Day suggests, and he hears echoes of this standard of proportionate retribution in Acts 13:6–12; 2 Tim 4:14; Rev 18.[172] From Day's perspective, the covenantal foundations of imprecation are as sturdy in the new covenant as they were in the old.

Turning his attention to Jesus' and Paul's commands of enemy love, Day argues that, while there exists a fundamental unity between the covenants, the New Testament nevertheless exhibits progression, working out more fully the implications of enemy love such that imprecatory speech occurs with less frequency and fervor than in the Old Testament.[173] Day maintains that Jesus' teaching in the Sermon on the Mount and Paul's exhortation in Rom 12:14 to lovingly bear with and bless enemies are not ethical innovations but are rather directives that intensify and more extensively apply the morality already present in the Old Testament.[174] This intensified ethic of enemy love is, Day reasons, the general or characteristic ethic of the Christian life, even as extreme circumstances warrant an extreme ethic that allows for imprecation.[175] This extreme ethic, Day claims, is reflected in the numerous instances of imprecatory language in the New Testament.[176] Such a distinction between a general Christian ethic that calls for perseverant blessing of enemies and an extreme ethic that permits cursing of enemies who are dramatically and dangerously recalcitrant in their opposition to God and his kingdom enables Day to hold together New Testament commands for enemy love and New Testament examples of enemy curses as discrete but equally valid dimensions of the overall Christian ethic, which

---

[172] Day, "Imprecatory Psalms," 123n96.

[173] Day, "Imprecatory Psalms," 143.

[174] Day, "Imprecatory Psalms," 143–60. Regarding Jesus' teaching in the Sermon on the Mount, Day maintains, "Jesus, then, rather than presenting a novel (or imposing even a foreign) interpretation on the Leviticus 19 passage, was both distilling and radicalizing the essence of the Old Testament teaching in this regard." Day, "Imprecatory Psalms," 153.

[175] Day, "Imprecatory Psalms," 159–60. "Paul, in Romans 12, is speaking in terms of principle, of the general characteristics and sentiments of a true Christian—in much the same way that Jesus speaks in the Sermon on the Mount. However, the Imprecatory Psalms, as do the other imprecatory passages of both the Old and New Testaments, arise out of extreme circumstances—circumstances which warrant the appeal to extreme ethics." Day, "Imprecatory Psalms," 159.

[176] Day cites as instances of imprecation Mark 11:14; Gal 1:8–9; Acts 13:10–11; 8:20; Rev 6:10. Day, "Imprecatory Psalms," 161–74.

take precedence in different circumstances.[177] Day therefore concludes that Christians encountering intense hostility and resolute unrepentance may faithfully follow the model of the imprecatory psalms, petitioning for divine vengeance against their foes in accord with the extreme ethic outlined in the New Testament.[178]

David Murray connects the judgment psalms to the *protoevangelium* of Gen 3:14–15, God's initial curse over both the serpent and his off-spring who follow in his ways.[179] Murray suggests that this original dec-laration of God's intent to judge the enemies of his kingdom is further developed in the Abrahamic covenant of Gen 12:3 and that together these form the covenantal background from which the psalms of ven-geance arise.[180] In making his case for the validity of Christian perfor-mance of the judgment psalms, Murray observes that the New Testament authors frequently quote the imprecatory psalms and offer their own petitions for divine judgment, and he suggests that Jesus himself implic-itly endorses imprecatory prayer in his teaching that disciples should pray, "Thy kingdom come."[181] The church's practice of the imprecatory

[177] Day seems to maintain that the general ethic of enemy love ought to persist until it is necessarily interrupted and superseded by the extreme ethic of imprecation: "By Christ's own witness and example, then, this enemy love is the attitude of readiness to show sustained and indiscriminate kindness. How-ever, if the enemy's cup of iniquity has become full to overflowing, so to speak, this love is *overtaken* by the demands of divine justice and vengeance. Jesus' approach, in this regard, is strikingly similar to the approach of the psalm-ists who penned such harsh words." Day, "Imprecatory Psalms," 154, empha-sis added; cf. Day, "Imprecatory Psalms," 184. According to this description, the Christian's extreme ethic is a divergence from—and not a manifestation of—enemy love. Nevertheless, Day repeatedly affirms that "in some fashion, the utterance of imprecation comports with the ethic of enemy-love and bless-ing, as expressed in either testament." Day, "Imprecatory Psalms," 175; cf. Day, "Imprecatory Psalms," 183.

[178] Day, "Imprecatory Psalms," 184. Peels, *Shadow Sides*, 104, similarly acknowledges that in the New Testament "the prayer of revenge is still heard in situations of emergency" but nevertheless recommends a spiritualized appro-priation of the imprecatory psalms for Christians.

[179] David P. Murray, "Christian Cursing?" in *Sing a New Song: Recovering Psalm Singing for the Twenty-First Century*, ed. Joel R. Beeke and Anthony T. Selvaggio (Grand Rapids: Reformation Heritage Books, 2010), 114.

[180] Murray, "Christian Cursing?"

[181] Murray, "Christian Cursing?" 115–18. Murray includes as New Tes-tament examples of imprecatory speech Matt 23:13–29; Gal 1:8–9; 5:11–12; 2 Tim 4:14; 1 Cor 16:22. Scholars endorsing a variety of readings of the

psalms is for Murray a reasonable response to God's covenant promises and the testimony of the New Testament.

Attempting to demonstrate how the permissibility of imprecation may coexist with the necessity of enemy love according to Christ's command, Murray argues for the potential simultaneity of a form of love and hate directed at the same person. He claims that Christians may hate their enemies and petition for their defeat insofar as they represent opposition to God and persecute his people while synchronously loving those very enemies and desiring their salvation.[182] Day agrees, asserting that this admittedly complex emotional stance is in fact an act of imitation of God's own simultaneous love and hate toward sinners.[183] From this perspective, enemy love and enemy imprecation are ethically compatible. Murray concludes with the suggestion that the most significant role the imprecatory psalms play is a Christological one: pointing the church to the certainty of Jesus' return as king and judge.[184] Following Adams, Murray considers the internal dynamics of such Christologically oriented prayer, contending that the practice of Christian imprecation will draw the believer into worship and patient confidence that God in Christ will keep his promises to consummate his kingdom.[185]

---

imprecatory psalms reference the second petition of the Lord's Prayer as relevant to the question of Christian imprecation, including McCann, *Theological Introduction*, 124; Walter Brueggemann and William H. Bellinger, Jr., *Psalms*, NCBC (New York: Cambridge University, 2014), 262; Broadhurst, "Should Cursing Continue?" 84; Vos, "Ethical Problem," 138; Adams, *War Psalms*, 52; Mennega, "Ethical Problem," 93.

[182] Murray, "Christian Cursing?" 117–18. Murray quotes John Piper, "Do I Not Hate Those Who Hate You, O Lord?" October 3, 2000, accessed March 20, 2017, http://www.desiringgod.org/articles/do-i-not-hate-those-who-hate-you-o -lord: "There is a kind of hate for the sinner (viewed as morally corrupt and hostile to God) that may coexist with pity and even a desire for their salvation."

[183] Day, "Imprecatory Psalms," 42–45. Like Murray, Day refers to the work of John Piper, citing Piper's *The Pleasures of God: Meditations on God's Delight in Being God* (Portland, Ore.: Multnomah Press, 1991), 66. Cf. the argument for the compatibility of enemy love and imprecation of Ibrahim S. Bitrus, "God Who Curses Is Cursed: Recasting Imprecation in Africa," *ILRS* 6 (2018): 44–46, who critiques Eurocentric methods of interpretation before offering an Afrocentric reading of the imprecatory psalms, though Bitrus explicitly states that the precise relationship between enemy love and imprecation lies outside the scope of his article. Bitrus, "God Who Curses Is Cursed," 45n28.

[184] Murray, "Christian Cursing?" 120.

[185] Murray, "Christian Cursing?" Murray quotes Adams, *War Psalms*, 33, 35.

E. Calvin Beisner's formulation of the covenantal continuity reading shares many of the contours of the approaches of Day and Murray,[186] but in addition to affirming the place of imprecatory prayer among Christians, Beisner offers pastoral guidelines to direct and delimit the practice of imprecation in the church. Beisner's concern is not merely *whether* Christians may pray the psalms of vengeance but *how* such prayer might faithfully be offered to God. Outlining his vision of Christian imprecation, Beisner maintains that imprecatory prayer may be presented to God exclusively by his covenant people,[187] who must be innocent in the situation,[188] and is properly directed only against those who spurn repeated invitations to repentance and exhibit evidence of hardened rebellion.[189] A correct petitioner and proper target, however, do not a faithful imprecation make, and Beisner additionally addresses the necessary motive, aim, and posture of Christian prayers for judgment. Such petitions, Beisner contends, must originate from a desire to see God's righteous law upheld, must have as their ultimate *telos* God's glory, and must arise from a spirit of penitent humility.[190]

Covenantal continuity readings are consistent with the same evangelical doctrines of Scripture and judgment that undergird many discontinuity readings. Demonstrating their coherence with and embeddedness in the theological and ethical framework established by God's voluntary and

[186] Beisner considers Old Testament commands for enemy love, New Testament examples of imprecation, and the implications of the second petition of the Lord's Prayer before concluding, "Imprecatory prayer, then—calling on God to curse his enemies (who consequently are the enemies of His people)—is approved by both Testaments. Christians may pray this way." E. Calvin Beisner, *Psalms of Promise: Celebrating the Majesty and Faithfulness of God*, 2nd ed. (Phillipsburg, N.J.: Presbyterian and Reformed, 1994), 174–79, quote 178–79.

[187] Beisner, *Psalms of Promise*, 179.

[188] Beisner, *Psalms of Promise*. Beisner does not envision total innocence as a prerequisite for imprecatory prayer, as do Bonhoeffer and Adams. Rather, he argues that imprecating Christians must be relatively innocent in the specific matter about which they are praying. Beisner sees this type of relative innocence reflected in David in Pss 7:8; 109:4–5, 22–25, 30–31.

[189] Beisner, *Psalms of Promise*, 179–80.

[190] Beisner, *Psalms of Promise*, 180–81. Beisner cites John Calvin, *Commentary on the Book of Psalms*, trans. James Anderson, Calvin's Commentaries 6 (repr., Grand Rapids: Baker Books, 2005), 2:283 (*sic*, the quote occurs at 4:283 in Calvin's discussion of Ps 109:16), who commends appeals to God's vengeance against the unrepentant on the condition that "our hearts are pure and peaceful." Cf. Bonhoeffer, "Sermon on a Psalm of Vengeance," 91.

self-imposed promissory commitments, proponents of continuity readings of the imprecatory psalms are able to unreservedly affirm the God-givenness and trustworthiness of the psalms of vengeance as inspired Scripture.[191] This perspective on Scripture influences conceptions of divine justice as well, since God's covenantal declarations of his intentions to exercise retributive justice are considered authoritative and unerring revelations of God's character and purposes in history.[192] Continuity advocates' commendation of Christian imprecation thus arises from the interrelated convictions that God's covenant promises and the imprecatory psalms ought to be received as the inspired word of God and that God will indeed exercise justice in accord with his stated mission to exact vengeance on impenitent unrighteousness proleptically in history and definitively at the consummation. Stated more simply, the continuity approach maintains that the Bible is God's inspired word and that God in Christ will administer retributive justice against every opponent of his kingdom. As argued above, such convictions are also consistent with many discontinuity readings of the imprecatory psalms. What distinguishes these oft-dogmatically similar continuity and discontinuity proposals, therefore, is not ultimately one's theological commitment regarding Scripture's inspiration but one's synthesis of these authoritative Scriptures. What separates these positions is not fundamentally one's doctrine of divine judgment, but one's vision of faithful Christian prayer at this moment in redemptive history in light of the shared conviction that God will administer retributive eschatological justice. The key distinction, then, is a matter of biblical-theological integration and not systematic theological dogma.

Continuity readings offer a coherent interpretation of the imprecatory psalms and a proposal for Christian performance that accounts for the relevant biblical data—particularly New Testament instances of imprecatory language[193]—and are thus not susceptible to a major objection raised against covenantal inferiority and discontinuity approaches. Questions may, however, be submitted to the continuity position, which reveal the potential for further exploration of significant dimensions of this reading

[191]   See, e.g., both Day, "Imprecatory Psalms," 29–30; Murray, "Christian Cursing?" 112, critique Lewis' reading of the imprecations as inconsistent with the doctrine of inspiration.

[192]   Cf. Murray, "Christian Cursing?" 117–18, 120; Beisner, *Psalms of Promise*, 178; Day, "Imprecatory Psalms," 6–13.

[193]   Day, "Imprecatory Psalms," 161–74; Murray, "Christian Cursing?" 116; Beisner, *Psalms of Promise*, 174–78.

and for more detailed examination of the implications of this interpretive framework for Christian appropriation of the judgment psalms.

In his detailed biblical-theological consideration of the imprecatory psalms, Day utilizes the transtestamental category of covenant to trace the consistency of God's promises and relational arrangements with his people throughout redemptive history, asserting that the covenant structures that legitimized imprecation for the psalmists remain valid for the church and therefore justify the practice of imprecation by Christians. Day acknowledges, however, that the New Testament's attitude toward and practice of imprecation is not identical to that demonstrated in the Old Testament but rather signals both similarity and progression.[194] Day attributes this progression—evident in his distinction between the Christian's general and extreme ethics—to the New Testament's "more frequent and explicit calls for kindness in anticipation of the eschatological judgment along with a more overt identification of fundamental enmities at the spiritual level."[195] But how does this progression relate to the covenantal continuity Day and others have identified? What redemptive-historical shifts take place with Christ's inauguration of the kingdom of God and establishment of the new covenant that might clarify the New Testament's simultaneously similar-yet-different practice of imprecation? Additional biblical-theological investigation into the developments in God's relationship with his covenant community, the character of the kingdom, and the implications for Christian action introduced by Jesus' accomplishments could give valuable context to the church's performance of the imprecatory psalms—clarifying *why* Christian practice of the imprecatory psalms at this stage of redemptive history is not merely a matter of straightforward appropriation of Israel's prayers.

The covenantal framework employed by proponents of continuity readings, which detects a fundamental unity between the testaments, allows for recognition of Christological significance within the imprecatory psalms. Discussing Jesus' relationship to the Old Testament, Day asserts that "the Old Testament propels us *toward* Christ, is summed up *in* Christ, and must be interpreted *through* Christ."[196] Day limits application of this Christological principle, however, to Jesus' relationship to the Old Testament law and does not explore how such a hermeneutic might inform

[194] Cf. Day, "Imprecatory Psalms," 3, 176.

[195] Day, "Imprecatory Psalms," 178.

[196] Day, "Imprecatory Psalms," 144. Day considers Luke 24:27, 44–45; John 5:39–40, 46, as supportive of this Christological hermeneutic.

Christian interpretation and practice of the judgment psalms.[197] Murray maintains that the imprecations' most significant function is to point the church to Jesus, but he restricts his focus to Jesus' role as the Christ who calls for and consummates God's judgment upon his enemies.[198] How else might the New Testament present Jesus as the fulfillment of the figures and themes of the imprecatory psalms? Recognition of these multivalent Christological dimensions has the potential to illuminate the New Testament's perspective on the imprecatory psalms.

Further, such a polyvalent Christological reading has the capacity to richly shape the internal and existential dynamics of the Christian practice of imprecation. Beisner suggests that faithful imprecation in the church requires a posture of critical self-awareness and humility, but he describes this posture as something that must be achieved *prior to* the commencement of imprecatory prayer and seems to associate it with a disposition of serenity.[199] But this seems an odd prerequisite: before one may pray the angry, visceral, tragedy-induced prayers of the Psalter, one must first arrive at internal equilibrium and sober self-understanding. Is it possible, however, that the imprecatory psalms might serve as a resource for *creating* a posture of peace and humility—that these psalms, in all their Christological significance, might direct us to the gospel in such a manner that the very performance of their prayers takes the petitioning community on a journey toward renewed assurance, virtue, and Christlike regard for the enemy? If so, then a posture of peace and humility is not so much a precondition as it is a fruit of faithful imprecation, as the church petitions in a manner distinctly formed by her hope in the Christ to whom the Psalter testifies.

In a unique iteration of the continuity proposal, Kit Barker utilizes speech-act theory to develop a theological interpretation of the imprecatory psalms, arguing that one aspect of the imprecations' illocutionary force as God's word is to invite Christians to mimetically imitate their prayers for divine justice.[200] Might speech-act theory clarify the continuity between psalmic imprecation and Christian performance where standard continuity readings have left questions? Like the treatments

---

[197]   Day, "Imprecatory Psalms," 143–55. Day's primary concern is to demonstrate the consistency between Jesus' command of enemy love and the ethical commands of the Old Testament.

[198]   Murray, "Christian Cursing?" 120.

[199]   Beisner, *Psalms of Promise*, 181.

[200]   Barker, *Imprecation as Divine Discourse*, esp. 127–57.

of Day, Murray, and Beisner, Barker's proposal is consistent with evangelical notions of scriptural inspiration and divine judgment,[201] but in distinction to these continuity proposals, Barker is less concerned with the theological and ethical structures of the covenants that render the imprecatory psalms morally justified for Israel and the church and focuses instead on the illocutionary force of the covenant Scriptures as divine speech acts that commend the imprecations for appropriation.[202] Barker suggests that the imprecatory psalms—by virtue of their inclusion in the edited canonical worship book of Israel and theological fit with the Psalter as a whole—are presented in their Old Testament context as right responses to injustice that invite *mimesis*,[203] and he further maintains that the illocutionary stance of the New Testament supports the illocutionary stance of the psalms.

In addition to noting that the New Testament itself includes imprecatory speech,[204] Barker contends that the New Testament illocutions typically deemed incompatible with imprecation are in fact commensurate with prayers for judgment. Specifically, Barker argues that imprecation is consistent with Jesus' prohibition of cursing because imprecatory prayer directed to God is a different speech act than a curse directed against a human being,[205] with Jesus' commands of forgiveness because forgiveness in the New Testament is contingent upon the wrongdoer's

---

[201] Barker, *Imprecation as Divine Discourse*, 92n78, explicitly states that "the understanding of inspiration presupposed in this project is one that ensures that the human authors always speak in ways that honour God such that God either appropriates their illocutions or, alternatively, authorizes or affirms their illocutions." Cf. Barker, *Imprecation as Divine Discourse*, 36–65. Barker's understanding of divine judgment flows from his conception of inspiration and is evident throughout his treatment of the imprecatory psalms and esp. Barker, *Imprecation as Divine Discourse*, 177, in his description of Jesus' role in eschatological judgment.

[202] See Barker, *Imprecation as Divine Discourse*, 128n2.

[203] Barker, *Imprecation as Divine Discourse*, 132–36. Cf. Barker, *Imprecation as Divine Discourse*, 107–26, where Barker lays the foundation for this treatment with a discussion of the primary illocutions of the Psalter and how the human speech acts of the Psalter are appropriated by God as divine discourse.

[204] Barker, *Imprecation as Divine Discourse*, 155–56.

[205] Barker, *Imprecation as Divine Discourse*, 151–53. Cf. the similar contentions of, e.g., Peels, *Vengeance of God*, 236–38; Broadhurst, "Should Cursing Continue?" 67–68; Bernardino, "Reconsideration of 'Imprecations,'" 63–65.

prior repentance,[206] and with Jesus' mandates of enemy love because love (as Day and Murray assert) may exist simultaneously alongside petitions for judgment.[207] For Barker, the psalms' original illocutionary invitation to imitation is therefore unchanged by the potential supervening illocutions of the new covenant Scriptures because imprecation is not cursing per se, and one may love one's enemy and extend the possibility of forgiveness on the condition of repentance while nevertheless praying for God's justice on the as-yet-impenitent perpetrator. In a detailed examination of two psalms, Barker suggests that the New Testament presents Jesus as the Son who will definitively judge God's enemies in Christological fulfillment of Psalm 137 and as the righteous sufferer and imprecator via intertextual reference to Psalm 69. These typological identifications, in his estimation, further validate Christians' vocalization of the imprecations as they hope in Jesus' judgment and follow the pattern of their suffering and imprecating Savior.[208]

Barker's innovative employment of speech-act theory is particularly illuminating in his examination of the Psalter's presentation of the imprecations as righteous responses and invitations for *mimesis* at a generic and canonical level and in the clear distinction he identifies between the illocutionary force of imprecatory requests and enemy curses. Further, Barker's attention to New Testament intertextuality with Psalm 69—how the New Testament applies the language and imagery of the psalm to Jesus—offers a promising method for interrogating the Christological significance of the imprecations, which could be fruitfully expanded to

---

[206] Barker, *Imprecation as Divine Discourse*, 137–50. Barker maintains that "forgiveness is an example of a strong speech act (i.e., strong illocution) that requires a context of penitence for it to be enacted." Barker, *Imprecation as Divine Discourse*, 138. Barker, however, recognizes that this is a contested position. See Barker, *Imprecation as Divine Discourse*, 140–45.

[207] Barker, *Imprecation as Divine Discourse*, 153–54. Barker claims that "it is clear that one cannot both forgive a wrongdoer and imprecate against them at the same time. The two illocutions are mutually exclusive, requiring different contexts. In the case of loving one's enemies, its mutual exclusivity with respect to imprecation is not as clear. It could be possible to act in love towards one's enemy, to have shown kindness towards them and to even desire their redemption while at the same time maintain a desire for God to be glorified, for justice to be done and for personal vindication." Barker, *Imprecation as Divine Discourse*, 154. Cf. Murray, "Christian Cursing?" 117–18; Day, "Imprecatory Psalms," 42–45.

[208] Barker, *Imprecation as Divine Discourse*, 158–211.

encompass all of the imprecatory psalms. It is less clear, however, that Barker's approach clarifies the intertwined theological and ethical questions left open by other continuity readings. Barker's argument that the New Testament's illocutions regarding cursing, forgiveness, and love do not invalidate Christian imprecation does not engage in the kind of constructive theological investigation that examines how the content of the imprecatory psalms' requests reflect a specific redemptive-historical context and how the different redemptive-historical location of the church might necessitate modification of some of their specific petitions and expectations. That is, even if one finds Barker's explanations of conditional forgiveness and the noncontradictory simultaneity of enemy love and imprecation ethically persuasive, Barker's contention that the New Testament does not negate imprecatory prayer does not sufficiently explore how the New Testament positively supplies a narrative and theological framework centered on the accomplishments of Christ that might reorient how Christians give voice to, for example, the psalms' frequently expressed expectations of graphic individual and communal involvement in meting out the vengeance of God.[209] Though Barker's incorporation of speech-act theory may beneficially focus inquiry into certain aspects of the imprecatory psalms, his conceptual prioritization of illocution to the neglect of a more robust theologico-ethical examination fails to significantly add to the standard covenantal continuity reading in a manner that brings into sharper relief the logic and shape of moral Christian practice of the imprecatory psalms.[210]

The defining questions for covenantal readings of the imprecatory psalms are: *How does the Bible fit together? How do the covenants relate to one another?* The diverse arrangements suggested in response serve to situate the psalms of vengeance in relation to God's revelation to and action with Israel and to situate the church—God's new covenant

---

[209] See, e.g., Ps 41:10, which petitions, "But you, O LORD, be gracious to me, and raise me up that I may repay them!" Cf. the communal expectations of Pss 58:10; 68:22–23. Does Barker's contention that the New Testament does not delegitimize the practice of imprecatory prayer entail that Christians may pray such petitions in their most straightforward sense?

[210] Cf. the critique of Richard S. Briggs, review of *Imprecation as Divine Discourse: Speech Act Theory, Dual Authorship, and Theological Interpretation*, by Kit Barker, *RBL* (2019), https://www.sblcentral.org/home/bookDetails/11582, that Briggs remains "unpersuaded that a theological interpretation is better served by a hermeneutical theory than a theological wrestling directly with the substantive (theological) issues."

community—in relation to the psalms, resulting in distinct proposals for Christian performance of the imprecations. Inferiority, discontinuity, and continuity frameworks provide disparate answers concerning the connection between the covenants and the consequent propriety of Christian imprecation, yet in spite of the differences between these positions, one characteristic remains constant: one's vision of the (dis)unity of the Bible plays a determinative role in shaping a vision of Christian prayer of the Psalter's judgment prayers.

Into the Hands of God:
Relinquishment Readings of the Imprecatory Psalms

Rather than foregrounding moral judgments (e.g., aberrant human sentiment), biblical categories (e.g., covenant), or the identity of the petitioner (e.g., the imprecations as prayers of Christ) to explain the imprecatory psalms and articulate a proposal for Christian appropriation, relinquishment readings consider the Psalter's judgment petitions primarily *as prayer* and consequently concentrate attention on the dynamic interaction through which the petitioner hands over vengeful emotion and action to God. Representative of this interpretive approach, Erich Zenger argues,

> As poetic prayers, the psalms of vengeance are a passionate clinging to God when everything really speaks *against* God. . . . These psalms are the expression of a longing that evil, and evil people, may not have the last word in history, for this world and its history belong to God. Thus, to use theological terminology, these psalms are realized theodicy: They affirm God by surrendering the last word *to God*. They give *to God* not only their lament about their desperate situation, but also the right to judge the originators of that situation. They leave *everything* in God's hands, even feelings of hatred and aggression.[211]

The central assertion of this perspective is that the psalms' violent pleas for vengeance are a prayerful means by which, in the presence of God, the psalmists relinquish violence and violent desire, placing their enemies and all rights to vengeance in the hands of the God who can be trusted to bring justice.[212] Relinquishment readings thus envision the imprecatory psalms

---

[211] Zenger, *God of Vengeance?* 79, emphasis original.

[212] Walter Brueggemann's explanation of Psalm 109 in *Praying the Psalms: Engaging Scripture and the Life of the Spirit*, 2nd ed. (Eugene, Ore.: Cascade, 2007), 67, nicely summarizes the relinquishment perspective: "The speech of vengeance is characteristically offered to God, not directly to the enemy. . . .

as profoundly cathartic and therapeutic acts of and aids for nonviolence, and proponents frequently emphasize these benefits while advocating for their inclusion in Christian prayer and liturgy.[213] Though scholars who favor the relinquishment approach offer varied proposals for understanding and engaging with the imprecations, a number of characteristics are typical of such treatments.

First, relinquishment readings consistently portray the desires for vengeance underneath the imprecatory psalms as ethically deficient, unfaithful, base, less-than-ideal sentiments that must be acknowledged and expressed in prayer in order to be surrendered to God. Patrick Miller argues that Jesus' commands of enemy love and example of forgiveness invalidate imprecation as a faithful option for the Christian church, though liberation from such vengeful thoughts and feelings may indeed require their prayerful expression to God.[214] Similarly, Walter Brueggemann maintains that we should not feel the vindictive desires manifested

---

That is, vengeance is transferred from the heart of the speaker to the heart of God." The discussion of Psalm 137 by Zenger, *God of Vengeance?* 48, helpfully represents this view as well, arguing that Psalm 137 "is an attempt, in the face of the most profound humiliation and helplessness, to suppress the primitive human lust for violence in one's own heart, by surrendering *everything* to God." Emphasis original. Cf. the similar formulation from a Jewish perspective by Jonathan Magonet, "Psalm 137: Unlikely Liturgy or Partisan Poem? A Response to Sue Gillingham," in *Jewish and Christian Approaches to the Psalms*, ed. Susan Gillingham (Oxford: Oxford University Press, 2013), 87–88.

[213]   See, e.g., Nancy deClaissé-Walford, "The Theology of the Imprecatory Psalms," in *Soundings in the Theology of the Psalms: Perspectives and Methods in Contemporary Scholarship*, ed. Rolf A. Jacobson (Minneapolis: Fortress, 2011), 90–92; McCann, *Theological Introduction*, 115–17; Ellen F. Davis, *Getting Involved with God: Rediscovering the Old Testament* (Lanham, Md.: Cowley, 2001), 23–28; Gordon Wenham, *The Psalter Reclaimed: Praying and Praising with the Psalms* (Wheaton, Ill.: Crossway, 2013), 134–45; Brueggemann, *Praying the Psalms*, 66–81. David Tuesday Adamo, "The Imprecatory Psalms in African Context," in *Biblical Interpretation in African Perspective*, ed. David Tuesday Adamo (Lanham, Md.: University Press of America, 2006), 150–51, after providing an Afrocentric interpretation of the imprecatory psalms and surveying their use by African churches, suggests that most African Christians would understand the imprecations as acts of nonviolence. Cf. Bitrus, "God Who Curses," 45–46.

[214]   Patrick D. Miller, *They Cried to the Lord: The Form and Theology of Biblical Prayer* (Minneapolis: Fortress, 1994), 301–3. Patrick D. Miller, "The Hermeneutics of Imprecation," in *Theology in the Service of the Church: Essays in Honor of Thomas W. Gillespie*, ed. Wallace M. Alston, Jr. (Grand Rapids: Eerdmans, 2000), 161, describes the thoughts expressed by the imprecations as "justifiable but not

in the psalmists' cries—desires that he understands as obviously contra-dictory to the Christian ethic[215]—but these undesirable desires never-theless belong in discourse with the God who can be trusted with our rage and with every issue of justice.[216] Konrad Schaefer proposes that the sentiments that motivate the imprecations emerge from humanity's sin-ful condition, referring to Ps 140:10 as an "unholy wish."[217] But because the articulation of such unholy wishes involves both emotional catharsis and recognition of God's role as guarantor of justice, Schaefer argues that imprecatory prayer should be included in liturgical settings rather than repressed and ignored.[218] From this perspective, the ethically problematic judgment psalms are not so much imitable models of pious prayer as they are pragmatically beneficial—even therapeutically necessary—prayers on the journey through and away from impious emotions.

Second, proponents of relinquishment readings routinely appeal to the apparent absence of violent action amid the violent speech of the imprecatory psalms, often accentuating the distinction between speech and action, as evidence that the psalmists' violence never exceeds the rhe-torical sphere as all rights to vengeance are transferred to God. David Blu-menthal maintains that psalmic prayers for divine retribution are neither acts of retribution themselves nor calls for human acts of retribution,[219] and Bernd Janowski argues that the psalms generally lack any indication of enactments of or plans for personal vengeance.[220] Page Kelly takes this

---

justifiable," which presumably means that they are understandable given the cir-cumstances but not morally approvable. Cf. Davis, *Getting Involved with God*, 25.

[215] Walter Brueggemann, *The Psalms and the Life of Faith*, ed. Patrick D. Miller (Minneapolis: Fortress, 1995), 268, on Psalm 109: "Obviously this voice contradicts the invitation of the gospel that we should love our enemies (Matt 5:43–48; Rom 12:17, 21)." Cf. Walter Brueggemann, *Spirituality of the Psalms* (Minneapolis: Fortress, 2002), 33.

[216] Brueggemann, *Psalms and the Life of Faith*, 278–79.

[217] Konrad Schaefer, *Psalms*, Berit Olam: Studies in Hebrew Narrative and Poetry, ed. David W. Cotter (Collegeville, Minn.: Liturgical Press, 2001), xl–xli, quote xli. Cf. Schaefer, *Psalms*, xxxix. Jerome F. D. Creach, *Violence in Scripture*, Interpretation: Resources for the Use of Scripture in the Church (Louisville: Westminster John Knox, 2013), 210, refers to the anger motivating imprecation as a "sign of human frailty."

[218] Schaefer, *Psalms*, xli.

[219] David R. Blumenthal, "Liturgies of Anger," *Cross Curr.* 52, no. 2 (2002): 189.

[220] Bernd Janowski, *Arguing with God: A Theological Anthropology of the Psalms*, trans. Armin Siedlecki (Louisville: Westminster John Knox, 2013),

assertion even further, claiming that retaliatory acts *never* attended the psalmists' violent petitions for justice.[221] Brueggemann explains,

> It is important to recognize that these verbal assaults of imagination and hyperbole are verbal. They speak wishes and prayers. But the speaker does not do anything beyond speak. The speech of vengeance is not to be equated with acts of vengeance. This community which respected and greatly valued language encouraged speech, destructive as it might be, in the place of destructive action. So far as we know, even in the most violent cries for vengeance, no action is taken.[222]

The imprecatory psalms are certainly violent rhetoric, Brueggemann argues, but they are only rhetoric—not commissions of, plans for, or incitements of violent acts—and such Godward rhetoric, he contends, in fact had the real effect for the psalmists of averting vengeful action by entrusting it to God, supplanting and offering an alternative to violent behavior.[223] Per this perspective, the psalmists speak violently, pray violently, and plead violently, but they never act violently, and this demonstrates that the speaking inhibits the acting by handing over all vengeful action to God. The absence of violent activity among the psalmists thus emerges as a particularly salient piece of data in support of the claim that the Psalter's imprecatory prayers represent a total ceding of violence to God. Stated negatively, if the psalmists are found to have expected or perpetrated violence, the credibility of this approach would be seriously undermined.

Third, interpreters who favor relinquishment readings tend to open the door for unexpected—perhaps more palatable—manifestations of divine justice. Brueggemann appeals to divine freedom, noting that if vengeance is solely the prerogative of God, then the form of that vengeance is also completely subject to God's discretion and may not align with the

---

125–26. Cf. the claim of Firth, *Surrendering Retribution*, 3, that the individual laments "reject all forms of human violence. Within the 'I' psalms only the violence that may be enacted by Yahweh is acceptable."

[221] Page H. Kelly, "Prayers of Troubled Saints," *RevExp* 81, no. 3 (1984): 380.

[222] Brueggemann, *Praying the Psalms*, 67. Cf. Walter Brueggemann, *From Whom No Secrets Are Hid: Introducing the Psalms*, ed. Brent A. Strawn (Louisville: Westminster John Knox, 2014), 97; *Psalms and the Life of Faith*, 278; *The Message of the Psalms: A Theological Commentary*, Augsburg Old Testament Studies (Minneapolis: Augsburg, 1984), 76.

[223] Brueggemann, *From Whom No Secrets Are Hid*, 99.

petitioner's hopes.[224] For Zenger, the ultimate *telos* of divine judgment is the restoration of justice, in which the whole network of relationships in the cosmos functions once again as originally intended, and he envisions this justice-aimed judgment not as tormenting or annihilating the wicked so much as "[confronting] the wicked with their injustice in such a way that they honor justice through their repentance."[225] In Zenger's estimation, punitive conceptions of divine judgment—perhaps, we might say, the type of judgment for which the psalmists hope—must be denounced as sadistic, masochistic, and psychologically harmful in the harshest of terms. Miller considers the point from a soteriological perspective, arguing that the cross is the definitive expression of divine justice against every enemy of righteousness, an expression that presumably renders superfluous the concept of eschatological justice as eternal punishment.[226] Though the means by which scholars approach the issue of divine justice vary, the effect is the same: to introduce a disjunction between what is requested in the psalms and how God may truly respond, calling into question the necessity of punitive and retributive notions of divine wrath and, by extension, the plausibility of eschatological vengeance as a potential manifestation of judgment. The imprecations are thus softened, their offense somewhat diminished, because the prayers and pray-ers may be more violently vengeful than the God to whom such prayers are offered. From this standpoint, the imprecatory psalms relinquish justice into the hands of a God who may defy the psalmists' (and even our) expectations. The imprecations cry out for divine justice in the most violent of terms, but divine justice in reality may not be so violent after all.

Characteristic articulations of the relinquishment reading therefore posit that the imprecatory psalms need be considered neither ethically nor theologically normative: the responses to suffering they present are not necessarily morally approvable, and the vision of God that they

---

[224] Brueggemann, *Message of the Psalms*, 86. Cf. Zenger, *God of Vengeance?* 72; Davis, *Getting Involved with God*, 27.

[225] Zenger, *God of Vengeance?* 64. Cf. Michael Jinkins, *In the House of the Lord: Inhabiting the Psalms of Lament* (Collegeville, Minn.: Liturgical Press, 1998), 63–64. Creach, *Violence in Scripture*, 163–91, devotes considerable space to examining Old Testament and New Testament texts dealing with divine vengeance and judgment and their interpretation in church history before concluding that "the final word is about restoration and renewal, not punishment." Creach, *Violence in Scripture*, 191.

[226] See Patrick D. Miller, Jr., *Interpreting the Psalms* (Philadelphia: Fortress, 1986), 152; *They Cried to the Lord*, 303. Cf. Brueggemann, *Praying the Psalms*, 79–81.

project and from which they cry is not necessarily dogmatically accurate.[227] Underneath such a conclusion is a doctrine of Scripture that renders the conclusion permissible. In a helpful expression of transparency and candor, Zenger straightforwardly declares, "That *both testaments* appeal for the violent power of God *and* for an end to violence recalls for us the fundamental theological truth that the Bible is not revelation in the sense of an immediate, verbal communication from God, but is '*the word of God in human words*.'"[228] For Zenger, the ethical inconsistency of Scripture reveals its identity as human reflection on encounters with the divine,[229] and this understanding of the Bible in turn supplies hermeneutical legitimation for the interpretive claim that the ethics and theology of the imprecations conflict with other portions of Scripture and are not necessarily binding on the church. This conception of the word of God shifts the revelatory function of Scripture—and in this case, particularly the psalms—away from enjoining a perspective on the life of faith and communicating truths about the character of God toward revealing the violent reality of the world in which sufferers have no other recourse but to imprecate.[230] A doctrine of Scripture that allows the interpreter to reject the ethical and theological normativity of the psalms alleviates much of the tension created by the presence of the imprecations in the canon, but it should be noted that this approach toward Scripture also gives rise to a hermeneutic where the Bible's claims may be quite easily dismissed as the (mistaken) response of human beings to their confrontation by God, a hermeneutic that may perhaps impede God's confrontation of us.

Nevertheless, proponents of relinquishment readings are often vehement in their insistence that the imprecatory psalms must be recovered as a vital dimension of Christian piety and liturgy.[231] Such recovery of Christian practice of the imprecations, advocates argue, will introduce a variety of psychological, spiritual, and social benefits to the church. Crucial

---

[227] Zenger, *God of Vengeance?* 92: "The psalms of enmity offer us neither a dogmatic doctrine of God nor a summary of biblical ethics."

[228] Zenger, *God of Vengeance?* 81, emphasis original.

[229] See Zenger, *God of Vengeance?* 84. Cf. Craigie, *Psalms 1–50*, 41.

[230] Zenger, *God of Vengeance?* 85.

[231] Zenger refers to elimination of the imprecations from the Roman Catholic Liturgy of the Hours as "an act of magisterial barbarism." Zenger, *God of Vengeance?* viii. Indeed, the entire argument of his *God of Vengeance?* is aimed at defending the place of imprecatory prayer in the church's liturgy. Cf. Wenham, *Psalter Reclaimed*, 143; Brueggemann, *Psalms and the Life of Faith*, 279.

to relinquishment readings is the claim that imprecatory performance provides an appropriate context for the cathartic release of intense emotion and the conscious yielding of all vengeance to God in a manner that liberates the petitioner for mercy and forgiveness.[232] Whereas the internalization and repression of rage only increases one's proclivities toward violence,[233] so it is argued, imprecatory prayer brings these most powerful human emotions into the presence of God, unburdening the Christian and entrusting the future to God such that the believer may endure in nonviolence.[234] Advocates of relinquishment readings thus understand Christian performance of the vengeance psalms as integral to psychological well-being, the exercise of specific virtues, and social responses that contribute to peace and reconciliation. Unethical prayer is proposed as an essential resource for ethical living.

Supporters of relinquishment readings, however, identify several additional effects of Christian appropriation of the imprecatory psalms. Zenger proposes that the psalms of enmity serve to sensitize believers to the reality of violence in society, the pain of oft-forgotten victims of injustice,[235] and their own participation in the world's structures and cycles of violence,[236] promoting the petitioner's knowledge of self, others,

[232]   Kevin J. Youngblood, "Don't Get Even, Get Mad! Imprecatory Prayer as a Neglected Spiritual Discipline: (Psalm 69)," *Leaven* 19, no. 3 (2011): 157; McCann, *Theological Introduction*, 115, 119–20; Creach, *Violence in Scripture*, 210; Brueggemann, *Spirituality of the Psalms*, 37–38. Brueggemann, *From Whom No Secrets Are Hid*, 99: "We might hope and wish that we would catch up to Jesus and his readiness to forgive. But it is clear that we have not arrived there yet. Still further, psalms such as Psalms 69 and 137 suggest that we will not arrive there before our deep dark secrets are brought to light, voiced, and expressed in God's presence—God, the one from whom no secrets are hid."

[233]   See, e.g., Hankle, "Therapeutic Implications," 277, who cites L. Roemer, B. T. Litz, S. M. Orsillo, and A. W. Wagner, "A Preliminary Investigation of the Role of Strategic Withholding of Emotions in PTSD," *J. Trauma. Stress* 14, no. 1 (2001): 149–56, which finds that withholding negative emotion as a coping strategy is associated with symptoms of PTSD.

[234]   Zenger, *God of Vengeance?* 79, 92. Cf. Elizabeth Achtemeier, *Preaching Hard Texts of the Old Testament* (Peabody, Mass.: Hendrickson, 1998), 109.

[235]   Cf. Robert Althann, "The Psalms of Vengeance against Their Ancient Near Eastern Background," *JNSL* 18 (1992): 11, who argues that the imprecatory psalms afford Christians the opportunity to enter into the feelings of those who have suffered injustice and thus to understand them.

[236]   Cf. John Mark Hicks, "Preaching Community Laments: Responding to Disillusionment with God and Injustice in the World," in *Performing the Psalms,*

and world.[237] McCann views the practice of imprecation as an opportunity to intercede for others—to imprecate on their behalf against their enemies—recognizing the plight of the global church and exhibiting solidarity with the marginalized and wounded body of Christ in the world.[238] Turning from the liturgical to the clinical setting, Dominick Hankle argues that the imprecatory psalms can facilitate the processing and healing of negative emotion in Christian counseling. Hankle maintains that the therapeutic utilization of the vengeance psalms will prevent the silencing of negative emotion, affirm the normalcy of the desires for violence that are natural to sinful humans, encourage release of these acknowledged desires to God, and allow for further self-examination and exploration of one's anger such that repentance is possible.[239] For advocates of relinquishment readings, the imprecatory psalms can be a richly beneficial resource in a diversity of contexts—personal, liturgical, and clinical.

Relinquishment readings of the vengeance psalms make a promising shift from strictly biblical and theological interrogations of the curses to consideration of the subjective dynamics of imprecatory prayer, helpfully focusing attention on the changes that take place within the believer who dares to bring her anger to God. This therapeutic turn, which approaches the imprecatory psalms as resources for healing and nonviolence, opens fruitful avenues for further research. Here, trauma theory may serve as an illuminating dialogue partner, shedding light on the personal and social effects of traumatic violence—which may in turn contribute to additional violent behavior—and offering a lens for exploring in more detail the healing potential of imprecatory psalms and their liturgical embodiment.[240] In

---

ed. Dave Bland and David Fleer (St. Louis: Chalice Press, 2005), 77; Steussy, "Enemy in the Psalms," 11; Ursula Sibler, "'Whatever Is in Parenthesis We Do Not Include in Our Prayers'!? The Problematic Nature of the 'Enemy Psalms' in Christian Reception," *Eur. Judaism* 46, no. 2 (2013): 121.

[237] Zenger, *God of Vengeance?* 74–76.

[238] McCann, *Theological Introduction*, 116–17. McCann supports this proposal with an extensive citation from James L. Mays, "A Question of Identity: The Three-Fold Hermeneutic of Psalmody," lecture delivered at Eden Theological Seminary, St. Louis, Mo., April 2, 1991. Cf. Wenham, *Psalter Reclaimed*, 143–45.

[239] Hankle, "Therapeutic Implications," 278–79.

[240] For applications of trauma theory to psalmic performance, see, e.g., Brent A. Strawn, "Trauma, Psalmic Disclosure, and Authentic Happiness," in *Bible through the Lens of Trauma*, ed. Elizabeth Boase and Christopher G. Frechette (Atlanta: SBL Press, 2016), 143–60; Christopher G. Frechette, "Destroying the Internalized Perpetrator: A Healing Function of the Violent Language

addition to encouraging and enacting the surrender of personal violence, how else might the justice psalms shape communities for wholeness and peace? The relinquishment approach opens the way for consideration of these heretofore largely underexamined dimensions of the imprecations.

Yet despite this auspicious direction, a few discernible weak spots emerge in typical articulations of the relinquishment perspective. Relinquishment readings generally characterize the desires that motivate the imprecations as ethically problematic, even antithetical to the teachings of Jesus. While the relinquishment reading is susceptible to many of the questions posed to positions that similarly evaluate imprecation as morally inappropriate for Christians,[241] this proposal raises novel ethical and liturgical concerns as well. Given that the longings for vengeance expressed in the imprecations are often deemed immoral and contradictory to Jesus' teachings, the relinquishment proposal's commendation of Christian imprecatory prayer seems something of a utilitarian concession to unfaithful desires. The worthy ends appear to justify the problematic means, a therapeutically pragmatic conclusion dependent upon the moral reasoning that prayers that ought not to be prayed because they are morally wrong in fact ought to be prayed because they have beneficial consequences. But is this an ethically satisfactory conclusion? If the imprecations are in fact morally deficient, do they really have a place in Christian prayer? Proponents of relinquishment readings maintain that the imprecatory psalms reveal that humanity's most undesirable desires

---

against Enemies in the Psalms," in *Trauma and Traumatization in Individual and Collective Dimensions: Insights from Biblical Studies and Beyond*, ed. Eve-Marie Becker, Jan Dochhorn, and Else K. Holt, SAN 2 (Göttingen: Vandenhoeck and Ruprecht, 2014), 71–84; Serene Jones, *Trauma and Grace: Theology in a Ruptured World* (Louisville: Westminster John Knox, 2009), 43–67; Rebecca W. Poe Hays, "Trauma, Remembrance, and Healing: The Meeting of Wisdom and History in Psalm 78," *JSOT* 41, no. 2 (2016): 183–204.

[241] E.g., does not the clear utilization of imprecatory language in Luke 18:1–8; Gal 1:8–9; 1 Cor 16:22; Rev 6:10 suggest that such language may be not only ethically appropriate but worthy of imitation? That Jesus, Paul, and the heavenly saints commended or employed imprecatory language in their own speech may indicate that they did not detect the ethical conflict with Jesus' teachings that advocates of relinquishment readings frequently do. If the anger that drives imprecation is in fact presented by Scripture as ethically praiseworthy, then perhaps such anger is not to be left behind, gotten over, or moved on from—as relinquishment proposals argue—so much as consciously engaged, cultivated in its appropriate forms and proportions, and aimed at its appropriate ends.

belong in conversation with God as the context in which such yearnings are most profitably disclosed.[242] But these proposals neglect to articulate precisely how such unethical expressions can permissibly enter into communion with the Lord whose ethical standards they defy, how Christians might properly beseech God from the very sentiments he allegedly condemns. Is prayer the one sphere of Christian existence where the commands of God need not apply, where disobedience to the call of Christ is a legitimate alternative?[243] The proposition that petitions may be simultaneously morally unacceptable to God and acceptable as prayer to the same God introduces a tension that requires further investigation and clarification if the conclusions of the relinquishment reading are to be considered ethically consistent and argumentatively persuasive.

From the perspective of liturgical performance, if one of the embedded and inescapable pedagogical functions of liturgy is to inculcate particular modes of relating to God[244]—if liturgical practice inevitably exerts a norming influence on the community—then the inclusion of ethically suspect prayers in the church's scripted performance seems to implicitly commend imprecation while explicitly condemning its generative states of heart in a disorienting confluence of incompatible messages. Why would the church

---

[242] Brueggemann, *Psalms and the Life of Faith*, 278–79; Zenger, *God of Vengeance?* 79.

[243] Jesus' emphasis on the ethical significance of the human heart—the affections, yearnings, and desires that drive and direct both speech and action—and warnings concerning eschatological accountability and judgment specifically for speech that arises from a wrongly oriented heart suggest that, even in prayer, there may indeed be sentiments Christians should not embrace and express to God, desires that—though they may be named and confessed—do not belong in God's presence as the propelling force of prayerful requests. Cf. Matt 12:33–37; 15:10–20. The condemnation of wrongly motivated prayer in Jas 4:1–4 supports the same conclusion.

[244] See Joel LeMon, "Saying Amen to Violent Psalms: Patterns of Prayer, Belief and Action in the Psalter," in Jacobson, *Soundings in the Theology of the Psalms*, 93, who adds to the motto *lex orandi, lex credendi* the phrase *lex agendi*, noting that how one prays not only affects what one believes but also how one subsequently lives in the world and in relation with God. Liturgical repetition inescapably involves ethical claims as to what is right and imposes ethical norms as to how a community ought to live. Cf. Paul Ramsey, "Liturgy and Ethics," *JRE* 7, no. 2 (1979): 139; James K. A. Smith, *Desiring the Kingdom: Worship, Worldview, and Cultural Formation*, vol. 1 of Cultural Liturgies (Grand Rapids: Baker Academic, 2009); *Imagining the Kingdom: How Worship Works*, vol. 2 of Cultural Liturgies (Grand Rapids: Baker Academic, 2013).

authorize through inclusion in its liturgy forms of communion with God that are merely pragmatically tolerable but fail to reach the ideal of ethical faithfulness? The coupling of a negative moral evaluation of imprecatory desire with a positive endorsement of the place of imprecation in the church's worship results in a proposal for Christian prayer that risks pedagogical inconsistency, potentially shaping Christians in practice for a piety that is denounced in teaching as contradictory to the commands of their Lord.[245] If the imprecatory psalms are to be recovered and the benefits of their practice embraced in the church's worship, a pedagogically coherent proposal is necessary, one that demonstrates the congruity of imprecatory prayer with faithful Christian ethics and considers with sufficient nuance the inherently formative, norming capacity of the liturgical context.

Furthermore, the standard claim among advocates of relinquishment readings that, among the psalmists, violent rhetoric replaced violent action raises important questions. As noted above, the alleged absence of instantiations and intentions of personal violence is regularly presented as evidence that the imprecatory prayers functioned for the psalmists as a complete ceding of vengeance to God. But does this accurately describe the imprecatory psalms' testimony and function? In a detailed exegetical analysis of the individual laments, David Firth contends that these psalms universally reject human violence while nevertheless noting that the psalmic figure of the Israelite king stands as an exception: "As the representative of Yahweh, the king exercises his right in violence."[246] Firth recognizes that in the psalms the king may act as the royal, human agent of divine violence as he protects the covenant community and enforces justice, presumably through military means. Janowski similarly acknowledges that the psalms contain references to royal violence, but he additionally concedes that

---

[245] This pedagogical inconsistency is evident in Schaefer's claim that imprecation has no place in individual Christian piety but may be profitably included in Christian liturgy. Schaefer, *Psalms*, xliv. But where else is individual Christian piety learned but in the liturgical practice of the gathered church? The assertion of Zenger, *God of Vengeance?* 92, that the imprecatory psalms are neither theologically nor ethically normative but ought to be recovered in the church's liturgical practice—practice that implicitly communicates and establishes communal norms—similarly suffers from an underdeveloped vision of the inescapably formative capacity and inherent claims of liturgical performance.

[246] Firth, *Surrendering Retribution*, 3. Cf. David G. Firth, "Cries of the Oppressed," in *Wrestling with the Violence of God: Soundings in the Old Testament*, ed. M. Daniel Carroll R. and J. Blair Wilgus, BBRSup 10 (Winona Lake, Ind.: Eisenbrauns, 2015), 76–77.

some psalms communicate the expectation that God's people will participate in the divine exercise of vengeance.[247] If the king, the military, and the wider community are understood by the psalmists as potential agents of divine vengeance, it seems reasonable to suggest that the psalmists, and the whole of Israel together with them, would have prayed the imprecations not as a total relinquishing of all human violence to God, but as a petition that God would enact a just violence, which may include appropriate forms of human agency.[248] The thesis that the imprecatory psalms function to promote nonviolence in Christians through the surrender of vengeance to God cannot rest on the inaccurate and overgeneralized claim that the psalmists eschewed all human violence. Arguments proposing the imprecations as resources for the Christian eschewal of violence cannot be substantiated by drawing a straight line from the experience of Israel to the experience of the church. Claims about the peacemaking potential of the imprecatory psalms must give due consideration to their context within the biblical history of God's unfolding action and the related theological expectations of the Old Testament, explore the shifts introduced by the inauguration of God's temple-kingdom in Jesus Christ, and demonstrate how the psalms' vision of human agency in divine violence is consistent with the Christian project of peace.

The tendency among interpreters to entertain the possibility of surprising, and consequently less offensive, manifestations of divine justice also calls for careful evaluation. Relinquishment readings often depict imprecatory prayer as a surrendering of vengeance to a God who will do justice in—at least from the psalmists' perspective—unforeseeable ways, and the net effect of this strategic move is to introduce a disjunction between the petitions for judgment and God's genuine (potentially more merciful) intentions for the wicked. There exists, however, a significant collection of scriptural texts—spanning both testaments—that

[247] Janowski, *Arguing with God*, 126n133. Janowski refers to Ps 18:47–48 as an instance of royal violence and Pss 58:10–11; 149:7 as instances of wider participation in divine vengeance. Cf. Joel M. LeMon, "Psalms," in *DSE*, 645; Steffen Jenkins, "Retribution in the Canonical Psalter" (PhD diss., University of Bristol, 2015), 135–37.

[248] Cf. LeMon, "Psalms," 645. When we consider the place of divinely authorized conquest and war in Israel's history, it becomes difficult to imagine that Israelites who prayed along with the psalmists would not have considered their own agency as at least a potential means God would use to answer their prayers for deliverance and justice.

ostensibly present a perspective on divine justice that is compatible with the psalmists' expectations. How might Brueggemann's view of God's unpredictable freedom interact with the apparent biblical testimony concerning God's covenantal commitment to curse his enemies?[249] How might Zenger's understanding of divine justice as restoration without retribution or Miller's vision of the cross as the exhaustive demonstration of divine vengeance engage with those scriptural texts in which the New Testament authors, and even Jesus himself, seem to assure Christians of a retributive form of eschatological justice that awaits the unrepentant?[250] For the vision of God and his relationship to imprecatory prayer proposed by relinquishment readings to be persuasive, especially at the level of the local church, its advocates must acknowledge and address those challenging biblical texts that appear to offer an alternative, even psalmic, perspective on divine judgment.

The typical conceptions of divine justice promoted in relinquishment readings elicit additional questions concerning the existential practice of imprecatory prayer. Such proposals encourage Christians to wholeheartedly beg God to exercise a vengeance that God is in fact unwilling to administer, and which *they believe* God is unwilling to administer. So there is an incongruity not only between what is requested by the petitioner and how God may act in response, but also between what is formally requested and what is genuinely anticipated within the petitioner herself. If God's judgment in truth bears no resemblance to the pleas of the imprecations, does this not reduce Christian performance of the imprecatory psalms to a cathartic theological fiction—a mere emotional release with little, if any, connection to divine reality? And if Christians are to petition for vengeance with the conscious expectation that God has no intention of acting in the manner requested—if they know that their requests

---

[249]   Several scholars offer detailed arguments that the psalmists' petitions are consistent with the Bible's overt declarations of judgment and are based upon divine promises through which the fully free God has bound and committed himself to a very specific course of action. See Day, "Imprecatory Psalms," 98–109, 138–42; Shepherd, "Place of the Imprecatory Psalms," 110–26; Laney, "Fresh Look," 41–42; Nehrbass, "Therapeutic and Preaching Value," 124–25; Alex Luc, "Interpreting the Curses in the Psalms," *JETS* 42, no. 3 (1999): 405–7.

[250]   Terence E. Fretheim, "God and Violence in the Old Testament," *WW* 24, no. 1 (2004): 18, notes that though "the New Testament commonly avoids such a charge . . . it, too, is filled with violent words and deeds, and Jesus and the God of the New Testament are complicit in this violence." Cf. Adams, *War Psalms*, 40–46.

defy God's character and purposes and consequently will never come to fruition—does not such a practice risk quickly descending into a theologically disingenuous, prayerfully inauthentic, and existentially divided simulacrum of prayer?[251] Indeed, can one truly hand over vengeance to a God who refuses to grasp it, and who is known to do so? The depictions of divine justice that soften the offense of the imprecatory psalms—which get God off the hook, as it were—thus give rise to new issues regarding the potentially conflicted posture that relinquishment readings invite Christians to inhabit in their prayer of these psalms of vengeance.

Distinctive among relinquishment readings is the recent dissertation of Daniel Nehrbass. Operating from traditional evangelical assumptions concerning the inspiration of Scripture and the nature of divine justice,[252] Nehrbass contends that the imprecatory psalms should be primarily understood as prayers of dependence, the intentional transference of personal vengeance to a God who will indeed execute just eschatological judgment upon the wicked who do not repent.[253] Unlike some articulations

---

[251] Recourse to speech-act theory may help clarify this point. Speech-act theorists regularly refer to the felicity conditions of speech acts, the contextual conditions that must be met in order for a speech act to be successful or felicitous. John R. Searle, *Speech Acts: An Essay in the Philosophy of Language* (New York: Cambridge University Press, 1969), 66, maintains that one of the felicity conditions of a request is the preparatory condition: the hearer must be able to perform the requested action, and the speaker must *believe* that the hearer is able to perform the requested action in order for the request to be felicitous. An imprecatory request offered by a speaker who does not believe God is able to exact the requested judgment—that God is bound by his character to *not* judge in the manner requested—fails to meet this preparatory condition and is therefore an infelicitous speech act.

[252] On Nehrbass' doctrine of Scripture, see Nehrbass, "Therapeutic and Preaching Value," 16–18. Nehrbass, "Therapeutic and Preaching Value," 140, describes divine judgment as satisfied in the cross of Christ even as the future expectation of eschatological judgment remains. Cf. Nehrbass, "Therapeutic and Preaching Value," 283.

[253] Nehrbass, "Therapeutic and Preaching Value," 11, 210. Firth, "Cries of the Oppressed," 88–89, briefly offers a similar proposal for Christian performance of the imprecatory psalms from an evangelical perspective. Cf. also the abbreviated treatment of John Goldingay, *Psalms: Volume 1, Psalms 1–41*, BCOTWP (Grand Rapids: Baker Academic, 2006), 66–67, who emphasizes the New Testament's apparent lack of discomfort with imprecation and the dynamics of relinquishment.

of the relinquishment reading,[254] Nehrbass approaches the imprecatory psalms as the inspired words of God, which are truthful and authoritative in all that they teach,[255] leading him to consider the imprecatory psalms as theologically normative in their doctrine of God,[256] to argue for their consistency with the wider witness of Scripture,[257] and consequently to commend them as an ethically permissible alternative for Christians.[258]

In Nehrbass' estimation, then, Christian performance of the imprecatory psalms is not ethically problematic yet pragmatically useful but is rather a therapeutically valuable dimension of faithful Christian piety with deep resources for healing anger and eschewing violence.[259] Despite these convictions, however, Nehrbass still fails to untangle the central ethical conundrum of the imprecatory psalms and illustrate precisely how the Christian practice of imprecation coheres with Jesus' calls for enemy love—a solution without which the church is unlikely to widely embrace liturgical performance of the imprecatory psalms.[260] And while he

[254] See, e.g., Zenger, *God of Vengeance?* 81, 84–85.

[255] See Nehrbass, "Therapeutic and Preaching Value," 17. Nehrbass recognizes the unique issues involved in claiming that the prayerful words of humans to God are God's revelatory words to humans, and he connects the truthfulness of the psalmic prayers to their pedagogical intent. That is, he understands them to be true and trustworthy in everything they intend to teach about God, humanity, and the world.

[256] Nehrbass, "Therapeutic and Preaching Value," 127–36.

[257] Nehrbass, "Therapeutic and Preaching Value," 124–27.

[258] Nehrbass, "Therapeutic and Preaching Value," 285. Nehrbass approvingly quotes James Sire, *Learning to Pray through the Psalms* (Downers Grove Ill.: InterVarsity Press, 2005), 164: "We can trust the psalmist not to mislead us into a prayer that in the final analysis would be incorrect to pray."

[259] Nehrbass, "Therapeutic and Preaching Value," 204–40.

[260] Nehrbass, "Therapeutic and Preaching Value," 124, 280, acknowledges that for many Christians the fundamental tension introduced by the imprecatory psalms is their apparent incongruity with Jesus' ethical teaching. However, rather than demonstrating how the imprecations might be consistent with Jesus' ethical teaching, Nehrbass instead labors to illustrate their consistency with other portions of Scripture. Nehrbass, "Therapeutic and Preaching Value," 124–36. Nehrbass contends, "Clearly neither Jesus nor his disciples saw imprecation as inherently inconsistent with the nature of the Messiah," but neglects to offer an ethical argument as to how or why this might be the case. Nehrbass, "Therapeutic and Preaching Value," 128. The closest Nehrbass comes to offering a resolution to this question is in his assertion that "the Sermon on the Mount . . . is not the only place that treatment of enemies is addressed, nor does it offer the one and only way to deal with them." Nehrbass, "Therapeutic and

suggests that homiletical instruction alone is insufficient as an instrument of communal transformation,[261] the necessarily limited scope of Nehrbass' research prevents him from exploring the formative potential of performance of the imprecatory psalms in less didactic, more participatory modes.

Nehrbass' treatment of the imprecatory psalms reveals that the fundamental claims of the relinquishment reading exhibit a remarkable flexibility. Scholars with competing conceptions of Scripture, Christian ethics, and divine justice are nevertheless able to agree that an essential dynamic of imprecatory prayer is the submission of personal violence to God. This flexibility suggests that acknowledgement and exploration of a relinquishment dimension in the imprecatory psalms is not limited to a particular theological circle or hermeneutical niche but may complement a variety of broader, more comprehensive attempts to understand and appropriate the psalms of vengeance—attempts that aim to fill in the gaps left by relinquishment readings alone and to plumb further into the resources for healing that the imprecatory psalms might offer.[262]

Assessing Available Avenues and Charting a Coherent Course

As evidenced by the preceding analysis, interpretation of the imprecatory psalms does not take place in a theological vacuum. That is, there is no pure, objective, presuppositionless evaluation or application of these difficult texts. Rather, certain theological convictions that the reader brings to the interpretive task—especially regarding the inspiration of the imprecatory psalms, and subsidiarily regarding the shape of God's justice and

---

Preaching Value," 283. Nehrbass, "Therapeutic and Preaching Value," 282–83, 288, proposes that the prescriptive speech of Christ's Sermon on the Mount addresses God's people differently than the descriptive speech of the Psalter, but he concedes that even this observation does not ultimately invalidate utilization of imprecatory speech in light of the presence of imprecations in the New Testament. Firth, "Cries of the Oppressed," 81, likewise recognizes this tension without a detailed ethical resolution. Goldingay, *Psalms: Volume 1*, 66–67, does not address the issue.

[261] Nehrbass, "Therapeutic and Preaching Value," 199.

[262] Many scholars incorporate dimensions of the relinquishment proposal into readings of the imprecatory psalms that foreground other concepts and categories. See, e.g., Murray, "Christian Cursing?" 118–19; Day, "Imprecatory Psalms," 92; Zuck, "Problem of the Imprecatory Psalms," 69; Weiser, *Psalms*, 431–32; Limburg, *Psalms*, 473; Adams, *War Psalms*, 45–46; Bonhoeffer, "Sermon on a Psalm of Vengeance," 91; Lessing, "Broken Teeth," 370; Barker, *Imprecation as Divine Discourse*, 177.

the (dis)unity of the Bible[263]—exercise considerable influence in shaping the possible theological and ethical conclusions one may reach.[264] This is not to suggest, however, that these three doctrinal positions determine the interpreter's readings, for scholars who give very similar answers on these issues nevertheless exhibit appreciable diversity in their proposed readings, only that previously held beliefs concerning inspiration, divine judgment, and the relationship between the testaments both sanction and limit the permissible hermeneutical moves any interpreter may consistently employ in assessing the imprecations.

Representatives of the aberrant human sentiment reading (e.g., Lewis) and the majority relinquishment reading (e.g., Zenger)[265] deny that the imprecatory psalms are themselves the inspired—and therefore truthful and authoritative—words of God.[266] A doctrine of Scripture that separates the words of the imprecatory psalms from the revealing word of God opens up hermeneutical maneuvers otherwise unavailable, making possible the conclusion that the psalms contain material that is both theologically non-normative and ethically deviant. Only if the imprecatory psalms do not address the church in their very words with the trustworthy and authoritative address of God can the interpreter plausibly and unproblematically contend that the vision of God (and God's justice) implicit in the psalms is theologically inaccurate and that the ethics exhibited and endorsed by the imprecations are inconsistent with the psalmists', and our,

[263] Cf. Gabriel Torretta, "Rediscovering the Imprecatory Psalms: A Thomistic Approach," *The Thomist: A Speculative Quarterly Review* 80, no. 1 (2016): 30.

[264] Undoubtedly relevant as well are the conscriptive practices of a given interpreter's liturgical tradition and sociocultural location, practices that reflect and reinforce a theologically charged vision of the world and that in turn make possible certain ways of cognitively reflecting on theological and ethical issues. See my "Introduction: The Conditions of Interpretation and the Tools of the Trade," in *Violent Biblical Texts: New Approaches*, ed. Trevor Laurence and Helen Paynter (Sheffield: Sheffield Phoenix Press, 2022).

[265] I utilize the phrase "majority relinquishment reading" to distinguish Nehrbass' evangelical relinquishment reading (briefly espoused by Firth and Goldingay as well) from the nonevangelical proposal most fully articulated by Zenger and supported by most other relinquishment proponents.

[266] Interestingly, Peter Craigie—an advocate of the aberrant human sentiment reading—is often identified with the evangelical tradition but avers that the imprecatory psalms "are not the oracles of God." Craigie, *Psalms 1–50*, 41. How coherently this claim aligns with an evangelical understanding of Scripture's inspiration is an open question.

moral obligations before God.[267] Stated positively, when the psalms are assessed as human words capable of theological and moral error, ascriptions of theological and moral error become valid interpretive judgments. Denying any traditional evangelical conception of the inspiration of the imprecations consequently diminishes the impetus for synthesizing how the cursing psalms might harmonize with the rest of the canon because, on this view, positing disharmony within the canon poses no real theological problem. While the aberrant human sentiment and majority relinquishment readings arrive at differing conclusions regarding the appropriateness of Christian performance of the imprecatory psalms, both readings attempt to take the sting out—reduce the offense—of the psalms of vengeance with the assurance that, whether one prays such prayers or not, the imprecatory psalms do not veraciously reflect the character and will of God or lay moral claim upon the church as his faithful divine discourse. But this particular resolution of the tension must be predicated on a prior formulation of the psalms' inspiration.

For interpreters who bring to the imprecatory psalms a traditional evangelical conviction regarding their authoritative truthfulness, evaluation of the psalmists' pleas as theologically erroneous or ethically aberrant is ruled out from the start. The corresponding presupposition that Scripture speaks as the unified word of a single divine author necessitates creative and critical deliberation on the manner in which the imprecations' ethics and portrait of God relate to the wider biblical witness. The requirements that evangelical readings of the psalms of vengeance affirm their theological and ethical faithfulness and demonstrate canonical coherence, however, leave evangelical interpreters with a noteworthy hermeneutical flexibility. An evangelical doctrine of inspiration is in fact consistent with every proposal reviewed above, with the exception of the aberrant human sentiment reading, and there is at least one significant evangelical representative of each of these positions.

Those evangelicals who distance the imprecatory psalms from the life and piety of the church do not do so with justifications that the words of the psalms are not the words of God or reflective of his intentions to

---

[267] I include the phrase "in their very words" because, while Lewis and Zenger deny that God's words are identifiable with the psalmists' words, they nevertheless affirm there is a type of revelation from God that occurs through the imprecatory psalms. In their understandings, what God intends to communicate through the psalms does not depend upon their theological or ethical normativity.

administer justice through divine vengeance. Rather, evangelical interpreters create this necessary distance through a variety of alternative methods, whether by placing the petitions on the lips of Jesus (Adams) or positing a relationship of inferiority (Zuck) or discontinuity (e.g., Laney, Kidner, Kline) between the old and new covenants.[268] In each case, the hermeneutical moves employed to address the ethical questions surrounding Christian performance of the imprecatory psalms and to qualify the church's relation to these prayers are compatible with a robust affirmation of the psalms' theological truthfulness and ethical faithfulness. Such proposals therefore reveal that while evangelical convictions do not necessitate seamless appropriation of the imprecatory psalms by the church, they certainly shape how interpreters may argue for their ethical impropriety for, or modified appropriation by, Christians.

Proponents of the covenantal continuity reading (e.g., Day) uphold a traditional evangelical doctrine of Scripture while maintaining that Christian practice of the imprecatory psalms is ethically warranted. The dogmatic assumption that Scripture is inspired, and thus a noncontradicting unity, requires that these interpreters demonstrate how such performance ethically coheres with Jesus' commands of enemy love. It is on this point that Nehrbass' evangelical iteration of the relinquishment proposal falls short, for Nehrbass asserts that the biblical testimony permits Christian performance of the imprecations without working out precisely how this licensing of imprecation does not contravene the commands of Christ. Nehrbass' position leaves the moral directives of Scripture in sharp tension without resolution, thereby rendering him susceptible to the charge that his conclusions are out of line with his own affirmations about Scripture. Advocates of the majority relinquishment reading endorse Christian practice of the imprecatory psalms as well, but their simultaneous insistence that such performance is morally problematic raises considerable concerns about the proposal's ethical and pedagogical consistency.

No less than the readings surveyed, the shape of the argument I put forward is circumscribed and stimulated by the theological assumptions with

---

[268]   Though they do not receive sustained attention here, evangelical scholars Johannes Vos and Alex Luc generate this requisite distance in creative ways as well. Vos, "Ethical Problem," appeals to specially revealed knowledge of election and reprobation as the morally decisive factor, and Luc, "Interpreting the Curses," reevaluates the type of speech act present in the imprecations, maintaining that the imprecatory psalms are declarative, prophetic judgment proclamations and not strictly petitionary requests. See Laurence, "Cursing with God," 56–81.

which I approach the imprecatory psalms. My evangelical conviction that Scripture speaks to the church as the inspired word of God—God's own address to his covenant people—commits me to receiving the testimony of the psalms as accurate representations of God's works, character, and will and to regarding the prayerful, pedagogical example of the imprecations as ethically faithful, covenantally appropriate piety. My perspective on the narrative unity of the Bible and the Christocentric focus of all of God's redemptive-historical workings prohibits recourse to the interpretive strategies of covenantal inferiority and discontinuity readings, which are grounded in different conceptions of the relationship between the Old and New Testaments, and instead necessitates hermeneutical engagement with the imprecatory psalms that accounts for their place in and contribution to this unified, Christocentric biblical narrative. And because my doctrine of Scripture assumes that the divine author speaks sans contradiction to his people, the onus is mine to demonstrate how my redemptive-historical reading of the psalms of vengeance and subsequent proposal for Christian performance may be reconciled with the ethics of Jesus' kingdom.

Taken together, the questions posed to each of the prominent proposals for interpreting and performing the imprecatory psalms point toward the requisite contours of a successful constructive proposal for Christian enactment of the psalms of vengeance. Any such proposal must address the lacunae and avoid the points of vulnerability identified in the existing body of research. We may therefore suggest the following criteria for a successful, coherent, and persuasive proposal for the interpretation and performance of the imprecatory psalms, criteria which will shape the proceeding investigation. The proposal must:

- Explore the imprecatory psalms in their redemptive-historical context—that is, in light of their location in the developing Christocentric narrative of Scripture and the theological expectations, ethical obligations, covenantal structures, and eschatological character related to that location—and must consider how the church's redemptive-historical location influences her relationship to such psalms.

- Account for the psalmic assumption that there are ethically appropriate forms of instrumental human agency in God's exercise of vengeance.

- Recognize and exhibit consonance with the pedagogical function of the Psalter for Israel and the apostolic church, providing a viable explanation for the psalms' instructive, piety-shaping performance by both communities.

- Interact with and offer a cogent rationale for New Testament instances of imprecatory speech.

- Examine New Testament citations of and allusions to the imprecatory psalms in order to clarify the polyvalent Christological significance of the imprecatory psalms.

- Address the internal, existential dynamics of ethically faithful imprecatory prayer, elucidating the requisite attitudinal postures and teleological aims of such prayer and how faithful practice of the imprecatory psalms works upon, directs, and develops the imprecator, especially in light of the redemptive-historical location of the church and the Christological significance of the imprecatory psalms.

- Examine how Christian practice of the imprecatory psalms relates to New Testament commands of enemy love.

- Exhibit ethical consistency. That is, conclusions that Christians ought to pray the imprecatory psalms should be grounded in ethical reasoning that finds such prayer morally faithful. If a proposal deems Christian performance of the imprecatory psalms to be ethically inappropriate, the proposal should not encourage such unethical forms of communion with God.

- Exhibit pedagogical consistency. That is, conclusions that Christian churches ought to include performance of the imprecatory psalms in the pedagogically charged rhythms of liturgical worship ought to be grounded in the judgment that such prayer assumes and imparts a correct theological understanding of God and is an ethically faithful practice. If a proposal concludes that imprecatory prayer misrepresents God and defies Christian ethical standards, the proposal should not encourage such prayer in liturgical worship.

- Exhibit existential consistency. That is, any proposal for Christian performance of the imprecatory psalms should meet the felicity conditions of requests, which include a belief by the petitioner that the hearer is able to perform the requested act. Endorsements of Christian practice of the imprecatory psalms should therefore promote the expectation within Christians that God is able to act in the manner requested without defying his character. If a proposal overtly discourages the expectation that God will act in accord with Christians' imprecatory petitions, the proposal should not encourage Christian performance of the imprecatory psalms, for such prayer would be existentially divided and fail to meet the conditions of a felicitous request.

Clearly, latent within our primary question—*How may the Christian church perform the imprecatory psalms in an ethically faithful manner?*—lie significant subsidiary questions regarding, among other things, the ethical evaluation of the judgment prayers in their psalmic context and the consonance of such petitions with God's action in Jesus Christ and with the consequent moral calling of the community that follows Jesus in faith. What characteristics must a method exhibit in order to address satisfactorily these questions and meet the stipulated criteria?

A fitting method must in the first place be *exegetical*.[269] Because this investigation focuses on Christian performance of the *imprecatory psalms*, ethical reflection must begin with the raw material provided by exegesis of the imprecatory psalms themselves, exegesis that seeks to identify and describe their discrete petitions, discursive force, theological claims, and constitutive themes.[270] I am not here interested in the morality of Christian prayer for divine judgment as a general category of behavior but in Christian

---

[269]   On the relationship between ethics and exegesis, cf., e.g., Charles E. Curran and Richard A. McCormick, eds., *The Use of Scripture in Moral Theology*, Readings in Moral Theology 4 (New York: Paulist Press, 1984); Oliver M. T. O'Donovan, "The Possibility of a Biblical Ethic," *TSF Bulletin* 67 (1973); Craig Bartholomew, Jonathan Chaplin, Robert Son, and Al Wolters, eds., *A Royal Priesthood? The Use of the Bible Ethically and Politically, A Dialogue with Oliver O'Donovan*, Scripture and Hermeneutics Series 3 (Grand Rapids: Zondervan, 2002); Charles H. Cosgrove, "Scripture in Ethics: A History," in *DSE*, 13–25; Bruce C. Birch, "Scripture in Ethics: Methodological Issues," in *DSE*, 27–34; Charles H. Cosgrove, *Appealing to Scripture in Moral Debate: Five Hermeneutical Rules* (Grand Rapids: Eerdmans, 2002). My focus here is specifically on the role of exegesis in investigating the ethics of Christian performance of particular Old Testament texts. My interest is not merely in ethics generally, or even Old Testament ethics, but in the ethics of Christian enactment of certain psalmic prayers, an interest that makes disciplined exegetical engagement indispensable.

[270]   On the relationship between exegesis and biblical theology, see D. A. Carson, "Systematic Theology and Biblical Theology," in *NDBT*, 91. Exegesis is analytical and descriptive, but Carson's discussion draws attention to the nonobjective character of this exercise. That is, exegesis always entails theological presuppositions and concomitant hermeneutical commitments. Cf. Kevin J. Vanhoozer, "Exegesis and Hermeneutics," in *NDBT*, 55.

prayer of the canonical judgment petitions of the Psalter.[271] Apart from careful exegetical attention to the imprecatory psalms, ethical deliberation on concepts like cursing and vengeance may quite easily import assumptions about the characteristic content, attitudes, and aims of imprecatory petition that reflect more the experiences, context, presuppositions, and moral predilections of the inquirer than they do the specific nuances and concerns of the imprecatory psalms. And because this investigation focuses on *Christian* performance of the imprecatory psalms, ethical reflection must take into account exegesis of those New Testament texts, directed at the new covenant community in light of the advent of Christ, that are relevant to the practice of the psalmic imprecations. These relevant New Testament texts include those that cite or allude to the imprecatory psalms, those that exhibit some form of imprecatory petition, as well as those that enjoin an enemy love that ostensibly invalidates prayers of vengeance. Failure to give such texts appropriate consideration will result in moral conclusions and pre/proscriptions that cannot be reconciled with the admittedly diverse data of the New Testament—data that, as the authoritative address of God, must have the final word in all matters of the church's life and faith.[272] An exegetical approach is thus necessary—but not in and of itself sufficient.

This is because a fitting method must also be *theological*. Indispensable as exegesis of both the imprecatory psalms and relevant New Testament passages may be, more is required for the development of an ethic of Christian performance of the psalmic imprecations than mere collation, combination, or comparative analysis of disparate biblical teachings and examples.[273]

---

[271] Of course, any examination of the ethics of Christian performance of the imprecatory psalms will have implications for the question of ethical Christian prayer for judgment more generally.

[272] In its theological ethics, the Reformed tradition to which I am indebted—while diverse in its own right—has considered exegesis of Scripture as integral to the ethical enterprise. See Dirkie Smit, "Reformed Ethics," in *DSE*, 663–64. Calvin's discussion of the moral law in *Institutes of the Christian Religion*, ed. John T. McNeill, trans. Ford Lewis Battles (Louisville: Westminster John Knox, 1960), 2.8, illustrates the relationship between Reformed convictions about biblical authority and exegetical consideration of Scripture in ethical reasoning. Calvin, in a manner followed by the Reformed confessions and catechisms, organizes his treatment around the Ten Commandments while also appealing to additional Old Testament and New Testament texts to elucidate the Christian's ethical obligations.

[273] Cf. Oliver O'Donovan, *Resurrection and Moral Order: An Outline for Evangelical Ethics*, 2nd ed. (Grand Rapids: Eerdmans, 1994), 182; Craig G.

Indeed, it is precisely because coherent consolidation of the discordant voices of the Psalter and the rest of Scripture, not least Jesus, has proven so elusive that the ethical question still generates so much attention from scholars and laypersons alike.[274] What is required is a theological framework within which the polyphonous biblical testimony may be integrated,[275] a theological framework that is able to explain such psalms' prayerful emergence and propriety within God's reality as well as the presence of imprecatory speech in the New Testament alongside apparently conflicting emphases on enemy love. Of course, some such framework is always already at work in the act of scriptural interpretation and moral reasoning about the Bible.[276] But this framework needs to be made explicit rather than permitted to operate unacknowledged so that the theological commitments and rationale shaping the interpreter's ethical synthesis of texts are themselves open to critical examination and may be shown to provide justification for the resultant moral conclusions, thereby avoiding the suspicion of hermeneutical arbitrariness. A distinctly theological approach to the ethical question makes possible integration of the diverse exegetical data that not only addresses whether and how the church may make the Psalter's imprecatory prayers her own but also demonstrates why such scriptural diversity exists, framing the seemingly divergent particularities of God's word within the determinative theological structures that make sense of them.

Bartholomew, introduction to Bartholomew et al., *Royal Priesthood?* 19–26; Allen Verhey, "Ethics in Scripture," in *DSE*, 5; Christopher J. H. Wright, *Living as the People of God: The Relevance of Old Testament Ethics* (Leicester: InterVarsity Press, 1983), 19; Walter C. Kaiser, Jr., *Toward Old Testament Ethics* (Grand Rapids: Academie Books, 1983), 4.

[274] Gilbert Meilander, "Ethics and Exegesis: A Great Gulf?" in Bartholomew et al., *Royal Priesthood?* 261, reflects more generally on the way the Bible, given its diversity, informs ethics: "Our reading of the Bible shapes moral and political insight not, usually, by proofs almost mathematical in character, but by something better described (in Mill's phrase from a quite different context) as considerations 'sufficient to determine the intellect.' The Bible is far too variegated a book for our use of it to be otherwise."

[275] See O'Donovan, *Resurrection and Moral Order*, 200.

[276] Verhey, "Ethics in Scripture," 5, asserts that "biblical ethics is inalienably theological." This inalienably theological character of biblical ethics means not only that ethics requires theological reflection in order to be approached correctly but that ethics always involves theological reasoning, whether the ethical interrogator recognizes it or not.

In this case, however, a properly theological method must be specifically *biblical theological*. Dogmatic categories alone are insufficient for adequately attending to the salient issues of the imprecatory psalms and their
Christian rehearsal.[277] Systematic theology logically organizes doctrine
and trades in atemporal concepts, but the ethical question of Christian
performance of Israelite prayers contains within it an inescapably temporal element: How ought God's covenant people *now*—that is, in response
to the epoch-altering revelation and accomplishments of Christ—pray the
imprecatory prayers of God's covenant people in the past?[278] While dogmatic formulations of, for example, divine sovereignty or the *imago Dei*
may indeed stimulate fruitful reflection on certain facets of the morality
of ecclesial imprecation, these categories on their own are ill-equipped
to consider the historical character of the question I am here posing.[279]
Theological engagement with the imprecatory psalms must come to the
task with the conceptual resources to account for the historical particu-
larity of these Old Testament petitions and the new historical moment in
which the church participates. Such engagement requires the conceptual
resources to reckon with the historically contingent contours of ethical
prayer to a God who not only is but who acts progressively in time and
space to make known his saving purposes and bring them to completion in a manner that calls forth various responses at various moments.

---

[277]   See my critique of Johannes Vos' privileging of the Reformed doctrine
of election in his examination of the ethics of Christian imprecation in "Cursing
with God," 79–80.

[278]   Wright, *Living as the People of God*, 24–26, argues that in both testaments, history has ethical significance, for God's redemptive work in the past
and his eschatological purposes for the future frame the moral agent's action
in the present. Wright notes that there is a continuity between Old Testament
and New Testament ethics in that both are rooted in the historical activity of
God (with its redemptive and eschatological dimensions) but also acknowledges that God has done something new in history in the person of Jesus. The
ethical intelligibility of the imprecatory psalms thus arises from the redemptive-
eschatological matrix created by God's historical involvement with Israel, and
ethical performance of these psalms by the church requires consideration of the
new redemptive-eschatological matrix that emerges from the life, death, and
resurrection of Jesus.

[279]   One could further argue that atemporal dogmatic categories alone are
incapable of adequately addressing *any* ethical question. See Stanley Hauerwas,
A Community of Character: Toward a Constructive Christian Social Ethic (Notre
Dame: University of Notre Dame Press, 1981), 98–100.

Biblical theology is that discipline concerned with the historical development of God's revelation and saving action,[280] and it is therefore a suitable discipline for investigating how the Psalter's old covenant cries might find voice in the new covenant church and the difference Jesus makes for the prayerful piety of his disciples. On this point the general approach of the various proponents of covenantal readings is quite right, even if their conclusions leave something to be desired, for their method for addressing the ethics of Christian prayer of the imprecations foregrounds a category (covenant) that introduces the temporal dimension of God's developing redemptive activity as a lens for understanding the judgment psalms and the church's relationship to them.

Further, a fitting method must be *ethically holistic*. This entails first that a methodology for exploring the ethics of Christian imprecation must attend to each of the aspects of the practice that Scripture identifies as morally significant and so address the whole person and the whole ethical life.[281] Even a cursory reading of the Bible reveals a God who not only issues divine commands to govern the actions of moral agents but also is deeply concerned with the affective aims and postures of the moral agent's heart—the intended *teloi* of human acts and the desires, attitudes, and dispositions from which such acts are committed.[282] Ethical inquiry that addresses these salient features of moral creaturely existence will consider act and agent; action, attitude, and aspiration; what the church is commanded by God to do as well as how (with what posture) and why (to

---

[280] Geerhardus Vos, *Biblical Theology of the Old and New Testaments* (Grand Rapids: Eerdmans, 1948), 16; Brian Rosner, "Biblical Theology," in *NDBT*, 4.

[281] See O'Donovan, *Resurrection and Moral Order*, 204–5.

[282] One need only consult Christ's Sermon on the Mount to observe these various morally significant dimensions of human behavior. Jesus regularly explicitly commands and prohibits specific acts (e.g., Matt 7:1–6), issues instructions regarding the proper goals of acts (e.g., Matt 6:1–18), and teaches that right desires and attitudes are essential to genuinely ethical living (e.g., Matt 5:21–48). Indeed, these dimensions are frequently quite difficult to unravel, for Jesus often commands internal postures of the heart that in turn reorient the goals of behavior, enjoining as the Christian's ethical duty a life of virtue aimed at proper ends. We would do well, then, to treat these aspects of Christian ethics as complementary, mutually informing, and highly interwoven. See Calvin, *Institutes*, 2.8.6, where Calvin maintains that God's jurisdiction covers the whole moral agent. Cf. O'Donovan, *Resurrection and Moral Order*, 204–7. Kaiser, *Toward Old Testament Ethics*, 7–10, demonstrates that this concern is evident in the Old Testament as well.

what end) she is called to ethically participate in God's world.[283] Accordingly, if I am to arrive at a holistically ethical proposal for Christian performance of the imprecatory psalms, my methodology must address each of the dimensions Christian Scripture upholds as ethically consequential. To fail to do justice to any of these aspects of the ethics of Christian imprecation would leave important questions unanswered and consequently would leave the church without the requisite guidance to perform these psalms with confidence regarding the ethical propriety of her petitions. Even worse, such failure could give the impression that the neglected aspects are morally insignificant for the ecclesial rehearsal of the imprecatory psalms, thereby legitimating modes of imprecatory prayer that are in fact highly problematic for the church's witness and formation. It is, after all, quite easy to imagine how the church might pray right prayers as regards their formal content and yet do so with improper (that is, sinful) goals or dispositions toward God and the enemy,[284] or alternatively how the covenant community might imprecate from appropriate attitudes toward proper ends while praying substantively incomplete prayers. An ethically holistic method—one that accounts for the various morally significant features of Christian imprecation—will yield conclusions that enable the church's confident, ethically faithful rehearsal of the imprecatory psalms while ensuring that this rehearsal is in every relevant aspect moral rehearsal that witnesses to the authority, character, and beauty of her Lord and his kingdom.

Second, an ethically holistic examination of Christian performance of the imprecatory psalms must attend to the person-altering, affection-generating dynamics of ecclesial imprecation. Ethics as a discipline is concerned not only with developing criteria that render practices morally permissible but also with the ways that practices act upon agents, forming

---

[283] Cf. Oliver O'Donovan, *Self, World, and Time*, vol. 1 of *Ethics as Theology* (Grand Rapids: Eerdmans, 2013), 18. See esp. John Frame, *The Doctrine of the Christian Life*, A Theology of Lordship (Phillipsburg, N.J.: P&R Publishing, 2008), 19–37. Hauerwas, *Community of Character*, 98—following Alasdair MacIntyre, "Theology, Ethics, and the Ethics of Medicine and Health Care: Comments on Papers by Novak, Mouw, Roach, Cahill, and Hartt," *J. Med. Philos.* 4, no. 4 (1979): 437—observes that "there is no inherent incompatibility between a *telos*, virtue, and law."

[284] This disjunction between formal speech and internal intention is precisely in view in the description of enemies in Ps 62:4: "They bless with their mouths, but inwardly they curse."

them as persons and cultivating new ways of being.[285] Ethical investigation of a given practice is therefore incomplete unless it includes investigation of how the practice teaches, trains, and disciplines the church to inhabit God's world. Consequently, a holistic ethical treatment of Christian enactment of the imprecatory psalms, in addition to discerning the fitting affective postures and aims of imprecatory prayer, must address the affective effects of Christian imprecation: how such enactment stimulates the affections—producing internal movements of emotion, intention, evaluation, and desire[286]—and thus reorients the imprecating agent in relation to God, world, and enemies in ethically significant ways that deter certain forms of action and commend new possibilities.[287] Given the understandable (and historically substantiated) concern that the imprecatory psalms could be enacted in a manner that exercises and

---

[285]   See D. E. Saliers, "Liturgy and Ethics: Some New Beginnings," *JRE* 7, no. 2 (1979): 174. Cf. Stanley Hauerwas and Samuel Wells, "Why Christian Ethics Was Invented," in *The Blackwell Companion to Christian Ethics*, ed. Stanley Hauerwas and Samuel Wells (Malden, Mass.: Blackwell, 2004), 37. Theological ethics must concern itself with the ethical formation that practices facilitate, asking not only "What ought we to do?" but also "How will doing what we ought to do help us be who we ought to be (and thus more readily do what we ought to do)?" As noted in "From System to Story: An Alternative Pattern for Rationality in Ethics," in *Truthfulness and Tragedy: Further Investigations in Christian Ethics*, by Stanley Hauerwas, with Richard Bondi and David B. Burrell (Notre Dame: University of Notre Dame Press, 1977), 36, the practices that flow from an ethically determinative story of the world in turn shape practitioners to relate to this storied world in particular ways. Theological ethics must account for the ways that narrative renders practices morally intelligible and the ways practices morally fashion practitioners for participation in the narrative.

[286]   On the affections, see the influential reflections of Saint Augustine, *City of God*, trans. Marcus Dods (New York: Modern Library, 1993), 14.6–9; Jonathan Edwards, *Religious Affections*, in vol. 2 of *Works of Jonathan Edwards*, ed. John E. Smith (New Haven: Yale University Press, 1959); and more recently the relevant discussions of Joshua Hordern, *Political Affections: Civic Participation and Moral Theology* (Oxford: Oxford University Press, 2013), 61–130; Gregory S. Clapper, "Affections," in *DSE*, 44–45; Martha C. Nussbaum, *Upheavals of Thought: The Intelligence of Emotions* (New York: Cambridge University Press, 2001), 19–88.

[287]   William C. Spohn, "Christian Spirituality and Theological Ethics," in *The Blackwell Companion to Christian Spirituality*, ed. Arthur Holder (Malden, Mass.: Wiley-Blackwell, 2011), 271, discusses the affection-shaping character of Christian spiritual practices in general, connecting the affections with the biblical image of the heart and describing them as "dispositions, abiding inclinations to act in certain ways."

reinforces self-justifying, vengeful, and potentially dangerous affections, a method that accounts for the affectively generative dimensions
of Christian imprecation is necessary to guard against sanctioning a
mode of imprecatory performance that deforms disciples and cultivates
dispositions that incline petitioners toward self-justification, bitterness,
vindictiveness, and even violence.[288] Further, attention to the affective
kinetics of Christian imprecation enables exploration of the ways that
the imprecatory psalms might function positively to stimulate ethically
faithful affections, and how these psalms might act upon Christians as
a means of grace to generate dispositions and desires consonant with
their calling.[289]

A Redemptive-Historical Ethic of Christian Imprecation

My approach to addressing the morality of Christian performance of the
imprecatory psalms may be described as an exercise in redemptive-historical
ethics. A redemptive-historical method for investigating the ethics of Christian imprecation interprets the psalmic petitions for judgment and reflects
upon the moral life of the church from within the framework of God's overarching story of the world. This story is immersive, a metanarrative that
structures, defines, and directs every dimension of human existence. As
such, the canonical narrative of God's redemptive works in history provides
the plot within which the dialogue of the imprecatory psalms may be properly interpreted and simultaneously sweeps up the church into a story that
comprehensively governs her participation in God's world, including her
practice of imprecatory prayer. The redemptive-historical narrative that elucidates the theo-logic and ethical coherence of the imprecatory psalms is on
this understanding the very narrative in which the church dwells, the very
narrative that dictates what counts as fitting and faithful action for Christians. A redemptive-historical-ethical method thus utilizes the redemptive-
historical story of God in Scripture as a lens for ethically understanding

---

[288] See Calvin, *Commentary on the Book of Psalms*, 4:275–6; Zenger, *God of
Vengeance?* 57–58. Cf. Barton, *Understanding Old Testament Ethics*, 73–74. The
potential for malformation (not only of the mind but also of the heart) requires
attention to how—by what process and with what results—the church is shaped
through her interaction with texts like the imprecatory psalms.

[289] Cf. the reflections on the ethically formative capacity of prayer by
Saliers, "Liturgy and Ethics," 182–86; Smith, *Imagining the Kingdom*, 176–77;
Debra Dean Murphy, *Teaching That Transforms: Worship as the Heart of Chris-
tian Education* (Grand Rapids: Brazos, 2004), 173–87.

what is happening in the psalmic cries for justice and what must happen in the church's imprecatory performance.

Ethics and narrative are inextricably connected. Story provides the categories and teleology from which moral claims emerge and within which they make sense. Alasdair MacIntyre describes the narrative shape of human existence, observing that human acts only become intelligible when situated within a story.[290] MacIntyre maintains that the human is "essentially a story-telling animal,"[291] one who not only renders intelligible the actions of others by means of narrative but who lives out a narrative and understands his or her life in narrative terms.[292] Consequently, the way for this story-telling animal to determine what counts as ethical action is to determine the narrative in which he or she is a character: "I can only answer the question 'What am I to do?' if I can answer the prior question 'Of what story or stories do I find myself a part?'"[293] Story provides both a past history and a vision of the future that impinge upon the present and, whether tacitly or through conscious reflection, frame considerations of how moral agents may ethically play their part as actors within the narrative.

In a manner consonant with MacIntyre's insights into the significance of story, narrative approaches to Christian ethics privilege story as a lens for exploring the content, conditions, and coherence of the moral life of the church. Stanley Hauerwas argues that ethics is inherently and inescapably narratival,[294] proposing that "our first moral question must be Of what history am I a part and how can I best understand it?"[295] One's situatedness within a narrative is determinative for ethical deliberation concerning what constitutes appropriate action. For Hauerwas, the issue is not whether a

[290] Alasdair MacIntyre, *After Virtue: A Study in Moral Theory*, 3rd ed. (Notre Dame: University of Notre Dame Press, 2007), 206–10. Cf. the contention of Stephen Crites, "The Narrative Quality of Experience," *JAAR* 39, no. 3 (1971): 291, that "the formal quality of experience through time is inherently narrative."

[291] MacIntyre, *After Virtue*, 216.

[292] MacIntyre, *After Virtue*, 212.

[293] MacIntyre, *After Virtue*, 216.

[294] Hauerwas, *Community of Character*, 98–99. Cf. Hauerwas, *The Peaceable Kingdom: A Primer in Christian Ethics* (Notre Dame: University of Notre Dame Press, 1983), 61; Hauerwas and Burrell, "From System to Story," in Hauerwas, with Bondi and Burrell, *Truthfulness and Tragedy*, 21.

[295] Hauerwas, *Community of Character*, 100; cf. Hauerwas, *Community of Character*, 10. Hauerwas regularly notes the influence of Alasdair MacIntyre on his work, so even when MacIntyre is not explicitly cited, it is not surprising to hear echoes of MacIntyre in the development of Hauerwas' arguments.

community's ethics is formed by a story,[296] but rather which story exercises such morally formative influence,[297] and the story that forms the Christian community is the story of God communicated by Scripture and most fully revealed in the story of Christ.[298] Hauerwas explains:

> There is no point outside our history where we can secure a place to anchor our moral convictions. We must begin in the middle, that is, we must begin within a narrative. Christianity offers a narrative about God's relationship to creation that gives us the means to recognize we are God's creatures. . . . We have a saving God, and we are saved by being invited to share in the work of the kingdom through the history God has created in Israel and the work of Jesus. Such a history completes our nature as well as our particular history by placing us within an adventure which we claim is nothing less than God's purpose for all of creation.[299]

The Christian Scriptures tell the story of what God is doing with and within his creation, a story that conscripts the church as participants in God's kingdom and "purpose for all of creation" and provides the requisite narrative anchor for her moral convictions, offering her a truthful vision of God's world.[300] The calling of the Christian community, then, is to live as befits characters in God's narrative,[301] and this living is only possible as the community is schooled in virtue, shaped in character, and supplied

[296] Hauerwas reflects on the definition of story and its place in Christian theology in "Story and Theology," in Hauerwas, with Bondi and Burrell, *Truthfulness and Tragedy*, 71–81. Cf. Stanley Hauerwas and L. Gregory Jones, eds., *Why Narrative? Readings in Narrative Theology* (Grand Rapids: Eerdmans, 1989).

[297] Hauerwas, *Community of Character*, 4; cf. Hauerwas and Jones, *Why Narrative?* 9–10, 99.

[298] Hauerwas and Jones, *Why Narrative?* 10: "For as H. R. Niebuhr argued, only when we know 'what is going on,' do we know 'what we should do,' and Christians believe that we learn most decisively 'what is going on' in the cross and resurrection of Christ." Cf. Hauerwas and Jones, *Why Narrative?* 149. In addition to noting that ethics as a discipline is necessarily narratival, Hauerwas, *Peaceable Kingdom*, 24–29, argues that Christian theological convictions take the form of narrative, further confirming the appropriateness of a narrative approach to Christian ethics.

[299] Hauerwas, *Peaceable Kingdom*, 62.

[300] Hauerwas and Jones, *Why Narrative?* 29. Cf. Hauerwas, "Vision, Stories, and Character," in *The Hauerwas Reader*, ed. John Berkman and Michael Cartwright (Durham, N.C.: Duke University Press, 2001), 165–70.

[301] Hauerwas, *Community of Character*, 49: "To be a disciple means to share Christ's story, to participate in the reality of God's rule."

with a new grammar for existence by the story of Jesus.[302] Hauerwas' narrative ethics thus involves moral reflection on the ways of being that correspond to God's story of Christ and the story-shaped practices that grow the church into faithful actors.[303]

This narrative-oriented approach to Christian ethics helpfully attends to the ineluctably storied character of human being, of moral deliberation, and of the Christian convictions that define the church's conceptions of God, self, and world.[304] Is it possible to order the basic sensibilities of narrative ethics toward the interpretation of the imprecatory psalms and their performance by Christians—to integrate the promising resources of a narrative framework for ethical inquiry with a textually focused approach that attends to the particularities of the psalms and the New Testament witness?

Redemptive-historical biblical theology offers a promising way forward. This discipline seeks to observe and interrogate the unity of Scripture and explore the relationship of discrete texts to other texts and to the wider Christocentric, canonical narrative of God's saving works in history,[305] describing the story of Scripture on its own terms and investigating

---

[302] The Christian narrative thus performs a double function, philosophically providing the narrative basis for Christian ethics and practically forming the church into the type of community that can faithfully participate in the narrative. Hauerwas, *Community of Character*, 67: "The narrative of scripture not only 'renders a character' but renders a community capable of ordering its existence appropriate to such stories. Jews and Christians believe this narrative does nothing less than render the character of God and in so doing renders us to be the kind of people appropriate to that character." Cf. Hauerwas, *Community of Character*, 35; *Peaceable Kingdom*, 94; Hauerwas and Burrell, "From System to Story," 36.

[303] See Hauerwas, *Peaceable Kingdom*, 69.

[304] Hauerwas' method is not, however, immune to critique. John Barton, *Ethics and the Old Testament* (London: SCM Press, 1998), 21–22, notes that, despite the priority granted to the Christian narrative in his ethics, Hauerwas pays precious little attention to the specific details of this narrative as communicated in Scripture. Brevard Childs, *Biblical Theology of the Old and New Testaments: Theological Reflection on the Christian Bible* (Minneapolis: Fortress, 1992), 665, levels a similar criticism, suggesting that Hauerwas' notion of story involves mostly "abstraction without specific biblical content."

[305] A salvation-historical approach to Old Testament theology is advanced by Gerhard von Rad, *Old Testament Theology*, 2 vols., OTL (Louisville: Westminster John Knox, 1962), though the problems with von Rad's strong distinction between Israel's history as chronicled by modern historical-critical scholarship and the history of divine acts as recorded in the Old Testament—e.g., the

how individual passages emerge from, contribute to, and are developed by this story. Redemptive-historical biblical theology thus provides exegetically grounded theological reflection on the story of Scripture, the story that Christians confess is the true and normative story of the entire world,[306] the story that frames and directs the church's moral life as she participates in God's reality.[307] Narrative ethics and redemptive-historical biblical theology are both concerned with God's narrative of the world and are consequently well-suited for union in a methodological marriage that yields the resources to address how Scripture presents God's story, how distinct texts relate to this story, and how this story informs and forms the church for ethical faithfulness.[308]

My practice of redemptive-historical ethics brings together biblical-theological examination of the imprecatory psalms in their relation to the Christocentric narrative of God's kingdom-restoring work in

---

methodological discussion of von Rad, *Old Testament Theology*, 1:106–15—have been well documented. See Walter Brueggemann, introduction to *Old Testament Theology*, 1:xxiv–xxvi. Of course, the difficulty this bifurcation of critical history and salvation history creates was not lost on von Rad: "The fact that these two views of Israel's history are so divergent is one of the most serious burdens imposed today upon Biblical scholarship." Von Rad, *Old Testament Theology*, 1:108. My conception of redemptive history, which receives the narrated canonical history as God's faithful recounting and interpretation of events, clearly departs on this point from von Rad and consequently does not suffer from the particular issues introduced by such a bifurcation.

[306] N. T. Wright, *The New Testament and the People of God*, vol. 1 of *Christian Origins and the Question of God* (Minneapolis: Fortress, 1992), 41–42. Cf. Michael W. Goheen, "The Urgency of Reading the Bible as One Story," *ThTo* 64 (2008): 470–73.

[307] On the totalizing nature of the Bible's storied claims upon reality, see Erich Auerbach, *Mimesis: The Representation of Reality in Western Thought* (1953; repr., Princeton, N.J.: Princeton University Press, 2003), 14–15; Allan J. McNicol, *The Persistence of God's Endangered Promises: The Bible's Unified Story* (London: Bloomsbury T&T Clark, 2018), 27–30.

[308] A number of scholars have observed the potential fruitfulness of biblical-theological reflection on the canonical story for Christian ethics. See, e.g., Craig G. Bartholomew and Michael W. Goheen, *The Drama of Scripture: Finding Our Place in the Biblical Story*, 2nd ed. (Grand Rapids: Baker Academic, 2014), 17–23; Bartholomew, *Introducing Biblical Hermeneutics: A Comprehensive Framework for Hearing God in Scripture* (Grand Rapids: Baker Academic, 2015), 51–84; Wright, *New Testament and the People of God*, 139–43; Edward W. Klink III and Darian R. Lockett, *Understanding Biblical Theology: A Comparison of Theory and Practice* (Grand Rapids: Zondervan, 2012), 107.

creation with narrative-oriented ethical consideration of how the church's location in this narrative governs her practice of the judgment psalms. This weds the insights and concerns of narrative ethics with the textual focus and scriptural synthesis of redemptive-historical biblical theology, and thereby ensures that moral inquiry into the ethical implications of the canonical story is adequately rooted in the canon's presentation of the story. Redemptive-historical ethics thus approaches the question of morally faithful Christian performance of the imprecatory psalms by investigating how the dominant themes and theology of the imprecations arise from the Bible's story, how they are developed as the story moves toward its culmination in Christ, and how this same story—now with plot advanced and theological structures brought to fulfillment by Jesus' advent—frames the moral life of the church and her performance of the vengeance psalms. A redemptive-historical-ethical method acknowledges that, to modify MacIntyre's adage, we can only answer the question, "How ought the church to pray the imprecatory psalms?" if we can answer the prior question, "Of what story are the imprecatory psalms and the church a part?" Scripture's Christocentric narrative renders the imprecatory psalms ethically intelligible and structures the church's intelligible ethical embodiment of their petitions.

Throughout this study, I make abundant reference to the redemptive-historical, canonical narrative of the temple-kingdom of God. There are as many syntheses of the grand story of Scripture as there are biblical theologians, but the broad framework I employ is indebted to the scholarship of evangelical biblical theologians such as Graeme Goldsworthy, Stephen Dempster, Thomas Schreiner, Craig Bartholomew, and Michael Goheen, who privilege the category of the kingdom of God as the organizing principle for their narratival reflection on salvation history, and the work of Michael Morales and G. K. Beale tracing the templing presence of God as a unifying theme in the biblical story.[309] In my framing of the scriptural

---

[309]   See esp. Graeme Goldsworthy, *Christ-Centered Biblical Theology: Hermeneutical Foundations and Principles* (Downers Grove, Ill.: InterVarsity Press, 2012); *According to Plan: The Unfolding Revelation of God in the Bible* (Downers Grove, Ill.: InterVarsity Press, 1991); *Gospel and Kingdom*, in *The Goldsworthy Trilogy* (Eugene, Ore.: Wipf and Stock, 2000); Stephen G. Dempster, *Dominion and Dynasty: A Theology of the Hebrew Bible*, NSBT 15 (Downers Grove, Ill.: InterVarsity Press, 2003); Thomas R. Schreiner, *The King in His Beauty: A Biblical Theology of the Old and New Testaments* (Grand Rapids: Baker Academic, 2013); Bartholomew and Goheen, *Drama of Scripture*; L. Michael Morales,

narrative,[310] I frequently utilize the (admittedly more cumbersome) language of the temple-kingdom of God rather than referring simply to the kingdom of God in order to foreground the profound interconnectedness of these concepts: the temple of God is the sacred site of God's royal presence from which he rules his kingdom, and the kingdom of God is the place where God reigns and resides with his covenant people.[311] Reference to the temple-kingdom calls attention to the manner in which each of the structures interpenetrates and illumines the other while simultaneously reinforcing that conceptualizations of God's kingdom must involve notions of holiness and sacred space typically associated with the divine presence, in addition to those of sovereignty and kingship. The temple-kingdom of God functions as a suitable lens for my approach to the redemptive-historical narrative in this study for two reasons.[312] First, a

---

Who Shall Ascend the Mountain of the Lord? A Biblical Theology of the Book of Leviticus, NSBT 37 (Downers Grove, Ill.: InterVarsity Press, 2015); G. K. Beale, *The Temple and the Church's Mission: A Biblical Theology of the Dwelling Place of God*, NSBT 17 (Downers Grove, Ill.: InterVarsity Press, 2004). The biblical-theological work of Herman Ridderbos, Geerhardus Vos, N. T. Wright, Peter Gentry, Stephen Wellum, James Hamilton, and numerous others also figures prominently in my redemptive-historical analysis.

[310] I am not here advocating that the theme of the temple-kingdom of God is *the* center of biblical theology—only that this theme is a valid and valuable organizing principle for synthesizing and understanding the narrative of Scripture and one that is well-suited for addressing the issues in question in this study. Other cross-canonical themes may likewise serve as helpful lenses for biblical-theological investigation, and the prioritization of diverse structures for framing the canonical story only contributes to fuller appreciation of the symphonic complexity of the Bible. See Andreas J. Köstenberger, "The Present and Future of Biblical Theology," *Them* 37, no. 3 (Nov 2012): 452–55.

[311] See Vern S. Poythress, *Theophany: A Biblical Theology of God's Appearing* (Wheaton, Ill.: Crossway, 2018), 26. My terminological conjunction is an attempt to push against what Nicholas Perrin, *Jesus the Temple* (Grand Rapids: Baker Academic, 2010), 7, identifies as the "widespread tendency to construe the temple, as one might expect, in very western—one might even say Protestant—terms" focusing on forgiveness and reconciliation with God rather than recognizing the temple as a "totalizing institution" that is both political and religious.

[312] John Bright, *The Kingdom of God: The Biblical Concept and Its Meaning for the Church* (New York: Abingdon, 1953), 7, suggests that "the concept of the Kingdom of God involves, in a real sense, the total message of the Bible. . . . To grasp what is meant by the Kingdom of God is to come very close to the heart of the Bible's gospel of salvation." Cf. Graeme Goldsworthy, "Kingdom of God," in *NDBT*, 620.

thematic emphasis on God's temple-kingdom conforms to the prominence of the themes of God's reign and residence in both the Psalter and in the New Testament's proclamation about Jesus.[313] Second, while the theme of the temple-kingdom of God overlaps considerably with the theme of covenant (a significant structuring principle for theological reflection in the Reformed tradition),[314] the theme of God's temple-kingdom draws specific attention to the concrete religious, legal, cultic, and social structures that organize the community and dictate the form of life within the covenant at various moments in the history of redemption.[315] We might say that the temple-kingdom of God is the shape of life under God's covenantal reign and in his covenantal presence in space and time,[316] and this perspective on the biblical storyline proves quite fruitful as a resource for illuminating the theo-logic of the psalmic petitions against enemies.

How can redemptive-historical ethics so described be applied to the question before us of moral Christian performance of the imprecatory

---

[313] On this convergence of themes in the Psalter and in Jesus' ministry, respectively, see Mays, *Lord Reigns*, 18–19; Perrin, *Jesus the Temple*, 149–82. On the significance of the kingdom in Jesus' teaching, see Herman Ridderbos, *The Coming of the Kingdom*, ed. Raymond O. Zorn, trans. H. de Jongste (Philadelphia: Presbyterian and Reformed, 1962), xi.

[314] See, e.g., WCF 7.1–6. Geerhardus Vos, frequently identified as the father of Reformed biblical theology in the twentieth century, advocated for a biblical theology organized around the theme of covenant. See Geerhardus Vos, *Biblical Theology*, 16. The title of Peter J. Gentry and Stephen J. Wellum, *Kingdom through Covenant: A Biblical-Theological Understanding of the Covenants* (Wheaton, Ill.: Crossway, 2012), is itself suggestive of the intimate connection between the themes of kingdom and covenant in the Bible.

[315] This attention to organizing structures under the covenant gives the theme of the temple-kingdom of God a certain suppleness, a flexibility, that is able to account for the changing shape of Israel's life and the particularities of God's purposes in each subsequent iteration of the kingdom even under the same covenant administration. E.g., the shape of God's rule over and among his temple-kingdom community develops through Israel's wilderness wanderings, the conquest of Canaan, the period of judges, and Saul's kingship, while Israel's relationship with God is all the while governed by the Abrahamic and Mosaic covenants. Cf. Ridderbos, *Coming of the Kingdom*, 22–23.

[316] The description of God's kingdom by Goldsworthy, *According to Plan*, 99, touches each of these dimensions: "The generation, or creation, of the heavens and the earth, of the whole universe and everything in it, centers on the people of God in the place where they are put to live under the loving guidance and rule of God. Adam and Eve living before God in the Garden of Eden provide us with the pattern of the kingdom of God."

psalms? What methodological moves will direct the journey from the psalmic prayers of Israel to the prayed psalms of the church? My approach begins with exploration of the psalms themselves, mapping the theological architecture of the narrative universe within the imprecatory psalms, the world of the text that the psalms construct and into which they induct supplicants. Claus Westermann proposes that psalms of lament characteristically feature three agents: God, lamenter, and enemy.[317] Modifying this threefold schema to reflect the particularities of the imprecations, a subgenre of the psalmic laments, I describe the narrative universe of the imprecatory psalms with reference to the three principal actors—characters—who inhabit this universe: the imprecating victim of injustice, the victimizer against whom imprecations are directed, and the divine judge to whom imprecations are offered. This descriptive work pieces together a theological sketch of God's cosmos and the web of relationships contained therein according to the imprecatory psalms.

With this analysis, I am concerned not only with identifying the defining features of these typical figures within the imprecatory psalms and the interplay of relations between them but also with examining the connection of these features and relationships to the progressing scriptural story of God and his temple-kingdom. To this end, I devote special attention to psalmic allusions to earlier Old Testament texts and interaction with cross-canonical themes associated with the temple-kingdom of God—how the imprecatory psalms take up, expand, modify, and apply the Old Testament narrative. Here I employ what Stefan Alkier refers to as a production-oriented perspective on biblical intertextuality, focusing investigation on discernible references within the imprecatory psalms to those Old Testament texts that presumably constitute the psalmists' encyclopedia of production.[318] Examination of such psalmic references to the

---

[317]   Claus Westermann, *Praise and Lament in the Psalms*, trans. Keith R. Crim and Richard N. Soulen (Atlanta: John Knox, 1981), 169.

[318]   Stefan Alkier, "Intertextuality and the Semiotics of Biblical Texts," in *Reading the Bible Intertextually*, ed. Richard B. Hays, Stefan Alkier, and Leroy A. Huizenga (Waco, Tex.: Baylor University Press, 2009), 10: "The *production-oriented* perspective inquires (in the sense of limited conceptions of intertextuality) about effects of meaning that result from the processing of identifiable texts within the text to be interpreted. Under the stipulations of the respective encyclopedia to which the text owes its existence, this perspective observes not only which texts are cited or referred to in some way but also the ways in which that occurs." Emphasis original. Alkier defines the encyclopedia of production as "the cultural framework in which the text

text and contours of the Old Testament story discloses how the psalmists describe their circumstances, articulate their hopes, and reflect on the significance of their experiences with the imagery, categories, and structures of preceding canonical material and in so doing situate themselves within the narrative of God's activity in redemptive history.

Here my engagement with the imprecatory psalms exhibits a theoretical affinity with concerns in the work of Paul Ricoeur, especially his characteristic focus upon "the world of the text"[319]—"the world the text unfolds before itself"[320]—and his attention to narrative. Ricoeur suggests not only that there is a necessary correlation between narrative and temporal human experience[321] but also that there is a fundamentally narrative structure to Scripture.[322] For Ricoeur, "Narrative not only externally frames, organizes, and realigns the various non-narrative components within the canon, it actually invades and transforms these non-narrative

---

is situated and from which the gaps of the text are filled." Alkier, "Intertextuality and the Semiotics of Biblical Texts," 9. Cf. G. K. Beale, *Handbook on the New Testament Use of the Old Testament: Exegesis and Interpretation* (Grand Rapids: Baker Academic, 2012), 40. On criteria for detecting intertextual references, see Richard B. Hays, *Echoes of Scripture in the Letters of Paul* (New Haven: Yale University Press, 1989), 21–33; cf. Beale, *Handbook*, 31–35. There is an unavoidable degree of subjectivity in the identification of intertextual references, especially when those references involve subtle evocations of texts, and conclusions concerning Old Testament echoes of the Old Testament will also invariably be shaped by a scholar's perspective on the relative dating and/or composition history of the texts in question. Nevertheless, these criteria provide a helpful framework for substantiating claims of intertextuality. While space does not permit a detailed examination of each imprecatory echo considered in this study, such criteria have informed my evaluations throughout.

[319] Paul Ricoeur, "Naming God," *Union Seminary Quarterly Review* 34, no. 4 (1979): 217.

[320] Paul Ricoeur, "Toward a Hermeneutic of the Idea of Revelation," *Harvard Theological Review* 70, no. 1/2 (1977): 23.

[321] See Paul Ricoeur, *Time and Narrative*, trans. Kathleen McLaughlin and David Pellauer (Chicago: University of Chicago Press, 1984), 1:52.

[322] Ricoeur, "Naming God," 220. James Fodor, *Christian Hermeneutics: Paul Ricoeur and the Refiguring of Theology* (New York: Oxford University Press, 1995), 235, summarizes: "There is an undeniable narrative shape to Scripture and, in that sense, narrative constitutes an encompassing genre. After all, both Jewish and Christian theologies are rooted in literary accounts based on the retelling of founding or epoch-making events."

elements."[323] Narrative even penetrates the Psalter: Ricoeur argues that the Bible's hymnic discourse takes up the story of God's acts in history in a manner that "elevates the story and turns it into an invocation."[324] Ricoeur's conception of the relationship between narrative and the other modes of biblical discourse, including those found in the psalms, means that "the intertextual movements within biblical discourse (between narrative and various other non-narrative elements) is a requirement *internal* to Scripture itself and not some theological exigency imposed from without."[325] Thus, attending to the world of the biblical text calls for appreciation of the text's inherent intertextuality, of the ways even non-narrative texts draw upon narrative elements in their presentation of a world. While my redemptive-historical reading of the imprecatory psalms is by no means Ricoeurian in every sense,[326] I seek to sensitively interrogate the psalms' intertextual overtures to the wider narrative substructure of Scripture in my exploration of the world poetically manifested by the text in a manner that is sympathetic to certain of Ricoeur's commitments.[327]

My redemptive-historical, narratival contextualization of the Psalter's judgment petitions has the additional benefit of grounding deliberation over the ethics of imprecation within the psalms (e.g., "Were the psalmists right to pray this way against their enemies?") in the narrative universe of the Psalter and the wider canon, allowing the world of the text to supply the salient categories for moral evaluation rather than imposing ethical paradigms that are rooted in a modern metanarrative that conflicts with

---

[323] Fodor, *Christian Hermeneutics*, 235. Cf. Richard Bauckham, "Reading Scripture as a Coherent Story," in *The Art of Reading Scripture*, ed. Ellen F. Davis and Richard B. Hays (Grand Rapids: Eerdmans, 2003), 39.

[324] Ricoeur, "Toward a Hermeneutic," 14. Cf. Paul Ricoeur, "Lamentation as Prayer," in André LaCocque and Paul Ricoeur, *Thinking Biblically: Exegetical and Hermeneutical Studies*, trans. David Pellauer (Chicago: University of Chicago Press, 1998), 213, 222–26.

[325] Fodor, *Christian Hermeneutics*, 235, emphasis original.

[326] E.g., I do not follow Ricoeur through the desert of criticism into a second naivete in the manner he describes in *The Symbolism of Evil*, trans. Emerson Buchanan (New York: Beacon Press, 1967), 349–51, and displays throughout *Thinking Biblically*. While not dismissing the contributions of historical-critical scholarship, I am far less sanguine about the capacity of historical-critical methods to adequately and accurately recreate the history that lies behind the biblical text.

[327] I borrow the language of the text's poetic manifestation of a world from Ricoeur, "Naming God," 219: texts "poetically manifest and thereby reveal a world we might inhabit."

the metanarrative of the Bible.[328] Framing the psalmists' cries for divine vengeance and vindication within the Old Testament story of the temple-kingdom of God affords the opportunity to discern how the imprecatory psalms exhibit a coherent theo-logic that makes moral sense within the narrative universe that they assume, allude to, and unfold. It also facilitates reflection upon how certain features of the psalmic prayers—namely, the immediacy of their requested judgments and their expectations of historical participation in the actualization of divine judgment—may be related to the eschatologically realized character of the temple-kingdom in Israel.

Having described the imprecations' theological topography and situated them in their redemptive-historical context, I proceed to examine how the New Testament narrates and reflects upon the works of God in Jesus Christ through interaction with and development of the text and constitutive themes of the imprecatory psalms. Specifically, I investigate New Testament citations of and allusions to the psalms of vengeance to determine how the New Testament authors portray various actors within the Christian-era scene of redemptive history with reference to the primary inhabitants of the imprecatory psalms' narrative world—as enacting the characteristics, roles, and destinies of the innocent imprecator, cursed enemy, and divine enactor of justice. This intertextually sensitive reading attends to the ways the New Testament authors present the Christian church's vocation in terms drawn from the figure of the imprecating psalmic petitioner and to their descriptions of the enemies of Christ and his temple-kingdom in the evocative hues of the psalmic enemy. I also focus attention on the New Testament's deployment of the imprecatory psalms to depict Jesus' identity and action as the antitypical fulfillment of each of the figures in the imprecations, thereby revealing a threefold Christological significance to the judgment psalms.[329] The result of this examination is an appreciation for how the New Testament communicates the events and meaning of God's kingdom-restoring action in Jesus from his first to his second advents as the extension and culmination of the imprecatory psalms' narrative world. I then utilize this allusively constructed narrative

---

[328] This tendency to evaluate the ethics of the Old Testament with categories reflective of thoroughly modern moral assumptions about, e.g., individual autonomy and freedom is evident across theological commitments.

[329] Due to space considerations, my discussions of New Testament uses of the imprecatory psalms generally include only those conclusions relevant to the argument of this book, though where necessary, I refer to detailed supporting evidence to substantiate my claims.

framework as a lens for reading the New Testament's several imprecatory speech acts. In so doing, I permit the New Testament to supply the intertextually resonant story—the narrative categories and *telos*—within which the New Testament's imprecatory speech acts may be theologically interpreted and ethically evaluated.

Scripture's redemptive-historical narrative of God's kingdom-restoring activity aids not only in discerning the theological and moral rationale undergirding the practice of imprecatory prayer in both testaments but also in connecting the New Testament's utilization and imitation of the imprecatory psalms with the ethical life of the Christian church. The Christocentric story of God's temple-kingdom that is communicated in the New Testament through intertextual reference to the imprecatory psalms, and that in turn renders intelligible the New Testament's own imprecatory speech acts, is the very story that bounds and governs the moral existence of the church. I treat this narrative as God's true story of the world, the story of reality in which the church is called to participate as a faithful actor. Taking cues from the New Testament's intertextual application of the imprecatory psalms, especially in its depictions of Christ's *ekklesia* and the various enemies of his temple-kingdom, I articulate how the church fits as a character into the redemptive-historical narrative that supplies a vocation, time, and *telos* that together determine what constitutes ethical Christian performance of the imprecatory psalms. I offer a proposal for ethical imprecation that coheres with the church's calling—the role she has been divinely granted—in God's narrative, her postresurrection and pre-*parousia* location in redemptive history, and God's covenant promises and purposes for his creation.

Such a redemptive-historically informed, narrative-oriented approach makes possible an ethically holistic perspective on Christian performance of the imprecatory psalms. This is because the narrative of God and his temple-kingdom is an immersive reality, enveloping and directing the whole disciple in a divinely rendered cosmos. This story gives the Christian more than explicit commands; it offers the Christian a history, what God has done for the church and world through Jesus Christ, and a future, a *telos* toward which God's purposes are advancing, that together call for fitting behaviors, affective postures, and intentional orientations in response. In God's story, disciples are conscripted—brought into the action—as participants in God's temple-kingdom as they are made participants in Christ through the Spirit, and this conscription has ethical implications for both the imprecatory act and the imprecating agent. I therefore examine the loves—the affective desires and corresponding teleological aims—that are fitting for Christian prayers for justice within God's ethically determinative narrative of the world. Of course, the most obvious challenge to any proposal for Christian performance of the imprecatory psalms arises from the New Testament's ethical prescriptions of enemy love. Attempting to bridge the apparent gap between imprecatory prayer and enemy love, I explore how my proposal for ethical Christian imprecation may be practiced as a legitimate manifestation of love toward the enemies of God's king and temple-kingdom—an exercise of love that prayerfully pursues the good for enemies who are committed to pursuing their own destruction in the continued destruction of others.

As I argued above, ethical analysis of a practice requires consideration of the ethical effects of the practice, of the practice's capacity to cultivate affections that may ethically form (or deform) practitioners. My redemptive-historical-ethical study accordingly turns from examination of the ethical features of faithful Christian enactment of the imprecatory psalms within God's narrative to examination of the ways that performance of the imprecatory psalms might act upon Christians by affectively reimmersing them in God's narrative. Leveraging the doctrine of union with Christ, I interrogate how Christians' union with the Christ who polyvalently fulfills the imprecatory psalms makes possible in the act of praying the imprecations an affective retracing of God's past accomplishments, present blessings, and future promises in Jesus Christ that stimulates in the petitioner the faith, hope, and love that properly flow from apprehension of God's works in Jesus. Inquiring into how performance of the imprecatory psalms inducts Christians into God's Christocentric narrative of the world and cultivates the affections, I maintain that Christian practice of the imprecatory psalms that is sensitive to their polyvalent Christological witness has the capacity to generate the very affective postures that are necessary for ethical Christian imprecation.

Bringing the Christian's Spirit-wrought union with Christ to bear on the performance of the imprecatory psalms permits me to examine the practice of these Christically rich prayers as a potently implicatory act as opposed to a bald recitation of Scripture, an act that carries the psalm-singing church to the foot of the cross and to the edge of the age to come in a manner that rehearses the gospel and engenders fitting affections even as it interrupts and reorients disordered desires, serving as a guard against and corrective to improper modes of imprecatory prayer. A redemptive-historical-ethical approach to Christian practice of the psalms of vengeance, then, addresses both what is required for faithful ecclesial performance of the imprecatory psalms in God's narrative as well as how prayerful performance of the imprecatory psalms may foster the affections integral to ethical faithfulness by renarrating reality according to the story of God.

Overall, this study situates the imprecatory psalms and the church within the Christocentric story of God's kingdom-restoring work in creation, the story that simultaneously clarifies the theological rationale and ethical propriety of the Psalter's cries and morally governs the new covenant community's embrace of those cries as her own. This approach to addressing the ethics of Christian performance of the imprecatory psalms grounds reflection in the exegetical particularities of the psalms and relevant New Testament texts, offers a theological framework for synthesizing the biblical testimony, attends to the temporal character of God's developing salvific activity in history, and generates an ethically holistic proposal that grants appropriate consideration both to the various morally significant features of ecclesial embodiment of the psalms of vengeance and to the ethically salient affective dynamics of Christian imprecation. A redemptive-historical-ethical treatment thus satisfies the criteria outlined above for a successful methodology for examining the question of ethically faithful Christian enactment of the imprecatory psalms. What remains is to put this approach to the test, to see if this strategy generates conclusions that chart a coherent and compelling path for the Christian church in her relationship with the psalmic petitions for judgment in the face of violence.

2

Cursing in the Psalms

The Imprecatory Psalms in Redemptive-Historical Perspective

O God, break the teeth in their mouths;
    tear out the fangs of the young lions, O LORD!
Let them vanish like water that runs away;
    when he aims his arrows, let them be blunted.
Let them be like the snail that dissolves into slime,
    like the stillborn child who never sees the sun. . . .
The righteous will rejoice when he sees the vengeance;
    he will bathe his feet in the blood of the wicked. (Ps 58:6–8, 10)

The unsuspecting reader who stumbles upon Psalm 58 may be tempted to ask, "What in the world is the psalmist praying here?" The undisguised violence of the accumulating requests, punctuated with the declaration that righteous feet will splash victoriously in enemy blood, simply cannot be integrated with the conceptions of faithful piety that most readers bring to the Psalter. The psalm elicits many responses—confusion, embarrassment, exasperation, discouragement, offense, outrage—but worship is not likely to be one of them. We might, however, more profitably pose a slightly revised question: "*In what world* is the psalmist praying here?"

The imprecatory psalms unfold a world[1]—a storied cosmos with a past, present, and future, a narrative universe with a structure, history, *telos*, and

---

[1]   Cf. James L. Mays, *The Lord Reigns: A Theological Handbook to the Psalms* (Louisville: Westminster John Knox, 1994), 6; Michael Jinkins, *In the House of the Lord: Inhabiting the Psalms of Lament* (Collegeville, Minn.: Liturgical Press, 1998), 1; Walter Brueggemann, *Israel's Praise: Doxology against*

inhabiting characters—and they artfully construct this world in large measure through intertextual appeal to the scriptural story of God's acts with and for Israel. The psalmists invoke the images, players, events, and conceptual categories of preceding portions of the biblical story in their theologically charged presentation of reality and thus locate themselves as actors within the narrative of God's works and ways in the world. As the narrative within which the psalmists consciously situate themselves, Israel's story of God is also the narrative within which the imprecators' identity and the moral status of their petitions for judgment are most appropriately discerned. Interrogation of the vengeance psalms' allusive references to the Bible's narrative of redemptive history, then, can fill in the substantive content of the story in which the praying psalmists believe they are participants and, in turn, can illuminate within this narrative framework the moral intelligibility of their violent prayers for judgment. My approach here reads the imprecatory psalms in the context of the scriptural story to which the psalms abundantly allude, appreciating how these allusions supply the storied matrix in which their requests make theological and ethical sense.[2]

Idolatry and Ideology (Philadelphia: Fortress, 1988), 6; *Abiding Astonishment: Psalms, Modernity, and the Making of History*, Literary Currents in Biblical Interpretation, ed. Danna Nolan Fewell and David M. Gunn (Louisville: Westminster John Knox, 1991), 21. Israel sings her way into the world, fashioning a cosmos in which to dwell by rehearsing the works and ways of God, learning the language of truthful existence through the grammar of prayer.

[2]   This investigation is not here concerned with historical-critical reconstructions of the precise events, political scenarios, or cultic rituals that may have given rise to the psalms, nor with redaction-critical hypotheses concerning editorial layers of composition and the theological purposes of tradents, stimulating as such studies may be. My redemptive-historical method shares with the canonical biblical theology of Brevard Childs a concern with the final canonical form and arrangement of Scripture and with the ways that prior canonical texts are taken up and interpreted in later texts. But Childs' canonical method is characterized by analysis of the ways a single text evidences theologically informed redaction over time. Thus, Childs' biblical-theological method is concerned not only with the final form of the text but also with the critically reconstructed historical process by which the text arrived at its final form, and this concern shifts the locus of his biblical theology from the testimony of the text to the theological developments evidenced by the possible compositional layers of the text. See esp. Brevard Childs, *Biblical Theology of the Old and New Testaments: Theological Reflection on the Christian Bible* (Minneapolis: Fortress, 1992), 70–71; cf. Edward W. Klink III and Darian R. Lockett, *Understanding Biblical Theology: A Comparison of Theory and Practice* (Grand Rapids: Zondervan, 2012), 143–45. My redemptive-historical method, on the other hand, focuses attention on the final form of the canonical

Our entry point for examining the theological architecture of the imprecatory psalms' narrative universe comes through the three principal characters who inhabit their world—the victimizing enemy against whom imprecation is directed, the imprecating victim who makes imprecatory petition, and the divine judge to whom imprecation is offered.[3] I describe the psalmists' poetic, ethical depiction of the characteristic traits and behaviors that distinguish each of these world-inhabiting agents. I further examine the status and action of these moral agents within the imprecations with reference to the temple-kingdom of God, reading the psalms of vengeance with an eye toward their thematic connections to God's royal reign and cultic residence, and I investigate their intertextual associations with extrapsalmic Old Testament texts that emphasize this motif and advance the scriptural narrative of the temple-kingdom. Investigation of the psalms' allusions to and echoes of the Old Testament story reveals how the psalmists detail their circumstances, express their hopes, and reflect on the significance of their experiences with the grammar of Scripture's narrative of God's acts in redemptive history and in so doing connect themselves—write themselves in—to this unfolding story.[4] As a picture

---

text in its function as a unified witness to God's purposes and works within history and does not grant critical hypotheses about the possible compositional development of the text methodological priority. When I speak of the canonical story of Scripture, I am referring to the narrative of God's works within redemptive history as related in the final form of those texts that compose the Christian canon and not importing the various meanings associated with Childs' canonical criticism.

3   Modifying the threefold schema of Claus Westermann, *Praise and Lament in the Psalms*, trans. Keith R. Crim and Richard N. Soulen (Atlanta: John Knox, 1981), 169. Cf. Christiane de Vos and Gert Kwakkel, "Psalm 69: The Petitioner's Understanding of Himself, His God, and His Enemies," in *Psalms and Prayers: Papers Read at the Joint Meeting of the Society of Old Testament Study and Het Oudtestamentisch Werkgezelchap in Nederland en België, Apeldoorn August 2006*, OtSt 55, ed. Bob Becking and Eric Peels (Leiden: Brill, 2007), 159–79.

4   Elaine A. Phillips, "Serpent Intertexts: Tantalizing Twists in the Tales," *BBR* 10, no. 2 (2000): 235, suggests that the process of interrogating intertextuality "presumes a degree of conceptual significance underlying observed lexical and thematic connections." The theological convictions that God is, that he has spoken in Scripture, and that this Scripture speaks with symphonic unity reflective of its singular divine author provides theological legitimation for examining the potentially meaningful thematic connections where intertextual associations are detected. In a helpful metaphor, Peter J. Leithart, *Deep Exegesis: The Mystery of Reading Scripture* (Waco, Tex.: Baylor University Press, 2009), 109–39, argues that texts function like jokes, requiring previous knowledge

gradually emerges of a psalmic world in which the enemy, imprecator, and divine judge fit in morally meaningful ways as players in the canonical story of God's temple-kingdom, I reflect upon how their roles, aims, and futures within this story inform and render intelligible the ethics of the Psalter's justice petitions, and I consider how the shape of God's temple-kingdom in Israel's scene of redemptive history might bear upon the shape of Israelite imprecation.[5]

Making sense of the imprecatory psalms requires making sense of the story of which they are a part. This redemptive-historical exploration of the ethics of the imprecations seeks to do just that, reading the judgment psalms through the biblical-theological lens of God's story of the world, surveying the storied world of the most violent psalms, and discerning the theological and moral rationale for their disquieting pleas for divine vengeance.

The Victimizing Enemy: Serpent Seed and Kingdom Foes

Developing a biblical-theological portrait of the enemy in the imprecatory psalms involves attending to three related questions. How do the impre-cations poetically depict the moral features and future of the enemy—the foe's characteristic traits, behaviors, and ultimate end in the designs of

---

from outside the text in order to "get it," and that intertextuality names the way texts appeal to outside knowledge of previous texts. Leithart, *Deep Exegesis*, 138:

> Interpreters must be well informed about the subject matter of the text. A reader of Virgil who is innocent of Homer will not get it, and a reader of Eliot who is not familiar with Dante, and Dante's readings of the Latin literary tradition, will not understand what Eliot is up to. The interpreter must have the relevant information at hand to get the joke, or, when he does not have that information, he must be able to find it. Of course, the best interpreters of jokes are the ones who have the relevant information at their fingertips, and do not have to do research to discover what the jokester intends to call to mind.

We might add that a reader of the psalms who is not familiar with Genesis will not get it and that the best interpreters of the psalms are those who have the Old Testament at their fingertips, primed to hear the intertextual connections and get in on the joke.

5   What follows is thus not a detailed exegetical analysis of every conceiv-able textual, grammatical, syntactical, and historical issue of the imprecatory psalms but rather a theologico-ethical and intertextually sensitive exposition in dialogue with the body of existing and able exegetical scholarship on the psalms, concentrating theological attention on the ethics of the psalms within their allusively constructed narrative world.

God? How do the imprecations allude to and appropriate the language and themes of extrapsalmic Old Testament texts in their portrayal of the enemy, particularly those related to the temple-kingdom of God? And what do these intertextual connections suggest about the enemy's theological significance and place within the redemptive-historical narrative of Scripture? Answering such questions will yield a theological and ethical composite that identifies the typical moral attributes and actions of the enemy and interprets this enemy as a character in the ongoing scriptural saga of God's temple-kingdom.[6]

But before turning to these questions, we must not overlook the simple yet profound fact that the psalms paint a cosmos in which enemies *are*, in which they exist. Psalmic piety is not a purely private affair wherein the only persons who come into view are the covenant people and the covenant God; the psalmist prays with eyes wide open, conscious of the wicked and the dangers they pose.[7] Pain, fear, anxiety, and anger impinge into Israel's communion with God in the person of the enemy and the responses such persons elicit. Opposition is thus a regular feature of the landscape of the world, woven into the fabric of Israelite prayer. The

---

[6]   Cf. the examinations of the psalmic enemy by, e.g., Hans-Joachim Kraus, *Theology of the Psalms*, trans. Keith Crim (Minneapolis: Augsburg, 1986), 125–34; Bernd Janowski, *Arguing with God: A Theological Anthropology of the Psalms*, trans. Armin Siedlecki (Louisville: Westminster John Knox, 2013), 97–120; William P. Brown, *Seeing the Psalms: A Theology of Metaphor* (Louisville: Westminster John Knox, 2002), 136–44; Westermann, *Praise and Lament in the Psalms*, 188–94; Sigmund Mowinckel, *The Psalms in Israel's Worship*, trans. D. R. Ap-Thomas (Oxford: Basil Blackwell, 1962), 1:196–200; Erhard S. Gerstenberger, "Enemies and Evildoers in the Psalms: A Challenge to Christian Preaching," *HBT* 4, no. 1 (1982): 61–77; Dennis Tucker, Jr., "Empires and Enemies in Book V of the Psalter," in *The Composition of the Book of Psalms*, ed. Erich Zenger, BETL 238 (Leuven, Belgium: Uitgeverij Peeters, 2010), 723–31; Tucker, "The Role of the Foe in Book 5: Reflections on the Final Composition of the Psalter," in *The Shape and Shaping of the Book of Psalms: The Current State of Scholarship*, ed. Nancy L. deClaissé-Walford, Ancient Israel and Its Literature 20 (Atlanta: SBL Press, 2014), 179–92. Even in these more detailed analyses, however, attention is almost exclusively granted to the explicit descriptions and metaphorical depictions of the enemy. What is missing is an appreciation of the way that psalmic intertextuality functions to characterize the enemy through allusive association with figures from prior episodes in the scriptural narrative, an appreciation that may stimulate ethical insight.

[7]   See Erich Zenger, *A God of Vengeance? Understanding the Psalms of Divine Wrath*, trans. Linda M. Maloney (Louisville: Westminster John Knox, 1996), 9–13.

imprecatory psalms generate a theological topography in which the faithful covenant community dwells and is known in relation to and in tension with the foes who oppose her.[8]

Intriguingly, the imprecations rarely identify with any precision the original referents against whom they are directed but rather ordinarily offer typical—and consequently transferrable—descriptions of the defining qualities of Israel's opponents.[9] The psalms are not so much concerned with naming the enemy as with characterizing the enemy. Marshaling the language of redemptive history, drawing on the evocative conceptual reservoir of prior scenes in Scripture's story, the imprecatory psalms present an allusively rich portrait of those whose acts stimulate in the faithful petitions for divine vengeance. The enemy in the present is understood and portrayed through reference to the enemy in the past. Who then is this enemy in the imprecatory psalms?

The Enemy Oppresses in Violence and Injustice

The enemies against whom the imprecating psalmists petition are by no means monolithic.[10] Psalms 35 and 109, for example, direct pleas against

---

[8]   Cf. James Luther Mays, *Psalms*, Interpretation: A Bible Commentary for Teaching and Preaching (Louisville: John Knox Press, 1994), 34.

[9]   See H. G. L. Peels, *The Vengeance of God: The Meaning of the Root NQM and the Function of the NQM-texts in the Context of Divine Revelation in the Old Testament*, OtSt 31 (Leiden: Brill, 1995), 243; Walter Brueggemann and William H. Bellinger, Jr., *Psalms*, NCBC (New York: Cambridge University, 2014), 361; Mays, *Psalms*, 272; Bernhard W. Anderson and Steven Bishop, *Out of the Depths: The Psalms Speak for Us Today*, 3rd ed. (Louisville: Westminster John Knox, 2000), 68. The general absence of historical referents enables utilization of psalmic enemy language across circumstances, contexts, and conflicts. Cf. Beth LaNeel Tanner, *The Book of Psalms through the Lens of Intertextuality*, Studies in Biblical Literature 26 (New York: Peter Lang, 2001), 52; Patrick D. Miller, Jr., *Interpreting the Psalms* (Philadelphia: Fortress, 1986), 22–26; Patrick D. Miller, *They Cried to the Lord: The Form and Theology of Biblical Prayer* (Minneapolis: Fortress, 1994), 83; Ursula Sibler, "'Whatever Is in Parenthesis We Do Not Include in Our Prayers'!? The Problematic Nature of the 'Enemy Psalms' in Christian Reception," *Eur. Judaism* 46, no. 2 (2013): 119; Kit Barker, *Imprecation as Divine Discourse: Speech Act Theory, Dual Authorship, and Theological Interpretation* (Winona Lake, Ind.: Eisenbrauns, 2016), 119. An obvious exception is the specific malediction against the Edomites and Babylonians in Ps 137:7–9 and the explicit reference to various nations in Psalm 83.

[10]   Reed Lessing, "Broken Teeth, Bloody Baths, and Baby Bashing: Is There Any Place in the Church for Imprecatory Psalms?" *ConJ* 32, no. 4 (2006): 368, observes that the imprecatory psalms can be grouped according to the nature

personal enemies, individuals known by the psalmist who intend him great harm.[11] Psalm 58 calls for judgment on societal enemies, judges who have abdicated their responsibility to administer justice and permitted wickedness to run rampant.[12] Psalm 83 begs for God's intervening vengeance against national enemies, hostile nations that direct their rage

---

of the enemy against whom they are directed: societal, national, or personal. I privilege Psalms 35; 58; 83; 109 in the ensuing discussion because they span this range of enemies found within the imprecatory psalms.

[11]   Psalms 35; 109 are both individual laments, utilizing first-person-singular terms to describe the experience of persecution. Psalm 35:13–14 makes it clear that the enemies were previously known to the psalmist. My use of the masculine pronoun "him" here is due to the superscriptional identification of Psalms 35; 109 as Davidic psalms. One need not ascribe to Davidic authorship of the psalms bearing his name in order to recognize that, in the final form of the Psalter, these psalms are ascribed to him and envision him as their prototypical speaker. Where appropriate, therefore, I speak of David as the author/actor/agent in these psalms. For helpful discussions of issues surrounding authorship of the psalms, cf. John Goldingay, *Psalms: Volume 1, Psalms 1–41*, BCOTWP (Grand Rapids: Baker Academic, 2006), 25–30; Geoffrey W. Grogan, *Psalms*, THOTC (Grand Rapids: Eerdmans, 2008), 34–39.

[12]   So Beth Tanner, "Psalm 58: How the Mighty Will Fall," in *The Book of Psalms*, by Nancy L. deClaissé-Walford, Rolf A. Jacobson, and Beth Laneel Tanner, NICOT (Grand Rapids: Eerdmans, 2014), 492–95; John N. Day, "The Imprecatory Psalms and Christian Ethics" (PhD diss., Dallas Theological Seminary, 2001), 86–91; J. Clinton McCann, Jr., *Psalms*, in vol. 4 of *NIB* (Nashville: Abingdon, 1996), 908; Samuel Terrien, *The Psalms: Strophic Structure and Theological Commentary*, ECC (Grand Rapids: Eerdmans, 2003), 440; Erhard S. Gerstenberger, *Psalms: Part 1, with an Introduction to Cultic Poetry*, FOTL 14 (Grand Rapids: Eerdmans, 1988), 233; Derek Kidner, *Psalms 1–72: An Introduction and Commentary*, TOTC 15 (Downers Grove, Ill.: InterVarsity Press, 1973), 226. The intended target of Ps 58:1 is debated. MT reads אֵלֶם ("silence")—a reading followed by Terrien, *Psalms*, 438; Gerstenberger, *Psalms: Part 1*, 233—but most scholars emend to אֵלִם, translating the term as either "gods" (ESV) or "rulers" (NIV). A translation decision alone, however, does not settle the issue, because "gods" can be understood as a reference to subordinate divinities—as in Richard J. Clifford, *Psalms 1–72*, AOTC, ed. Patrick D. Miller (Nashville: Abingdon, 2002), 273–75—or to human rulers or judges responsible for representing God in their administration of justice (cf. Exod 21:6; 22:8–9 NIV). McCann, *Psalms*, 908; Kidner, *Psalms 1–72*, 226, argue that wicked human beings are clearly in view in v. 3, suggesting that human beings are also the referent of vv. 1–2. The scholars initially cited above differ on the appropriate translation of v. 1, reflecting the whole range of options, but nevertheless concur that the psalm is focused on human judges or authorities.

against Israel as a collective.[13] Nevertheless, these various types of enemies are all united by violence, injustice, and bloodshed. This is no mere tautology: while it may be true that all enemies are definitionally oppositional, the enemies in the imprecatory psalms are cast as active in their antagonism, dangerously hungry in their unrelenting desire to do evil.

The enemy, in the most concise of terms, is devoted to unjust violence. In Psalm 35, the enemies pursue the psalmist (v. 3), seeking after his life and plotting evil (v. 4) without cause (v. 19). Their attacks are unprovoked, their quest to ensnare irrational, as they return evil for good (v. 12) and celebrate the psalmist's painful misfortune (v. 26). In a world where malice, though always immoral, is sometimes understandable, the psalmist testifies—bewilderment palpable—that these "are wrongfully my foes" (v. 19). A similar dynamic is present in Psalm 109, where the enemy responds to overtures of love with hatred and accusation (vv. 3–5, 20, 25, 29), seeking to condemn the psalmist to death (v. 31).[14] The nations of Psalm 83

---

[13]   Brueggemann and Bellinger, *Psalms*, 360, observe that Psalm 83 is a community lament. Cf. Hermann Gunkel, *The Psalms: A Form-Critical Introduction*, Biblical Series 19, trans. Thomas M. Horner (Philadelphia: Fortress, 1967), 32. Verses 3–4 explicitly identify the people of Israel as a nation as the target of hostility.

[14]   David G. Firth, *Surrendering Retribution in the Psalms: Responses to Violence in Individual Complaints*, PBM (Eugene, Ore.: Wipf & Stock, 2005), 36, maintains that the accusations against the psalmist in Psalm 109 "probably reflect a capital crime." Cf. Mitchell Dahood, *Psalms III: 101–150*, AB (Garden City, N.Y.: Doubleday and Company, 1970), 99; Frank-Lothar Hossfeld and Erich Zenger, *Psalms 3: A Commentary on Psalms 101–150*, Hermeneia, ed. Klaus Baltzer, trans. Linda M. Maloney (Minneapolis: Fortress, 2011), 129–30. The most debated issue surrounding Psalm 109 is whether the imprecations of vv. 6–19 are the psalmist's words against his enemy or a quotation of the accusations the enemy has leveled against the psalmist. Compare ESV with NRSV, which inserts "they say" before the text of v. 6, a phrase that does not appear in MT. On the quotation hypothesis and various arguments in favor of the proposal, see Zenger, *God of Vengeance?* 59–60; Hossfeld and Zenger, *Psalms 3*, 128–30; Robert Alter, *The Book of Psalms: A Translation with Commentary* (New York: W. W. Norton and Company, 2007), 391–92. Against the quotation hypothesis, see Terrien, *Psalms*, 746; Day, "Imprecatory Psalms," 132–35; Dahood, *Psalms III*, 102; John H. Eaton, *Kingship in the Psalms*, SBT 32 (London: SCM Press Ltd, 1976), 81; Brueggemann and Bellinger, *Psalms*, 473–74. John Goldingay, *Psalms: Volume 3, Psalms 90–150*, BCOTWP (Grand Rapids: Baker Academic, 2008), 279–80, opts for the quotation hypothesis but rightly notes that this reading does little to avoid the discomfort that often accompanies imprecatory speech in the mouth of the psalmist, pointing out that v. 20

aim at nothing less than the extermination of Israel from earth and memory (v. 4), desiring to dispossess them from the land given them by God (v. 12).[15] The "gods" of Psalm 58 fail to judge rightly and instead deal out violence in the land (vv. 1–2).[16]

The wickedness of the enemy in the imprecatory psalms is a comprehensive wickedness. The whole body is committed to evil: hands distribute injustice and grasp for the poor (58:2; 71:4);[17] feet chase the weak (35:3; 109:16); eyes watch for the moment of vulnerability (10:8; 56:6; 71:10); mouths, lips, tongues spew forth false speech (109:2–4). The whole self is committed to evil: arrogance and violence bubble up from the heart (58:2; 10:6; 55:15) as imaginations hatch predatory plots (35:4; 31:13; 59:5) and bodies take destructive action.[18] Indeed, the whole life is committed to evil: evildoers never rest from their quest to harm (55:10; 74:22–23; 140:2), and the injustice practiced in the present is depicted by the psalmist in some cases as but the latest point on a trajectory of wickedness that began in the womb (58:3).[19]

(to which I would add v. 29 as well) is the psalmist's plea that the requests of vv. 6–19 be turned on the accusing enemy. In what follows, I treat Ps 109:6–19 as the words of the psalmist.

[15]   The desire to take possession of the land is placed in v. 12 in the mouths of Israel's past enemies, but the logic of the psalm turns on the similarity of Israel's past and present enemies: the psalmist requests that God repeat his past deeds in the present because the present enemies repeat the wickedness of the past. Cf. McCann, *Psalms*, 1010.

[16]   Psalm 58:2 claims that the hands of the wicked deal out violence בָּאָרֶץ ("on earth," ESV, NASB, NRSV), but John Goldingay, *Psalms: Volume 2, Psalms 42–89*, BCOTWP (Grand Rapids: Baker Academic, 2007), 201n2, observes that "in the land" is also an acceptable translation and that "either way, the focus will be on the land of Israel."

[17]   "Hand" is frequently used metonymically in the psalms. The "hand of the enemy/wicked" (e.g., Pss 31:8, 15; 71:4; 82:4; cf. 55:20) refers to the enemy with a particular emphasis on the enemy's agency to affect and their power to control the psalmist. Note the contrast in Ps 31:15, where the psalmist trusts that his times are in God's hands even as he petitions for deliverance from the hands of enemies.

[18]   This internal-to-external movement of wickedness is poetically described in Ps 7:14 in terms of childbearing. What begins inside grows up until it makes its way out into the world.

[19]   In Psalm 55, the enemy's shift toward evildoing against the psalmist is accompanied by the shock of betrayal as a once close companion is revealed to be a traitorous oppressor. Yet even here, the psalm depicts the enemy as continually devoted to destruction in the present, never granting victims a moment's reprieve (vv. 10, 15).

While the enemy may certainly be engaged in overt acts of physical or military violence—as in Psalm 83—this is by no means the only, or even the most prominent, manifestation of violence to which the psalmists are subjected. A common, though perhaps easily overlooked, form of violence in the imprecatory psalms is verbal violence.[20] Slander (140:11), false accusation (35:11, 21; 109:4, 20, 25, 29), mockery (35:15–16, 26; 109:25), and deceitful speech (35:20; 58:3; 109:2) expose the psalmists to emotional turmoil (35:12; 109:22), legal peril (109:31),[21] and the relational alienation that follows closely behind a tarnished reputation (69:8).[22] The enemy's words have power, not in some magical sense, but in the sense that they elicit enormous social consequences. They create a new and toxic social reality, one that is not grounded in truth, and the psalmist is forced to dwell in the unstable relational world created by his foes' falsehoods.[23] Such speech endangers the psalmist's name certainly, but it also imperils his very life, whether drowning him under the psychological stress of unjust accusation, compromising his participation in the common life of the community, or opening him to severe legal punishment in the court

[20] Cf. Miller, *They Cried to the Lord*, 82; Kraus, *Theology of the Psalms*, 129–30. Verbal violence and sins of speech against the psalmist appear overtly in Psalms 3; 5; 7; 10; 12; 31; 35; 40; 55; 58; 59; 69; 70; 71; 109; 119; 137; 140. The prevalence of complaints against verbal violence should not come as a surprise once we consider that harmful speech against another is quite often the easiest, and most socially acceptable, form of violence to commit. Those who would not dare exhibit physical violence may have no trouble destroying with their words. Those who lack the courage to speak maliciously to the target of their accusations may have no trouble speaking so to another, eagerly attentive party.

[21] On the legal character of the conflict and juridical terminology in Psalm 109, cf. Firth, *Surrendering Retribution*, 36, 40–41; Dahood, *Psalms III*, 99; Terrien, *Psalms*, 746; Goldingay, *Psalms: Volume 3*, 280–81; Hossfeld and Zenger, *Psalms 3*, 129–30.

[22] Cf. Mays, *Psalms*, 231. The public nature of slander and accusation, and hence their relational effects, should be kept in mind even when consequences of alienation are not explicitly outlined. The frequent reference in the psalms to shame and dishonor as a result of accusatory words (e.g., Pss 31:17–18; 69:4–8, 19–20) also points to the psalmists' concern with the public and relational fallout from unjust speech. On the social significance of shame and honor within Israel, cf. Timothy S. Laniak, *Shame and Honor in the Book of Esther*, SBLDS 165 (Atlanta: Scholars Press, 1998), 7–34.

[23] Anyone who has been the subject of slanderous gossip or false accusation understands all too well the disorientation, fear, and sense of powerlessness that accompanies the recognition that one's relationships have been corrupted by unjust, untruthful speech.

of law.[24] In this context, the enemy's nefariously multiform violence is suf-focating. Every step feels perilous, for one never knows where the hidden net lies (35:7), and there is no way of escape through either space or time, for the enemy encircles (109:3) and shows no sign of relenting.

Throughout the imprecations, the psalmists employ bestial metaphors to communicate the extent of the enemies' savagery and the terrors they induce.[25] They are lions on the prowl, teeth bared, hungry for blood and ready to consume the faithful as prey (7:2; 10:8–9; 17:12; 35:17; 58:6). They are serpents, venom dripping in anticipation of the deadly strike (58:4–5; 140:3). When these brutal enemies "open wide their mouths" (35:21a), there is the momentary question of whether their intention is to vomit accusation (35:21b) or swallow the psalmist alive (35:25)—but whether out or in, the result is violence. Such animalic descriptions should not be understood as attempts to dehumanize the enemy or diminish their responsibility for their actions.[26] The imprecatory psalms can hardly be accused of failing to hold enemies accountable for their misuse of moral agency! These carnivorous comparisons rather stretch language to cap-ture the inhumanity and inhumaneness of very human beings. They are a tragic indication of the degree to which violence has settled to the level of instinct, poetic portrayals of the enemy's unpredictability, single-mindedness, and bondage to bloody appetites,[27] descriptors that evoke the dreadful panic of life in the presence of humans who are no longer recog-nizable as such, at least not as the humans they once were.[28]

Unique among the imprecations is Psalm 82. This Asaphite psalm directs its indictment and prayer for judgment against a societal enemy, but the enemy is the gods of the divine council, and the society under assault is the non-Israelite nations over which they have been permitted to rule! Though an Israel amid or in the aftermath of exile is almost certainly

[24]   See Firth, *Surrendering Retribution*, 39–42, 72–75, 140–41.

[25]   Kraus, *Theology of the Psalms*, 130–31; Janowski, *Arguing with God*, 114–20; Brown, *Seeing the Psalms*, 136–44. On "monstering" the enemy as an act of identity-creation and as a response to trauma in the Old Testament, see Brandon R. Grafius, "Text and Terror: Monster Theory and the Hebrew Bible," *CBR* 16, no. 1 (2017): 34–49.

[26]   *Contra* Brown, *Seeing the Psalms*, 144.

[27]   Cf. Brueggemann and Bellinger, *Psalms*, 261.

[28]   This is particularly poignant in Ps 35:13–16 (cf. Ps 55:12–14). The psalmist knew and treated with love those who would become his enemies, only to find them gathering around him with gnashing teeth, inviting strangers to take part in the ceaseless wildness.

to be counted among "the weak and the needy" (v. 4) who require rescue,[29] the psalm does not concern itself exclusively with the condition of the covenant people but pleads for relief for all of the weak, fatherless, destitute, and afflicted under the gods' (temporary) jurisdiction. Yet even here, the animating concern remains the same: the gods—and the human agents and institutions through which they exercise their governance over the nations[30]—oppress the innocent and rule in injustice, defying God's will for creation and the human beings who inhabit it. Even when the psalms take aim at the heavens, even when they take aim at the plight befalling other peoples, they set their petitionary sights on the violent enemies of justice in the world.

The Enemy Threatens the Temple-Kingdom

The significance of the enemy's violent oppression in the imprecatory psalms is not limited simply to its destructive consequences for the nation, community, and individual. Within the theological universe of the Psalter, such aggression is presented more broadly as opposition to God's acts and intentions within history, to the temple-kingdom of God's reign and residence that God is establishing through Israel in faithfulness to his covenant promises and for the blessing of the nations.[31]

---

[29]   The devastation of exile looms large in the Asaph collection of Psalms 73–83, making it quite natural to read Psalm 82's cry in its canonical location from the perspective of routed Israel. Cf. W. Dennis Tucker Jr. and Jamie A. Grant, *Psalms, Volume 2*, NIVAC (Grand Rapids: Zondervan Academic, 2018), 215–16.

[30]   See Frank-Lothar Hossfeld and Erich Zenger, *Psalms 2: A Commentary on Psalms 51–100*, Hermeneia, ed. Klaus Baltzer, trans. Linda M. Maloney (Minneapolis: Fortress, 2005), 330.

[31]   Mays, *Lord Reigns*, 12–22, argues that the reign of God—God's kingship—is the theological center of the Psalter. Gerald Henry Wilson, *The Editing of the Hebrew Psalter*, SBLDS 76 (Chico, Calif.: Scholars Press, 1985), 207–28, argues that the five books of the Psalter are structured in a manner that develops the theme of kingship, beginning with the introduction of the Davidic covenant in Psalm 2 and concluding with the eternal kingship of God over his people in Psalms 145–150. Cf. Gerald H. Wilson, "King, Messiah, and the Reign of God: Revisiting the Royal Psalms and the Shape of the Psalter," in *The Book of Psalms: Composition and Reception*, ed. Peter W. Flint and Patrick D. Miller, VTSupp 99 (Boston: Brill, 2005), 404–5. In both form and content—structure and substance—the Psalter foregrounds the theme of the kingship and kingdom of God. Of course, as I have argued previously, God's kingship over his people is intimately linked to his covenantal presence with

The kingdom-threatening character of the enemy is apparent in Psalm 83, in which the conspiring nations make their aspirations known: "Come, let us wipe them out as a nation; let the name of Israel be remembered no more!" (v. 4). This might be understood as generic political rivalry and military invasion but for the fact that a nation (גּוֹי) and name (שֵׁם) are precisely what God promised to Abraham (Gen 12:2)—and in that order. The enemies' announcement of purpose situates them at cross-purposes with the divine purpose to establish a kingdom family for the blessing of all the families of the earth.[32] This imminent battle between earthly empires involves God, for the nations rise against his "treasured ones" (v. 3)—the people upon whom God has set his covenantal love, with whom God has promised to dwell, over whom God reigns as sovereign king. The nation of Israel is the temple-kingdom of God—"God's people in God's place under God's rule"[33] and in God's presence—in this psalmic moment of redemptive history,[34] and to attack Israel is to attack the kingdom of God on earth. The would-be assailants "cut a covenant"

---

his people: he is enthroned at Zion and exercises royal authority from his temple. Reading the imprecatory psalms through the lens of God's temple-kingdom is therefore no imposition of some external concern but rather corresponds with the concerns of the Psalter itself.

[32]   On the contours of the Abrahamic covenant, see Gen 12:1–3; 17:1–8; 22:15–18. God's promise to Abraham establishes a covenantal relationship with Abraham's offspring (the people of Israel), a line from which kings will arise, that will result in the blessing of all the nations of the earth. Cf. T. D. Alexander, *From Paradise to Promised Land: An Introduction to the Pentateuch*, 2nd ed. (Grand Rapids: Baker Academic, 2002), 120–22. Meredith G. Kline, *Kingdom Prologue: Genesis Foundations for a Covenantal Worldview* (Eugene, Ore.: Wipf and Stock, 2006), 326–40, suggests that the Abrahamic covenant is God's promise to restore the kingdom lost in Eden, a promise that includes a king, a kingdom people, and a kingdom land that will bring universal blessing. Cf. Thomas R. Schreiner, *The King in His Beauty: A Biblical Theology of the Old and New Testaments* (Grand Rapids: Baker Academic, 2013), 17.

[33]   Graeme Goldsworthy, *Gospel and Kingdom*, in *The Goldsworthy Trilogy* (Eugene, Ore.: Wipf and Stock, 2000), 54.

[34]   On the covenant community of Israel as the kingdom of God at this stage of redemptive history, see Craig G. Bartholomew and Michael W. Goheen, *The Drama of Scripture: Finding Our Place in the Biblical Story*, 2nd ed. (Grand Rapids: Baker Academic, 2014), 45–117; Peter S. Gentry and Stephen J. Wellum, *Kingdom through Covenant: A Biblical-Theological Understanding of the Covenants* (Wheaton, Ill.: Crossway, 2012), 594–95. This is a major theme throughout the Psalter, where Israel is regularly presented as the people over and with whom God reigns—the kingdom of God. Cf. Mays, *Lord Reigns*, 12–22;

(בְּרִית יִכְרֹתוּ, v. 5) in opposition to the covenant-cutting God and his covenant kingdom, fashioning themselves as an alternative covenant community, the anticovenant people.[35] And in plotting to take by force "the pastures of God" (v. 12), these competing kingdoms strive to seize the land divinely deeded to Israel, the very land in which God resides as king among his people. In the psalmist's address to God, he thus fittingly refers to these enemies not as Israel's enemies, but as "your enemies" and "those who hate you" (v. 2),[36] for in seeking to exterminate God's kingdom, they have allied themselves against God himself, opposed his workings in history, and sought to annihilate the vessel through whom God promised in the Abrahamic covenant to extend kingdom blessing to the whole world.[37] In other imprecations—e.g., Psalms 74; 79—the external enemies targeted by the psalmists' petitions are explicitly those who have defiled and destroyed the temple in which God royally resides and slaughtered the people with whom he dwells, assaulting the covenant kingdom that has God's templing presence at its center.

The temple-kingdom of God is threatened from without, certainly, but the threat dwells within as well. Structurally, Psalm 58 communicates the enemies' opposition to God and his kingdom by contrasting the gods who judge wrongly in v. 1 with the God who surely judges on earth in v. 11: the end of the psalm answers with God's reign the problem of the gods' reign introduced at the beginning of the psalm.[38] The wicked rulers of Psalm 58 pervert the cause of justice and fail to judge uprightly, dealing out violence "in the land" (בָּאָרֶץ, v. 2). The land of Israel, the

---

J. Clinton McCann, Jr., *A Theological Introduction to the Book of Psalms: The Psalms as Torah* (Nashville: Abingdon, 1993), 41–50.

[35] Cf. Goldingay, *Psalms: Volume 2*, 577; Hossfeld and Zenger, *Psalms 2*, 342; Zenger, *God of Vengeance?* 42; Marc Brettler, "Images of YHWH the Warrior in Psalms," *Semeia* 61 (1993): 149; J. H. Eaton, *Psalms: Introduction and Commentary*, TBC (London: SCM Press Ltd, 1967), 208.

[36] Cf. Kraus, *Theology of the Psalms*, 127; Kidner, *Psalms 73–150: An Introduction and Commentary*, TOTC 16 (Downers Grove, Ill.: InterVarsity Press, 1975), 331; Terrien, *Psalms*, 594.

[37] See Konrad Schaefer, *Psalms*, Berit Olam: Studies in Hebrew Narrative and Poetry, ed. David W. Cotter (Collegeville, Minn.: Liturgical Press, 2001), 203. The extermination of Israel spells the extermination of the people through whom the Abrahamic promises are to come to pass. Zenger, *God of Vengeance?* 41, suggests that if Israel vanishes, God himself "will also 'vanish.'" While this ought not to be pressed in any ontological sense, it is true that if Israel vanishes, God's redemptive activity and covenantal purposes to restore his kingdom are ostensibly thwarted, calling God himself into question.

[38] Cf. McCann, *Psalms*, 909; Zenger, *God of Vengeance?* 36.

place of God's presence, the physical territory wherein God reigns over his people, is filled not with righteousness and justice—and the peace, security, and flourishing that would accompany them—but with violent injustice and the oppression, fear, and languishing that follow when unrighteousness proliferates in the halls of power. As McCann states, "In short, the governance of the wicked . . . is a reign of terror, the antithesis of the reign of God."[39] Overrun with inequity and in defiance of God's law, Israel under the leadership of the wicked fails to enjoy the social blessings of her kingdom identity, which accompany faithfulness and justice, forsakes her calling to live as a "kingdom of priests and a holy nation" (Exod 19:6) that witnesses to the beauty of life in God's ruling presence among the nations,[40] and risks incurring the covenant curses of a God who promises to judge evil even when it lurks within his kingdom.[41] Indeed, in Deut 16:18–20, Israel's inheritance of and existence in the land where God will dwell among them is conditioned upon the justice of their appointed leaders:

> You shall appoint judges and officers in all your towns that the LORD your God is giving you, according to your tribes, and they shall judge the people with righteous judgment. You shall not pervert justice. You shall not show partiality, and you shall not accept a bribe, for a bribe blinds the eyes of the wise and subverts the cause of the righteous. Justice, and only justice, you shall follow, that you may live and inherit the land that the LORD your God is giving you.

The life, vocation, and preservation of the temple-kingdom of God are in jeopardy.

---

[39] McCann, *Psalms*, 908.

[40] See G. K. Beale, *The Temple and the Church's Mission: A Biblical Theology of the Dwelling Place of God*, NSBT 17 (Downers Grove, Ill.: InterVarsity Press, 2004), 117.

[41] Note the conditionality of Exod 19:5–6: "Now therefore, *if you will indeed obey my voice and keep my covenant*, you shall be my treasured possession among all peoples, for all the earth is mine; and you shall be to me a kingdom of priests and a holy nation." Emphasis added. Exodus 23:6–8 explicitly includes the administration of justice for the poor among Israel's covenantal obligations. Cf. Lev 19:15; Deut 16:18–20; 27:19; Bruce C. Birch, *Let Justice Roll Down: The Old Testament, Ethics, and Christian Life* (Louisville: Westminster John Knox, 1991), 176–82. The prophets regularly prosecute Israel and warn of the impending judgment of God for her neglect of justice. Cf. Isa 5:7, 22–23; Amos 5:6–24; Birch, *Let Justice Roll Down*, 259–69.

Abundant thematic and lexical connections exist between Psalm 58 and the Song of Moses in Deuteronomy 32[42]—connections that will be interrogated below—and certain of these resonances further confirm the kingdom-threatening character of the enemy in Psalm 58. In Deuteronomy 32, Moses sings as a witness against Israel and her future idolatry (cf. Deut 31:16–22) of the Lord's faithfulness, the people's unfaithfulness, God's judgment in the form of invading nations, and God's eventual judgment upon the nations that were his instrument of judgment against Israel.[43] The nations whom the Lord sends in judgment on Israel are described as teeth-baring beasts and venomous serpents (vv. 24, 33), but God will cleanse the land with bloody vengeance such that his people may rejoice (vv. 41–43).[44] Intriguingly, Psalm 58 applies this imagery not to the nations but to the wicked rulers of Israel: the Israelite authorities are the serpents (vv. 4–5) and lions (v. 6), and they are the enemies to be cleansed by God's bloody vengeance for the joy of the righteous (v. 10).[45] Psalm 58 ironically reapplies the imagery of Deuteronomy 32 in a manner that evocatively equates Israel's judges with the marauding nations, placing them in the same conceptual space as pagan armies. As a threat to the temple-kingdom, the Israelites who wield injustice are indistinguishable from militaries marching with swords on the borders of the land.

The enemies in the intensely personal laments of Psalms 35 and 109, too, endanger the temple-kingdom of God. Much like the societal injustice of Psalm 58, the virulent spread of murderous wickedness and lethally sinful speech against the poor, the needy, and the innocent imperils the

---

[42] Day, "Imprecatory Psalms," 98–105; McCann, *Psalms*, 909; Terrien, *Psalms*, 441.

[43] On the structure of Deuteronomy 32, see Walter Brueggemann, *Deuteronomy*, AOTC (Nashville: Abingdon, 2001), 277–82; Ronald E. Clements, *The Book of Deuteronomy*, in vol. 2 of *NIB* (Nashville: Abingdon, 1998), 527–28.

[44] MT v. 43 reads הַרְנִינוּ גוֹיִם עַמּוֹ, rendered by NIV and NASB, "Rejoice, O nations, with his people."

[45] Cf. Day, "Imprecatory Psalms," 104–5. Day observes that the imagery of Deuteronomy 32 is expanded "to include ungodly oppressors in general—even if they are among God's own people." Day, "Imprecatory Psalms," 104n51. However, he stops short of interrogating what this ironic reapplication of motifs reserved for the nations in Deuteronomy 32 rhetorically suggests about the Israelite rulers. The use of Deuteronomy 32 in Psalm 58 is not so much a matter of the expansion of images as of surprising role reversal—the elite among the covenant people are characterized as the pagan nations upon whom God's judgment is guaranteed.

integrity of God's covenant people—the witness, the joy, and the sustained covenantal blessing of the kingdom of God.[46] The wicked who speak not peace (שָׁלוֹם, 35:20) but against the quiet in the land are a "threat to the very fabric of God's kingdom values."[47] If God's temple-kingdom may be likened to the renewal of Edenic *shalom*,[48] the bloodthirsty pursuit of the righteous that compromises the *shalom* of his people (cf. 35:27) is an enacted contradiction of this expectation and calling.[49] And if unconfronted unholiness is permitted to run rampant in Israel, the community's continuation in the place of God's presence is in question: "You shall therefore keep all my statutes and all my rules and do them, that the land where I am bringing you to live may not vomit you out" (Lev 20:22).

But more specifically, in their canonical form, both Psalms 35 and 109 bear the Davidic superscription לְדָוִד ("of David"), suggesting at the very least that while every Israelite may pray these words, the king is the prototypical petitioner envisioned by these psalms.[50] The Israelite king

---

[46]   The premier covenantal stipulation against sinful speech is the ninth command of Exod 20:16; Deut 5:20, but other portions of the law address this issue as well. The use of the phrase "malicious witnesses" in Ps 35:11 echoes the same phrase in Exod 23:1, where God's law prohibits the Israelite from conspiring with the wicked to act as a malicious witness. David's complaint in Ps 109:20 that false accusers speak against his life recalls the legislation of Lev 19:16: "You shall not go around as a slanderer among your people, and you shall not stand up against the life of your neighbor: I am the LORD."

[47]   Beth Tanner, "Psalm 35: Fight for Me, Save Me," in deClaissé-Walford, Jacobson, and Tanner, *Book of Psalms*, 337.

[48]   As in, e.g., Exod 15:17–18; Num 24:5–6; Deut 8:7–10; Josh 5:10–15; Isa 11:1–10; 51:1–4; Ezek 36:33–38. Stephen G. Dempster, *Dominion and Dynasty: A Theology of the Hebrew Bible*, NSBT 15 (Downers Grove, Ill.: InterVarsity Press, 2003), 147–48, draws out the Edenic parallels in the description of the prosperity and justice of the kingdom under Solomon's reign in 1 Kings 3–4. Cf. Schreiner, *King in His Beauty*, 17.

[49]   Cf. Mays, *Psalms*, 34–35.

[50]   See Peter C. Craigie and Marvin E. Tate, *Psalms 1–50*, 2nd ed., WBC 19 (Grand Rapids: Zondervan, 2004), 33–35; Grogan, *Psalms*, 34–39, for able summaries of views regarding the significance of לְדָוִד as a superscription. Mays, *Psalms*, 13: "The result of attributions and cross-references was to make David the patron and prototypical case of the piety of dependence and trust represented by the psalms, especially the prayers. David became the example and teacher of psalmic piety, as Solomon did of proverbial wisdom." Of the psalms containing imprecatory speech, a Davidic superscription heads Psalms 3; 5; 7; 9; 11; 12; 17; 28; 31; 35; 40; 41; 54; 55; 56; 58; 59; 68; 69; 70; 86; 109; 139; 140; 141; 143; 144. Wilson, *Editing of the Hebrew Psalter*, 143, maintains that the Davidic superscriptions of the psalms

is simultaneously the mediator of God's kingship and the premier representative of the people;[51] the kingdom is in a sense carried in his flesh. An assault on the king—the very type described in Psalms 35; 109—is de facto an assault on the kingdom.[52] Further, God's covenant with David (2 Sam 7:1–17), wherein the Lord promises to establish a house for his name and a never-ending kingdom through David's royal offspring, connects Israel's temple-kingdom hopes specifically to the Davidic line. All of God's covenant promises to Israel are channeled into the figure of the Davidic king.[53] In this redemptive-historical context, the attacks against the life of the Davidic monarch must be understood as attacks on the fruition of the promised temple-kingdom of God,[54] for if the Davidic line is severed, who

---

encouraged personal appropriation by individual Israelites: "The implication is: If David responded to such events by expressing himself in a ps, then what better way for me to respond to similar conflicts in my own life than to appropriate the words of his classical utterance?" Cf. Howard N. Wallace, "King and Community: Joining with David in Prayer," in Becking and Peels, *Psalms and Prayers*, 267–77.

[51]   See Eaton, *Kingship in the Psalms*, 136; cf. Mays, *Psalms*, 33; David P. Murray, "Christian Cursing?" in *Sing a New Song: Recovering Psalm Singing for the Twenty-First Century*, ed. Joel R. Beeke and Anthony T. Selvaggio (Grand Rapids: Reformation Heritage Books, 2010), 115; Jace Broadhurst, "Should Cursing Continue? An Argument for Imprecatory Psalms in Biblical Theology," *AJET* 23, no. 1 (2004): 81; Chalmers Martin, "Imprecations in the Psalms," *PTR* 1, no. 4 (1903): 547; J. Carl Laney, "A Fresh Look at the Imprecatory Psalms," *BSac* 138 (1981): 43. Whereas many recognize that the Israelite king represented the people such that an attack on the king was an attack on the whole kingdom, we might intriguingly reframe the question to ask, To what extent does this representative dynamic work the other way? Might it be that an unjust attack against an individual Israelite is simultaneously an attack against the king who represents her (a la Acts 9:4)? If such were the case, then the individual who took David's words on her lips through the psalms would experience a deep resonance with the royal cries. David's complaint of unmerited assault would be reasonably applied to the predicament of the individual represented by the king.

[52]   Illuminating in this regard is the prayer of Psalm 20, which has the congregation petitioning the God who rules from his sanctuary in Zion to deliver the anointed Davidic king in the day of trouble. As Goldingay, *Psalms: Volume 1*, 305–6, rightly observes, the congregation hopes to celebrate in the king's salvation (v. 5) because the people as a whole are implicated in the conflict directed against the king. An attack on the king is an attack on the temple-kingdom that he leads and represents.

[53]   See Dempster, *Dominion and Dynasty*, 143. Within the Psalter, Psalm 72 connects the Davidic king with the fulfillment of the Abrahamic covenant.

[54]   Cf. Harry Mennega, "The Ethical Problem of the Imprecatory Psalms" (ThM thesis, Westminster Theological Seminary, 1959), 61.

then will bring the longed-for kingdom? God's covenant ostensibly fails.[55] The enemies in Psalms 35; 109 are thus enemies of the kingdom, and in their wicked ravings against the king, the eschatological hope of Israel hangs in the balance.

Whether the enemies dwell outside of Israel or in her midst, whether they occupy the seats of power or antagonize through interpersonal malice, the enemies within the imprecatory psalms threaten the holiness, prosperity, peace, witness, and the very existence of the temple-kingdom of God in the world. Even where the enemy in the imprecations is not an overt antagonist to Israel *per se*,[56] concerns about God's reign and residence are never out of view. The Psalter is unequivocal: creation as a whole is fashioned to be the cosmic house of God (104:1–5),[57] the Lord intends to fill the earth with the glory of his holy presence (72:19; cf. 57:5, 11),[58] and he will rule as king over the entire cosmos within which he wills to dwell (82:8). Unholy injustice anywhere is, therefore, an impediment to the temple-kingdom that God purposes to progressively establish everywhere.

The Enemy Is the Serpent Seed

The unjust, violent, oppressive combatants against God's temple-kingdom are not, however, portrayed as discrete, unconnected iterations of animosity. Rather, the imprecatory psalms draw upon the grammar of Scripture's developing story to present the enemies of God's kingdom as united by a vicious familial bond. They are the seed of the serpent, striking at the heel of God's people, ever in enmity with the kingdom line of promise.[59]

---

[55]   Hence the Old Testament preoccupation with the Davidic line. See Dempster, *Dominion and Dynasty*, 151–56, 225–27.

[56]   As in, e.g., Psalms 82 and 104.

[57]   McCann, *Psalms*, 1097; Tucker and Grant, *Psalms, Volume 2*, 496; David G. Barker, "The Waters of the Earth: An Exegetical Study of Psalm 104:1–9," *Grace Theological Journal* 7, no. 1 (1986): 69–70; Norman C. Habel, "He Who Stretches Out the Heavens," *CBQ* 34, no. 4 (1972): 425–29. See my "'Let Sinners Be Consumed': The Curious Conclusion of Psalm 104," in *Violent Biblical Texts: New Approaches*, ed. Trevor Laurence and Helen Paynter (Sheffield: Sheffield Phoenix Press, 2022).

[58]   Elsewhere in the Old Testament, cf. Num 14:21; Isa 11:9; Hab 2:14. This thread of the biblical narrative receives further attention below.

[59]   For a survey and discussion of serpent- and dragon-related imagery in ANE literature and its possible influence upon the imagery of the Old Testament, see John Day, *God's Conflict with the Dragon and the Sea: Echoes of a Canaanite Myth in the Old Testament* (New York: Cambridge University Press, 1985), esp. 7–18.

Genesis 3:15—often referred to as the *protoevangelium*—has traditionally been interpreted as God's initial promissory announcement of salvation and judgment following the serpent's temptation of Adam and Eve and the original pair's fall into sin.[60] As part of his curse upon the deceiving serpent, God declares,

> I will put enmity between you and the woman,
> and between your offspring and her offspring;
> he shall bruise your head,
> and you shall bruise his heel.

Stephen Dempster explains the significance of this text for the ensuing biblical narrative of redemptive history:

> God curses the serpent, and contained within the curse is literally a seed of hope for humanity: there will be enmity between the seed of the woman and the seed of the snake; the woman's seed will strike the serpent on the head while the latter will strike a blow to the former. In light of the immediate context, the triumph of the woman's seed would suggest a return to the Edenic state, before the serpent had wrought its damage, and a wresting of the dominion of the world from the serpent. Just as the woman was built from the man to complete the old creation, so a seed will be built from the woman with the task of restoring the lost dominion of the old creation to its rightful heirs.[61]

---

[60] See R. A. Martin, "The Earliest Messianic Interpretation of Genesis 3:15," *JBL* 84 (1965): 425–27, on the possible messianic significance of the LXX translation of Gen 3:15. John Skinner, *Genesis*, ICC (New York: Charles Scribner's Sons, 1910), 80–81, discusses messianic readings of Gen 3:15 in Jewish literature. For examples of the interpretation of Gen 3:15 in the Christian tradition, see Irenaeus, *Against Heresies*, vol. 1 of *ANF*, ed. Alexander Roberts, James Donaldson, A. Cleveland Coxe (Buffalo: Christian Literature Publishing Company, 1885), 3.23.7; John Calvin, *Commentaries on the First Book of Moses Called Genesis*, vol. 1 of Calvin's Commentaries (Grand Rapids: Baker Books, 2005), 1:168–71; Ryan M. McGraw, "'The Foundation of the Old Testament': John Owen on Genesis 3:15 as a Window into Reformed Orthodox Old Testament Exegesis," *JRT* 10 (2016): 3–28; Louis Berkhof, *Systematic Theology* (Grand Rapids: Eerdmans, 1939), 293–94; Herman Bavinck, *Reformed Dogmatics*, ed. John Bolt, trans. John Vriend (Grand Rapids: Baker Academic, 2003), 3:221; Vos, *Biblical Theology of the Old and New Testaments* (Grand Rapids: Eerdmans, 1948), 42–44.

[61] Dempster, *Dominion and Dynasty*, 68.

On this reading, Gen 3:15 serves as a paradigmatic text that sets the trajectory for the story that follows, a tale of two seeds in perpetual conflict until the woman's seed deals a victorious head blow against the serpent that reestablishes the Edenic temple-kingdom fractured at the fall.[62] James Hamilton traces the scriptural references to Gen 3:15 and compellingly demonstrates that the Old Testament—including the Psalter—regularly appeals to this complex of images,[63] casting the antagonism between God's covenant people and their enemies in serpentine, head-crushing, foot-stomping, dust-licking terms that theologically link Israel's experience with the promise of the *protoevangelium*.[64] The kingdom-threatening enemy of the psalmic imprecations certainly fits the serpent seed motif on a thematic-theological level—every unholy intruder in the place of God's presence is, so to speak, a serpent in God's garden—but do the psalms of

[62] Cf. Gentry and Wellum, *Kingdom through Covenant*, 627; Vos, *Biblical Theology*, 42–44; Bartholomew and Goheen, *Drama of Scripture*, 42; Dempster, *Dominion and Dynasty*, 69.

[63] James Hamilton, "The Skull-Crushing Seed of the Woman: Inner-Biblical Interpretation of Genesis 3:15," *SBJT* 10, no. 2 (2006): 30–54; "The Seed of the Woman and the Blessing of Abraham," *TynBul* 58, no. 2 (2007): 253–73. Cf. Walter Wifall, "Gen 3:15—A Protevangelium?" *CBQ* 36, no. 3 (1974): 361–65; Thomas R. Schreiner, "Editorial: Foundations for Faith," *SBJT* 5, no. 3 (2001): 2–3; Phillips, "Serpent Intertexts," 233–45. James M. Hamilton, Jr., *God's Glory in Salvation through Judgment: A Biblical Theology* (Wheaton, Ill.: Crossway, 2010); Schreiner, *King in His Beauty*; Dempster, *Dominion and Dynasty*, repeatedly draw attention to references to Gen 3:15 and its related themes in their biblical-theological engagements with the Old Testament (Dempster) and the whole canon (Hamilton, Schreiner). Hamilton, *God's Glory in Salvation through Judgment*, 77, detects allusions to Gen 3:15 in Pss 2:9; 44:5; 58:4–6, 10; 60:12; 68:21–23; 72:4, 9; 74:12–14; 89:10, 23; 91:11–13; 108:13; 110:6; 137:9. Hamilton was kind enough to share with me an early draft of what would eventually become James M. Hamilton, Jr., *Psalms*, 2 vols., EBTC (Bellingham, Wash.: Lexham Academic, 2021), which develops these themes as well.

[64] Hamilton, "Skull-Crushing Seed," 34–42. In line with his recognition of a variety of themes and motifs associated with Gen 3:15, Hamilton, *God's Glory in Salvation through Judgment*, 77, argues that scholars have failed to appreciate the Old Testament references to Gen 3:15 because of a too-narrow approach that only looks for explicitly repeated terms or phrases rather than recognizing that "themes can be developed with synonymous terms," expanded with conceptually related imagery. Especially with a paradigmatic text like Gen 3:15, overt lexical repetition is not a sine qua non of potential intertextual echo—just as biblical allusions to an epochal event like the exodus do not require the recycling of specific keywords.

vengeance themselves make this connection?[65] Close inspection reveals that the imprecatory psalms interact not infrequently with the imagery and expectations of Gen 3:15, drawing upon serpent-related imagery and themes, in overt and subtle ways, in their portrayals of the enemy.[66]

---

[65] Of course, to phrase the question this way raises questions about the relative dating of Gen 3:15 (and a potential J document more broadly) and the Psalter. Amid the varied and competing iterations of the documentary hypothesis that have emerged (see Alexander, *From Paradise to Promised Land*, 7–94), offering markedly different dates for J, Gordon J. Wenham, *Genesis 1–15*, WBC 1 (Nashville: Thomas Nelson, 1987), xlii–xlv, suggests that the literary form of Genesis likely dates from between 1250 and 950 BC (excepting the obvious editorial revisions) with J as its main redactor and reliably preserves oral traditions that are in fact much older. John H. Sailhamer, *The Meaning of the Pentateuch: Revelation, Composition and Interpretation* (Downers Grove, Ill.: InterVarsity Press, 2009), 200–206, contends for a compositional approach to Mosaic authorship; cf. Tremper Longman III, *How to Read Genesis* (Downers Grove, Ill.: IVP Academic, 2005), 43–57. On such understandings, the account related in Genesis 3 would have been readily available to the composers and compilers of the Psalter, and given the foundational nature of the Genesis 3 account, one should not be surprised to find that this cosmogonic narrative supplies the language, imagery, and categories for the psalmists' presentation of the world. Hamilton, *God's Glory in Salvation through Judgment*, 77, similarly suggests that Gen 3:15's "announcement of judgment on the serpent provides the fundamental imagery that is reused and interpreted throughout the rest of the Old Testament." Arguing from a critical perspective, Wifall, "Gen 3:15," 363, contends that Gen 3:15 arises from a Davidic background that is further reflected in, e.g., Psalms 8; 72; 89; 110, and this shared Davidic milieu commends reading these texts in connection with one another. See also Catherine L. McDowell, *The Image of God in the Garden of Eden: The Creation of Humankind in Genesis 2:5–3:24 in Light of the* mīs pî pīt pî *and* wpt-r *Rituals of Mesopotamia and Ancient Egypt*, Siphrut 15 (Winona Lake, Ind.: Eisenbrauns, 2015), 189–99, who problematizes notions that this text is a necessarily late composition.

[66] Murray, "Christian Cursing?" 114, conceptually links the imprecatory psalms to Gen 3:14–15, but only in the briefest of terms. Hamilton, *God's Glory in Salvation through Judgment*, 288–89, considers Psalm 137 through the lens of Gen 3:15 before linking the enemy in the imprecations to the serpent motif: "Psalm 137 envisions salvation through judgment for God's glory in vibrant colors tinged with Genesis 3:15, blessing the one who will arise to crush the seed of the serpent, visiting the judgment of God on the enemies of God and simultaneously delivering God's people (Ps. 137:8–9). The language of these imprecatory psalms is harsh (dashed heads against rock, broken teeth, etc.), but it is justly fierce, corresponding to the depth of wickedness displayed by those who would join the serpent against God."

Psalm 58:3–5 explicitly likens the unjust Israelite judges to venomous serpents,[67] but the potential serpent seed associations run deeper. These enemies
are depicted as wicked offspring—"estranged from the womb" (v. 3)—serpents
(נָחָשׁ, v. 4; cf. Gen 3:1) who multiply violence among the "children of man" (בְּנֵי
אָדָם, v. 1; cf. Gen 4:8–9; 5:2–4).[68] Two lines stand in conflict as serpentine
offspring abuse the children of אָדָם, and the enemies' mouths, like the original serpent's, are the organs of destruction, wherein lies their poison. This
application of serpent imagery is intriguing because the primordial serpent
destroys not with literal venom but with deceptive speech, with false words.
The serpent is the archetypal liar, and the liars of Psalm 58 are serpents that
share a family resemblance.[69] Verse 6 petitions God to "break the teeth in their
mouths," and v. 10 anticipates the righteous bathing their feet in the enemies'
blood, images that together evoke the head-striking and foot-stomping vision
of Gen 3:15, with the psalmist's enemies filling the role of the serpent.[70]

I noted above that Psalm 58 alludes heavily to the Song of Moses
in Deuteronomy 32, and among the parallels between these texts are a
concern with the cleansing of the land (Deut 32:43; Ps 58:2), references
to the teeth of beasts (Deut 32:24; Ps 58:6), serpentine descriptions of
enemies (Deut 32:24, 32–33; Ps 58:4–6),[71] assurances of God's vengeance
(Deut 32:41, 43; Ps 58:10), the rejoicing of God's people (Deut 32:43; Ps
58:10), images of head-striking and enemy blood (Deut 32:42; Ps 58:6,
10),[72] and a focus on the exclusivity of God among the gods (Deut 32:39;
Ps 58:1, 11).[73] Significantly, Deuteronomy 32 reaches a climax when the
nations characterized as venomous serpents, as "things that crawl in the
dust" (v. 24, echoing Gen 3:14),[74] are struck in the skull and when God

---

[67]　See Adam E. Miglio, "Imagery and Analogy in Psalm 58:4–9," *VT* 65
(2015): 116–17.

[68]　Cf. Schaefer, *Psalms*, 143.

[69]　Cf. Jesus' denunciation in John 8:44.

[70]　Hamilton, "Skull-Crushing Seed," 41; cf. Hamilton, *God's Glory in Salvation through Judgment*, 76.

[71]　Cf. Karolein Vermeulen, "Eeny Meeny Miny Moe Who Is the Craftiest
to Go?" *JHS* 10 (2010): 4.

[72]　Cf. Ps 68:20–23, which integrates allusions to Deut 32:39, 42, with
imagery of Israelite feet stomping in blood.

[73]　Terrien, *Psalms*, 441, observes parallels with Deut 32:28, 33, 35, 42, 43.
Cf. Day, "Imprecatory Psalms," 103–5.

[74]　Cf. Daniel I. Block, *Deuteronomy*, NIVAC (Grand Rapids: Zondervan,
2012), 761n75; Jack R. Lundbom, *Deuteronomy: A Commentary* (Grand Rapids:
Eerdmans, 2013), 891.

spills blood "from the long-haired heads of the enemy" (v. 42).[75] Not only does Psalm 58 deploy the motifs of Gen 3:15 in its description of the enemy, but it also utilizes the language and themes of a Deuteronomy 32 text, rich with reverberations of the *protoevangelium* in its own right, that presents Israel's enemies as the serpent seed in order to depict, with surprising irony, Israel's rulers as serpents whose heads will be crushed by the judgment of God.

Psalm 83:3 signals the serpentine character of the surrounding nations in its description of their "crafty" (from ערם; cf. Gen 3:1) plans.[76] Like the crafty serpent scheming for the destruction of God's kingdom people in the garden of his presence, the nations plot the extermination of God's covenant nation in the land to obstruct God's purposes for history.[77] The requests of Ps 83:9–12 allusively appeal to this same matrix of images, holding up individuals and nations from Judges 4–8—where serpent themes abound—as past examples of the divine judgment that the psalmist desires in the present. In the Judges narrative, the defeat of Jabin king of Canaan is secured when Jael drives a tent peg into the temple of his army commander Sisera (4:21–22) and is memorialized as Deborah celebrates in song Jael's head-crushing victory (5:26) and requests that all God's enemies might perish in this manner

[75]   Sailhamer, *Meaning of the Pentateuch*, 36–37, argues that Deuteronomy 32–33 is one of the four major poetic seams (along with Genesis 49; Exodus 15; Numbers 23–24) in the structure of the Pentateuch, suggesting that each of these poems consciously takes up and expands the themes of Genesis 1–11:

> Central to this connection is the identification of the future warrior of Genesis 3:15 with the messianic king of the larger poems. Along with that is the identification of the nature of the warfare in the remainder of the Pentateuch with the battle between the 'seed of the woman' and the 'seed of the serpent' in Genesis 3:15. . . . This consistent pattern of usage of the poems as interpretation is intentional and extends to the scope of the whole Pentateuch. The fact that the poems have been extended and linked to the king from the house of Judah (David) suggests that their intent is to identify the king in the poems as a messianic figure. The messianic hope begins to emerge from these poems along with the eternal reign of God as king.

Sailhamer, *Meaning of the Pentateuch*, 242. One need not agree with every element of Sailhamer's thesis about the macrostructure and composition of the Pentateuch to appreciate his sensitivity to the intertextual connections of these major poetic texts, including Deuteronomy 32, with the early chapters of Genesis.

[76]   Cf. Goldingay, *Psalms: Volume 2*, 575.

[77]   Cf. Kidner, *Psalms 73–150*, 331.

(5:31)[78]—a request echoed in Ps 83:17.[79] When in the ensuing episode Midian encroaches unbidden into and lays waste to Israel's land (6:3–6),[80] the Lord promises that Gideon will strike the Midianites (6:16), the Ephraimites present the heads of the princes Oreb and Zeeb to Gideon (7:25), and Gideon slays the kings Zebah and Zalmunna such that Midian "raised their heads no more" (8:28).[81] Drawing on the narrative of God's head-smiting judgments in redemptive history, Ps 83:9–12 begs that God will crush the heads of the crafty serpent nations in the same way he shattered serpent skulls in former days. The nations "who hate you have raised their heads" (v. 2; cf. Judg 8:28)[82]—Midian redivivus, poised snakelike and ready to strike—but the psalmist pleads that they too will be struck to raise their heads against God's kingdom no more.

The concluding prayer of Psalm 83 further alludes to the Song of the Sea in Exodus 15 with the request that the coalition headlined by Edom and Moab be dismayed (Ps 83:17; cf. Exod 15:15)[83] so that the God "whose name is the LORD" (Ps 83:18; cf. Exod 15:3) may be acknowledged. Intriguingly, Moses' song announces that the Lord "shatters the enemy" (v. 6)—an Egyptian foe already cast as a serpent empire (Exod 4:3–4)[84]—in order to plant his people on his sanctuary mountain (v. 17), harkening back to

[78] On the relation of Judges 4–5 to the serpent themes of Gen 3:15, see Hamilton, "Skull-Crushing Seed," 35; *God's Glory in Salvation through Judgment*, 156. It is possible that the account of Jael alludes to Num 24:17, another text that develops serpent-related themes. John Sailhamer, "Creation, Genesis 1–11, and the Canon," *BBR* 10, no. 1 (2000): 98–99, observes that the same Hebrew term used in Num 24:17 to describe the crushing of Moab's forehead is employed in Judg 5:26 to describe Jael's shattering of Sisera's temple.

[79] Hossfeld and Zenger, *Psalms 2*, 340.

[80] Brettler, "Images of YHWH," 149n11, entertains the possibility that Ps 83:12 references Judg 6:3–6.

[81] Dempster, *Dominion and Dynasty*, 132, suggests of the liberating work of Israel's judges generally, "This is not only a realization of the royal-conquest motifs in Genesis 1 but also a fulfilment of the promise as the seed of the woman establishes dominion by defeating oppression." Cf. Schreiner, *King in His Beauty*, 120–22. Hamilton, "Skull-Crushing Seed," 35, argues that Judges 9 continues the serpent-striking imagery with the account of the crushing of Abimelech's head, which further suggests that reading the early chapters of Judges through the lens of Gen 3:15 is warranted.

[82] Cf. Hossfeld and Zenger, *Psalms 2*, 341; Goldingay, *Psalms: Volume 2*, 575; Beth Tanner, "Psalm 83: God, Arise against Our Enemies," in deClaissé-Walford, Jacobson, and Tanner, *Book of Psalms*, 647n8.

[83] Cf. McCann, *Psalms*, 1010; Goldingay, *Psalms: Volume 2*, 583.

[84] Göran Larsson, *Bound for Freedom: The Book of Exodus in Jewish and Christian Traditions* (Peabody, Mass.: Hendrickson, 1999), 36.

the serpent-shattering, temple-kingdom restoring promise of Gen 3:15.[85] It is possible then—especially in light of the concentration of serpent seed references throughout Psalm 83—that Exodus 15, in addition to Judges 4–8, serves as a mediating text through which Psalm 83 conceptualizes the enemy as the serpent seed and petitions for God's crushing judgment on the basis of the *protoevangelium*.[86] The psalm appears to make intertextual appeal to passages united by serpent seed associations to situate Israel's current experience within the story of Israel's conflict against the offspring of the serpent through the ages.[87]

[85] Sailhamer, *Meaning of the Pentateuch*, 36–37; Afolarin Olutunde Ojewole, "The Seed in Genesis 3:15: An Exegetical and Intertextual Study" (PhD diss., Andrews University Seventh-Day Adventist Theological Seminary, 2002), 300–301; Hamilton, *God's Glory in Salvation through Judgment*, 77; "Skull-Crushing Seed," 38.

[86] Psalm 35 may also draw upon enemy-serpent themes via allusions to Exodus 15 and Deuteronomy 32. Psalm 35:3 asks for God to be revealed as the psalmist's salvation (cf. Exod 15:2); v. 10 emphasizes the incomparability of God by asking, "Who is like you?" (cf. Exod 15:11); and v. 24 pleads for vindication so that enemies are not permitted to entertain their delusions of supremacy (cf. Deut 32:36–38).

[87] There may yet be more to the serpent motif in Psalm 83. I find it intriguing that several of the nations listed (Edom, Moab, Amalek, and Asshur) are also grouped together in the Balaam account of Numbers 24, which includes the promise of a king who shall shatter the nations (v. 8) and crush the forehead of Moab (v. 17). Deuteronomy 23:3–6 links Ammon with Moab's guilt in hiring Balaam, and Judg 3:13—immediately preceding the account of Judges 4–8 appealed to so explicitly in Psalm 83—narrates Ammon and Amalek joining with Moab against Israel. On the allusions to Gen 3:15 in Numbers 24, see Hamilton, "Skull-Crushing Seed," 34, 38; "Seed of the Woman," 263–66; Dempster, *Dominion and Dynasty*, 116–17. Sailhamer, "Creation, Genesis 1–11, and the Canon," 99, claims that if Numbers 24 indeed alludes to Genesis 3, then "it suggests the serpent and his 'seed' in Gen 3:15 are to be identified with Israel's historical enemies, the Moabites and Edomites." Philistia, in its archetypal battle against Israel in 1 Samuel 17, is represented by a giant clad in armor of scales and fatally struck in the forehead, and 2 Sam 22:39–43 employs feet-stomping, enemy-crushing language to describe David's defeat of the Philistines. Cf. Hamilton, "Skull-Crushing Seed," 38; Dempster, *Dominion and Dynasty*, 144. Could it be that Psalm 83 draws upon serpent themes not only with its petitions for judgment, but also with its very selection of named enemy nations? Schaefer, *Psalms*, 203; Brueggemann and Bellinger, *Psalms*, 361; Kidner, *Psalms 73–150*, 331–32, draw attention to the symbolic import of the geographical arrangement of the nations in Psalms 83, which encircle Israel on all sides. Hossfeld and Zenger, *Psalms 2*, 342: "The nations and tribes that are named are emblematic for the world of nations experienced *and* feared by Israel throughout its

The psalms that imprecate against personal enemies likewise cast the enemy in serpentine terms. This is perhaps most evident in Psalm 140, a Davidic lament where the enemies, whose tongues are "sharp as a serpent's" (נָחָשׁ, v. 3), take aim at the psalmist's feet (v. 4), and the psalmist calls for judgment on the opponents' head (vv. 9–10)[88] so that the slanderers whose words are venom are not "established in the land" (v. 11)—in the place of God's ruling presence (v. 13) over and with his people.[89] In addition to this significant concatenation of images, it is also worth observing the place of Psalm 140 within the final Davidic collection of the psalter (Psalms 138–145). Read together, Psalms 140–145 "moves from a repeatedly intensified plea made in virtually eschatological distress to an image of paradisiacal happiness in 144:12–15 and to the praise of the universal kingdom of Yhwh in Psalm 145."[90] What is more, this paradisiacal happiness that culminates David's pleas within the collection in Ps 144:12–15 is an invocation of the blessing of Edenic renewal. Sons are like plants (נְטִעַ; cf. נטע, Gen 2:8) in a garden and daughters are like pillars in a temple-palace (v. 12)—reminiscent of the original temple-garden—and the promises of Edenic fruitfulness and security in the land in Deut 28:3–8 come to fruition.[91] The canonical progression of Psalms 140–144 thus petitions against serpentine enemies in a manner that leads up to the hope of Edenic restoration. With Psalm 140, the elements and expectations of Gen 3:15—snakes, feet, sinful speech, judgment, broken

---

history, the nations and tribes in whose midst Israel lived." Emphasis original. This makes sense on a poetic level, and the possibility of serpentine allusions in the selection of nations is compatible with this reading.

[88]   Verse 9 begins with ראשׁ (cf. Gen 3:15), which in connection with the reference to serpents in v. 3 recalls the initial Edenic promise of deliverance. Cf. Ps 3:7 for another instance of head-oriented judgment in an imprecation against a personal enemy.

[89]   Cf. Schreiner, *King in His Beauty*, 277.

[90]   Erich Zenger, "The Composition and Theology of the Fifth Book of Psalms, Psalms 107–145," *JSOT* 80 (1998): 95.

[91]   See Nancy L. deClaissé-Walford, "Psalm 144: Content Are the People Whose God Is the Lord," in deClaissé-Walford, Jacobson, and Tanner, *Book of Psalms*, 988; Goldingay, *Psalms: Volume 3*, 688–89; McCann, *Psalms*, 1256. Noting the use of אָדָם, Brueggemann and Bellinger (*Psalms*, 601) suggest that Psalm 144 may be read "as a reflection on the reality of the king as 'Adam' (v. 3)" in connection with Genesis 1–2, a claim that is consistent with an Edenic motif. Th. Booij, "Psalm 144: Hope of Davidic Welfare," *VT* 59 (2009): 180, also observes the similarity of language between Ps 144:12–15 and Ezek 34:23–31; 37:24–27, which are prophetic descriptions of future abundance under a renewed Davidic rule that conspicuously surround the promise of Edenic renewal in Ezek 36:35.

heads, and the liberation of God's temple-kingdom—emerge in the imprecatory psalms yet again.

Examples of such features in the imprecatory psalms could be multiplied. Psalm 68 announces that God will strike the hairy crown of his enemies' heads (v. 21) and have his people strike their feet in the foes' blood (v. 23), weaving together imagery of the *protoevangelium* with an allusion to the long-haired, bloodied heads of serpentine invaders from Deut 32:42 in a manner reminiscent of Psalm 58.[92] Psalm 72 pleads for oppressors to be crushed (v. 4) and enemies made to lick the dust (עָפָר, v. 9; cf. Gen 3:14).[93] In Psalm 74, the Lord's head-crushing, serpent-breaking acts of old (vv. 13–14) are recounted in prayer so that God will remember, arise, and destroy the enemy again.[94] And in Psalm 137, the psalmist anticipates the shattering of the Babylonian offspring, the seed of the nation that violently intruded into the land of God's presence and laid bare his dwelling.[95]

Less overt, but nevertheless suggestive, is the Davidic imprecation of Psalm 109.[96] The canonical placement of Psalm 109 between Psalms 108 and 110 in the final form of the Psalter bolsters the conceptual linkage of

---

[92]   Martin Klingbeil, *Yahweh Fighting from Heaven: God as Warrior and as God of Heaven in the Hebrew Psalter and Ancient Near Eastern Iconography*, OBO 169 (Fribourg, Switzerland: University Press Fribourg Switzerland, 1999), 125n348. Hamilton, "Skull-Crushing Seed," 37, reads Psalm 68 as an allusion to Gen 3:15; cf. Ojewole, "Seed in Genesis 3:15," 326–28. Deuteronomy 32 appears to serve as a thematic locus from which both Psalms 58 and 68 draw and as a mediating text through which both psalms appeal to the imagery of Gen 3:15.

[93]   Wifall, "Gen 3:15," 363; Hamilton, "Skull-Crushing Seed," 39; "Seed of the Woman," 269–70; Ojewole, "Seed in Genesis 3:15," 330; Sailhamer, *Meaning of the Pentateuch*, 501.

[94]   Hamilton, "Skull-Crushing Seed," 41; *God's Glory in Salvation through Judgment*, 285; Phillips, "Serpent Intertexts," 239.

[95]   Hamilton, *God's Glory in Salvation through Judgment*, 288–89; "Skull Crushing Seed," 39.

[96]   There may be echoes of Deut 32:26 in Ps 109:15 and of Deut 32:27, 39 in Ps 109:27. Cf. Hossfeld and Zenger, *Psalms 3*, 135, who observe a thematic connection between Ps 109:27 and Deut 32:39. If this is the case, then Psalm 109 (like Psalm 58, considered above) may resonate with the language of a Deuteronomy 32 text that paints Israel's enemies as the seed of the serpent headed toward head-cracking divine judgment and thereby subtly draw this characterization and expectation into the psalm's evocative depiction of the enemy.

the enemy with the serpent seed. In the "planned composition"[97] that is the Davidic triad of Psalms 108–110, Psalm 108 contrasts God's promise of Israel's supremacy among the enemy nations with her present experience, Psalm 109 expands the call for divine intervention against David's enemies, and Psalm 110 subsequently announces God's answering judgment against all of the king's enemies through the coming victory of the Davidic anointed.[98] When Psalms 108–110 are approached as a consciously edited whole, the boundaries separating the psalms, though present, become porous, permitting thematic associations to traverse back and forth between the individual psalms. A canonical reading that is sensitive to the placement of Psalm 109 in the Davidic trilogy interprets the king's personal enemies within Israel in the central psalm as of a kind with the national enemies of Psalm 108 and those adversaries destined for judgment in Psalm 110,[99] and the triptych moves from recognition of the kingdom-threatening foe without to imprecation upon the kingdom-threatening foe within and finally to assurance of judgment against every kingdom-threatening foe.

What significance might this canonical arrangement have for the characterization of the enemy in Psalm 109? Psalms 108 and 110 employ imagery that is by now familiar, as God in Psalm 108 casts his shoe upon Edom (v. 9) and treads down the enemies of Israel (v. 13)[100] and in Psalm 110 makes the enemies of the anticipated Davidic king his footstool (v. 1)[101] and promises that he will shatter kings (v. 5) and "the head" (ראש, v. 6).[102] The beginning and ending of the Davidic trilogy depict the enemies of the king as the seed

---

[97]   Zenger, "Composition and Theology of the Fifth Book of Psalms," 89–90.

[98]   Cf. Hossfeld and Zenger, *Psalms 3*, 136.

[99]   Tucker, "Empires and Enemies," 727–30, argues that the canonical placement of Psalm 109 between Psalms 108 and 110 frames its cries to the extent that Israel may have taken up David's personal imprecations as corporate prayers against external enemies. Cf. Hossfeld and Zenger, *Psalms 3*, 136–37.

[100]   Hamilton, "Skull-Crushing Seed," 40.

[101]   Wifall, "Gen 3:15," 363; Matthew Habib Emadi, "The Royal Priest: Psalm 110 in Biblical-Theological Perspective" (PhD diss., Southern Baptist Theological Seminary, 2016), 126–32.

[102]   NRSV, KJV, NET, OJB translate v. 6 with "head(s)." On the various connections between Psalm 110 and Gen 3:15, see Dempster, *Dominion and Dynasty*, 200; Emadi, "Royal Priest," 157–60; Ojewole, "Seed in Genesis 3:15," 334–35. Hamilton, "Skull-Crushing Seed," 37, includes a summary of additional intertextual resonances in Psalm 110—among them Gen 49:10; Num 24:8, 17; Judg 5:26—many of which take up the themes of Gen 3:15 in their own right.

of the serpent, framing David's imprecatory cry in its canonical location and thematically coloring the king's deceitful, lying, covenant-breaking, unholy enemies in Psalm 109 with the serpentine hues of Psalms 108 and 110.[103]

The cumulative force of the theological reverberations of Gen 3:15 and its related complex of themes and images in the imprecatory psalms substantiates the conclusion that the enemy in the psalms of vengeance is presented as the seed of the serpent, aggressively antagonistic against God's purposes in and for his temple-kingdom in the world. In the storied world of the imprecatory psalms, the enemy is depicted as a character in the ongoing narrative of serpentine opposition against the temple-kingdom of God, and this characterization—as will become evident below—has ramifications for discerning the moral rationale of the imprecations in the context of the canonical story.

The Enemy Is Destined for Judgment and Destruction, or Not?

The biblical-theological presentation of the enemy as the serpent seed implicitly communicates the enemy's certain future. The psalmists' decision to identify the enemy allusively and theologically as the offspring of the serpent situates the enemy within a narrative moving inevitably toward God's promised judgment on the serpents who strike at his temple-kingdom people. In this sense, the utilization of serpentine images and themes is itself a defiant act of courageous hope oriented toward the future: God has promised that the serpent's head will be crushed, and to portray the enemy in serpentine terms in the midst of the experience of unjust violence is subtly yet unmistakably to say something about the enemy's destiny. At times, this motif moves into outright declarations of the enemy's fate—the wicked will be tread underfoot (58:10; 68:22–23) and struck on the head by God (3:7; 68:21), and their violence will descend upon their own skulls (7:14–16)[104]—but even where it does not, the narrative-invoking capacity of intertextual reference brings this future to the horizon of expectation.[105]

Explicit statements of the enemy's destiny abound in the imprecatory psalms, complementing the pleas for divine vengeance with proclamations that such vengeance is coming. As Kraus observes, "The

---

[103]   See Schreiner, *King in His Beauty*, 272. Cf. Wilson, *Editing of the Hebrew Psalter*, 221; Emadi, "Royal Priest," 99–100.

[104]   Hamilton, "Skull-Crushing Seed," 49n43, posits that the frequent Old Testament image of evil returning upon the heads of the wicked (as in Ps 7:16) could be related to the wider motif of judgment applied to the serpent's head.

[105]   See Paul E. Koptak, "Intertextuality," in *DTIB*, 333–34, on intertextuality's capacity to relate the individual scriptural scene to the broader biblical-theological story and, relatedly, to rhetorically characterize a person or situation.

result which the victim prays for can be seen on the periphery of the prayer songs."[106] The enemy's future is simultaneously begged for and confidently known, hopefully proclaimed.[107] Boastful foes will not stand before God's eyes but will be destroyed (5:5–6), humbled (55:19), driven away (68:1–2). God will cast those who would threaten the integrity of his temple-kingdom into the pit (55:23), deliver them to Sheol (9:17), discard them like dross (119:119), tear them down to be built up no more (28:5). Indeed, the destruction of enemies bookends the Psalter in its canonical form, as Psalms 1 and 2 announce that the wicked will perish (1:4–6) and be dashed by God's anointed (2:9), and Psalm 149 envisions God's people executing the judgment written against the kings and kingdoms that oppose God and God's (149:6–9).[108] The imprecatory psalms are thus consistent with the Psalter as a whole in their presentation of the destiny of the enemy.[109]

And yet while the destiny of the enemy is certain, it is less certain that those who are enemies in the present will remain enemies always. Repentance is possible,[110] a turning of heart that diverts the agent's path away from the inevitability of judgment. Psalm 7:12–13 expresses this relationship in the negative:

> If a man does not repent, God will whet his sword;
>> he has bent and readied his bow;
> he has prepared for him his deadly weapons,
>> making his arrows fiery shafts.

"If a man does not repent, God will whet his sword," but if he does repent, the readied sword will return to its sheath, the bent bow will slacken.[111] This potentiality that judgment might redirect the enemy to seek God's name is the psalmist's plea in Ps 83:16,[112] because the destiny of a particular enemy

---

[106] Kraus, *Theology of the Psalms*, 133.

[107] Cf. Martin, "Imprecations in the Psalms," 551; Miller, *They Cried to the Lord*, 127–30.

[108] Cf. Zenger, *God of Vengeance?* 12–13.

[109] Cf. Schreiner, *King in His Beauty*, 426; Bernardino, "Reconsideration of 'Imprecations,'" 42–44.

[110] A theme introduced into the Psalter by the invitation of Ps 2:12, however one elects to translate the text.

[111] Goldingay, *Psalms: Volume 1*, 149–50. Steffen G. Jenkins, *Imprecations in the Psalms: Love for Enemies in Hard Places* (Eugene, Ore.: Pickwick, forthcoming), 147–50.

[112] See, e.g., Brueggemann and Bellinger, *Psalms*, 362; McCann, *Psalms*, 1010; Tanner, "Psalm 83," in deClaissé-Walford, Jacobson, and Tanner, *Book of*

in a particular moment is, from the petitioner's perspective, undecided.[113] The enemy is destined for judgment and destruction, unless of course this enemy is not. Insofar as impenitent wickedness will be avenged, the future of the enemy as a general class is sealed; insofar as repentance is ever within the realm of possibility, the future of the individual enemy is a graciously open question.

The Innocent Imprecator: Suffering Priest-Kings and Sons of God

With a biblical-theological portrait of the enemy in view, we may turn to discerning how the petitioner in the imprecatory psalms—the praying target of the enemy's aggression—is presented and connected to the story of God's temple-kingdom in ways that inform the ethics of the psalmists' prayers for vengeance. How do the imprecatory psalms characterize the moral status, experience, and future of the petitioner? How do they echo previous scenes in the scriptural story, and what do these intertextual resonances suggest about the relationship of the requests to God's covenant promises and the trajectory of the biblical narrative? What desires are expressed in the imprecatory psalms as motives behind the pleas, and are these desires ethically appropriate in the psalmists' place within God's story? How is the imprecator depicted as a character in the developing canonical drama, and how does this role illuminate the ethics of imprecatory prayer against the enemy in the psalmists' redemptive-historical moment? As these questions are addressed, as the imprecatory psalms are read through the lens of the biblical narrative of the temple-kingdom of God, the theological and ethical rationale for their cries and expectations will come more crisply into focus, sharpened against the backdrop of the story in which they participate.

The Imprecator Suffers Unjustly

That the imprecator's suffering at the hands of the enemy is unjust and undeserved is the corollary, the flip side, of the recognition that the enemy's attacks are a violent injustice. Much of what was observed above regarding

---

Psalms, 648; Zenger, *God of Vengeance?* 43; Goldingay, *Psalms: Volume 2*, 582; Daniel Simango, "An Exegetical Study of Imprecatory Psalms in the Old Testament" (PhD diss., North-West University, 2011), 163.

[113] *Contra* the assertion of Johannes G. Vos, "The Ethical Problem of the Imprecatory Psalms," *WTJ* 4 (1942): 137; Mennega, "Ethical Problem," 87, that the psalmists knew by divine revelation that the targets of their prayers were reprobate in the secret counsels of God.

the enemy's injustice is applicable here and need not be repeated, but a few points are worthy of attention. In both Psalms 35 and 109, the petitioner forthrightly declares his innocence of wrongdoing against those who seek his life (cf. 59:3–4). The psalmist's good is met with evil, his love with hatred, his sympathetic compassion with unceasing mockery and false accusation (35:12–16; 109:3–5). Enemy speech flies against "the quiet in the land" (35:20)—those who, at the very least, pose no active threat to others. The nets that the enemy has set for the petitioner's feet seek to ensnare "without cause" (35:7), and the predatory bestial imagery that describes the enemy by contrast depicts the imprecator as prey (35:17). The conflict within these psalms is, thus, not one between evenly matched opponents of comparable character who are similarly committed to the contest but one between persons separated by a chasmic moral difference and power differential (35:10; 109:16, 22), one of whom has dragged the other unwillingly into the fray (109:3).

In Psalm 58, the unjust rulers deal out violence, but the imprecator is presented as one among the righteous who heretofore have borne the brunt of animalic power abuses (vv. 4–6), who have been deprived of justice but will yet rejoice and be rewarded when God comes in judgment (vv. 10–11).[114] Psalm 83 depicts the encircling international alliance as an unprovoked attempt to strip Israel from the land that is her home by divine promise (v. 12), an uninstigated conspiracy to ensure that her very memory fades into oblivion (v. 4) from a coalition populated by several nations whom Israel was divinely prohibited from seeking to dispossess.[115] These psalms are representative of the vengeance psalms as a whole: there is not a single psalm of imprecation that gives the impression that the imprecator is complicit in the enemy's injustice. Rather, the pleas for vengeance universally arise from those whose hands are clean in the matter at hand.[116]

That is not to say that the victims of injustice in the imprecatory psalms are entirely guiltless, devoid of sin. Inclusion of self-conscious acknowledgments of the psalmists' personal failings before God within the judgment prayers prohibits entertainment of any notion of sinless perfection in reality

---

[114]   John Shepherd, "The Place of the Imprecatory Psalms in the Canon of Scripture," *Chu* 111, no. 1 (1997): 42. Cf. Zenger, *God of Vengeance?* 37.

[115]   Goldingay, *Psalms: Volume 2*, 580, insightfully points to Deut 2:1–23, which prohibits attempted dispossession of Edom, Moab, and Ammon.

[116]   Cf. Shepherd, "Place of the Imprecatory Psalms," 42; E. Calvin Beisner, *Psalms of Promise: Celebrating the Majesty and Faithfulness of God*, 2nd ed. (Phillipsburg, N.J.: Presbyterian and Reformed, 1994), 179.

or naïve hubris in self-conception (69:4–5; 79:8; 143:2).[117] The issue is not total innocence, but relative innocence—not absolute blamelessness, but blamelessness in the conflict in view—such that the imprecator may legitimately claim before God that the enemies are "wrongfully my foes" and "hate me without cause" (35:19).[118] The psalmic portrait of the petitioner who calls out to God for justice is not one of an antagonistic aggressor who cries foul when a foe responds in kind. Neither is it of an imprecator who blithely assumes God will paper over his own iniquity while holding opponents to account. No, the psalmic portrait of the petitioner is of one who owns personal guilt, welcomes God's rightly judgmental gaze upon heart and life (7:3–5, 8; 139:1–6, 23–24),[119] and yet boldly maintains innocence, pleading as a righteous victim of another's aggressive antagonism who has done nothing to warrant the lethal threat posed by the enemy.[120]

The Imprecator Pleads for the End of Violence, Public Vindication, and Covenant Justice

The defining feature of the imprecatory psalms, and the feature that generates the most interpretive consternation, is their pleas for divine judgment against the enemy who unjustly attacks the innocent petitioner. Exploration of this element of the imprecatory psalms—what they specifically request and how they appeal to past episodes in the scriptural story—demonstrates their conceptual links to the redemptive-historical narrative of God's temple-kingdom restoring activity in the world and reveals the narrative-formed theo-logic that ethically legitimates within that world their discomfort-inducing cries.

---

[117] *Contra* William L. Holladay, *Long Ago God Spoke: How Christians May Hear the Old Testament Today* (Minneapolis: Fortress, 1995), 304. See also Kraus, *Theology of the Psalms*, 156–57.

[118] Kraus, *Theology of the Psalms*, 154–55: "The 'righteous' person is the one who is innocent. This is anything but self-righteousness. The person is suffering through slander and false accusations." Cf. Shepherd, "Place of the Imprecatory Psalms," 42–43; J. W. Wenham, *The Goodness of God* (London: InterVarsity Press, 1974), 159; Gert Kwakkel, *According to My Righteousness: Upright Behavior as Grounds for Deliverance in Psalms 7, 17, 18, 26 and 44*, OtSt 46 (Leiden: Brill, 2002).

[119] Cf. Kwakkel, *According to My Righteousness*, 37–39; Craigie and Tate, *Psalms 1–50*, 100–101.

[120] In Ps 141:3–4, the imprecator longs for a personal integrity that extends even into the future, untainted by wicked participation with the evil against whom he pleads.

It is important to note from the outset that the psalmists are engaged in prayer—that is, these psalms are not curses *per se*. As many scholars have recognized, a curse is a speech act directed toward an enemy with the intention of releasing power and thereby effecting the reality spoken. The pleas of the imprecatory psalms, however, are petitions directed toward and offered to God.[121] The imprecatory psalms, then, are engaged in a fundamentally different mode of discourse than curses proper. In the Psalter, it is invariably the enemy who curses (10:3, 7; 59:12; 109:17–18, 28). The psalmist, by contrast, declares, "I give myself to prayer" (109:4).[122] As will become clear below, the cursing psalms are worthy of the name insofar as they petition on the basis of God's own covenantal curses for the cursing

[121]   Anderson and Bishop, *Out of the Depths*, 74 (citing Claus Westermann, *A Thousand Years and a Day* [Philadelphia: Fortress, 1962], n.p.), discuss the significance of this distinction:

> In the ancient world, as in some cultures today, it was believed that the word spoken in curse released a power, or spell, which was automatically effective. . . . As long as one believed in the power of verbal vengeance, prayer was unnecessary. Claus Westermann explains, "The distinctiveness of the curse lies in the fact that it is aimed directly, without any detour via God, at the one it is meant to hit. A curse is a word of power which the swearer released without any recourse to God." The Psalter, it is true, contains traces of ancient curse formulas (e.g., Ps 58:6–9) that echo traditional language used in cultic ceremonies of covenant renewal, but no longer are they curses in the proper sense. They are prayers to God, who obtains vindication in God's own way and in God's own time.

Anderson also points to Helmer Ringgren, *The Faith of the Psalmists* (Philadelphia: Fortress, 1963), 31–32. Cf. Robert Althann, "The Psalms of Vengeance against Their Ancient Near Eastern Background," *JNSL* 18 (1992): 2–4; Peels, *Vengeance of God*, 236–38; Broadhurst, "Should Cursing Continue?" 67–68; Bernardino, "Reconsideration of 'Imprecations,'" 63–65; Barker, *Imprecation as Divine Discourse*, 151–53. *Contra*, e.g., Mowinckel, *Psalms in Israel's Worship*, 2:48–52; Ragnar C. Teigen, "Can Anything Good Come from a Curse?" *Lutheran Quarterly* 26, no. 1 (1974): 46.

[122]   Exodus 22:28 explicitly commands, "You shall not . . . curse [אָרַר] a ruler of your people," which further suggests the imprecatory psalms ought not be understood as curses. The psalms do not hesitate to cry for judgment against wicked authorities in Israel (e.g., Ps 58). If one posits that such prayers are curses and that the psalmists recognized them as curses, this creates the implausible scenario that the psalmists—and later compilers of the Psalter—intentionally established within Israel's liturgical worship an act that explicitly transgresses God's revelation delivered at Sinai, encouraging just the sort of behavior that would imperil Israel's blessing in the land of God's presence.

of the wicked—for God's covenant curses to be rightly enacted—but they do so as prayers and not as unmediated, inherently effectual speech acts.

Most immediately, the imprecations beg God for the interruption and cessation of the enemy's violence,[123] which will mean the deliverance of the innocent.[124] This is apparent in Ps 7:9, where the psalmist openly requests that the evil of the lionlike, soul-rending wicked come to an end.[125] Elsewhere, the imprecator prays in metaphorical language for broken teeth, excised fangs, blunted arrows (58:6–7), shattered arms (10:15),[126] and divided tongues (55:9),[127] petitioning God to thwart the instruments of the enemy's aggression, to render the tools of violence ineffective. A toothless beast is not capable of nearly so much destruction. Psalm 35 pleads that the foes would be turned back—defeated and disappointed—in their evil endeavors (v. 4; cf. 40:14; 129:5), that their deadly desires would not come to violent fruition (v. 25; cf. 140:8), longing for a divine interruption of the enemies' plans that redirects them and prevents their intended carnage from reaching its full potential. The supplications of Ps 83:9–18 for the destruction, scattering, and shaming of armies bent on eliminating Israel demonstrate the same logic: God's judgment is the means by which the threat against his temple-kingdom might be quelled, the means by which the looming specter of violence might be eradicated.[128] Of course, the call for God to confront and subdue the violent enemy (17:13) takes its most extreme form in requests for the death of the devastator, as in the prayers of Pss 54:5; 55:15; 58:8; 69:28; 104:35; 109:8–9. In situations where the enemy represents an imminent danger to the life of the innocent, God's sovereignty over life and death may interrupt violence by interrupting the mortal existence of the violent themselves. The petitions for divine vengeance against the enemy hope for a delivering judgment that will

---

[123] See Jenkins, *Imprecations in the Psalms*, 143–45; Jerome F. D. Creach, *Violence in Scripture*, Interpretation: Resources for the Use of Scripture in the Church (Louisville: Westminster John Knox, 2013), 194–95. Cf. Zenger, *God of Vengeance?* 11.

[124] Lessing, "Broken Teeth," 369; Roy Ben Zuck, "The Problem of the Imprecatory Psalms" (ThM thesis, Dallas Theological Seminary, 1957), 74–75; Day, "Imprecatory Psalms," 8.

[125] Cf. Mays, *Psalms*, 63.

[126] Craigie and Tate, *Psalms 1–50*, 125; cf. Kidner, *Psalms 1–72*, 89.

[127] Schaefer, *Psalms*, 137, notes the allusion to the Babel episode of Gen 11:6–9, where confused speech thwarts ungodly schemes.

[128] McCann, *Psalms*, 1011; cf. Mays, *Psalms*, 272.

neutralize the unjust violence that characterizes the attacker's intentions and actions so that, as Ps 10:18 envisions, "man who is of the earth may strike terror no more."[129]

Along with the life-saving abolition of the enemy's violence, the imprecator petitions for personal and public vindication, calling for divine action that demonstrates the imprecator's innocence and the undeserved nature of the opponent's attacks.[130] The cries "Vindicate me!" (cf. 17:2; 54:1) and, negatively phrased, "Let me not be put to shame!" (cf. 31:1, 17; 69:6; 71:1; 74:21) plead for God to show on the world stage that the psalmist is in the right, that the enemies, however they have sought to justify their aggression ("He is a liar!" "He is a danger!" "He is a menace!" "He must be dealt with!") are in the wrong.[131] In Psalm 35, the imprecator, maligned by baseless accusations, requests a visible and dramatic reversal—vindication of the innocent and humiliation of the guilty accusers:

> [23] Awake and rouse yourself for my vindication,
>   for my cause, my God and my Lord!
> [24] Vindicate me, O LORD, my God,
>   according to your righteousness,
>   and let them not rejoice over me!
> [25] Let them not say in their hearts,
>   "Aha, our heart's desire!"
> Let them not say, "We have swallowed him up."
>
> [26] Let them be put to shame and disappointed altogether
>   who rejoice at my calamity!
> Let them be clothed with shame and dishonor
>   who magnify themselves against me![132]

---

[129]   Rolf A. Jacobson, "Psalm 9/10: The Power and Presence of God," in deClaissé-Walford, Jacobson, and Tanner, *Book of Psalms*, 143: "The psalm ends with the affirmation that God judges the wicked for the very purpose of protecting the innocent—there is no separation between the two actions."

[130]   Anderson and Bishop, *Out of the Depths*, 70.

[131]   It is worth considering that, whether or not such justifications were ever explicitly uttered, the sheer act of violence carries with it the implication that the attack is justified, even if only from the attacker's perspective. This is perhaps why, when targets of an unprovoked act of aggression, we are not merely hurt by the immediate effects of the act but also by what we fear the act "says" about us.

[132]   Cf. Goldingay, *Psalms: Volume 1*, 501. Walter Brueggemann, "Psalm 109: Three Times, 'Steadfast Love,'" *WW* 5, no. 2 (1985): 153–54, offers interesting reflections on the public nature of justice in Psalm 109.

Where the injustice of the enemy has made the righteous a public mockery, the imprecator pleads for God to publicly set the record straight. Where false words elicit deadly consequences, the imprecator pleads that the liberating truth be made manifest. The imprecator prays for a vindicating judgment from God upon the wicked that unmasks their deception and issues an authoritative "No!" to their insinuations about the psalmist's character, repairing his reputation and restoring his status as an honorable member of the community.

These specific requests for the end of violence and the vindication of the righteous, however, are expressions of an appeal to something more basic: the covenantal justice of God.[133] This justice is not some universal principle of desert or equity, the terms of which might be agreed upon by all people in all times and places,[134] but a justice that derives its particular shape, content, and rationale from the narrative history of God's dealings with Israel. In covenant, God has committed himself by promise to future action on behalf of his people and has defined what constitutes just recompense for the wicked, and through both overt reference and allusive echo, the imprecatory psalms petition for this narrative-dependent, covenantally determined form of justice from God. The imprecations plead for God to do precisely what he has promised to do,[135] to exercise justice according to the parameters he has established. "Have regard for the covenant" (74:20) is in this respect the fundamental request of the imprecatory psalms, but more often this generic request emerges as an appeal to a specific episode in or aspect of God's covenantal relationship with Israel.

---

[133]   Peels, *Vengeance of God*, 212: "The call for God's vengeance is none other than a prayer to YHWH, in this time of most extreme, heaven-irritating need, to act as King and Judge in accordance with his own word (Exod 22:23; 34:7; Ps 99:8); avenging and restoring justice, to protect his covenant people." Cf. Janowski, *Arguing with God*, 125.

[134]   On the existence of competing conceptions of justice and the relationship of these conceptions to the histories and forms of life of particular communities, see Alasdair MacIntyre, *Whose Justice? Which Rationality?* (Notre Dame: University of Notre Dame Press, 1988).

[135]   Cf. Peels, *Vengeance of God*, 241; Allan M. Harman, "The Continuity of the Covenant Curses in the Imprecations of the Psalter," *RTR* 54, no. 2 (1995): 70; John Shepherd, "The Place of the Imprecatory Psalms in the Canon of Scripture," *Chu* 111, no. 2 (1997): 117; Laney, "Fresh Look," 41; Alex Luc, "Interpreting the Curses in the Psalms," *JETS* 42, no. 3 (1999): 405; Daniel Michael Nehrbass, "The Therapeutic and Preaching Value of the Imprecatory Psalms" (PhD diss., Fuller Theological Seminary, 2012), 124–25.

Several scholars suggest that the Abrahamic covenant establishes the ultimate theological basis for the Psalter's imprecations,[136] but the prevalence of *protoevangelium*-related imagery in the vengeance psalms suggests that Gen 3:15 in fact provides the primal promissory foundation for the psalmists' requests for divine judgment.[137] The echoes of Gen 3:15 in the imprecatory psalms not only characterize the enemy as the serpent seed and situate the psalmists' present conflict within the story of serpentine antagonism against the temple-kingdom of God, as argued above, but also recall and rely upon the divine guarantee of a certain future in which the serpent seed is crushed underfoot and the fractured kingdom restored. "He shall bruise your head" presents a promise, a speech act from God that sets the trajectory of Israel's history and determines what God's people may reasonably expect from him. When the imprecatory psalms plead for God to break the teeth of venomous serpents (58:6), trample upon the wicked (68:30; cf. vv. 21, 23), crush oppressors such that they eat dust (72:4, 9), and smite the heads of crafty nations as he did in the past (83:9–12), they do so on the basis of God's commitment that the seed of the serpent will be shattered beneath the feet of the seed of the woman, taking their cues—deriving their content—from Gen 3:15. Indeed, given the regularity with which the enemy is described in serpentine terms, it is possible to read every plea for judgment, even those that do not explicitly reference the imagery of Gen 3:15, through the lens and logic of the *protoevangelium*, conceptually framed by the narrative expectation that God will indeed smash the serpent seed. The imprecations beg God to bring about that future which he has declared is coming, to enact that just judgment upon serpents' skulls which he has bound himself by promise to deliver.

In the developing narrative of Scripture, the Abrahamic covenant further specifies how the initial promise of Gen 3:15 will come to fruition, channeling the expectation of a serpent-crushing royal seed into the line of Abraham.[138] This association of the *protoevangelium* with the Abrahamic covenant is reflected in Psalm 72, where the psalmist petitions for an Israelite monarch who will crush oppressors (v. 4) and make enemies

---

[136]   See, e.g., Laney, "Fresh Look," 42; Day, "Imprecatory Psalms," 84; Shepherd, "Place of the Imprecatory Psalms," 115.

[137]   Cf. Murray, "Christian Cursing?" 114; Mennega, "Ethical Problem," 53–56; Kidner, *Psalms 73–150*, 331.

[138]   T. Desmond Alexander, "Royal Expectations in Genesis to Kings: Their Importance for Biblical Theology," *TynBul* 49, no. 2 (1998): 205; Schreiner, *King in His Beauty*, 17.

lick the dust (v. 9) such that his name endures forever and all nations find their blessing in him (v. 17; cf. Gen 12:2–3).[139] The request for judgment upon enemies is couched as a request for the manifestation of the promises of Genesis 3 and 12 through the Davidic king.[140] Other imprecations, too, draw upon the language of God's covenant with the first patriarch as they call for justice against the enemy. In Gen 12:3, God proclaims that he will bless those who bless Abram and curse those who curse Abram, a promise echoed in the petition of Ps 109:17 ("He loved to curse; let curses come upon him!") and the confident declaration of Ps 109:28 ("Let them curse, but you will bless!").[141] The psalmist appeals to the Abrahamic promise in his request for and anticipation of a divine vengeance that will mean the cursing of the wicked and the blessing of the faithful. Psalm 83:4 portrays the enemy coalition as those who threaten the name and nation God committed in Gen 12:2 to make great and bless, thereby framing the pleas for vengeance that follow as requests for God to make good on his word to Abraham by thwarting their murderous efforts. In Gen 15:1, God commits himself to act as Abram's shield (מָגֵן), an image utilized in Pss 3:3; 7:10; 119:114 to link the imprecations within each psalm with the covenantal promise of divine defense,[142] and the request of Ps 35:1–2 for God to take up his מָגֵן and fight against the psalmist's enemies may similarly allude to Gen 15:1 in its call for God's justice. God's word to Abraham in the redemptive-historical past provides a theological rationale in the

---

[139]   Hamilton, "Seed of the Woman," 269–70; Dempster, *Dominion and Dynasty*, 196; Schreiner, *King in His Beauty*, 260–61.

[140]   On the Davidic covenant as a further channeling of the promises of the *protoevangelium* and the Abrahamic covenant into the royal line of David, see Hamilton, "Seed of the Woman," 268; Schreiner, *King in His Beauty*, 157.

[141]   Day, "Imprecatory Psalms," 140; Mays, *Psalms*, 349.

[142]   Cf. James Limburg, *Psalms*, Westminster Bible Companion, ed. Patrick D. Miller and David L. Bartlett (Louisville: Westminster John Knox, 2000), 22; Mitchell Dahood, *Psalms I: 1–50*, AB (Garden City, N.Y.: Doubleday and Company, 1966), 16–17. Intriguingly, the only other use of מָגֵן in the Pentateuch occurs in Deut 33:29, the concluding verse of Moses' blessing over Israel, where he refers to the Lord as Israel's shield just before proclaiming that Israel will tread upon the backs of her enemies, bringing together images from Gen 3:15 and 15:1. 2 Samuel 22 also similarly combines shield imagery characteristic of the Abrahamic covenant with imagery drawn from Gen 3:15, describing David's military victories in foot-trampling terms (vv. 39–43). Cf. Wifall, "Gen 3:15," 363; Hamilton, "Skull-Crushing Seed," 40; Dempster, *Dominion and Dynasty*, 144.

psalmic present for petitions for judgment against those who would harm the life of God's covenant kingdom.[143]

The imprecatory psalms likewise appeal to the covenantal curses and requirements of justice inscribed in the Mosaic legislation and its principle of proportionate retribution (*lex talionis*) in their requests for divine vengeance.[144] The psalmist's claim in Ps 94:6 that the enemies murder the widow, sojourner, and fatherless recalls God's concern for this oppressed triad throughout Deuteronomy: God promises to execute justice on their behalf (10:18), forbids the perversion of justice against them (24:17), and curses anyone who does them harm (27:19).[145] Psalm 94:6 thus signals that the enemies against whom the imprecator prays are precisely those menaces to the *shalom* of the temple-kingdom who are already under the covenantal curse of God.[146] The psalmist affirms to God, "You rebuke the insolent, accursed ones, who wander from your commandments" (Ps 119:21),[147] recalling the comprehensive curse of Deut 27:26 upon "anyone who does not confirm the words of this law by doing them,"[148] and the imprecations' frequent characterizations of the enemy as depriving the needy of justice (e.g.,

---

[143]   Many scholars argue that the Abrahamic covenant provides the covenantal context from which the imprecations arise, though this contention is less often supplemented by careful consideration of the ways in which the imprecations themselves take up the language of the Abrahamic covenant. See Shepherd, "Place of the Imprecatory Psalms," 115; Laney, "Fresh Look," 41–42; Brian Doyle, "Psalm 58: Curse as Voiced Disorietation," *Bijdragen* 57, no. 2 (1996): 145; Lessing, "Broken Teeth," 368–69; James E. Adams, *War Psalms of the Prince of Peace: Lessons from the Imprecatory Psalms* (Phillipsburg, N.J.: Presbyterian and Reformed, 1991), 73; Murray, "Christian Cursing?" 114; Harman, "Continuity of the Covenant Curses," 68; Kevin J. Youngblood, "Don't Get Even, Get Mad! Imprecatory Prayer as a Neglected Spiritual Discipline: (Psalm 69)," *Leaven* 19, no. 3 (2011): 155.

[144]   The *lex talionis* is outlined in Exod 21:23–25; Lev 24:17–22; Deut 19:21.

[145]   Cf. Hossfeld and Zenger, *Psalms 2*, 454.

[146]   Interestingly, Meredith G. Kline, *Treaty of the Great King: The Covenant Structure of Deuteronomy, Studies and Commentary* (Grand Rapids: Eerdmans, 1963), 123, connects the curses of Deuteronomy 27 to the original curse upon the serpent. Read in this way, those cursed in Deuteronomy 27—and in turn imprecated against in Psalm 94—are the seed of the serpent who share in the serpent's cursing due to their participation in the serpent's campaign to pollute and fragment the temple-kingdom of God.

[147]   Cf. Pss 119:126: "It is time for the LORD to act, for your law has been broken."

[148]   Hossfeld and Zenger, *Psalms 3*, 268, point to the curses of Deut 27:15–26 as a whole as the background for the concept in this verse.

10:18; 72:4; 82:3–4; 140:12) and deceptively plotting violence against the innocent (e.g., 10:8; 35:7; 69:4; 94:20–21; 140:4–5) resonate with the curses of Deut 27:17–19, 24–25 against just such offenders.[149] Read within the covenantal framework supplied by the Deuteronomic curses, the imprecators' prayers against unrepentant transgressors of God's law emerge as petitions for judgment upon those internal threats to the life of the temple-kingdom whom God has already committed himself to judge.[150]

Appeals to the Mosaic code are perhaps most concentrated in Psalm 109. While the echoes of the Deuteronomic curse certainly reverberate in David's circumstances,[151] the scenario of unjust accusation against the poor envisioned by this psalm (cf. vv. 3–5, 22) is further addressed in Exod 23:6–7, where God prohibits the perversion of justice against the poor (v. 6) and declares that he will not acquit the wicked who seek the life of the righteous by false charges (v. 7). In light of God's assurance of justice in Exod 23:7, the petition for those who speak evil against the psalmist's life (Ps 109:20) to "come forth guilty" (Ps 109:7) may be read as a rather

---

[149] Gerhard von Rad, *Deuteronomy: A Commentary*, OTL (Philadelphia: Westminster, 1966), 167–69, offers a number of insightful observations about the curses of Deuteronomy 27 that are germane to the imprecatory psalms. First, the covenant community offers its "Amen" to each curse, which not only signals agreement with God's wrath but further commits the community to participate in God's verdict by breaking fellowship with such lawbreakers. The imprecator may thus be understood as upholding his "Amen," praying against the injustices of the enemy in a manner that instantiates his commitment to God's law. Second, the curses focus on secret practices—sins more likely to escape detection of officials charged with carrying out justice, whether because they occur in private or because they prey upon the weak who are more vulnerable to injustice. In the imprecatory psalms, the secret and deceptive character of the enemies' violence, as well as the power differential between powerful attacker and vulnerable attacked, are often brought to the fore, and it is precisely because their injustice has escaped legal detection that the psalmist cries to God to expose the enemies' schemes and ensure that justice comes to pass. Cf. Kline, *Treaty of the Great King*, 124. On the representative character of the curses, see Earl S. Kalland, "Deuteronomy," in vol. 3 of *EBC* (Grand Rapids: Zondervan, 1992), 163; J. A. Thompson, *Deuteronomy: An Introduction and Commentary* (Leicester: InterVarsity Press, 1974), 266. This representative interpretation seems to be confirmed by the comprehensive concluding curse of Deut 27:26.

[150] Cf. Shepherd, "Place of the Imprecatory Psalms," 115–18; Adams, *War Psalms*, 57–59.

[151] Esp. the curses of Deut 27:19, 24–25 upon those who pervert justice against the weak and secretly seek the life of the innocent. The characterization of the enemy in Psalm 109 fixes the foe squarely under the Deuteronomic pronouncements of God's covenantal curse.

straightforward application of God's legislative word.[152] The mandates of Deut 19:16–21 also speak to the imprecator's circumstances, requiring that false witnesses have done to them what they meant to do to the innocent as a specific instantiation of the *lex talionis*.[153] Consonant with this conception of justice, the prayer of Psalm 109 carefully signals that the judgments requested parallel the intended effects of the enemy's evil: a wicked foe for the wicked foe (vv. 2, 6), an accuser for the accuser (vv. 4, 6, 20), curses for the curser (vv. 17–18), a void of kindness for one devoid of kindness (vv. 12, 16),[154] poverty for the pursuer of the poor (vv. 10–11, 16), death for him who sought death for others (vv. 8–9, 16, 20).[155] The imprecations of Psalm 109 are thus legitimated and limited by the covenant law of God's kingdom,[156] the Mosaic legislation that dictates the shape of justice among the people over whom God reigns. Deuteronomy's talionic stipulations concerning false witnesses frame the appeals of Psalms 35 and 69 against lying accusers as well,[157] and in other imprecatory psalms, the

[152] A similar dynamic is at play in Ps 139:20. The psalmist states that God's enemies "take your name in vain," clearly alluding to Exod 20:7. The imprecation of Ps 139:19 is thus grounded in v. 20 in the covenantal promise that God will judge those who misuse his name.

[153] See Firth, *Surrendering Retribution*, 41; J. W. Rogerson and J. W. McKay, *Psalms 101–150*, The Cambridge Bible Commentary (Cambridge: Cambridge University Press, 1977), 59–60, both of whom point to the case of Naboth in 1 Kings 21 as an example of the possible effects of false accusation, including the confiscation of property and death. Cf. McCann, *Psalms*, 1126; Allen P. Ross, *A Commentary on the Psalms: Volume 3 (90–150)*, KEL (Grand Rapids: Kregel Academic, 2016), 335.

[154] Brueggemann and Bellinger, *Psalms*, 474; Brueggemann, "Psalm 109," 149–51.

[155] See the detailed survey of talionic parallels within Psalm 109 by Day, "Imprecatory Psalms," 137. Cf. McCann, *Psalms*, 1126; Bernardino, "Reconsideration of 'Imprecations,'" 102–4; Simango, "Exegetical Study," 221.

[156] Firth, *Surrendering Retribution*, 142, observes that the *lex talionis* and its specialized application in cases of false accusation limit the retribution requested while being "built upon a conception of justice that is rooted in Israel's legal traditions."

[157] Youngblood, "Don't Get Even," 155, concludes of Psalm 69 that "the prayer conforms exactly to the retributive principle outlined" in Deut 19:16–19. Gordon J. Wenham, *Psalms as Torah: Reading Biblical Songs Ethically*, Studies in Theological Interpretation (Grand Rapids: Baker Academic, 2012), 170, detects an allusion to Deut 19:16–17 in Ps 35:11. On Psalm 35 and the *lex talionis*, see Brueggemann and Bellinger, *Psalms*, 174; Firth, *Surrendering Retribution*, 73–75; Shepherd, "Place of the Imprecatory Psalms," 41–42.

requests for proportionate retribution are explicit: "Give to them according to their work and according to the evil of their deeds; give to them according to the work of their hands; render them their due reward" (28:4; cf. 94:2; 137:8). The petitions present God's principles back to him, calling for justice according to God's own terms.

What is requested from God in the imprecatory psalms makes moral sense within the redemptive-historical narrative of God's covenant kingdom, drawing upon the story of God's promises to preserve and protect his temple-kingdom from those who would threaten her and the conception of justice that governs the community over whom God rules. In the narrative world of the imprecatory psalms, the pleas that sound so barbaric to modern ears are in fact consistent with God's covenantal commitments, his stated purposes for history, and his demands of justice in his kingdom. The content of the petitions is ethically justified within the storied cosmos that the psalms of vengeance inhabit and project.

The Imprecator Petitions from Love

The imprecations plead for the end of violence, public vindication, and the manifestation of God's covenant justice, but why? That is, what desires, motives, and loves give rise to these petitions for divine vengeance? Of course, the internal psychology of the psalmist is not available to the interpreter for analysis, but in addition to disclosing their intentions with regular explicit declarations of purpose, the psalmists orient their prayers toward certain goals, toward desired states of affairs, and these aspirational indicators—these overt and embedded teleological aims—may be considered as textual evidence of the affections that prompt the cries for justice.[158]

The imprecator curses chiefly from love of God.[159] "For your name's sake" is a repeated motivation for God's petitioned action in the

---

[158] Consider the relationship between love and *telos* as suggested by James K. A. Smith, *Desiring the Kingdom: Worship, Worldview, and Cultural Formation*, vol. 1 of Cultural Liturgies (Grand Rapids: Baker Academic, 2009), 52: "We are the sorts of animals whose love is aimed at different ends or goals (Greek: *teloi*). As intentional, love always has a target, something that it intends or aims at. So as we inhabit the world primarily in a noncognitive, affective mode of intentionality, implicit in that love is an end, or *telos*." To discern the psalmists' *teloi*, then, is to discern the psalmists' loves.

[159] See Wenham, *Goodness of God*, 164; Murray, "Christian Cursing?" 115. Cf. Ringgren, *Faith of the Psalmists*, 27–36; Mowinckel, *Psalms in Israel's Worship*, 1:204–5.

imprecatory psalms (79:9; 109:21; 143:11), calling upon the Lord of history to demonstrate the manifold excellencies of his character—his power, justice, covenant faithfulness—in order that he might be glorified and exalted. Praise of God on the lips of his delivered saints is the envisioned end of God's judgment upon the threatening enemy (5:11; 7:17; 9:14; 35:9-10, 18, 27-28; 40:16; 109:30), the future in which the imprecator desires to participate, the future made possible by God's avenging action. The imprecations are born from and oriented toward worship of God.

But it is not just the righteous who will behold the glory of God in his liberating judgment. The imprecator pleads for a demonstration of justice that will confront the enemy with his finitude (9:20) and result in recognition of the ultimately undeniable kingship of God (58:11; 59:13; 83:18; 109:27).[160] When the enemy scoffs at God (74:10, 18, 22; 79:9-10; 139:20), calling his character and being into question, the psalmist imprecates with the goal that God will defend his cause and vindicate himself, silencing the blasphemous claims of the wicked "for the glory of [his] name" (79:9).[161] The imprecator even dares to hope that the self-vindication of God would cause his foes to seek his name (83:16), graciously turning detractors into instruments of praise.[162] The psalms' prayers for judgment have as their *telos* the ever-enduring glory of God (104:31)—an earth that is full of God's glory (72:19), no longer polluted with the sinful violence that defames his name (104:35)[163]—a *telos* that finds its origin in Godward love.

The imprecator is concerned with the glory of God primarily, but not exclusively, for the psalmist curses from love of God's temple-kingdom as

---

[160] Cf. Althann, "Psalms of Vengeance," 6-7; Zuck, "Problem of the Imprecatory Psalms," 74-75; Laney, "Fresh Look," 41; Shepherd, "Place of the Imprecatory Psalms," 41.

[161] Cf. Walter Brueggemann, *The Message of the Psalms: A Theological Commentary*, Augsburg Old Testament Studies (Minneapolis: Augsburg, 1984), 72; Martin, "Imprecations in the Psalms," 544; Eric Peels, *Shadow Sides: The Revelation of God in the Old Testament* (Carlisle, UK: Paternoster, 2003), 97-98; Vos, "Ethical Problem," 134; Luc, "Interpreting the Curses," 405; Meredith G. Kline, *The Structure of Biblical Authority*, 2nd ed. (Eugene, Ore.: Wipf & Stock, 1997), 161; Zuck, "Problem of the Imprecatory Psalms," 74; Wenham, *Goodness of God*, 161-64.

[162] Cf. Goldingay, *Psalms: Volume 2*, 582; Kidner, *Psalms 73-150*, 333; Laney, "Fresh Look," 41; Grogan, *Psalms*, 148; McCann, *Psalms*, 1010; Tanner, "Psalm 83," in deClaissé-Walford, Jacobson, and Tanner, *Book of Psalms*, 648; Limburg, *Psalms*, 283.

[163] See Kraus, *Theology of the Psalms*, 128.

well.[164] That is, the imprecations reflect a desire not only for God's manifestation and exaltation but also for the preservation, peace, and prosperity of the people over whom God reigns in the land of his presence.[165] Indeed, in the imprecatory psalms, these two loves are complementary: the imprecator longs for God's name by longing for God's action on behalf of the community who bears that name, praying in love for king and kingdom.[166]

The psalmists' kingdom-directed love is evident in the pleas of Psalm 83 for the proactive protection of God's covenant people in God's land from dispossession and extermination (vv. 3–5, 12), as well as in the retrospective malediction of Ps 137:7–9, arising as it does from a self-maledictory oath of allegiance to Jerusalem (vv. 5–6), the city of God.[167] The cries for justice in Psalms 74 and 79 petition for a divine answer to the destruction of Zion's sanctuary and the congregation that organizes its life around God's temple presence, and Psalm 69 overtly states that the psalmist's zeal for God's holy house is the origin of the enemy's assaults (v. 9) before begging for a judgment that effects the salvation of Zion and the people who dwell there with God (vv. 35–36; cf. v. 6).[168] The imprecation against unjust judges in Psalm 58 pursues via prayer the elimination of violence in the land (v. 2)— which compromises the life and witness of God's kingdom people—and aims at the joy of the righteous when they behold the vengeance of God (vv. 10–11). Psalms 35 and 109, though Davidic imprecations against personal

---

[164]   Kline, *Structure of Biblical Authority*, 161; cf. Martin, "Imprecations in the Psalms," 546; Peels, *Vengeance of God*, 243.

[165]   Cf. David R. Blumenthal, "Liturgies of Anger," *Cross Curr.* 52, no. 2 (2002): 195.

[166]   E.g., in Psalm 83 the psalmist pleads, contrary to the enemy's intentions, that the nation that knows God as covenant king (vv. 3–4) would dwell securely in the land where God dwells (vv. 9–12), desiring the deliverance of God's temple-kingdom through judgment upon those that threaten her as the very means by which God's character might be magnified (vv. 13–18). Love of God's kingdom is here a subsidiary love that complements and serves, but does not displace, love of God the king. The requested judgment that is salvation for the kingdom is simultaneously vindication for God, and to desire the glory of the covenant-making king is to simultaneously desire the good of the kingdom whom he has covenanted to bless.

[167]   Zenger, *God of Vengeance?* 50: "The appeal to the God who protects a just world order is rooted, for those who pray Psalm 137, in the recollection of the love of YHWH for Zion/Jerusalem/Israel experienced in history. Therefore the passionate language of the psalm is the expression of passionate love—and can be properly understood and comprehended only by those who love."

[168]   See esp. Goldingay, *Psalms: Volume 2*, 338.

enemies, nevertheless exhibit a love that extends beyond the psalmist's self, seeking the blessedness of the quiet in the land (35:20)[169] and the liberation of the poor and brokenhearted (109:16) from those who neither speak nor enact peace.[170] And insofar as the survival of the temple-kingdom depends upon the survival of the Davidic king that mediates God's rule over her, the Davidic imprecations for the king's personal deliverance are simultaneously pleas for the deliverance of the kingdom that he leads and represents.

The yearned-for end of these psalms is a renewed sociality that instantiates the kingdom, that embraces and lives into the holy form of life that characterizes God's reign over and with his people. The imprecator wants rescue for the weak and fatherless (82:3–4; cf. 10:8–11), defense of the needy and their children (72:4, 12–14), covenant faithfulness where "the dark places of the land are full of the habitations of violence" (74:20), rejoicing for those whose refuge is God (5:11),[171] the routing of the wicked so that the kingdom might flourish "with no cry of distress in our streets" (144:14; cf. vv. 5–6, 12–15).[172] In each case, the love-born *telos* of the imprecations is the justice and joy, the safety, stability, and *shalom* of the temple-kingdom of God. The petitions for vengeance for the sake of the kingdom are expressions of kingdom love.

Is it possible, though, that in addition to desiring the glory of God and the good of the temple-kingdom, the imprecator curses from love even of

---

[169]   Tanner, "Psalm 35," in deClaissé-Walford, Jacobson, and Tanner, *Book of Psalms*, 336–37, observes that in pitting themselves against *shalom* and the quiet in the land, the enemies "have contempt for the very things God values. These ones are a threat to the very fabric of God's kingdom values." The psalmist's petition on behalf of *shalom* and the quiet in the land is alternatively a prayer for God's temple-kingdom and the values that sustain its communal life.

[170]   See Brueggemann and Bellinger, *Psalms*, 474.

[171]   In such instances where the psalmist desires the Godward praise of God's people, the complementarity of love of God and love of God's kingdom is again evident. The joy of God's kingdom community abounds to the glory of God; God is exalted in the exultation of his people. To pray toward the end of worship is to desire the good of the kingdom and the glory of the king, to love both the God who reigns and the community over whom he reigns. Cf. Mays, *Psalms*, 58.

[172]   The descriptions of blessing in Ps 144:12–15 that will follow after God's delivering judgment echo the promises of quasi-Edenic fruitfulness and security in the land in Deut 28:3–8. Cf. deClaissé-Walford, "Psalm 144," in deClaissé-Walford, Jacobson, and Tanner, *Book of Psalms*, 988; Goldingay, *Psalms: Volume 3*, 688–89; McCann, *Psalms*, 1256. Other indications of kingdom-oriented love in the imprecatory psalms may be found in, e.g., Pss 10:16–18; 55:9–11; 59:6; 140:11.

the enemy? The Old Testament enjoins enemy love as a necessary aspect of the ethical life of faith (Exod 23:4–5; Lev 19:17–18; Prov 24:17–18; 25:21–22),[173] but do the imprecatory psalms manifest this love in their cries for judgment? I suggest that the answer is *yes*, that—while admittedly less apparent than the psalmists' love of God and kingdom—the imprecations are consistent with enemy love insofar as they petition for ends consonant with the enemy's good, and in some cases they overtly express this love.[174]

A significant initial piece of data is the psalmist's own testimony concerning his love for his enemies. David recounts in Ps 35:12–14 the love he exhibited toward those who would abuse him: he had done them good (v. 12), mourning at their sickness with an intensity normally reserved for the most intimate of relationships (vv. 13–14).[175] Similarly, David claims in Ps 109:4–5 that the hatred demonstrated by his enemies is the incommensurate response to his own exercise of love, and rather than returning false accusation for false accusation—rather than engaging in the same sort of unjust, destructive behavior as his enemies—David gives himself to prayer (v. 4), most likely the very prayer preserved in the psalm. Psalm 109:4–5 suggests not only that David's previous relationship with his would-be accusers was characterized by love but also that his response of prayer is consistent with, an extension of, his previous posture, a refusal to participate in the type of unjust and violent hatred exercised by his enemies.[176]

---

[173] Janowski, *Arguing with God*, 122–24; Shepherd, "Place of the Imprecatory Psalms," 111; Laney, "Fresh Look," 38–39; Bernardino, "Reconsideration of 'Imprecations,'" 22–23; Craigie and Tate, *Psalms 1–50*, 41; Wenham, *Goodness of God*, 158–59; Beisner, *Psalms of Promise*, 174; *contra* Zuck, "Problem of the Imprecatory Psalms," 60–63.

[174] *Contra*, e.g., Rogerson and McKay, *Psalms 101–150*, 59; Miller, *They Cried to the Lord*, 302–3; Walter Brueggemann, *The Psalms and the Life of Faith*, ed. Patrick D. Miller (Minneapolis: Fortress, 1995), 268. Craigie and Tate, *Psalms 1–50*, 41, recognizes that the Old Testament mandates enemy love but maintains that the imprecations run afoul of this prescription.

[175] Cf., e.g., Simango, "Exegetical Study," 77; Tanner, "Psalm 35," in deClaissé-Walford, Jacobson, and Tanner, *Book of Psalms*, 336; Allen P. Ross, *A Commentary on the Psalms: Volume 1 (1–41)*, KEL (Grand Rapids: Kregel Publications, 2011), 770–71; Limburg, *Psalms*, 115.

[176] See John Calvin, *Commentary on the Book of Psalms*, trans. James Anderson, Calvin's Commentaries 6 (repr., Grand Rapids: Baker Books, 2005), 4:272–73. The explanation of Zenger, *God of Vengeance?* 60–61 is also instructive:

> In this extreme distress, he or she *will not and cannot* retaliate with the same weapons. Instead, the one who prays appeals to the God of mercy

The calls of Pss 7:8; 139:23–24 for God to search and judge the psalmist's innermost being for even a modicum of unrighteousness in the matter at hand—calls that follow imprecatory petitions[177]—further indicate that the imprecator detects no incompatibility between God's law of love and his practice of pleading for justice.

This self-proclaimed love for the enemy is further exhibited in the aims of the imprecations, the sought-after ends of the requested judgments, which often include the enemy's recognition of and turning toward God. Most apparently, Ps 83:16 asks for God to fill the assaulting nations with shame "that they may seek your name, O Lord." The imprecator's stated hope is that divine vengeance will provoke those who have pursued God's people to instead pursue God in the pattern of his people. This is nothing less than a plea for the enemy's repentance and conversion, that those devoted to the destruction of the temple-kingdom would become its citizens.[178] More subtle is the declaration of Ps 7:12 that God will follow

and blessing to save—to save the one against whom these enemies are fighting without cause, and who has practiced the love demanded by Leviticus 19 (cf. the echoes of Lev 19:17–18 in v. 5). The devout one ruptures the vicious circle of violence with the cry, "In return for my love they accuse me—but I am a prayer!" This prayer is our very psalm itself!

Though Zenger defends the quotation hypothesis regarding vv. 6–19, I am nevertheless sympathetic to his reading of vv. 4–5. It is intriguing that the commands of Exod 23:4–5 requiring loving beneficence toward an enemy is immediately followed by God's prohibition of perverting justice against the poor and his declaration that he will not acquit the wicked who level such false charges in Exod 23:6–7, a text which I argued above may provide part of the covenantal background for Psalm 109. It is possible that the juxtaposition of these two themes in Exodus 23 informs the psalmist's conviction that his recourse to prayer on the basis of Exod 23:6–7 is not at odds with the love enjoined by Exod 23:4–5.

[177] This is especially striking in Psalm 139, where the psalmist's call for God to slay the wicked and declaration of hatred against those that hate God in vv. 19–22 is immediately followed by the invitation for God to search him for any grievous way in vv. 23–24.

[178] Cf. Marvin E. Tate, *Psalms 51–100*, WBC 20 (Waco, Tex.: Word Books, 1990), 348–49; Walter C. Kaiser, Jr., "The People of Psalm 83," *BSac* 174 (2017): 264–65; Tanner, "Psalm 83," in deClaissé-Walford, Jacobson, and Tanner, *Book of Psalms*, 648; Artur Weiser, *The Psalms: A Commentary*, OTL, trans. Herbert Hartwell (Philadelphia: Westminster, 1962), 564; Limburg, *Psalms*, 283; Brueggemann and Bellinger, *Psalms*, 362; McCann, *Psalms*, 1010; Goldingay, *Psalms: Volume 2*, 582; Grogan, *Psalms*, 148; Kidner, *Psalms 73–150*, 333; Allen P. Ross, *A Commentary on the Psalms: Volume 2 (42–89)*, KEL (Grand Rapids:

through in judgment "if a man does not repent" (cf. 55:19), punctuating the imprecation of v. 9 for God to "let the evil of the wicked come to an end" with the desirable possibility that the wicked might bring their own evil to an end through penitence, that the wrath that God expresses every day (v. 11)[179] might turn the enemy from his ways before more drastic judgments are necessary.[180] Psalm 141:6 confidently envisions judgment upon "their judges"—likely the influential leaders of the wicked—as the means by which the psalmist's enemies hear and receive his pleasant words, framing the imprecatory plea of v. 10 with the expectation that God's vengeance will have remedial effects that prompt opponents to join with him in devotion to and dependence upon God.[181] A similar framing is present in Psalm 40, where the announcement that "many will see and fear, and put their trust in the LORD" (v. 3) because of God's delivering deeds in the past sets up the cries for present deliverance in vv. 13–15: perhaps the petitioned intervention will not only bolster the faith of the righteous but also stimulate the fear of the Lord in those who have put their trust elsewhere in opposition to God (cf. v. 4).[182]

The repentance- and worship-inducing effects of divine judgment appear to be in view in the prayer of Ps 68:28–31 as well:

> [28] Summon your power, O God,
>   the power, O God, by which you have worked for us.
> [29] Because of your temple at Jerusalem
>   kings shall bear gifts to you.

Kregel Academic, 2013), 746–47; Terrien, *Psalms*, 595; Denise Dombkowski Hopkins, *Psalms: Books 2–3*, ed. Linda M. Maloney, Wisdom Commentary 21 (Collegeville, Minn.: Liturgical Press, 2016), 318; Hossfeld and Zenger, *Psalms 2*, 344–45, though they argue that v. 16b (HT 17b) is a redactional insertion, Hossfeld and Zenger, *Psalms 2*, 340.

[179] Following the translation of NIV of זֹעֵם. *HALOT* 1:277 glosses this use in Ps 7:11 (HT 12) as "a God showing indignation," and NIV captures this sense of God's demonstration of his indignation better than, e.g., ESV ("a God who feels indignation") or NASB, NRSV ("a God who has indignation").

[180] Cf. Goldingay, *Psalms: Volume 1*, 149.

[181] Cf. Hossfeld and Zenger, *Psalms 3*, 560; Kidner, *Psalms 73–150*, 508; Goldingay, *Psalms: Volume 3*, 657–58. On some of the translation issues associated with vv. 6–7, see McCann, *Psalms*, 1244. The reading I propose is consistent with the rendering of ESV, NASB, NIV, and even the NRSV, despite its differences.

[182] Cf. Grogan, *Psalms*, 94; McCann, *Psalms*, 843; Mays, *Psalms*, 167. On the relationship between past (vv. 1–10) and present (vv. 11–17) in Psalm 40, see McCann, *Psalms*, 842; Goldingay, *Psalms: Volume 1*, 568; Brueggemann and Bellinger, *Psalms*, 198.

[30] Rebuke the beasts that dwell among the reeds,
the herd of bulls with the calves of the peoples.
Trample underfoot those who lust after tribute;
scatter the peoples who delight in war.
[31] Nobles shall come from Egypt;
Cush shall hasten to stretch out her hands to God.

The requests for God to summon his power and to rebuke, trample, and scatter the peoples are followed by confident declarations that the kings and nobles of the nations shall come into God's presence with outstretched hands bearing gifts, and the sequential structuring of the psalm suggests that here—as in Ps 68:18, where God's victorious ascension to Zion following judgment leads to his reception of gifts "even among the rebellious"—the revelation of God's delivering judgment against the enemies of his temple-kingdom is envisioned as a key means by which God will draw the nations to his temple and to himself in worship.[183] In various imprecatory psalms, then, the imprecator either explicitly requests or implicitly anticipates that divine judgment would instigate reformation, bringing enemies to repentance and faith-filled fellowship with God for his glory and their good. Indeed, from a canonical perspective, every imprecatory plea is conditioned by the Psalter's introductory call for God's enemies to "kiss the Son, lest he be angry, and you perish in the way" (2:12), an exhortation that holds out repentance as the most desirable of potential responses of the wicked to the reality of God's judgment.[184]

And yet, even if God's action does not have a converting influence upon the enemy, the imprecator's petitions for judgment may still be understood as requests for the enemy's good, requests of love. This conception of imprecation as an act of love depends upon the recognition that the enemy's unimpeded continuation of and descent into violence is detrimental not only to the innocent he assaults, but to himself as well. To journey unconfronted down the path of wickedness is to compound sin upon sin and incur greater degrees of guilt before God, to be confirmed and hardened in one's self-aggrandizing delusions, to become the kind of

---

[183]   Cf. Ps 72:10–11, 15, which petitions that the "royal son" (v. 1) who crushes the oppressor (v. 4) would receive homage and gifts from the kings of the nations.

[184]   On Psalm 2 as an introduction to the canonical Psalter, see McCann, *Theological Introduction*, 41–50.

person for whom violence is increasingly easy and instinctual.[185] Every new egregious act is yet one more act with which the enemy must live as he carries a personal history in which he has been the unjust destroyer of lives. Recent work on moral injury, focusing largely on combat veterans, has explored the ways that acts of violence may have profoundly detrimental effects not only for the victims of violence but also for its perpetrators, as the transgressive nature of the violent act shatters the agent's self-conception, inhibits trust, and provokes a variety of problematic psychological and behavioral responses.[186] In a 2007 study of perpetrators of violent crimes, 45.7 percent reported experiencing intrusive memories of their offenses, and 5.7 percent exhibited symptoms of PTSD.[187] Doing violence does something to human beings.[188] While not equating victims and victimizers, such research sheds light on the very real ways in which victimizers may in some sense be victims of their own violence.

From this perspective, the imprecator's prayers may be read as petitions to spare the enemy the disintegrating and agonizing moral, spiritual, and psychological effects of further violence by neutralizing his capacity to reap destruction (58:6–7), refusing to give him the distorted desires of his heart (35:4, 25), challenging his self-exaltation (9:20; 59:12–13; 140:8), and disappointing his murderous schemes (40:14–15)—in short, by interrupting his violence in judgment. Rather than revealing an absence of enemy love, such prayers may be received as evidence that the psalmist loves the

[185]   This is simply to acknowledge the character and habit-forming quality of practice. See the discussion of Smith, *Desiring the Kingdom*, 55–62. In "Theology Takes Practice: *Fare Forward* Interviews James K. A. Smith," *Fare Forward*, December 4, 2013, accessed May 17, 2022, http://farefwd.com/index .php/2020/12/16/theology-take-practice/, Smith observes that the practice of vice has a similar capacity to "de-form" persons.

[186]   See, e.g., Jonathan Shay, "Moral Injury," *Psychoanalytic Psychology* 31, no. 2 (2014): 182–91; Jeremy D. Jinkerson, "Defining and Assessing Moral Injury: A Syndrome Perspective," *Traumatology* 22, no. 2 (2016): 122–30; Warren Kinghorn, "Combat Trauma and Moral Fragmentation: A Theological Account of Moral Injury," *JSCE* 32, no. 2 (2012): 57–74.

[187]   Ceri Evans et al., "Intrusive Memories in Perpetrators of Violent Crime: Emotions and Cognition," *J. Consult. Clin. Psychol.* 75, no. 1 (2007): 134–44.

[188]   Bernhard Giesen, "The Trauma of Perpetrators: The Holocaust as the Traumatic Reference of German National Identity," in *Cultural Trauma and Collective Identity*, ed. Jeffrey C. Alexander et al. (Berkeley: University of California Press, 2004), 112–54, considers how the perpetration of violence may traumatically affect entire communities and societies, using post-Holocaust Germany as a case study.

enemy enough to petition God for his good even when the enemy does not want the good for himself,[189] to desire for the enemy a momentary pain in the present that will prevent a deeper pain in the future.[190]

But what of the cries for the enemy's death (e.g., 54:5; 55:15; 58:7–8; 69:28; 104:35; 109:8–9)? How could these possibly be the prayerful fruit of enemy love? For those hell-bent on inducing as much terror as possible, who press forward in bloodthirsty violence with a callous disregard for the devastation they inflict upon others and themselves, the divine withdrawal of life may be understood as a merciful last resort, a sovereignly administered preventative that restrains the enemy from adding to his iniquity, bearing responsibility for yet more horrific injustice, sinking even further into inhumanity.[191] The imprecator's petitions demonstrate an unwillingness to let the enemies harm themselves in their harming of others, calling

---

[189] Cf. Oliver O'Donovan, *Resurrection and Moral Order: An Outline for Evangelical Ethics*, 2nd ed. (Grand Rapids: Eerdmans, 1994), 229. Love of the enemy-neighbor perceives his divinely instituted *telos*—the end for which he was made by God—and prays, in the midst of all the vicissitudes of disordered existence, that the enemy would be graciously prevented from pursuing his own destruction and disintegration, that his life and experience would be moved in the direction of the righteousness and peace in which he (and others) might prosper.

[190] This conception of love resonates with the portrait of true friendship in Prov 27:6 (cf. Prov 26:28; 28:3; 29:5). Israel's wisdom literature presents the unwillingness to confront a person with the danger of their folly—even when such unwillingness masquerades as ostensibly kind speech—as a failure of love that only does the individual more harm. This is analogous to the relationship of love and discipline in parenting (e.g., Prov 13:24), where genuine concern for the well-being of a child is willing to expose the child to the brief and controlled pain of discipline in order to save the child from the pain of a life committed to foolishness and rebellion. Cf. Lev 19:17 and the reflections of Nicholas Wolterstorff, *Justice in Love*, EUSLR (Grand Rapids: Eerdmans, 2011), 197.

[191] Something of this dynamic is present in the reflections of Sue Klebold, *A Mother's Reckoning: Living in the Aftermath of Tragedy* (New York: Crown Publishers, 2016), 17, on her response to hearing that her son Dylan was actively perpetrating the 1999 shooting at Columbine High School in Littleton, CO: "Like mothers all over Littleton, I had been praying for my son's safety. But when I heard the newscaster pronounce twenty-five people dead, my prayers changed. If Dylan was involved in hurting or killing other people, he had to be stopped. As a mother, this was the most difficult prayer I had ever spoken in the silence of my thoughts, but in that instant I knew the greatest mercy I could pray for was not my son's safety, but for his death." A mother's love for her son fuels the painful, tragic prayer that he mercifully be stopped in death. This is imprecation born of love.

upon God to interrupt their malevolence in a manner that, when considered in light of the manifold injurious effects of violence on the violent, is strangely consistent with love—a prayer for the enemy's good.

But, it may be objected, the psalmist explicitly declares his hate toward the enemy in a text like Ps 139:21–22. Surely love is absent from such prayers!

> [21] Do I not hate those who hate you, O LORD?
>   And do I not loathe those who rise up against you?
> [22] I hate them with complete hatred;
>   I count them my enemies.

We ought first to recognize that this psalm, like others (e.g., 31:6; 119:113), holds out a certain form of hate as a virtue to be adopted and imitated—not a vice to be avoided.[192] This is consistent with the evaluation of Ps 15:4, where the question of v. 1 concerning who may enter God's tent and dwell on his holy hill is answered with a description of one "in whose eyes a vile person is despised" (cf. 26:5). There is a type of hate that is a precondition for, and not an inhibition to, access to the sacred space of Yahweh's holy presence. Perhaps in spite of our instinctive sense that hate and love are mutually exclusive affections, "hate" (שָׂנֵא) may refer to a condition of disapproval, aversion, rejection, distancing, or separation that does not necessarily include the vindictive desire for ill, which would be the antithesis of love.[193] As Peels observes, "Hatred always creates a distance, yet it does not always imply malicious intentions."[194] Indeed, just as one may desire just judgment for the sake of the enemy's true good, one may conceivably hate—that is, reject, disapprove of, experience aversion toward—the agent whose vicious acts spell his own and others' harm from a commitment to the agent's ultimate flourishing. Elsewhere, the unimpeachable God of love is said to hate evildoers (5:5–6; 11:5) without any suggestion that this might contradict his holy character, and analogously, the psalmist may hate his enemies in a manner consistent with and rooted in love. We might even say that there is kind of hate that is only possible for those who love, a hate that is angrily opposed to a person precisely because the person

---

[192]   See Goldingay, *Psalms: Volume 3*, 638.

[193]   Cf. E. Lipiński, "*śānē*," *TDOT*, 14:164.

[194]   Eric Peels, "'I Hate Them with Perfect Hatred' (Psalm 139:21–22)," *TynBul* 59, no. 1 (2008): 38. Peels' careful analysis is worth consulting in its entirety (pp. 35–46).

is acting in ways that inflict self-harm and thus fail to lay hold of that God-determined good that is desired for the person by the lover.[195] In this sense, there are circumstances in which the one who truly loves *must* hate. This does not suggest by any means that all forms of hate are ethically consistent with the demands of love, for disordered love will give rise to disordered (and so unethical) hate. One must love rightly in order to hate rightly, but there are times when one must hate truly in order to love fully.

The Imprecator Is the Royal-Priestly Son of God

I argued previously that, within the storied world of the imprecatory psalms, the enemy is allusively presented as the serpent seed, familially connected to the primeval opponent of God's temple-kingdom and destined for head-crushing destruction. But the matrix of images and echoes that situates the enemy within a broader narrative framework simultaneously casts the imprecator as a corresponding player within that same narrative. If the enemy is the serpentine offspring striking at the heel of God's people, then the imprecator is the Adamic son of God, the seed of the woman who wages war against the serpent as royal priest and priestly king. The imprecator is portrayed—sometimes quite straightforwardly, though more often through intertextual reference—as a character whose God-given role in the story enjoins certain obligations, determining what constitutes appropriate and ethical action. Evaluation of the imprecator's prayers thus requires consideration of the imprecator's place within the canonical narrative upon which the imprecatory psalms draw in their depiction of the cosmos, the canonical narrative that supplies the script and moral logic against which the imprecator's words may be measured.

The beginnings of the scriptural story in Genesis 1–2 depict the whole creation as the temple of the divine king—the place where God wills to establish his royal presence with and over his people—and the garden in Eden's east as the primal microcosmic sanctuary upon the earth.[196] Into

---

[195]   Cf. John L. McKenzie, "The Imprecations of the Psalter," *American Ecclesiastical Review* 111, no. 2 (1944): 90–93.

[196]   The linguistic and conceptual parallels between Genesis 1–2 and Old Testament descriptions of cultic space have been well-surveyed. See esp. Beale, *Temple and the Church's Mission*, 66–80; Gordon J. Wenham, "Sanctuary Symbolism in the Garden of Eden Story," in *I Studied Inscriptions from before the Flood*, ed. R. S. Hess and D. T. Tsumara (Winona Lake, Ind.: Eisenbrauns, 1994), 399–404; L. Michael Morales, *Who Shall Ascend the Mountain of the Lord? A Biblical Theology of the Book of Leviticus*, NSBT 37 (Downers Grove, Ill.: InterVarsity Press, 2015), 40–42; Kline, *Kingdom Prologue*, 47–49; John H. Walton, *Genesis*, NIVAC

this garden sanctuary Adam is placed as the son of God, bearing God's image and likeness,[197] commissioned as a royal priest who mediates God's kingship (Gen 1:26–28) and serves and guards the Lord's residence (Gen 2:15).[198] This Adamic priest-king is tasked with exercising dominion in worship of God, subduing the earth to expand the boundaries of God's garden-temple across the whole earth,[199] and protecting the land in which God dwells from unwelcome intruders. On this final point, Beale argues, "It is apparent that priestly obligations in Israel's later temple included the duty of 'guarding' unclean things from entering (cf. Num 3:6–7, 32, 38; 18:1–7), and this appears to be relevant for Adam, especially in view of the unclean creature lurking on the perimeter of the Garden and who then enters."[200] The royal-priestly office of the son of God thus comprises a

---

(Grand Rapids: Zondervan, 2001), 147–50; Richard Davidson, "Earth's First Sanctuary: Genesis 1–3 and Parallel Creation Accounts," *AUSS* 53, no. 1 (2015): 65–89; Jon D. Levenson, *Sinai and Zion: An Entry into the Jewish Bible* (New York: HarperOne, 1985), 142–45; Moshe Weinfeld, "Sabbath, Temple, and the Enthronement of the Lord—The Problem of the Sitz im Leben of Genesis 1:1–2:3," in *Melanges biblique et orientaux en l'honneur de M. Henri Cazelles*, AOAT 212, ed. André Caquot and Mathias Delcor (Kevelaer: Butzon and Bercker, 1981), 501–12.

[197]   See McDowell, *Image of God*, 131–37; Kline, *Kingdom Prologue*, 45–46; Gentry and Wellum, *Kingdom through Covenant*, 194–95. Cf. Luke 3:38.

[198]   The Hebrew of Gen 2:15 describes Adam's task with עבד and שׁמר, often translated "to work it and keep it." Beale, "Eden, the Temple, and the Church's Mission in the New Creation," *JETS* 48, no. 1 (2005): 7–8, observes that these words "can easily be, and usually are, translated 'serve and guard.' When these two words occur together later in the OT, without exception they have this meaning and refer either to Israelites 'serving and guarding/obeying' God's word (about 10 times) or, more often to priests who 'serve' God in the temple and 'guard' the temple from unclean things entering it (Num 3:7–8; 8:25–26; 18:5–6; 1 Chr 23:32; Ezek 44:14)."

[199]   Cf. Beale, *Temple and the Church's Mission*, 81–87; Walton, *Genesis*, 185–87.

[200]   Beale, *Temple and the Church's Mission*, 69. Beale notes that priests in ancient pagan temples were tasked with similar guarding responsibilities before continuing,

> Adam's priestly role of "guarding" (*šāmar*) the garden sanctuary may also be reflected in the later role of Israel's priests who were called "guards" (1 Chr 9:23) and repeatedly were referred to as temple "gatekeepers" (repeatedly in 1 and 2 Chronicles and Nehemiah: e.g., 1 Chr 9:17–27) who "kept watch [*šāmar*] at the gates" (Neh 11:19), "so that no one should enter who was in any way unclean" (2 Chr 23:19). Consequently, the priestly role in both the Garden and later temple was to "manage" it by maintaining its order and keeping out uncleanness.

juridical element, a responsibility to guard the temple-kingdom by expelling any encroaching unholy creature and to subdue the earth by progressively casting out everything unfit for God's holy presence such that creation attains its end as the consummate house of the Lord.

From this angle, the fall of man in Genesis 3 involves not only disobedience to the divine command but with it a failure to fulfill the role of the son of God to protect the temple-kingdom and exercise judgment upon the serpent by driving it out of Eden.[201] God's response to this failure in the *protoevangelium* of Gen 3:15 is to declare enmity between the two lines and to promise a seed from the woman who will answer the calling of the son of God, definitively judging the serpent for the restoration of the kingdom, so that God's people might dwell under his rule and in his presence as holy priests, worshiping kings, faithful sons of God. This first iteration of the gospel does not abrogate the Adamic vocation but announces its continuation and ultimate fulfillment: as the seed of the serpent ever strikes at the seed of the woman, her offspring will oppose the serpent seed as sons of God who embrace their royal-priestly calling until the premier seed-son wins the decisive victory.[202]

Developing this theme, the Pentateuch identifies Israel as the son of God (Exod 4:22–23; Deut 14:1)[203] who is a "kingdom of priests" (Exod 19:5–6).[204] The seed of Abraham—the whole covenant community—is called by God to take up the Adamic mantle as a royal-priestly son who, in addition to guarding the holiness of the camp and cutting off all

---

[201] Cf. Kline, *Kingdom Prologue*, 86; Beale, *Temple and the Church's Mission*, 87; Peter J. Leithart, *Defending Constantine: The Twilight of an Empire and the Dawn of Christendom* (Downers Grove, Ill.: IVP Academic, 2010), 333–34.

[202] Kline, *Kingdom Prologue*, 132, maintains that Eve's enmity toward the serpent is linked with the "renewal in her of the image of God," but does not expand upon the ways this makes use of the son of God motif previously introduced within the narrative. Biblical-theological treatments of Genesis 1–3 regularly note the royal-priestly dimensions of the image/son of God and read Gen 3:15 as a promise of kingdom restoration but have largely neglected the ways in which the promised seed of Gen 3:15 draws upon the conceptualization of the son of God earlier in the Genesis narrative. A notable exception is Leithart, *Defending Constantine*, 334, who rightly observes that the promise of the delivering seed of the woman is the promise of a true Adam, a son of God who fulfills the royal-priestly calling originally given to Adam.

[203] It is noteworthy that God in Exod 4:23 commands Pharaoh to let Israel go so that his son may serve (from עבד, the same root as in Gen 2:15) him.

[204] On the Adamic character of Israel as a royal priesthood, cf. Schreiner, *King in His Beauty*, 36; Gentry and Wellum, *Kingdom through Covenant*, 322.

corruption, subdues the land (Num 32:22, 29; Josh 18:1)[205] and drives the serpent seed from the place where God has purposed to dwell with his people. Indeed, the conquest of Canaan is presented as an exercise in Israelite sonship: the royal priesthood, entering a new Eden from the east,[206] is to perform the work Adam failed to accomplish, expelling the unclean, serpentine nations from the land so that God might reside among his kingdom community in holiness.[207]

The Davidic king, as the premier representative of God's kingdom of priests, is also called a son of God.[208] God's covenant with the king explicitly characterizes his offspring as sons of God (2 Sam 7:14), and throughout 2 Samuel 6–10, David acts as a priest-king, dressed in priestly garb (6:14), making offerings (6:17), blessing the people (6:18),[209] seeking to

---

[205] The same root is used in these texts to describe Israel's subduing of the land (כבשׁ) as in the Adamic commission of Gen 1:28. Intriguingly, Num 32:20–22 depicts Israel's going to war in the land of Canaan as the means by which God will drive out the nations and the land will be subdued. Israel subdues the land as the royal-priestly son of God by expelling the nations from the land of God's presence in judgment.

[206] In Gen 3:24, an angel and flaming sword are placed at the east of Eden to guard the land from the sons of God who failed to guard the land themselves. In Josh 5:13–15, the sword-bearing angel stationed at the east of Canaan aids the son of God in driving out the serpentine nations from the land of God's presence. This episode presents Israel as the Adamic son of God, reentering the Edenic land as a royal priesthood to do what Adam did not. Cf. Dempster, *Dominion and Dynasty*, 128.

[207] On this reading of the Canaanite conquest, see esp. Kline, *Kingdom Prologue*, 86–87; G. K. Beale, *The Morality of God in the Old Testament*, Christian Answers to Hard Questions (Philadelphia: Westminster Seminary Press; Phillipsburg, N.J.: P&R Publishing, 2013), 10–11. Dempster, *Dominion and Dynasty*, 127, notes the parallels between Gen 1:28; Josh 18:1 and draws attention to the allusions to Gen 3:15 in Josh 10:24–26, where Joshua instructs the chiefs of the men of war to put their feet on the necks of the enemy. Within the Joshua narrative, Israel is depicted as the seed of the woman who strikes with her foot the head of the serpent seed and in so doing subdues the land as the image-bearing son of God.

[208] Cf. Scott W. Hahn, *Kinship by Covenant: A Canonical Approach to the Fulfillment of God's Saving Promises*, The Anchor Yale Bible Reference Library (New Haven: Yale University Press, 2009), 196–97.

[209] See Scott W. Hahn, *The Kingdom of God as Liturgical Empire: A Theological Commentary on 1–2 Chronicles* (Grand Rapids: Baker Academic, 2012), 57–61, on David's royal-priestly characterization in 1 Chronicles 15–16 and Deborah W. Rooke, "Kingship as Priesthood: The Relationship between the

build a dwelling place for God in the land (7:2), and subduing the enemies of the kingdom (8:1–10:19).[210] Psalm 2 frames the Psalter's portrait of the Davidic monarch with the divine decree, "You are my son" (v. 7), and declaration that this son of God will guard the kingdom from outside aggressors and extend God's domain throughout the earth by exercising shattering judgment upon the nations (vv. 8–9).[211] Subsequent psalms expand upon this motif,[212] depicting the Davidic anointed as the son of God (72:1; 89:26) who, as priest and king (110:2, 4),[213] protects the kingdom of God's presence by subduing the land (18:47; 144:1–2), driving out the wicked (18:34–42; 41:10; 101:5, 8), and crushing the serpent seed in accord with the *protoevangelium's* promise of a faithful, victorious, Adamic son of God (18:38; 60:8–12; 72:4, 9; 89:23; 108:9–13; 110:1, 6).[214]

In their rendering of the world, the imprecatory psalms appeal to this narrative and import these categories, portraying the imprecator as the royal-priestly son of God who—in line with his calling—aims to guard the kingdom where God dwells by petitioning for judgment upon the unholy serpent seed that threatens God's people in God's place and who, at times, endeavors to extend the boundaries of God's dwelling on earth. The

---

High Priesthood and the Monarchy," in *King and Messiah in Israel and the Ancient Near East: Proceedings of the Oxford Old Testament Seminar*, ed. John Day, JSOTSup 270 (Sheffield: Sheffield Academic Press, 1998), 187, on 1 Kings 8; 12; 2 Kings 16 in addition to 2 Samuel 6 as instances of "the unmistakably cultic duties undertaken" by Israel's kings.

[210]   2 Samuel 8:11 uses the same root as Gen 1:28 (כבש) to describe David's subduing of the enemy nations. On the Adamic characterization of David's action, see Hamilton, *God's Glory in Salvation through Judgment*, 171–72. In 1 Chron 22:18–19, David states that the subduing of the land through military victory over its inhabitants makes possible the construction of the sanctuary as a house for God's name. Driving out the enemy from the land prepares the way for God's temple presence with his people.

[211]   Hamilton, "Skull-Crushing Seed," 39, links the language of Ps 2:7, 9 to Gen 3:15 and the promise of sonship in 2 Sam 7:14.

[212]   Cf. G. K. Beale, *A New Testament Biblical Theology: The Unfolding of the Old Testament in the New* (Grand Rapids: Baker Academic, 2011), 75–81, on the Adamic character of the Israelite king in the Psalter.

[213]   Cf. Hahn, *Kinship by Covenant*, 193; Kraus, *Theology of the Psalms*, 111. Eaton, *Kingship in the Psalms*, 172–77, explores the priestly quality of kingship in the psalms and links the king's judicial role to his priestly function.

[214]   Cf. Wifall, "Gen 3:15," 363; Hamilton, "Seed of the Woman," 269–70; "Skull-Crushing Seed," 37–40.

imprecations are prayed in the voice of the son of God, whose God-given vocation in the progressing story of Scripture ethically legitimates and even obligates such prayer. The imprecator's status as son of God is foregrounded in Psalm 72, which, bearing a Solomonic superscription, begins with the plea in v. 1, "Give the king your justice, O God, and your righteousness to the royal son!"[215] This son of God petitions that he will be enabled to secure the justice and prosperity of the people by crushing the oppressor (vv. 2–4) and that he will enjoy a worldwide dominion characterized by flourishing and peace as his enemies are made to lick the dust (vv. 7–9)[216] so that the whole earth might be filled with God's glory (v. 19). With language reminiscent of Gen 1:28; 3:15, the royal-priestly son prays that he will fulfill the duties of his office—guard the kingdom from unclean intrusions, expand its borders across the earth, judge the serpent seed, secure dominion, and cultivate the world for the holy presence of the God who lives and reigns among his kingdom people[217]—and the prayer itself is an exercise of this office, a petitionary means of inhabiting his calling.

The Davidic imprecations exhibit a similar dynamic. In Psalm 58, David calls for judgment against the serpents (vv. 4–6) guilty of perverting justice and filling the land with violence (v. 2), exercising in prayer his royal-priestly prerogative to protect God's temple-kingdom from the serpents that threaten it from within.[218] The allusions to Gen 3:15 that position the unjust judges as the seed of the serpent simultaneously position the imprecator in opposition to them as the seed of the woman, the

---

[215] The "prayers of David" (Ps 72:20) in Books I–II of the Psalter are book-ended by son of God language in Ps 2:7 and Ps 72:1.

[216] See Sailhamer, *Meaning of the Pentateuch*, 501.

[217] Cf. Beale, *Temple and the Church's Mission*, 153–54; Hamilton, "Seed of the Woman," 269–70; *God's Glory in Salvation through Judgment*, 284; McCann, *Psalms*, 963. In Psalm 104, the description of creation in temple-related terms is brought to a climax with the call of v. 35 for the consumption of the sinful wicked from the earth so that the glory of God might endure forever (v. 31). Like Psalm 72, Psalm 104 endeavors to prayerfully subdue the earth as the holy house of Yahweh by driving out the wicked through supplication. See Laurence, "Let Sinners Be Consumed."

[218] Kraus, *Theology of the Psalms*, 126–27, argues of the psalms more generally that the king is the agent who brings God's judgment upon enemies before observing, "If in defeating his foes the king acts as the representative and agent of Yahweh, the situation is the same for the execution of punishment which the domestic ruler metes out to 'the wicked in the land,' and to those who do evil in the city of Yahweh (Ps 101:8)."

snake-striking son of God.[219] Psalm 58's above-surveyed references to Deuteronomy 32 fill out the portrait of David: as serpents whose heads are destined for smashing, Israel's leaders are in reality no different from the invading nations about whom Moses sang, and their reign of terror is as defiling and horrific as military subjugation. With his judgment prayer, David subdues "the nations" within Israel as he subdued the nations without (1 Chron 22:18), driving out "the nations" from God's holy people and his holy land in a petitionary recapitulation of the conquest, which was itself a cleansing of new Edenic ground. Interestingly, David not only petitions as the son of God but in v. 10 also requests that the whole covenant community would act as the son of God, bathing their feet in the blood of the wicked, treading upon the serpents in kingdom-liberating judgment.[220]

Psalm 68 opens with the declaration that God will scatter and drive away the wicked for the joy of the righteous (vv. 1–3)[221] before announcing that God will strike his enemies' heads (v. 21) and recording God's assurance that he will take action so that "you may strike your feet in their blood" (v. 23). David presents the judgment of God upon the seed of the serpent as being wrought through the agency of the son of God according to the expectations of the *protoevangelium*, and he (and, it seems, Israel with him) is this son.[222] The imprecator writes himself into the story, interpreting his role in relation to the enemies of the kingdom through the lens of Israel's canonical narrative. The imprecation of v. 30—requesting

---

[219]   Hamilton, *God's Glory in Salvation through Judgment*, 76–77; "Skull-Crushing Seed," 41.

[220]   Kidner, *Psalms 1–72*, 228, compares this verse with Isa 63:1–6, where God is appalled that no one has joined him in the exercise of judgment. Cf. Schaefer, *Psalms*, 143.

[221]   With clear echoes of Moses' prayer in Num 10:35 for God to arise and scatter his enemies as Israel journeyed toward Canaan, led by the holy presence of God. The psalm thus opens with an intertextual reference to Moses' prayerful agency in God's theophanic preservation of the community with whom he resided, repurposing the language as an affirmation that God will theophanically preserve the community with whom he resides in the land of his presence. The specific phrase utilized in Num 10:35 (קוּמָה יְהוָה) is used in the imprecations of Pss 3:7; 7:6; 9:19; 10:12; 17:13, where the psalmists recapitulate Moses' prayerful agency by calling upon God to protect his temple-kingdom by driving away enemies with his holy presence.

[222]   Hamilton, "Skull-Crushing Seed," 37; cf. Ojewole, "Seed in Genesis 3:15," 326–28.

that God rebuke, trample, and scatter those who delight in war—turns the psalm's confident proclamations into supplications as David asks that the serpentine enemy be crushed underfoot to endanger God's sanctuary-kingdom no more. As the royal-priestly son of God, then, David in Psalm 68 embraces his calling to guard the temple-kingdom both in his imprecatory prayer on the kingdom's behalf and in his anticipation that he will lead Israel as God's instrumental means of striking the serpent that encroaches upon God's people in the place where God resides and rules. The Davidic king's allusive, narratively informed portrayal through-out the Psalter, and specifically within the imprecatory psalms, suggests that, even where such characterizations are not as prominent, the Davidic imprecations should be heard as arising from the lips of the son of God, the priestly king divinely authorized to protect the temple-kingdom and subdue those who would do it harm.[223]

This characterization of the imprecator applies to communal impreca-tions as well, to those non-Davidic imprecatory psalms that offer prayers in the voice of the Israelite people as a whole, because within the devel-oping scriptural story Israel—no less than the Davidic king—is called as a royal-priestly son of God. In the communal cry of Psalm 74, "the enemy has destroyed everything in the sanctuary" (v. 3), and this defiling of the place of God's presence prompts Israel to recall God's snake-smiting acts in the past (vv. 13–14) as they plead for him to defend his cause on the basis of the covenant once again (vv. 20–23).[224] Playing the part of the son of God, the imprecating community labors through prayer to cleanse the land of violence by seeking God's head-crushing judgment upon the ser-pent that has infested the kingdom.[225]

---

[223] In Psalm 140, the imprecation against the serpentine enemy (vv. 3, 8–11) culminates in the hope of the upright dwelling securely in the land of God's presence (vv. 11, 13), and in Psalm 144, the Davidic imprecation of v. 6 is oriented toward the Edenic renewal of vv. 12–15. These are royal-priestly peti-tions for the judgment of the enemy that seek to effect the restoration of God's temple-kingdom.

[224] The same dynamic is at work in Psalm 80, where the imprecating community—note the first-person plural language—recounts God's driving out of the nations from the land (vv. 8–9) before beseeching him to have regard for "the son whom you made strong for yourself" (v. 15) and bring judgment once again upon the nations (v. 16). As the psalm invokes Israel's identity as the son of God, the imprecator takes action as the son of God, praying for the expulsion of the enemy from the land.

[225] Cf. Psalm 79, where the imprecating community recounts the nations' serpentine infestation of Israel's land and defilement of the temple (vv. 1–4)

Something similar seems to be taking place in Ps 137:7–9. The community reminds God of Edom's part in the destruction of his temple-city before uttering a blessing in anticipation of the one who shall shatter (נפץ) the children—the seed—of Babylon, calling for crushing judgment on those who defiled the place of God's presence. That the anticipated seed-shatterer is in fact the Davidic son of God is suggested by the only other occurrence of נפץ in the Psalter at 2:9, where the Davidic anointed shatters the nations like a potter's vessel.[226] If this interpretation is correct, then Psalm 137 has the Israelite community functioning as the son of God (pleading for shattering judgment upon the serpent seed that has attacked the kingdom) as she prays for an Israelite king who will function as the son of God (actually administering the shattering judgment upon the kingdom's serpentine defilers).[227]

The concentration of serpentine allusions in Psalm 83 likewise casts the community as an implicit foil, the seed-son at enmity with the serpent seed set on claiming "the pastures of God" (v. 12). Guarding the kingdom against the crafty enemy (v. 3), the imprecator begs God to do to the present foe what he did in the past when he delivered his kingdom through the skull-smashing activity of Jael, Gideon, and the Ephraimites (vv. 9–12),

---

before calling for divine vengeance. Verse 10 alludes to Deut 32:43, linking the invading nations with the serpentine invaders of Deuteronomy 32 and the requested judgment with God's cleansing of the land in vengeance. As in Psalm 74, the community in Psalm 79 imprecates against serpentine intruders who have assaulted the temple-kingdom, guarding the kingdom and cleansing the land in prayer as a son of God.

[226] The Davidic identity of the blessed seed-shatterer is also suggested by the canonical placement of Psalm 137 in the Psalter. Psalm 137:9 immediately gives way to the final Davidic collection in the Psalter (Psalms 138–145) such that by its very organization, the Psalter presents the Davidic anointed as the answer to Psalm 137. Cf. the reflections of Zenger, "Composition and Theology of the Fifth Book of Psalms," 96; Wilson, *Editing of the Hebrew Psalter*, 221–22.

[227] It is worth noting that the petitions of Psalm 137 are, like the imprecations of other psalms, rooted in prior promises concerning God's action. Isaiah 13:16 prophesies that Babylon's infants will be dashed in pieces, and Isa 14:20–23 records God's declaration that he will cut off Babylon's name and descendants so that the wicked offspring of the wicked cannot rise, possess, and fill the earth. Elsewhere in the Psalter, Pss 21:10; 37:28 announce the Lord's intention to destroy the seed of the wicked from the earth. Psalm 137's prayer turns these assurances into requests, pleading for the promised elimination of the line of the wicked so that the viciously unholy are no longer a threat to God's temple-kingdom in the world.

members of Israel who drove out the serpent in royal-priestly fashion.[228] In a manner analogous to Solomon's prayer for God to "give the king your justice" (Ps 72:1), Israel ostensibly prays that she would be empowered to fulfill her kingdom-protecting vocation as the son of God,[229] and she begins to step into this vocation by virtue of her prayer for God's expulsive vengeance upon the serpent seed so that God's people might live at peace with their divine and present king.

In the narrative universe of the imprecatory psalms, the imprecator—whether king or community—is presented as the son of God faithfully executing his task to guard (and, at times, extend) the place of God's holy presence by striking the serpent's seed underfoot and driving out the enemy through prayer. The imprecating psalmist is not merely one human praying against another human within a purely immanent frame of reference but is rather an office-bearer possessed of a divine commission, a character in God's story whose divinely authorized task within the narrative is to mediate judgment, protect the place in which, and community with whom, God resides in holiness, and press the bounds of the temple-kingdom to the very ends of the earth. The psalmist knows of Yahweh that "evil may not dwell with you" (Ps 5:4) in the sacred space God has set apart for his dwelling, and he consequently requests of bloodthirsty transgressors that the Lord "cast them out" (Ps 5:10)—expel them from the place of his holy presence. The justice psalms may thus be heard as the battle-prayers of a royal priesthood engaged in the Bible's most basic conflict, an element of the son of God's war against the serpent, his seed, and every corrupting unholiness that vitiates the blessedness, sanctity, and consummation of the temple-kingdom of the Lord.

The redemptive story of which the imprecator is part renders the pleas of the imprecatory psalms not only morally intelligible but ethically justified—a righteous actualization of the imprecator's role within

---

[228] Dempster, *Dominion and Dynasty*, 132, observes that the record of conquest in Judges (including the accounts referred to by Psalm 83) "is not only a realization of the royal-conquest motifs in Gen 1 but also a fulfillment of the promise as the seed of the woman establishes dominion by defeating oppression."

[229] While commentators are generally quite quick to point out that Psalm 83 asks God to do in the present what he did in the past, there is far more hesitation in acknowledging that this makes the petition of v. 9 a request that God would empower Israel for military victory, for that is precisely what he did in the Judges 4–8 narrative to which this psalm makes explicit reference. The psalm holds up as a historical model for God instances when he used Israel as his agent of judgment.

God's unfolding drama. Stated negatively, to fail to seek the expulsion of the venomous wicked from the land would be an abdication of a divinely commissioned duty, a misguided ad-lib departure from the son of God's God-scripted character. A Psalter without imprecation—while perhaps more palatable for many modern readers—would represent a gross dereliction of duty, a sinful rejection of God's call, by the son of God. The canonical narrative of God's purposes for and works in the world thus makes moral sense of the imprecatory psalms and ethically legitimates their cries for divine vengeance. Additionally, this biblical-theological exploration of the imprecator's identity as royal-priestly son of God elucidates why the imprecator regularly expresses the expectation that human beings will participate in God's vengeance as instruments of his judgment.[230] Mediation of God's judgment against God's enemies for the sake of God's temple-kingdom is an essential aspect of the mission of God's son in God's story.

The Imprecator Is Destined for Deliverance and Joy

Within the storied cosmos of the imprecatory psalms, the imprecator whose prayers and identity are rooted in the redemptive-historical past has a covenantally ensured future as well. That is, the narrative of God's action and purposes in the past, which structures and defines the imprecator's requests and vocation in the present, simultaneously stretches out into a future for God's kingdom people, a future whose certainty is grounded in the authority of God's promise and reinforced in the imprecator's prayers. In the midst of vehement cries for justice, for the fulfillment of God's covenant promises and of creation's *telos*, the imprecator thus presses forward in time, pulling the firmness of what shall be into the instability of what is, and expresses the confident expectation that, despite present appearances to the contrary, his destiny—and the destiny of all God's people with him—is secure.[231]

---

[230] In the imprecatory psalms, this expectation is present in 41:10; 58:10; 68:22–23; 72:4; 137:8–9; 144:1–2. Elsewhere in the Psalter, see 18:31–42, 47; 44:5; 60:9–12; 75:10; 101:5, 8; 108:10–13; 110:5–6; 118:10–13; 149:6–9.

[231] On the destiny of the righteous in the psalms more generally, see Jerome F. D. Creach, "The Destiny of the Righteous and the Theology of the Psalms," in *Soundings in the Theology of the Psalms: Perspectives and Methods in Contemporary Scholarship*, ed. Rolf A. Jacobson (Minneapolis: Fortress, 2011), 49–61. Creach notes that the future of the righteous is introduced as a theme in Ps 1:1–3. Creach, "Destiny of the Righteous and the Theology of the Psalms," 51.

The jubilant declaration of Ps 69:35–36 is representative of a chorus of future-oriented assurances that answer the imprecatory psalms' requests with affirmations of God's deliverance:

[35] For God will save Zion
and build up the cities of Judah,
and people shall dwell there and possess it;
[36] the offspring of his servants shall inherit it,
and those who love his name shall dwell in it.

God's people will possess, inherit, and dwell in God's place under his loving rule as Zion—the archetypal temple-city of God[232]—enjoys the divine king's saving intervention (cf. 12:5, 7). The Lord "will not forsake his people" (94:14), those he has made his own possession through covenant, but will hear the cries of his people, do justice for the oppressed, and see to it that "the nations perish from his land" (10:16; cf. vv. 17–18)[233] so that his kingdom might be free from the terror the enemy provokes. This anticipated communal future is particularized and applied to the individual as well. Praying in the first person, the psalmist asserts that God will preserve (40:11),[234] save (55:16), and revive (71:20–21) *me*, meeting the imprecator with steadfast love so that he might look in triumph upon his enemies (59:10). God, called upon to act on the psalmist's behalf, characteristically stands at the right hand of the needy (109:31), poised to save.[235] The psalms that petition for deliverance simultaneously declare that deliverance is on the way.

And this covenantally ensured deliverance from the enemy is a deliverance into the existential joy of life with God. The Lord's vengeance, his liberation of his temple-kingdom from the corruption of oppressive violence, and his vindication of his name and his people will fuel the

---

[232] Within the psalms, Zion is the place of God's temple dwelling (e.g., 68:16) and from which the anointed Davidic king mediates the kingship of God (e.g., 2:6)—the place of God's royal presence among his people. Cf. Grogan, *Psalms*, 268–71.

[233] Cf. Jacobson, "Psalm 9/10," in deClaissé-Walford, Jacobson, and Tanner, *Book of Psalms*, 143; Limburg, *Psalms*, 31; Brueggemann and Bellinger, *Psalms*, 66.

[234] God's certain preservation is turned outward in Ps 55:22 as a word of hopeful instruction: "Cast your burden on the LORD, and he will sustain you; he will never permit the righteous to be moved."

[235] Goldingay, *Psalms: Volume 3*, 288: "The public testimony presupposes that such action on Yhwh's part is the rule rather than the exception."

rejoicing of the righteous (58:10; 68:3).[236] When God executes justice and drives out the unholy from the land, the once-afflicted will offer thanksgiving and dwell in God's presence (140:12–13), untroubled by the wicked who previously threatened the peace of God's kingdom. The upright will behold God's face in covenantal communion (11:7),[237] an assurance that the imprecator in Ps 17:15 claims for himself: "As for me, I shall behold your face in righteousness; when I awake, I shall be satisfied with your likeness."[238] The world of the imprecatory psalms is one in which the innocent imprecator is fated for fellowship before the face of God, bound for a future of fullness and joy in the presence of the king who reigns in love over his people.

The Divine Judge: Cosmic King and Covenant Keeper

The third actor in the relational triad of the imprecatory psalms is God, the divine judge to whom the imprecator's prayers are offered. The Creator is a character, indeed the primary character, in the world of the text—present, active, possessed of a history of action, and committed to particular ends—and, when situated within the narrative universe of the psalms of vengeance, the fittingness of his character and acts comes into focus. How is God's role as judge of the enemy depicted as a function of his royal relationship to his people—his kingship over and with his temple-kingdom? How do the imprecatory psalms characterize this judging God with reference to previous episodes of redemptive history, establishing both continuity with the canonical narrative of God's past action and expectations for his future action? And what is God's self-appointed destiny in the storied cosmos of the imprecations? Consideration of these questions will illuminate the ways the imprecatory psalms present the divine judge of the imprecations, like the enemy and imprecator, as a player within his narrative of his purposes for his temple-kingdom, a character whose judgment is rendered intelligible by the scriptural story to which the psalms appeal.

---

[236] See Peels, *Vengeance of God*, 218.

[237] Mays, *Psalms*, 76.

[238] McCann, *Psalms*, 741, picks up on an allusion to Moses' intimate communion with God, pointing specifically to Num 12:8 where Moses is said to behold the תְּמוּנָה ("form," ESV) of the Lord, the same term that appears in Ps 17:15 ("likeness," ESV). Brueggemann and Bellinger, *Psalms*, 92, suggest that language "connotes divine presence or theophany in the temple." Psalm 17 describes the imprecator's future in terms of fellowship with the tabernacling presence of God among his people.

The Judge Is the Cosmic Warrior-King

The imprecatory psalms, as prayers for divine vengeance, cry out to God as the judge under whose jurisdiction the enemy falls, whose prerogative it is to administer justice. The psalmists address God as the "judge of the earth" (94:2; cf. 58:11) and the "righteous judge" (7:11), characterizing him as the ultimate and trustworthy juridical authority over the cosmos.[239] As judge, God is called upon both to render and to enact his judgments upon the guilty and for the sake of the innocent, to weigh the demands of justice and deliver retribution, and his refusal to acquit the wicked is manifested in his punitive action against them (cf. 69:27).[240] But God's judgeship within the imprecatory psalms is inseparable from his role as sovereign king.[241] Psalm 9 portrays God as seated upon his eternal throne, issuing his just judgments as the universal king who reigns from Zion (vv. 4, 7–8, 11–12), and other imprecatory psalms follow suit, depicting God's judicial activity as a function of his royal sovereignty (e.g., 5:2; 10:16–18; 55:19; 74:12). Within the universe of the imprecations, the holy king who dwells in his temple-sanctuary and sits enthroned in heaven (cf. 11:4; 68:24; 80:1) is the God who renders judgment—hearing the cause of the righteous, deciding in wisdom and equity and steadfast love, exercising vengeance, and upholding justice in his kingdom. God thus rules in a double sense: his judicial ruling in the cases presented to him within the imprecations is one means by which he royally rules over the affairs of creation and his covenant people. The gavel belongs to the divine hand that holds the scepter. God's royal office authorizes his juridical action. The judge of the cosmos is the cosmos' king.

And this divine judge who is the cosmic king is simultaneously depicted as a conquering warrior. As king, God not only sits in judgment as the final arbiter of justice but also rises for battle against the enemies of his kingdom.[242] Peels' observation about the Old Testament's portrait of God generally is true of the imprecatory psalms specifically: "God is

---

[239] Hossfeld and Zenger, *Psalms 2*, 453.

[240] Cf. Peels, *Vengeance of God*, 234.

[241] Cf. Vern S. Poythress, *Theophany: A Biblical Theology of God's Appearing* (Wheaton, Ill.: Crossway, 2018), 39; Peels, *Vengeance of God*, 280. On the kingship of God in the psalms, see Robert D. Rowe, *God's Kingdom and God's Son: The Background to Mark's Christology from Concepts of Kingship in the Psalms*, AGJU 50 (Leiden: Brill, 2002), 14–24; Kraus, *Theology of the Psalms*, 24–27.

[242] As Poythress, *Theophany*, 76, states, "God as the great king over Israel wages war to defend Israel against enemies."

the King who reigns in majesty and deserves all tribute. This King is the Judge who gives laws, speaks justice and pronounces sentence. The King is the Warrior who takes up weapons to free his people. King, Judge, and Warrior are one."[243] The divine sovereign is the "God of hosts" (59:5; 69:6; 80:4, 7, 14, 19) who leads his armies in war,[244] protecting the kingdom against all threats.[245] Dressed for battle, the God to whom the psalmists cry is armed with sword (7:12; 17:13) and bow (7:12–13; 144:6), spear and javelin, shield and buckler (35:2–3)—equipped to attack the enemy and to offer refuge for the faithful. The royal judge is a warrior-king.[246]

The imprecatory psalms reinforce this divine warrior-king motif via intertextual allusion to God's victorious judgments at prior points in redemptive history, allusions that in turn supply a narrative background for the psalmists' portrayal of God. Unlike more overt descriptions of God as king, judge, and warrior, such intracanonical overtures serve as indirect yet highly condensed means of introducing and integrating information about God's identity into the psalms, framing the psalmic portrait of God within a wider scriptural story that reveals the pattern and logic of divine action. As discussed previously, the Song of the Sea in Exodus 15 and the Song of Moses in Deuteronomy 32 are frequently echoed in the imprecatory psalms, and these resonances connect the psalmists' God with the God of Israel's past, drawing upon those texts' characterizations of God as royal warrior.[247] The prayer of Ps 35:3 ("Say to my soul, 'I am

---

[243] Peels, *Vengeance of God*, 277. Cf. Tremper Longman III and Daniel G. Reid, *God Is a Warrior*, Studies in Old Testament Biblical Theology (Grand Rapids: Zondervan, 1995), 44; P. F. Theron, "The 'God of War' and His 'Prince of Peace,'" *NGTT* 45, nos. 1–2 (2004): 120; Patrick D. Miller, "God the Warrior: A Problem in Biblical Interpretation and Apologetics," in *Israelite Religion and Biblical Theology: Collected Essays*, JSOTSup 267 (Sheffield: Sheffield Academic Press, 2000), 362.

[244] Cf. Hossfeld and Zenger, *Psalms 2*, 314–15; Hans-Joachim Kraus, *Psalms 1–59: A Commentary*, trans. Hilton C. Oswald (Minneapolis: Augsburg, 1988), 85–86; Mitchell Dahood, *Psalms II: 51–100*, AB (Garden City, N.Y.: Doubleday and Company, 1968), 68–69.

[245] Patrick D. Miller, Jr., *The Divine Warrior in Early Israel*, Harvard Semitic Monographs 5 (Cambridge, Mass.: Harvard University Press, 1973), 174, observes that God's role as warrior is always in service of his kingship, maintaining that "it is the establishment of Yahweh's eternal rule and sovereignty that is the ultimate goal of Yahweh's wars." Cf. Peels, *Vengeance of God*, 281–82.

[246] Cf. McCann, *Psalms*, 668.

[247] On the presentation of the divine warrior in Exodus 15, see Longman and Reid, *God Is a Warrior*, 32; Miller, *Divine Warrior*, 113–17.

your salvation!'") turns the declaration of Exod 15:2 ("The LORD . . . has become my salvation") into a plea, begging for the God of the Exodus—the "man of war" (Exod 15:3) who "will reign forever and ever" (Exod 15:18) and plant his people in his sanctuary dwelling (Exod 15:17)—to reprise his kingdom-liberating battle against the Egyptians in the psalmist's own experience.[248] When Psalm 83 calls God to terrify and dismay Edom, Moab, and the enemy nations (vv. 15, 17; cf. Exod 15:15) so that they may know that he "whose name is the LORD" (v. 18) is Most High, the psalmist takes up the language of Exod 15:3 ("The LORD is a man of war; the LORD is his name"), invoking the memory of the divine warrior-king in his petition for God to make war against Israel's current foes and demonstrate his sovereignty once again.[249] Similarly, the concentration of allusions to Deuteronomy 32 in Psalm 58 surveyed in detail above establishes continuity between the God who promised to wage bloody war against enemies of the kingdom and the God who hears the psalmist's prayer, implicitly importing God's self-description as a sword-bearing, arrow-firing, head-cracking avenger of his kingdom people (cf. Deut 32:39–43) into the psalm's depiction of the divine judge over unjust judges.

Other imprecations appeal to the language and imagery of Israel's battle march toward Canaan, especially the Mosaic prayer of Num 10:35. As Israel journeyed toward the promised land, the ark of the covenant would go before them, and Moses would pray, "Arise, O LORD (קוּמָה יְהוָה), and let your enemies be scattered, and let those who hate you flee before you." Like a king leading his army to battle, God led Israel against her enemies, preserving the kingdom community with whom he dwelt and driving away the unholy nations with his holy presence.[250] Psalms 3:7; 7:6; 9:19; 10:12; 17:13 replicate the precise introductory phrase from Num 10:35 when they petition, "Arise, O LORD" (קוּמָה יְהוָה), echoing the Mosaic invocation and framing their requested judgments as a continuation of God's campaign to scatter the enemy with his royal presence and preserve the community over and with whom he reigns (cf. Pss 74:22; 82:8, where

---

[248] Cf. Craigie and Tate, *Psalms 1–50*, 286. Note also the allusion to Exod 15:11 in Ps 35:10; cf. Kidner, *Psalms 1–72*, 161.

[249] Brian D. Russell, *The Song of the Sea: The Date of Composition and Influence of Exodus 15:1–21*, Studies in Biblical Literature 101 (New York: Peter Lang, 2007), 120–24, argues that Exodus 15 figures heavily in the Asaphite psalms, concluding, "The Song of Moses and the Israelites functioned as an authoritative traditum of Israel's foundational events from which the Asaphites drew inspiration."

[250] Longman and Reid, *God Is a Warrior*, 39.

the phrase is קוּמָה אֱלֹהִים).[251] The allusion is even more direct in Ps 68:1: "God shall arise, his enemies shall be scattered; and those who hate him shall flee before him!"[252] In each of these psalms, the imprecator calls upon God as the warrior-king who defended his tabernacle-camp with his holy presence on the way to the land, pleading with him to take up the task of defending his temple-kingdom with his holy presence within the land—to expel the enemy and cleanse the land so that he might dwell in purity and blessedness with his people.[253] The theophanic descriptions of God's judgment in the imprecatory psalms—storms howling (68:7–8; 83:13, 15; 144:5–7; cf. 58:9), fire consuming (68:2; 83:14), glory shining forth (80:1; 94:1), and the wicked perishing before the presence of God (9:3; 80:16; cf. Ps 5:4–6)—may be understood as variations on this theme,[254] the royal warrior-judge driving out every threat to his kingdom with his holy appearing in order that his people might flourish in the land where his glory resides.

The imprecatory psalms thus do not present or pray to a God for whom judgment is a foreign activity but a God whose identity as king, judge, and warrior is consistent with the exercise of vengeance and whose narrative history with Israel demonstrates a commitment to judgment for the sake of his temple-kingdom.

The Judge Is the God of the Covenant

Earlier, I demonstrated that the imprecatory psalms petition for the covenantal justice of God, regularly appealing to the promises and structures of God's covenant relationship with Israel in their pleas for vengeance. But while these references to the covenant situate the psalmists' cries within the story of God's purposes for his people, they simultaneously fill out the psalmic portrait of the divine judge. Allusions to God's covenants specify that, within the narrative universe of the imprecatory psalms, "this Judge

---

[251] Cf. Craigie and Tate, *Psalms 1–50*, 74; Kraus, *Psalms 1–59*, 141; Goldingay, *Psalms: Volume 1*, 113.

[252] Miller, *Divine Warrior*, 104–5; Hossfeld and Zenger, *Psalms 2*, 164; Dahood, *Psalms II*, 134; Brueggemann and Bellinger, *Psalms*, 295.

[253] Poythress, *Theophany*, 353, discussing the warrior motif in Psalm 3: "The warrior language in the Psalms should be seen as an expression of the intensive presence of God, coming to judge his enemies and the enemies of his people."

[254] Mays, *Psalms*, 92, observes, "The genre [of theophany] is used in different kinds of psalms to speak of and present the irresistible power and the passionate active zeal of the Lord in defending his people and advancing his rule in the world."

is not neutral. He is the God of the covenant who will not permit his people and inheritance . . . to be trampled with impunity."[255] The recipient of prayer—the highest authority—is not merely *a* deity; he is *this* deity, the covenant-making God of Israel's history who has bound himself by promise to a *telos* and a teleologically informed justice.[256]

Several typical features of the imprecatory psalms reveal and reinforce the covenantal bond between the divine warrior-king and the psalmist. Throughout the imprecations, the psalmist utilizes the covenantal name of God—יְהוָה, the self-appellation God revealed to Moses in Exod 3:15—particularizing the distributor of vengeance as "the LORD (יְהוָה), the God of your fathers, the God of Abraham, the God of Isaac, and the God of Jacob" and establishing a continuity of identity between the God who reigns in the psalmic present and the God who was promised in the patriarchal past.[257] Similarly, the psalmists frequently appeal to God's חֶסֶד,[258] his steadfast love and enduring faithfulness to the people to whom he has committed himself in covenant.[259] With remarkable economy of language, the designation of God as יְהוָה and attribution of חֶסֶד together implicitly recall the whole complex of the Lord's covenantal commitments—pulling them onto the horizon of the psalms—and confirm his character as the cosmic judge who can be depended upon to act in accordance with his

[255] Peels, *Vengeance of God*, 210.

[256] Cf. Rowe, *God's Kingdom and God's Son*, 22.

[257] See Mays, *Psalms*, 30. Of the psalms containing imprecatory petitions, only Psalm 82 lacks a reference to יְהוָה.

[258] See, e.g., 5:7; 17:7; 31:7, 16, 21; 40:10, 11; 59:10, 16, 17; 69:13, 16; 86:5, 13, 15; 94:18; 109:21, 26; 119:41, 64, 76, 88, 124, 149, 159; 143:8, 12; 144:2.

[259] Cf. Grogan, *Psalms*, 279–80. On the relationship between God's חֶסֶד and the concept of covenant, see the technical studies of Nelson Glueck, *Ḥesed in the Bible*, ed. Elias L. Epstein, trans. Alfred Gottschalk (Cincinnati: Hebrew Union College Press, 1967), 70–102; Katharine Doob Sakenfeld, *The Meaning of Hesed in the Hebrew Bible: A New Inquiry* (Eugene, Ore.: Wipf and Stock, 1978), 233–39; *Faithfulness in Action: Loyalty in Biblical Perspective*, Overtures to Biblical Theology (Philadelphia: Fortress, 1985), 39–89; Gordon H. Clark, *The Word "Hesed" in the Hebrew Bible*, Bloomsbury Academic Collections Biblical Studies: Biblical Languages (London: Bloomsbury Academic, 2015), 128–32, 267–68; Robin Routledge, "Ḥesed as Obligation: A Re-Examination," *TynBul* 46, no. 1 (1995): 186–88; Kraus, *Theology of the Psalms*, 43–45. Though the precise translation and definition of the term is a matter of much debate, God's commitment, faithfulness, loyalty, kindness, and steadfast love toward Israel are summarized and structured by his covenant promises to them.

word.[260] Even something as seemingly mundane as the use of possessive language presents the God of the imprecatory psalms as a king in covenant with the psalmist. God is "my God" (e.g., 35:24; 83:13; 109:26) and "our God" (40:3; 68:20; 94:23), and Israel is "your people" (e.g., 28:9; 79:13; 83:3; 94:5), "his people" (28:8; 68:35; 94:14; 125:2). In the world of the imprecations, imprecator and judge belong to one another in indissoluble covenant relation.[261]

The abundant echoes and images in the imprecatory psalms—overt and oblique alike—of specific covenantal promises in God's history with Israel likewise portray the divine judge as one who has unremittingly pledged himself to the preservation of his kingdom people and the exaction of just vengeance upon every enemy that threatens her and, through her, his purposes for all creation.[262] Yahweh is the God of the *protoevangelium*, the smasher of snake heads who vows that the serpent's crown will be crushed beneath the foot of his royal-priestly son (58:3–6, 10; 68:21–23, 30; 72:4, 9; 74:13–14; 83:3; 137:9; 140:3).[263] The Lord is the God of the Abrahamic promise, committed to making Abraham's family a nation from which kings shall arise for the blessing of the world and to cursing those who seek the harm of his treasured people (3:3; 7:10; 35:1–2; 72:17; 74:20; 83:4; 109:17, 28; 119:114). The judge of the imprecations is the God of the Mosaic legislation, the lawgiver who curses and will not acquit the murderous slanderers of the weak, innocent, and righteous and who mandates proportionate retribution for injustice within his kingdom (e.g., 28:4; 35:11; 94:2, 6; 109; 119:21; 137:8–9; 139:19–20). In light of God's covenantally informed identity in the psalms of vengeance, it should come as no surprise that the psalmists' requests are so regularly interspersed with faith-full declarations of God's certain action (e.g., 17:6; 40:11; 58:10; 68:1–2, 21–23; 69:35–36) and doxological affirmations of God's goodness (e.g., 3:3; 9:9–12; 28:8; 31:19; 86:5), which exude confidence that this judge will indeed answer on the imprecator's behalf.

---

[260] Sakenfeld, *Meaning of Hesed*, 238–39. Cf. Anderson and Bishop, *Out of the Depths*, 54.

[261] Cf. Rowe, *God's Kingdom and God's Son*, 16; Goldingay, *Psalms: Volume 1*, 128.

[262] Cf. Peels, *Vengeance of God*, 284–87.

[263] All references to psalmic allusions to God's covenantal promises in this paragraph have been explored in detail above. The covenantal echoes that communicate something about the identities of the enemy and imprecator simultaneously communicate something about the identity of God the judge.

The God of the imprecatory psalms is thus the covenant God of Israel—lovingly oriented toward the protection, preservation, and prosperity of his covenant kingdom, willfully constrained by the power of a promise to a *telos* from which he will not waver. With their allusions to the covenants, the psalmists depict God as the judge who has proleptically ruled against the wicked in his promises to avenge injustice—whose verdict is already in, so to speak—and signal that this divine judge is none other than the God who revealed his character and purposes at Eden, Ur of the Chaldeans, and Sinai. The reverberations of God's covenant commitments in the imprecatory psalms present the Lord of the cosmos as the guarantor of judgment, a God more zealous about the exercise of vengeance than even the psalmists themselves, a king who cannot fail to defend his temple-kingdom from present and future opposition because of his promissory word in the past.

The Judge Is Destined for Glory

In the narrative universe of the imprecatory psalms, the divine judge—like the enemy and imprecator—possesses a certain future. As the psalmists appeal to God's redemptive-historical deeds and promises in their requests for their covenant warrior-king to act in the present, they also extrapolate from God's prior participation in his narrative into the not-yet, envisioning what is to come for the God who is both author and protagonist of the story of his temple-kingdom. The sovereign of history who has destined the enemy for judgment and the imprecator for joyful deliverance has appointed a future for himself as well, a future characterized by recognition of his lordship, gratitude for his works, worship of his name—in a word, glory. The imprecations' storied cosmos is moving irrepressibly toward its culmination, at which point the King of Glory will be seen and celebrated in all his splendor.

Psalm 58:10–11 declares that when God acts in his judicial role as royal warrior, exacting his promised judgment upon the enemy for the liberation of his kingdom, he will be met with the praise of his people and the acknowledgement of all humanity:

> [10] The righteous will rejoice when he sees the vengeance;
>   he will bathe his feet in the blood of the wicked.
> [11] Mankind will say, "Surely there is a reward for the righteous;
>   surely there is a God who judges on earth."

God the avenger of injustice will be the recipient of his kingdom's rejoicing, and whether or not a watching mankind trusts and delights in the God who judges the earth, they will at very least no longer be able to ignore him or suppress the truth of his identity.[264] God's assured hearing and answering of the psalmists' prayers in judgment will result in the glad exultation of the righteous (68:3), thanksgiving to God's name (140:12–13),[265] praise that goes on forever from generation to generation (79:13) as God is the source of his people's satisfaction (17:15).[266] As surely as God will keep his promises, he will be glorified in the Godward joy of his people.

And yet the imprecations testify to a more expansive glory that awaits God, one that shall include the allegiance of the very nations that have in history defied God and assaulted his kingdom.[267] Kings and nobles will come to the temple in Jerusalem bearing gifts for God as the nations stretch out their hands in worship (68:29, 31). Psalm 86:8–10 announces that the Lord's unparalleled majesty among the gods will finally be seen and savored throughout the earth: "All the nations you have made shall come and worship before you, O Lord, and shall glorify your name" (v. 9), engaging in the same God-exalting worship in which the Davidic imprecator anticipates participating forever (v. 12).[268] The scene in Psalm 86 is of a multinational congregation gathered in God's presence, Davidic king and Gentile kingdoms worshiping the God of Israel together. The Lord "shall inherit all the nations" (82:8), and a world that at times within the psalms seems to be on the verge of unraveling will be the blessed realm

---

[264]   See Clifford, *Psalms 1–72*, 276; Kraus, *Psalms 1–59*, 536; Kidner, *Psalms 1–72*, 228.

[265]   Cf. Terrien, *Psalms*, 884. Schaefer, *Psalms*, 330, observes that "the upright will thank God and dwell in a world governed by the divine presence."

[266]   Schaefer, *Psalms*, 40–41: "In contrast to people content with this present life, the psalmist will only be satisfied with God's company in the temple."

[267]   In this regard, the imprecatory psalms exhibit the same eschatological expectation as the rest of the Psalter. Rowe, *God's Kingdom and God's Son*, 24, describes the Psalter's vision of the universal reign of God over the nations, noting, "While this may have been represented as a present reality in the cult, its realisation is in the future." Cf. Grogan, *Psalms*, 290–95; Wilson, *Editing of the Hebrew Psalter*, 207–28; McCann, *Theological Introduction*, 41–50; David C. Mitchell, *The Message of the Psalter: An Eschatological Programme in the Book of Psalms* (Newton Mearns, Scotland: Campbell Publications, 2003).

[268]   Verses 9 and 12 both utilize the Piel of כבד to describe the nations' and the psalmist's activity in relation to God's שֵׁם. They share the same future with God. McCann, *Psalms*, 1021: "The psalmist embodies personally the response of the nations."

of the divine king who need rise no more as a warrior in judgment, for there will be no unholy intruder in the land. The psalms that yearn, "May the whole earth be filled with his glory" (72:19), answer back that this global glory of God is coming indeed.

Eschatology and Imprecation

Making sense of the imprecatory psalms requires making sense of the story of which they are a part. The imprecatory psalms unfold a world in which the three primary actors—enemy, imprecator, and judge—are united by a shared story. Through intertextual reference to the canonical narrative of Israel's history with God, the psalmists connect their world and the figures who inhabit it to the progressing drama of God's kingdom-restoring action in his creation. The enemy is the kingdom-threatening serpent seed, an unholy intruder in the land of God's presence devoted to a violence and injustice that compromises the character and continued existence of the people over and with whom God reigns. The imprecator is the royal-priestly son of God, an innocent victim of the enemy's injustice who embraces the Adamic vocation to guard and expand the temple-kingdom where God royally resides and drive out the seed of the serpent in covenantally inflected prayers of love. The divine judge is the warrior-king and covenant-keeper, a God who goes to battle for his kingdom, scattering the enemy from his dwelling place with his royal presence and preserving the life and integrity of his people in faithfulness to his covenant promises.

Within this storied cosmos, where the psalmic present is depicted as inextricably linked to the redemptive-historical past and covenantally ensured future, the biblical narrative of God's purposes to reestablish his fallen temple-kingdom provides the necessary framework for evaluating the ethics of the psalmists' cries for divine judgment against the enemy. The psalms' petitions for vengeance are not the "devilish"[269] and "diabolical"[270] ravings of "ferocious, self-pitying, barbaric men"[271]; they are not "the cruel vindictiveness of an intolerant religious fanaticism"[272]; neither are they the "justifiable but not justifiable"[273] emblems of the "crudest level

---

[269] C. S. Lewis, *Reflections on the Psalms* (San Diego: Harcourt Brace Jovanovich, 1958), 20.

[270] Lewis, *Reflections on the Psalms*, 21.

[271] Lewis, *Reflections on the Psalms*, 24.

[272] Weiser, *Psalms*, 432.

[273] Patrick D. Miller, "The Hermeneutics of Imprecation," in *Theology in the Service of the Church: Essays in Honor of Thomas W. Gillespie*, ed. Wallace M. Alston Jr. (Grand Rapids: Eerdmans, 2000), 161.

of human nature."[274] They are rather the prayers of the divinely commissioned son of God that the covenant king would exercise justice and expel the serpentine enemy from the place where the Lord resides and reigns for the life and joy of the temple-kingdom of God—prayers that are consistent with the narrative-determined identity of each actor, with the imprecator's calling and God's covenants, with the structures and *telos* of God's story of the world.

But a final observation is in order. The imprecatory psalms are also consistent with their time within God's story—the *when* of their particular location in redemptive history, the act that they inhabit within the developing drama—and the corresponding eschatological character of God's temple-kingdom in Israel. That is, the specific shape and content of these prayers for the kingdom against the enemies of the kingdom to the covenant God of the kingdom by priest-kings tasked with defending and extending the kingdom are connected to the form of God's kingdom in the psalmists' place in the history of redemption. In the psalmic moment of the biblical narrative, the kingdom of God is very much a physical reality: "God's people in God's place under God's rule"[275] is a physical nation in the physical land of promise where God dwells in the physical temple edifice and his anointed reigns from a physical throne.[276] The temple-kingdom is thus eschatologically realized, proleptically actualized in space and time, providing a material template for the reign of God that will arrive in full over the course of the Christocentric narrative of Scripture only with Jesus' first and second advents.[277] In Israel, God is present among his people in a discrete place on earth with discernible borders; the kingdom is organized as a political monarchy in which the maintenance of justice and protection of the covenantal *polis* are mandated by God and necessary to its continued survival and faithful witness; and the inbreaking of divine judgment against covenant breakers within and competing kingdoms without, whether directly from God or mediated through the judicial and military structures of Israel, is a regular feature of the kingdom that reveals and

---

[274] Schaefer, *Psalms*, xxxix.

[275] Goldsworthy, *Gospel and Kingdom*, 54.

[276] Even in those imprecatory psalms lamenting the loss of the kingdom, the destruction of the temple, and the desolation of exile (e.g., Pss 74; 79; 137), the psalmists hope for the reestablishment of a kingdom that is every bit as physical as the one over which David reigned.

[277] See Vos, *Biblical Theology*, 126; Graeme Goldsworthy, *Christ-Centered Biblical Theology: Hermeneutical Foundations and Principles* (Downers Grove, Ill.: InterVarsity Press, 2012), 148; Kline, *Kingdom Prologue*, 340–45.

instantiates God's wrath against sin while simultaneously demonstrating the moral character and upholding the existence of the kingdom of God.[278] The pattern of the temple-kingdom, which will be inaugurated in the life, death, and resurrection of Christ and consummated at his *parousia*, is here tangibly and typologically revealed in history as the children of Abraham dwell in the land of Israel with the temple presence of God under the Davidic monarchy and serve the temple-kingdom through military and juridical means.

Recognition of this eschatologically realized character of God's temple-kingdom in Israel helps bring the imprecatory psalms further into focus, for the royal-priestly son of God fulfills his vocation to defend and extend the kingdom in prayer in a manner that aligns with the nature of the temple-kingdom he is called to serve. That is, the imprecations are consonant with and reflective of the structures and calling of God's kingdom as a physical, political, revelatory entity.[279] The urgent petitions for God to act now to execute covenant justice and eliminate the wicked as

---

[278] *Contra* proponents of covenantal discontinuity readings that appeal to the concept of intrusion, e.g., Kline, *Structure of Biblical Authority*, 154–64; Mennega, "Ethical Problem," 80–84; Harman, "Continuity of the Covenant Curses," 71–72; Beale, *Morality of God*, 17–30. The intrusion thesis argues that God's eschatological judgment periodically intrudes into the era of common grace, temporarily suspending "the ethics of the present age because the ethics of the future age project from that age back into the present." Beale, *Morality of God*, 18. I propose, however, that what these scholars interpret as intrusive interruptions into the normal order of things are in fact the normal order of things in Israel, a typical feature of the temple-kingdom of God as it is manifested at that point within redemptive history. God's purpose to establish a physically structured kingdom that reveals the shape of his coming reign authorizes Israel to administer covenantal justice inside her borders, to drive out the nations from the land, and to utilize military measures to defend herself against outside aggressors.

[279] Several scholars argue that the petitions for divine justice in the midst of history in the imprecatory psalms reflect the more limited eschatological vision of the Old Testament, wherein justice—if it is to happen at all—must happen in the present world, a vision that is expanded in the New Testament. See, e.g., Anderson and Bishop, *Out of the Depths*, 74–75; Shepherd, "Place of the Imprecatory Psalms," 44–45; Kidner, *Psalms 1–72*, 40; Peels, *Vengeance of God*, 214; Mays, *Lord Reigns*, 38–39; Westermann, *Psalms*, 68–69. But this is to frame the issue negatively, in terms of what the psalmists lack in comparison with the authors of the New Testament. To connect the content and emphases of the imprecations to the eschatologically realized character of the kingdom of God in the Old Testament, however, is to frame the issue positively, in terms of God's purposes for and structuring of his kingdom in the psalmists' location within God's redemptive-historical narrative. Cf David G. Firth, "Cries of the Oppressed," in *Wrestling with*

internal and external threats to the kingdom are pleas for the realization in fact of a temple-kingdom that is eschatologically realized in principle, for the establishment and actualization of the kingdom as a faithful, corporeal (and eventually global) manifestation of the reign of God on earth. The requests that human agents be empowered to physically (and perhaps violently) administer and participate in God's judgment, to drive out the wicked from the land of God's presence, and to prepare the world as the temple of Yahweh are prayers that God's kingdom of priests would rightly function in her time and place as an authorized agent of divine justice in history that concretely manifests God's rule. When the imprecator pleads for the preservation, flourishing, and expansion of the temple-kingdom through God's just exaction of vengeance, he prays "thy kingdom come" in Old Testament dialect,[280] and his conceptualization of both the kingdom and the manner of its coming is inflected by the particularities of the architecture of God's temple-kingdom in his redemptive-historical location. Eschatology and imprecation are therefore intimately related: the immediacy and expectations of the psalms' imprecatory prayers on behalf of the kingdom are contingent upon the eschatological character of the kingdom, the degree to which the kingdom physically irrupts into human history at the psalmists' point in the story of God's kingdom-restoring work in the world. Following from this, when the eschatological shape of the temple-kingdom changes, so too must change the shape of imprecatory prayer for the kingdom by the citizenry of the kingdom.

When the imprecatory psalms are morally evaluated through the lens of the kingdom-oriented scriptural narrative to which the psalmists themselves appeal—a narrative that reveals both the imprecator's divinely commissioned vocation to protect the temple-kingdom and the kingdom's character as an eschatologically realized political structure in Israel—the petitions for divine vengeance against those who would destroy the temple-kingdom of God emerge as ethically intelligible, morally faithful prayers that cohere with God's purposes and the imprecator's identity in God's authoritative story of reality.

---

the Violence of God: Soundings in the Old Testament, ed. M. Daniel Carroll R. and J. Blair Wilgus, BBRSup 10 (Winona Lake, Ind.: Eisenbrauns, 2015), 81.

[280] Cf. McCann, Theological Introduction, 124; Broadhurst, "Should Cursing Continue?" 84–85; Vos, "Ethical Problem," 138; Adams, War Psalms, 52; Mennega, "Ethical Problem," 93; Murray, "Christian Cursing?" 117–18.

3

Cursing and Christ

The Imprecatory Psalms and The New Testament

"Give me justice against my adversary."

If one were to attempt to capture the essence of the imprecations in a single, simple plea, it would likely sound something like this. The psalms are full of petitions that give voice to permutations of this basic longing. But can Christians pray this kind of prayer? For many, the reflexive impulse to answer in the negative is grounded in a Christological conviction: *that prayer—so reminiscent of the imprecatory psalms—doesn't sound like the Jesus I see in the New Testament.* Jesus, so we tend to reason, is concerned with forgiveness and mercy and enemy love, not with justice or judgment or desires for the divine redress of harmful wrongs. To turn the page to the second testament means ostensibly to turn from the piety of the Psalter.

In reality, the above prayer sounds exactly like the Jesus of the New Testament because it *is* the Jesus of the New Testament. In Luke 18:3, amid a parable intended to encourage perseverance in prayer (v. 1), Jesus' model petitioner cries out for justice against her adversary, and the Lord concludes his teaching with a promise and a call for his disciples to do the same: "And will not God give justice to his elect, who cry to him day and night? Will he delay long over them? I tell you, he will give justice to them speedily. Nevertheless, when the Son of Man comes, will he find faith on earth?" (vv. 7–8). Perhaps the relationship between the New Testament's Jesus and the imprecatory psalms is not as apparent or adversarial as is typically conceived. Perhaps the New Testament's vision of God's world and faithful human action within it is not as divergent from the imprecatory psalms' as we might initially suspect.

Like the imprecatory psalms, the New Testament unfolds a theologically charged world through intertextual reference to Israel's Scriptures.[1] By allusively drawing upon the Old Testament, the New Testament authors establish continuity between the work of God in Christ and the story of Israel while simultaneously developing that story toward an unanticipated culmination in Jesus of Nazareth and the community that bears his name.[2] Intriguingly, the imprecatory psalms themselves serve

[1]   C. H. Dodd, *According to the Scriptures: The Sub-Structure of New Testament Theology* (New York: Charles Scribner's Sons, 1953), is frequently credited with sparking renewed interest in the New Testament use of the Old Testament, on which cf. Barnabas Lindars, *New Testament Apologetic: The Doctrinal Significance of the Old Testament Quotations* (Philadelphia: Westminster, 1961); D. A. Carson and H. G. M. Williamson, eds., *It Is Written: Scripture Citing Scripture, Essays in Honour of Barnabas Lindars* (Cambridge: Cambridge University Press, 1988); *CNTOT*; Steve Moyise, "Intertextuality and the Study of the Old Testament in the New Testament," in *The Old Testament in the New Testament: Essays in Honor of J. L. North*, ed. Steve Moyise, JSNTSup 189 (Sheffield: Sheffield Academic Press, 2000), 14–41; Richard B. Hays, *Echoes of Scripture in the Gospels* (Waco, Tex.: Baylor University Press, 2016). On the New Testament's use of the Psalter, see, e.g., Steve Moyise and Maarten J. J. Menken, eds., *The Psalms in the New Testament*, The New Testament and the Scriptures of Israel (London: T&T Clark International, 2004); Margaret Daly-Denton, *David in the Fourth Gospel: The Johannine Reception of the Psalms*, AGJU 47 (Leiden: Brill, 2000); Stephen P. Ahearne-Kroll, *The Psalms of Lament in Mark's Passion: Jesus' Davidic Suffering* (Cambridge: Cambridge University Press, 2007).
In this expanding field, studies have focused attention on a variety of stimulating issues. On the hermeneutical strategies employed by the New Testament authors in their appropriation of the Old Testament, cf. G. K. Beale, ed., *The Right Doctrine from the Wrong Text? Essays on the Use of the Old Testament in the New* (Grand Rapids: Baker Academic, 1994); Donald Juel, *Messianic Exegesis: Christological Interpretation of the Old Testament in Early Christianity* (Philadelphia: Fortress, 1988); Matthew Scott, *The Hermeneutics of Christological Psalmody in Paul: An Intertextual Enquiry*, SNTSMS 158 (New York: Cambridge University Press, 2014). On the rhetorical function of intertextual reference, see Christopher D. Stanley, *Arguing with Scripture: The Rhetoric of Quotations in the Letters of Paul* (New York: T&T Clark International, 2004); Lindars, *New Testament Apologetic*. On the possibility of an earlier tradition of Christological interpretation of the Old Testament, see Dodd, *According to the Scriptures*; Richard B. Hays, "Christ Prays the Psalms: Paul's Use of an Early Christian Exegetical Convention," in *The Future of Christology: Essays in Honor of Leander E. Keck*, ed. Abraham J. Mahlerbe and Wayne A. Meeks (Minneapolis: Fortress, 1993), 122–36.
[2]   See esp. Richard B. Hays, *Reading Backwards: Figural Christology and the Fourfold Gospel Witness* (Waco, Tex.: Baylor University Press, 2014), 5. What Hays claims of the evangelists can be extended to the other writers of the New

as a frequent source of the New Testament's Old Testament appeals—a referential reservoir of categories, images, structures, roles, and themes to which the New Testament returns time and again in its recounting of and reflection upon God's climactic action for the world in Jesus Christ. As a result, the New Testament story evocatively depicts various actors in the Christian-era scene of redemptive history with reference to the inhabitants of the imprecatory psalms' narrative world—including Christ's human enemies, Satan, the Christian church, God the Father, and Jesus himself—investing agents and their actions with theological and narrative significance. A reasonable first step toward discerning how the imprecatory psalms bear witness to Jesus and relate to his followers, then, is to attend closely to the ways that the New Testament Scriptures apply the imprecatory psalms as a lens for understanding both. Indeed, the New Testament authors intertextually resource the psalms of vengeance in a manner that, among other things, clarifies the church's identity and calling and presents Jesus' person and work as the polyvalent (and perhaps surprising) fulfillment of the imprecatory psalms. Of course, the New Testament's dependence upon, adaptation of, and contribution to the redemptive-historical structures and story, which figure prominently in the imprecatory psalms, are not limited to discernible references to discrete imprecatory texts. They may also take the form of broader interaction with the imprecations' constitutive themes, whether through the deployment of standard biblical language and concepts or intertextual connection with texts outside the imprecatory psalms.[3] Accordingly, where intertextual resonances suggest important correspondences between an aspect of the imprecations and God's action in Jesus—where they "tip off" the interpreter to pay

---

Testament as well. Cf. Steve Moyise and Maarten J. J. Menken, "Introduction," in Moyise and Menken, *Psalms in the New Testament*, 1. The Old Testament supplies the encyclopedia of the New Testament, "the cultural framework in which the text is situated and from which the gaps of the text are filled." Stefan Alkier, "Intertextuality and the Semiotics of Biblical Texts," in *Reading the Bible Intertextually*, ed. Richard B. Hays, Stefan Alkier, and Leroy A. Huizenga (Waco, Tex.: Baylor University Press, 2009), 9.

[3] Roy E. Ciampa, "Scriptural Language and Ideas," in *As It Is Written: Studying Paul's Use of Scripture*, SBLSymS 50, ed. Stanley E. Porter and Christopher D. Stanley (Atlanta: SBL Press, 2008), 41–57, discusses Paul's "general use of biblical language and ideas, when he is not citing, alluding to, or echoing specific Old Testament text(s)." Quote, 41. Ciampa recognizes that the New Testament may interact with the Old Testament without interacting with a single, discrete, easily identifiable Old Testament text.

attention to the New Testament's development of a particular theme—I pull on those thematic threads and explore how the New Testament integrates and expands upon those motifs. When the New Testament's connections with and developments of the imprecatory psalms' storied cosmos are interrogated and synthesized, a biblical-theological narrative framework emerges—a way of telling the story of Jesus according to the grammar and logic of the Psalter's justice psalms.

What is more, the New Testament engages in its own imprecatory speech acts—petitions for divine vengeance against enemies—in texts like Luke 18:1–8; Gal 1:8–9; 5:12; 1 Cor 16:22; Rev 6:9–10. Exegeted in isolation, these may seem like uncharacteristic, morally inexplicable interruptions of petitionary pettiness. When the New Testament's own intertextually resonant story, however, is permitted to supply the narrative framework for ethically evaluating the New Testament's imprecatory speech acts, the moral intelligibility of the New Testament's pleas for judgment may come more clearly into focus. As in the imprecatory psalms, the New Testament's imprecators act as characters within the unfolding story of God's temple-kingdom, characters whose actions are rendered ethically comprehensible and shown to be ethically faithful given their identity and calling inside the narrative that the New Testament itself both invokes from the imprecatory psalms and articulates afresh.

I have repeatedly suggested that the ethical status of Scripture's imprecatory speech acts is most fruitfully investigated within the constraints of Scripture's unfolding story. Like the imprecatory psalms, the New Testament supplies the narrative framework within which its imprecatory pleas are most properly assessed. This chapter explores the ways the New Testament weaves the storied world of the imprecatory psalms—its characters, expectations, themes, and narrative background—into its own Christocentric story of the world and in so doing situates the imprecatory petitions that arise within its pages as ethically intelligible acts in the narrative of God's purposes to bring his temple-kingdom in Christ.

Echoes of the Imprecator: Innocent, Suffering Son(s and Daughters) of God

The New Testament tells the story of Jesus and his church in the register of the imprecatory psalms, echoing their text and expanding upon their themes in its theologically resonant narrative of God's action in Christ. In particular, the New Testament writers allusively appeal to and develop the figure of the psalmic petitioner, and they depict the identity, calling, and future of Jesus and his community through these echoes of the imprecator. How does Jesus embody and fulfill the character, vocation, experience, and destiny of the imprecator in the psalms? And how does the New Testament in turn present the church in these terms, as inhabiting the place of the psalmic supplicant?

Thick within the evangelists' portraits of Jesus is the motif of the innocent Davidic sufferer, drawn to a considerable extent from the contours of the Davidic petitioner in the imprecatory psalms. Especially in his passion account, Mark allusively pulls from the imprecatory psalms in his descriptions of Jesus' suffering.[4] Jesus is betrayed by a close friend and confidante who eats bread at his table (14:18; cf. Ps 41:9) and is delivered into the hands of sinners (14:41; cf. Pss 71:4; 140:4).[5] His opponents, who by stealth (14:1; cf. Ps 10:7–8)[6] seek after his life (14:55; cf. Ps 54:3), unjustly target him with false speech (14:57; cf. Ps 35:11),[7] and Jesus becomes the object of head-wagging derision (15:29; cf. Ps 109:25) and mockery (15:29–30; cf. Pss 35:21; 40:15; 70:3) in his humiliating execution. Mark's inclusion of the seemingly innocuous detail that Jesus

---

[4]   On Mark's use of the psalms of lament more generally in his passion narrative, see esp. Ahearne-Kroll, *Psalms of Lament in Mark's Passion*, though I am not persuaded by his argument that David in the psalms of lament "challenges God's role in his suffering . . . [and] finally attempts to shame God to act on his behalf only because he is suffering" and that Mark's appeals to the psalms of lament in his narration of Jesus' passion "includes a challenge to God's role in his suffering and death." Ahearne-Kroll, *Psalms of Lament in Mark's Passion*, 38.

[5]   Cf. Joel Marcus, *The Way of the Lord: Christological Exegesis of the Old Testament in the Gospel of Mark* (Louisville: Westminster John Knox, 1992), 173. Rikk E. Watts, "Mark," in *CNTOT*, 235, observes that "Mark's passion narrative is replete with echoes of the 'righteous sufferer' psalms," and his list of references includes several imprecatory psalms, which I discuss here. Cf. the list of citations and echoes of the individual lament psalms in Mark by Adela Yarbro Collins, "The Appropriation of the Psalms of Individual Lament by Mark," in *The Scriptures in the Gospels*, ed. C. M. Tuckett, BETL 131 (Leuven: Leuven University Press, 1997), 227n21.

[6]   Cf. Rikk Watts, "The Psalms in Mark's Gospel," in Moyise and Menken, *Psalms in the New Testament*, 42. Marcus, *Way of the Lord*, 172, observes suggestive lexical similarities between LXX Ps 9:28–29 and Mark 14:1, namely the terms δόλος and ἀποκτείνω.

[7]   *Contra* R. T. France, *The Gospel of Mark*, NIGTC (Grand Rapids: Eerdmans, 2002), 604n13. I find the use of ἀναστάντες in both LXX Ps 34:11 and Mark 14:57 a likely indicator of allusion here. Cf. Marcus, *Way of the Lord*, 173; Watts, "Psalms in Mark's Gospel," 42.

was offered sour wine (15:36; cf. Ps 69:21), a detail repeated in each Gospel's report of the crucifixion,[8] becomes within this intertextual milieu a confirmation of Jesus' identity as the innocent accused, all the more referentially powerful for its apparently tangential quality in Mark's account. The interpretive ear that is attuned to the melody of the Psalter cannot help but detect in the Markan minor key of Christ's crucifixion the recapitulation and intensification of the pattern of the righteous Davidide, the Davidic anointed whose righteousness and undeserved sorrows both exceed that of his psalmic forebear.[9] Intriguingly, Mark may also allude to Ps 74:19 ("Do not deliver the soul of your dove to the wild beasts") in his narration of Jesus' baptism and wilderness temptation (1:9–13), where the Spirit-dove descends upon Jesus before driving him out among the wild animals,[10] evocatively associating Jesus with Israel as a whole and his sufferings with her exile among the nations.[11] If this is in fact what Mark is doing, then his Gospel links the righteous Christ's agonies to the violence lamented in both the individual and communal imprecations, presenting Jesus' sufferings as the extension and culmination of David's and all Israel's:[12]

Where Mark leans on allusion, John and Luke utilize quotations of the imprecatory psalms in addition to subtler echoes to solidify the identification between the crucified Christ and the innocent Davidic sufferer of the psalms of vengeance. In John's Gospel, Jesus quotes Ps

---

[8]   Matt 27:34, 48; Luke 23:36; John 19:28–29. Hays, *Echoes of Scripture in the Gospels*, 140–41, argues that Matthew amplifies the citation from Mark by including key terms from LXX Ps 68:22.

[9]   Mark's theme may in fact begin far earlier in his narrative. Collins, "Psalms of Individual Lament," 235–36, notes that the motif of alienation from family found in Ps 69:8 is applied to Jesus in Mark 3:21.

[10]   The juxtaposition of dove and wild beast imagery in both texts is suggestive, and Mark 1:13 uses the same Greek term (θηρίον) as LXX Ps 73:19.

[11]   David B. Capes, "Intertextual Echoes in the Matthean Baptismal Narrative," *BBR* 9 (1999): 47–49, proposes that Ps 74:19 may be in the background of the dove imagery in Matthew's baptismal account, identifying Jesus with suffering Israel as the one who brings Israel's story to fulfillment. Capes is quite right about the intertextual significance in Matt 3:16, but Mark's reference to both key images in Ps 74:19—the dove and the wild animals—makes his intertextual connection even more resonant than Matthew's.

[12]   On the wider motif of Jesus as Israel, see esp. N. T. Wright, *The New Testament and the People of God*, vol. 1 of *Christian Origins and the Question of God* (Minneapolis: Fortress, 1992), 406.

41:9 (13:18) and Ps 69:4 (15:25)[13] when reflecting on the necessity of his ignominious fate, explicitly stating that in his experience the Scriptures' witness to David's betrayal by a bread-sharing friend and reception of causeless hatred will be fulfilled. The allusive characterization of Jesus as "troubled [ἐταράχθη] in his spirit" in John 13:21, pregnant with the memory of David's cries in Pss 31:9; 55:4,[14] only reinforces the connection established in the quotations, that in Jesus' suffering unto death, David's unmerited sufferings are somehow being brought to their climactic completion.[15] Luke's passion account has Jesus quoting Ps 31:5 from the cross just before breathing his last—"Father, into your hands I commit my spirit" (23:46)—taking David's words on his lips, confidently entrusting himself to God in the midst of great distress in the hope that vindication awaits on the other side of shame.[16] This quotation does more than align Jesus with David's righteous suffering;[17] it simultaneously aligns Jesus with David's expectation of divine deliverance. Jesus' David-esque faithfulness is in view in Rom 15:3 as well, where Paul quotes Ps 69:9 with Christ as the implied speaker: David's claim to suffer for his godliness finds fullest expression in the sinless one upon whom fell the deadly reproaches of those who

---

[13]   The same phrase occurs in Ps 35:19 as well, but the quotation of Ps 69:9 earlier in John 2:17 suggests that Ps 69:4 is more likely the alluded text here. Cf. Hays, *Echoes of Scripture in the Gospels*, 338; Köstenberger, "John," in *CNTOT*, 493–95; Daly-Denton, *David in the Fourth Gospel*, 201–8.

[14]   Where ἐταράχθη is used in LXX Pss 30:10; 54:5, creating a discernible lexical link between the texts. There may be another allusion to Ps 31:9 in John 12:27. Cf. Köstenberger, "John," in *CNTOT*, 488. Daly-Denton, *David in the Fourth Gospel*, 255–57, argues that the psalmic text in view is Psalms 42–43, but I find it more likely in context that, following the Davidic quotation in John 13:18, the psalmic David continues to be the echoed referent in John 13:21.

[15]   Like Mark, John 7:5 may allude to the Davidic imprecator's experience of familial alienation in, e.g., Ps 69:8. Cf. Daly-Denton, *David in the Fourth Gospel*, 129–30.

[16]   Cf. Peter Doble, "The Psalms in Luke-Acts," in Moyise and Menken, *Psalms in the New Testament*, 113. Recall that in Luke's Gospel, Jesus has by this point explicitly predicted that resurrection will follow his death. Cf. Luke 9:22; 18:33.

[17]   Luke also quotes Pss 69:25; 109:8 in Acts 1:20. I consider that passage below, but here it is worth pointing out that the attribution of enemy language to Judas places Jesus in the conceptual space of the imprecator, the innocent sufferer who receives the enemy's treachery.

reproached God.[18] This intertextual presentation of Jesus by multiple New Testament authors portrays him as the righteous sufferer of the imprecatory psalms, the innocent *par excellence* who receives unjust violence to the highest degree, the long-awaited king whose Davidic royalty is ironically yet fittingly revealed in his participation in the pattern of David's blameless sorrows.

Other New Testament references to the imprecations emphasize not Jesus' Davidic suffering but his Davidic role as the royal-priestly son of God, the anticipated king who guards and extends God's temple-kingdom and mediates God's judgment against God's enemies. This begins to emerge in Matthew's infancy narrative—in terms echoing Solomon's prayer from Ps 72:10–11, 15, for the kings of the nations to bring gifts and fall down before the royal son—as the Evangelist recounts the μάγοι from the east falling down before, offering gifts to, and worshiping the Christ child (2:11).[19] Matthew's intertextual narration invests this act of homage with an added layer of theological meaning, as the revelation of God's answer to the pleas of Psalm 72. The adoration of the magi is the unveiling of the son of God who will judge with righteousness (Ps 72:2), crush the oppressor (Ps 72:4, 9),[20] and exercise dominion from sea to sea (Ps 72:8) as the whole earth is filled up as a temple with the כְּבוֹד of God (Ps 72:19).[21]

---

[18]   In context, the quotation of Ps 69:9 in Rom 15:3 functions as an illustration of Jesus' sacrificial refusal to please himself, but the coherence of Paul's pedagogic example depends upon identification of Jesus with the righteous sufferer of Psalm 69. Cf. Hays, "Christ Prays the Psalms," 122–36; Sylvia C. Keesmaat, "The Psalms in Romans and Galatians," in Moyise and Menken, *Psalms in the New Testament*, 156. Jesus' devotion to God in his self-sacrifice is highlighted in the allusion to Ps 40:6 in Eph 5:2 and the quotation of Ps 40:6–8 in Heb 10:5–7, though the element of innocent suffering at the hands of enemies is not present in these texts.

[19]   Craig L. Blomberg, "Matthew," in *CNTOT*, 5. Blomberg observes that there may also be an allusion to Isa 60:6. Cf. Hays, *Echoes of Scripture in the Gospels*, 176. R. T. France, *The Gospel of Matthew*, NICNT (Grand Rapids: Eerdmans, 2007), 76, detects allusions to both texts. These potential allusions are thematically complementary, not mutually exclusive.

[20]   Stephen G. Dempster, *Dominion and Dynasty: A Theology of the Hebrew Bible*, NSBT 15 (Downers Grove, Ill.: InterVarsity Press, 2003), 232, connects the star rising in the east (Matt 2:2) with the star of Num 24:17 that crushes the enemy's head. Matthew's birth narrative brings together allusions to serpent-crushing themes from multiple Old Testament texts.

[21]   There is a possible allusion to Ps 72:17 ("May his name endure forever, his fame continue as long as the sun! May people be blessed in him, all nations call

When John describes Jesus' expulsion of corrupt sellers and moneychangers from the temple, he observes that the disciples remembered the words of Ps 69:9: "Zeal for your house will consume me" (John 2:17). In Psalm 69, the enemies act in opposition to the temple, opposing David because of David's loving concern for God's house (v. 9), and in so doing fill the land of God's holy presence with unholy, predatory injustice.[22] David responds by "cleansing God's dwelling place" in prayer, driving out by imprecation (vv. 22–28) those aligned against God's temple, king, and people (cf. v. 6) in the confidence that God will save Zion (vv. 34–36), the temple-city in which he resides. Sharing King David's priestly passion for God's house, Jesus not only commits himself to suffer like David for the sake of righteousness,[23] but also takes upon himself the Davidic mantle of the son of God. In the temple, Jesus does in action what the Davidic psalmist does in (imprecatory) prayer: he guards the place of God's holy presence by driving out the wicked,[24] enacting his vocation as the Adamic son of God in the mold of David,[25] symbolically announcing his purpose to renew

---

him blessed!") in Luke 1:48, where Mary declares that all generations will call her blessed. Mary will be blessed by all generations as the vessel through which God delivers the king—the son of God—who will be blessed by all nations.

[22]   Note that the enemies in Psalm 69 endanger the temple-kingdom in multiple, interrelated ways. They not only act against the temple, but in their opposition to David's temple zeal they also unjustly threaten the Davidic king who is the heir of God's temple-kingdom promises and who represents the Israelite community with whom God intends to dwell.

[23]   As John Goldingay, *Psalms: Volume 2, Psalms 42–89*, BCOTWP (Grand Rapids: Baker Academic, 2007) 343–44, explains, the psalmist's zeal for the temple in Ps 69:9 is likely presented as a reason for his opponents' attacks. The faithful psalmist suffers because of his love for God's house, a love that may have included critiques of the temple worship of his contemporaries. The quotation of Ps 69:9 in John 2:17 transfers this characterization to Jesus, depicting him as the righteous temple-lover who receives opposition for his faithfulness. This point is emphasized by Köstenberger, "John," in *CNTOT* 433–34; cf. Daly-Denton, *David in the Fourth Gospel*, 128.

[24]   Note that the imprecatory pleas of Ps 69:22–28 are followed by the affirmations of vv. 35–36: "For God will save Zion and build up the cities of Judah, and people shall dwell there and possess it; the offspring of his servants shall inherit it, and those who love his name shall dwell in it." The *telos* of the psalmist's prayer is the blessedness of Zion, the temple-kingdom of God, the people of God in the land of God's presence.

[25]   Note that the temple's structure and ornamentation deliberately recall Eden. See esp. G. K. Beale, *The Temple and the Church's Mission: A Biblical Theology of the Dwelling Place of God*, NSBT 17 (Downers Grove, Ill.: InterVarsity

sacred space and to ensure that God's people may dwell in God's presence free of the disruptive hostility of the ungodly.[26] The citation of Ps 69:9 illuminates Christ's cleansing of the temple as the zealous act of the royal-priestly son of God, come to restore God's temple-kingdom.[27]

The conceptualization of Jesus as the mediator of God's victorious judgment arises emphatically in Col 2:15. Though this verse contains no discernible allusion to a single psalmic text,[28] it is noteworthy that Paul's description of God's accomplishments in Christ reads like a response to the petitions of the imprecatory psalms: God "disarmed the rulers and authorities (cf. Pss 7:9; 10:15; 55:9; 58:6–7) and put them to open shame (cf. Pss 31:17; 35:4, 26; 40:14; 70:2; 71:13; 83:16–17; 86:17; 109:29; 119:78; 129:5), by triumphing over them in him (cf. Pss 58:10; 59:10; 68:22–23;

Press, 2004), 66–75. Eden is the first temple, and the temple is a renewed Eden. When the symbolic significance of the space in which this event transpires is kept in view, Christ's driving out of the corrupt from the temple becomes a symbolic enactment of Adam's calling to guard the place of God's presence from the serpent by expelling the intruder from the garden-temple.

[26] Daly-Denton, *David in the Fourth Gospel*, 123, suggests that Zech 14:21, with its expectation of comprehensive holiness among God's people accompanied by a trader-less temple, may provide relevant background to Jesus' clearing of the temple as well.

[27] In Psalms of Solomon 17, petition is made for a son of David who will reign over Israel, purge Jerusalem of the nations, and drive out sinners so that unrighteousness may no longer dwell in Israel's midst, expelling and subduing the enemy in royal-priestly fashion. Cf. Daly-Denton, *David in the Fourth Gospel*, 97–98; Nicholas Perrin, *Jesus the Temple* (Grand Rapids: Baker Academic, 2010), 21–29. This is of interest for two reasons. First, it demonstrates that within the intertestamental period, messianic expectation continued to develop along the trajectory I proposed in the previous chapter, with a royal-priestly son of God driving out the unclean from the place of God's presence and thus defending the temple-kingdom of God. Second, as background to John's account, it provides one more layer of resonance through which Jesus' action in the temple may be interpreted as carrying symbolic messianic significance, acting out in the temple theater the role of the anticipated unrighteousness-expelling son of God. On the royal overtones of Jesus' actions in the temple more generally, see N. T. Wright, *Jesus and the Victory of God*, vol. 2 of *Christian Origins and the Question of God* (Minneapolis: Fortress, 1996), 427–28, 490–93. Of course, the twist of John's narrative is that the priest-king who cleanses the place of God's presence so that God may dwell with his people is himself the temple incarnate, the true temple of God on earth. Cf. John 2:18–22.

[28] Though I wonder if Ps 68:18 might provide background for Paul's description in Col 2:15. This seems reasonable, especially given the likely allusion to Ps 68:16 in Col 1:19 and Paul's quotation of Ps 68:18 in Eph 4:8.

72:4, 9; 137:8–9; 144:1–2)." In the events of Good Friday and Easter Sunday, when God canceled the church's record of debt by nailing it to the cross and raising Jesus from the dead (Col 2:12–14), Christ defended God's kingdom from the enemy rulers and authorities—disempowering them, exposing them, conquering them in his death and resurrection—so that God's people might be free from their terror and threats.[29] Preaching in the Areopagus, Paul argues that in Jesus, one might say, God will one day finish what he started. Paul borrows the language of divine judgment from Ps 9:8, declaring that God "has fixed a day on which he will judge the world in righteousness by a man whom he has appointed" (Acts 17:31).[30] God, who "judges the world with righteousness" (Ps 9:8), will definitively exercise his eschatological judgment through the man Jesus, who, as God's son, is the appointed human mediator of God's just vengeance upon the wicked (cf. Ps 72:2).[31] In the imprecatory psalms, the son of God defends and extends the temple-kingdom in prayer, at times explicitly petitioning for God's aid in driving the violent enemy from the land of God's presence. In the New Testament, Jesus fulfills this role as the true and faithful son of God, protecting the temple-kingdom and defeating her enemies through his death, resurrection, and imminent *parousia*, which will consummate the cosmic temple of Yahweh.

When Jesus' identity, experience, and action as the innocent, suffering son of God are understood through the lens of the imprecatory psalms—a lens that the New Testament itself supplies—Jesus' resurrection comes into focus as the eminently comprehensible next step in the story of the Davidic Messiah. The imprecating son of God in the psalms begs for

[29]   On the logical progression of Col 2:14–15, see esp. Peter T. O'Brien, *Colossians, Philemon*, WBC 44 (Waco, Tex.: Word Books, 1982), 124–29.

[30]   Similar language occurs in Pss 67:4; 96:13; 98:9.

[31]   It is possible that the description of Jesus in Rev 19:11 ("in righteousness he judges") includes an allusion to Ps 72:2 ("May he judge your people with righteousness"), drawing upon the psalm's plea for a royal son who rightly mediates divine judgment, though I argue below that the primary allusion is to the divine role of righteous judgment in, e.g., Ps 9:8. The likelihood that a Davidic son of God motif supplies part of the background of this verse is bolstered by an allusion to Ps 2:9 in Rev 19:15. Cf. G. K. Beale, *The Book of Revelation: A Commentary on the Greek Text*, NIGTC (Grand Rapids: Eerdmans, 1999), 949–51, 961–63. If, as seems plausible, Rev 19:11 conjures both the son of God and the divine judge from the psalms, then the verse functions something like an intertextual affirmation of Christ's humanity and divinity, an intertextual hypostatic union.

public vindication from the enemy's violent accusations and attacks,[32] a divinely authored demonstration of the psalmist's righteousness, and confidently declares that God in his steadfast love and faithfulness will indeed deliver him,[33] rescuing him from the threat of death and exalting him over his foes. In his resurrection, the Christ who suffered as the blameless son of God after the pattern of the imprecatory psalms receives the vindication and exaltation for which the psalmist hoped in faith (cf. Col 2:15; Heb 5:7). This point is made in the second clause of the very sentence of Paul's Areopagus sermon referenced above: God "has fixed a day on which he will judge the world in righteousness by a man whom he has appointed; and of this he has given assurance to all by raising him from the dead" (Acts 17:31). The resurrection is the Father's public assurance that Jesus is the royal-priestly son of God through whom his judgment will be mediated to the world, the divine answer to and reversal of the slander and injustice of a world that put to death its true king.[34] Indeed, it is highly likely that the repeated echoes of the imprecatory psalms (and other psalmic laments) in the Gospels' accounts of Jesus' innocent suffering are intended to generate a narrative expectation of vindication, to point with intertextual subtlety to the future beyond the crucifixion, hinting that the Christ who embodies the depths of psalmic suffering will be delivered to the heights of psalmic joy.[35] The Christ who experiences the treachery of Ps 41:9 (John 13:18; cf. Mark 14:18) also receives the exaltation and juridical prerogative of Ps 41:10: "Raise me up, that I may repay them!"[36] Jesus, then, brings to completion the whole portrait of the imprecator in the

---

[32]   E.g., Pss 17:2; 31:1, 17; 35:23–26; 54:1; 69:6; 71:1; 74:21.

[33]   E.g., Pss 12:5, 7; 40:11; 55:16; 59:10; 71:20–21.

[34]   Commenting on Paul's assertion in Rom 1:3–4 that Jesus "was descended from David according to the flesh and was declared to be the Son of God in power according to the Spirit of holiness by his resurrection from the dead," N. T. Wright, *The Resurrection of the Son of God*, vol. 3 of *Christian Origins and the Question of God* (Minneapolis: Fortress, 2003), 244, argues, "Israel's God, the creator, had reversed the verdict of the court, in reversing the death sentence it carried out. Jesus really was the king of the Jews; and, if he was the Messiah, he really was the lord of the world." Cf. Wright, *Resurrection of the Son of God*, 451, where Wright connects Acts 17:31 with Rom 1:4.

[35]   Cf. David W. Pao and Eckhard J. Schnabel, "Luke," in *CNTOT*, 399; Watts, "Psalms in Mark's Gospel," 43–44; Kelli S. O'Brien, *The Use of Scripture in the Markan Passion Narrative*, LNTS 384 (New York: T&T Clark, 2010), 193–94.

[36]   Marcus, *Way of the Lord*, 183.

psalms—the righteous, suffering son of God who is rescued from violence and vindicated before the world.

And yet the New Testament, especially the intensely allusive book of Revelation, also depicts the church—those who are in Christ by faith, the citizens of God's new covenant kingdom—with reference to the psalmic imprecator, as inhabiting the conceptual space of the petitioner in the psalms of vengeance. Luke casts Stephen's execution in Acts 7 in the hues of psalmic suffering, drawing attention to his opponents' gnashing teeth (v. 54; cf. Ps 35:16) and his prayer, "Lord Jesus, receive my Spirit" (v. 59), an echo of Jesus' prayer from the cross (Luke 23:46), which is itself a quotation of Ps 31:5.[37] Following in the footsteps of David and David's greater son, Stephen suffers in righteousness and expresses his confidence that vindication from the king, and not raging from the wicked, will be the final word over him.

In Rev 11:9–10, John describes the suffering of the church, herself the temple-city of God (vv. 1–2), as two slaughtered witnesses whose bodies go unburied while earth dwellers merrily rejoice over their demise.[38] The imagery alludes to Ps 79:3–4, where the nations in their defiling of Jerusalem and the temple slay, expose, and mock the people of Israel: "They have poured out their blood like water all around Jerusalem, and there was no one to bury them. We have become a taunt to our neighbors, mocked and derided by those around us."[39] With intertextual dexterity, John connects the tribulations of the church with Israel's sorrows, characterizing Christians' persecution as a continuation of the nations' unjust and violent opposition against the temple-kingdom of God, the people among whom

[37]   Cf. I. Howard Marshall, "Acts," in *CNTOT*, 571–72; Luke Timothy Johnson, *The Acts of the Apostles*, SP 5 (Collegeville, Minn.: Liturgical Press, 1992), 139–40.

[38]   On the identification of the two witnesses as the church, see Robert H. Mounce, *The Book of Revelation*, rev. ed., NICOT (Grand Rapids: Eerdmans, 1997), 217; Beale, *Book of Revelation*, 572–75; Wilfrid J. Harrington, *Revelation*, SP 16 (Collegeville, Minn.: Liturgical Press, 1993), 123; Craig R. Koester, *Revelation: A New Translation with Introduction and Commentary*, AYB 38A (New Haven: Yale University Press, 2014), 496–97.

[39]   Grant R. Osborne, *Revelation*, BECNT (Grand Rapids: Baker Academic, 2002), 428: "The pattern in the psalm, with the defilement of the temple (=Rev 11:2a) and the trampling of Jerusalem (=Rev 11:2b), followed by the death of the saints (=Rev 11:8–9) and the rejoicing of the persecutors (=Rev 11:10), fits Rev 11:1–10 quite well."

he dwells.[40] Something similar is likely at work in Rev 12:14–17, where the portrayal of the church's divinely orchestrated preservation from the Satanic serpent-dragon echoes the exodus imagery of Ps 55:6–8.[41] There, David in his anguish prays,

> [6] And I say, "Oh, that I had wings like a dove!
> I would fly away and be at rest;
> [7] yes, I would wander far away;
> I would lodge in the wilderness; *Selah*
> [8] I would hurry to find a shelter
> from the raging wind and tempest."

When the Revelator figuratively envisions the church as a woman being given eagles' wings so that she might flee the serpent, fly into the wilderness, and there find protection from the dragon's flood (12:14–16), and simultaneously casts the church as the woman's offspring upon whom the serpent-dragon still wages war (12:17), he weaves together echoes of Psalm 55 with clear allusions to the *protoevangelium*.[42] The author fashions the church as the seed of the woman who remains the target of the serpent's animosity and yet experiences the exodus-like deliverance and safety for which the Davidic imprecator pleaded in the midst of attack. The church and her sufferings thus come into focus in John's presentation as part of a narrative that begins in Genesis, extends through the psalms, and reaches all the way into the covenant community's antagonism-laced

---

[40]   Beale, *Book of Revelation*, 595, observes that both Rev 11:7 and LXX Ps 78:2 refer to the beast(s) (θηρίον), contributing one more layer of lexical resonance between the texts.

[41]   Beale, *Book of Revelation*, 669; G. K. Beale and Sean M. McDonough, "Revelation," in *CNTOT*, 1126. There are a host of possible Old Testament echoes in these few verses of Revelation 12, notable among them Exod 19:4; Deut 32:10–11. But the details of Rev 12:14–17—the giving of (and not just bearing upon) wings, the woman's flying from persecution, the wilderness as the destination of refuge, the preservation from watery destruction—all find concentrated parallel in Ps 55:6–8.

[42]   Echoes of Genesis 3 are especially evident in Rev 12:9, 17, but the whole complex of imagery in Revelation 12—woman, serpent-dragon, and seed—recall the promises of Gen 3:15. See Paul S. Minear, "Far as the Curse Is Found: The Point of Revelation 12:15–16," *NovT* 33, no. 1 (1991): 71–77. Cf. Brian K. Blount, *Revelation: A Commentary*, NTL (Louisville: Westminster John Knox, 2009), 235; Mounce, *Book of Revelation*, 242n12; Harrington, *Revelation*, 135.

present.[43] She, like Israel and David and Jesus before her, is a suffering son of God, buffeted by (but never abandoned to) enemies at enmity with God and his kingdom.

The church also takes up the speech of the imprecatory psalms, praying to God for judgment upon her enemies in language that is drawn from and evokes the psalms of vengeance. This is perhaps most evident in Rev 6:9–10, where "the souls of those who had been slain for the word of God and for the witness they had borne . . . cried out with a loud voice, 'O Sovereign Lord, holy and true, how long before you will judge and avenge our blood on those who dwell on the earth?'" The heavenly saints cry out, "How long?"—the question posed to God repeatedly in the imprecations (cf. Pss 35:17; 74:10; 79:5; 80:4; 94:3)—desiring like the psalmic petitioner to see God's vindicating vengeance manifested in history.[44] The request for the divine avenging of blood alludes more specifically to Ps 79:10: "Why should the nations say, 'Where is their God?' Let the avenging of the outpoured blood of your servants be known among the nations before our eyes!"[45] In the prayer of Rev 6:10, departed Christians inhabit the words of the imprecator, pleading for God to reveal his God-ness and pour out judgment upon those who defile and devour the place and people of his presence.[46] Less overt, but suggestive nonetheless, are the allusions to Ps

[43]   I consider the intertwining of references in Rev 12:14–17 to the *proto-evangelium* and the imprecator in the psalms to be no small evidence that my reading of the imprecatory psalms is at very least consistent with the inner-biblical exegesis of the scriptural Apocalypse.

[44]   Cf. Peter J. Leithart, *Revelation 1–11*, ITC (New York: Bloomsbury T&T Clark, 2018), 306.

[45]   Cf. Stephen Pattemore, *The People of God in the Apocalypse: Discourse, Structure, and Exegesis*, SNTSMS 128 (Cambridge: Cambridge University Press, 2004), 84. Beale, *Book of Revelation*, 392–93, notes that Rev 6:8 mentions the "wild beasts of the earth" (τῶν θηρίων τῆς γῆς) in very similar phrasing to LXX Ps 78:2 (τοῖς θηρῖοις τῆς γῆς).

[46]   Beale, *Book of Revelation*, 393, argues that Rev 6:10 may allude to Deuteronomy 32 in its description of God as holy and true (cf. LXX Deut 32:4) and affirmation of divine avenging of the blood of his children (Deut 32:43). I find this to be quite likely, as I previously suggested that Ps 79:10 is itself an allusion to Deut 32:43. Cf. Alan S. Bandy, "Vengeance, Wrath and Warfare as Images of Divine Justice in John's Apocalypse," in *Holy War in the Bible: Christian Morality and an Old Testament Problem*, ed. Heath Thomas, Jeremy Evans, and Paul Copan (Downers Grove, Ill.: IVP Academic, 2013), 111. As demonstrated earlier, Deuteronomy 32 serves as an important intertextual locus for the imprecatory psalms in their development of the image of the kingdom-threatening,

141:2 in Rev 5:8; 8:3–4. Petitioning for personal preservation and judgment upon the wicked, the Davidic psalmist begs, "Let my prayer be counted as incense before you" (Ps 141:2). Revelation 5:8; 8:3–4 employ this image, depicting the prayers of the saints as incense that rises before God.[47] What is more, the incense prayers of the saints are, like the psalmist's, prayers for divine vengeance: their content is revealed as it ascends from the altar in Rev 6:10,[48] and Rev 8:5 presents God's judgment as his response to the prayerful incense of 8:3–4.[49] Within the Apocalypse, the saints pray in the pattern of the imprecatory psalms, standing in the place of the imprecator as they echo the Psalter in their incense pleas for just divine action in history. The church of John's vision petitions as priest-kings, participating by supplication in the advent of God's judgment. They guard the ecclesial temple-kingdom and subdue the earth as sacred space through petition, driving out the enemy in prayer for vindication and vengeance, so that the whole creation—unmarred by ungodly violence—may be the place of God's holy, ruling presence with his people.[50]

The church that prays as a royal priesthood, however, also *acts* as a royal priesthood, mediating divine judgment not only through petition

---

serpentine enemy and the confident expectation of head-crushing vengeance from the divine royal warrior who cleanses his land of the wicked. It is intriguing that John's depiction of judgment-requesting Christians echoes Psalm 79, with its pleas for vengeance against those who have lethally intruded into the land of God's temple dwelling, as well as Deuteronomy 32, evoking further associations with the serpentine enemy who must be cleansed from the land. The mediated allusion to Deuteronomy 32 through Psalm 79 subtly connects the saints' petitions with the original conflict of Gen 3:15 and with the royal-priestly vocation of God's son through the ages as a (prayerful) participant in his land-cleansing judgment.

47   Christopher C. Rowland, "The Book of Revelation: Introduction, Commentary, and Reflections," in vol. 12 of *NIB* (Nashville: Abingdon, 1998), 630; Alan Johnson, "Revelation," in vol. 12 of *EBC* (Grand Rapids: Zondervan, 1981), 489.

48   See Richard Bauckham, "Prayer in the Book of Revelation," in *Into God's Presence: Prayer in the New Testament*, ed. Richard M. Longenecker (Grand Rapids: Eerdmans, 2001), 252–71.

49   Catherine Gunsalus González and Justo L. González, *Revelation*, Westminster Bible Companion (Louisville: Westminster John Knox, 1997), 62.

50   As Revelation 20–22 makes clear, the *telos* of God's judgment is the restoration of the cosmos and the consummation of his temple-kingdom. In the progression of John's Apocalypse, the saints' prayers for judgment contribute toward this cultic, kingdom-oriented end.

but also through eschatological participation as an agent through whom God's vengeance comes to fruition upon the opponents of his kingdom. The expectation of human, royal-priestly participation in the exercise of judgment occurs frequently in the imprecatory psalms (e.g., Pss 41:10; 58:10; 68:22–23; 72:4; 137:8–9; 144:1–2) and is applied to Christians in the New Testament. Alluding to the benediction of Ps 137:8 ("O daughter of Babylon, doomed to be destroyed, blessed shall he be who repays you with what you have done to us!"), Rev 18:6 narrates a voice from heaven that calls God's people to exact just retribution upon Babylon: "Pay her back as she herself has paid back others."[51] The avenging covenant community of Revelation 18 acts as the answer to the anticipations of the imprecating covenant community in Psalm 137, filling the role of the human mediator of God's talionic eschatological justice.[52] The final defeat of the anti-kingdom of God—the consummate expulsion of the sinful enemy from the world that will be God's royal home with his people—involves the church as an instrument of divine judgment.

Despite some objections to the contrary,[53] the passage is consistent with John's development of the church's identity elsewhere in the

[51]   Cf. Steve Moyise, "The Psalms in the Book of Revelation," in Moyise and Menken, *Psalms in the New Testament*, 241; Leonard L. Thompson, *Revelation*, ANTC (Nashville: Abingdon, 1998), 168. Osborne, *Revelation*, 641, suggests that Jer 50:29 is the principal alluded text, but that "Jeremiah could well have been alluding to Ps 137:8."

[52]   On the church as the addressee of the command of Rev 18:6, see esp. Paul Middleton, *The Violence of the Lamb: Martyrs as Agents of Divine Judgement in the Book of Revelation*, LNTS 586 (New York: T&T Clark, 2018), 231–35; Susan M. Elliott, "Who Is Addressed in Revelation 18:6–7?" *BR* 40 (1995): 98–113. Cf. John M. Court, *Myth and History in the Book of Revelation* (Atlanta: John Knox, 1979), 143. Pattemore, *People of God in the Apocalypse*, 104, agrees that God's people are the addressees of the command but suggests that "there is no unambiguous call for Christian militancy which would be at odds with the mode of victory of the people of God in 12:11, that of self-sacrificial witness." I find this assertion quite difficult to square with the text and allusions of Revelation 18. One need not fashion a disjunction between martyrial witness and participation in eschatological judgment, for in Revelation, it is those who conquer through faithful witness in this age who will be vindicated agents of divine judgment at the end of the age. On this, Middleton, *Violence of the Lamb*, 188–235, on Christian martyrdom and participation in God's wrath is focused and helpful.

[53]   See, e.g., David A. deSilva, *Seeing Things John's Way: The Rhetoric of the Book of Revelation* (Louisville: Westminster John Knox, 2009), 266; Blount, *Revelation*, 330; Koester, *Revelation*, 700.

Apocalypse. John's opening doxology introduces believers in Rev 1:6 as a people that has been made by Jesus a kingdom and priests, restored in Christ to the original human vocation and the royal-priestly status of the sons and daughters of God.[54] Those who conquer by persevering in faith will share in Jesus' messianic authority over the nations and will rule them with a rod of iron (2:26–27), participating in the prerogatives of the son of God in Ps 2:8–9.[55] Those ransomed by the Lamb have been made "a kingdom and priests to our God, and they shall reign on the earth" (5:10), and they follow Jesus as the armies of heaven when he appears to make war and tread the winepress of God's fury (19:14; cf. 17:14).[56] In Rev 20:4–6, John sees "thrones, and seated on them were those to whom the authority to judge was committed" (v. 4) as slaughtered saints are granted to reign as priests (v. 6) with Christ and take part in judging their oppressors and God's enemies.[57] Repeatedly in Revelation, then, John presents the church as priest-kings, the sons and daughters of God who at Christ's coming will subdue the earth, drive out the wicked, and exercise dominion as mediating agents of God's victorious, kingdom-consummating judgment—fulfilling humanity's Adamic calling, fulfilling the hopes of the imprecatory psalms.

---

[54]   Aside from the reference to "servants" in Rev 1:1, the royal and priestly imagery of v. 6 is the first descriptor of the church in the Apocalypse. Commentators unanimously affirm that v. 6 alludes to Exod 19:6, often pointing out that the identity of the church as a kingdom and priests in the fashion of Israel entails mediation of God's presence via cruciform witness to the world. This is by no means wrong, only incomplete, for it neglects the juridical dimension of the royal-priestly calling throughout the Old Testament and elsewhere in Revelation.

[55]   Middleton, *Violence of the Lamb*, 225; Elliott, "Who Is Addressed in Revelation 18:6–7?" 102.

[56]   See Middleton, *Violence of the Lamb*, 227–28. Cf. Elliott, "Who Is Addressed in Revelation 18:6–7?" 102. Adela Yarbro Collins, "The Political Perspective of the Revelation to John," *JBL* 96, no. 2 (1977): 247–48, views Rev 14:4; 17:14 as indications that "the author was aware of the tradition that the elect would fight in the last battle."

[57]   Middleton, *Violence of the Lamb*, 229–30, follows David E. Aune, *Revelation*, WBC 52C (Nashville: Thomas Nelson, 1998), 1087–88, in arguing that the wording of Rev 20:4 parallels the description of the souls of the martyrs under the altar in Rev 6:9 such that the judging of Rev 20:4 is presented as the answer to the cry of Rev 6:10. Cf. Koester, *Revelation*, 785. Middleton, *Violence of the Lamb*, 230: "The martyrs cried out for vindication and vengeance (6:10) and John now shows how that will be achieved. Their tormentors will be destroyed and the martyrs take part in their judgment."

"Or do you not know that the saints will judge the world? . . . Do you not know that we are to judge angels?" So inquires Paul in 1 Cor 6:2–3, confirming the church's participatory place in God's judgment of heaven and earth.[58] His letter to the Romans concludes with the empowering reminder that God "will soon crush Satan under your feet" (Rom 16:20), an allusion to the *protoevangelium* that characterizes Christ's community as the seed-son who will enjoy foot-stomping, head-shattering triumph over the serpentine enemy of God's kingdom, precisely the aspiration of Pss 58:10; 68:21–23.[59] Perhaps this is why, as Paul states in Rom 8:19, "creation waits with eager longing for the revealing of the sons of God"—not only because the curse on the ground will be unwound with resurrection but because the sons and daughters of God will enact their vocation to cleanse God's world from every unholy influence, setting it free from its bondage to corruption so that it may be the holy dwelling of God.[60] Even

[58]   Gordon D. Fee, *The First Epistle to the Corinthians*, rev. ed., NICNT (Grand Rapids: Eerdmans, 2014), 255. Cf. William F. Orr and James Arthur Walther, *I Corinthians: A New Translation*, AB 32 (Garden City, N.Y.: Doubleday and Company, 1976), 194; Hans Conzelmann, *1 Corinthians: A Commentary on the First Epistle to the Corinthians*, trans. James W. Leitch, ed. George W. MacRae, Hermeneia (Philadelphia: Fortress, 1975), 104–5; Anthony C. Thiselton, *The First Epistle to the Corinthians: A Commentary on the Greek Text*, NIGTC (Grand Rapids: Eerdmans, 2000), 425–27.

[59]   On the allusion to Gen 3:15 and the eschatological character of the envisioned crushing, cf. Mark A. Seifrid, "Romans," in *CNTOT*, 692; Douglas J. Moo, *The Epistle to the Romans*, NICNT (Grand Rapids: Eerdmans, 1996), 932–33; Frank J. Matera, *Romans*, Paideia Commentaries on the New Testament (Grand Rapids: Baker Academic, 2010), 344; Thomas R. Schreiner, *Romans*, BECNT (Grand Rapids: Baker Academic, 1998), 804–5. While not suggesting that there is an explicit intertextual link between Psalms 58; 68 and Rom 16:20, I think it eminently plausible that Paul's reading and utilization of the *protoevangelium* has been mediated through the lens and expectations of the Psalter, which envisions the covenant community participating in the action of God and God's Davidic anointed to crush the serpentine enemy's head underfoot. Cf. Robert Jewett, *Romans: A Commentary*, ass. Roy D. Kotansky, ed. Eldon Jay Epp, Hermeneia (Minneapolis: Fortress, 2007), 994. Derek R. Brown, "'The God of Peace Will Shortly Crush Satan Under Your Feet': Paul's Eschatological Reminder in Romans 16:20a," *Neot* 44, no. 1 (2010): 1–14, argues for an allusion to Ps 110:1, though I find his contention that the influence of Gen 3:15 on Rom 16:20 is unlikely unpersuasive, especially in light of my argument in the previous chapter that Ps 110:1 is itself a text that resonates with the *protoevangelium*.

[60]   This seems to me consonant with the overtures to Genesis 3 in this passage and further clarifies why Paul would make "the revealing of the sons of

Jesus affirms that his followers will share in his royal authority, treading on "serpents and scorpions, and over all the power of the enemy" (Luke 10:19) in their gospel witness,[61] and sitting on thrones and "judging the twelve tribes of Israel" (Matt 19:28) in the eschaton.[62] The New Testament depicts the church as enacting the expectations of the imprecator in the psalms, mediating divine judgment upon the enemies of Christ's kingdom as the royal-priestly sons and daughters of God.

In her suffering, her prayer, her active participation in divine judgment, and also in her joyous eschatological worship, the church fills out the pattern of the psalmic imprecator. After requesting judgment upon his enemies, David commits, "I will sing a new song to you, O God; upon a ten-stringed harp I will play to you" (Ps 144:9; cf. 40:3), and the 144,000 in Rev 14:2–3 celebrate God's delivering judgment in the pattern of the psalmist, worshipping God with a voice "like the sound of harpists playing on their harps, and they were singing a new song."[63] In Ps 86:9, the Davidic psalmist envisions the peoples of the earth gathering with him in praise and declares, "All the nations you have made shall come and worship before you, O Lord, and shall glorify your name." In Rev 15:4, the church celebrates the delivering judgment of God,[64] taking up the imprecator's song: "All nations will come and worship you,

---

God" the object of creation's anticipation rather than appealing more simply to a concept such as resurrection or restoration. Cf. Jewett, *Romans*, 512, and esp. N. T. Wright, "Romans," in vol. 10 of *NIB* (Nashville: Abingdon, 2002), 596–97.

[61] Cf. James Hamilton, "Skull-Crushing Seed of the Woman: Inner-Biblical Interpretation of Genesis 3:15," *SBJT* 10, no. 2 (2006): 42; Pao and Schnabel, "Luke," in *CNTOT*, 318; I. Howard Marshall, *The Gospel of Luke*, NIGTC (Grand Rapids: Eerdmans, 1978), 429. Like Paul in Rom 16:20, it is likely that Jesus is utilizing *protoevangelium* imagery refracted through the lens of the Psalter. In fact, Jack P. Lewis, "The Woman's Seed (Gen 3:15)," *JETS* 34, no. 3 (1991): 303, argues that Paul's statement may have Luke 10:19 in the background.

[62] On Christian participation in judgment and the significance of the allusion to Dan 7:22 in Matt 19:28, see France, *Gospel of Matthew*, 743–44. Cf. Stanley Hauerwas, *Matthew*, BTCB (Grand Rapids: Brazos, 2006), 175–76; David L. Turner, *Matthew*, BECNT (Grand Rapids: Baker Academic, 2008), 475–76.

[63] See Blount, *Revelation*, 267. Cf. Rowland, "Book of Revelation," 664. Beale, *Book of Revelation*, 735–36.

[64] Adela Yarbro Collins, *The Apocalypse*, NTM 22 (Wilmington, Del.: Michael Glazier, 1979), 107. Cf. George Eldon Ladd, *A Commentary on the Revelation of John* (Grand Rapids: Eerdmans, 1972), 205; Beale, *Book of Revelation*, 784. *Contra* Mounce, *Book of Revelation*, 285.

for your righteous acts have been revealed."[65] The worship the psalmist offered in advance of God's vengeance becomes the worship the saints offer in the wake of God's vengeance. Because God's "righteous acts have been revealed," the church sings David's future hope as her impending present, on the cusp of realization. Similarly, the heavenly multitude's thrice-repeated hallelujah in Rev 19:1–4, her doxological response to God's eschatological judgment, echoes the הַלְלוּ־יָהּ of Ps 104:35, which follows after the psalmist's imprecatory call for sinners to be consumed from the earth.[66] Where psalmic praise rises in the hope of world-clearing judgment, the church's praise rises because of its actualization in history. Indeed, the multitude's justification for her joy in Rev 19:2 puts the plea of Ps 79:10 (and, it should be noted, Rev 6:10) into the aorist: God "has avenged . . . the blood of his servants."[67] Prospective petition becomes retrospective jubilation as the church worships God for his judgment. And this church who gives thanks for God's wrath in the grammar of the imprecatory psalms will experience the beatific destiny to which the imprecator looked forward. "They will see his face. . . . They will need no light of lamp or sun, for the Lord God will be their light, and they will reign forever and ever" (Rev 22:4–5). The New Testament ends with reigning priest-kings beholding the face of God in covenantal communion (cf. Pss 11:7; 17:15),[68] his glorious countenance shining upon them (cf. Pss 31:16; 80:3, 7, 19; 119:135),[69] the cultic culmination of the imprecator's highest longing—to dwell in the presence of God.

[65]   Moyise, "Psalms in the Book of Revelation," in Moyise and Menken, *Psalms in the New Testament*, 235–36, argues that Ps 86:8–10 is the key allusion in Rev 15:3–4.

[66]   Cf. Philip Mauro, *The Patmos Visions: A Study of the Apocalypse* (Boston: Hamilton Bros., 1925), 506; Beale, *Book of Revelation*, 926–7; Blount, *Revelation*, 341; Rowland, "Book of Revelation," 695. Recall that Psalm 104 depicts God's creation in cultic, temple-laden terms before concluding with a royal-priestly imprecation, a thematic matrix consistent with the movement of Revelation 19–22 from judgment to restored temple-cosmos.

[67]   Osborne, *Revelation*, 665; Beale, *Book of Revelation*, 928–29.

[68]   Cf. J. P. M. Sweet, *Revelation*, Westminster Pelican Commentaries (Philadelphia: Westminster, 1979), 312; Blount, *Revelation*, 399; Beale, *Book of Revelation*, 1113–14; Harrington, *Revelation*, 216.

[69]   Beale, *Book of Revelation*, 1115: "The repeated prayer of OT saints was that God would reveal his presence by 'shining the light of his countenance' on them (Num 6:25–26; Pss 4:6; 31:16; 67:1; 80:3, 7, 19; 119:135; *Pesikta Rabbati* 1.2). This prayer is consummately answered in Rev 22:5."

The New Testament thus integrates the defining features of the psalmic imprecator into its presentation of Christ and his church and their place in the story of God's purposes to restore his temple-kingdom on earth. In the New Testament's interaction with the imprecations' text and themes, Jesus emerges as the innocent, suffering son of God who enjoys deliverance and vindication through resurrection and disempowers the enemies of God's temple-kingdom, ultimately driving them from the place of God's dwelling in consummative judgment. And Christians are characterized as innocent, suffering sons and daughters of God, too. Bearing the enmity of God's foes, the royal-priestly church serves as a mediator of judgment, guarding the temple-kingdom and cleansing creation now by petitioning for divine vengeance and at the *parousia* by actively participating in God's eschatological justice that the cosmos may be filled with God's glory—the temple-kingdom where she worships and lives in God's holy presence forever.

Echoes of the Enemy: Crushed Serpents and Cursed Kingdom Foes

But what of the enemy? In the narrative world of the imprecatory psalms, so I have argued, the enemy is characterized as the serpent's seed, violently and unjustly opposed to God's temple-kingdom and fated for divine judgment. To whom does the New Testament intertextually apply the psalmic descriptions of the enemy? And how does the New Testament's allusive and thematically resonant narration of and reflection upon God's works in Jesus present these Christian-era foes as filling the role and fulfilling the destiny of the enemy in the psalms of vengeance?

Given the extent to which the Gospels frame Jesus as the righteous Davidic sufferer with the imagery and language of the imprecatory psalms, it is unsurprising that his deadly antagonizers are described with echoes and evocations of the psalmic enemy. Indeed, most of the intertextual instances discussed above that depict Jesus as the antitypical oppressed innocent serve a dual function, simultaneously casting those lethally committed to his downfall as the tormenting enemy of the imprecatory psalms. That is, the same allusion that says something about Jesus says something about Jesus' enemies, about their theological significance in the unfolding events of redemption. Christ claims that the Jewish religious leaders' opposition toward him fulfills "the word that is written in their Law" from Ps 69:4: "They hated me without a cause" (John 15:25). With this quotation, Jesus pulls the psalmic world into his messianic present, not only affirming his identity as the Davidic "me" but also correspondingly characterizing the religious elite as the hate-filled "they," sinfully opposed to God's king and kingdom. The chief priests, scribes, elders, and whole council in the leadup to Christ's passion operate by stealth to kill (Mark 14:1; cf. Ps 10:7–8), ruthlessly seeking Jesus' life (Mark 14:55; cf. Ps 54:3), and theirs are the sinful hands into which the true David is delivered (Mark 14:41; cf. Pss 71:4; 140:4).[70] False witnesses rise up against him at the behest of the Jewish leadership (Mark 14:57; cf. Ps 35:11), incorporated into their unjust scheme to put Jesus to death. These intertextual associations with the enemy in the imprecations resonate thematically with Jesus' identification of the Jewish authorities as the serpent seed in John 8:44, offspring of the devil who participate in his murderous lies and animosity toward the son of God (cf. Matt 3:7; 12:34; 23:33; Luke 3:7).[71] The primordial conflict that extended from Eden into the Psalter wages on in the religious establishment's falsehoods and animosity toward the Christ.[72] The Israelite coalition continues and climactically instantiates the pattern of the vicious, serpentine enemy of the imprecatory psalms, violently and deceptively devoted to the destruction of the innocent anointed king over God's kingdom.

The evangelists also particularize their echoes of the psalmic enemy, narrowing their referent to a single individual: Judas Iscariot. In John's narration of Jesus' final night, Jesus explicitly identifies Judas as the fulfiller of Ps 41:9: "But the Scripture will be fulfilled, 'He who ate my bread has lifted his heel against me'" (John 13:18; cf. Mark 14:18).[73] Jesus thus characterizes Judas as the supreme antitype of the enemy in the imprecatory psalms, the singular person who brings the paradigm of the

[70]   Cf. Watts, "Psalms in Mark's Gospel," 42.

[71]   Maarten J. J. Menken, "Genesis in John's Gospel and 1 John," in *Genesis in the New Testament*, ed. Maarten J. J. Menken and Steve Moyise, LNTS 466 (New York: Bloomsbury T&T Clark, 2012), 91. Cf. James M. Hamilton Jr., *God's Glory in Salvation through Judgment: A Biblical Theology* (Wheaton, Ill.: Crossway, 2010), 411; Köstenberger, "John," in CNTOT, 458.

[72]   This is consistent with my reading of Jesus' cleansing of the temple in John 2:13–17 as a recapitulation of Adam's vocation in Eden. John 2 supplies a lens very early in John's Gospel for interpreting Jesus' conflict with the religious leadership of Israel in terms of the Adam-serpent conflict in Genesis 3, terms to which Jesus quite overtly appeals in John 8.

[73]   Daly-Denton, *David in the Fourth Gospel*, 197, observes that "in John 13:26–27, Jesus engages Judas in an enactment of Ps 40:10 [ET 41:9] by dipping a ψωμίον and handing it to him." Cf. Köstenberger, "John," in *CNTOT*, 487.

bread-breaking betrayer of the Davidic king to its redemptive-historical climax. In Luke's postascension account, Peter quotes two imprecatory psalms to explain the necessity of Judas' death and apostolic replacement following his treason. "For it is written in the Book of Psalms, 'May his camp become desolate, and let there be no one to dwell in it'; and 'Let another take his office'" (Acts 1:20; citing Pss 69:25; 109:8). The traitor's suicide and Matthias' installation into his vacated office are in Peter's understanding a fulfillment of Scripture, "which the Holy Spirit spoke beforehand by the mouth of David concerning Judas" (Acts 1:16), as the imprecator's specific prayers for divine judgment upon his enemies become actualized in the history of Judas, the enemy of Jesus.[74]

But the New Testament's utilization of enemy imagery from the imprecatory psalms is not limited to those groups and individuals personally involved in the betrayal, arrest, and crucifixion of Christ. Both Jesus and Paul expand the figure of the psalmic enemy to encompass the whole of national Israel. The weeping Jesus laments over Jerusalem and announces that her enemies "will crush you to the ground (ἐδαφιοῦσίν), you and your children within you" (Luke 19:44, NRSV), echoing the yearning malediction of Ps 137:9 against Babylon: "Blessed shall he be who takes your little ones and dashes (ἐδαφιεῖ, LXX Ps 136:9) them against the rock!"[75] Jesus' allusive declaration of judgment intertextually positions the epicenter of the Israelite kingdom as the serpentine Babylonian oppressor—aligned in her Christward antipathy with the psalmic enemy who rages against God's temple-kingdom, aligned in her destiny with the serpent seed who will be crushed by God. Offering scriptural justification for his claim that Israel has undergone a hardening from God, Paul quotes in Rom 11:9–10 David's imprecatory prayers against his oppressors from

---

[74]   Cf. Darrell L. Bock, *Acts*, BECNT (Grand Rapids: Baker Academic, 2007), 85–87; Lindars, *New Testament Apologetic*, 102–3; Marshall, "Acts," in *CNTOT*, 530; Hans Conzelmann, *Acts of the Apostles*, ed. Eldon Jay Epp and Christopher R. Matthews, trans. James Limburg, A. Thomas Krabel, and Donald H. Juel, Hermeneia (Philadelphia: Fortress, 1987), 11–12; Doble, "Psalms in Luke-Acts," 116. Note that the citation in Acts 1:20 could reasonably be interpreted as evidence that Luke does not accept the quotation hypothesis in his reading of Psalm 109.

[75]   Cf. Pao and Schnabel, "Luke," in *CNTOT*, 356–57; Joseph A. Fitzmyer, *The Gospel According to Luke (X–XXIV)*, AB 28A (Garden City, N.Y.: Doubleday and Company, 1985), 1258; Marshall, *Gospel of Luke*, 718–19; Luke Timothy Johnson, *The Gospel of Luke*, SP 3 (Collegeville, Minn.: Liturgical Press, 1991), 299.

Ps 69:22–23 that God would "let their table become a snare" and "let their eyes be darkened so that they cannot see."[76] Consistent with his later use of Ps 69:9 as reflective of the experience of Jesus (Rom 15:3), Paul here suggests that the Davidic psalmist's prayers for judgment against his enemies have been answered in God's eye-darkening judgment upon the people of Israel, who in their rejection of God's Messiah have made themselves the enemies of David's ultimate heir.[77] With an intertextual irony worthy of the psalms, Jesus and Paul—like David in Psalm 58—apply Old Testament language about ungodly opponents of God's kingdom to Israelites, revealing that Israel as a corporate entity has stepped into the role of the unjust enemy in the continuing story of the temple-kingdom and that the petitioned vengeance of God from Psalms 69 and 137 is breaking into the world upon the covenant people that has rebelled against the reign of the promised covenant king.

The religious leaders who pursued Jesus; the apostle who betrayed Jesus; the nation who rejected Jesus—these adversaries of Christ are depicted as inhabiting the part played by the violent oppressor of God's king and kingdom in the imprecatory psalms, acting out and amplifying the character in the New Testament's new chapter of the redemptive-historical drama. The theological significance of their treachery and, in the case of Judas and Israel, the intelligibility of their reception of judgment are communicated via allusive reference to the enemy in the storied world of the vengeance psalms. And yet the New Testament authors also leverage the imprecations' enemy imagery to narrate and reflect upon the enemies of Christ's temple-kingdom people, the church—her human and spiritual enemies alike.

After Stephen's testimony before the Sanhedrin, Luke reports that the members of the council "ground their teeth at him" (Acts 7:54), evoking the teeth-gnashing hatred of David's detractors in Ps 35:16.[78] In 1 Cor 3:17, Paul pronounces, "If anyone destroys God's temple, God will destroy him. For God's temple is holy, and you are that temple." Recalling the nations of Ps 79:1 that "have defiled your holy temple," Paul connects anyone who harms the holy ecclesial temple-people among whom God dwells with the marauders who desecrated his dwelling in Jerusalem. Their modus

---

76   See Seifrid, "Romans," in *CNTOT*, 670, for a detailed survey of the relationship between Paul's quotation and LXX Ps 68:23–24.

77   Keesmaat, "Psalms in Romans and Galatians," 155. Cf. Moo, *Epistle to the Romans*, 682–83; Schreiner, *Romans*, 588–89.

78   Cf. Marshall, "Acts," in *CNTOT*, 571.

operandi is the same, and the temple-defending vengeance for which the psalmist prayed (cf. 79:6, 10) will be their same fate as well.[79] Addressing a Thessalonian church that has suffered at the hands of her countrymen (1 Thess 2:14–16), Paul reminds the saints that "sudden destruction will come upon" unbelievers at the dawning of the day of the Lord (1 Thess 5:3). Paul's description of the coming judgment echoes the imprecatory plea of Ps 35:8—"Let destruction come upon him when he does not know it!"[80]—for the judgment the psalmist desired will finally come to fruition at the *parousia* when God destroys those who oppose him and oppress his people.[81] In 2 Thess 1:6, Paul reminds this same church that is suffering for the kingdom of God (v. 5) that "God considers it just to repay with affliction those who afflict you," alluding to the benediction of Ps 137:8 upon the one who justly judges Babylon and "repays you with what you have done to us!"[82] The agents afflicting these Christians participate in the

[79]   On the thick temple imagery throughout 1 Corinthians 3, which connects the church with the garden-temple of God, see Beale, *Temple and the Church's Mission*, 245–50.

[80]   Scholars typically have not noted an allusion to Ps 35:8 in 1 Thess 5:3, this is not entirely surprising given that 1) Paul is not following the more easily comparable Greek of LXX 34:8, which differs from the Hebrew text, and 2) there are other allusions in this cluster of verses, most of which come through at a higher volume than the allusion to Ps 35:8 (e.g., "the day of the Lord," coming "like a thief in the night," "peace and security," "labor pains"). Nevertheless, Paul's statement in 1 Thess 5:3—especially since it is destruction that comes upon unbelievers—appears to correspond with the MT of Ps 35:8 quite nicely.

[81]   Many—e.g., Jeffrey A. D. Weima, *1–2 Thessalonians*, BECNT (Grand Rapids: Baker Academic, 2014), 348–51; Gordon D. Fee, *The First and Second Letters to the Thessalonians*, NICNT (Grand Rapids: Eerdmans, 2009), 189; Frederick W. Weidmann, *Philippians, 1 and 2 Thessalonians, and Philemon*, Westminster Bible Companion (Louisville: Westminster John Knox, 2013), 151–52; Abraham Smith, "The First Letter to the Thessalonians," in vol. 11 of *NIB* (Nashville: Abingdon, 2000), 726—suggest that Paul's mention of those who talk of peace and security refers to those aligned with Rome and its imperial propaganda, introducing to v. 3 a contrast between competing kingdom communities.

[82]   Gene L. Green, *The Letters to the Thessalonians*, PNTC (Grand Rapids: Eerdmans, 2002), 286; Weima, *1–2 Thessalonians*, 465, note the lexical similarity between 2 Thess 1:6 and Ps 137:8, but they maintain that the primary allusion is to Isaiah 66, where ἀνταποδίδωμι occurs in vv. 4, 6, with a related form in v. 15. There may indeed be a link with Isaiah 66, especially in light of the likely allusions to Isaiah 66 elsewhere in 2 Thessalonians 1. However, though 2 Thess 1:6 and LXX Ps 136:8 are only lexically united by a single verb (ἀνταποδίδωμι), the syntactical and logical

same kingdom-combating dynamics as Israel's Babylonian tormentors, and the talionic recompense the psalmist sought from God, Paul avers, will be poured out upon the enemies of Christ's kingdom community. In each of these texts, it is the church's flesh-and-blood enemies—her human foes—whose actions and destiny are depicted in terms culled from the psalmic enemy.

This intertextual rendering of the church's human opponents in the hues of the imprecator's enemies continues in John's Apocalypse. The allusions to Psalm 79 in the martyrs' imprecatory inquiry of Rev 6:10 (cf. 79:10), the description of the church's suffering in Rev 11:9–10 (cf. Ps 79:3–4), and the heavenly multitude's celebration of manifested judgment in Rev 19:2 (cf. Ps 79:10) each situate the violent, blood-spilling enemies of God's *ekklesia* as inhabiting the role of temple-defiling, servant-slaying, kingdom-infiltrating nations that devastated Israel in the redemptive-historical past.[83] "Those who dwell on the earth" (Rev 6:10; 11:10)[84] and "the great prostitute" (Rev 19:2) Babylon—the church's enemies viewed in their oppressive capacity as individuals and as a systemic collective—extend the invading nations' animosity against God's temple-kingdom and thus become the objects of the church's imprecatory prayer (Rev 6:10) and God's vindicating vengeance (Rev 19:2; cf. Rev 18:6),[85] experiencing the anticipated future of the psalmic enemy. In Rev 14:10, those who worship the beast, aligning their allegiance with the political powers that persecute God's people, will drink wrath-wine from the cup of God's anger and will be tormented with fire and sulfur (cf. Rev 21:8),

construction of Paul's phrase—with its somewhat untidy affirmation of repaying to an enemy that which the enemy did to God's people—appears indebted to the flow of Ps 137:8. Compare 2 Thess 1:6 (ἀνταποδοῦναι τοῖς θλίβουσιν ὑμᾶς θλῖψιν; lit. "to repay those who afflict you affliction") with Ps 137:8 (שֶׁגָּמַלְתְּ לָנוּ אֶת־גְּמוּלֵךְ שֶׁיְשַׁלֶּם־לָךְ; lit. "who repays you your recompense you recompensed to us") and LXX Ps 136:8 (ὡς ἀνταποδώσει σοι τὸ ἀνταπόδομά σου ὃ ἀνταπέδωκας ὑμῖν; lit. "who will repay you your repayment which you repaid to us").

[83]   Cf. discussions of the allusions to Psalm 79 by Osborne, *Revelation*, 428; Beale, *Book of Revelation*, 392–93, 595.

[84]   Beale, *Book of Revelation*, 290, argues that "τοὺς κατοικοῦντας ἐπὶ τῆς γῆς ('those dwelling on the earth') is a technical term throughout Revelation for unbelieving idolaters, who suffer under various forms of retributive tribulation." Cf. Mounce, *Book of Revelation*, 148–49.

[85]   The echoes of Ps 79:10 in Rev 19:2 and of Ps 137:8 in Rev 18:6 both depict Babylon the great as an oppressive invader who terrorizes God's kingdom and receives the petitioned judgment originally aimed against the historical Babylon in the psalms.

their fate the enactment of the imprecator's hope that fire and sulfur would be the portion of the enemy's cup (Ps 11:6).[86] Revelation 19:20 details the beast itself, along with the false prophet—that is, the world's oppressive systems and those who participate in and contribute to the violence of the state and encourage obsequence to its totalizing claims[87]—being "thrown alive" (ζῶντες), recalling David's request that his enemies "go down to Sheol alive" (Ps 55:15; ζῶντες, LXX Ps 54:16),[88] into the lake of fire and sulfur (cf. Ps 11:6). Once again, the judgment requested against the enemy in the imprecatory psalms is manifested in the eschatological judgment exercised against the church's oppressors. The Apocalypse concludes with "the dogs" and all manner of sinners left outside the gates of the restored temple-city of God (Rev 22:15). Psalm 59:6, 14 lamented the wicked incessantly "howling like dogs and prowling about the city" as a ritually unclean and violent threat, but in Rev 22:15, the dogs no longer lurk hungrily around the city's exterior. The unclean are consigned to their alienation—banished from the land of God's reign, never to threaten the holy temple-kingdom again.[89]

---

[86] Cf. Middleton, *Violence of the Lamb*, 170n136; Beale, *Book of Revelation*, 760; Blount, *Revelation*, 275.

[87] On the beast and false prophet in Revelation as representing systems of violent state coercion against the church and economic, political, social, and religious pressure to comply with the state's idolatrous aspirations a la Rome and the imperial cult, see Collins, *Apocalypse*, 89–98; Beale, *Book of Revelation*, 681–718; Koester, *Revelation*, 580–606; on the two beasts in Revelation 13, Jürgen Roloff, *The Revelation of John: A Continental Commentary*, trans. John E. Alsup (Minneapolis: Fortress, 1993), 161: "John wishes to characterize all the institutions, people, and forces that promote the religious veneration of the empire and its power, focused chiefly in the cult of the Caesar."

[88] Interestingly, Ps 55:15 alludes to the judgment following Korah's rebellion in Num 16:30, 33—a judgment that removes the unholy (cf. Num 16:5) from the camp where God dwells. Something similar happens on a cosmic scale in Rev 19:20.

[89] The multiple points of correspondence between the texts—1) dogs 2) located on the outside 3) of God's city 4) as a (non)threat—make Psalm 59 a likely candidate as a source of John's imagery. There is, however, an ironic reversal involved in the echo of Ps 59:6, 14. The dogs who powerfully prowled outside the city are now relegated to the outside of a city that dwells in security and peace. The dogs who looked in from the outside with evil intentions are now left on the outside looking in. As far as Hays' criterion of satisfaction in *Echoes of Scripture in the Letters of Paul* (31) is concerned—the ability of a potential echo to generate a satisfying reading of the alluding text—I find that this potential intertextual reference succeeds.

The spiritual enemies of Christ's church share in the lot of her human foes as recipients of the enemy-directed retribution of the imprecatory psalms. Paul promises that Satan, the arch-spiritual opponent of God's temple-kingdom throughout redemptive history, will be crushed under Christians' feet (Rom 16:20), blending the *protoevangelium*'s expectations of head-shattering judgment upon the serpent with the imprecatory psalms' affirmations that judgment on the serpentine wicked will be meted out through the feet of God's covenant community (Pss 58:10; 68:21–23). The humanly mediated foot-stomping vengeance that the imprecations declare will come to the serpent seed becomes in Paul's hopeful exhortation the eschatological portion of the diabolical father whose image they bear. The fiery, sulfuric punishment drawn from Ps 11:6 and allotted to the human worshipers of the beast (Rev 14:10) and to the beast and false prophet (Rev 19:20) is in Rev 20:10 exacted against the devil when he is "thrown into the lake of fire and sulfur." The devil who deceived the nations to march against the saints (Rev 20:7–9), the enemy at work underneath every other enemy of the church, receives with them the climactic eschatological judgment that finally answers the pleas and anticipations of the imprecations.

The New Testament thus draws upon the figure of the enemy in the judgment psalms to evocatively describe the character, action, theological significance, and destiny of the various opponents that array themselves against God's temple-kingdom—the historical enemies of king Jesus and the human and spiritual enemies of Jesus' church across time. This intertextual portrayal presents the Christian-era enemies of God's kingdom as continuing the fundamental conflict that animates the imprecatory psalms and as definitively reaping the vengeance that the imprecatory psalms pray for and guarantee is coming. Every antagonizer of and threat to God's temple-kingdom will be justly neutralized, punished, driven from the new creational world where God will reign among his people.

And yet the New Testament's deployment of enemy imagery from the imprecations is more diverse still, for Paul universalizes the psalms' concept of the enemy to include all of humanity, even those who belong to Christ's kingdom by faith. Supporting his contention that "all, both Jews and Greeks, are under sin" (Rom 3:9), Paul offers a catena of Old Testament citations comprising several imprecatory psalms:

[13] "Their throat is an open grave;
they use their tongues to deceive" (Ps 5:9).

"The venom of asps is under their lips" (Ps 140:3).[90]
[14] "Their mouth is full of curses and bitterness" (Ps 10:7).[91]

Here the psalmists' descriptions of the enemy—focusing on the deceptive, violent, serpentine nature of the enemy's speech—is expanded to encompass every human being; Paul indicts the whole world as participants in the psalmic foes' opposition toward God and corresponding violence.[92] In Paul's argument, the righteous are not those who have never been numbered among God's law-breaking enemies (3:19–20), but those law-breaking enemies who have been "justified by his grace as a gift, through the redemption that is in Christ Jesus, whom God put forward as a propitiation by his blood, to be received by faith" (3:24–25). God's kingdom is populated with adversaries turned citizens, rebels made children, who have been reconciled to the Father by the death of the Son "while we were enemies" (5:10). This linking of Christians with the enemy in the imprecations occurs again in 2 Cor 2:14. Paul gives thanks that God "in Christ always leads us in triumphal procession,"[93] echoing God's "leading a host of captives in [his] train" in Ps 68:18.[94] Paul envisions himself, and the

[90]   Cf. Jas 3:8, where James similarly describes all humanity as naturally possessing a tongue that is "full of deadly poison." Dan G. McCartney, *James*, BECNT (Grand Rapids: Baker Academic, 2009), 192, argues that James borrows the image from Pss 58:3–4; 140:3. Cf. Peter H. Davids, *The Epistle of James*, NIGTC (Grand Rapids: Eerdmans, 1982), 145; Scot McKnight, *The Letter of James*, NICNT (Grand Rapids: Eerdmans, 2011), 289–90; Martin Dibelius, *James: A Commentary on the Epistle of James*, rev. Heinrich Greeven, trans. Michael A. Williams, ed. Helmut Koester, Hermeneia (Philadelphia: Fortress, 1976), 201.

[91]   On Paul's Old Testament citations in Rom 3:10–18, see Seifrid, "Romans," in *CNTOT*, 616–18; Moo, *Epistle to the Romans*, 202–4; Jewett, *Romans*, 261–62.

[92]   Moo, *Epistle to the Romans*, 202–3. Cf. Schreiner, *Romans*, 167–68; Jewett, *Romans*, 261–62.

[93]   Paul here uses θριαμβεύω, the same verb he utilizes in Col 2:15 to describe Jesus' triumph over demonic powers.

[94]   Many interpreters find a reference here to the Roman practice of the triumphal procession. See, e.g., Scott J. Hafemann, *Suffering and the Spirit: An Exegetical Study of II Corinthians 2:14–3:3 within the Context of the Corinthian Correspondence*, WUNT 2/19 (Tübingen: Mohr, 1986), 18–39. While this culturally available image would almost certainly figure into Paul's description, I find it surprising that very few interpreters consider the possibility of an allusion to Ps 68:18. For a notable exception, see J. M. Scott, "The Triumph of God in 2 Cor 2.14: Additional Evidence of Merkabah Mysticism in Paul," *NTS* 42 (1996): 268–70. Given Paul's penchant for echoing Psalm 68 in Colossians and

entire church with him, in the place of the psalmic foe, led by Jesus as a conquered enemy in the train of God's victorious procession. But in Paul's creative appropriation of this image, Christians are not subjugated, unwilling prisoners vanquished in judgment (cf. Col 2:15); they are a different kind of enemy entirely. Christians are those repentant enemies of God whose rebellion has been overcome by grace, former opponents who now joyfully follow as servant-slaves of the king.[95] Paul's allusion portrays the church as enemies made captive, but she is a happy captive whose captivity to Jesus is salvation and life.

But in what may be the most surprising intertextual application of enemy language from the imprecatory psalms, Jesus too is depicted as inhabiting the role of the cursed kingdom foe. In Luke 12:50, after stating that he has come to cast the fire of judgment on the earth,[96] Jesus announces, "I have a baptism to be baptized with, and how great is my distress until it is accomplished!" This combination of fire and flood imagery occurs in the (by now familiar) petition of Ps 11:6 that God would rain coals on the wicked and make fire and sulfur the portion of their cup, and Jesus' allusively pregnant words evoke the impression that he too will be inundated in the fiery judgment that is properly directed at the wicked: "Jesus himself then shares in the judgment which is to come upon the world."[97] Christ's imminent baptism intertextually and theologically locates him in the position of the psalmic enemy, bearing the flaming flood of divine vengeance in the place of the violent adversaries of God's kingdom. This same psalm text lies in the background of the cup sayings in the Gospels. Jesus asks an eager James and John if they can drink the cup that he drinks or be baptized with the baptism with which he is baptized (Mark 10:38; cf. Matt 20:22), again uniting cup and flood imagery in a manner reminiscent of the raining coals and

---

Ephesians, it seems plausible that his reference to a Roman triumphal procession simultaneously draws upon the parallel imagery of Psalm 68, especially since in 2 Cor 2:14 and Ps 68:18 it is God who leads the captives.

95   Murray J. Harris, *The Second Epistle to the Corinthians: A Commentary on the Greek Text*, NIGTC (Grand Rapids: Eerdmans, 2005), 245.

96   Cf. Marshall, *Gospel of Luke*, 546–47; Darrell L. Bock, *Luke*, BECNT (Grand Rapids: Baker Academic, 1996), 2:1191–92. This theme is introduced in Luke 3:16–17.

97   Marshall, *Gospel of Luke*, 547. In considering the allusion to Ps 11:6, Marshall follows Gerhard Delling, "ΒΑΠΤΙΣΜΑ ΒΑΠΤΙΣΘΗΝΑΙ," *NovT* 2, no. 2 (1957): 106. Cf. Pao and Schnabel, "Luke," in *CNTOT*, 332.

blazing cup apportioned to the enemy in Ps 11:6.[98] In Gethsemane, Jesus requests that the Father "remove this cup from me" (Mark 14:36; Luke 22:42; cf. Matt 26:39), expressing his fear even as he acknowledges his fate to drink up the wrath of God.[99] Jesus' echoes of the imprecatory psalms plant him in the conceptual space of the enemy, interpreting his impending crucifixion as an experience of the kind of divine judgment appropriate to the opponents of God's kingdom. In the New Testament's Christologically polyvalent utilization of the imprecations, the cross that is the undeserved suffering and foe-disarming victory of the innocent son of God is simultaneously divine wrath upon the Christ who stands in the place of God's enemies.[100]

This intertextual linking of Christ's death with God's enemy-aimed vengeance in the imprecations supplies an intriguing lens through which to view the portrait of Jesus' suffering developed elsewhere in the New Testament. If Jesus' allusive invitation to read his baptism-cup in connection with the psalmic adversary is accepted, multiple aspects of Christ's passion may be found to exhibit striking parallels with the psalmists' petitions for and descriptions of divine judgment against the enemy. Wicked men and accusers stand against Jesus (Mark 14:55–59; 15:3; cf. Ps 109:6), and when he is tried, he comes forth guilty (Mark 14:64; cf. Ps 109:7). The Lord is struck in the face (Matt 26:67; John 18:22; cf. Pss 3:7; 58:6) and upon the head (Mark 15:19; Matt 27:30; cf. Pss 68:21; 74:13–14), the

---

[98] James R. Edwards, *The Gospel According to Mark*, PNTC (Grand Rapids: Eerdmans, 2002), 322, references Ps 11:6 as one of several Old Testament texts that contribute to the cup of wrath motif. Cf. C. E. B. Cranfield, "The Cup Metaphor in Mark xiv. 36 and Parallels," *ExpTim* 59, no. 5 (1948): 137–38. While the judgment cup image indeed appears quite frequently in the Old Testament, the appeal to both a cup and a baptism in Mark 10:38 suggest that Ps 11:6 is a particularly probable candidate as the chief alluded text. Delling, "ΒΑΠΤΙΣΜΑ ΒΑΠΤΙΣΘΗΝΑΙ," 106, argues that, in view of the imagery of Ps 11:6, the seemingly contradictory images in Luke 12:49–50; Mark 10:38 are in fact unsurprising.

[99] Walter W. Wessel and Mark L. Strauss, "Mark," in vol. 9 of *EBC* (Grand Rapids: Zondervan, 2010), 951, note that the cup of Mark 14:36 "is the same one Jesus referred to in 10:38–39—the cup of the wrath of God," and detect the influence of Ps 11:6 among other texts. Though if my argument that Ps 11:6 is in the allusive foreground of Mark 10:38 is correct, its reverberations should still be heard in Mark 14:36. Cf. Hans F. Bayer, *Jesus' Predictions of Vindication and Resurrection*, WUNT 2/20 (Tübingen: Mohr, 1986), 70–85.

[100] Cf. Dietrich Bonhoeffer, "Sermon on a Psalm of Vengeance—Psalm 58," in *Meditating on the Word*, trans. and ed. David M. Gracie, 84–96 (Cambridge, Mass.: Cowley, 1986), 94.

recipient of the crown-battering punishment designated in the psalms against God's serpentine opponents. Jesus is exposed to shame and humiliation (Mark 15:16–20, 29–32; Acts 8:33;[101] Heb 12:2; cf. Pss 31:17; 35:4, 26; 40:14–15; 70:2; 71:13; 83:16–17; 86:17; 109:29; 119:78; 129:5) and ultimately put to death, blotted out of the book of the living (Mark 15:37; Acts 8:33; cf. Pss 58:8; 69:28; 104:35; 109:8–9). Following his declaration from Deut 27:26 that everyone who does not abide by the law is cursed, Paul explicitly argues in Gal 3:13 that Jesus' crucifixion was a subjection to the covenant curse for the sake of covenant breakers: "Christ redeemed us from the curse of the law by becoming a curse for us—for it is written, 'Cursed is everyone who is hanged on a tree'" (citing Deut 21:23).[102] The psalms characterize the imprecators' enemies as those who already bear the Deuteronomic curse, and they petition for the revelation of judgment within that covenantal framework (e.g., Pss 94:6; 119:21, 126),[103] but at Golgotha, it is the blameless Christ who bears—becomes—the Deuteronomic curse, judged as an accursed enemy on behalf of accursed enemies.[104] Indeed, Jesus "suffered outside the gate" (Heb 13:12), expelled in

[101] Noting that Acts 8:32–33 connects the "good news about Jesus" (v. 35) with the suffering servant of Isa 52:13–53:12 (cf. 1 Pet 2:22–25), Hamilton, "Skull-Crushing Seed," 42, proposes that the crushing of the servant by God for sin in vv. 5, 10 echoes the *protoevangelium*. The servant receives the crushing due to a people that has lived like the serpent seed. If we bring these two strands together—Jesus as the Isaianic servant and the Isaianic servant's crushing as theologically linked with Gen 3:15—then it could be argued that the New Testament's association of Jesus with the Isaianic servant presents Christ as taking upon himself the crushing vengeance of God against the serpent seed so that sinners who have walked in the way of the serpent seed might be acquitted and healed.

[102] On the intertextually and theologically dense text of Gal 3:10–13, cf. Moisés Silva, "Galatians," in *CNTOT*, 795–800; Richard N. Longenecker, *Galatians*, WBC 41 (Dallas: Word Books, 1990), 116–123; F. F. Bruce, *The Epistle to the Galatians*, NIGTC (Grand Rapids: Eerdmans, 1982), 157–67; Douglas J. Moo, *Galatians*, BECNT (Grand Rapids: Baker Academic, 2013), 201–14; J. Louis Martyn, *Galatians*, AB 33A (New York: Doubleday, 1997), 307–21. For a detailed rhetorical analysis of this text within its context in Galatians, cf. Kjell Arne Morland, *The Rhetoric of Curse in Galatians: Paul Confronts Another Gospel*, Emory Studies in Early Christianity (Atlanta: Scholars Press, 1995), 181–233.

[103] In the previous chapter, I argued that these psalm texts appeal to the curses of Deut 27:15–26, which in turn furnishes the text to which Paul alludes (Deut 27:26) when describing the curse upon those for whom Jesus became a curse (Gal 3:10).

[104] See Thomas R. Schreiner, *Galatians*, ZECNT (Grand Rapids: Zondervan, 2010), 217; Longenecker, *Galatians*, 122; Moo, *Galatians*, 214. Cf. James

his execution from the temple-city of God—like the sacrifices that atoned for Israel's uncleanness (Heb 13:11; cf. Lev 16) and like the unclean enemy who is driven in the imprecations from the land of God's presence.[105] "Jesus Christ died the death of the godless,"[106] occupying the place of psalmic enemy, enduring the cursed, expulsive judgment due covenant breakers and kingdom combatants.

In the New Testament's narration of the story of God's temple-kingdom, then, the enemy from the imprecatory psalms emerges as a remarkably flexible intertextual figure, allusively evoked to describe and theologically situate a variety of actors in the new covenant scene of redemptive history. Jesus is inundated by the covenantal justice of God at the cross, bearing the judgment due the psalmic enemy, and Christians are depicted as former participants in the enemy's opposition who now gladly follow the resurrected Lord as conquered foes. The adversaries who persist in their violent antipathy to Jesus and his people, however, continue the imprecated enemies' serpentine war against God's temple-kingdom and will reap at the consummation that divine vengeance for which the beleaguered psalmist prayed.

Echoes of the Divine: Covenant King and Coming Cosmic Judge

No less than the imprecating son of God and the cursed kingdom enemy, the divine judge from the imprecatory psalms is intertextually summoned into the New Testament's narrative of Christ's temple-kingdom. That is,

---

D. G. Dunn, *The Epistle to the Galatians*, BNTC (Peabody, Mass.: Hendrickson, 1993), 178. As many have noted, Paul omits the words "by God" in his citation of Deut 21:23 in v. 13, but the most compelling reasoning for this is that the omission creates a neat parallelism between his citations of Deut 27:26 in v. 10 and Deut 21:23 in v. 13 that emphasizes Christ's entrance into the very curse that condemns those who fail to uphold God's law. The verbal parallelism between the citations underscores the theological parallelism between Jesus' experience and the lawbreaker's condemnation.

[105] This thematic connection between the unclean enemy expelled from the land and the sacrifice that carries Israel's uncleanness out of the land is present in Leviticus 16–18. Whereas Leviticus 16 details the priestly duty to take the sacrifice that bears Israel's iniquities outside the camp, Lev 18:27–28 states that the previous inhabitants of the land were vomited out because of their abominations, which rendered the land unclean. The Day of Atonement may thus be interpreted as an Adamic priestly exercise, ritually driving out impurity from the land so that Israel may continue to dwell with the holy presence of God. Cf. Dempster, *Dominion and Dynasty*, 107–9.

[106] Bonhoeffer, "Sermon on a Psalm of Vengeance," 94.

the New Testament tells the story of God's continuing kingdom-restoring action in the world by allusively appealing to the role, character, and expectations of the covenantal warrior-king in the psalms of vengeance. How does the New Testament characterize the identity, activity, and future of the Father of Jesus in continuity with the God of the imprecations? How does Jesus himself play the part of the divine judge in the New Testament's intertextual narration, answering the psalmists' pleas for justice? Attending to these questions illuminates the ways in which the New Testament's witness to the judgment of God and the end of history testifies in the grammar of the imprecatory psalms and actualizes the kingdom-defending vengeance for which they long.

Across the New Testament, God is depicted as the certain administrant of cosmic judgment in terms drawn from the imprecations' portrait of the divine arbiter between the psalmists and their enemies. Echoing the psalmist's confession, "I am afraid of your judgments" (Ps 119:120)—a confession that follows his consideration of God's wrath upon the wicked (Ps 119:119)—Jesus exhorts his disciples in Luke 12:5, "Fear him who, after he has killed, has authority to cast into hell. Yes, I tell you, fear him!"[107] Jesus' allusive stirring of this canonical memory not only commends the psalmist's fear as an imitable posture before God but simultaneously associates his fear-worthy Father, possessed of authority to cast into hell, with the God whom the psalmist feared, the God of judgment who discards like dross all the wicked of the earth (Ps 119:119). Paul proclaims at the Areopagus that God "has fixed a day on which he will judge the world in righteousness" (Acts 17:31), turning David's confidence that the Lord "judges the world in righteousness" (Ps 9:8) into a future-oriented declaration that this righteous judgment will be definitively unveiled at the last day. The apostle's descriptions of eye-darkening judgment on Israel (Rom 11:9–10; cf. Ps 69:22–23),[108] sudden destruction that will come upon unbelievers (1 Thess 5:3; cf. Ps 35:8), and talionic affliction for the

---

[107] NA27 identifies this allusion.

[108] Intriguingly, while Paul quotes an imprecatory psalm to scripturally justify God's judgment on Israel, he alludes to another imprecatory psalm to affirm God's covenantal commitment to Israel when he echoes Ps 94:14 ("For the LORD will not forsake his people") just a few verses earlier in Rom 11:2: "God has not rejected his people whom he foreknew." Paul connects both God's covenant faithfulness to and his just judgment against Israel to the imprecations' portrait of God. Cf. Keesmaat, "Psalms in Romans and Galatians," 153–55.

church's afflicters (2 Thess 1:6; cf. Ps 137:8) each weave into pastoral discourse allusions to the imprecatory psalms that depict God's present or future juridical action against opponents of his temple-kingdom in terms of the judgments requested of God in the past. As these texts situate the enemies of Jesus and his church in the place of the psalmic enemy, they simultaneously present God's judgments as exhibiting continuity with the imprecators' theological portrait and expectations of God.

In 1 Pet 5:7, Peter encourages a suffering church to respond to God by "casting all your anxieties on him" in the certainty that God will exalt them at the proper time (v. 6). Peter's exhortation draws upon Ps 55:22— "Cast your burden on the LORD"[109]—a call to faithful reliance upon God that concludes David's imprecatory prayer and rises from the assurance that God will judge the enemy and vindicate his people.[110] Peter's republication of David's words thus appears to appeal not only to the psalmic text but also to the wider themes of divine judgment and vindication in the psalm,[111] pulling the psalmist's vision of God onto the horizon of his exhortation, calling the church to engage in the psalmic action of faithful dependence precisely because God remains the psalmic God who judges evil and vindicates the righteous.[112]

The Apocalypse, with its characteristic emphasis on divine judgment, likewise frames God's identity and acts in terms borrowed from the imprecatory psalms. John sees God "seated on the throne" in heaven (Rev 4:2), confirming God's cosmic royal authority and power

---

[109] 1 Peter 5:7 parallels the terminology of LXX Ps 54:23 in its use of ἐπιρίπτω and μέριμναν. Cf. Thomas R. Schreiner, *1, 2 Peter, Jude*, NAC 37 (Nashville: Broadman and Holman, 2003), 241; John H. Elliott, *1 Peter: A New Translation with Introduction and Commentary*, AB 37B (New York: Doubleday, 2000), 851; Paul J. Achtemeier, *1 Peter: A Commentary on First Peter*, ed. Eldon Jay Epp, Hermeneia (Minneapolis: Fortress, 1996), 339, esp. n56.

[110] Notably, Ps 55:22 is not only preceded by affirmations of vindication and deliverance (vv. 16–19) but is also immediately followed by v. 23: "But you, O God, will cast them down into the pit of destruction; men of blood and treachery shall not live out half their days. But I will trust in you."

[111] Cf. Schreiner, *1, 2 Peter, Jude*, 241.

[112] This raises an interesting question. In Psalm 55, David's call for Israel to cast her burden on the Lord is likely an exhortation to engage in the type of burden-casting imprecatory prayer that he has just modeled in the body of the psalm. See Goldingay, *Psalms: Volume 2*, 177. With his allusive exhortation for the marginalized church to cast her burdens on the Lord, might Peter be commending this type of prayer as well?

to issue judgment with the heavenly throne imagery of Ps 11:4.[113] It is this enthroned God who receives the imprecatory plea of Rev 6:10 (cf. Ps 79:10) and the incense prayers of Rev 8:3–4 (cf. Ps 141:2) and who ultimately answers them by manifesting his wrath, "for he has judged the great prostitute . . . and has avenged on her the blood of his servants" (Rev 19:2; cf. Ps 79:10). As the Apocalypse echoes the imprecatory psalms, it projects a vision of God as a royal judge who receives and responds to the church's vengeance prayers in accord with the psalms' testimony and expectations regarding his character and works of judgment. Revelation 16:1 records a loud voice from the temple instructing angels to "pour out on the earth the seven bowls of the wrath of God," depicting God's action as bringing to pass the requests of Ps 69:24 ("Pour out your indignation upon them, and let your burning anger overtake them") and Ps 79:6 ("Pour out your anger on the nations that do not know you").[114] The final judgment of the dead "according to what they had done" (Rev 20:12, 13) recalls David's plea in Ps 28:4: "Give to them according to their work and according to the evil of their deeds; give to them according to the work of their hands; render them their due reward."[115] In the Revelator's narration of history's culmination, God does what the imprecator asked, taking account of the deeds of the wicked and judging them with justice. Reverberating with Ps 10:16's declaration of God's enemy-clearing, eternal reign—"The LORD is king forever and ever (LXX Ps 9:37, βασιλεύσει κύριος . . . εἰς τὸν αἰῶνα τοῦ αἰῶνος); the nations perish from his land"—Rev 11:15 envisions the consummation of the kingdom when God cleanses his world of all opposition and establishes his never-ending rule: "The kingdom of the world has become the kingdom of our Lord and of his Christ, and he shall reign forever and ever (βασιλεύσει εἰς τοὺς αἰῶνας τῶν αἰώνων)."[116] The New Testament's

---

[113] Cf. Koester, *Revelation*, 360; NA27. Beale, *Book of Revelation*, 320, points out that, in Revelation, judgments frequently come forth from the throne of God, identifying 6:1–8, 16; 8:3–6; 16:17 as examples.

[114] Cf. Matthew Streett, *Here Comes the Judge: Violent Pacifism in the Book of Revelation*, LNTS 462 (New York: T&T Clark, 2012), 103; Osborne, *Revelation*, 578–79; Beale, *Book of Revelation*, 812–13; Roloff, *Revelation*, 188.

[115] Cf. NA27; Blount, *Revelation*, 373; Beale, *Book of Revelation*, 1033.

[116] NA27 lists a variety of possible allusions in Rev 11:15, including Ps 10:16; Dan 2:44; 7:14, 27. Cf. Thompson, *Revelation*, 128; Blount, *Revelation*, 220; Osborne, *Revelation*, 441–42; Beale, *Book of Revelation*, 611–12. While

intertextual appeals to the imprecatory psalms in its presentation of God cumulatively communicate that *that* God is *this* God. The divine avenger to whom the psalmists pray is the warrior-king who will judge the world. The God of the imprecations is the Father of Jesus.

And yet the psalmic descriptors of God in the imprecations are also applied within the New Testament to Jesus himself. Psalm 68 serves as an important intertext in New Testament reflection upon the meaning of Jesus' first coming, especially the description of God's former victory over his enemies and ascension to his temple throne in Zion in vv. 16–18:

> [16] Why do you look with hatred, O many-peaked mountain,
> at the mount that God desired for his abode,
> yes, where the LORD will dwell forever?
> [17] The chariots of God are twice ten thousand,
> thousands upon thousands;
> the Lord is among them; Sinai is now in the sanctuary.
> [18] You ascended on high,
> leading a host of captives in your train
> and receiving gifts among men,
> even among the rebellious, that the LORD God may dwell there.

LXX Ps 67:17 reads ὃ εὐδόκησεν ὁ θεὸς κατοικεῖν ἐν αὐτῷ, and in Col 1:19, Paul utilizes this language to characterize Jesus: "For in him (ἐν αὐτῷ) all the fullness of God was pleased (εὐδόκησεν) to dwell (κατοικῆσαι)."[117] Paul's echo evocatively identifies Christ as the holy temple presence of God on earth in whom God's royal dwelling among his people is restored.[118] I argued previously that the image of a God-led triumphal procession of Christians in 2 Cor 2:14 alludes to the host of captives in God's train in Ps 68:18, but it should be acknowledged here that in Paul's conception God leads his former enemies turned joyful captives "in Christ," with Jesus occupying the place of

---

each of these potential intertexts is united by themes of God's overcoming of enemies to establish his royal presence among his people, and while the echoes are by no means mutually exclusive, Rev 11:15 bears the most lexical similarity to the phrasing of LXX Ps 9:37.

[117] See Christopher A. Beetham, *Echoes of Scripture in the Letter of Paul to the Colossians*, BIS 96 (Boston: Brill, 2008), 143; G. K. Beale, "Colossians," in *CNTOT*, 856.

[118] Beetham, *Echoes of Scripture in the Letter of Paul to the Colossians*, 153; Beale, "Colossians," in *CNTOT*, 857. Cf. Scot McKnight, *The Letter to the Colossians*, NICNT (Grand Rapids: Eerdmans, 2018), 161.

the conquering divine king.[119] In Eph 4:8, Paul overtly references Ps 68:18 in his teaching on Jesus' ascension and conferring of gifts to the church: "Therefore it says, 'When he ascended on high he led a host of captives, and he gave gifts to men.'" Drawing upon the psalmic depiction of God's triumphal temple enthronement—wherein the divine warrior-king not only defeats his enemies and receives gifts (v. 18) but also "from his sanctuary . . . gives power and strength to his people" (v. 35)—Paul theologically frames Jesus as the ascending God who, after vanquishing his foes through death and resurrection, takes his heavenly throne and grants gifts to his temple-kingdom.[120] Peter makes a similar intertextual move at Pentecost, proclaiming that Jesus was "exalted at the right hand of God, and having received from the Father the promise of the Holy Spirit, he has poured out this that you yourselves are seeing and hearing" (Acts 2:33). The key movements of Psalm 68—exaltation to the throne, reception of gifts, and subsequent distribution of gifts—are allusively resourced as a lens for understanding Jesus' ascension and his reception and giving of the Spirit as the accomplishment and consequence of the victorious enthronement of God.[121] Each of these texts intertextually presents Jesus as inhabiting

[119]   Cf. Scott, "Triumph of God," 272; George H. Guthrie, 2 Corinthians, BECNT (Grand Rapids: Baker Academic, 2015), 164.

[120]   Timothy G. Gombis, "Cosmic Lordship and Divine Gift-Giving: Psalm 68 in Ephesians 4:8," NovT 47, no. 4 (2005): 375, persuasively argues that Paul is "appropriating the narrative movement of the entire psalm." Gombis responds to the influential argument of, e.g., W. Hall Harris III, The Descent of Christ: Ephesians 4:7-11 and Traditional Hebrew Imagery, AGJU 32 (Leiden: Brill, 1996), that the citation serves as part of an anti-Moses polemic (based on the Targum of Psalm 68) and demonstrates that the divine warrior motif leveraged in the quotation of Ps 68:18 fits with the themes of divine battle and victory throughout Ephesians. Cf. William N. Wilder, "The Use (or Abuse) of Power in High Places: Gifts Given and Received in Isaiah, Psalm 68, and Ephesians 4:8," BBR 20, no. 2 (2010): 185-200; Frank S. Thielman, "Ephesians," in CNTOT 824; Seth M. Ehorn, "The Use of Psalm 68(67).19 in Ephesians 4.8: A History of Research," CBR 12, no. 1 (2012): 96-120.

[121]   On the allusion to Ps 68:18, cf. Lindars, New Testament Apologetic, 51-59. As is the case with the allusion to Ps 68:18 in Eph 4:8, several interpreters read Acts 2:33 as an allusion to Moses ascending Sinai and giving the Torah to men in the Targum of Ps 68:18. E.g., Wilfred L. Knox, The Acts of the Apostles (Cambridge: Cambridge University Press, 1948), 85-86; G. K. Beale, "The Descent of the Eschatological Temple in the Form of the Spirit at Pentecost, Part 2: Corroborating Evidence," TynBul 56, no. 2 (2005): 69-72. On the problems

the role of God in Psalm 68, and taken together, they tell a story in which Christ temples as the presence of God among his people, overcomes the enemies of his dominion as the divine warrior-king, ascends in triumph to his throne in heaven, and dispenses gifts upon the inaugurated temple-kingdom over whom he reigns and with whom he resides by his Spirit. Indeed, a fundamental longing of the imprecatory psalms—that the holy warrior-king would drive out his enemies so that his people might flourish in the ruling presence of God—finds an initial answer in Jesus' first advent.[122]

Elsewhere, the New Testament appeals to the imprecatory psalms' portrait of God to describe Jesus' exercise of judgment. John the Baptist announces of the Christ that "the chaff he will burn with unquenchable fire" (Luke 3:17), appropriating imagery that resonates with the imprecatory pleas of Ps 83:13–15 to make the enemies of God's temple-kingdom "like chaff before the wind" and to pursue them "as fire consumes the forest."[123] The theophanic flame judgment upon the enemy chaff that is requested in Psalm 83—and referenced frequently in the Old Testament in

---

with this reading, see Darrell L. Bock, *Proclamation from Prophecy and Pattern: Lucan Old Testament Christology*, LNTS 12 (Sheffield: Sheffield Academic Press, 1987), 182–83; Harold W. Hoehner, *Ephesians: An Exegetical Commentary* (Grand Rapids: Baker Academic, 2002), 527. There is certainly a new Moses typology at work in the events of Pentecost. However, given that the focus of Acts 2:32–36 is on the exaltation of Jesus to a position of royal authority that reveals his identity as "both Lord and Christ" (v. 36) and that Peter's sermon has already applied an Old Testament text about God to Jesus (Joel 2:32 in Acts 2:21), I find it much more compelling to interpret Peter's allusion to Ps 68:18 as contributing to the association between Jesus' ascension and God's victorious enthronement.

[122]   Though there is no clear allusion, the account in Acts 8:26–40 of the conversion of "an Ethiopian, a eunuch, a court official of Candace, queen of the Ethiopians, who was in charge of all her treasure" (v. 27) resonates with the promise of Ps 68:31—"Cush [that is, Ethiopia] shall hasten to stretch her hands out to God." Cf. Marshall, "Acts," in *CNTOT*, 573. Read through the lens of Psalm 68 (a lens for interpreting Christ's ascension already supplied by Acts 2:33), the Ethiopian's conversion may be understood as an initial turning of the nations in homage to Christ as a result of Jesus' heavenly enthronement over his inaugurated kingdom. Jesus won victory over the enemies of his kingdom by his death and resurrection and, having taken his throne in his ascension, now receives the first offering of the nations' allegiance.

[123]   Cf. Pao and Schnabel, "Luke," in *CNTOT*, 279.

connection with God's vengeance upon the wicked[124]—is here attributed to Jesus.[125] The Son of Man declares of himself in Matt 16:27 that when he comes in his Father's glory, "he will repay each person according to what he has done," taking in his own hands the divine prerogative of distributing talionic justice (cf. Ps 28:4).[126] Paul reminds the Thessalonians that "the Lord is an avenger" (1 Thess 4:6), appropriating the language of Ps 94:1 ("O LORD, God of vengeance") to describe the Lord Jesus as the requiter of unrighteousness.[127] In his ensuing discussion of Christ's return, Paul states of unbelievers that "sudden destruction will come upon them" (1 Thess 5:3), envisioning Jesus' *parousia* as manifesting the judgment requested of God in Ps 35:8 ("Let destruction come upon him when he does not know it!"). Readdressing Christ's return in 2 Thessalonians 1, Paul details Jesus as "inflicting vengeance on those who do not know God" (v. 8), casting Jesus' appearing in the mold of the psalmist's plea for God to pour out his anger on the nations "that do not know you" (Ps 79:6).[128] The apostle goes on to describe Jesus' expulsion of the wicked from his glorious presence at his second advent (v. 9) "when he comes on that day to be glorified in his saints (ἐν τοῖς ἁγίοις αὐτοῦ), and to be marveled at (θαυμασθῆναι) among all who have believed" (v. 10) and in so doing allusively associates Christ with the marvelous, avenging God of LXX Ps 67:36 (θαυμαστὸς ὁ θεὸς ἐν τοῖς ἁγίοις αὐτοῦ; lit., "Marvelous is God in his holy ones").[129] And in 2

---

[124] Pao and Schnabel, "Luke," in *CNTOT*, 279, Pao and Schnabel point to Mal 4:1; Isa 29:5–6; Obad 18 as instances of chaff and fire imagery utilized to depict divine judgment. Examples could be multiplied: e.g., Isa 5:24; 47:14; Joel 2:5; Nah 1:6–10.

[125] See Vern S. Poythress, *Theophany: A Biblical Theology of God's Appearing* (Wheaton, Ill.: Crossway, 2018), 44, on the parallel text in Matt 3:12.

[126] Cf. Blomberg, "Matthew," in *CNTOT*, 55; Turner, *Matthew*, 412.

[127] Paul's ἔκδικος κύριος parallels the θεὸς ἐκδικήσεων κύριος of LXX Ps 93:1. See Jeffrey A. D. Weima, "1–2 Thessalonians," in *CNTOT*, 877–78. Cf. Fee, *First and Second Letters to the Thessalonians*, 151; Charles A. Wanamaker, *The Epistles to the Thessalonians*, NIGTC (Grand Rapids: Eerdmans, 1990), 156; I. Howard Marshall, *1 and 2 Thessalonians*, New Century Bible Commentary (Grand Rapids: Eerdmans, 1983), 112.

[128] Cf. Weima, "1–2 Thessalonians," in *CNTOT*, 884; Marshall, *1 and 2 Thessalonians*, 177–78; Ernest Best, *A Commentary on the First and Second Epistles to the Thessalonians*, BNTC (London: Adam & Charles Black, 1972), 259–60.

[129] Cf. Fee, *First and Second Letters to the Thessalonians*, 261–62; Wanamaker, *Epistles to the Thessalonians*, 230–31; Weima, "1–2 Thessalonians," in *CNTOT*, 885–86.

Tim 4:14, Paul takes comfort in the wake of Alexander's harmful action that "the Lord will repay him according to his deeds," proclaiming that the divine talionic retribution of Ps 28:4 will be meted out by "Christ Jesus, who is to judge the living and the dead" (v. 1).[130]

Revelation continues to develop the portrait of Jesus as divine judge through allusion to the imprecatory psalms. Where Ps 69:28 ascribes to God the authority to blot persons out of the book of the living, Jesus assumes this very authority for himself when he promises to every Sardisian Christian who conquers that he "will never blot his name out of the book of life" (Rev 3:5).[131] The imprecatory incense prayers for wrath upon the church's tormentors, drawn from Ps 141:2 and presented to God in Rev 8:3–4, are in Rev 5:8 offered to the Lamb before whom the twenty-four elders fall. Revelation 19:11–16 records John's vision of Jesus—called Faithful and True (v. 11), King of kings and Lord of lords (v. 16)[132]—leading the armies of heaven as a divine warrior-king (v. 14), "and in righteousness he judges" (v. 11), this phrase an evocation of God's righteous judgment in Ps 9:8.[133] At the Apocalypse's conclusion, Jesus announces with an echo of God's proportional retribution in Ps 28:4 that he is coming soon "to repay each one for what he has done" (Rev 22:12).[134] With its manifold resonances with the imprecatory psalms, the New Testament that portrays Jesus as the human son of God who mediates God's judgment simultaneously presents him as the divine judge of the cosmos, the warrior-king who with his second coming consummates the judgment and the kingdom that he inaugurated with his first.[135]

---

[130]   Philip H. Towner, "1–2 Timothy and Titus," in *CNTOT*, 908–9. Cf. George W. Knight III, *The Pastoral Epistles: A Commentary on the Greek Text*, NIGTC (Grand Rapids: Eerdmans, 1992), 467–68.

[131]   Cf. Mounce, *Revelation*, 96; Beale, *Book of Revelation*, 281; Koester, *Revelation*, 314–15; Blount, *Revelation*, 71.

[132]   Both of these names attributed to Jesus are titles for God. Cf. 3 Macc 2:11; LXX Dan 4:37; and the comments by Beale, *Book of Revelation*, 950, 963–64.

[133]   Cf. NA27; Koester, *Revelation*, 753; Beale, *Book of Revelation*, 950–51; Osborne, *Revelation*, 680.

[134]   Blount, *Revelation*, 407; Osborne, *Revelation*, 788, acknowledge that Ps 28:4 is likely one of several texts supplying the background of Rev 22:12. Cf. NA27.

[135]   Additional New Testament texts allude to the imprecatory psalms in a manner that intertextually presents Jesus as occupying the place of God. E.g.,

The imprecatory psalms testify that the future of the divine judge is one in which he receives thanksgiving, worship, and glory for his prayer-answering vengeance on behalf of his temple-kingdom, and the New Testament alludes to the imprecations to describe the praise offered to God in the wake of his acts of judgment. The 144,000 of Rev 14:2–3 sing with harp-like voices a new song and rejoice over God's judgment, rendering the sort of thankful adulation David vowed to offer in response to God's delivering wrath (Ps 144:9). Where Ps 86:9 joyfully anticipated that all the nations would one day come and worship God, the church in Rev 15:4 responds to God's climactic judgments at history's consummation by singing the imprecator's words as an unfolding reality: "All nations will come and worship you, for your righteous acts have been revealed." In response to his liberating vengeance, the saints worship God by delighting in the nations' soon-to-be-realized worship of God. The threefold hallelujah that follows the eschatological manifestation of God's judgment in Rev 19:1–4 echoes the הַלְלוּ־יָהּ prompted in Ps 104:35 by the psalmist's cry for the consumption of sinners from the earth, praising the Lord in psalmic register for definitively clearing the world of wickedness. And in Rev 21:24, the "kings of the earth will bring their glory into" the new Jerusalem, the realized temple-city of God, offering the multinational worship Ps 68:29 foretold when it declared, "Because of your temple at Jerusalem kings shall bear gifts to you."[136] God's future, according to the New Testament, is indeed one characterized by praise, thanksgiving, and adoration, wherein the worship offered and anticipated in the imprecatory psalms is given voice in the exultation of God's kingdom people and redounds to the glory of the God who exercises justice upon his enemies, clears all uncleanness from the place of his royal presence, and reigns over and with his covenant community forever.

Before moving on, we would be well served to review in broad strokes the story that the New Testament narrates through intertextual reference to and thematic development of the imprecatory psalms and the diverse ways that its authors frame the characters in this Christian act of God's redemptive-historical drama within the roles of the principal actors of the imprecations' narrative world. This story may be recounted from three

---

Matt 14:30 (Ps 69:1–2); Mark 2:8 (Ps 139:23); Luke 21:33 (Ps 119:160); Rom 9:5 (Ps 41:13); Rev 2:6 (Ps 139:21).

[136] While the primary alluded text in Rev 21:24 is almost certainly Isa 60:3–5, the imagery resonates with Ps 68:29 as well. Cf. NA27; Beale, *Book of Revelation*, 1100.

different but complementary angles, each of which foregrounds one of the figures of the imprecatory psalms:

- As the royal-priestly son of God *par excellence*, the innocent Christ suffers injustice in his death and is vindicated by his resurrection. With his dying and rising, Jesus initially subdues the enemies of the temple-kingdom and at his return will mediate God's judgment upon the wicked, expelling them from the land where God dwells so that God's people may live in peace under God's reign. Until then, the suffering church enacts her vocation as the sons and daughters of God by guarding the temple-kingdom and subduing the earth as sacred space in prayer—driving out the enemy through prayer for God's vindicating vengeance, awaiting the last day when she shall participate in the actualization of divine judgment as a priest-king of God.

- The violently unjust enemies—the schemers against Jesus, the antagonists of his church, and the spiritual foes of God's people—continue the serpent seed's opposition to God's temple-kingdom and will experience divine eschatological judgment when God definitively expels them from the place of his royal presence. Jesus, however, receives in his crucifixion the judgment curse due to God's enemies, and Christians are those enemies who by faith have become joyful captives of Christ.

- With his first coming, Jesus acted as the divine warrior-king to decisively defeat the foes of his kingdom, ascend to his heavenly throne, and pour out blessing upon his temple people, and with his second coming, Jesus will exercise talionic justice and vengeance against God's enemies as the cosmic judge. On that last day, God too will arise and answer his church's petitions by judging the world in righteousness, and he will receive the praises of his people and the glory of the nations as he dwells in his renewed temple-city—the new heavens and new earth, the consummated kingdom of God.

These angles on Scripture's unfolding redemptive-historical narrative draw attention to the figural flexibility and Christological polyvalence of the New Testament's intertextual appropriation of the imprecatory psalms: each of the principal actors in the imprecations' narrative world is allusively resourced to portray multiple actors in the New Testament's redemptive-historical narration, and Jesus is depicted as climactically filling the roles and destinies of all three. Jesus embodies the figure of the enemy, the son of God, and the divine judge—enduring God's wrath, experiencing suffering before vindication and mediating God's judgment as a human priest-king, and exacting vengeance as the divine warrior-king. From this perspective, the cross of Christ is simultaneously his bearing of the covenantal curse on behalf of God's enemies, his unjust murder at the hands of God's enemies, his royal-priestly disempowering of God's enemies, and his divine victory over God's enemies. And in his *parousia*, Jesus will complete his work as the human mediator and divine administrant of cosmic justice, expelling the wicked from the land and making the world the kingdom where God dwells in unobstructed joy, peace, and covenantal communion with his people forever.

Imprecatory Speech Acts in the New Testament

Having examined in detail the New Testament's deployment of the text and themes of the imprecatory psalms in its narration of and reflection upon God's kingdom-restoring action in Jesus, including the ways the New Testament draws upon the roles of the various actors within the imprecations' storied world to frame the characters in the Christian era of redemptive history, we can now employ the narrative perspective generated by the preceding analysis as a lens for theologically and ethically interpreting the imprecatory speech acts of the New Testament. How do the New Testament's imprecatory speech acts mirror the contours of the psalms' petitions for justice? How does the redemptive-historical narrative surveyed above illuminate the roles occupied and acted out in the requests for divine judgment that arise in Jesus' teaching and the Christian authors' writing? And how does this scriptural story supply a moral logic that renders ethically intelligible the imprecatory petitions recorded, modeled, and encouraged within the New Testament?

Give Me Justice against My Adversary: Luke 18:1–8

"And he told them a parable to the effect that they ought always to pray and not lose heart" (Luke 18:1). In this prayer-stimulating, courage-inducing parable, Jesus recounts a widow's unrelenting petition to an unjust judge: "Give me justice against my adversary" (v. 3). Though the judge is prompted to act by love of neither God nor humanity (cf. Luke 10:27),[137] he at last grants her justice out of self-preservation so that her continual pleading will not expose his injustice and jeopardize his position of influence (vv. 4–5).[138] With the unjust judge's internal dialogue still

---

[137]   Cf. Donald Penny, "Persistence in Prayer: Luke 18:1–8," *RevExp* 104 (2007): 739.

[138]   Cf. John Mark Hicks, "The Parable of the Persistent Widow (Luke 18:1–8)," *ResQ* 33, no. 4 (1991): 217–18; Marshall, *Gospel of Luke*, 672–73; François

ringing, Jesus asks, "And will not God give justice to his elect who cry to him day and night?" (v. 7), affirming that God will indeed give justice to the people with whom he is in covenant (v. 8).[139] Jesus concludes with a question, inquiring whether the Son of Man will find faith on earth when he comes, ending where v. 1 began, with a focus on the necessity of persistent prayer to God for justice as his followers wait for the revelation of the Son of Man, the consummation of the temple-kingdom of God, and the manifestation of perfect judgment.[140]

The exemplary widow of this parable suffers unjustly and requests justice against her adversary, petitioning the judge to take up her cause in a manner that makes public the wrongdoing of the offender, vindicates the widow's innocence, eliminates the threat of ongoing oppression, and renders due punishment to the offender.[141] She is, in Jesus' parabolic scene, an imprecator, pleading that her adversary's injustice would not continue

---

Bovon, *Luke 2: A Commentary on the Gospel of Luke 9:51–19:27*, trans. Donald S. Deer, ed. Helmut Koester, Hermeneia (Minneapolis: Fortress, 2013), 534.

[139] Scholars differ over whether ἐν τάχει ("quickly") is best understood in the sense of "suddenly" (e.g., Bovon, *Luke 2*, 536–37) or "soon" (e.g., John Nolland, *Luke 9:21–18:34*, WBC 35B [Dallas: Word Books, 1993], 870). Regardless of which sense one prefers, the main thrust of Jesus' statement is that God will certainly give justice. The term ἐκλεκτός in v. 7 occurs in, e.g., LXX Pss 88:4, 20; 104:6, 43; 105:5, 23 to describe those in covenant with God, those chosen for relationship with God. Cf. Pao and Schnabel, "Luke," in *CNTOT*, 349; Herman Hendrickx, *The Parables of Jesus: Studies in the Synoptic Gospels* (San Francisco: Harper and Row, 1986), 223.

[140] These themes are linked in Dan 7:13–14, which likely provides the Old Testament background for Jesus' self-appellation, and they are linked as well in the immediately preceding account of Jesus' teaching (Luke 17:20–37), where a discussion of the kingdom of God is followed by an extended statement regarding the coming of the Son of Man in judgment. Cf. Pao and Schnabel, "Luke," in *CNTOT*, 349; Hicks, "Parable of the Persistent Widow," 221.

[141] Cf. Bovon, *Luke 2*, 533; E. Earle Ellis, *The Gospel of Luke*, rev. ed., NCB (London: Oliphants, 1974), 213; Benjamin B. Warfield, "The Importunate Widow and the Alleged Failure of Faith," *ExpTim* 25, no. 3 (1913): 70–71. Nolland, *Luke 9:21–18:34*, 868, argues that the widow's request "could be a call for vengeance, but an appeal for protective or restorative justice is permitted by the language and is much more in keeping with the widow image." However, the almost universally acknowledged resonance of this text with Sir 35:17–25, where God answers the cries of widows with crushing judgment and shattering vengeance, suggests the opposite. Given the allusive association with the petitioning widows of Sir 35:17–25, the widow image in Jesus' parable makes it more likely—not less—that the justice requested is a full-orbed justice that includes juridical punishment.

unacknowledged and unabated but would be interrupted and rectified by authoritative judicial action, paralleling in her relentless requests the concerns of the justice prayers that are typical of the imprecatory psalms. Given that even the unjust judge eventually capitulates to the widow's beseeching, Jesus declares that God—not the kind of judge who must be badgered into self-protective action—will at the coming of the Son of Man certainly give justice to his chosen ones who follow in the pattern of the imprecating widow and cry to him for justice day and night.[142] The juxtaposition of this parable with Jesus' teaching on his disciples' desire for and the nature of the Son of Man's return (Luke 17:22-37) further suggests that the vindicating justice for which his people pray,[143] and which God will bring, includes the destruction of the wicked that Jesus associates with his advent (Luke 17:26-30).[144] The Son of Man is, in Daniel 7, a simultaneously priestly and royal figure—one who enters the heavenly temple on clouds like incense and receives everlasting dominion over all the nations of the earth—and Jesus' adoption of this title constitutes a self-identification as the eschatological priest-king who will fulfill the original Adamic commission.[145] Jesus

[142] See Bovon, *Luke 2*, 535; Joel B. Green, *The Gospel of Luke*, NICNT (Grand Rapids: Eerdmans, 1997), 642; R. C. H. Lenski, *The Interpretation of St. Luke's Gospel* (Minneapolis: Augsburg, 1946), 895–96.

[143] The elect's cries for justice seem to link back to Luke 17:22, where Jesus tells his disciples that in coming days they "will desire to see one of the days of the Son of Man" before describing the destruction upon the wicked that will accompany his coming. In the flow of Luke 17:22–18:8, then, the disciples' desire for the Son of Man's coming in liberating judgment, which Jesus asserts will not be instantly gratified (17:22), will one day come to fruition, a promise that ought to stimulate the disciples' perseverant prayer for God's avenging justice and the Son of Man's return (18:7–8). They therefore ought not lose heart but rather continue in prayer (18:1) for the justice of God and the advent of the Son of Man and his kingdom.

[144] Though there is debate over the meaning of ἐκδικέω within Jesus' parable, the wider context of Luke 17:20–37 clarifies any potential ambiguity over the nature of God's giving of justice as the true judge in the extraparabolic world. Jesus' immediately preceding teaching on the coming of the Son of Man must be permitted to illuminate what is involved in the granting of divine justice at the coming of the Son of Man in Luke 18:8. The inclusion of a retributive sense in the ἐκδίκησις of vv. 7–8 agrees with the use of the term in other NT texts where avenging is clearly in view (e.g., Luke 21:22; Acts 7:24; Rom 12:19; 2 Thess 1:8; 1 Pet 2:14; Heb 10:30).

[145] See esp. Nicholas Perrin, *Jesus the Priest* (Grand Rapids: Baker Academic, 2018), 168–84.

therefore holds out the assurance of God's liberating and avenging judgment when the royal-priestly Son of Man comes to definitively establish his world-encompassing kingdom (cf. Dan 7:13–14) as a motivation for his followers to persevere in prayer for justice.[146] Like the imprecatory psalms, which ground their petitions for vengeance in the covenantal promises of God's kingdom-restoring judgment, the prayers of Christ's disciples for divine justice are to be galvanized by the hopeful certitude that God will indeed make his temple-kingdom a creation-wide reality and exercise vindicating vengeance against the adversaries of his people. Jesus' final question communicates that such prayers for God's justice against believers' enemies are evidence of the faith the Son of Man desires to find when he comes: Jesus desires his disciples' desires for divine justice.[147]

With the parable of Luke 18:1–8, Jesus thus exhorts his followers to continually engage in a type of prayer that bears all the marks of the psalmists' imprecations—to petition the covenant God and judge of the world to give justice to his chosen ones, vindicating their righteousness and judging the wicked, enervated by the eschatological expectation that justice will be theirs when God's priest-king acts to consummate his kingdom.[148] Interpreted through the lens of the scriptural story I have outlined, Jesus the royal priest calls his disciples to unflaggingly pray as royal-priestly sons and daughters of God, defending in prayer the people over and with whom God reigns from the oppression of the enemy, begging God to interrupt, expose, and expel the unjust who terrorize the innocent and compromise the *shalom* of the temple-kingdom in the assurance that this is precisely what he intends to do.[149] And insofar as the petitioned justice of the Son of Man includes the consummation of all creation as the temple-kingdom of

[146]   Cf. Marshall, *Gospel of Luke*, 676; Pao and Schnabel, "Luke," in *CNTOT*, 293; Joseph A. Fitzmyer, *The Gospel According to Luke (I–IX)*, AB 28 (Garden City: Doubleday and Company, 1981), 211.

[147]   On prayer as the fruit of the desired faith of v. 8, cf. Marshall, *Gospel of Luke*, 676; Hendrickx, *Parables of Jesus*, 229; Hicks, "Parable of the Persistent Widow," 221.

[148]   Cf. David P. Murray, "Christian Cursing?" in *Sing a New Song: Recovering Psalm Singing for the Twenty-First Century*, ed. Joel R. Beeke and Anthony T. Selvaggio (Grand Rapids: Reformation Heritage Books, 2010), 117; Marti J. Steussy, "The Enemy in the Psalms," *WW* 28, no. 1 (2008): 9.

[149]   Dorothy Jean Weaver, "Luke 18:1–8," *Int* 56, no. 3 (2002): 319: "As Luke sees it, *justice is the name for God's action in the world to make right what is wrong. And prayer is the name for the collaboration of humans in that act of God.*" Emphasis original. Prayer for the manifestation of divine justice through God's singular priest-king is one way the royal-priestly sons and daughters of God

God, disciples' justice prayers participate in the subduing of the earth and its cleansing from unholiness to be sacred space for the holy presence of the Lord. Read within this redemptive-historical narrative, Christians' widow-like practice of crying out to God day and night for justice and Christ's commendation of this imprecatory practice become ethically comprehensible, aligning with the God-ordained *telos* of history and Christians' God-given vocation as judgment-mediating, kingdom-defending, enemy-expelling priest-kings in God's drama of redemption.

Let Them Be Accursed: Galatians 1:8–9; 5:12; 1 Corinthians 16:22

Though the nature of the threat posed by the Judaizers to the Galatian churches is never specifically spelled out, this much is certain: Paul considers their foregrounding of the foreskin in the practice of circumcision as tantamount to preaching "a different gospel" (1:6), one that enslaves by, in a bitter irony, freeing its adherents from Christ (5:1–4).[150] With their distorting of the gospel, the Judaizing enemies trouble the Christian community (1:7), jeopardizing the faith, witness, joy, and identity of God's temple-kingdom people, the *ekklesia* over whom Jesus reigns and with whom his Spirit resides.

Against anyone who preaches an anti-gospel gospel, Paul states, "Let him be accursed" (ἀνάθεμα ἔστω, 1:8, 9). Paul includes himself in this imprecation—"But even if we . . . should preach to you a gospel contrary" (v. 8)—welcoming, like the imprecator in the psalms (e.g., Pss 7:3–5, 8; 139:1–6, 23–24), God's examination and just judgment should his own conduct warrant condemnation,[151] regarding himself as a potential object of divine wrath.[152] And like the psalmists' imprecations, the apostolic

---

participate in the judgment of God for the sake of the temple-kingdom and the world in this time before the time of eschatological justice.

[150] Note the play on words in 5:1–4: Christ has come to set free; the Judaizers reimpose a yoke of slavery; those who follow them are devastatingly freed (καταργέω, v. 4) not from slavery, but from Christ. On the probable character of the Judaizers' teaching, see John M. G. Barclay, "Mirror-Reading a Polemical Letter: Galatians as a Test-Case," *JSNT* 31 (1987): 73–93. Cf. Longenecker, *Galatians*, xcviii.

[151] Cf. Martinus C. de Boer, *Galatians: A Commentary*, NTL (Louisville, Westminster John Knox, 2011), 47; Hans Dieter Betz, *Galatians: A Commentary on Paul's Letter to the Churches in Galatia*, Hermeneia (Philadelphia: Fortress, 1979), 52–53; Martyn, *Galatians*, 114.

[152] Betz, *Galatians*, 54, suggests that the *anathema* amounts essentially to excommunication, but while excommunication of offenders would be a

anathema is theologically predicated upon the preceding reality—the already-announced, authoritative declaration—of God's covenantal curse against those who rely on works of the law (Gal 3:10) and are severed from Christ (Gal 5:4). In psalmic fashion, Paul appeals for covenantal justice, asking only for that accursing judgment God has already promised to execute, upon those who already bear God's curse. Both the character and the target of Paul's imprecatory petition are covenantally determined by and grounded in God's prior promises.

The term ἀνάθεμα is a frequent LXX rendering of חֵרֶם that refers to a thing devoted or consecrated to God and removed from ordinary use[153]— whether by destruction or transfer to the exclusive ownership of God. The term is applied to unclean Israel and her idolatrous cities (e.g., Josh 7:12; Deut 13:15)[154] as well as Canaanite cities and materials in the context of holy war and conquest (e.g., Num 21:2–3; Josh 6:17).[155] It is thematically associated with Israel's royal-priestly task to guard the purity of and drive out uncleanness from the people among whom and the land in which God makes his holy, royal dwelling.[156] Read against this septuagintal background,

consistent ecclesial response to those who fall under the *anathema*, Moo, *Galatians*, 80, is correct in arguing that "what is involved is nothing less than suffering the judicial wrath of God," not least because excommunication cannot be primarily in view if the offending agent is "an angel from heaven" (Gal 1:8). Cf. Schreiner, *Galatians*, 87–88; Longenecker, *Galatians*, 17; Ronald Y. K. Fung, *The Epistle to the Galatians*, NICNT (Grand Rapids: Eerdmans, 1988), 47–48. At any rate, a strong distinction between excommunication and divine wrath is unwarranted. If church discipline is indeed one means by which God manifests his judgment in the world (à la 1 Cor 5:5) and identifies those who apart from repentance will subsequently bear eschatological judgment, then there is no conflict in understanding Paul's *anathema* as a petition for divine judgment that includes but is not exhausted by ecclesial excommunication.

[153]   Cf. J. Behm, "ἀνατίθημι, προσανατίθημι, ἀνάθεμα, ἀνάθημα, κατάθεμα, ἀναθεματίζω, καταθεματίζω," in *TDNT*, 1:354, and the conceptual contours of John H. Walton and J. Harvey Walton, *The Lost World of the Israelite Conquest: Covenant, Retribution, and the Fate of the Canaanites* (Downers Grove, Ill.: IVP Academic, 2017), 169–78.

[154]   Cf. Morland, *Rhetoric of Curse*, 81–97, esp. 94. The verb חרם is used to describe the mandated fate of individual Israelites who sacrifice to other gods in Exod 22:20 and is translated in LXX with ὀλεθρεύω.

[155]   On the LXX background of ἀνάθεμα, cf. de Boer, *Galatians*, 45; Moo, *Galatians*, 80; Schreiner, *Galatians*, 87–88; Longenecker, *Galatians*, 17. *Contra* Bruce, *Galatians*, 83.

[156]   Cf. G. K. Beale, *The Morality of God in the Old Testament*, Christian Answers to Hard Questions (Philadelphia: Westminster Seminary Press;

Paul's petition for divine judgment upon the corrupters of Christ's church may be understood as a petition for the ecclesial expulsion and eschatological destruction of those who, like serpents, would infiltrate and defile the kingdom community that is the temple of God's presence.[157] Paul's *anathema* undoubtedly functions at a rhetorical level as more than a request, warning the Galatians against following such teachers into wrath and urging them to regard and separate from the Judaizers as accursed,[158] but the apostolic "let them be" is certainly not less than a request.[159] In asking for the judgment of the church's deadly troublers, Paul petitions as a priest-king and son of God, guarding God's temple-kingdom from the serpentlike enemies who threaten her life, peace, holiness, and flourishing.

In Gal 5:12, Paul expresses his desire regarding these same enemies, "I wish those who unsettle you would emasculate themselves!" "A little leaven leavens the whole lump" (v. 9), and the Judaizers have introduced their uncleanness into the church, polluting God's community with their sinfully seductive celebration of circumcision. Paul's wish may at first appear to be little more than coarse jest or bitter sarcasm,[160] but in light

---

Phillipsburg, N.J.: P&R Publishing, 2013), 10–11; Meredith G. Kline, *Kingdom Prologue: Genesis Foundations for a Covenantal Worldview* (Eugene, Ore.: Wipf and Stock, 2006), 86–87; Dempster, *Dominion and Dynasty*, 127; Hamilton, *God's Glory in Salvation through Judgment*, 141–42.

[157] In 2 Cor 11:3–4, Paul explicitly compares false apostles who bring a εὐαγγέλιον ἕτερον ("different gospel," cf. Gal 1:6) to the serpent who entered the first garden-temple to deceive and destroy. Later in the same passage (vv. 13–15), Paul calls these pseudo-apostles servants of Satan whose end in judgment will match their wicked works. In both Gal 1:6–9 and 2 Cor 11:3–4, 13–15, Paul addresses false teachers preaching a different gospel, one contrary to the true gospel the church received from Paul. The characterization of these false teachers in 2 Corinthians 11 as deceptive serpents and servants of Satan who will be judged by God is consistent with his call in Gal 1:8–9 that the false teachers be expelled in judgment from God's temple-kingdom community.

[158] Cf. Morland, *Rhetoric of Curse*, 163–65.

[159] Gordon P. Wiles, *Paul's Intercessory Prayers: The Significance of the Intercessory Prayer Passages in the Letters of St. Paul* (New York: Cambridge University Press, 1974), 129, characterizes Paul in his utterance of the *anathema* as "an intercessor before God." Cf. Ernest De Witt Burton, *A Critical and Exegetical Commentary on the Epistle to the Galatians*, ICC (New York: Charles Scribner's Sons, 1920), 28; Franz Mußner, *Der Galaterbrief*, HTKNT 9 (Freiburg: Herder, 1974), 60–61.

[160] Cf. Betz, *Galatians*, 270; Longenecker, *Galatians*, 233–34. Recognition of the important cultural and scriptural background to Paul's wish fills out the

of the practice throughout Galatia and Phrygia of castrating priestly *galli* for service in the Cybeline goddess cult and the Deuteronomic prohibition of the emasculated and those with severed genitalia from entering the Lord's assembly (Deut 23:1),[161] Paul's imprecatory desire in fact turns on a far more subtle and ironic logic. Against the teachers who would cut others' members by circumcision in a manner that cuts recipients off from Christ (Gal 5:4), Paul wishes that they would cut their members completely in a manner that, according to their own adherence to the Mosaic code, cuts them off from the covenant community and simultaneously exposes them as the functional equivalent of a pagan priesthood committed to ritual castration.[162] The apostle voices his psalm-like desire that the enemies of the church would be revealed in their shameful, true colors (e.g., Pss 35:4, 26; 40:14–15) and experience a talionic turning of their sin upon their own heads (e.g., Pss 7:15–16; 140:9), that the severing they inflict on others would be inflicted upon them, so that the leaven that is the Judaizers would be removed, cleansed, cut off from the lump that is the people of God. Galatians 5:12 is, in this way, a yearning for the protection of God's temple-kingdom and the expulsion of her unclean antagonizers, a yearning fit for a son of God.

Paul concludes 1 Corinthians with an imprecatory *anathema* in 16:22 similar to those in Gal 1:8–9: "If anyone has no love for the Lord, let him be accursed (ἤτω ἀνάθεμα). Our Lord, come (Μαράνα θά)!"[163] Paul has already affirmed in 3:17 that God will destroy any who, like the invading nations of Ps 79:1, destructively defile the holy temple of God that is the Corinthian

---

interpreter's appreciation of Paul's sophisticated, though admittedly graphic, statement.

[161] See James R. Edwards, "Galatians 5:12: Circumcision, the Mother Goddess, and the Scandal of the Cross," *NovT* 53, no. 4 (2011): 319–37. The relevance of Deut 23:1 is widely acknowledged: e.g., Frederick W. Weidmann, *Galatians*, Westminster Bible Companion (Louisville: Westminster John Knox, 2012), 112; Dieter Lührmann, *Galatians: A Continental Commentary* (Minneapolis: Fortress, 1992), 98; Craig S. Keener, *Galatians*, NCBC (New York: Cambridge University Press, 2018), 242–43.

[162] See Carl E. DeVries, "Paul's 'Cutting' Remarks about a Race: Galatians 5:1–12," in *Current Issues in Biblical and Patristic Interpretation: Studies in Honor of Merrill C. Tenney Presented by His Former Students*, ed. Gerald F. Hawthorne (Grand Rapids: Eerdmans, 1975), 115–20. Cf. Burton, *Galatians*, 289.

[163] Fee, *First Epistle to the Corinthians*, 837. Wiles, *Paul's Intercessory Prayers*, 154, suggests 1 Cor 16:22 ought to be regarded "like the corresponding passage in Galatians, as a type of negative intercessory wish-prayer."

church and in 6:9–10 that the unrepentantly unrighteous will not inherit the kingdom of God. The request for the accursing of those who have no love for the Lord is thus once again predicated upon the covenantal certainty of divine judgment against those who defy God and wreak havoc upon the community among whom he takes up royal residence: Paul asks for precisely that which he has already confirmed will come to pass.[164] Acting as a royal-priestly son of God,[165] the apostle invokes God's cleansing, expulsive judgment against the church's enemies whose unholiness threatens the life of God's temple-kingdom people—rich with septuagintal reverberations of the *anathema* upon those entities that would pollute the people and place of God's presence. Indeed, Paul has already exhorted the community, "Purge the evil person from among you" (5:13), applying God's command for Israel to execute those who corrupt his dwelling place (cf. Deut 13:5; 17:7, 12; 21:21; 22:21–23; 24:7) to the Corinthians' requisite excommunication of the unrepentant in their midst. With this instruction in the background, Paul in 16:22 pleads for a promised judgment that has its initial communal affirmation, symbolic declaration, and proleptic instantiation in the church's disciplinary driving out of the unholy.[166] Intriguingly, Paul immediately follows his request for God's kingdom-preserving judgment with a *maranatha* cry for Christ's eschatological appearing, the *parousia* that will mean the final judgment of the wicked, the blessedness of the righteous, and the consummation of the kingdom.[167] In the flow of 1 Cor 16:22, the call for God's accursing of the church's antagonizers—their removal from the midst

[164] On the relation between 16:22 and other judgment texts in 1 Corinthians, cf. Morland, *Rhetoric of Curse*, 174; Fee, *First Epistle to the Corinthians*, 837n29; Wiles, *Paul's Intercessory Prayers*, 151–53.

[165] Cf. Wiles, *Paul's Intercessory Prayers*, 154.

[166] As in Gal 1:8–9, ecclesial separation from the offender is included in but does not exhaust the divine judgment for which the Pauline *anathema* aims, especially in light of the *maranatha* that follows in 1 Cor 16:22. The expulsive discipline of the church is an ecclesial casting out of the one who will be eschatologically cast out, and Paul's petition encompasses both. From this perspective, one way the church embraces her vocation as the royal-priestly son of God is by driving out in excommunication those who threaten God's temple-kingdom, acting as an agent of God's judgment in the world.

[167] Cf. Thiselton, *First Epistle to the Corinthians*, 1348–52; Fee, *First Epistle to the Corinthians*, 838–39; Craig S. Keener, *1–2 Corinthians*, NCBC (New York: Cambridge University Press, 2005), 142; Richard B. Hays, *First Corinthians*, Interpretation (Louisville: John Knox Press, 1997), 292; Raymond F. Collins, *First Corinthians*, SP 7 (Collegeville, Minn.: Liturgical Press, 1999), 614; Anders Eriksson, "Fear of Eternal Damnation: *Pathos* Appeal in 1 Corinthians 15 and

of Christ's *ekklesia* and eschatological destruction—leads quite naturally into a call for the return of Christ, which is the cleansing of the world, the sanctifying of heaven and earth as the place of God's royal dwelling with his covenant people.[168]

How Long Before You Will Judge? Revelation 6:9–10

The final relevant imprecatory speech act in the New Testament occurs in Rev 6:9–10. John sees under the altar "the souls of those who had been slain" (v. 9) for God's word and their witness and hears their psalmically resonant cry, "O Sovereign Lord, holy and true, how long (cf. Pss 35:17; 74:10; 79:5; 80:4; 94:3) before you will judge and avenge our blood (cf. Ps 79:10) on those who dwell on the earth?" Though framed as a question, the martyrs' cry does not anticipate a numerical answer—as if they are interested in the precise number of days that must elapse—but rather expresses a desire to see God's vindicating vengeance manifested against the violent oppressors of his people, an interrogative locution with petitionary illocutionary force.[169] The martyrs' prayer is thus an imprecatory speech act, asking God in the language of the imprecatory psalms to justly judge those who prey upon his church. Just as the petitioner of Psalm 79 prays for judgment against the enemies that have come into God's inheritance, defiled his holy temple-city (v. 1), and spilled his servants' blood (vv. 2–3), the heavenly martyrs step into the imprecator's role and call for divine wrath against the tormentors that would pour out the blood of his people and destroy God's temple-kingdom community. In this, the martyrs pray as the royal-priestly sons and daughters of God that they are (cf. Rev 2:26–27; 5:10; 20:4–6), guarding God's temple-kingdom from the violent wicked who seek her devastation, begging for the just expulsion of God's enemies from God's world so that the entire cosmos may be the place of God's holy, royal dwelling with his people. Indeed, God's answer to the martyrs' prayer is to give them a white robe—to

---

16," in *Paul and* Pathos, ed. Thomas H. Olbricht and Jerry L. Sumney, Symposium (Atlanta: SBL Press, 2001), 121–22.

[168] See C. F. D. Moule, "A Reconsideration of the Context of *Maranatha*," *NTS* 6, no. 4 (1960): 307–10. Cf. Thiselton, *First Epistle to the Corinthians*, 1349; Roy E. Ciampa and Brian S. Rosner, "I Corinthians," in *CNTOT*, 748; David E. Garland, *1 Corinthians*, BECNT (Grand Rapids: Baker Academic, 2003), 773–74; C. K. Barrett, *A Commentary on the First Epistle to the Corinthians*, HNTC (New York: Harper and Row, 1968), 398.

[169] Cf. Leithart, *Revelation 1–11*, 306; Beale, *Book of Revelation*, 392. Osborne, *Revelation*, 284: "As the only prayer of supplication in the Apocalypse . . . it is important to realize that it is an imprecatory prayer for vengeance."

dress them in priestly vestment—that they might rest in expectation of riding as a priestly army with Jesus in Rev 19:14.[170]

The martyrs' prayer is not, however, the prayer of the martyrs only, but of the church on earth as well.[171] In the movement of the Apocalypse, the record of the martyrs' cry for vengeance from under the altar in 6:9–10 specifies the content of the incense "prayers of the saints" in 5:8, an image that is further developed in 8:3–5 when the incense "prayers of all the saints" (v. 3) rise from the altar to God and are answered with God's theophanic judgment (v. 5).[172] The whole people of God—the living and the dead—takes up the imprecatory prayer offered by the martyrs, petitioning as priest-kings in defense of God's temple-kingdom and in pursuit of a world free of sin and violence where God's ruling presence will fill the earth and ever reside among his covenant people. In so doing, the church in Revelation acts as a prayerful agent of judgment, active through supplication in the revelation of God's wrath upon the enemies of his Christ and kingdom.[173] The vengeance petition of Rev 6:9–10 thus supplies a model for the ongoing prayer of Christ's body on earth,[174] and Rev 8:3–5, by simply

[170]   See Beale, *Book of Revelation*, 961; Leithart, *Revelation 1–11*, 307. Cf. Peter J. Leithart, *Revelation 12–22*, ITC (New York: Bloomsbury T&T Clark, 2018), 279.

[171]   *Contra* Beale, *Book of Revelation*, 392; Robert Thomas, *Revelation 1–7: An Exegetical Commentary*, Wycliffe Exegetical Commentary (Chicago: Moody, 1992), 522–23.

[172]   On the relationship between Rev 5:8; 6:9–10; 8:3–5, cf. Blount, *Revelation*, 113, 163–64; Osborne, *Revelation*, 259; Koester, *Revelation*, 435; Beale, *Book of Revelation*, 357–58, 455–57; Johnson, "Revelation," 469. On Rev 8:3 including the earthly church in the imprecatory prayer of 6:9–10, cf. Mounce, *Book of Revelation*, 175; J. Ramsey Michaels, *Revelation*, IVPNTC (Downers Grove, Ill.: InterVarsity Press, 1997), 118; Gerhard A. Krodel, *Revelation*, ACNT (Minneapolis: Augsburg, 1989), 194–95. The entire argument of Bauckham, "Prayer in the Book of Revelation," 252–71, is instructive.

[173]   See Mounce, *Book of Revelation*, 175; Michaels, *Revelation*, 118; Martin Kiddle, *The Revelation of St. John*, MNTC (New York: Harper and Brothers, 1940), 146. Cf. Middleton, *Violence of the Lamb*, 231.

[174]   G. B. Caird, *A Commentary on the Revelation of St John the Divine*, BNTC (London: Adam & Charles Black, 1966), 85. Cf. Harrington, *Revelation*, 104. Though he does not include 6:9–10 in his study, Robert S. Smith, "Songs of the Seer: The Purpose of Revelation's Hymns," *Them* 43, no. 2 (2018): 197, claims that Revelation's hymn texts serve a pedagogical function to model how the church ought to respond amid tribulation, and his observation may be applied to the nonhymnic, imprecatory petition of 6:9–10.

narrating the incense rising before God's throne, assumes that such petitions will indeed be offered in the prayers of all the saints.[175]

Conclusion

The New Testament narrates and reflects upon God's kingdom-restoring action in Jesus through frequent intertextual appeal to the narrative world of the imprecatory psalms, exhibiting both a figural flexibility and a Christological polyvalence in its evocative application of the imprecations' roles, imagery, and themes to actors in the Christian-era act of God's redemptive-historical drama. Jesus inhabits the place of each of the three principal figures in the imprecatory psalms: he suffers in righteousness before experiencing vindication and mediates God's judgment in his first and second comings as the royal-priestly son of God; he bears the divine judgment curse at the cross on behalf of God's enemies; he wins victory over his foes by his death, resurrection, and ascent to the heavenly throne and will definitively administer covenantal justice at his *parousia* as the divine judge and warrior-king. The church, once serpentine enemies characterized by rebellion against God, have been made happy captives of Jesus, joyfully following in his train, and have been restored to their Adamic vocation as priest-kings, sons, and daughters of God. As such, God's new covenant people mediate God's judgment in the world—guarding God's temple-kingdom and subduing the earth by driving out the unclean—through prayer in this age, awaiting the eschatological day when the sons and daughters of God will join the Son of God in actualizing God's vengeance and preparing the cosmos as sacred space. Those enemies who persist in their opposition to God's king and kingdom, refusing to become willing captives of the Christ who bore the covenant curse, will bear the curse themselves, receiving God's talionic justice as they are expelled from the land, the city, the temple-kingdom, the new creational home where God will dwell over and with his people.

The New Testament not only alludes to and echoes the imprecatory psalms in its presentation of God's story of the world; it also engages in its own imprecatory speech acts. Significantly, in those few texts where imprecatory petitions explicitly occur, the New Testament reflects positively upon the practice: Jesus issues a parabolic, messianic endorsement of Christian prayer for divine justice; Paul engages in apostolic imprecation; and the heavenly saints of John's Apocalypse model imprecatory prayer in which all the saints of God are depicted as participating. Read

---

[175] Bauckham, "Prayer in the Book of Revelation," 263.

within the redemptive-historical narrative framework supplied by the New Testament's own evocative interaction with the imprecatory psalms, the New Testament's imprecatory speech acts (and apparent moral commendation of such speech acts) are rendered ethically intelligible, aligning with the *telos* of God's purposes for history and the church's God-given vocation in God's story of reality. The royal-priestly sons and daughters of God, whose divinely granted role it is to mediate God's judgment in their tending and extending of God's temple-kingdom—driving out all wickedness in service and preparation of sacred space—embrace this calling in their imprecatory prayers. They petition on the basis of God's covenantal promises for the interruption, exposure, and judgment of the enemies of God's kingdom, which will mean the vindication, blessedness, and peace of God's people in the place of God's ruling presence. The New Testament's imprecatory speech acts are priest-king prayers for covenant justice that plead for God to do what God has already committed himself to do, indeed what he has assured the world he will do by raising Jesus from the dead (Acts 17:31), and with such pleas Christ's *ekklesia* faithfully enacts her vocation as the sons and daughters of God—she prays "in character"—within God's narrative.

Of course, certain ethically salient questions have yet to be addressed: How does the eschatological character of Christ's kingdom in the church's era of redemptive history influence the shape of Christian performance of the imprecatory psalms? How does such prayer comport with the New Testament's commands for enemy love? What are the proper objects, aims, and accompanying affections of Christian performance of the psalmic imprecations? How ought ecclesial imprecation take into account the Christological polyvalence of the vengeance psalms, praying evangelically—in response to God's salvific action in Christ—for God's judgment? And how might such redemptive-historically sensitive performance of the imprecatory psalms shape the internal, affective dynamics of the petitioner, acting upon the church even as the church enacts the psalms?

With this and the previous chapter, we have laid the biblical-theological groundwork for a narrative framework within which these questions may be fruitfully explored. So it is to this focused ethical treatment of Christian vocalization of the vengeance psalms that we now turn.

4

Cursing in Christ

Ethically Faithful Christian Performance
of the Imprecatory Psalms

Give the king your justice, O God,
　　and your righteousness [LXX Ps 71:1, δικαιοσύνην] to the royal son!
May he judge your people with righteousness [δικαιοσύνη],
　　and your poor with justice!
Let the mountains bear prosperity for the people,
　　and the hills, in righteousness [δικαιοσύνη]!
May he defend the cause of the poor of the people,
　　give deliverance to the children of the needy,
　　and crush the oppressor! (Ps 72:1–4)

Blessed are those who hunger and thirst for righteousness
[δικαιοσύνην], for they shall be satisfied. (Matt 5:6)

Within the imprecatory psalms, cries for the manifestation of God's righteousness in history are a regular feature of the justice prayers of the violently oppressed. That Yahweh sits enthroned forever and "judges the world with righteousness" (9:8)[1] grounds the hope that God shall administer judgment over the nations. Divine righteousness is the characteristic to which the psalmists appeal in their pleas for vindication from the enemy's false and deadly accusations (35:24) and for deliverance from the hand of the wicked (71:2). God's righteousness—actualized in the reign of the Israelite king—is the object of Solomon's longing (72:1–4), a righteousness that defends the downtrodden, gives rescue to the needy, and executes just

---

[1]　See also Pss 96:13; 98:9; cf. Ps 67:4.

judgment upon the predators of God's people. The imprecatory psalms are the prayer-pangs of those who hunger and thirst for righteousness. With this psalmic ache after righteousness rumbling in the background,[2] Jesus' fourth Beatitude may be heard as a declaration of blessedness not merely over those who yearn to embody personal righteousness but, more than that, over those who yearn for the righteousness of God to break into the world with a justice that rights wrongs, judges the wicked, and liberates the faithful for uninhibited life with God.[3] Beyond Luke 18:1–8, the fourth Beatitude grants dominical sanction to the desire for Yahweh's righteous judgment, the very desire that lies at the heart of the imprecatory psalms, and Jesus assures the justice-starved that these desires shall be sated.

There is more involved, however, in working out the ethics of Christian performance of the imprecatory psalms than a blanket declaration that such prayer constitutes a morally licit practice. Even the most innocuous forms of prayer are susceptible to abuse and may be directed toward unethical ends—praise may be enacted as an attempt at divine bribery, confession as an ironic flex of pious self-awareness for others, thanksgiving as a response to receiving gifts from God that have become idols of the heart—and the illicit exercise of licit prayers can reinforce affections and reify ways of being and relating to God that bend, distort, malform disciples in vice rather than shaping them for virtue. In this regard, the imprecatory psalms may be particularly dangerous prayers. We must, then, turn attention to Christian imprecation as a moral act and the imprecating Christian as a moral agent. We must inquire both how the Christian church may ethically perform the imprecatory psalms in light of her vocation and time within God's story of the world and how in turn these Christologically rich psalms might act upon the imprecating church.

---

[2]   The terminology of hungering (πεινάω), thirsting (διψάω), being satisfied (χορτάζω) in Matt 5:6 resonates strongly with the language of LXX Ps 106:5, 9 (ET 107:5, 9). In Psalm 107, God's satisfaction of those who hunger and thirst is an image connected with his restoration of Israel from exile (v. 3)—his reestablishment of his people in the land where he will dwell. With this echo evoking the themes of Psalm 107, Jesus' statement about hungering and thirsting for righteousness and being satisfied by God may aim to conjure associations with that divine judgment which releases his people from oppressive captivity and secures God's temple-kingdom for life in his holy presence.

[3]   Cf. Robert H. Gundry, *Matthew: A Commentary on His Handbook for a Mixed Church under Persecution*, 2nd ed. (Grand Rapids: Eerdmans, 1994), 70; D. A. Carson, "Matthew," in vol. 8 of *EBC* (Grand Rapids: Zondervan, 1984), 134.

Here, I utilize the biblical-theological reading of Scripture developed over the preceding two chapters as the narrative framework for ethically reflecting on what constitutes fitting and faithful Christian performance of the imprecatory psalms. As the authoritative story of reality,[4] the Bible's redemptive-historical narrative that renders ethically intelligible the imprecatory speech acts of both testaments simultaneously functions as the ethically determinative story within which the church lives and offers her petitions to God—the story whose categories and *telos* norm the church's practice of prayer and everything else.[5] Taking cues from the New Testament's intertextual application and development of the figures and structures of the imprecatory psalms in its communication of God's works in Christ, I address several salient questions: In this theologically charged and allusively resonant story of the world, who is the proper petitioning agent of imprecatory prayer? Who are the appropriate objects of petitions for judgment? For what types of divine judgment are Christian imprecations to plead? How does the eschatological character of God's temple-kingdom in this time between the advents of Jesus affect how the church may pray the imprecatory prayers of Israel? From what loves ought Christian imprecation to proceed, and toward what corresponding ends ought it be directed? And how are these teleologically oriented affections consonant with the New Testament's, including Jesus', ethical prescriptions of enemy love and proscriptions of cursing (e.g., Matt 5:44; Luke 6:27–28; Rom 12:14)? Ultimately, I seek to articulate an ethical mode of imprecatory performance that is a means by which Christians guard the temple-kingdom of God's holy presence—the church—and participate with properly directed love in subduing the serpentine wicked, clearing the creational land so that the whole earth may be the place where God rules over and dwells among his covenant people forever, thereby faithfully executing their calling from God as characters in his narrative.

[4]   Recall N. T. Wright, *The New Testament and the People of God*, vol. 1 of *Christian Origins and the Question of God* (Minneapolis: Fortress, 1992), 41–42.

[5]   John R. Stumme, "Inhabiting the Christian Narrative: An Example of the Relationship between Religion and the Moral Life," *Journal of Lutheran Ethics* 3, no. 1 (2003), https://www.elca.org/JLE/Articles/896, observes, "The Christian narrative is the biblical narrative," while also affirming that any rendering of this normative narrative is "partial and selective"—that is, it necessarily involves a process of synthesizing the scriptural data into a coherent and relevant narrative whole. That synthetic integration of the biblical data was the task of the previous two chapters, an endeavor that now opens the way for reflection on the way of life that is appropriate for the church that inhabits that narrative.

Of course, the potential for misuse of the imprecatory psalms is considerable.[6] Few human beings in the throes of violence are likely to instigate imprecatory prayer from ideal affections, and even in serene conditions, unreflective, self-assured enactment of the vengeance psalms could conceivably beget a self-deception that assumes one's judgment petitions are ethical when they in fact reflect and reinforce hazardously disordered desires. Therefore, it is necessary to attend not only to the way God's narrative of redemptive history supplies the requisite context for reflection upon the conditions for ethical ecclesial imprecation but also to the way prayerful enactment of the imprecatory psalms—so rich with polyvalent Christological significance—might move the imprecator on an affection-altering journey through God's Christocentric story in the very act of praying the psalmic imprecations.

Having previously surveyed the New Testament's portrayal of Jesus as the multidimensional fulfiller of the imprecatory psalms, here my concern is how these Christological associations influence the internal dynamics of Christian performance of the imprecatory psalms. The doctrine of union with Christ names and explicates that Spirit-wrought reality by which Christians are legally and vitally, covenantally and existentially connected to Jesus such that what is true of him is true of them as well.[7] With recourse to this doctrine, I consider how performance of the Christically fertile imprecatory

---

[6]   See, e.g., Erich Zenger, *A God of Vengeance? Understanding the Psalms of Divine Wrath*, trans. Linda M. Maloney (Louisville: Westminster John Knox, 1996), 57–58, who surveys ways that Psalm 109 has been historically abused to legitimate antisemitism and as a quasi-magical means of "praying people to death." Cf. the warnings of Harry Mennega, "The Ethical Problem of the Imprecatory Psalms" (ThM thesis, Westminster Theological Seminary, 1959), 90; Ellen F. Davis, *Getting Involved with God: Rediscovering the Old Testament* (Lanham, Md.: Cowley, 2001), 23; Dominick D. Hankle, "The Therapeutic Implications of the Imprecatory Psalms in the Christian Counseling Setting," *JPT* 38, no. 4 (2010): 277.

[7]   On the Reformed understanding of union with Christ, cf. WCF 26.1; WLC 66; John Calvin, *Institutes of the Christian Religion*, ed. John T. McNeill, trans. Ford Lewis Battles (Louisville: Westminster John Knox, 1960), III.1.1; Louis Berkhof, *Systematic Theology* (Grand Rapids: Eerdmans, 1939), 447–53; Herman Bavinck, *Reformed Dogmatics*, ed. John Bolt, trans. John Vriend (Grand Rapids: Baker Academic, 2003), 3:591–92; and more recently, e.g., Sinclair B. Ferguson, *The Holy Spirit*, Contours of Christian Theology (Downers Grove, Ill.: InterVarsity Press, 1996), 100–113; J. Todd Billings, *Union with Christ: Reframing Theology and Ministry for the Church* (Grand Rapids: Baker Academic, 2011); Michael Horton, *The Christian Faith: A Systematic Theology for Pilgrims on the Way* (Grand Rapids: Zondervan, 2011), 587–619.

psalms implicates the petitioner—affectively retracing the contours of God's story and ushering the supplicant to the foot of the cross and the edge of the age to come—and in so doing reorients the praying heart in a manner that cultivates a faith and hope that engender love. From this perspective, Christian embodiment of the imprecatory psalms is not merely an affective moral practice that must cohere with God's narrative but also a morally affecting practice in which the praying subject engages in a dynamic rehearsal of God's Christocentric narrative, a narrativizing practice that reimpresses the story upon the petitioning agent and consequently stimulates the very internal conditions necessary for their ethical enactment, even when such conditions are not initially present. Praying the imprecatory psalms in union with Christ functions as the transformative means by which Christians learn to pray the imprecatory psalms in faith, hope, and love, and as a training ground for virtue and faithfulness in a world full of unholy violence.

My aim is to offer a proposal that delineates the characteristics of ethical Christian imprecation and that simultaneously explores how ecclesial embrace of the imprecatory psalms may work upon the petitioner as the prayerful means of grace by which the postures necessary for right imprecatory practice are generated. This approach confronts the tumultuous affectional realities of suffering and addresses how the imprecatory psalms may be ethically recovered as God's gift to the church amid them—as prayers that have the capacity to cultivate ethical dispositions and move the praying agent, who begins with immoral affections, toward the faith, hope, and love that are pleasing to God, consistent with the call of Christ, oriented toward the good of others, and fitting in God's story of the world. The result is a vision of Christian performance of the imprecatory psalms that commends the vengeance psalms to Christ's disciples as prayers that may indeed be offered to God in confidence of their moral propriety within his narrative, even in the midst of the affective turbulence that almost inevitably accompanies experiences of violence and precedes prayers for vengeance.

Imprecating in Character:
The Agents, Objects, and Content of Christian Imprecation

The redemptive-historical narrative of God's works in the world renders ethically intelligible the judgment petitions of the imprecatory psalms and the New Testament's imprecatory speech acts, and it is within this same narrative that the Christian church finds herself as a moral agent—the recipient of a God-given identity and concomitant calling to which she must be faithful, a time in which she must act, and a *telos* with which her life in God's world must conform. Christians are thrust into the action of God's story as characters, and consequently the fidelity of any act must be evaluated by its coherence with the Christian's role and location within God's ethically normative narrative of history. With this section, I examine how the morally determinative structures of God's redemptive-historical story dictate the formal shape of ethical Christian performance of the imprecatory psalms. Drawing upon the preceding two chapters' redemptive-historical and ethical framing of the imprecatory psalms and analysis of the New Testament's intertextual development of their inhabiting figures, I here demonstrate the church's relationship to the constitutive features of the imprecations and elucidate the ethical claims made by the scriptural story upon the church's practice of the imprecatory psalms regarding the permissible agents, objects, and content of Christian judgment prayers.

The Agents of Christian Imprecation

Who is the proper petitioning agent of imprecatory prayer? The imprecator in the psalms is presented as the innocent, suffering son of God, a royal priest—besieged by the unwarranted violence of the enemy—who is commissioned by God to guard and extend the temple-kingdom of God's dwelling and mediate God's judgment upon the serpentine wicked, a priest-king who faithfully embraces his vocation by praying for divine vengeance upon the enemies of God's kingdom. Two ethically salient features of the agent of imprecation arise from this identification. Vocationally, the imprecator plays a specific role in God's story—is cast as a particular character—as a son of God who has been divinely called as a royal priest to protect God's temple-kingdom from assailing serpents and expand its bounds throughout creation. Circumstantially, the imprecator is a righteous sufferer, one who is the relatively innocent target of unprovoked aggression. The moral agent who would take up the royal-priestly prayers of the righteous, suffering psalmists as her own prayers before God must meet both the vocational and the circumstantial conditions.

The New Testament regularly depicts the church with recourse to the language and imagery of the imprecatory psalms in order to present the citizens of Christ's new covenant community as royal-priestly sons and daughters of God who, like the imprecator in the psalms, are inheritors of the original Adamic calling and are therefore tasked with defending God's temple-kingdom and driving out the serpentine enemy from the land that God has claimed as his royal dwelling. Christians are those former enemies of God's king and kingdom (Rom 3:13–14), now made happy captives of Jesus (2 Cor

2:14), who have been restored in Christ to the true human vocation as sons and daughters of God (Rom 8:19) and a kingdom of priests (Rev 1:6; 5:10; 20:4–6), protectors of the place where God reigns over and with his people (Rev 6:9–10) and serpent-crushing mediators of God's land-cleansing judgment (Luke 10:19; Rom 16:20; Rev 18:6). The church's divinely granted office, a sharing in the royal priesthood of the Son of God to which she is united, invests her with the authority to protect God's temple-kingdom in prayer. Accordingly, Jesus exhorts his followers to pray for the revelation of God's justice (Luke 18:1–8); Paul petitions for the expulsive destruction of serpents preying upon the church (Gal 1:8–9; 1 Cor 16:22; cf. Gal 5:12); and the saints in heaven and on earth join in prayer for God's avenging upon the blood-shedding oppressors of his people (Rev 5:8; 6:9–10; 8:3–5). The role that the psalmists played in God's narrative, the role that authorized them to pray for God's judgment upon those devoted to the decimation of God's temple-kingdom, is thus the very role granted to the Christian church. This role not only legitimates her practice of enemy-subduing prayer within God's story of the world but obligates her to take up the imprecatory psalms in opposition to the serpent seed who would infiltrate and destroy God's ecclesial temple-kingdom and who must be expelled if the creation is to fulfill its appointed destiny as the glorious, royal residence of God with his people. Who may pray for—and thus prayerfully participate in—God's judgment? Only those who by repentance and faith in Christ have been divinely reinstated to their identity and vocation as priest-kings; only those to whom it has been given to mediate God's judgment as his sons and daughters.[8] But for those to whom it has been given, the prayerful exercise of this vocation is a duty as ethically binding as the calling is irrevocable.

Yet, that the imprecatory psalms are the prayerful prerogative of the sons and daughters of God does not entail that every son or daughter of God will in every circumstance be permitted to pray the Psalter's

---

[8]   Intriguingly, then, the answer to the common question to the imprecatory psalms, "May Christians pray them?" is that *only* Christians may pray them. Cf. E. Calvin Beisner, *Psalms of Promise: Celebrating the Majesty and Faithfulness of God*, 2nd ed. (Phillipsburg, N.J.: Presbyterian and Reformed, 1994), 179, who argues that only "those who are keepers of [God's] covenant" may pray the imprecations, which presumably means the new covenant community in this time since Christ's first advent. While this covenantal framing is certainly consistent with my own proposal, I find that appeal to the concept of vocation within God's narrative—a calling from God that imposes a purpose to be pursued in action—offers a thicker account of the moral legitimacy of Christian imprecation than the broader concept of covenant.

vengeance prayers. The explicit content of the judgment psalms places an inherent limit on the potential agent of imprecation. The imprecatory psalms, even as they humbly acknowledge the reality of the petition-er's sin (69:5; 143:2), include with their requests for judgment manifold descriptions of the causeless character of the enemies' attacks (35:7, 12, 19; 109:3–5; 119:161) and the baselessness of their accusations (35:20–21; 69:4; 109:4; 119:69), declarations of personal righteousness (9:4; 17:1–5), invitations for God's moral examination (7:8; 139:23–24), and self-imprecations should the psalmist be guilty of that over which he indicts the wicked (7:3–5). Only the petitioner who is similarly innocent of wrongdoing may without dishonesty, dissimulation, or self-contradiction utter such prayers to God.[9] Gordon Wenham describes praying the psalms as engaging in "commissive speech acts: the psalms as prayers are really a

---

[9]   Cf. Beisner, *Psalms of Promise*, 179. James E. Adams, *War Psalms of the Prince of Peace: Lessons from the Imprecatory Psalms* (Phillipsburg, N.J.: Presby-terian and Reformed, 1991), 102; Dietrich Bonhoeffer, "Sermon on a Psalm of Vengeance—Psalm 58," in *Meditating on the Word*, trans. and ed. David M. Gracie, 84–96 (Cambridge, Mass.: Cowley, 1986), 86–87, also attend to the requirement of innocence, but in their contention that only Jesus is sufficiently innocent to pray the imprecations, they conflate the relative innocence that is the concern of the psalms with the absolute innocence that may only be predicated of Jesus. Jerome F. D. Creach, *Violence in Scripture*, Interpretation: Resources for the Use of Scrip-ture in the Church (Louisville: Westminster John Knox, 2013), 194, argues that the imprecatory psalms concern "violence done to the poor and lowly" and that there-fore "imprecation has its proper setting in the struggle for justice to be done for the powerless; this means then that the imprecatory psalms can only be prayed rightly by and on behalf of the powerless." Of course, many of the imprecatory psalms are placed on the lips of the Israelite king, a figure who identifies as "poor and needy" (e.g., Pss 35:10; 41:17; 109:22) even as his office confers a significant degree of social and political power. Nevertheless, the king protests against the lies uttered and injus-tices committed against him, which endanger his life undeservedly—he petitions as an innocent sufferer. It is certainly the case that the experience of unjust aggression necessarily involves a power differential between the wicked who would use power to pursue and the righteous who are the objects of such unwarranted and seemingly inescapable attacks (even when the righteous one is an otherwise powerful figure), and some of the imprecatory psalms indeed cry out against injustice from positions of profound powerlessness (e.g., Psalm 137). However, to foreground the condi-tion of powerlessness *per se* without attending to the moral differential between the unrighteous, unjust aggressor and the innocent recipient of unprovoked animosity is to oversimplify the psalms' testimony, to misidentify the characteristic quality of the suffering and the sufferer in the imprecatory psalms, and consequently to mis-locate the circumstantial condition for performance of the imprecatory psalms.

series of vows"[10] that commit the petitioner to the commitments made by the psalmists. In the case of the imprecatory psalms, this commissive quality of psalmic prayer requires that the petitioner be able to commit to the psalmists' commitments of personal righteousness in the matter at hand.[11] To plead with God, "Hear a just cause, O LORD. . . . Give ear to my prayer from lips free of deceit!" (Ps 17:1) when one's cause is unjust and one's lips have deceived is to implicitly communicate a state of affairs that is patently untrue. To lament, "They repay me evil for good" (Ps 35:12), when one's assailants are merely responding in kind to the petitioner's own initiating aggression is to explicitly mischaracterize the conditions surrounding one's request for redress. To pray, "O LORD my God, if I have done this, if there is wrong in my hands . . . let the enemy pursue my soul and overtake it" (Ps 7:3, 5), when there is indeed wrong in one's hands toward the enemy is to engage in a dangerously self-defeating mode of discourse, to call down divine judgment on one's own head. Thus, it is exclusively those Christian priest-kings able with the psalmists to affirm their relative innocence in the precipitating conflict who may take up the Psalter's prayers for vengeance. In the mouth of an aggressor, the psalmists' prayers for justice on behalf of the suffering righteous become something very different: prayers for divine intervention on behalf of one oppressor over and against another. Significantly, when the New Testament records imprecatory speech acts (Luke 18:1–8; Gal 1:8–9; 5:12; 1 Cor 16:22; Rev 6:9–10), it in every instance presents the petitioners as those suffering under unjust antagonism and never as agents complicit in evil.

The fitting agent of imprecation is therefore a petitioner whose vocation and circumstances align with the imprecator in the psalms, a royal-priestly son or daughter of God in Jesus Christ who is innocent in relation to the enemy, the righteous target of unprovoked violence.

The Objects of Christian Imprecation

Who are the appropriate objects of Christian petitions for judgment? That is, against whom may the innocent, suffering sons and daughters of

[10]   Gordon Wenham, *The Psalter Reclaimed: Praying and Praising with the Psalms* (Wheaton, Ill.: Crossway, 2013), 28. Cf. Kit Barker, *Imprecation as Divine Discourse: Speech Act Theory, Dual Authorship, and Theological Interpretation* (Winona Lake, Ind.: Eisenbrauns, 2016), 117.

[11]   See Wenham, *Psalter Reclaimed*, 26. Cf. Davida Charney, "Maintaining Innocence Before a Divine Hearer: Deliberative Rhetoric in Psalm 22, Psalm 17, and Psalm 7," *BibInt* 21, no. 1 (2013): 62.

God pray the imprecatory psalms? The enemy who is the object of the psalmic petitioner's pleas for divine vengeance is portrayed as the seed of the serpent, the violently unjust opponent of God's temple-kingdom who—whether from inside or outside the covenant community—threatens the flourishing, witness, and existence of God's people and, unless he turns in repentance from his wickedness, is destined for head-crushing, foot-stomping, expulsive judgment. The God-given vocation of the son of God authorizes and requires him to participate in God's judgment of such serpentine enemies, tending and extending God's temple-kingdom by clearing the land of his presence by prayer. Determining the proper objects of Christians' royal-priestly prayers requires determining the characters in this postresurrection, pre-*parousia* era of redemptive history who in serpentine fashion oppose God's reign and oppress God's people, the actors whom God has promised to eschatologically judge and expel from the world where he will rule over and with his people, the players whom Christians are tasked with prayerfully driving out of the land where God will reside. The New Testament's narration of and reflection upon God's continuing work in Jesus intertextually appeals to the imprecatory psalms in its depiction of the spiritual, human, and systemic enemies of God's Messiah and his ecclesial temple-kingdom—a depiction that does not exempt Christians themselves—characterizing each of these figures in the violent, serpentine, covenantally cursed hues of the imprecator's enemies. In the church's scene of God's story, the spiritual, human, and systemic enemies of Christ's kingdom inhabit the role of the enemy in the imprecatory psalms and participate in the serpent seed's aggressive antagonism to God's people and purposes in the world, rendering them the fitting objects of the imprecatory prayers of the Christian sons and daughters of God. And insofar as the Christian's indwelling sin corrupts the individual and corporate body, which is the temple of God, imitating the serpent's unclean intrusion into God's dwelling place, the Christian's own persisting unholiness too becomes a proper object of his or her imprecation.

The New Testament describes the spiritual enemies of the church—Satan and the demonic forces of the kingdom of darkness—as being engaged in violent battle against the temple-kingdom of God. Though the Lord Jesus, the church's premier priest-king, has disarmed, shamed, and triumphed over the rulers and authorities in his debt-canceling death and resurrection (Col 2:15), the devil yet "prowls around like a roaring lion, seeking someone to devour" (1 Pet 5:8). He furiously makes war on the people of God as the archetypal serpent-dragon (Rev 12:13–17)—the original serpent whose image the serpent seed bears (Rev 12:9)—working for the destruction of the community over and with whom God reigns in Christ by his Spirit. If guarding God's temple-kingdom from those who would harm her is essential to the task of the sons and daughters of God, then Satanic spiritual forces are a necessary object of Christians' imprecatory prayer. Indeed, Paul exhorts the Ephesians to actively engage in war, dressing for spiritual battle against a spiritual enemy and "praying at all times in the Spirit, with all prayer and supplication" (Eph 6:18) for the saints: "Put on the whole armor of God, that you may be able to stand against the schemes of the devil. For we do not wrestle against flesh and blood, but against the rulers, against the authorities, against the cosmic powers over this present darkness, against the spiritual forces of evil in the heavenly places" (Eph 6:11–12). Though Paul here says nothing explicitly about imprecatory prayer, his description of persistent prayer on behalf of the saints as a means of war against the church's spiritual enemies exhibits more than a little similarity to my description of imprecation as kingdom-protecting, enemy-expelling petition.[12] The demonic powers scheme for the devastation of Christ's church, and the priest-kings whose commission it is to protect God's temple-kingdom must therefore wage war against the devil's hordes in prayer.[13]

Ecclesial imprecation against Satan and wicked spiritual forces is, further, consistent with the *telos* to which God's story of history is moving. Applying

---

[12] Cf. Frank Thielman, *Ephesians*, BECNT (Grand Rapids: Baker Academic, 2010), 434; Rudolf Schnackenburg, *Ephesians: A Commentary*, trans. Helen Heron (Edinburgh: T&T Clark, 1991), 281.

[13] On the spiritual enemies of the church as proper objects of imprecatory prayer, see, e.g., Kevin J. Youngblood, "Don't Get Even, Get Mad! Imprecatory Prayer as a Neglected Spiritual Discipline: (Psalm 69)," *Leaven* 19, no. 3 (2011): 157; John Shepherd, "The Place of the Imprecatory Psalms in the Canon of Scripture," *Chu* 111, no. 2 (1997): 125; H. G. L. Peels, *The Vengeance of God: The Meaning of the Root NQM and the Function of the NQM-texts in the Context of Divine Revelation in the Old Testament*, OtSt 31 (Leiden: Brill, 1995), 245; Eric Peels, *Shadow Sides: The Revelation of God in the Old Testament* (Carlisle, UK: Paternoster, 2003), 104; Mennega, "Ethical Problem," 89; Alex Luc, "Interpreting the Curses in the Psalms," *JETS* 42, no. 3 (1999): 409; Tremper Longman III, *How to Read the Psalms* (Downers Grove, Ill.: InterVarsity Press, 1988), 139–40; James L. Mays, *The Lord Reigns: A Theological Handbook to the Psalms* (Louisville: Westminster John Knox, 1994), 38; Derek Kidner, *Psalms 1–72: An Introduction and Commentary*, TOTC 15 (Downers Grove, Ill.: InterVarsity Press, 1973), 46–47; Ragnar C. Teigen, "Can Anything Good Come from a Curse?" *Lutheran Quarterly* 26, no. 1 (1974): 49; William L. Holladay, *Long Ago God Spoke: How Christians May Hear the Old Testament Today* (Minneapolis: Fortress, 1995), 309–11.

the wrathful fate of the enemy in the imprecatory psalms to the devil, the New Testament testifies that God will crush the Satanic serpent under the feet of the sons of God (Rom 16:20; cf. Ps 58:10; 68:21–23) and throw him into the lake of fire and sulfur (Rev 20:10; cf. Ps 11:6). When Christians direct their performance of the imprecatory psalms against the spiritual enemies of the church, they not only embrace their calling to defend God's temple-kingdom from her violent, serpentine antagonists and drive them from the creation where God will dwell in holiness. They also—like the psalmists—petition for the vengeance God has promised to administer against the foes he has promised to judge, praying in line with God's revealed purposes for his world. In the church's chapter of God's narrative, then, the spiritual powers committed to assaulting God's people are fitting objects of ecclesial imprecation.

Spiritual enemies are not, however, the only enemies who seek to infiltrate, corrupt, and ravage God's new covenant temple-kingdom and are consequently not the exclusive targets of faithful Christian imprecation.[14] Significantly, in every imprecatory speech act in the New Testament, the object of the petition is a human being, the exemplary widow of Jesus' parable cries for justice against a human adversary (Luke 18:3). Paul requests the *anathema*-expulsion of human teachers who distort the gospel and lead the church to desert her true Lord (Gal 1:6–9; cf. Gal 5:12). The heavenly saints pray for vengeance against blood-shedding humans, "those who dwell on the earth" (Rev 6:10). The New Testament's imprecatory speech acts are not aimed solely at the wicked as a generic class, as if nonspecificity were a requisite characteristic of faithful imprecation,[15] nor are they directed against humans' sin or the effects of their sin, as if the impersonality of the imprecatory object were a critical ethical feature.[16] They are rather requests

---

[14]   *Contra*, e.g., Longman, *How to Read the Psalms*, 139–40; Kidner, *Psalms 1–72*, 46–47; Shepherd, "Place of the Imprecatory Psalms," 125; Teigen, "Can Anything Good Come from a Curse?" 49; Luc, "Interpreting the Curses," 409; Mays, *Lord Reigns*, 38; Youngblood, "Don't Get Even," 157.

[15]   *Contra* Johannes G. Vos, "The Ethical Problem of the Imprecatory Psalms," *WTJ* 4 (1942): 137; Mennega, "Ethical Problem," 87; Adams, *War Psalms*, 53; Peels, *Vengeance of God*, 246.

[16]   *Contra* Robert Althann, "The Psalms of Vengeance against Their Ancient Near Eastern Background," *JNSL* 18 (1992): 10; C. S. Lewis, *Reflections on the Psalms* (San Diego: Harcourt Brace Jovanovich, 1958), 32; Peter C. Craigie and Marvin E. Tate, *Psalms 1–50*, 2nd ed., WBC 19 (Grand Rapids: Zondervan, 2004), 41. Barker, *Imprecation as Divine Discourse*, 131, critiques the common notion that Christians are to pray against sin and not sinners. Cf. Carroll Stuhlmueller, *Psalms 1 (Psalms 1–72)*, Old Testament Message 21 (Wilmington, Del.: Michael Glazier, 1983), 314.

for judgment against objects that are in several cases particular—the widow's adversary, the false teachers troubling the Galatians—and in every case personal, imprecating against humans who utilize their agency for sin and are culpable for the destructive effects. The royal-priestly sons and daughters of God must protect God's temple-kingdom and drive out all uncleanness from the world that God has claimed for his royal presence, and when human beings array themselves against God's people in league with the Satanic serpent—whether endangering the church from within or without—they join the serpent as proper objects of the church's imprecatory prayer. Such petitions align with God's stated purposes—praying with the teleological current of God's redemptive-historical narrative—for God promises that, in his story of the world, the judgments requested in the imprecatory psalms will be poured out upon the serpent's human seed. The temple's destroyers will be destroyed (1 Cor 3:17; cf. Ps 79:1, 6, 10); the church's afflicters will be repaid with affliction (2 Thess 1:6; cf. Ps 137:8); the kingdom's opponents will drink the cup of his wrath-wine and experience the torment of fire and sulfur (Rev 14:10; cf. Ps 11:6); and the cosmos will be the residence of a holy God with holy humans. Christian imprecation against human enemies who participate in the animosity of the psalmic, serpentine enemy is thus consistent with the church's vocation and the divinely orchestrated *telos* of God's narrative.

Insofar as human systems, and not merely individuals, contribute to the violent oppression of the church, they too become the fitting objects of Christian imprecation.[17] In the book of Revelation, Babylon, the beast, and the false prophet symbolically represent the systems and structures of the world in their idolatrous, coercive, repressive, brutal opposition to God's reign and people.[18] The complex interaction of a society's institutions,

---

[17]   Cf. Roy Ben Zuck, "The Problem of the Imprecatory Psalms" (ThM thesis, Dallas Theological Seminary, 1957), 78. Zephania Kameeta, *Why, O Lord? Psalms and Sermons from Namibia* (Geneva: World Council of Churches, 1986), 48, models imprecation that acknowledges the individual and systemic character of human violence in his adaptation of Ps 137:7–9:

Remember, Lord, what the oppressors did
    the day they turned us into refugees . . .
Happy is the man who pays you back
    for what you have done to us—
who takes your rotten system of apartheid
    and smashes it against a rock.

[18]   See Richard Bauckham, *The Theology of the Book of Revelation*, New Testament Theology (New York: Cambridge University Press, 1993).

policies, practices, persons, and values has the capacity to exert profound political, military, economic, social, and religious pressures upon Christ's *ekklesia*, especially when the state begins making totalizing claims upon its citizens. The Apocalypse repeatedly observes that these systems are leveraged by the Satanic dragon to wage a bloody war on the saints who refuse to offer their fundamental allegiance to any political or spiritual power besides Jesus (e.g., Rev 13:1–18; 17:1–6).[19] Systemic violence participates in the serpent's age-old conflict against God's temple-kingdom, and God will judge these systems and the people who animate them in the pattern of the requested judgments against the psalmic enemy. He will avenge upon Babylon "the blood of his servants" (Rev 19:2; cf. Ps 79:10) and throw the beast and false prophet "alive into the lake of fire that burns with sulfur" (Rev 19:20; cf. Pss 11:6; 55:15). Christian imprecation against the systems and structures, the institutions and forces that assault God's people and corrupt the world where he wills to dwell in holiness is therefore to be evaluated as an ethically faithful deployment of the church's royal-priestly vocation that pleads in line with the promised *telos* of God's narrative.

It is important to note, however, that spiritual, human, and systemic enemies need not violently assault God's church *per se* in order to violently oppose his kingdom and defile his world. Even when the enemies' sights are set on non-Christians, any and every act of murderous, deceptive, and oppressive predation upon the innocent is an act of defiance against the righteous character of the holy kingdom that God wills to establish on the earth, a proliferation of the pattern of the kingdom of darkness in the cosmic house of the Lord. The perpetrators fill with unholy, unjust violence the creation that God has claimed as his eschatological temple. Every spiritual, human, and systemic agent engaged in wicked assault upon the innocent—whether the target is the church or the mosque, a minority community or an entire nation—opposes God's reign, rebels against the way of the king, and corrupts the world that God has purposed to make his sacred dwelling. The priest-kings tasked with prayerfully subduing the earth and driving out the unclean enemy from the land where God will establish his holy presence are accordingly right to make all such enemies of God's temple-kingdom the objects of their expulsive, imprecatory prayers.[20]

---

[19]   On the beasts of Revelation 13, cf. G. K. Beale, *The Book of Revelation: A Commentary on the Greek Text*, NIGTC (Grand Rapids: Eerdmans, 1999), 691–92, 717.

[20]   Cf. the argument of Barker, *Imprecation as Divine Discourse*, 179, advocating for Christian imprecation against every kind of extreme violence, "for all those who are suffering horrific oppression."

And yet, if it is the story-determined duty of the sons and daughters of God to prayerfully protect the temple-kingdom and petition for the expulsion of every unclean thing from the land of God's royal presence, then there is one more necessary object of Christian imprecation: the indwelling sin of the Christian individual and community.[21] The sons and daughters of God are God's former enemies, captives of the conquering Christ (2 Cor 2:14; cf. Ps 68:18) of whom it was once rightly predicated, "Their throat is an open grave; they use their tongues to deceive. The venom of asps is under their lips" (Rom 3:13; cf. Pss 5:9; 140:3). What is true of the enemy in the imprecations was once true of the Christian—the present follower of Christ was once a participant with all of fallen humanity in the serpent's deceptive, venomous antagonism toward God—and, as the Westminster Confession of Faith states, "This corruption of nature, during this life, doth remain in those that are regenerated."[22] The image of the enemy still rears its head in the Christian's heart; the flesh still wars against the Spirit (Gal 5:17); there is an idolatrous uncleanness that must yet be driven out of that temple of God, which is the individual believer's body and the communal body of believers (1 Cor 6:19; 2 Cor 6:14–7:1); and still-sinful Christians are accordingly intensely capable of corrupting the life, flourishing, and witness of the holy temple-kingdom community in resolutely serpentine fashion.

Drawing on this complex of themes, Paul rehearses the promise that "we are the temple of the living God" (2 Cor 6:16)[23] and exhorts the Corinthians, "Let us cleanse ourselves from every defilement of body and spirit, bringing holiness to completion in the fear of God" (2 Cor 7:1), a project of sanctification whose pursuit may be well served through self-directed, temple-cleansing, imprecatory prayer. Indeed, the operative logic of

---

[21] Cf. the discussions of self-directed imprecation by Lewis, *Reflections on the Psalms*, 136; Augustin [*sic*], *Saint Augustin: Expositions on the Book of Psalms*, ed. A. Cleveland Coxe, vol. 8 of *NPNF*, ed. Philip Schaff, trans. J. E. Tweed, T. Scratton, H. M. Wilkins, C. Marriott, and H. Walford (New York: Christian Literature Company, 1888), 137.12; Youngblood, "Don't Get Even," 157; Holladay, *Long Ago God Spoke*, 309–16.

[22] WCF 6.5.

[23] Victor Paul Furnish, *II Corinthians*, AB 32A (Garden City, N.Y.: Doubleday and Company, 1984), 363, rightly notes that the temple to which Paul is referring here is "the whole people of God, the Christian community" and draws attention to similar imagery in 1 Cor 3:16; Eph 2:21, acknowledging also that 1 Cor 6:19 particularizes the identification of God's temple with the individual believer's body. Cf. Alfred Plummer, *A Critical and Exegetical Commentary on the Second Epistle of St Paul to the Corinthians*, ICC (Edinburgh: T&T Clark, 1915), 208–9.

excommunication—oriented as it is toward the restoration of the believer through repentance (1 Cor 5:5)—is that the believer's impenitent sin may prove so endangering and destabilizing that the community must be protected, that those who belong to Christ by faith may so live like unclean leaven that they must for a time be cleansed from the Lord's holy lump (1 Cor 5:6–7): "Purge the evil person from among you" (1 Cor 5:13).[24] The sons or daughters of God who would truly fulfill their calling to guard the place of God's royal presence from every unholy intrusion must therefore direct imprecatory prayer against their own corruption individually and collectively, petitioning for the expulsion of the indwelling sin in oneself and in the wider community—"my" sin and "our" sin—that corrupts bodies and threatens the covenant body, both of which are the Spirit's temple-dwelling. Christians' remaining unholiness becomes the object of their own imprecatory petitions not as a means of evading forms of imprecation directed against other enemies,[25] but precisely because their sin, like the sinful enemy, is unfit for God's temple—precisely because their sin always carries the potential of destructively aligning them against God's kingdom community with the serpentine enemy who is also the fitting object of their judgment prayers. This mode of imprecation, too, coheres with God's *telos* for his world, for his story is moving toward a new creation temple-kingdom where "nothing unclean will ever enter" (Rev 21:27),[26] where those who dwell with God are "raised in glory" to "bear the image of the man of heaven" (1 Cor 15:43, 49; cf. Rom 8:29–30), transformed into his likeness by his appearing (1 John 3:2; Phil 3:21; Col 3:4),[27] made holy inhabitants of the city of God.

As the royal-priestly prayers of the sons and daughters of God, ethical Christian imprecation may have as its object the spiritual, human,

---

[24]   Cf. Brian S. Rosner, *Paul, Scripture and Ethics: A Study of 1 Corinthians 5–7*, AGJU 22 (Leiden: Brill, 1994), 61–81.

[25]   For Lewis, *Reflections on the Psalms*, 136; Youngblood, "Don't Get Even," 157; Holladay, *Long Ago God Spoke*, 309–16, the suggestion that imprecatory prayer may be directed against one's own sinful nature is part of a larger strategy of eschewing imprecatory prayer where the object is one's human enemies.

[26]   Cf. Beale, *Book of Revelation*, 1101. This of course suggests that those who do inhabit the new Jerusalem have been definitively cleansed, made holy for the presence of God.

[27]   Cf. Robert W. Yarbrough, *1–3 John*, BECNT (Grand Rapids: Baker Academic, 2008), 178. Note that in 1 John 3:2–3, the promise that Christians will be made like God at his future appearing supplies a motivation for the present work of purification. The present task aligns with the future hope; the future hope makes reasonable the present task.

and systemic enemies of God's king and kingdom as well as the imprecating agent's own temple-defiling uncleanness. There may exist, then, a simultaneous multiplicity of referent in the Christian's practice of the imprecatory psalms wherein a single prayer may be uttered with several intended objects. "Break the arm of the wicked and evildoer" (Ps 10:15) may, in the heart and on the lips of the Christian, take aim at Satan and spiritual forces, particular human antagonists, violently oppressive systemic structures, and the believing individual's and community's temple-corrupting sin in an affectively complex, intentionally polyvalent Godward supplication.

The Content of Christian Imprecation

For what types of divine judgment are Christians to plead? For what forms of divine action may the innocent, suffering sons of God petition as they direct their performance of the imprecatory psalms against the variegated enemies of God's temple-kingdom in this time between Christ's advents? The imprecator in the psalms seeks to prayerfully protect and expand God's temple-kingdom—driving out the serpentine wicked from the land of God's dwelling—by pleading for the interruption and cessation of the enemy's violence, the public vindication of the righteous, and the manifestation of God's covenant justice. The content of the imprecatory prayers offered by Christian sons and daughters of God—the forms of vengeance they seek from God in their vocalization of the imprecatory psalms—must exhibit these same characteristics if God's royal priests in Christ are to fulfill their calling to guard the ecclesial temple-kingdom and cleanse the world of everything unclean by prayer in a manner that coheres with the basic requests of the psalms themselves. By petitioning for divine action that leads to repentance, temporal judgment that thwarts the violence of the wicked by whatever just means necessary, and eschatological judgment that definitively and justly brings an end to all evil and makes the world the dwelling of God's royal presence, the church exercises her calling to protect God's temple-kingdom and expel the serpent's seed in ways that plead for the interruption of violence, the vindication of the righteous, and the realization of God's justice in various iterations. With petitions for these specific forms of divine judgment, the church embraces her vocation in God's narrative of the world, defending and cleansing the place of God's presence and participating in the movement of the narrative and the world toward its God-appointed end.

The first form of judgment for which Christians ought to petition is that action of God within history that effects the repentance and conversion of the enemies of his kingdom.[28] This is not, it should be noted, a softening evasion of the psalms' pleas for judgment, for conversion is within the New Testament a thoroughly violent affair, involving nothing less than the divinely mediated crucifixion of the old human being and its animating desires (Gal 2:20; 5:24), a judgment of death upon sin that leads to life (Rom 6:8; 2 Tim 2:11), a making captive that begets true freedom (2 Cor 2:14). John Donne famously captures something of the violence involved in the divine reorientation of the human heart:

> Batter my heart, three person'd God; for, you
> As yet but knocke, breathe, shine, and seeke to mend;
> That I may rise, and stand, o'erthrow mee, and bend
> Your force, to breake, blowe, burn and make me new.[29]

The psalmists already express the desire and hopefully acknowledge the possibility that God's judgment upon the enemy might stimulate repentance (Ps 83:16; cf. Pss 7:11–13; 40:3; 141:6), but for Christians who themselves have experienced the merciful judgment—the violent grace—of conversion, it is particularly appropriate to orient the imprecations' petitions for vengeance before all else toward the overcoming of the enemy's animosity in repentance. Such prayer is properly evangelical, a fitting response to the evangel of Christ by which the imprecating agent has been made an enemy-turned-citizen of God's kingdom through Jesus' representative reception of judgment. This evangelical mode of imprecation is also redemptive-historically warranted, for the church's chapter of God's story is the age in which the gospel goes forth in the power of the Spirit, bringing foes by grace into the fold of God. To petition for intervening divine action that leads to repentance, then, is to petition in a manner that resonates with the Christian's existential experience of grace—desiring for the other the joyful mercy one has received—and the gracious character of this present time in God's narrative, this inaugurated eschatological moment, this time of patience that makes room for repentance before the consummation of judgment (2 Pet 3:9–10).[30]

---

28 Cf., e.g., Adams, *War Psalms*, 59–61; Bonhoeffer, "Sermon on a Psalm of Vengeance," 96; Shepherd, "Place of the Imprecatory Psalms," 125; Longman, *How to Read the Psalms*, 138–40; Peels, *Vengeance of God*, 245–46.

29 John Donne, "Holy Sonnet XIV," in *The Complete Poetry and Selected Prose of John Donne*, ed. Charles M. Coffin (New York: Modern Library, 2001), 264.

30 Cf. Peels, *Vengeance of God*, 245–46. I offer a more focused analysis below of the inaugurated eschatological character of the kingdom of God during the church age and its ethical implications for Christian imprecation.

Prayer for God to bring about the conversion of the enemy faithfully answers the calling of the sons and daughters of God to guard the Lord's temple-kingdom and drive out the serpentine wicked while addressing the imprecatory psalms' characteristic concerns. The enemy's repentance interrupts the violence of the enemy's antagonism, breaking the teeth that were once devoted to devouring the innocent (cf. Ps 58:6) and shattering the arm that formerly grasped for the righteous (cf. Ps 10:15), turning them back from the evil they devised (cf. Ps 35:4) and rendering inert the threat they posed to the kingdom through a transfer of allegiance. The enemy's repentance vindicates the rightness of the righteous he previously pursued by acknowledging the wrongness of the pursuit and joining with the righteous in humble worship of God. The enemy's repentance satisfies God's covenant justice, for the Christ called upon by faith in the enemy's conversion is the Christ who was cast out and covenantally cursed for sinners (Gal 3:13; Heb 13:12) precisely so that God might be just and the justifier of the ungodly (Rom 3:26). When the imprecatory psalms are oriented toward conversion, God's priest-kings in Christ guard the kingdom by praying for enemies to enter the kingdom and drive out the serpentine wicked by praying for the serpentine wicked to become faithful children in the family of God.

Such prayers for God to act in such a way as to effect the repentance of the enemy are properly directed at the human enemies of God's temple-kingdom. There is, after all, no scriptural indication that God's spiritual enemies are even capable of repentance, and Christians are nowhere commanded to pray on their behalf or seek their good.[31] Insofar as potentially penitent human beings inhabit, animate, shape, and implement the systemic structures of human society, petition for the repentant reformation of such structures is a legitimate mode of prayerful protection of God's temple-kingdom and cleansing of God's world from a violent enemy that exhibits the capacity for transformation. And prayer for God's repentance-inducing action may be directed against the Christian's self and community as the royal priest of God guards the holiness of the individual and corporate body within which God dwells and reigns by pleading that God

---

[31]   Shepherd, "Place of the Imprecatory Psalms," 125; Longman, *How to Read the Psalms*, 138–40, rightly argue that petitioning for the repentance of human enemies is in fact a means of petitioning for the downfall of spiritual enemies. Conversion is, after all, a wresting of human subjects from the dominion of darkness (Col 1:13), an attack against the hegemonic pursuits of Satan's kingdom.

would expose, mortify, and reorient even those sinful dimensions of life that are hidden from the imprecating agent's own view.[32]

The second form of judgment for which Christians ought to petition is that temporal judgment by which God interrupts the kingdom-threatening violence of the wicked by any means just and necessary. While the church offers her imprecatory prayers with a priority of intention toward the conversion of her human enemies, this intended form of judgment does not exhaust the possible content of ethical imprecation. There is a wider intention—a state of affairs wherein the enemy's violence has been brought to an end such that God's temple-kingdom may flourish in and fill the earth, and the world is liberated from the plague of serpentine hostility—of which the enemy's conversion is but the eminently desirable, but not exclusive, expression. Scripture and experience alike suggest that there will be scenarios wherein the foes of God's reign will not be deterred by the call to conversion, and the church (like the psalmists) is in no epistemic position to know ahead of time which of her enemies will relent in repentance.[33] From the imprecating Christian's perspective, every

---

[32]   Thus Ps 7:9 takes on something of the character of Ps 19:12–14. "Oh, let the evil of the wicked come to an end" is given voice in the Christian's heart like the prayer,

Who can discern his errors?
  Declare me innocent from hidden faults.

Keep back your servant also from presumptuous sins;
  let them not have dominion over me!

Then I shall be blameless,
  and innocent of great transgression.

Let the words of my mouth and the meditation of my heart
  be acceptable in your sight,
  O Lord, my rock and my redeemer.

[33]   On the Christian petitioner's ignorance of God's secret purposes, cf. Mennega, "Ethical Problem," 87, 94; Adams, *War Psalms*, 53; Vos, "Ethical Problem," 137–38. Interestingly, for each of these scholars, the Christian's lack of definite knowledge about who will and will not repent is appealed to in order to discourage imprecatory prayer against particular enemies, lest the Christian pray for a judgment against an enemy that is out of step with God's eternal decrees: Christians should petition against no particular enemy because any particular enemy may be elect. I contend, however, that the Christian's ignorance of God's eternal decrees requires that the Christian be prepared to pray for violence-interrupting, temporal judgment upon every enemy—that the Christian leave open the possibility in each instance of imprecatory prayer that

enemy is a potential penitent and simultaneously one who may require temporal intervention in order to be diverted from his deadly designs. If the royal priests of the new covenant community are to guard God's temple-kingdom and cleanse the land of every serpentine enemy, then, they must petition with the psalmists that God would manifest his just judgment within time and space in whatever manner is required to thwart the destructive antagonism of the kingdom's foes, even as they privilege conversion as the chiefly sought means of intervention: "Oh, let the evil of the wicked come to an end" (Ps 7:9).

The psalmists regularly pray that God would disappoint (35:4, 25–26; 40:14; 129:5) and disempower (10:15; 55:9; 58:6–7), confront and subdue (17:13), and even bring about the death of the enemy (58:8; 69:28; 104:35; 109:8–9) in their service of God's temple-kingdom. Significantly, however, the psalmists regularly signal that their pleas are legitimated and limited by the *lex talionis* (e.g., 109): they ask God to intervene against the enemy in ways that are justly proportionate to the enemy's sins (cf. 28:4; 94:2). In the same way, the sons and daughters of God in Christ must beg the judge of heaven and earth to preserve his people, protect the place of his royal dwelling, and move the cosmos toward its holy end by exercising temporal vengeance that frustrates the destructive schemes of the wicked, up to and including the death of those lethally opposed to his reign. They simultaneously constrain their petitions to forms of temporal vengeance that constitute a proportional and just response according to God's law of talionic retribution. A failure to pray for God to do whatever is necessary to stop the enemy from raging against the kingdom and polluting his world with violence would be an abdication of the calling of the sons and daughters of God; a failure to pray for God to do what is proportionally

---

God's intervention in history may be the only way that any particular enemy's oppression will come to an end. This is the opposite effect of that proposed by the above scholars: Christians should petition for divine action including just and necessary temporal judgment upon every enemy because any enemy may require divine inhibition in order to be stopped. The fundamental issue is not what form of prayer will perfectly align with God's hidden and unknowable decrees (a concern conspicuously absent from the Psalter), but what form of prayer is required for Christians to uphold their calling as sons and daughters of God in their present epistemic condition. Given the Christian's inability to know whether any particular enemy will repent according to God's eternal decrees, her mandate to protect God's temple-kingdom necessitates an expansion of the content of imprecation to include those just and necessary means of temporal judgment that will interrupt the enemy's violence should they reject the call to repentance.

just in his obstruction of the enemy would be a perpetuation of injustice unfit for God's holy temple-kingdom.

Thus, while petitions for the enemy's death may be ethically warranted—namely, when the enemy vehemently and violently seeks the death of the innocent—they will not be ethically warranted in every circumstance. Here, Paul's (nonlethal) imprecatory desire in Gal 5:12 is instructive: against enemies who threaten to cut Christians so as to cut them off from Christ, Paul expresses the talionic wish that they would cut themselves so as to be exposed in their falsehood and cut off from the community, pleading for a proportional protection of the *ekklesia*. Such petitions for proportional and necessary temporal judgment are a prayerful means by which the church seeks the interruption of the enemy's aggression for the deliverance of the innocent, as well as the exposure and overthrow of evil in a vindicating reversal for the righteous, in accord with God's promises to sustain his people and with his standards of covenant justice. With these pleas, the church thereby executes her vocation to guard the temple-kingdom from those enemies who threaten the peace, witness, flourishing, and life of God's people and to drive out the serpent's seed from the land in which he purposes to eternally rule in a manner consonant with the fundamental pursuits of the imprecatory psalms.

This form of imprecatory prayer is fittingly directed against every type of enemy. Human beings, systemic powers, and spiritual entities may violently oppress the innocent, and the calling of God's royal priests in Christ to protect the temple-kingdom from and cleanse the land of the serpentine enemy requires that Christians petition for God to take just action in history to interrupt the raging of each of these classes of enemy by whatever means necessary. The psalmic pleas for broken teeth, torn fangs, and blunted arrows (58:6–7) may for the Christian serve as a prayer for the effective, talionic, temporal disempowering of any and every foe devoted to the destruction of the kingdom—whether false teachers within the church, violent individuals without, repressive regimes, unjust structures, or the demonic forces of darkness. Even Christians themselves are the proper objects of such prayers. To the extent that the indwelling sin of the Christian individual and church always renders God's own people a possible threat to the witness and life of the covenant community, the vocation to faithfully guard the temple-kingdom enjoins the obligation to pray that God would do whatever is required in order to expose and frustrate Christians' latent capacity to wreak havoc like a serpent in the garden. "Break the arm of the wicked" (Ps 10:15) is thus rightly prayed as "Break the arm of the human, systemic, and spiritual enemies of your kingdom" and "Break my arm, too—expose, disappoint, inhibit us however you must—in order to keep your people from participating in the destructive violence of the wicked."

The third form of divine judgment for which Christians ought to petition is the eschatological judgment that with the coming of Christ brings an end to all unrighteousness, consummates the temple-kingdom of God on earth, and definitively manifests God's covenant justice against the wicked.[34] In the New Testament, Jesus exhorts his followers to pray for eschatological justice until the day the Son of Man returns in glory to administer it in full (Luke 18:1–8); Paul follows his *anathema* request in 1 Cor 16:22 with a *maranatha* cry for Jesus' *parousia* as the consummate answer to his petition for the expulsion of the wicked; the martyrs of Rev 6:9–10 beg for an avenging, which God answers in the course of the Apocalypse with proleptic judgments in history and, finally, with the eschatological unveiling of his perfect justice. The New Testament's imprecatory speech acts thus indicate that petitions for eschatological judgment against the enemies of God's kingdom are fitting prayers for the priest-kings of God. Elsewhere, Christians are instructed and assumed to eagerly anticipate Jesus' coming (e.g., Luke 12:35–40; Titus 2:13; 2 Tim 4:8; Rev 22:20), and these instructions and assumptions implicitly suggest that Christians correspondingly are to long for the definitive judgment upon the wicked, which Jesus' coming entails.[35] Insofar as God has already committed himself to pour out final judgment at the appearing of Christ, imprecatory prayers for eschatological justice are petitions for the judgment God has irrevocably promised to render—such imprecation is an "Amen, so let it be" to the word of God, a response of faith and affirmation to God's revelation of his intentions and his *telos* for history.

The eschatological vengeance of God upon the enemies of his kingdom is the consummate interruption of violence, a cessation of hostility never again to be followed by a resumption of aggression. Christ's

---

[34] Cf. Peels, *Vengeance of God*, 246; Longman, *How to Read the Psalms*, 140; Shepherd, "Place of the Imprecatory Psalms," 125; John Mark Hicks, "Preaching Community Laments: Responding to Disillusionment with God and Injustice in the World," in *Performing the Psalms*, ed. Dave Bland and David Fleer (St. Louis: Chalice Press, 2005), 77; John N. Day, "The Imprecatory Psalms and Christian Ethics" (PhD diss., Dallas Theological Seminary, 2001), 175.

[35] See J. W. Wenham, *The Goodness of God* (London: InterVarsity Press, 1974), 167–68; Longman, *How to Read the Psalms*, 140; Shepherd, "Place of the Imprecatory Psalms," 125.

second advent is the eternal vindication of the righteous, the ultimate divine unmasking of the wickedness of the wicked that is the universal revelation and glorious exaltation of the righteous. And the victorious return of Christ the king is God's final and most complete answer to his covenant promises to crush the serpent, curse those who curse Abraham, cast out law breakers, and repay the guilty exactly what their evil works deserve. Petitions for eschatological judgment align with the imprecatory psalms' basic requests for the termination of violence, the vindication of the innocent oppressed, and the revelation of covenantal justice and are consistent with the calling of the sons and daughters of God to prayerfully protect the temple-kingdom and expel the serpent seed from the land where God will reside in glory, holiness, and peace with his redeemed people forever.

Requests for God's eschatological vengeance are appropriately directed at the spiritual, human, and systemic enemies of the kingdom. Every form of opposition will be eradicated from God's new creational temple-kingdom with the *parousia* of Christ, and every form of opposition is thus a fitting target of prayer for God's expulsive, kingdom-consummating justice. Such prayers may also be directed against Christians' indwelling sin as petitions for the final, sin-destroying, temple-cleansing glorification of believers that God assures shall accompany Jesus' second coming (1 John 3:2; Phil 3:21; Col 3:4). The Lord promises to make the believing community the holy temple-city of God (Rev 21:2–3), each member finally and fully fit to reside and minister in the presence of the holy king (Rev 22:3–5), and the church's *maranatha* prayer is in part a plea for the Lord to hasten the day when her sin shall be driven away and she shall be truly clean. Christian prayer for God's eschatological clearing of every unclean thing from the land of his eternal dwelling ought to take aim, then, at the persons, structures, and spiritual forces violently opposed to God and at those parts of the disciple's and the church's divided hearts that remain obstinately opposed to God as well.

The sons and daughters of God in Christ, therefore, ought to orient their performance of the imprecatory psalms toward petitions for divine action leading to repentance and conversion, temporal judgments that interrupt the violence of the wicked by any just means necessary, and eschatological judgment that irreversibly eradicates all opposition to God's reign and consummates his temple-kingdom in the earth. Such petitions cohere with Christians' royal-priestly vocation to guard the temple-kingdom and cleanse the land of the unclean wicked and with the imprecatory psalms' prayerful pursuit of covenantal justice that ends violence and vindicates the righteous. It should be further observed that each of these ethically permissible forms of requested judgment finds implicit commendation in the second petition of the Lord's Prayer: "Thy kingdom come" pleads for the manifestation of God's reign on earth, a manifestation that progressively emerges as believers are sanctified to reflect the character of the kingdom, sinners are converted to join the kingdom, and violent enemies are interrupted from opposing the kingdom, and that definitively materializes in history with the consummating return of Christ.[36] Calvin's summary of the second petition is illuminating:

> Therefore, no others keep a lawful order in this petition but those who begin with themselves, that is, to be cleansed of all corruptions that disturb the peaceful state of God's Kingdom and its purity [sanctifying self-imprecation]. Now, because the word of God is like a royal scepter, we are bidden here to entreat him to bring all men's minds and hearts into voluntary obedience to it [repentance and conversion]. . . . Afterward we should descend to the impious, who stubbornly and with desperate madness resist his authority. Therefore, God sets up his Kingdom by humbling the whole world, but in different ways. For he tames the wantonness of some, breaks the untamable pride of others. We must daily desire that God gather churches unto himself from all parts of the earth; that he spread and increase them in number; . . . on the other hand, that he cast down all enemies of pure teaching and religion; that he scatter their counsels and crush their efforts [temporal judgment]. . . . But its fullness is delayed to the final coming of Christ when, as Paul teaches, "God will be all in all" (1 Cor 15:28) [eschatological judgment].[37]

The second petition of the prayer Jesus taught his disciples to pray thus bears all the marks of royal-priestly prayer, a suppliant participation in the various forms of judgment by which God prospers his temple-kingdom and thwarts its antagonizers in history and ushers the world toward its

---

[36] Several scholars draw attention to the affinities between the imprecatory psalms and the second petition of the Lord's Prayer. See, e.g., Murray, "Christian Cursing?" 117–18; J. Clinton McCann, Jr., A Theological Introduction to the Book of Psalms: The Psalms as Torah (Nashville: Abingdon, 1993), 124; Jace Broadhurst, "Should Cursing Continue? An Argument for Imprecatory Psalms in Biblical Theology," AJET 23, no. 1 (2004): 84–85; Vos, "Ethical Problem," 138; Adams, War Psalms, 52; Mennega, "Ethical Problem," 93.

[37] Calvin, Institutes, III.20.42.

appointed eschatological end as the holy dwelling of God with humanity. As the imprecatory psalms are "thy kingdom come" in Israelite grammar, so the second petition is implicit Christian imprecation, and when Christians take up the imprecatory psalms to beg for repentance and conversion, temporal judgment, and eschatological justice, they obey the command of their Lord, "Pray then like this" (Matt 6:9).

Eschatology and Christian Imprecation

How does the eschatological character of the temple-kingdom of God in this time between Jesus' advents affect how the church may pray Israel's imprecatory prayers? Stated alternatively, how does the shape of God's kingdom in the church's time within God's narrative—the particular way in which God's reign is manifested in the world in this postresurrection, pre-*parousia* scene of redemptive history—influence the manner in which she guards the kingdom and endeavors to cleanse God's world for the consummation of the kingdom through prayer? I have argued that the immediacy of the imprecatory psalms' petitions for the inbreaking retribution of God against the wicked and their requests and expectations that human beings would be divinely empowered to execute God's vengeance upon the enemy was related to the realized eschatological character of God's temple-kingdom in Israel. The kingdom existed as a physical nation with a physical temple edifice in which divine judgment upon internal and external threats to the kingdom, whether directly from God or mediated through the structures of Israelite society, was a regular feature that concretely revealed the pattern and righteousness of God's rule and in which the Israelite king and community were authorized to actualize God's just judgments in history. The psalmists, accordingly, pray for the realization in fact of a kingdom that is eschatologically realized in principle, and they pray that God will mobilize his people to faithfully act as agents of his wrath in the world.

In the church's scene of God's story, the eschatological character of the temple-kingdom has shifted; the kingdom is inaugurated, not realized, as the ascended Christ reigns over his multinational spiritual community from heaven and dwells with her by his Spirit, delaying the consummation of judgment and the physical instantiation of his reign and patiently welcoming even violent enemies to become citizens by grace. This shift in the eschatological character of the temple-kingdom requires a shift in the shape of the imprecatory prayers offered by those Christian priest-kings tasked with defending the kingdom and clearing God's land of all uncleanness. This renders appropriate a clearer foregrounding of repentance as the principally intended form of desired divine action against enemies and an eschatologizing of ecclesial expectations of human actualization of divine vengeance against the enemies of God's kingdom.

The kingdom of God in the church's time is eschatologically inaugurated, simultaneously already present and not yet consummated, established in history and awaiting its ultimate completion.[38] God's reign is already present insofar as Jesus has triumphed over his enemies through his death and resurrection (Col 2:13–15), ascended his heavenly throne in victory (Eph 4:8), and poured out his Holy Spirit to mediate his royal presence and the blessings of salvation among his temple-people (Acts 2:33). God's kingdom is not yet consummated, however, insofar as the kingdom still awaits physical instantiation in the world, to be accomplished at the return of Christ when he will administer perfect justice, expel every form of opposition from his creation, and rule bodily over and with his resurrected community of royal priests forever. This inaugurated eschatological character—this already-not-yet tension in the present shape of God's temple-kingdom in the world—results in several unique and interrelated features of the kingdom in the church's moment of redemptive history. First, Christ rules spiritually over his kingdom from heaven such that, unlike the kingdom in Israel, the kingdom in the church age exists as a transnational, spiritual communion that cannot be identified with any political nation, civil magistrate, human monarchy, or bounded physical territory.[39] Where Israel existed as a nation alongside the nations, the kingdom of Christ given political expression in the church is a community called to permeate every nation without itself being a nation.

Second, God's inbreaking judgment in history, a regular feature of the realized kingdom in Israel, has been to a considerable degree delayed—suspended—until the *parousia* when Jesus will execute God's

---

[38]   See the classic treatments of inaugurated eschatology in the New Testament by Herman Ridderbos, *The Coming of the Kingdom*, ed. Raymond O. Zorn, trans. H. de Jongste (Philadelphia: Presbyterian and Reformed, 1962); George Eldon Ladd, *The Presence of the Future: The Eschatology of Biblical Realism* (Grand Rapids: Eerdmans, 1974). Cf. Anthony A. Hoekema, *The Bible and the Future* (Grand Rapids: Eerdmans, 1979), 1–75.

[39]   See Peels, *Vengeance of God*, 246; George Eldon Ladd, *The Gospel of the Kingdom: Scriptural Studies in the Kingdom of God* (Grand Rapids: Eerdmans, 1959), 22–23.

just vengeance upon the world in full (cf. 1 Cor 15:24–25).[40] In Israel God frequently took direct action against covenant breakers, the law institutionalized punitive judgment against offenders, and the military waged holy war as an expression of God's wrath against the nations as God manifested the justice and righteousness of his reign in history. But the present time is one characterized by divine patience and grace wherein God's enemies are permitted to reside in the world that God has claimed for his dwelling (Matt 13:24–30; Rev 12:17)[41] and to violently rage against his temple-kingdom as sinners are granted the opportunity to repent (2 Pet 3:9–10), enter the kingdom by faith, and escape the revelation of God's expulsive judgment on the last day.[42]

Third, the royal-priestly sons and daughters of God in Christ are to serve as human mediators of God's judgment in the world in a manner consonant with the inaugurated character of the temple-kingdom in their time. Whereas Israel mediated God's judgment and participated in the realized establishment of his kingdom in part by actively executing vengeance upon the internal and external threats to God's temple-kingdom, Christians will not actively participate in the expulsion of the enemy until they are revealed as the sons and daughters of God (Rom 8:19) and join Jesus at his kingdom-consummating coming in definitively driving out every serpentine uncleanness from the land where God will eternally rule and reside (Matt 19:28; Rom 16:20; 1 Cor 6:2–3; Rev 2:26–27; 17:14; 18:6; 19:14; 20:4–6). As Jesus informed Pilate, "My kingdom is not of this world. If my kingdom were of this world, my servants would have been fighting"

---

[40]   Of course, the New Testament testifies that God's judgment continues to irrupt into history: e.g., the deaths of Ananias and Sapphira in Acts 5:1–11; the striking down of Herod in Acts 12:20–23; the illness and death of Corinthians around the Lord's Table in 1 Cor 11:29–32; and the testimony of the Apocalypse that God's judgments are manifest in history until the climactic judgment of Christ's return. But while God's judgment continues to operate in history, the inbreaking of such judgment is not an integral feature of the present inaugurated kingdom as it was in the realized kingdom of Israel, where threats to the kingdom were to be totally, decisively, and immediately expelled in the execution of divine justice. The total and decisive revelation of God's judgment that liberates his kingdom to flourish without threat awaits the consummation of Christ's *parousia*.

[41]   Cf. Ridderbos, *Coming of the Kingdom*, 106–13, 136–41.

[42]   Ridderbos, *Coming of the Kingdom*, 148–55, observes that the postponement of final judgment in the inaugurated kingdom supplies the context for the preaching of grace and repentance.

(John 18:36).[43] Until the *parousia*, the sons and daughters of God mediate divine judgment against God's enemies—guarding the temple-kingdom and cleansing the land—through nonviolent means. They mortify the sin that corrupts the temple-body (2 Cor 7:1). They exercise the church discipline that cleanses the temple-kingdom from corruption (1 Cor 5:1–13).[44] They expose the worldliness of the world and reveal God's verdict on unrighteousness through faithful witness to the way of Christ's kingdom (Eph 5:7–14; Phil 1:28; 2 Thess 1:5).[45] They wage war against the kingdom of darkness and enter the land God has claimed for his kingdom in the ministry of word and sacrament (Luke 10:19; Matt 28:18–20; 2 Cor 10:3–6).[46] And they pray for the revelation of God's violence-ceasing

[43]   On the eschewal of violence as related to the spiritual, as opposed to politically instantiated, character of Christ's kingdom in the present age, cf. Andreas J. Köstenberger, *John*, BECNT (Grand Rapids: Baker Academic, 2004), 528, esp. n39; Ernst Haenchen, *John 2: A Commentary on the Gospel of John Chapters 7–21*, trans. Robert W. Funk, ed. Robert W. Funk with Ulrich Busse, Hermeneia (Philadelphia: Fortress, 1984), 179; Marianne Meye Thompson, *John: A Commentary*, NTL (Louisville: Westminster John Knox, 2015), 380; Barnabas Lindars, ed., *The Gospel of John*, NCB (London: Oliphants, 1972), 558–59. Cf. also John Bright, *The Kingdom of God: The Biblical Concept and Its Meaning for the Church* (New York: Abingdon, 1953), 199–200; Hoekema, *Bible and the Future*, 212–13.

[44]   Cf. Meredith G. Kline, *Kingdom Prologue: Genesis Foundations for a Covenantal Worldview* (Eugene, Ore.: Wipf and Stock, 2006), 86–87; David H. Wenkel, "Kingship and Thrones for All Christians: Paul's Inaugurated Eschatology in 1 Corinthians 4–6," *ExpTim* 128, no. 2 (2016): 67–69.

[45]   See Stanley Hauerwas, *The Peaceable Kingdom: A Primer in Christian Ethics* (Notre Dame: University of Notre Dame Press, 1983), 100; Oliver O'Donovan, *The Desire of the Nations: Rediscovering the Roots of Political Theology* (New York: Cambridge University, 1996), 258.

[46]   Jesus' commission of his disciples in Matt 28:18–20 to go into the world baptizing and teaching to observe all his commands, bolstered by the knowledge of his presence, resonates with echoes of the Lord's commission of Joshua-led Israel in Josh 1:1–9 to go into the land and observe all the law Moses commanded, encouraged by the promise of the Lord's continual presence. Cf. 2 Chron 36:23, where Cyrus proclaims he has been given authority to build a house for God at Jerusalem and invokes God's presence with his people. Jesus is building God's house in the world, and the Great Commission is a commission for a new conquest as God's enemies are driven from the world over and in which he shall reign through the gospel ministry of the church. Paul's statement in 2 Cor 10:3–6 is conceptually similar, describing the apostle's nonviolent ministry of the gospel in language drawn from Israel's land-clearing conquest in the Old Testament.

judgment upon all unrighteousness (Luke 18:1–8; Gal 1:8–9; 5:12; 1 Cor 16:22; Rev 6:9–10; 8:3–5; cf. Eph 6:18). Each of these forms of human participation in God's judgment aligns with the not-yet-consummated character of God's kingdom and the nature of the present time as an era of gracious patience and delayed vengeance. God's priest-kings presently mediate his judgment in peace, for it is the peacemakers—and not the violent—whom the Lord blesses and calls the sons and daughters of God (Matt 5:9).[47]

The prayerful battle against the enemies of God's kingdom waged by the royal-priestly members of God's kingdom must be conducted in a manner that aligns with the inaugurated eschatological character of God's kingdom. Which is to say, the current shape of God's kingdom in the world determines what constitutes a fitting prayerful defense of the kingdom and petitionary pursuit of a cleansed world that is coterminous with the kingdom by those sons and daughters of God in Christ who are citizens and agents of the kingdom. I argued above that Christians' performance of the imprecatory psalms must reflect the inaugurated eschatological character of the temple-kingdom by prioritizing divine action eliciting repentance and conversion as the principally desired form of judgment upon the enemies of the kingdom. Though the psalmists periodically express a longing for or expectation of the enemy's conversion (Pss 7:11–13; 40:3; 83:16; 141:6), their petitions typically foreground desires for temporal manifestations of judgment that bring an end to the life-endangering threats posed by the wicked and contribute to the concrete instantiation of the temple-kingdom in the world. Cries such as "Oh that you would slay the wicked, O God!" (Ps 139:19), "Let sinners be consumed from the earth, and let the wicked be no more!" (Ps 104:35), and "Let them be like the snail that dissolves into slime" (Ps 58:8) far outnumber explicit statements about the enemy's repentance in the imprecations, and this prayerful prioritization of temporal judgment coheres with the realized eschatological character of the kingdom in Israel in which the revelation of divine vengeance upon covenant-breaking wickedness within history was a regular feature. In a time, however, characterized not by immediate manifestations of divine judgment but by a gracious postponement of the consummate revelation

---

[47]   Donald A. Hagner, *Matthew 1–13*, WBC 33A (Dallas: Word Books, 1993), 94, contends that this proclamation is directed against those who, like the Zealots, desired to bring the kingdom through violence and militarism. Only those who seek to guard the kingdom and clear the land for the holy dwelling of God in peace faithfully embrace the calling of the sons of God in this age.

of wrath that gives space for repentance, the church prays in line with the character of the present temple-kingdom when she intends every psalmic prayer for judgment first as a prayer that God in this era of patience would break, shatter, interrupt, and slay the enemy by crucifying them with Christ through faith. God still works directly and through instrumental means in this redemptive-historical moment to restrain evil and exercise temporal judgment on the wicked (e.g., Acts 5:1–11; 12:20–23; 1 Cor 11:29–32; Rom 13:4; Rev 6:1–8; 8–9), and he will work at the consummation to judge his enemies with perfect justice, and the church accordingly prays for his evil-restraining, kingdom-protecting action in the midst of history and his earth-cleansing justice at the end of history. But the consummation-delaying, gracious character of the kingdom of God in this chapter of God's story leads to a reordering of intention in Christian imprecation through which the judgment of conversion is desired above and before, though not to the exclusion of, all other forms of judgment.

The inaugurated eschatological character of the temple-kingdom also requires modification of ecclesial expectations of active participation in the administration of divine judgment in Christian performance of the imprecatory psalms. The psalmists frequently anticipate that the human son of God—whether the Davidic king or Israelite community—will participate in the violent manifestation of God's wrath upon the serpentine threats to God's temple-kingdom (Pss 41:10; 58:10; 68:22–23; 72:4; 137:8–9; 144:1–2)[48] in a manner consistent with the realized character of the kingdom in Israel and with Israel's concomitant calling to actualize God's judgment as a royal-priestly son of God. The sons and daughters of God in Christ, however, will not participate in the active execution of divine vengeance upon the wicked until the eschatological appearing of Jesus, the human priest-king *par excellence*. Psalmic expectations of human mediation of God's violent judgment consequently must be transposed into the Christian key of the already–not yet, anticipated and requested not as an element of the church's royal-priestly vocation in the present course of history but as a feature of her eschatological vocation to be embraced only at the kingdom-consummating *parousia* of her Lord. At the end of the age, God will indeed crush the Satanic serpent under the feet of his people (Rom 16:20); Christians will ride into victory with Jesus as he strikes down the nations and treads the winepress of God's wrath (Rev 19:14); God's human priest-kings will pay back Babylon with talionic justice (Rev

---

48   Similar expectations occur throughout the Psalter: e.g., Pss 18:31–42, 47; 44:5; 60:9–12; 75:10; 101:5, 8; 108:10–13; 110:5–6; 118:10–13; 149:6–9.

18:6; cf. Ps 137:8–9); the sons and daughters of God will judge and reign with the Son of God (Rev 2:26–27; 20:4–6). When the church takes up the Psalter's royal-priestly prayers as her royal-priestly prayers, petitioning for her own active agency with Christ in the foot-stomping, head-crushing, serpent-shattering, enemy-subduing vengeance of God, she accordingly must pray for the unveiling of that agency as an eschatological reality rather than an agency to be exercised in the present time. In the Christian's mouth, "Raise me up, that I may repay them" (Ps 41:10) and all similar prayers must be prayers for juridical participation in the eschatological tomorrow rather than the historical today.

Christian imprecation that is consistent with the church's time in God's narrative—with the inaugurated eschatological character of God's temple-kingdom—will thus prioritize divine action leading to the enemy's repentance in requests for judgment and will eschatologize expectations and requests for the church's active participation with Jesus in the consummate manifestation of God's justice. Such prayer aligns with the nature of the church's redemptive-historical location as an age of gracious patience prior to the realization of God's vengeance in the world on the last day, a day when Christians will be finally and gloriously revealed in their status as the sons and daughters of God and authorized to mediate God's definitive enemy-expelling judgment as Christ clears the earth of every serpentine intruder so that God may dwell in holiness and peace with his people forever.

Christian Imprecation and the Law of Love

Ethical Christian performance of the imprecatory psalms must exhibit the proper agents, objects, and content in a manner that coheres with the church's calling and time in God's narrative, but these previously identified features—though necessary—are not sufficient, for ethical Christian practice requires appropriate agential postures and affective orientations as well. Isaiah and Jesus alike observed that the external conditions of piety may be met with a heart yet far from God.[49] From what loves, then, ought Christian imprecation to proceed, and toward what corresponding ends ought it be directed? That is, what are the fitting objects and aims of affective desire for the sons and daughters of God in Christ who embrace their calling to guard the temple-kingdom and cleanse the world in prayerful action? Relatedly, how are these teleologically oriented affections consonant with the New Testament's, including Jesus', ethical prescriptions of enemy love and proscriptions of cursing (e.g., Matt 5:44;

---

[49]   Matt 15:8; Mark 7:6; Isa 29:13.

Luke 6:27–28; Rom 12:14)? Whereas thus far we have examined the form of ethical Christian imprecation as a moral act, here we grant particular attention to the imprecating moral agent, inquiring about the internal postures of heart required for ethical Christian imprecation, the necessary loves that give rise to and are reflected in the ultimate *teloi* of right prayer.

Christian imprecatory prayer must be born from loves consistent with the purposes, works, and commands of God, loves that aim for those goals for which God aims in his narrative of the world and that God has explicitly directed his covenant people to pursue. Consequently, ethical performance of the imprecatory psalms by God's royal priesthood in Christ must arise from—and is in turn necessitated by—affections characterized by love of God, God's temple-kingdom, God's creation, and God's enemies and ordered toward the good of each. Imprecation that does not proceed from such loves, though it may be offered by the proper agents against the proper objects with the proper content, will fail to meet the standards of ethical imprecation for characters in God's story of the world.[50] What is more, where such loves are permitted to grow up into maturity and bear the fruit of action, they must bear the fruit of imprecatory prayer.

Christian performance of the imprecatory psalms must arise chiefly from love of God, having as its supreme *telos* the vindication, exaltation, and magnification of God's glory.[51] Imprecatory prayer—as petition for God's just, kingdom-guarding, expulsive judgment upon every serpentine antagonism that defies his holy character, contravenes his purposes, and corrupts his creation—is consistent with love of God insofar as it pleads for the confirmation of his righteousness, faithfulness, and sovereignty in history, but such prayer must have love of God as its active, attending affection as well.[52] According to Jesus, the first and great commandment is

---

[50]   Calvin, *Institutes*, III.20.29, maintains that "prayer itself is properly an emotion of the heart within [*cordis affectum*], which is poured out and laid open before God, the searcher of hearts." He continues, "From this, moreover, it is fully evidence that unless voice and song, if interposed in prayer, spring from deep feeling of heart, neither has any value or profit in the least with God. But they arouse his wrath against us if they come only from the tip of the lips and from the throat, seeing that this is to abuse his most holy name and to hold his majesty in derision." Calvin, *Institutes*, III.20.31. Cf. Karl Barth, *Prayer*, ed. Don E. Saliers, trans. Sara F. Terrien (Louisville: Westminster John Knox, 2002), 19.

[51]   Cf. Beisner, *Psalms of Promise*, 181.

[52]   That is, it is not sufficient for the content of imprecatory prayer to be consistent with love of God. The imprecating agent must affectively exhibit love of God in the offering of such prayer for the act to be ethical.

to "love the Lord your God with all your heart and with all your soul and with all your mind" (Matt 22:37), a comprehensive framing that claims the whole human person for love of God,[53] and Paul instructs the Corinthians, "So, whether you eat or drink, or whatever you do, do all to the glory of God" (1 Cor 10:31), commending the worshipful apprehension and revelation of God's glorious character as the supreme end of all human action (cf. 1 Cor 6:20).[54] Imprecatory prayer, as part of the "whatever you do," must seek God's glory, and as an operation of heart, soul, and mind, must have Godward love as its originating affection. The imprecatory psalms themselves, with marked regularity and explicitness, express a desire for God to act "for your name's sake" (79:9; 109:21; 143:11) so that he might be rightly recognized and praised by covenant community and enemy alike (e.g., 7:17; 9:14; 40:16; 58:11; 83:16–18), and the Christian who would make these prayers her own engages in a commissive speech act that performatively pledges her affections as aligning with the psalmists' God-exalting love.[55]

Indeed, God's ethically determinative narrative of the world is ordered toward the manifestation and adoration of his glory: Christians are elected and redeemed by God in Christ "to the praise of his glory" (Eph 1:12, 14; cf. v. 6); all things, existing from and through him, are simultaneously directed to him, an affirmation that elicits from Paul the fitting doxology, "To him be glory forever" (Rom 11:36); and the consummation of creation and God's works within it, the goal toward which God's story is moving, is the Godward worship of his saints in the renewed cosmos where God will reign over and with his people (Rev 22:3). Only when Christians' royal-priestly prayers for the kingdom-protecting, land-clearing judgment of God are affectively oriented in love toward God's glory—the vindicating and acknowledgment-inducing exhibition of his holy character in his just confrontation of wickedness—do they cohere with the commands of Scripture, the stated ends of the imprecatory psalms, and God's own aims within his narrative of history. The priest-king in Christ who pleads for judgment from any other first love practices a surreptitious idolatry in the form of faithful imprecatory prayer,

---

[53] See R. T. France, *The Gospel of Matthew*, NICNT (Grand Rapids: Eerdmans, 2007), 846; Carson, "Matthew," 464.

[54] Cf. WLC Q. 1: "What is the chief and highest end of man? Man's chief and highest end is to glorify God, and fully to enjoy him forever."

[55] See the discussions of commissive speech acts by Wenham, *Psalter Reclaimed*, 22–35; Barker, *Imprecation as Divine Discourse*, 117.

honoring God with the lips while nurturing a wayward heart (cf. Matt 15:8; Isa 29:13). Conversely, the son or daughter of God who refuses to plead for judgment in the form of faithful imprecatory prayer, to petition God to vindicate his character, purposes, and promises in justice, has—consciously or not—permitted some foreign love to displace God as first love and has allowed some lesser aim to displace the revelation of God's glory in the world as chief aim.[56]

Christian performance of the imprecatory psalms must also arise from love for God's temple-kingdom, love that seeks as its end the preservation, peace, purity, prosperity, and proliferation of the community over and with whom God reigns in Christ by his Spirit. Imprecatory prayer, petitioning as it does for the protection of God's temple-people and the eschatological consummation of God's kingdom throughout the earth, is consistent with a kingdom love that pursues the kingdom's good, but for any particular act of Christian imprecation to be ethical, the prayer that is formally consistent with kingdom love must in fact affectively arise from kingdom love. In the paradigm of Christian desire that is the Lord's Prayer, the longing made petition that immediately follows the hallowing of God's name is for the coming of God's kingdom (Matt 6:9–10). Jesus' teaching indicates that Christian prayer ought to desire the kingdom, which is to say that Christian prayer is to pour forth as an expression of love for the kingdom of God. Of course, kingdom love is neither opposed to nor in competition with love for God but is a distinct yet inseparable iteration of love for God: to love God and to desire his glory is to love the kingdom that God loves and over which he rules and to desire its continued existence, witness, and expansion in the world. Just as "your kingdom come" proceeds from "hallowed be your name," love of God flows into and finds expression in love for the temple-kingdom that proclaims and demonstrates God's glory and through which God manifests his kingship and accomplishes his purposes in history.[57]

The psalmists' pleas reflect a love for the temple-kingdom, prayerfully oriented toward the good of the kingdom as the psalmists beg for the protection of God's covenant people (e.g., Ps 83:1–5), the removal of violence from the land (e.g., Ps 58:2, 6–7), the joy of the righteous (cf. Pss 5:11; 58:10), and the instantiation of a temple-kingdom characterized

---

[56]   Cf. Adams, *War Psalms*, 47.

[57]   See Calvin, *Institutes*, III.20.35, on the glory of God as the chief aim of the entire Lord's Prayer and its particular relation to the first three petitions.

by justice, abundance, and security where there is "no cry of distress in our streets" (Ps 144:14; cf. vv. 12–13, 15; Pss 72:1–4; 82:3–4). Once again, the commissive quality of prayerful enactment of the psalms implicates the imprecating agent, obligating the priest-king who prays the imprecatory psalms to exhibit the affections and desire the ends given voice in the psalmists' petitions. The Christian imprecator who would petition for the kingdom performatively commits herself to desiring the good of the kingdom in love, and the imprecator who would petition for the kingdom apart from kingdom love renders his prayerful speech an affectionless farce that pursues the kingdom in word only.

Like the imprecatory psalms, the sweeping scriptural narrative of God's action in history is directed toward the establishment and blessedness of God's temple-kingdom in the world.[58] God creates the world and commissions humanity to spread his temple-kingdom throughout the earth (Gen 1:28); God promises to restore his kingdom when it is fractured by sin (e.g., Gen 3:15; 12:1–3); God redeems and calls Israel to live in holiness and faith as a "kingdom of priests" (Exod 19:6) in his presence; God sends Jesus into his creation to announce and inaugurate the kingdom of God in the world by triumphing over every opposing power in his death, resurrection, and ascension and by giving his Spirit to his people (Acts 2:33; Eph 1:20–23; Col 2:13–15; Rev 1:5–6); and God brings his story to its culmination in a world filled with his glory as the temple-kingdom where he dwells in eternal *shalom* with his covenant community (1 Cor 15:24–28; Rev 21:1–4). This is the story within which Christians act and pray, a story that renders kingdom love both fitting and necessary for the faithful characters who inhabit its world. If the temple-guarding, kingdom-extending prayers of the sons and daughters of God in Christ are to align with God's purposes and works within God's narrative, then they must emerge from affections aimed in the direction of God's aims, from love for God's kingdom that desires the good of God's kingdom. Apart from such

---

[58] Cf., e.g., Graeme Goldsworthy, *Gospel and Kingdom*, in *The Goldsworthy Trilogy* (Eugene, Ore.: Wipf and Stock, 2000); Craig G. Bartholomew and Michael W. Goheen, *The Drama of Scripture: Finding Our Place in the Biblical Story*, 2nd ed. (Grand Rapids: Baker Academic, 2014); Thomas R. Schreiner, *The King in His Beauty: A Biblical Theology of the Old and New Testaments* (Grand Rapids: Baker Academic, 2013); Stephen G. Dempster, *Dominion and Dynasty: A Theology of the Hebrew Bible*, NSBT 15 (Downers Grove, Ill.: InterVarsity Press, 2003); G. K. Beale, *The Temple and the Church's Mission: A Biblical Theology of the Dwelling Place of God*, NSBT 17 (Downers Grove, Ill.: InterVarsity Press, 2004).

love, the imprecating agent desires at cross-purposes with the God who is the author of the controlling story in which the agent is a mere player, but where such love is present, prayer for the divine justice that preserves the temple-kingdom and brings it to consummation must follow.[59]

In addition to love of God and kingdom, Christian performance of the imprecatory psalms must issue from love of God's creation, both the natural creation that is God's handiwork and the human creatures who bear his image. As royal-priestly prayer that seeks the cleansing of God's world from every unholy, corrupting influence and that petitions for the interruption of the wicked in their unjust attacks against innocent human beings—no matter who the innocent may be—the petitions of Christian imprecation are consonant with love for God's creation that desires the good of the world and image bearers threatened by his enemies' raging. And yet again, as with the other requisite loves surveyed, consonance with love of creation does not of itself ethical prayer make, as the imprecating agent must affectively exercise this love for any specific act of imprecatory prayer to be ethically faithful.

The scriptural narrative makes clear that God loves his created world and intends its ultimate renewal and restoration.[60] God crafts the cosmos and takes up residence in Eden as his garden-temple, commissioning his royal priests to subdue the earth and extend the boundaries of his holy dwelling throughout the earth (Gen 1:28). The Lord purposes to make his home in the land he grants to Israel, "a land that the LORD your God cares for" (Deut 11:12), as she answers her calling to drive out serpentine uncleanness, and in his law God mandates that his people steward land and livestock in ways that support their flourishing (e.g., Exod 20:10; Lev 25:1–12), promising that the faithful fruitfulness of his kingdom people

[59]   Which is to say, a failure to protect and press forward the temple-kingdom in prayer evidences a failure to love the temple-kingdom rightly. Cf. Mennega, "Ethical Problem," 92.

[60]   For diverse treatments of God's love for the earth and the concomitant ethical obligation of Christians to love the earth, cf., e.g., Steven Bouma-Prediger, *For the Beauty of the Earth: A Christian Vision for Creation Care* (Grand Rapids: Baker Academic, 2010), 111–29; Holmes Rolston III, "Loving Nature: Christian Environmental Ethics," in *Love and Christian Ethics: Tradition, Theory, and Society*, ed. Frederick V. Simmons with Brian C. Sorrells (Washington, D.C.: Georgetown University Press, 2016), 313–31; John Frame, *The Doctrine of the Christian Life*, A Theology of Lordship (Phillipsburg, N.J.: P&R Publishing, 2008), 743–45; Norman Wirzba, *From Nature to Creation: A Christian Vision for Understanding and Loving Our World*, The Church and Postmodern Culture (Grand Rapids: Baker Academic, 2015), 18–24.

will be attended with the abundant fruitfulness of the kingdom land (e.g., Lev 25:18–22; Deut 28:1–14). Jesus' death and resurrection effect not only the salvation of human beings but the resurrection of the entire created order that was subjected to futility because of sin (Rom 8:19–22), a new heaven and earth that will be the temple-dwelling of God with redeemed humanity (Rev 21:1–5) when the appointed time arrives for God's "destroying the destroyers of the earth" (Rev 11:18). The *telos* of God's story is a natural world liberated from the bondage of sin and the corruption of violence as the holy habitation of God with humanity, a *telos* that must orient the desire of his royal-priestly characters if they are indeed to live and pray with the grain of God's story. As the sons and daughters of God fulfill their narrative vocation by petitioning for the cleansing of the created world from every unholy intrusion, it is fitting and necessary for them to do so from a love for the earth that God loves and redeems, the earth that he will one day live in and reign upon and fill with his glory, desiring its freedom and completion.[61] And, as with love of God and kingdom, love of God's world—a world that is quite often a forgotten victim of the injustice and violence of the wicked—must drive the Christian into land-cleansing imprecatory prayer.

But to love God's creation is to love the human beings God has created in his image as well, and here I am especially concerned with those human beings whose life and peace are jeopardized by the violence of the wicked. In Jesus' teaching, the second great commandment upon which, along with love of God, all the Law and Prophets depend is to "love your neighbor as yourself" (Matt 22:39; cf. Rom 13:8–10; Gal 5:14; Jas 2:8).[62] Prompted by a lawyer's self-justifying query—"And who is my neighbor?"—the Lord recounts the parable of the good Samaritan, a vignette that famously centers attention not on the identity of the neighbor but on the moral agent's responsibility to exhibit neighborliness, to

[61]   Oliver O'Donovan, *Resurrection and Moral Order: An Outline for Evangelical Ethics*, 2nd ed. (Grand Rapids: Eerdmans, 1994), 236, suggests, "Love of the material world is good if it is built upon a recognition of what material goods are and what they are for." While this principal has manifold particular applications in the Christian agent's relation to discrete objects in God's world, at the highest level, the material world is for the holy dwelling of God with his people, and a good love of the material world will be built upon this recognition and desire its fruition.

[62]   As France, *Gospel of Matthew*, 846, bluntly observes, "The neighbor is everyone." Cf. Douglas J. Moo, *The Epistle to the Romans*, NICNT (Grand Rapids: Eerdmans, 1996), 813, on Rom 13:8.

live as a neighbor in love, even across ethnic and religious lines, to every human being whose need confronts and lays claim upon the agent (Luke 10:25–37).[63]

Within the contours of God's narrative, such love is not only obedience to the divine command but is also a recognition of and imitative participation in God's love toward humanity and as such is an expression of love for God.[64] God created human beings in his image (Gen 1:26–27), investing them with a peculiar and inalienable dignity that merits the loving attention and honor of every other image bearer.[65] Sent in love by the Father, the Son through whom the world was made entered the world in love, taking on the flesh and nature of humanity so that any human who would turn to him in repentant faith might experience the blessing of life with God (John 1:9–10; 3:16; 1 John 4:9–10). In his life, Jesus loved human beings in action—men and women, adults and children, able-bodied and disabled, healthy and ill, Jew and Gentile, those who followed him and those who did not—and in his death, Jesus exhibited a love for human beings greater than which no human can embody (John 15:13). Christian characters in God's story of the world, beneficiaries of God's love in Christ toward humanity, play and pray their part well only when they love the image bearers that God loves and follow in the loving example of Christ. Imprecatory prayers that petition for the interruption of God-defying, innocent-assaulting violence wherever it is found, that ask God to effect peace and justice for his oppressed human creatures as he drives out all serpentine unholiness from his world, must therefore proceed from affections of love for God's image bearers. And when confronted with the suffering of the innocent at the hands of the violent wicked—which, in the media-saturated context of the digital age, is an almost constant phenomenon—true neighborliness demands a love for those human beings in need that seeks their good, a love that refuses to merely pass them by but instead desires their preservation and

---

[63]   Cf. O'Donovan, *Resurrection and Moral Order*, 239–40, on the Lucan parable and its implications for the ethics of neighbor love, as well as David Lyle Jeffrey, *Luke*, BTCB (Grand Rapids: Brazos, 2012), 148–51.

[64]   Gene Outka, *Agape: An Ethical Analysis*, Yale Publications in Religion 17 (New Haven: Yale University Press, 1972), 44, observes that "normally beliefs concerning God's action in creation and redemption are invoked to emphasize that the neighbor is the object of divine love. Love for God thus implies conformity in loving what He loves."

[65]   See Calvin, *Institutes*, II.8.40.

flourishing and bears the fruit of loving action in imprecatory prayer on their behalf.[66]

Thus far, I have argued that Christian performance of the imprecatory psalms—which as kingdom-protecting and world-cleansing prayer is consistent in its pleas with love of God, temple-kingdom, and creation—must affectively arise from and is in turn necessitated by love of God, temple-kingdom, and creation that desires the good particularly suited to each. The Christian imprecator whose prayer does not flow from such love fails to live into the affective orientation proper to characters in God's story. And love that fails to engage in imprecatory prayer has been cut short, interrupted before growing up to maturity in prayerful action, and thus represents a failure to grab hold in love of the resources of prayer commended to the church by God for the pursuit of his glory, the *shalom* of his temple-kingdom, and the flourishing of his human and nonhuman creation. Imprecation must be born of love, and love that does not give birth to imprecation is incomplete at best.

But what of love for the image-bearing neighbor who is the enemy?[67] Is the task of imprecatory prayer—which I have suggested is not only an essential element in the Christian's royal-priestly calling to defend the temple-kingdom and subdue the enemy but also a necessary fruit of the Christian's moral obligation to love God, his kingdom, and his creation—a duty in conflict with the Christian's duty to love the human enemy? Or is it possible that Christian performance of the imprecatory psalms that petitions for divine

[66]   In his exposition of the sixth commandment, Calvin, *Institutes*, II.8.39, describes what is enjoined in God's prohibition of murder in similar terms: "We are accordingly commanded, if we find anything of use to us in saving our neighbors' lives, faithfully to employ it; if there is anything that makes for their peace, to see to it; if anything harmful, to ward it off; if they are in danger, to lend a helping hand." Imprecatory prayer, as an ethically permissible resource ever available to Christians to serve human beings in need, is thus a duty of love for Christians commanded to seek their neighbors' good in whatever ways open to them. Such prayer is of use in the saving of our neighbors' lives, makes for their peace, wards off their harm, and serves as a help in the midst of danger and is therefore to be faithfully employed for their good. Calvin, *Institutes*, II.8.40: "Again, unless you endeavor to look out for his safety according to your ability and opportunity, you are violating the law with a like heinousness."

[67]   Paul Ricoeur, "Love and Justice," *Philos Soc Critic* 21, no. 5/6 (1995): 33, refers to love of the enemy as the "extreme form" of love for one's neighbor. The call to love the enemy is a more specific (and demanding) expression of the general call to love the image bearing human neighbor rather than an altogether distinct moral obligation.

judgment against the human enemies of God's temple-kingdom may in fact prove to be a surprising manifestation of enemy love that desires and pursues in prayerful action the enemy's good? My contention here is that ethical Christian imprecation must and indeed can proceed from enemy love, that Christians praying for judgment upon the enemy must obey the New Testament prescriptions of enemy love and that each of the potential forms of judgment requested in Christian imprecation is a possible and legitimate iteration of desire for the good of the enemy.

The New Testament is unequivocal about the place of enemy love in the Christian ethic. In Matthew's account of the Sermon on the Mount, Jesus commands his followers, "Love your enemies and pray for those who persecute you" (Matt 5:44). The command is expanded in Luke's Sermon on the Plain: "Love your enemies, do good to those who hate you, bless those who curse you, pray for those who abuse you" (Luke 6:27–28). Paul echoes the words of Christ when he exhorts in Rom 12:14, "Bless those who persecute you; bless and do not curse them," and in 1 Thess 5:15, "See that no one repays anyone evil for evil, but always seek to do good to one another and to everyone." Peter joins the chorus of commendations of enemy love in 1 Pet 3:9: "Do not repay evil for evil or reviling for reviling, but on the contrary, bless, for to this you were called, that you may obtain a blessing."[68] Taken together, these New Testament texts enjoin Christians to reject cursing and retaliation—refusing to repay evil for evil—and to instead love those who oppose them by seeking the good of the enemy in action and speech.[69]

At first blush, the explicit proscription of cursing in Rom 12:14 would appear to invalidate Christian performance of the imprecatory psalms—the "cursing psalms"—as an ethically acceptable action for the followers of Christ. Here, however, it is essential to recall that the cursing psalms are not curses proper; that is, they are not unmediated, inherently effectual speech acts aimed at harnessing and directing power for

[68]   On the relationship between Jesus' teaching on enemy love and the prescriptions of enemy love elsewhere in the New Testament, see John Piper, 'Love Your Enemies': Jesus' Love Command in the Synoptic Gospels and in the Early Christian Paraenesis, SNTSMS 38 (Cambridge: Cambridge University Press, 1979), 49–65.

[69]   Cf. William Klassen, "'Love Your Enemies': Some Reflections on the Current Status of Research," in The Love of Enemy and Nonretaliation in the New Testament, ed. Willard M. Swartley (Louisville: Westminster John Knox, 1992), 1–31.

ill against a human being.[70] The imprecatory psalms are rather prayers directed to God that petition God to act on the basis of his covenant commitments to judge the wicked. Whereas curses attempt to manipulate and autonomously control divine power, the imprecatory psalms consciously submit and defer to the will and agency of God in their requests for Yahweh to act according to his promises and sovereign purposes. The cursing psalms ask God to bring his covenant curses to fruition; they do not curse the enemy directly. Accordingly, Christian performance of the imprecatory psalms, as prayer toward God and not unmediated speech toward the enemy intended to automatically release power for the enemy's harm, is a different class of speech act entirely and therefore is not prohibited by the New Testament's prohibition of cursing.[71]

Of course, this clarifying distinction, significant as it may be, does not settle the question, for the New Testament requires that Christians love their enemies positively by engaging in action that seeks their good and in speech that seeks God's blessing and beneficial operation on their behalf.[72] In order for Christian imprecation to be affirmed as ethically warranted, it must be demonstrated that psalmic prayer for divine judgment upon the human enemies of God's temple-kingdom by the sons and daughters of

---

[70] F. Büchsel, "ἀρά, καταράομαι, κατάρα, ἐπικατάρατος, ἐπάρατος," in *TDNT*, 1:449: "A curse is a directly expressed or indicated utterance which in virtue of a supernatural nexus of operation brings harm by its very expression to the one against whom it is directed." Cf. Warren Carter, "Love Your Enemies," *WW* 28, no. 1 (2008): 16.

[71] Cf. Barker, *Imprecation as Divine Discourse*, 152–53. *Contra* Piper, 'Love Your Enemies,' 129, who conflates the act of cursing with the desire for an enemy to be cursed by God, which I argue below may in fact be an expression of a desire for divine action that effects the enemy's good.

[72] BDAG, "εὐλογέω," 408, glosses the key term for bless as it occurs in Luke 6:28; Rom 12:14 as "to ask for bestowal of special favor, esp. of calling down God's gracious power." Cf. I. Howard Marshall, *The Gospel of Luke*, NIGTC (Grand Rapids: Eerdmans, 1978), 81; Darrell L. Bock, *Luke*, BECNT (Grand Rapids: Baker Academic, 1994), 1:589; John Nolland, *Luke 9:21–18:34*, WBC 35B (Dallas: Word Books, 1993), 294, on the overlapping character of the commands to bless and pray for the enemy in Luke 6:28. Blessing the enemy is a form of prayer, and offering a prayer on behalf of the enemy is a form of blessing, and my reference to prayer that seeks God's blessing and beneficial action for the enemy's good is intended to encompass petitionary speech to God that is consistent with both commands. It should be noted that, while "bless" and "curse" specifically denote modes of speech, they may also function as synecdoche in Jesus' teaching to refer to any acts that seek good or ill, respectively.

God in Christ can be offered in obedience to the call to do good to, bless, and pray for the enemy from love that desires the good of the enemy—that it may be a form of prayerful action that pursues the enemy's welfare in deed and that petitions for the enemy's welfare in Godward speech.

Imprecatory prayer that intends and petitions for divine action effecting the enemy's repentant conversion may function as an exercise of enemy love that desires and pursues the enemy's good.[73] The highest good that any human can experience is the good of reconciliation with God. The supreme blessing that any human can receive is the gracious gift of fellowship with the divine king and membership in his kingdom. Christian imprecation, as I argued above, prioritizes the enemy's conversion as the principally desired form of judgment upon the enemy, praying that God would thwart the plans and capacities of the wicked to multiply violence by breaking them in repentance, crucifying them with Christ, making them new—turning them from serpents who attack God's people and corrupt God's world into citizens and priest-kings of the temple-kingdom over and with whom God reigns. As such, Christian imprecation as petition for conversion is a form of prayerful action that aims at the enemy's good in God, a potential iteration of love that desires the blessing and welfare of the opponents of God's temple-kingdom,[74] and the agent who loves her enemy will pray that God bring the enemy into his fold through repentance and faith as the desire for the enemy's good grows up into action that pursues that good from God.[75]

Imprecatory prayer that intends and petitions for temporal judgment that interrupts the violence of the wicked by whatever just means necessary is also consonant with the demands of enemy love. To pray that God would confront and impede the enemy's vicious antagonism is to prayerfully pursue a state of affairs in which the enemy is no longer permitted to descend into a violence and inhumanity that destroys both the innocent and the enemy himself. As previously noted, the enemy's

---

[73] Cf. Adams, *War Psalms*, 59–61; Longman, *How to Read the Psalms*, 138–40; Peels, *Vengeance of God*, 245–46.

[74] Adams, *War Psalms*, 61, contends, "No judgment is too great if it drives people to seek the true God in Jesus Christ. We must learn to pray with this understanding for evil men today." Because judgment that prompts repentance—even severe judgment—is in fact blessing, prayer for such repentance-inducing judgment is in fact prayer for blessing.

[75] Cf. Piper, 'Love Your Enemies', 129, 143–44; France, *Gospel of Matthew*, 225–26.

unobstructed movement along the path of violent oppression is a compounding of sin that incurs greater degrees of guilt before God. It confirms and hardens the enemy in self-exalting delusions of invincibility and immunity. It habituates the enemy to violence in a manner that makes predatory desire and action against the innocent in opposition to God an increasingly instinctive dimension of the enemy's character.[76] And it constructs a personal history of unjust victimizing action with which the enemy must live, a personal history of action that may traumatically haunt and intrude upon the victimizer as well as the victim. Without diminishing the harm that the enemy does to the innocent targets of his aggression, it must be acknowledged that the enemy's violence harms the perpetrator, too, introducing injurious spiritual, moral, and quite possibly psychological and physiological effects that militate against the enemy's flourishing in God's world. To pray that God would act within history to stop the enemy from destroying himself with the violence that destroys others is to pray that God would act to spare the enemy from the multifaceted harm of his own rebellion—it is to pray for the good of an agent that is wholeheartedly committed to pursuing ill for himself as he pursues ill for others.[77]

Even death—that ultimate interruption—may be a sovereign mercy, a gracious blessing, insofar as it prevents the enemy from falling further into inhumanity, becoming responsible for further atrocity, exposing himself to a still more severe judgment from the God who promises to repay the wicked according to their works with talionic justice.[78] Prayer for just judg-

---

[76] See Elizabeth R. Moberly, *Suffering, Innocent and Guilty* (London: SPCK, 1978), 75–78, on punishment as an attempted arresting of a process of moral deterioration that endeavors to avert the punished agent from the harmful moral effects of his action, though her focus is on punishment as symbolic expression rather than, as I am principally concerned with here, the way that judgment may actively interrupt the agent's ability to continue pursuing such self-deteriorating wrongs.

[77] Prayer for God's temporal interruption of the enemy's purposes and actions is a way of regarding the enemy in love "as one whose ultimate good must be pursued even when his proximate interest must be denied." O'Donovan, *Resurrection and Moral Order*, 234.

[78] That God eschatologically judges the enemies of his kingdom with a severity proportional to the enemies' sin is suggested by the many New Testament talionic texts I surveyed in chap. 3 (e.g., Matt 16:27; 2 Tim 4:14; Rev 18:6; 20:12, 13; 22:12) and by Jesus' teaching in, e.g., Matt 11:20–24; Luke 12:47–48. See esp. Bavinck, *Reformed Dogmatics*, 4:713–4. Cf. Berkhof, *Systematic Theology*, 733–34;

ment up to and including the death of the lethally wicked is considerably more difficult to understand as an act of love so long as ethical deliberation concerning the enemy's welfare is restricted to the purely immanent frame, so long as purely immanent notions of human well-being are the only ones operative. But if a God who judges proportionally to the offender's offense is permitted to shatter the immanent frame, then petitions for God to cut down the offender before he sows more destruction, becomes increasingly deformed, and heaps further judgment upon his head becomes a perhaps surprising expression of the loving pursuit of the offender's true good. To be sure, the enemy's mortal death is by no means an absolute good, but the imprecatory psalms and the evening news alike bear witness that there exist tragic circumstances where the enemy's death may be a relative good, a state of affairs that is relatively better for the enemy than the alternative of his unmitigated continuation in reckless evil. While Christian priest-kings principally intend the enemy's conversion, the imprecatory prayer that intends God's violence-thwarting temporal judgment by whatever means just and necessary may be a plausible exercise of love that longs and acts for the welfare—rather than the continuing disintegration and exacerbated condemnation—of the enemy.[79] The prayer that must be born of enemy love indeed can be.[80] And love of the enemy requires that, rather than being content to see their enemies destroy themselves in their destruction of the innocent, the sons and daughters of God take prayerful action to petition God to bless and benefit their enemies by keeping them from the harms they have devoted themselves to chasing.

But is it even conceivable that enemy love could pray for the eschatological judgment of the enemy? I suggested earlier that Christian imprecation properly petitions, in the pattern of the New Testament (e.g., 1 Cor 16:22;

D. A. Carson, *The Gagging of God: Christianity Confronts Pluralism* (Grand Rapids: Zondervan, 1996), 533; Emma Disley, "Degrees of Glory: Protestant Doctrine and the Concept of Rewards Hereafter," *JTS* 42, no. 1 (1991): 82–85.

[79] *Contra* Day, "Imprecatory Psalms," 159–60.

[80] I am not arguing here that enemy love may exist simultaneously and without contradiction alongside a desire for the enemy's temporal judgment in the manner of Murray, "Christian Cursing?" 117–18; Day, "Imprecatory Psalms," 154–55; Daniel Michael Nehrbass, "The Therapeutic and Preaching Value of the Imprecatory Psalms" (PhD diss., Fuller Theological Seminary, 2012), 128; Shepherd, "Place of the Imprecatory Psalms," 122–23; Frame, *Doctrine of the Christian Life*, 342. I am rather arguing that a desire for the enemy's temporal judgment may itself be an expression of enemy love that desires the good of the violent opponent.

Rev 22:20), for Christ's return in glory, which entails the definitive cessation of violence, cleansing of God's world, manifestation of divine justice, and consummation of the temple-kingdom on earth. Such petitions must arise from love for the enemy, but how can prayer for eschatological judgment—the irreversible, eternal, and thoroughly just condemnation, punishment, and expulsion of the wicked from God's restored temple-kingdom—be a pursuit of the enemy's good that without affective contradiction desires that good? Advocates of annihilationist conceptions of eschatological judgment, sometimes referred to as conditional immortality, argue that God's vengeance involves the destruction, extinguishment, and extinction of the wicked and consequently may contend that, like the temporal judgment of death, such eschatological judgment is an exercise of love that brings to a merciful end an existence defined by inveterate rebellion against God and the disintegrating bondage of sin,[81] one that honors the freedom of the enemy to will and choose nonexistence rather than repentant life with God.[82] Imprecation that intends eschatological judgment upon the enemy would then be a prayerful pursuit of the goods of nonexistence (as opposed to continued misery) and freedom (as opposed to coercion).

For those affirming with the Westminster Larger Catechism that God's punishment of the wicked in the world to come involves "everlasting separation from the comfortable presence of God, and most grievous torments in soul and body, without intermission, in hellfire forever,"[83] eschatological judgment may yet be framed as a loving respect of the enemy's freedom to willfully reject life with God,[84] but recourse

---

[81] Cf. Gregory A. Boyd, *The Crucifixion of the Warrior God: Interpreting the Old Testament's Violent Portraits of God in Light of the Cross* (Minneapolis: Fortress, 2017), 2:787.

[82] See, e.g., Jonathan L. Kvanvig, *The Problem of Hell* (New York: Oxford University Press, 1993), 135–61, esp. 153; Nigel G. Wright, "A Kinder, Gentler Damnation?" in *Rethinking Hell: Readings in Evangelical Conditionalism*, ed. Christopher M. Date, Gregory G. Stump, and Joshua W. Anderson (Cambridge: Lutterworth Press, 2014), 228–33. For a brief introduction to this perspective on eschatological judgment, see Glenn A. Peoples, "Introduction to Evangelical Conditionalism," in Date, Stump, and Anderson, *Rethinking Hell*, 10–24.

[83] WLC Q. 29; cf. WCF 33.2.

[84] Christopher D. Marshall, "Divine and Human Punishment in the New Testament," in Date, Stump, and Anderson, *Rethinking Hell*, 220, outlines the logic of love in the conditional immortality perspective: "To enjoy such union [with God], people must participate in God's perfection. This requires their full and free cooperation, a willing submission to God that cannot be

is unavailable to the compelling notion that final judgment is an act of love that extinguishes in mercy the sin-bound enemy. Nevertheless, in light of the traditional Reformed theological presupposition that the God who is love (1 John 4:16), and thus always acts in love, effects without internal contradiction the everlasting judgment of the wicked,[85] it should not be surprising that there are additional considerations regarding the relationship between enemy love and eschatological judgment that must be taken into account.

First, the just expulsion of the wicked from the world resurrected as the temple-kingdom of God's holy presence ensures that agents committed to violence are unable to continue violating God's creation, his people, and, in the process, themselves—viciously acting in contradiction to the order of creation and in egregious defiance of their creaturely *telos* within it, experiencing and striding with every violent step ever deeper into the deformation and disordered existence of sin.[86] God's enemy is mercifully restrained from persisting in the violence that harms the self as it harms others; from becoming an increasingly habituated transgressor of God,

---

coerced. Some may shrink from such surrender and choose instead radical separation from God. Out of love for them, God must honor their freedom of choice. It would be unloving and unjust to force them against their will to take up eternal residence in God's kingdom, which for the stubbornly impenitent would be an experience of hell." There is very little about the core contentions of this description that could not be affirmed by a proponent of the traditional Reformed conception of eschatological judgment. Additionally, I am not aware of any decisive theological or scriptural reason to surmise that the wicked in hell experience a transformation of heart by which they begin to love and desire God, especially in light of Reformed confessional convictions about the state of the will in bondage to sin and the gracious divine action necessary to overcome it (e.g., WCF 9.3–4). Cf. Carson, *Gagging of God*, 533–34. On this understanding, everlasting eschatological judgment is a continuous honoring of the agent's continuing willful rejection of God.

[85]   Cf. the juxtaposition of theological descriptors in WCF 2.1. My claim here is distinct from the attempted harmonizations of judgment and love that claim eschatological judgment of the wicked is an expression of love for those oppressed by the wicked but not for the wicked themselves, a position that seems to raise significant theological issues. See, e.g., Tony Lane, "The Wrath of God as an Aspect of the Love of God," in *Nothing Greater, Nothing Better: Theological Essays on the Love of God*, ed. Kevin J. Vanhoozer (Grand Rapids: Eerdmans, 2001), 167.

[86]   Cf. Eleonore Stump, "Dante's Hell, Aquinas's Moral Theory, and the Love of God," *CJP* 16, no. 2 (1986): 195–98. For a critique of Stump's proposal, see Kvanvig, *The Problem of Hell*, 123–30.

corrupter of earth, and perpetrator of human beings; from writing in action a personal narrative that unceasingly grows as tragic new chapters of unjust atrocity are perpetually added. By preventing the wicked from committing new acts of (self-)destructive violence, the expulsive eschatological justice of God serves the good of the enemy as well as that of God's name, kingdom people, and creation.

Second, God's judgment honors the wicked person as a moral agent whose actions have transcendent significance and who is responsible for the life lived.[87] In judgment, God does not treat the wicked as instinct-driven animals who cannot be held accountable for their decisions and acts, excusing them from responsibility in a paternalistic and condescending obliteration of agency, even when their action is more bestial (cf. Pss 7:2; 10:8–9; 17:12; 35:17; 58:4–6) than human. Judgment bestows a peculiar dignity upon the human being as God answers the life of the wicked with a *yes* in affirmation of their identity as a moral agent and the significance of their moral action, which is a simultaneous *no* to their violent exercise of moral agency. In this manner, eschatological judgment serves the good of the enemy by recognizing and responding to, rather than effacing, his agency, responsibility, and capacity for moral action as an image-bearing human being who is accountable to God.

Third, eschatological judgment is a definitive confrontation of the wicked with the truth of who they have become and the gravity of the evil they have committed, a confrontation that destroys the self-justifying delusions in which they have lived, a confrontation in which they can do no other than reckon with the sinfulness of their sin against a holy God and innocent bearers of his image.[88] Psalm 10 describes the self-deception

---

[87]   Robert Spaemann, *Persons: The Difference Between 'Someone' and 'Something,'* trans. Oliver O'Donovan, Oxford Studies in Theological Ethics (Oxford: Oxford University Press, 2006), 233, cites G. W. F. Hegel, *Philosophy of Right*, trans. T. M. Knox (Oxford: Clarendon, 1952), §100, in his discussion of political punishment: "Yet punishment, as Hegel said, is 'the honouring of the offender,' i.e. as a person.... Even life imprisonment can be understood in principle as the effacement of guilt, an address to the person as a person, not merely a measure for dealing with him or with the situation. His place as a subject is not eliminated." *Contra* Walter Moberly, *The Ethics of Punishment* (Hamden, Conn.: Archon Books, 1968), 158. I am arguing that this honoring of the person as a person that takes place in political punishment takes place in eschatological punishment as well.

[88]   Moberly, *Suffering, Innocent and Guilty*, 114, considers that God's final judgment "may be viewed as *the statement of what we have become and are*. It is no longer something imposed *ab extra* or a partial critique of one's actions.

that energizes the violence of the wicked: he boasts of the misdirected desires that fuel his renunciation of God and predation of the weak (v. 3); he pursues the poor in arrogance (v. 2) and in pride says, "There is no God" (v. 4); his prosperity in wickedness pushes the reality of divine judgment out of sight (v. 5); he imagines his life inviolably secure, saying within his heart, "I shall not be moved; throughout all generations I shall not meet adversity" (v. 6); he assures himself, "God has forgotten; he has hidden his face, he will never see it. . . . You will not call to account" (vv. 11, 13). The enemy dwells in a world constructed of falsehoods, a world in which there is no God to see or judge and no repercussion or accountability for evil action, a world in which the enemy is powerfully immune to adversity and the idolatrous loves that incite violence are fundamentally misvalued as worthy of boasting. When God in Christ brings his talionic recompense with him "to repay each one for what he has done" (Rev 22:12), however, the enemy's false world will fall—the truth of heart and deed will be revealed (Luke 12:2), the wicked will recognize Jesus as Lord and judge (Acts 17:31; Phil 2:9–11), and the violent in their existential encounter with God's righteous verdict and perfect justice will inescapably encounter the meaning and magnitude of the injustice they perpetrated, celebrated, and rationalized. If apprehension of the truth is a qualitatively better condition than delusion in perpetual falsehood—and I contend that it is[89]—then eschatological judgment serves the good of the

---

Rather it is an intrinsic judgment, a complete critique of all that one is. What one has *done* is but symptomatic of what one has *become*." Though I do not here suggest that final judgment can be reduced to a communicative act, I nevertheless agree that one significant dimension of final judgment is this communicative and revelatory capacity.

[89]   Though it is only an analogous comparison, Scripture indicates that love for another will seek the other's apprehension of the truth over and against perpetual self-deception, even when loving confrontation of the other with the truth involves the other's experience of pain. E.g., Ps 141:5; Prov 9:8; 25:12; 27:6; Ecc 7:5. Analogously, eschatological judgment can be conceived of as a loving confrontation with the truth of those who have unremittingly rejected, suppressed, and renarrated the truth to legitimate their violence. Describing what he refers to as reprobative punishment—that is, punishment that symbolically expresses disapproval—Nicholas Wolterstorff, *Justice in Love*, EUSLR (Grand Rapids: Eerdmans, 2011), 197, contends, "When reprobative punishment is exercised properly, it's an intrinsic good in the life of punisher and wrongdoer. . . . Of course the hard treatment which is a component of reprobative punishment is, as such, a diminution of the wrongdoer's wellbeing, But the entire package is a good in his life—not an evil imposed to redress an evil. Recall

enemy as God breaks through the enemy's self-deception and ineludibly discloses the true state of affairs.

Taken together, these considerations suggest that Christians' imprecatory prayers for the Lord's coming and the consummation of God's expulsive judgment of the unrepentant wicked may in fact be offered in enemy love that desires and pursues the good of the enemy who has failed to desire and pursue the good for himself but has implacably desired and pursued that which effects his own harm. In petitioning for eschatological justice, Christian imprecation must be born of enemy love, and indeed it can be when affectively aimed at the affirmation of the enemy's freedom, the restraint of the enemy's self-destructive violence, the honoring of the enemy's dignity as a moral agent, and the confrontation of the enemy with the truth of his violent injustice within God's reality. Christian obedience to the Jesus of Luke 6, who commands his disciples to love their enemies by acting and praying for their good, therefore does not necessarily entail disobedience to the Jesus of Luke 18, who exhorts his disciples to pray for the divine justice to be revealed with the coming of the Son of Man.

Each of the potential forms of judgment requested in Christian performance of the imprecatory psalms, then—repentance and conversion, temporal judgment that interrupts violence by whatever means just and necessary, and eschatological judgment—are potential iterations of the enemy love that Jesus declares must be the originating affection of Christians' response to their oppressors.[90] "Christian cursing"—prayer for the judgment of God in faithfulness to his covenant promises—is a prayer of blessing, a petition for the enemy's welfare. What is more, the Christian who desires the good for the enemy who does not desire the good for himself will bear the fruit of loving action in prayer chiefly

---

that Moses cited reproving one's neighbor as an example of loving the neighbor (Leviticus 19:17)." Though Wolterstorff has particularly in mind human forms of punishment, it seems to me that God's eschatological judgment (and indeed his temporal judgment as well) can be conceptualized as a good of the enemy along analogous lines.

[90]   *Contra*, e.g., Patrick D. Miller, *They Cried to the Lord: The Form and Theology of Biblical Prayer* (Minneapolis: Fortress, 1994), 303; Walter Brueggemann, *The Psalms and the Life of Faith*, ed. Patrick D. Miller (Minneapolis: Fortress, 1995), 268; Walter Brueggemann, *Spirituality of the Psalms* (Minneapolis: Fortress, 2002), 33; J. W. Rogerson and J. W. McKay, *Psalms 101–150*, The Cambridge Bible Commentary (Cambridge: Cambridge University Press, 1977), 59; Luc, "Interpreting the Curses," 409; James Limburg, *Psalms*, Westminster Bible Companion, ed. Patrick D. Miller and David L. Bartlett (Louisville: Westminster John Knox, 2000), 284.

for his repentant renewal in Christ and secondarily, given the enemy's committed pursuit of his own destruction in the violent destruction of others, for divine action to impede the enemy's assaults and manifest perfect justice with the *parousia* of Christ. Consequently, love of God, temple-kingdom, and creation and the faithful enactment of the disciple's vocation as a priest-king in God's narrative—ethical obligations the both of which require imprecatory prayer—do not fundamentally conflict with or contradict the disciple's moral duty to love her enemy. The son or daughter of God in Christ need not choose between mutually exclusive callings as if trapped in an impenetrable moral dilemma, for the imprecatory prayer that must arise from love of God, temple-kingdom, creation, and enemy indeed can, and when these loves are permitted to mature into action, they will generate imprecatory prayer for the particular good of each discrete object of love.

Of course, the requirement that Christian performance of the imprecatory psalms arise from these loves means that imprecation must not be born of a vindictive desire to inflict pain or harm on the human enemy as an end in itself, and neither may it function as a means of pursuing, protecting, or avenging the loss of idolatrous objects of affection that have no place in the Christian life. Here, a modification of Paul's reflection in 1 Cor 13:1–3 is in order: if I pray in the words of faithful psalmists and heavenly saints, but have not love, I am nothing.

The Affective Dynamics of Christian Imprecation

Having examined the conditions of ethical Christian performance of the imprecatory psalms, the requisite features of faithful imprecation in God's narrative of the world, we are prepared to consider the other side of the question: the ethical effects of such prayer, the affection-generating dynamics of Christian imprecation.[91] Given the rather easily imagined ways that a too-hasty, overconfident, unreflective enactment of psalmic judgment petitions could descend into an idolatrous, self-justifying, utterly unjust practice of prayer that reinforces and reifies improper dispositions of heart,[92] it is necessary to address how enactment of the imprecatory

---

[91]   Cf. the brief considerations of, e.g., Davis, *Getting Involved with God*, 28; Marti J. Steussy, "The Enemy in the Psalms," *WW* 28, no. 1 (2008): 11; Zenger, *God of Vengeance?* 68–69; Nehrbass, "Therapeutic and Preaching Value," 102–3; Adams, *War Psalms*, 84; McCann, *Theological Introduction*, 117; Holladay, *Long Ago God Spoke*, 308–9.

[92]   See Zenger, *God of Vengeance?* 57–58. John Calvin, *Commentary on the Book of Psalms*, trans. James Anderson, Calvin's Commentaries 6 (repr., Grand

psalms might affectively act upon the Christian, offer safeguards against unethical, malformative, and potentially dangerous misuse, and positively cultivate virtue.

In chapter three, I surveyed the New Testament's intertextual appropriation of the imprecatory psalms to demonstrate that Jesus Christ is presented as the polyvalent fulfillment of the three principal inhabitants of the imprecatory psalms' narrative world: he is simultaneously the righteously suffering son of God, the accursed substitute for the enemies of God, and the divine judge who executes justice as the cosmic warrior-king. Here, utilizing the doctrine of union with Christ as the Spirit-wrought reality by which Christians are covenantally and existentially connected to Jesus such that what is true of him is true of them as well, I inquire how prayerful performance of the imprecatory psalms that is sensitive to their Christological polyvalence might act upon the Christian petitioner, stimulating an affective retracing of the contours of God's Christocentric narrative, implicating the imprecator within that narrative, cultivating a faith in God's past redemptive action and a hope in God's future consummating action that reorient faulty affections and engender a present love for God, his temple-kingdom, his creation, and his enemies.

Notably, consideration of the way enactment of the imprecations acts upon the praying agent acknowledges the psychological, spiritual, and affectional complexity of prayer. Prayer is not a static exercise, a mere vocalization of speech with no residual effect on the speaker, but a person-engaging practice in which desires are expressed, truths rehearsed, realities confronted, and petitioners changed. The Westminster Confession of Faith recognizes prayer as a means of grace by which God increases and strengthens faith,[93] and Reformation-era theologies of petitionary

---

Rapids: Baker Books, 2005), 4:275–76, famously warns against taking up the imprecatory psalms (particularly Psalm 109) in selfishness, spite, and injustice before describing his awareness of abuses of the imprecations:

> How detestable a piece of sacrilege is it on the part of the monks, and especially the Franciscan friars, to pervert this psalm by employing it to countenance the most nefarious purposes! If a man harbor malice against a neighbour, it is quite a common thing for him to engage one of these wicked wretches to curse him, which he would do by daily repeating this psalm. I know a lady in France who hired a parcel of these friars to curse her own and only son in these words.

[93]   WCF 14.1.

prayer frequently emphasized the subjective, affection-orienting effects of prayer,[94] affirming with Calvin that God has ordained prayer "not so much for his own sake as for ours."[95] Having developed ethical criteria for Christian performance of the imprecatory psalms, my analysis seeks now to attend to these subject-altering, affection-stirring dimensions of imprecatory performance as an ethically formative practice.

What is more, this line of inquiry pursues the possibility of ethical imprecation amid the affectional vicissitudes, which in real human experience often serve as the starting point for prayer, moving from my previous examination of ideal ethical prayer to an investigation of the process by which prayer might become ethical in the less-than-ideal dispositional conditions in which sufferers often find themselves. Such an exploration seeks to recover practice of the imprecatory psalms as an ethically legitimate exercise amid the existential realities of suffering's chaos for those petitioners whose affections, understandably roiled and thrown into disarray by unjust violence, do not begin in model, well-ordered ethical proportion. If the imprecations are to serve as an ethically permissible practice for individuals in the throes of violent suffering and its effects, then what is required is an ethical perspective on their performance that accommodates the potentially immoral initial conditions that may accompany suffering and evaluates the ethics of imprecatory prayer in terms of where the dynamic affective process ends, rather than where it begins.[96]

---

[94] Christopher Woznicki, "What Are We Doing When We Pray? Rekindling a Reformation Theology of Petitionary Prayer," *CTJ* 53, no. 2 (2018): 319–43, helpfully interacts with the thought of John Calvin, Heinrich Bullinger, Wolfgang Musculus, and Peter Martyr Vermigli.

[95] Calvin, *Institutes*, III.20.3. See also John Kelsay, "Prayer and Ethics: Reflections on Calvin and Barth," *HTR* 82, no. 2 (Apr. 1989): 169–84; Ronald S. Wallace, *Calvin's Doctrine of the Christian Life* (Edinburgh: Oliver and Boyd, 1959), 271–95.

[96] An important characteristic of my approach thus concerns where one locates the ethically determinative moment of imprecatory prayer. For those who establish moral criteria as the precondition for imprecation, the ethically determinative moment is the moment imprecatory prayer begins. My approach, however, locates the ethically determinative moment at the conclusion of imprecatory prayer, permitting the subject-altering, affective dynamics of imprecatory prayer space to act upon the imprecating agent prior to rendering a conclusion concerning the moral propriety of the prayer. This perspective asks where the imprecator's affections culminate just before the "amen" of prayer rather than asking where the imprecator's affections commence before the transformative effects of prayer have begun to operate.

Toward this end, I endeavor to evocatively describe the almost instantaneous internal associations that may accompany Christian enactment of the Christically rich imprecatory psalms, fully aware that in seeking to communicate about these complex affective processes I am pressing against the limits of the capabilities of language. I am not, to be clear, making a claim about what will actually take place within a given imprecating Christian, whose experience of imprecation will naturally be influenced by a host of variables, but about what has the potential to take place within the imprecating Christian when the imprecatory psalms are permitted to direct the petitioner to Christ according to their polyvalent Christological witness. Imprecatory performance in union with Christ has the capacity to elicit a renewed sense of solidarity with the innocently suffering and vindicated son of God, the curse-bearing substitute for enemies, and the divine judge, which reinforces the contours of God's redemptive-historical narrative and the Christian's place within it, arousing faith in God's past action and hope in God's future faithfulness. This narrative-shaped faith and hope, which grab hold in the present of the promise of God's past and future, respectively,[97] stimulate love for God, his temple-kingdom, his creation, and his enemies, making possible and prompting an affective orientation that desires the good suited to each. Christian performance of the imprecatory psalms in union with the Christ who polyvalently fulfills them may thus serve as a dynamic means of grace by which unfitting (and potentially destructive) affections are destabilized, interrupted, and redirected and through which the affections of love required for ethical imprecation—and a life of witness more broadly—are generated.

Christian Imprecation in Union with Christ

The Christian performer of the imprecatory psalms, the disciple who would inhabit the speech of the Psalter's judgment prayers, is immediately confronted with the figure of the psalmic imprecator: his voice, sufferings, turmoil, hopes, and requests for God's just intervention. In such enactment,

---

[97] On faith and hope, see Calvin, *Institutes*, III.2.41–42. My utilization of these terms in what follows seeks to highlight the backward- and forward-oriented—the past- and future-facing—character of faith and hope, respectively, and I accordingly treat faith as that affection that rests upon the promise attached to God's past working in history and hope as that affection that reaches forward in anticipation to the future on the basis of that promise. Cf. Frame, *Doctrine of the Christian Life*, 27.

the Christian takes upon her own lips the prayers of psalmists who suffer in innocence, hope in the certainty of vindication from God, and exercise their vocation as royal-priestly sons of God to guard the kingdom and clear the land of serpentine uncleanness. For the petitioner sensitive to the ways the New Testament applies this role to Jesus, to the ways Jesus climactically recapitulates and culminates the psalmist's experience, this confrontation with the imprecator becomes a prayerful encounter with Christ. The frequent declarations of innocence and laments over unjust suffering draw the praying Christian to the cross, where the righteous sufferer *par excellence* bore the injustice of lies, shame, and violence in his human flesh all the way to death. The prayers for and confident expectations of God-effected vindication usher the believer to the third day, when God issued his vindicating declaration over the righteous Christ by raising him from the dead, and to the last day when Christ shall be revealed in the truth of his glory before the eyes of a world that did not receive him. The royal-priestly requests that seek to protect the temple-kingdom and mediate the expulsive vengeance of God against serpentine intruders transport the Christian's imagination to the true son of God, who in his dying and rising struck the death blow against every opposing power on behalf of his kingdom people and who in his coming again will comprehensively cleanse God's world of every unholy intruder as the definitive human mediator of God's just judgment.

For the performer of the imprecatory psalms who is united to Christ, this affective journey from the psalmic imprecator to the psalm-fulfilling Christ is an immersive, self-implicating journey that renarrates the Christian's own past, present, and future according to the history, activity, and destiny of Jesus. The imprecating Christian encounters in the suffering Christ the innocent human who on her behalf already endured and exhausted the ignominy and violence of the world, with whom she has already died, with whom her life is safely hidden in God from every violent threat (cf. Col 3:3).[98] The Christ to whom she is united therefore knows in body and soul the pain and temptation provoked by injustice and so in this and every future moment is able to sympathize in his high priestly intercession before God (Heb 4:15–16) even as he shares his Spirit to be present in her experience of suffering. Christ's solidarity and attendance with the petitioner introduces a new reality into the isolating loneliness of victimization.[99] At

---

[98]   Cf. Jerry L. Sumney, *Colossians: A Commentary*, NTL (Louisville: Westminster John Knox, 2008), 181; J. Todd Billings, *Rejoicing in Lament: Wrestling with Incurable Cancer and Life in Christ* (Grand Rapids: Brazos, 2015), 107–9.

[99]   See Billings, *Rejoicing in Lament*, 160–65.

the same time, the prayer of imprecation that thrusts the disciple into the sufferings of Christ pushes her into the sufferings of her fellow Christians and the wider world.[100] Wrapped up into Christ, the oppressed disciple is through him united to every other member of Jesus' ecclesial body. Bound not only to Adam the first human but also to Jesus the true human, the petitioning Christian shares in the humanity of every image bearer. The affective journey to the victimized Christ that renews solidarity with Jesus in the Christian's experience of victimization simultaneously renews solidarity with the church and all humanity, opening the imprecating disciple's attention outward to the victimization of the ecclesial and human family to whom she is differently but nonetheless intimately connected in Jesus.

The victimized Christ, however, is the vindicated Christ, and the psalmic cry for vindication that propels the believer toward Jesus' vindication in his resurrection and *parousia* confirms to the believer his own vindication as well. Faith hears in God's resurrection of Jesus a vindicating declaration of righteousness over the one united to him (Rom 4:24–25), and hope looks in assurance to vindication from God on the day his saints are glorified together with Christ (Rom 8:17; Col 3:4; 1 John 3:1–2).[101] The affective rehearsal of Christ's past and future royal-priestly judgment upon his enemies evokes a secure rest in the promise that Jesus' sacrificial death and triumphant resurrection exposed and defeated the true enemies of the supplicant who belongs to Christ, no matter how violently they yet rage. And it enervates an empowering, agency-renewing vision that the believer, a son or daughter of God in the Son of God, will participate as a priest-king with Jesus in executing God's eschatological justice and even now mediates that judgment in the very act of imprecatory prayer. The confrontation with the imprecating psalmist, which is a confrontation with the living Christ, is a confrontation with the Christian's true identity in Christ—a confrontation that provokes a fresh affective apprehension of Jesus' compassionate safeguarding and intercession and presence, the suffering Christian's solidarity with every sufferer, the petitioner's current and imminent vindication, the enemy's judgment in Christ's resurrection,

---

[100] Cf. the appeals for solidarity with the suffering by Adams, *War Psalms*, 84; McCann, *Theological Introduction*, 117; Holladay, *Long Ago God Spoke*, 308–9.

[101] Cf. Bernhard W. Anderson and Steven Bishop, *Out of the Depths: The Psalms Speak for Us Today*, 3rd ed. (Louisville: Westminster John Knox, 2000), 74–75.

and the Christian's role in actively mediating that judgment in this age and at Christ's return. Imprecation in Christ thus cultivates a faith-full reappropriation of the accomplishments of Jesus' passion and hopeful confidence in the future, which Christ's passion renders certain.

In the enactment of the imprecatory psalms, the Christian also encounters the psalmic enemy, the serpentine figure within the psalms' narrative world who elicits the psalmists' laments over violent injustice, prayerful petitions for God's liberating justice, and celebratory affirmations of future judgment. The imagination saturated in the New Testament's allusive portrait of Jesus, however, meets in the enemy an evocative witness to the curse-bearing Christ who received the covenantal justice of God in the place of sinners.[102] As the Christian cries out in psalmic speech against the enemy for stricken heads and judgment cups, for covenant curses and expulsion from the land of God's presence, she is affectively transported to Christ's trial and crucifixion, where Jesus was judged as the enemy—struck on face and head, given to drink the cup of God's wrath, made a curse upon the tree, expelled from the city and the land of the living.

Vitally connected to Christ by his Spirit, the Christian imprecator confronts anew in the judgment of Jesus the judgment of the Christian's own person.[103] The requested judgments of the psalms, judgments that Jesus bore on behalf of the petitioning Christian, are understood as judgments properly directed at the Christian himself: the praying disciple is compelled to know himself in the crucifixion of Christ as a sinner, an enemy of God, deserving of every judgment that his psalmic prayers call out for against his enemy. The son or daughter of God in Christ who prays the imprecatory psalms against the enemy prays in the same breath, "The judgment of God ought rightly to fall on me." In the petition for judgment against the enemy, the Christian is arrestingly reacquainted with his own wickedness

---

[102] Cf. the varied discussions of the imprecatory psalms' connection to Christ's reception of divine vengeance by Brueggemann, *Praying the Psalms*, 80; McCann, *Theological Introduction*, 120; Miller, *They Cried to the Lord*, 303; Bonhoeffer, "Sermon on a Psalm of Vengeance," 93–94; *Prayerbook of the Bible: An Introduction to the Psalms*, ed. Geffrey B. Kelly, trans. James H. Burtness, vol. 5 of *Dietrich Bonhoeffer Works* (Minneapolis: Fortress, 1996), 175; Adams, *War Psalms*, 43; Wenham, *Goodness of God*, 168–72; Christopher B. Hays, "How Shall We Sing? Psalm 137 in Historical and Canonical Context," *HBT* 27 (2005): 54.

[103] Cf. Dietrich Bonhoeffer, *Ethics*, ed. Clifford J. Green, trans. Reinhard Krauss, Charles C. West, and Douglas W. Stott, vol. 6 of *Dietrich Bonhoeffer Works* (Minneapolis: Fortress, 2005), 134.

and desert of divine vengeance, a reacquaintance that necessarily prompts humility, circumspection, personal repentance, and indeed a sense of solidarity with the wicked enemy under the penetrating gaze of God.[104]

Imprecatory performance in union with Christ is thus an inherently destabilizing act, a dynamic mode of prayer that provokes the imprecating Christian to confess his sinfulness, question his motives, acknowledge the commonality between himself and the enemy, and assess his all-too-easily excused complicity in the very violence he wishes to be eradicated. In this way, imprecation in Christ guards the petitioner from leveraging the imprecatory prayer as his own unreflective act of violence and injustice, from praying against the enemy's speck before attending to the log that impedes his own vision. Like the Lord's Prayer, the imprecatory "thy kingdom come!" precedes and stimulates the penitent "forgive us our debts," which in turn alters the posture in which the disciple offers his kingdom-protecting prayer, turning imprecation first against the indwelling sin of the self and only then against the sinful enemy. But even as the Christian recognizes himself in the enemy and in the accursed Christ to whom he is united, the crucifixion that uncovers his liability to judgment simultaneously reveals that in the cross his judgment has been administered and spent.[105] The divine vengeance so richly merited has been channeled onto the crucified Christ, and the petitioner who revisits Golgotha in the course of imprecatory prayer finds there a stimulus for faith that the judgment that fell upon Jesus no longer rests upon the Christian and for hope that gracious deliverance—not wrath—awaits the one already judged in Christ.

Entering into the psalmic triad of relations as she takes up the prayerful speech of the imprecations, the Christian performer who petitions with the psalmist against the enemy addresses her pleas to God, the divine judge and cosmic warrior-king. The recipient of imprecatory prayer is characterized throughout the vengeance psalms as the covenant-keeping God of Israel, the universal sovereign who in the redemptive-historical past marched to war on his people's behalf and can be trusted to make good on his promises by arising in judgment and administering justice against the intrusive oppressors of his temple-kingdom. Following the

---

[104] Cf. the suggestions of Bonhoeffer, "Sermon on a Psalm of Vengeance," 94; *Prayerbook of the Bible*, 175; Nehrbass, "Therapeutic and Preaching Value," 102–3; Zenger, *God of Vengeance?* 68–69; Steussy, "Enemy in the Psalms," 11; Davis, *Getting Involved with God*, 28–29; Hays, "How Shall We Sing?" 54–55.

[105] Cf. Bonhoeffer, "Sermon on a Psalm of Vengeance," 94; *Prayerbook of the Bible*, 175.

Christological contours of the New Testament's intertextual narration of God's works in Jesus, the Christian petitioner encounters in the divine judge of the imprecatory psalms the Christ who is himself the God of judgment. As the divine warrior-king, Jesus in his first coming vanquished his foes by his death and resurrection, ascended in victory to the throne of his heavenly temple, and poured out gifts upon the inaugurated kingdom over whom he reigns and with whom he dwells by his Spirit. In his second coming, Jesus will act as the judge of all the earth, definitively cleansing the world of all unrighteousness in his administration of talionic justice upon his enemies. The Christian who rediscovers this Christ in the affective movement of imprecatory prayer simultaneously rediscovers herself in union with Christ: seated in the heavenly places with and in Jesus as a sharer in his royal authority over every power in this age and the age to come (Eph 2:6; cf. 1:20–21), granted to presently participate in the benefits of Christ's conquering as a citizen in his kingdom, destined for an eternity of unimpeded worship and peace in God's holy presence when Jesus the judge consummates his victory over every threat to the Christian petitioner and his temple-kingdom. Imprecation in union with Christ thus stimulates a faith that receives and rests upon the divine triumph of Jesus' dying, rising, and ascending and a hope that confidently anticipates the just judgment of Christ the warrior-king.[106] The prayer born in the midst of violence leads the disciple's imagination and affections to the divine judge who acts for her and in whom she lives, giving birth to the faith and hope that may securely affirm that because the Lord and king has already conquered, he surely "will rescue me from every evil deed and bring me safely into his heavenly kingdom" (2 Tim 4:18).

Christian Imprecation and the Fruit of Love

Christian performance of the imprecatory psalms in union with the Christ who fulfills the roles of innocent and suffering son of God, accursed enemy, and divine judge ushers the petitioner on a polyvalent, implicatory, affective journey through the narrative of God's work in Jesus and in so doing cultivates correspondingly polyvalent forms of faith and hope. Faith and its necessary corollary hope are themselves requisite affections for ethical

---

[106] Cf. Murray, "Christian Cursing?" 120. *Contra* St. Augustine, *The Enchiridion on Faith, Hope and Love*, ed. Henry Paolucci (Chicago: Henry Regnery Company, 1961), VIII: "It is true that a thing which is not an object of hope may be believed. What true Christian, for example, does not believe in the punishment of the wicked? And yet such an one does not hope for it."

action (Rom 14:23; Heb 11:6).[107] For a failure of faith in Christ is a failure to rightly relate to God, receive the self,[108] and render the world that entails an animating trust in some alternative idol. And a failure of hope is a failure to recognize the extension of God's work and promise forward in time that entails a false and idolatrous refashioning of the future.[109] Insofar as Christian imprecation in union with Christ generates the affections of faith and hope, the practice stimulates affections indispensable to its ethical enactment. But faith and hope are affections that also make possible and empower the affection of love, which among the three is "the greatest of these" (1 Cor 13:13).[110] Faith in God's past and hope in God's future come together to frame the horizons of action, to reconfigure the narratival reality within which the moral agent dwells and deliberates, enabling reception of and response to God and his world in a love that apprehends, rejoices in, and desires what is good.[111] Christian imprecation in union with Christ, generating the affections of faith and hope in its self-implicating rehearsal of God's Christocentric narrative of the world, from this faith and hope may bear in the petitioner the fruit of love, a love that interrupts disordered and destructive desire and rightly redirects it toward God, God's temple-kingdom, God's creation, and God's enemies.

Christian performance of the imprecatory psalms, which must be born from love for God, has the capacity to stimulate love for God. In the affective bombardment that attends imprecatory prayer in union with Christ, the petitioning believer is immersively confronted with the multifaceted grace of God's gift in Jesus. Every good benefit secured for the Christian in Jesus' work as the suffering son of God, accursed substitute for enemies, and divine judge "is from above, coming down from the Father of lights" (Jas 1:17), a testimony to the loving faithfulness of the God who is himself the supreme benefit secured for the Christian in Jesus' work. The practice of imprecation that leads the Christian to faith in what God has done in Christ and to hope in what God will yet do in Christ properly begets love for the God who is the source and end, the giver and the gift, of the liberation, salvation, and life that are in Christ (cf. Luke 7:47). The praying

---

[107]   Cf. WCF 16.7.

[108]   See Oliver O'Donovan, *Self, World, and Time*, vol. 1 of *Ethics as Theology* (Grand Rapids: Eerdmans, 2013), 21.

[109]   O'Donovan, *Self, World, and Time*, 19–23, 173–78.

[110]   See Calvin, *Institutes*, III.2.41–42, on the relations of faith, hope, and love.

[111]   Cf. O'Donovan, *Resurrection and Moral Order*, 250.

disciple affectively reencounters the sweeping history of God's covenant-keeping mercy in the very process of praying for the manifestation of his covenant-keeping mercy such that imprecation blossoms—like so many of the imprecatory psalms (e.g., 7:17; 28:6–7; 54:6; 69:34–36; 79:13; 109:30)—into thanksgiving for God's works and praise of God's name. Christian imprecation as worship-inducing communion with God in Christ becomes a means of obeying the Pauline exhortations to "in everything by prayer and supplication with thanksgiving let your requests be made known to God" (Phil 4:6) and to "rejoice always, pray without ceasing, give thanks in all circumstances; for this is the will of God in Christ Jesus for you" (1 Thess 5:16–18). And because the affective dynamics of imprecatory prayer draw the Christian into worshipful apprehension of God's character, activity, and supreme worthiness of praise, the disciple who begins praying from any other chief love than the love of God, with any other principal aim than the glory of God, experiences in the practice of imprecation a challenge to and reorientation of affection. The prayer that commenced in idolatry, by the time the amen is uttered, is offered in love for the God of the gospel as a petitionary pursuit of his glory in the earth.[112]

Christian imprecation must arise from love of God's temple-kingdom and creation as well, and this kingdom- and creation-oriented desire is, together with the love of God, cultivated in the enactment of the imprecatory psalms. Imprecatory performance in union with Christ affectively rehearses God's costly commitment to assume humanity, enter into his creation, purchase the liberation of the cosmos, and inaugurate his temple-kingdom through Christ's first advent. At the same time, Christian imprecation impresses on the imprecating heart God's infallible promise to consummate his kingdom in Christ's second coming, to make the entire created world the temple of God's royal dwelling with a renewed and res-urrected humanity. The affective journey of imprecatory prayer recounts and reencounters in faith and hope the love of God for his temple-kingdom and his natural and human creation, nourishing the petitioner's love for the things the beloved God loves, aiming the petitioner's affections in the direction of God's affections, stimulating a desire for the good of the king-dom and creation whose good God in Christ has so sacrificially pursued. Christian imprecation has the potential to effect a mimetic love of God, a

---

[112] Augustine, *Enchiridion*, 140, observes more generally that "lust dimin-ishes as love grows," suggesting that inordinate loves are brought into right pro-portion as Godward love increasingly characterizes the affections.

love for God that cannot help but imitate and participate in his love for his temple-kingdom and creation.[113]

These affections for God's temple-kingdom and creation are activated in Christian practice of the imprecatory psalms in other, often deeply intertwined, ways as well. As the praying Christian experiences afresh the unmerited gift of welcome into Jesus' kingdom, this affective affirmation of the beauty and goodness and desirability of Christ's kingdom instigates a desire for his kingdom—that his temple-kingdom people would be preserved and prospered in this age to proclaim and demonstrate the way of the king and to expand throughout the earth, that his kingdom would finally reach its creation-filling completion in the eschaton. Insofar as a desire for the progress and consummation of the temple-kingdom involves a desire for peace to flourish, human beings to be reconciled to God, and the created world to be freed from the corruption of sinful violence, the love for God's kingdom enervated in imprecatory performance is an affection that simultaneously aims in love for the good of God's human and natural creation.

Yet further still, as the Christian imprecator tastes anew the blessing of God's loving liberation from her oppressors in Christ, God's gracious love toward her stirs a gracious love within her that yearns for the liberation of the church and all humanity from their oppressors, transforming her into a vessel of love that channels forward what she has received and desires that others would know the merciful protection of the God who has definitively protected her in Jesus. This outward turn in love toward the disciple's ecclesial and human families is only intensified by the renewed solidarity that the imprecating believer experiences with the body of Christ and humanity at large in her renewed solidarity with the suffering Jesus. For the Christian who approaches the imprecatory psalms blissfully unburdened by any personal enemies, this Christically mediated connection opens the possibility that imprecatory prayer might be enacted against the enemies who threaten God's covenant family and his human offspring.[114] For the Christian painfully cognizant of enemies devoted to

---

[113]   G. K. Beale, *We Become What We Worship: A Biblical Theology of Idolatry* (Downers Grove, Ill.: InterVarsity Press, 2008), interacts with the scriptural theme of what I am here referring to as mimetic love, of worship's capacity to form imitators and images of the object of worship, arguing in summary, "What people revere, they resemble, either for ruin or restoration." Beale, *We Become What We Worship*, 16.

[114]   Cf. McCann, *Theological Introduction*, 116; Wenham, *Psalter Reclaimed*, 143–45.

her destruction, the prayer that commences as a profoundly personal cry may yet grow to encompass others in love—Christians and non-Christians alike—as the imprecating imagination is drawn through Christ to the sufferers with whom her own flesh is variously bound. Kingdom-protecting, world-cleansing imprecatory prayer, when performed in union with Christ, has the potential to energize love for the temple-kingdom God has inaugurated and promised to consummate in Christ, for the created world God has redeemed in Jesus and promises to fill with his templing glory, and for the humanity Christ took into himself and invites to enjoy his presence. These multifaceted, love-generating dynamics ensure that the petitioning heart that follows the imprecatory psalms through the Christocentric narrative to which they testify, though its first word perhaps be born of selfish myopia or malice, will have its false affections interrupted and directed toward the kingdom and creation of God.

In addition to cultivating an ethically necessary love for God, his temple-kingdom, and his creation, Christian performance of the imprecatory psalms in union with Christ has the capacity to engender the love for human enemies that is required for ethical imprecatory prayer. First, imprecatory prayer evokes enemy love by drawing the imprecator into loving imitation of God's love of his enemies. That is, as Christian enactment of the imprecatory psalms cultivates love for God, the mimetic character of Godward love will follow the beloved God in his love for his enemies. Imprecation in union with Christ imaginatively retraces the gracious action of the Son of God to bear the judgment of God in the place of the enemies of God so that God's enemies might become his children. The imprecating Christian who encounters the love-inducing beauty of God in the affective rehearsal of God's works in Christ also encounters God's sacrificial love for his enemies, and this affective encounter directs the petitioner's desire along the trajectory of the desires of the preeminently desirable God. Invigorated in love for God, the praying disciple adopts the objects of love of the ultimate Object of love, imitating God's enemy love in mimetic love for God.

Second, Christian performance of the imprecatory psalms elicits enemy love by stimulating solidary identification with the enemy. The affective journey of imprecatory prayer in union with Christ confronts the petitioning Christian with his own judgment as an enemy in the judgment of the Christ who stood in the place of enemies. This confrontation provokes in the Christian not only repentance—an opportunity for conscious self-examination and confession of any idolatrous, potentially dangerous, affections as the petitioner recognizes his continuing capacity for injustice against others and rebellion against God, an opportunity to turn the imprecatory prayer inward at his own temple-defiling sinfulness—but also a sense of solidarity, a concarnational affinity, with the very enemy against whom his imprecatory prayer is directed. Discovering himself as a rightful object of God's wrathful justice, the Christian imprecator can no longer entertain the tempting delusion of the enemy's fundamental otherness, stoking pride and justifying mercilessness with the comforting lie that the enemy is essentially different in his capacity for sinful violence and desert of judgment.[115] Rather, knowing himself and his enemy as guilty together in the tribunal of God, acknowledging himself as profoundly capable of destructive violence like his enemy, seeing himself in the face of the enemy, the pride and mercilessness that may have dominated the imprecating Christian's affections are subverted and replaced with humility and compassion, with sympathy and understanding.[116] The enemy may consequently be received as a human being—as undeniably human as the imprecator himself—whose condition and rationale for action may be compassionately conceived because the imprecator recognizes the same potential and impulses within his own heart and character. The Christian performer of the imprecatory psalms thus finds in their affectively dynamic enactment a motive to love the enemy-neighbor as he loves himself, to desire and prayerfully pursue the good of the enemy with whom he identifies in solidarity, for the enemy-neighbor is in reality more like him than his initial appraisal may have suggested.

Third, Christian imprecation through the psalms cultivates enemy love by affirming the imprecator's identity as an enemy who has received grace from God. The affective rehearsal of God's gracious work in Christ that takes place in Christically sensitive imprecatory performance not only indicts the petitioner as an enemy judged by God in the judgment of Christ but also reconfirms the petitioner's status as a recipient of God's unmerited favor in

---

[115] Miroslav Volf, *Exclusion and Embrace: A Theological Exploration of Identity, Otherness, and Reconciliation* (Nashville: Abingdon, 1996), 84, describes the benefits of "recognition of solidarity in sin," contending that "it pricks the balloon of the self-righteousness of perpetrator and victim alike and protects all from perpetuating evil in the name of presumed goodness." See Volf, *Exclusion and Embrace*, 123–24, for Volf's suggestion that the imprecatory psalms stimulate this recognition of solidarity in a manner that makes possible forgiveness and love.

[116] Cf. Steussy, "Enemy in the Psalms," 12; Zenger, *God of Vengeance?* 68.

Christ. Having been spared the unremitting divine wrath that could have justly fallen on her, and having received undeserved blessing from God, the imprecating Christian is compelled to no longer view the enemy through the matrix of pure desert in the awareness that God has looked upon her through the matrix of grace.[117] Instead, the praying disciple—reacquainted with her own merciful movement from condemnation to reconciliation in Jesus—has her existence renarrated such that yearning for the enemy's gracious blessing is the only fitting affective response to God's work, for anything less would be a surd, an existential denial of the goodness of God's action toward her. In the enactment of the psalmic imprecations, the Christian discerns that unmerited blessing is a pivotal good of her own life and therefore a good worthy of pursuit in her life on behalf of the undeserving enemy. Grace received by the Christian as an enemy begets grace bestowed by the Christian to the enemy. The imprecatory prayer that might emerge from a vindictive desire for the enemy's ill, then, has the capacity to confront the imprecator with God's gracious pursuit of her good in Christ in a way that stifles her misdirected desire and grows within her a love that graciously longs for the good of her enemy. Thus, the petition for judgment merely for the sake of the enemy's suffering becomes in the process of prayer a petition for judgment for the sake of the enemy's welfare, supremely for the judgment of grace that is conversion and secondarily for the interrupting judgment that secures the enemy's good by inhibiting the enemy's self-destructive decline into wickedness.

Fourth, imprecatory prayer empowers enemy love by freeing the petitioner from the compulsion to exact violence. As many have observed, imprecation as prayer to God for his just judgment upon the enemy is itself a handing-over, a relinquishing, of all rights to vengeance to the God who can be trusted to bring justice. But more than this, imprecation as a dynamic practice that affectively reencounters God's works in Christ confirms to the petitioning believer that the God to whom vengeance is ceded has initiated vengeance and will consummate it through the agency of the Son and sons and daughters of God. The faith in Jesus' defeat of every opposing power at the cross and the hope in Jesus' and his ecclesial priest-kings' expulsive judgment of every enemy at his *parousia* that are cultivated in imprecatory performance render the petitioner's retributive violence superfluous, opening the Christian to the possibility of patient endurance that waits in confidence for God's just action

---

[117]   See Volf, *Exclusion and Embrace*, 85.

(Rom 12:19).[118] The death blow for evil has already been struck, and the eschatological day is drawing near. The imprecating Christian who internalizes these assurances about his past and future can in the present say *no* to personal vengeance and *yes* to perseverance in peace toward his enemies without fear that his refusal to execute violence spells the demise of justice.[119]

Further, the believer who has been accused, humiliated, alienated, targeted as an allegedly deserving object of hatred by the enemy's violence rediscovers in the Christically resonant rehearsal of imprecatory prayer that his vindication has been accomplished in Jesus' resurrection from the dead and will be manifested before the world when he is glorified with Christ at the end of history. The compulsion to justify oneself through violence in the wake of violence—to vindicate oneself through the victimization of the victimizer—is tamed by the reawakened reality of a better vindication from God. The imprecating Christian is liberated from the compulsion to commit violence not merely by cathartically relinquishing vengeance to God but by being affectively enveloped in a narrative in which God has begun and will complete his vindicating justice in Christ. Faith and hope wrap the praying disciple in the story of God's justice and God's vindication, freeing the believer from the recourse to violence in the name of either, empowering the endurance necessary for the patient witness of love that wills the enemy's good and answers aggression with peace. United to Christ, the imprecating Christian can follow Jesus in his refusal to answer violence with violence as he follows Jesus in "entrusting himself to him who judges justly" (1 Pet 2:23).[120]

---

[118]   Cf. Murray, "Christian Cursing?" 120.

[119]   Volf, *Exclusion and Embrace*, 302, describes the necessity of hope in divine vengeance for the present eschewal of personal vengeance: "Without entrusting oneself to the God who judges justly, it will hardly be possible to follow the crucified Messiah and refuse to retaliate when abused. The certainty of God's just judgment at the end of history is the presupposition for the renunciation of violence in the middle of it."

[120]   Murray, "Christian Cursing?" 121, posits that Jesus was silently praying the imprecatory psalms from the cross as he died. As I observed previously, Luke 23:46 depicts Jesus as quoting Ps 31:5—"Father, into your hands I commit my spirit!"—a declaration that recalls the psalmist's confident entrusting of himself to the God who gives vindication. According to Luke's account, then, Jesus indeed had at least one imprecatory psalm in his heart and mind as he suffered upon the cross, an imprecatory psalm that testifies to the truth of God's trustworthy

Fifth, and in many ways the culmination of the above surveyed dynamics, Christian performance of the imprecatory psalms cultivates enemy love by freeing the petitioner for forgiveness. The precise definition of forgiveness has proved notoriously difficult to pin down,[121] but here I use the term to refer to the affective shift toward a wrongdoer that relinquishes any claim to personal retaliation or revenge or requital, foreswears vindictive desire and ill will, and commits to pursuing the offender's good in love.[122] To leverage the accounting metaphor foregrounded by Jesus in Matt 6:12; 18:23–35; Luke 7:41–50; 11:4, forgiving a wrongdoer entails regarding the offender no longer as one's debtor and refusing to exact repayment for the propitiatory assuagement of the victim's wrath, resentment, and hostility.[123] Accordingly, forgiveness forsakes not only overt acts of retributive violence but also the malicious desire for the enemy's commensurate and compensatory harm as well as the embittered psychological rehearsal of the enemy's wrongs, which continually holds the offender as a debtor and is itself a subtle punishing of the wrongdoer.[124]

Prayers in Christ for the enemy's judgment may facilitate the Christian's exercise of this forgiveness. Immersed through the practice of imprecatory prayer in a narrative that stimulates faith in God's forgiveness on account of Christ's curse-bearing judgment on her behalf and

---

and just judgment, consistent with the claims of 1 Pet 2:23 that Jesus "continued entrusting himself to him who judges justly" in his passion.

[121]   See Nigel Biggar, "Forgiveness in the Twentieth Century: A Review of the Literature, 1901–2001," in *Forgiveness and Truth: Explorations in Contemporary Theology*, ed. Alistair McFadyen and Marcel Sarot (New York: T&T Clark, 2001), 181–217; Wolterstorff, *Justice in Love*, 165–71.

[122]   Cf. the definitions of Charles L. Griswold, *Forgiveness: A Philosophical Exploration* (New York: Cambridge University Press, 2007), 33–43; Wolterstorff, *Justice in Love*, 170; Jeffrie G. Murphy, "Forgiveness," in *Encyclopedia of Ethics*, ed. Lawrence C. Becker and Charlotte B. Becker, 2nd ed. (New York: Routledge, 2001), 1:561; Jerome Neu, "On Loving Our Enemies," in *The Ethics of Forgiveness: A Collection of Essays*, ed. Christel Fricke (New York: Routledge, 2011), 132.

[123]   Cf. Barker, *Imprecation as Divine Discourse*, 138, and the rich descriptors of forgiveness in WLC Q. 194.

[124]   Notably, this account of forgiveness does not require the offender's penitence as a prerequisite. On unilateral forgiveness, see Trudy Govier, *Forgiveness and Revenge* (New York: Routledge, 2002), 62–77. Cf. Matt 18:21–22; Luke 6:27–31; 11:4; 1 Pet 3:9, which do not identify the offender's repentance as a precondition to the forgiveness that foregoes retaliation and commits to the enemy's good in love. *Contra* Barker, *Imprecation as Divine Discourse*, 137–50.

hope in Jesus' and his church's certain eschatological mediation of God's perfectly just judgment against wickedness, the Christian imprecator undergoes an affective priming for humble, loving forgiveness in the present. The beneficiary of God's forgiveness in Christ, the Christian imprecator finds the sins of the enemy against her—however truly violent and egregious—relativized in the light of her own forgiven rebellion against God, displaced from its apparent ultimacy and thus rendered forgivable, and her fresh apprehension of God's forgiveness toward her generates a mimetic and fitting forgiveness that refuses to demand repayment from her enemy, granting the enemy the gift given the Christian by God (cf. Matt 18:21–35; Col 3:13).[125] And assured that God will indeed bring about a vengeance untainted by pettiness, idolatry, injustice, or perspectival finitude through the agency of Christ and the sons and daughters of God in him, the empowering certainty of God's judgment releases the praying disciple from attempting to administer retribution against the enemy and from the conscious obsession that replays the offense,[126] nourishes the grudge, wishes harm, and ever regards the enemy as one from whom payment must be exacted.

Christian imprecation, then, as a resonant affirmation of God's past and future for the disciple, opens to the petitioning believer a world in which

---

[125] See Bonhoeffer, *Prayerbook of the Bible*, 175; L. Gregory Jones, *Embodying Forgiveness: A Theological Analysis* (Grand Rapids: Eerdmans, 1995), 162; Todd Pokrifka-Joe, "Probing the Relationship between Divine and Human Forgiveness in Matthew: Hearing a Neglected Voice in the Canon," in McFadyen and Sarot, *Forgiveness and Truth*, 165. The reminder of Hauerwas, *Peaceable Kingdom*, 89, is appropriate: "We must remember that our first task is not to forgive, but to learn to be the forgiven," for only in the Christian's recognition of her forgivenness will she be sustained in the task of forgiveness.

[126] The language of conscious obsession here is intentional and refers to the voluntary rehearsal of wrongs that may attend nontraumatic forms of suffering. I am distinguishing this from the involuntary, intrusive remembering that is associated with violent trauma. See Bessel A. van der Kolk and Alexander C. McFarlane, "The Black Hole of Trauma," in *Traumatic Stress: The Effects of Overwhelming Experience on Mind, Body, and Society*, ed. Bessel A. van der Kolk, Alexander C. McFarlane, and Lars Weisaeth (New York: Guilford Press, 1996), 9–10; Bessel A. van der Kolk, *The Body Keeps the Score: Brain, Mind, and Body in the Healing of Trauma* (New York: Penguin Books, 2015), 66–71; Bessel A. van der Kolk and Onno van der Hart, "The Intrusive Past: The Flexibility of Memory and the Engraving of Trauma," in *Trauma: Explorations in Memory*, ed. Cathy Caruth (Baltimore: Johns Hopkins University Press, 1995), 172–73; Judith Lewis Herman, *Trauma and Recovery* (New York: BasicBooks, 1992), 37–42.

forgiveness is possible—a forgiveness that eschews both personal vengeance in action and vindictive desire in affection, releasing the disciple to perceive and respond to the enemy in love that pursues his good. In the language of the Lord's Prayer, the imprecatory "thy kingdom come" both precedes and stimulates not only the "forgive us our debts" of repentance but also the "as we forgive our debtors" of love. The psalmic prayer for judgment—even one that may initially arise from a yearning for the enemy's suffering as commensurate payment for the suffering inflicted upon the petitioner—leads the supplicant to the polyvalent Christ to whom the imprecations witness. And far from reifying bitter vindictiveness or underwriting plans for retributive violence, such Christically attentive prayer interrupts these faulty affections and promotes a forgiveness without which enemy love cannot be sustained, a forgiveness of the enemy's wrongs that transforms the prayer for judgment into one that seeks the enemy's welfare in the judgment of God.[127] Christian performance of the imprecatory psalms is therefore an ethical mode of prayer for the sons and daughters of God in Christ that empowers the affective posture of love that its ethical enactment requires by stimulating forgiveness of the enemy's wrongs against the petitioner.[128]

---

[127] Several scholars have argued that forgiveness is not incompatible with a desire for punishment. See, e.g., Govier, *Forgiveness and Revenge*, 175n9; Margaret R. Holmgren, *Forgiveness and Retribution: Responding to Wrongdoing* (New York: Cambridge University Press, 2012), 43; Murphy, "Forgiveness," in Becker and Becker, *Encyclopedia of Ethics*, 1:561. The conception of forgiveness I have proffered entails a refusal to pray for divine judgment from a vindictive desire for the offender's ill, as a retaliatory petition aimed at the enemy's harm. There is nothing about this conception of forgiveness, however, that renders it incompatible with actively desiring God's just judgment for the enemy's good. If imprecation, as I have argued, can indeed be an exercise of enemy love, then there is no intractable conflict between the forgiveness that rejects revenge and malice and the prayer for judgment that seeks the enemy's well-being through God's converting or, if necessary, violence-interrupting action.

[128] Cf. the discussions of imprecatory practice and forgiveness, which offer a very different formulation of the relationship between the two, by Walter Brueggemann, *From Whom No Secrets Are Hid: Introducing the Psalms*, ed. Brent A. Strawn (Louisville: Westminster John Knox, 2014), 99; Creach, *Violence in Scripture*, 210; McCann, *Theological Introduction*, 120; Miller, *They Cried to the Lord*, 303; Youngblood, "Don't Get Even," 157; Walter Brueggemann and William H. Bellinger, Jr., *Psalms*, NCBC (New York: Cambridge University, 2014), 477.

I have attempted to offer an evocative and detailed exploration of the affective kinetics of Christian performance of the imprecatory psalms in union with the Christ who polyvalently fulfills them, maintaining that Christian prayer that is sensitive to the Christological significance of the psalmic imprecations will usher the petitioner along a dynamic journey through the narrative of God's work in Jesus that cultivates a faith in God's past and hope in God's future, which together bear the fruit of love for God, his temple-kingdom, his creation, and his enemies. It is unlikely that any individual Christian imprecator will experience all of the above proposed agent-implicating associations in a single instance of imprecatory performance, at least not at a conscious level. Nevertheless, I have endeavored to articulate what is possible within the heart of the disciple who permits prayer of the imprecatory psalms to follow the psalms' multidimensional witness to Jesus Christ to the foot of his cross and the edge of the eschatological age to come.

Though prayer for divine judgment upon one's enemies is ever a dangerous calling—liable to sinful abuse and capable of reinforcing misdirected affections, especially in the affective turbulence of violent suffering—the Christically oriented mode of imprecatory performance that I have surveyed functions as its own safeguard, interrupting unethical and idolatrous desires and aiming the imprecator's affections toward the proper objects of love. Consequently, Christian imprecation that arises from unfitting affections cannot continue unchallenged, for the multifaceted encounter with Jesus that attends imprecation in union with Christ exposes inordinate desire, renarrates the Christian's existence, and stimulates love born of faith and hope. Entered into in this manner, Christian performance of the imprecatory psalms generates the very ethical affections that are required for ethically faithful Christian imprecation, for while the disciple's judgment prayer may not commence in love, the affection-altering dynamics of imprecatory prayer in union with Christ will exert an unrelenting force upon the disciple to end there, offering an "amen" in love renewed. Augustine famously prayed, "Grant what Thou dost command, and command what Thou wilt,"[129] and through Christically rich prayer of the imprecatory psalms, God gives what he commands, the dispositions of heart that are required for imprecatory prayer in conformity with the law of love.

---

[129] Augustine, *Confessions*, 2nd ed., trans. F. J. Sheed, ed. Michael P. Foley (Indianapolis: Hackett Publishing, 2006), 10.29.

Conclusion

With this chapter, I have examined how Christians might ethically enact the imprecatory psalms and how the imprecatory psalms might ethically act upon imprecating Christians. I have proposed a model for Christian imprecatory performance that is ethically consistent with disciples' vocation, redemptive-historical location, and call to love within God's ethically determinative story of the world, and I have articulated how performance of the Christologically polyvalent imprecatory psalms in union with Christ stimulates the very affections necessary for ethical imprecation.

The proper agents of ethically faithful imprecatory prayer are Christians who suffer in righteous innocence, restored in Christ to their vocation as royal-priestly sons and daughters of God called to protect God's temple-kingdom and cleanse the world through the expulsion of the serpentine wicked so that the earth may be the royal dwelling place of God with his people. The proper objects of Christian imprecation are the spiritual, human, and systemic enemies of God's king and kingdom and the Christian individual's and community's indwelling, temple-defiling uncleanness. Depending upon the object of imprecation, the proper content of imprecatory enactment may include divine action that effects the enemy's repentant conversion, temporal judgment that interrupts the enemy's violence through any just means necessary, and eschatological judgment that definitively instantiates the covenant justice of God.

Because Christians are priest-kings of an inaugurated kingdom—a kingdom that is already established and not yet consummated—they must pray the imprecatory psalms with a priority of intention granted to the enemy's conversion in this present age of gracious patience and eschatologize psalmic expectations of and pleas for active human mediation of divine vengeance, awaiting and requesting the *parousia* of Christ in which they will participate as royal priests in the execution of God's justice upon the enemy. Christians' imprecatory petitions must arise from affections that are consistent with the works, purposes, and commands of God, affections characterized by love for God, his temple-kingdom, his creation, and his enemies. Consonant with the New Testament's prescriptions of enemy love, the various judgments requested in Christian imprecation may be petitionary expressions of a desire for and pursuit of the good of the enemy who is violently and (self-)destructively committed to opposing God and his temple-kingdom.

The imprecatory psalms that must be enacted in accord with God's ethically determinative story have the capacity to act upon the Christian petitioner who makes their prayers her own by instigating an affective retracing of the story of God's works in Jesus. Performed in union with the Christ who fulfills the roles of petitioner, enemy, and divine judge in the imprecatory psalms, the Psalter's requests for vengeance stimulate within the performer an agent-implicating rehearsal of Christ's accomplished and promised action that cultivates faith and hope. Together, faith in God's past and hope in God's future reframe the imprecating Christian's vision of the world and the horizons of action, making possible a love in God's present that desires and pursues the good suited to God, his temple-kingdom, his creation, and his enemies.

In practice, these affective dynamics entail that the petitioner who commences psalmic imprecation with disordered loves experiences in the very process of Christically sensitive imprecation an exposure of, challenge to, and redirection of unethical desire toward the proper objects of affection. Thus, imprecatory performance in union with Christ safeguards the Christian's prayer for judgment from continuing in and reinforcing idolatrous, unethical, and potentially dangerous dispositions as Christologically oriented enactment of the imprecatory psalms functions as a means of grace by which God fashions the affections required to ethically pray the psalms of vengeance and, indeed, to live as faithful and virtuous witnesses in God's world.

Conclusion

Cursing with God

> Then the angel showed me the river of the water of life, bright as crystal, flowing from the throne of God and of the Lamb through the middle of the street of the city; also, on either side of the river, the tree of life with its twelve kinds of fruit, yielding its fruit each month. The leaves of the tree were for the healing of the nations. No longer will there be anything accursed, but the throne of God and of the Lamb will be in it, and his servants will worship him. They will see his face, and his name will be on their foreheads. And night will be no more. They will need no light of lamp or sun, for the Lord God will be their light, and they will reign forever and ever. (Rev 22:1–5)

At the beginning of the Bible's story, God planted his image-bearers in a sanctuary garden and commissioned them as royal priests to service and guard the place of his presence and to subdue the earth as sacred space, extending the bounds of God's holy dwelling until it filled up creation as the house of the Lord. At the end of the Bible's story, the cosmos is consummated as God's garden-temple, and the humanity created to be a royal priesthood continues to serve as a royal priesthood into eternity. The sons and daughters of God reign as royal heirs forever and ever, and they worship as priests, welcomed into the glorious and most holy presence of the Lord never to depart again, every one of them bearing on their foreheads the name of God after the pattern of the high priests of old (cf. Exod 28:36–38). Between the bookends of Genesis 1 and Revelation 22, the sons and daughters of God are to embrace the royal-priestly calling for which they were created and to which they are destined. They are to tend and extend God's sanctuary—guarding his dwelling place, driving out unholiness, subduing the land, preparing the entire creation as sacred space for Yahweh's holy presence. And from the kingdom of Israel to the kingdom of Christ, one way God's royal priesthood enacts that calling is through prayer.

Imprecatory Prayer in the Story of God

The imprecatory psalms are royal-priestly prayers. They are petitions in the voice of the son of God—whether the Israelite community or the Israelite king—pleas that exercise in prayer the Adamic vocation to protect God's temple-kingdom, drive out the unholy, subdue the wicked, and make the earth the sanctuary of Yahweh's glory. Through intertextual appeal to Israel's Scriptures, the imprecatory psalms unfold a storied cosmos within which the psalmists' prayers for divine judgment are ethically intelligible. The enemy is the serpent seed, unholy corrupters of sacred space whose violence threatens the temple-kingdom over and with whom God reigns and resides, and the imprecator seeks to drive out the wicked by supplication to the divine judge, the cosmic warrior-king, the covenant-keeper who has promised justice for Israel. Within the allusively constructed narrative world of the imprecatory psalms, the psalmists' cries for judgment emerge as a faithful enactment of their royal-priestly calling as the son of God that coheres with God's cultic *telos* for creation—his purpose to dwell in holiness with his people and to cultivate the whole creation as his sacred sanctuary.

Far from leaving the imprecatory psalms and their piety behind, the New Testament exhibits a multidimensional interaction with and development of the text and themes of the imprecatory psalms in its narration of and reflection upon God's kingdom-restoring works in Christ. The New Testament authors regularly appeal to the inhabitants of the imprecatory psalms' narrative world to depict the characteristics, actions, and futures of various actors in the Christian-era scene of redemptive history. Notably, the New Testament allusively presents Jesus as the antitypical fulfillment of each figure in the imprecatory psalms even as it evocatively portrays the enemies of Christ and his temple-kingdom as the extension and culmination of the psalmic enemy and Christians as inheritors of the role of the royal-priestly imprecator, prayerfully guarding the temple-kingdom and subduing the earth by driving out the unholy serpent seed from the place that God has claimed for his royal dwelling. But the New

Testament that tells its story by echoing the imprecatory psalms also contains its own imprecatory speech acts—commended by Jesus, performed by an apostle, prayed by the saints in heaven. Read through the lens of the intertextually resonant narrative framework generated by the New Testament's allusive interaction with the imprecatory psalms, these instances of Christian imprecation display a discernible theological and ethical rationale. Like the imprecatory psalms themselves, these New Testament imprecations against the enemies of God's temple-kingdom are a morally fitting enactment of the royal-priestly vocation of the sons and daughters of God.

The story of Scripture that situates the imprecatory prayers of both testaments is simultaneously the story within which Christians live as characters, the story that governs the church's moral existence. Consequently, any proposal for ethical Christian performance of the imprecatory psalms must account for Christians' vocation and location within God's teleologically oriented and ethically determinative narrative of the world. Christians are sons and daughters of God in the Son of God, restored in Christ to their royal-priestly calling and heirs of the primal commission to tend and extend God's sanctuary dwelling, and imprecatory prayer is an exercise of that divinely granted office. Accordingly, innocently suffering Christians are to petition as priest-kings for justice against the human, systemic, and spiritual enemies of Jesus and his temple-kingdom as well as against the petitioner's and the ecclesial community's temple-corrupting sin.

Depending upon the intended objects, Christian imprecation may include requests for the merciful judgment of conversion, temporal judgment that interrupts violence through whatever just means necessary, and eschatological judgment that consummates both God's covenantal justice and God's creation as his temple-kingdom. The inaugurated eschatological character of God's temple-kingdom in the church's time in redemptive history renders fitting in Christian imprecation a priority of intention granted to petitions for conversion and an eschatologizing of the psalmists' expectations of human actualization of God's vengeance. Ethical imprecatory performance, however, requires right affections in addition to right actions. Christian imprecation can and must be born from love for God, his temple-kingdom, his creation, and his enemies that is directed toward the good suited to each. Significantly, prayers for the conversion, temporal interruption, and eschatological judgment of the violently wicked may all be plausible expressions of enemy love, which desire and pursue the good of those who seek their own harm in their harming of others. There is, therefore, no necessarily intractable conflict between Christ's command to love the enemy and his command to pray like the persistent widow for God's justice.

Prayerful performance of the imprecatory psalms is a means by which Christians may—and must—exercise their vocation as royal priests in God's narrative of the world. At the same time, performance of the imprecatory psalms that is attentive to their polyvalent Christological witness has the potential to immerse petitioners within God's Christocentric narrative in a manner that cultivates affections of faith, hope, and love. The Christian united to the Christ to whom the imprecatory psalms bear multidimensional witness may experience in imprecatory performance an immersive rehearsal of the story of God's works in Jesus. This narrativizing reinduction into God's story has the capacity to cultivate a faith and hope that give rise to love for God, his temple-kingdom, his creation, and his enemies—the very affections required for ethical Christian imprecation. As the church enacts the imprecatory psalms, the imprecatory psalms in turn act upon the church, generating in disciples the affections appropriate to God's narrative by conscripting disciples into that narrative, stimulating the affective conditions necessary for ethical Christian imprecation and for a life of faith and virtue. The psalmic practice whose ethical intelligibility is derived from God's story in turn rehearses God's story in a manner that forms Christians for ethical prayer and participation in that story.

Paths for Future Research

This study, in addition to proposing an answer to the question of Christian performance of the imprecatory psalms, opens up promising pathways for future research in several domains that might fruitfully follow from its methods and conclusions.

In my treatment of the imprecatory psalms, I have foregrounded the related themes of the temple-kingdom of God and humanity's royal-priestly vocation in my articulation of Scripture's unified narrative of redemptive history, and I have attempted to demonstrate that this rendering of the biblical story helps to make theological and moral sense of the Psalter's violently graphic prayers against the violent enemies of God. If this biblical-theological framing is deemed a constructive contribution to the theo-ethical interpretation of the imprecatory psalms—one that brings clarity and coherence to these frequently perplexing texts—then this reading of the scriptural narrative and its capacity to illuminate the theological and ethical rationale of divinely sanctioned biblical violence more broadly warrants additional investigation. Situating diverse issues such as the capital punishments of the Mosaic legislation, the logic of *herem* and the conquest of Canaan, discrete iterations of divine judgment in the Old Testament, and even Jesus' teaching on and participation in judgment in the New Testament within a narrative framework that is teleologically oriented toward the establishment of God's holy temple-kingdom on earth, that attends to cultic conceptions of sacred space, and that is sensitive to the royal-priestly character of the human mediation of divine judgment might generate new insights that not only disclose the comprehensibility of sanctioned violence in the biblical story but that also aid the Christian church in relating to the Bible's violent texts as she embraces her calling as a peaceful kingdom of priests.

The conclusion that the imprecatory psalms are an ethically permissible and necessary component of faithful Christian prayer also commends further research into the proper form and the formational effects of their liturgical embodiment in the church's communal worship. Ecclesial recovery of the imprecatory psalms in ritualized worship requires—beyond a conviction regarding their ethical propriety—careful attention to the concrete and creative ways communities might perform the imprecatory psalms through chant, song, individual or collective reading, adapted responsive prayer, and the other forms psalmic rehearsal might take in various liturgical traditions as well as to the liturgical promptings that might facilitate participants' understanding and ethical exercise of the imprecations.[1] Especially within those traditions that have substantially edited or excised outright the imprecatory psalms from their worship books, disciplined reflection on and development of liturgies that familiarize communities with the imprecatory psalms, instruct on their ethical enactment, and give corporate voice to their petitions is essential if the costly loss of imprecation is to be rectified in the church catholic.[2]

A liturgical turn in scholarly investigation of the imprecations could also contribute to a deepened appreciation of the effects of imprecatory performance,

---

[1]   For a helpful discussion of psalm settings and the pedagogical value of liturgical framing, see John D. Witvliet, *The Biblical Psalms in Christian Worship: A Brief Introduction and Guide to Resources*, Calvin Institute of Christian Worship Liturgical Studies Series (Grand Rapids: Eerdmans, 2007), 69–130; John Witvliet, "The Biblical Psalms in Christian Worship," October 25, 2012, Kavanagh Lecture, Yale Institute of Sacred Music, New Haven, Conn., accessed April 16, 2019, https://divinity.yale.edu/news-and-media/videos/biblical-psalms -christian-worship.

[2]   An appreciative allusion to Walter Brueggemann, "The Costly Loss of Lament," *JSOT* 36 (1986): 57–71. I provide a sample liturgy of imprecation that seeks to accomplish these aims in the appendix.

expanding my treatment of the affective dynamics of Christian imprecation into a phenomenological examination that addresses how liturgical enactment of the imprecatory psalms inducts the body into a physiologically, socially, and theologically charged dramatic rehearsal. Research into the formative capacity of liturgical imprecation could shed light on the potential for such psalmic performance to conscript worshippers into God's story, recast viscerally held conceptions of reality, and shape instincts for faithfully inhabiting God's world by co-opting the physical and social bodies of the body of Christ.[3]

This study may offer intriguing possibilities for trauma-informed approaches to the imprecatory psalms as well. Trauma readings frequently interpret biblical texts as the writings, reflections, and recovery attempts of traumatized communities in a manner that affirms their therapeutic utility for victims of trauma while relativizing the theological normativity of those depictions of God, which are more disconcerting to modern, Western moral sensibilities.[4] Christopher Frechette explains:

> Recognizing a biblical text as a trauma narrative provides a rationale for doing two things: dismissing the presumption that a given biblical portrayal of God or people must stand on its own in a universal sense and allowing that some such portrayals may have limited beneficial therapeutic functions, as well as potentially harmful "side effects" for which correctives may emerge within a larger symbolic program.[5]

---

[3]   See James K. A. Smith, *Imagining the Kingdom: How Worship Works*, vol. 2 of Cultural Liturgies (Grand Rapids: Baker Academic, 2013), who interacts with the work of Maurice Merleau-Ponty and Pierre Bourdieu in his development of a liturgical phenomenology. Cf. M. Therese Lysaught, "Eucharist as Basic Training: Liturgy, Ethics, and the Body," in *Theology and Lived Christianity*, ed. David M. Hammond (Mystic, Conn.: Twenty-Third Publications, 2000), 257–86; "Love and Liturgy," in *Gathered for the Journey: Moral Theology in Catholic Perspective*, ed. David Matzko McCarthy and M. Therese Lysaught (Grand Rapids: Eerdmans, 2007), 24–42; Philip Kenneson, "Gathering: Worship, Imagination, and Formation," in *The Blackwell Companion to Christian Ethics*, ed. Stanley Hauerwas and Samuel Wells (Malden, Mass.: Blackwell, 2004), 53–67.

[4]   Christopher G. Frechette and Elizabeth Boase, "Defining 'Trauma' as a Useful Lens for Biblical Interpretation," in *Bible through the Lens of Trauma*, ed. Elizabeth Boase and Christopher G. Frechette (Atlanta: SBL Press, 2016), 17. For a survey of the emergence of trauma theory as an interpretive lens within biblical studies, see David G. Garber Jr., "Trauma Theory and Biblical Studies," *CBR* 14, no. 1 (2015): 24–44.

[5]   Christopher G. Frechette, "The Old Testament as Controlled Substance: How Insights from Trauma Studies Reveal Healing Capacities in Potentially Harmful Texts," *Int* 69, no. 1 (2015): 34.

Frechette interprets the imprecatory psalms accordingly, reading these prayers as aids for trauma victims in the process of recovery that do not necessarily bind interpreters to their portraits of God.[6] I have argued, however, that the imprecatory psalms are theologically and ethically consistent with the overarching redemptive-historical narrative of Scripture, opening the way for a trauma-informed hermeneutic that recognizes and explores the potential traumatic origins and therapeutic utility of the imprecations while simultaneously upholding the theological normativity of their representations of God's behavior and character. Might it be that the imprecatory psalms' therapeutic capacity for trauma survivors can be understood as a product of their invitation into the truthful realities of God—that the imprecations hold out hope for healing precisely because they bear witness to the unexpected God in whom healing is found? Such a theologically oriented approach to trauma hermeneutics might stimulate productive treatments of the imprecatory psalms and other violent texts even as it commends trauma as an interpretive lens to scholarly circles in which, perhaps due to theological reservations, trauma-informed readings have received relatively less attention.

Further, my analysis of the narrativizing affective dynamics of Christian imprecation might contribute to more detailed research into the therapeutic potential of imprecatory performance for survivors of trauma. Judith Herman offers a three-stage schema to describe the characteristic progression of traumatic recovery that includes establishing safety, remembering and mourning through construction of a trauma narrative that promotes reinterpretation of the event, and reconnecting with ordinary life,[7] and several scholars have utilized this schema to investigate the imprecatory psalms as prayerful scripts that facilitate survivors' movement through the recovery process.[8] No existing examination, however,

---

[6]   See Christopher G. Frechette, "Destroying the Internalized Perpetrator: A Healing Function of the Violent Language against Enemies in the Psalms," in *Trauma and Traumatization in Individual and Collective Dimensions: Insights from Biblical Studies and Beyond*, ed. Eve-Marie Becker, Jan Dochhorn, and Else K. Holt, SAN 2 (Göttingen: Vandenhoeck and Ruprecht, 2014), 71.

[7]   Judith Lewis Herman, *Trauma and Recovery* (New York: BasicBooks, 1992), esp. 155–213.

[8]   Cf. Brent A. Strawn, "Trauma, Psalmic Disclosure, and Authentic Happiness," in Boase and Frechette, *Bible through the Lens of Trauma*, 143–60; Frechette, "Destroying the Internalized Perpetrator"; Serene Jones, *Trauma and Grace: Theology in a Ruptured World* (Louisville: Westminster John Knox, 2009), 43–67.

has accounted for the capacity of imprecatory enactment to immerse petitioners in an affective rehearsal of the thoroughly Christocentric story of God's works to which the psalms bear witness, and attention to these dynamics could generate innovative accounts of the potential for imprecatory performance to foster a sense of security, renarrate the survivor's life and world, and reintegrate the survivor into a meaning-full reality. If, as I suggested above, research ensues on the body-inducting, formational effects of liturgical performance of the imprecatory psalms, such work could profitably interact with developing body-oriented conceptualizations of trauma and recovery to explore how the body that "keeps the score"[9] of trauma is involved and permitted to experience the world anew in the sensory-rich ritual of liturgical imprecation.[10]

Reopening the Imprecatory Psalms

So, to revisit my wife's question one final time, what are we supposed to do with the imprecatory psalms?

We read them in their intertextual connection with the ethically determinative narrative of Scripture. We follow their figures and themes into the allusively resonant New Testament and discern their polyvalent fulfillment in Jesus. We pray them in loving exercise of our God-ordained vocation as priest-kings in Christ and permit their witness to stimulate in us faith, hope, and love. We "curse" with God—that is, we ask our Father to enact the judgment curses he has already declared and to administer his promised justice for the sake of his temple-kingdom in a world marred by unholy violence. In so doing, we embrace and grow into the high calling of the sons and daughters of God.

---

[9] Bessel A. van der Kolk, *The Body Keeps the Score: Brain, Mind, and Body in the Healing of Trauma* (New York: Penguin Books, 2015). Cf. Bessel A. van der Kolk, Alexander C. McFarlane, and Lars Weisaeth, eds., *Traumatic Stress: The Effects of Overwhelming Experience on Mind, Body, and Society* (New York: Guilford Press, 1996).

[10] Cf. Jones, *Trauma and Grace*, 64. Shelly Rambo, *Spirit and Trauma: A Theology of Remaining* (Louisville: Westminster John Knox, 2010), 123: "In traditional therapies, the story is recovered. If a person who survives trauma can put words to that experience, the process of healing can take place. In more body-oriented therapies, the process of making visible is somatic. A person literally learns to move in the world again, rather than being paralyzed by it." Cf. van der Kolk, *Body Keeps the Score*, 3, 63–64. The type of phenomenological investigation of liturgical imprecation for which I advocated above shares with scholarship on trauma a concern with, e.g., embodiment, narrative, imagination, and prereflective conceptions of the world and thus could serve as a fruitful resource for work on psalmic performance and traumatic healing.

Appendix
Cursing in Corporate Worship

A Sample Liturgy of Imprecation

With this appendix, I offer a complete liturgy of imprecation—a template for ethical embodiment of the imprecatory psalms in ecclesial corporate worship—that reflects the liturgical practices of the evangelical Presbyterian community in which I minister. While the liturgy does not represent the precise elements, order, or musical preferences of every community, my intention is to provide an order of worship whose basic outline exhibits considerable overlap with various liturgical traditions and is therefore adaptable for diverse contexts.

Given the taming or total excision of the imprecatory psalms in many streams of Christian worship and the resultant lack of familiarity (and comfort) with their enactment by many Christians, the supplied liturgy foregrounds the imprecatory psalms without assuming any prior experience with their prayerful appropriation. That is, this liturgy aims to guide the congregation through ethical and affectively engaged performance of the imprecatory psalms as if for the first time.[1] Accordingly, the liturgy emphasizes themes

---

[1]   Toward this end, the included script for responsive imprecatory prayer seeks to model the wide variety of petitions and associations that the imprecatory psalms may prompt in the praying Christian. For communities becoming increasingly familiar with the practice of ethical imprecation in union with Christ, liturgical performance of the imprecatory psalms may at times privilege one particular mode of prayer aimed at a specific form of kingdom-threatening violence and utilize a psalm that is particularly suited for that type of petition. For example, Psalm 58 could be prayed against vicious church leaders who prey upon the flock of God; Psalm 83 could be directed against persecutors of the

that resonate throughout the imprecatory psalms—unjust oppression and violence, divine kingship and judgment, merciful deliverance and restoration, sacred space and royal priesthood—generating a discernible thematic unity from opening call to closing benediction, and imprecatory psalms are incorporated into several liturgical moments to demonstrate the range of responses they might fittingly evoke. The specific liturgical framings and scripted prayers I include aim to facilitate embodiment of the psalmic prayers for justice that coheres with the ethical conclusions I reached regarding the church's redemptive-historical vocation, the proper objects and content of imprecatory prayer, and the affective dynamics of Christologically sensitive imprecation. Given the graphic language and potentially distressing themes of the imprecatory psalms, leaders adopting this liturgy may be well-advised to make the community aware in advance of the texts and topics that will be engaged—perhaps in the preceding worship gathering or a weekly communication—thereby giving congregants the opportunity to meet and discuss questions with a church leader and to make a measured and informed decision concerning their participation in the liturgy.

In the liturgy of imprecation that follows, bulleted and italicized text designates each element in the movement of the liturgy. Plain text indicates words to be spoken or prayed by the liturgical leader, and congregational speech is in bold. Portions of the liturgy in which the gathered community is encouraged to stand in body or spirit are signaled by an asterisk (*), and those in which kneeling in body or spirit is appropriate are marked with a cross (†). The text included in brackets under the heading "Preparation for Worship" is intended to be displayed visibly or printed in the order of worship to inform the congregation of the issues that will be addressed in the liturgy and to prompt worshipers' prayer prior to the call to worship. Where I suggest songs for congregational singing, I also include additional options that match the liturgical moment and themes. My goal with these proposals is not to offer an exhaustive catalog of liturgical options but more modestly to submit representative examples of hymns, worship songs, and musical psalm settings that give expression to the truths, affections, themes, and speech acts suitable for a liturgy of imprecation. These musical options are no less contextually informed than the rest of

___

global church; Psalm 137 could be taken up as a plea for Jesus' eschatological advent and kingdom-consummating justice. Liturgical imprecation does not in every instance need to capture all the dimensions of faithful imprecatory performance, but it may prove helpful at the outset to practice the dynamic multivalence of imprecatory prayer in the ways the provided liturgy models.

the decisions that go into construction of a liturgy, and traditions that, for example, practice psalmic chant or incorporate unrepresented musical styles will undoubtedly have no trouble aggregating further candidates for inclusion in their own contexts.

Preparation for Worship

[As we worship today, we will hear and think, pray and sing about the violence and injustice of our world, the suffering and vindication of our Savior, and the judgment and victory of our God. If at any point you desire to step outside, feel free to do so, and elders will be available to talk or pray throughout the service. In preparation for worship, let us pray:

Loving Father, as we gather for worship this day, grant us humility to hear and receive your word, courage to confront the injustice in us and in the world, and faith to call out and cling to you as we return to your promises. Through Christ our Lord. Amen.]

Call to Worship and Greeting

Let us hear our gracious God and king as he calls us to worship him this day:

O kingdoms of the earth, sing to God;
    sing praises to the Lord,
to him who rides in the heavens, the ancient heavens;
    behold, he sends out his voice, his mighty voice.
Ascribe power to God,
    whose majesty is over Israel,
    and whose power is in the skies.
Awesome is God from his sanctuary;
    the God of Israel—he is the one who gives power and
    strength to his people.
Blessed be God! (Ps 68:32–35)

Blessed be the LORD, the God of Israel,
    who alone does wondrous things.
Blessed be his glorious name forever;
    may the whole earth be filled with his glory!
    Amen and Amen! (Ps 72:18–19)

The grace of the Lord Jesus Christ and the love of God and the fellowship of the Holy Spirit be with you all. (2 Cor 13:14)
    And also with you.

Prayer of Invocation

God and Father of our Lord Jesus Christ, you gave us your Son, the beloved one who was rejected, the Savior who appeared defeated. Yet the mystery of his kingship illumines our lives. Show us in his death the victory that crowns the ages, and in his broken body the love that unites heaven and earth. We ask this through your Son, our Lord Jesus Christ, who lives and reigns with you in the unity of the Holy Spirit, one God, forever and ever. Amen.[2]

Song of Adoration*

- "Psalm 96"[3]

- Additional options: "This Is My Father's World,"[4] "Sing to the King,"[5] "Authority of Christ,"[6] "Praise to the Lord, the Almighty,"[7] "O Worship the King"[8]

Scripture Reading

The word of the Lord from Psalm 11:

[1] In the LORD I take refuge;
how can you say to my soul,
    "Flee like a bird to your mountain,
[2] for behold, the wicked bend the bow;
    they have fitted their arrow to the string
    to shoot in the dark at the upright in heart;
[3] if the foundations are destroyed,
    what can the righteous do?"
[4] The LORD is in his holy temple;
    the LORD's throne is in heaven;
    his eyes see, his eyelids test the children of man.
[5] The LORD tests the righteous,
    but his soul hates the wicked and the one who loves violence.

---

2   *The Worship Sourcebook* (Grand Rapids: Calvin Institute of Christian Worship, Faith Alive Christian Resources, Baker Books, 2004), 676–77.

3   "Psalm 96," in *Trinity Psalter* (Pittsburgh: Crown and Covenant, 1994), 82.

4   Maltbie D. Babcock, "This Is My Father's World," Public Domain.

5   Billy J. Foote and Charles Silvester Horne, "Sing to the King," sixsteps Music, worshiptogether.com songs, 2003.

6   Jeff Bourque, "Authority of Christ," from *Songs for the Book of Luke*, The Gospel Coalition (CD), 2013.

7   Joachim Neander, "Praise to the Lord, the Almighty," Public Domain.

8   Robert Grant, "O Worship the King," Public Domain.

[6] Let him rain coals on the wicked;
>fire and sulfur and a scorching wind shall be the portion of
>>their cup.

[7] For the LORD is righteous;
he loves righteous deeds;
>the upright shall behold his face. (Ps 11:1–7)[9]

This is the word of the Lord.
Thanks be to God.

Preparation for Confession

In this psalm, David prays, telling God about the taunts of his enemies, rehearsing the Lord's holiness and commitment to righteousness, and asking his king to do justice—to pour out his holy judgment on those who love violence. Perhaps our first instinct is to put ourselves in David's position and pray against the violence and injustice of the world. If we are honest with ourselves, however, if we take a moment to examine our own hearts and lives, we begin to recognize that the judgment David requests is the judgment that ought rightly to fall on us, our injustice, our subtle and obvious forms of violence. But the good news of the gospel is that Jesus took our place: the Judge of the universe became the judged so that we who were God's enemies might be made God's children. At the cross, Jesus experienced the flood of God's judgment and took the cup of God's wrath as a substitute for unjust, violent people like us. The cross shows us the deadly seriousness of our sin, and it sets us free to confess our sin without fear, secure in the promise that we belong to God by grace. So now let us kneel in body or spirit and approach our holy king in prayer, confessing our sin together.

Confession of Sin†

Our Father, holy king, lover of righteousness, tester of hearts, judge of the world, we confess that we are often quick to accuse others of injustice and quicker to excuse it in ourselves. We harbor anger at the wrongs of others without acknowledging the wickedness in us. Expose our unrighteousness, grant us true repentance, and drive out all that is unholy from our hearts and lives.

---

[9] The translation utilized in this sample liturgy (ESV) is the one used throughout the book and in the corporate worship of the church where I serve. Communities opting for gender-neutral language in corporate worship may substitute, e.g., the NRSV of the texts I have included.

When we have afflicted others, whether by our own power or by our silent support of systems that oppress, enslave, and crush, **break us, Lord.**

When we have perplexed others and purposely confused them for our own gain or driven them to despair, **break us, Lord.**

When we have persecuted others, casting them out of our community unjustly, leaving them forsaken and alone, **break us, Lord.**

When we have nurtured violence in heart and speech and act by feeding bitterness, speaking without love, and harming neighbors who bear your image, **break us, Lord.**

Then broken, we carry in our bodies the death of Jesus so that the life of Jesus may be made visible in our bodies; **make us, Lord.**

With the power that belongs only to you, make us into your holy treasure; **make us, Lord.**

We are the clay, and you are the Potter. We are the work of your hands; **make us, Lord.**

Do not be exceedingly angry, and do not remember our iniquity forever. Now consider, for the sake of Christ, we are by grace your people. **Make us, Lord, through Jesus Christ, our Lord. Amen.**[10]

Let us take a moment to silently and individually confess our sins to God.

Assurance of Pardon*

Now rise to your feet as you are able, lift up your heads, hold out your hands, dear children of God, and receive the promise of your Father's gracious, forgiving, reconciling love toward you:

Jesus suffered outside the gate in order to sanctify you through his own blood. God shows his love for us in that while we were still sinners,

---

[10]   The responsive portion of this prayer of confession is adapted from *Worship Sourcebook*, 103–4.

Christ died for us. Since, therefore, we have now been justified by his blood, much more shall we be saved by him from the wrath of God. For if while we were enemies we were reconciled to God by the death of his Son, much more, now that we are reconciled, shall we be saved by his life. Jesus loves you and has freed you from your sins by his blood and made you a kingdom, priests to his God and Father. (Based on Heb 13:12; Rom 5:8–10; Rev 1:5–6)

Thanks be to God.

Song of Thanksgiving and Praise*

- "Let Us Love and Sing and Wonder"[11]
- Additional options: "Jesus! What a Friend for Sinners,"[12] "Hallelujah! What a Savior,"[13] "Your Great Name,"[14] "My Redeemer's Love,"[15] "Psalm 32"[16]

Apostles' Creed

Let us now confess the Christian faith, together with God's church in every time and place. Church, what do we believe?

We believe in God the Father Almighty, the Maker of heaven and earth, and in Jesus Christ, his only Son, our Lord, who was conceived by the Holy Spirit, born of the Virgin Mary, suffered under Pontius Pilate, was crucified, dead, and buried; he descended into hell. The third day he arose again from the dead; he ascended into heaven, and sits at the right hand of God the Father Almighty; from there he shall come to judge the living and the dead.

[11]   John Newton and Laura Taylor, "Let Us Love and Sing and Wonder," Laura Taylor Music, 2001.

[12]   John Wilbur Chapman and Rowland Prichard, "Jesus! What a Friend for Sinners," Public Domain.

[13]   Philip P. Bliss, "Hallelujah! What a Savior," Public Domain.

[14]   Krissy Nordhoff and Michael Neale, "Your Great Name," Integrity's Praise! Music, TwoNords Music, 2008.

[15]   Mark Altrogge, Jordan Kauflin, and Joel Sczebel, "My Redeemer's Love," Sovereign Grace Worship (ASCAP), Sovereign Grace Praise (BMI), 2012.

[16]   "Psalm 32," in *Trinity Psalter*, 24. Another suitable musical setting of Psalm 32 is Chrétien Urhan and Edward F. Rimbault, "How Blest Are They Whose Trespass," in *Psalms for All Seasons: A Complete Psalter for Worship* (Grand Rapids: Calvin Institute of Christian Worship, Faith Alive Christian Resources, Brazos, 2012), 207, an adaptation of Chrétien Urhan, "How Blest Is He Whose Trespass," in *The Psalter with Responsive Readings* (Pittsburgh: United Presbyterian Board of Publication, 1912), 73, Public Domain.

We believe in the Holy Spirit; the holy catholic church; the communion of saints; the forgiveness of sins; the resurrection of the body; and the life everlasting. Amen.

Catechism

Wherein did Christ's humiliation consist?

Christ's humiliation consisted in his being born, and that in a low condition, made under the law, undergoing the miseries of this life, the wrath of God, and the cursed death of the cross; in being buried, and continuing under the power of death for a time. (Westminster Shorter Catechism Q. 28)

Wherein consisteth Christ's exaltation?

Christ's exaltation consisteth in his rising again from the dead on the third day, in ascending up into heaven, in sitting at the right hand of God the Father, and in coming to judge the world at the last day. (Westminster Shorter Catechism Q. 29)

What benefits do believers receive from Christ at the resurrection?

At the resurrection, believers, being raised up in glory, shall be openly acknowledged and acquitted in the day of judgment, and made perfectly blessed in the full enjoying of God to all eternity. (Westminster Shorter Catechism Q. 38)

- Additional options: Westminster Larger Catechism Q. 89–90, Westminster Confession of Faith Chap. 33, Heidelberg Catechism Q. 50–52, Belgic Confession Art. 37, London Baptist Confession Chap. 32, Thirty-Nine Articles II–IV

Preparation for Imprecation

We live in a world full of violence and injustice, where the wicked oppress the innocent, oppose God's kingdom, and corrupt God's creation. Rather than holding in our anger and pain or taking vengeance into our own hands, God invites us to pray—to cry out to him to keep his promises to execute judgment, to protect his people, and to finally make his world his holy dwelling. From the very beginning of the Bible's story, God has called his sons and daughters to live as royal priests who guard his temple-kingdom, drive out unholiness, and subdue the earth as the holy house of the Lord. When we pray for justice in the face of violence, we are praying in line with God's promises and stepping into our God-given calling.

This may seem an inappropriate prayer for Christians, but consider that this intuition might owe more to our cultural assumptions than to Scripture. Jesus holds up the persistent widow as a model of faithful prayer as she pleads, "Give me justice against my adversary." The apostle Paul requests that false teachers in the church would be accursed—exposed, expelled, and judged. And the martyrs in heaven cry out to God with a prayer from the psalms, "How long before you will judge and avenge our blood?"

Indeed, the Psalter is full of prayers for God's covenant-keeping, kingdom-protecting, evil-expelling judgment. So as we confront the reality of violence in the world—and perhaps even the experience of injustice in our own lives—we the church on earth follow in the pattern of the church in heaven and take up the prayers that God has given, pleading in gospel-formed humility, zeal, and love for his justice and the spread of his temple-kingdom throughout the earth.

Prayers of Imprecation*

Let us pray for God's promised justice, guided by Psalm 58:

> Do you indeed decree what is right, you gods?
> > Do you judge the children of man uprightly?
> No, in your hearts you devise wrongs;
> > your hands deal out violence on earth.

O Lord, you have called humanity as your image-bearers to exercise dominion in faith and to walk in obedience, justice, and love, but we have filled your creation with sin. Each of us devises wrongs in our hearts and contributes in word and deed to the violence of the world.

> The wicked are estranged from the womb;
> > they go astray from birth, speaking lies.
> They have venom like the venom of a serpent,
> > like the deaf adder that stops its ear,
> so that it does not hear the voice of charmers
> > or of the cunning enchanter.

Wicked people align themselves against you and your kingdom, opposing your ways and oppressing your people. Worldly systems prey upon the vulnerable, assault the church, and multiply injustice. Satan, that ancient serpent, and the demonic forces of dark-

ness wage war against your children, your gospel, your purposes for peace. But Jesus is acquainted with our grief, suffering the oppression of wickedness in his death. Through his priestly intercession, hear our prayer, and by his Spirit, attend to our need.

O God, break the teeth in their mouths!

Where we attack others, reveal to us our sin and drive out our corruption in faith and repentance. In your mercy, break the teeth in our mouths, that we may live faithfully as your children.

Tear out the fangs of the young lions, O LORD!

We have tasted your grace toward your enemies in Jesus, and we ask you to bring our enemies to repentance. Tear out their fangs by giving them mouths that confess Jesus as Lord. Make the roaring lions to be faithful sheep in your flock, O Lord!

Let them vanish like water that runs away;
    when he aims his arrows, let them be blunted.
Let them be like the snail that dissolves into slime,
    like the stillborn child who never sees the sun.

Thwart the purposes of the evil one. Interrupt the hostility of worldly powers. In your love, bring a merciful end to the violence of the wicked, that the enemies of your kingdom may no longer destroy themselves in their destruction of your beloved creatures and creation, that man who is of the earth may strike terror no more.

Sooner than your pots can feel the heat of thorns,
    whether green or ablaze, may he sweep them away!

Come quickly, Lord Jesus, to execute perfect justice for every sin that has not been covered by your cross through repentant faith. Come quickly, Lord Jesus, to wipe away your people's tears, to sweep away all unrighteousness from your world, to rule the nations with justice, to fill the earth with your glory. Come quickly, Lord Jesus!

The righteous will rejoice when he sees the vengeance;
    he will bathe his feet in the blood of the wicked.

Jesus Christ the righteous has triumphed over sin in resurrection, and we rejoice now that our life is safely hidden in Christ with God. Our Lord Jesus will return to judge the world, and we will rejoice when you, O God of peace, soon crush Satan under our feet.

Mankind will say, "Surely there is a reward for the righteous;
   surely there is a God who judges on earth."

When Christ comes with vindication for your children and vengeance for your enemies, all the earth will know your promises are true and bow the knee to Jesus saying, "Surely there is a reward for the righteous; surely there is a God who judges the earth." Through Christ our Lord, amen.

Let us continue our prayer in song.

- "Psalm 58"[17]

- Additional options: "O Great God and Lord of the Earth,"[18] "O God, Do Not Be Silent (Psalm 83),"[19] "Hear, O Lord, My Urgent Prayer,"[20] "Psalm 3,"[21] "Come, Sing to God with All Your Heart"[22]

In all this, we pray as our Lord Jesus taught us:

Our Father in heaven, hallowed be your name. Your kingdom come, your will be done, on earth as it is in heaven. Give us this day our daily bread, and forgive us our debts, as we forgive our debtors. And lead us not into temptation, but deliver us from evil. For yours is the kingdom and the power and the glory, forever. Amen.

Sermon Text Reading

Hear the word of the Lord:

And he told them a parable to the effect that they ought always to pray and not lose heart. He said, "In a certain city there was a judge

---

[17]   "Psalm 58," in *Trinity Psalter*, 47.

[18]   John L. Bell and Guillermo Cuellar, "O Great God and Lord of the Earth," in *Lift Up Your Hearts: Psalms, Hymns, and Spiritual Songs* (Grand Rapids: Faith Alive Christian Resources, 2013), 293. Special thanks to John Witvliet of the Calvin Institute of Christian Worship for pointing me to this setting of Psalm 94.

[19]   Wendell Kimbrough, "O God, Do Not Be Silent (Psalm 83)," Wendell Kimbrough (BMI), 2017.

[20]   Marie J. Post and Timothy Hoekman, "Hear, O Lord, My Urgent Prayer," in *Psalms for All Seasons*, 26. This is a setting of Psalm 5.

[21]   "Psalm 3," in *Trinity Psalter*, 2.

[22]   Ruth C. Duck, "Come, Sing to God with All Your Heart," in *Psalms for All Seasons*, 50–51. This setting of Psalm 9 includes optional stanzas for Psalm 10 as well.

who neither feared God nor respected man. And there was a widow in that city who kept coming to him and saying, 'Give me justice against my adversary.' For a while he refused, but afterward he said to himself, 'Though I neither fear God nor respect man, yet because this widow keeps bothering me, I will give her justice, so that she will not beat me down by her continual coming.'" And the Lord said, "Hear what the unrighteous judge says. And will not God give justice to his elect, who cry to him day and night? Will he delay long over them? I tell you, he will give justice to them speedily. Nevertheless, when the Son of Man comes, will he find faith on earth?" (Luke 18:1–8)

This is the word of the Lord.

Thanks be to God.

- Additional options: Any imprecatory psalm could be inserted here. A combined reading of Psalm 79 and Revelation 6:9–11 would allow for preaching of the psalm alongside the heavenly martyrs' prayerful appropriation of the psalm. 2 Timothy 4:14–18 could be utilized to explore the various implications of divine justice for Paul's response to affliction. Texts that address issues of suffering, judgment, and restoration are also appropriate.

Sermon

Preparation for the Lord's Table

The Lord Jesus on the night when he was betrayed took bread, and when he had given thanks, he broke it, and said, "This is my body, which is for you. Do this in remembrance of me." In the same way also he took the cup, after supper, saying, "This cup is the new covenant in my blood. Do this, as often as you drink it, in remembrance of me." For as often as you eat this bread and drink the cup, you proclaim the Lord's death until he comes. (1 Cor 11:23–26)

So come, all you who trust Christ and have been baptized into his body, and receive in your bodies God's sign and seal of Christ's work for you. Jesus was betrayed by his friends and slain by the world, so we are never alone in our sorrow. Jesus offered his body and blood in place of sinners, so we have peace with God by grace. Jesus will come again to renew the world in justice, so we feast together now in anticipation of that heavenly feast in the presence of our God and king.

Let us pray: We do not presume to come to this your Table, O merciful Lord, trusting in our own righteousness, but in your manifold and great mercies. We are not worthy so much as to gather up the crumbs under your Table, but in your steadfast love you bid us come for the sake of Jesus.

We bless your name and give you thanks for this meal, which nourishes us with your many and great promises in the body and blood of Christ and which testifies to our failing hearts that we are yours, united to your Son in faith. Grant us rest in Christ's sacrificial work on our behalf. Grant us comfort in Christ's sympathetic intercession and presence with us by his Spirit. Grant us hope in Christ's return to abolish evil forever and consummate his holy kingdom of peace and joy. Strengthen us to live as befits your kingdom of priests—aggrieved by injustice, desirous of your reign, perseverant in prayer—until Jesus comes to make us and all things new. Through Christ our Lord, **amen.**[23]

Administration of the Lord's Table
Songs of Gospel Celebration*

- "O Church Arise"[24]

- "Come, Lord Jesus, to Redeem Us"[25]

- Additional options: "Even So Come,"[26] "A Mighty Fortress Is Our God,"[27] "Guide Me O Thou Great Jehovah,"[28] "Psalm 98,"[29] "Give Praise to Our God"[30]

Benediction*

Extend your hands, you saints of the Lord, and receive your Father's blessing:

> Blessed are the people whose God is the Lord! You are a chosen race,
> a royal priesthood, a holy nation, a people for his own possession,

---

[23]   The opening of this prayer is modified from "The Order for the Administration of the Lord's Supper or Holy Communion," in *The Book of Common Prayer and Administration of the Sacraments and Other Rites and Ceremonies of the Church* (New York: Oxford University Press, 1928), 82.

[24]   Stuart Townend and Keith Getty, "O Church Arise," Thankyou Music, 2004.

[25]   Gary A. Parrett, "Come, Lord Jesus, to Redeem Us," 2002.

[26]   Chris Tomlin, Jason Ingram, and Jess Cates, "Even So Come," S. D. G. Publishing, sixsteps Songs, Worship Together Music, Open Hands Music, So Essential Tunes, Chrissamsongs Inc., Go Mia Music, Vistaville Music, 2015.

[27]   Martin Luther, "A Mighty Fortress Is Our God," Public Domain.

[28]   William Williams and Jeremy Casella, "Guide Me O Thou Great Jehovah," 2037 Music (ASCAP), 2002.

[29]   "Psalm 98," in *Trinity Psalter*, 83.

[30]   "Give Praise to Our God," in *Psalms for All Seasons*, 992. This is a setting of Psalm 149 and is adapted from Henry J. Gauntlett, "The Promise of Victory," in *The Psalter with Responsive Readings*, 349, Public Domain.

that you may proclaim the excellencies of him who called you out of darkness into his marvelous light. The Lord bless you and keep you; the Lord make his face to shine upon you and be gracious to you; the Lord lift up his countenance upon you and give you peace. (Ps 144:15; 1 Pet 2:10; Num 6:24–26)

Sending*

Now, go out to proclaim and demonstrate, to pray for and participate in, the coming of Christ's kingdom to an often-violent world. As God's royal priests and temple dwelling, let us cleanse ourselves from every defilement of body and spirit, bringing holiness to completion in the fear of God. Beloved, never avenge yourselves, but leave it to the wrath of God. And looking to the certain hope of Christ's return, continue steadfastly in prayer, being watchful in it with thanksgiving. Go in peace. **Amen**. (Based on 2 Cor 7:1; Rom 12:19; Col 4:2)

Bibliography

Achtemeier, Elizabeth. *Preaching Hard Texts of the Old Testament*. Peabody, Mass.: Hendrickson, 1998.

Achtemeier, Paul J. *1 Peter: A Commentary on First Peter*. Edited by Eldon Jay Epp. Hermeneia. Minneapolis: Fortress, 1996.

Adamo, David Tuesday. "The Imprecatory Psalms in African Context." In *Biblical Interpretation in African Perspective*, edited by David Tuesday Adamo, 139–53. Lanham, Md.: University Press of America, 2006.

Adams, James E. *War Psalms of the Prince of Peace: Lessons from the Imprecatory Psalms*. Phillipsburg, N.J.: Presbyterian and Reformed, 1991.

Ahearne-Kroll, Stephen P. *The Psalms of Lament in Mark's Passion: Jesus' Davidic Suffering*. Cambridge: Cambridge University Press, 2007.

Alexander, T. Desmond. *From Eden to the New Jerusalem: An Introduction to Biblical Theology*. Grand Rapids: Kregel Publications, 2008.

———. *From Paradise to Promised Land: An Introduction to the Pentateuch*. 2nd ed. Grand Rapids: Baker Academic, 2002.

———. "Royal Expectations in Genesis to Kings: Their Importance for Biblical Theology." *TynBul* 49, no. 2 (1998): 191–212.

Alexander, T. Desmond, Brian S. Rosner, D. A. Carson, Graeme Goldsworthy, eds. *New Dictionary of Biblical Theology*. Downers Grove, Ill.: InterVarsity Press, 2000.

Alkier, Stefan. "Intertextuality and the Semiotics of Biblical Texts." In *Reading the Bible Intertextually*, edited by Richard B. Hays, Stefan Alkier, and Leroy A. Huizenga, 3–22. Waco, Tex.: Baylor University Press, 2009.

Alter, Robert. *The Book of Psalms: A Translation with Commentary*. New York: W. W. Norton and Company, 2007.

Althann, Robert. "The Psalms of Vengeance against Their Ancient Near Eastern Background." *JNSL* 18 (1992): 1–11.

Altrogge, Mark, Jordan Kauflin, and Joel Sczebel. "My Redeemer's Love." Sovereign Grace Worship (ASCAP), Sovereign Grace Praise (BMI), 2012.

Anderson, Bernhard W., and Steven Bishop. *Out of the Depths: The Psalms Speak for Us Today*. 3rd ed. Louisville: Westminster John Knox, 2000.

Asuma, Samuel Onchonga. "Speech Ethics in the Hebrew Psalter." PhD diss., Southern Baptist Theological Seminary, 2012.

Auerbach, Erich. *Mimesis: The Representation of Reality in Western Thought*. 1953. Princeton, N.J.: Princeton University Press, 2003.

Augustine. *City of God*. Translated by Marcus Dods. New York: Modern Library, 1993.

———. *Confessions*. 2nd ed. Translated by F. J. Sheed. Edited by Michael P. Foley. Indianapolis: Hackett Publishing, 2006.

———. *The Enchiridion on Faith, Hope and Love*. Edited by Henry Paolucci. Chicago: Henry Regnery Company, 1961.

———. *Saint Augustin: Expositions on the Book of Psalms*. Edited by A. Cleveland Coxe. Vol. 8 of *NPNF*. Edited by Philip Schaff. Translated by J. E. Tweed, T. Scratton, H. M. Wilkins, C. Marriott, and H. Walford. New York: Christian Literature Company, 1888.

Aune, David E. *Revelation*. WBC 52C. Nashville: Thomas Nelson, 1998.

Babcock, Maltbie D. "This Is My Father's World." Public Domain.

Bachl, Gottfried. "Das Gericht." *Christ in der Gegenwart* 45 (1993): 397.

Bandy, Alan S. "Vengeance, Wrath and Warfare as Images of Divine Justice in John's Apocalypse." In *Holy War in the Bible: Christian Morality and an Old Testament Problem*, edited by Heath Thomas, Jeremy Evans, and Paul Copan, 108–29. Downers Grove, Ill.: IVP Academic, 2013.

Barclay, John M. G. "Mirror-Reading a Polemical Letter: Galatians as a Test-Case." *JSNT* 31 (1987): 73–93.

Barker, David G. "The Waters of the Earth: An Exegetical Study of Psalm 104:1–9." *Grace Theological Journal* 7, no. 1 (1986): 57–80.

Barker, Kit. "Divine Illocutions in Psalm 137: A Critique of Nicholas Wolterstorff's 'Second Hermeneutic.'" *TynBul* 60, no. 1 (2009): 1–14.

———. *Imprecation as Divine Discourse: Speech Act Theory, Dual Authorship, and Theological Interpretation*. Winona Lake, Ind.: Eisenbrauns, 2016.

Barrett, C. K. *A Commentary on the First Epistle to the Corinthians*. HNTC. New York: Harper and Row, 1968.

Barth, Karl. *Prayer*. Edited by Don E. Saliers. Translated by Sara F. Terrien. Louisville: Westminster John Knox, 2002.

Bartholomew, Craig G. *Introducing Biblical Hermeneutics: A Comprehensive Framework for Hearing God in Scripture*. Grand Rapids: Baker Academic, 2015.

———. Introduction to Bartholomew et al., *Royal Priesthood?* 1–45.

Bartholomew, Craig G., Jonathan Chaplin, Robert Son, and Al Wolters, eds. *A Royal Priesthood? The Use of the Bible Ethically and Politically, A Dialogue with Oliver O'Donovan*. Scripture and Hermeneutics Series 3. Grand Rapids: Zondervan, 2002.

Bartholomew, Craig G., and Michael W. Goheen. *The Drama of Scripture: Finding Our Place in the Biblical Story*. 2nd ed. Grand Rapids: Baker Academic, 2014.

Bartholomew, Craig G., Colin Greene, and Karl Möller, eds. *After Pentecost: Language and Biblical Interpretation*. Scripture and Hermeneutics Series 2. Grand Rapids: Zondervan, 2001.

Barton, John. *Ethics and the Old Testament.* London: SCM Press, 1998.

———. *Understanding Old Testament Ethics: Approaches and Explorations.* Louisville: Westminster John Knox, 2003.

Bauckham, Richard. "Prayer in the Book of Revelation." In *Into God's Presence: Prayer in the New Testament,* edited by Richard M. Longenecker, 252–71. Grand Rapids: Eerdmans, 2001.

———. "Reading Scripture as a Coherent Story." In *The Art of Reading Scripture,* edited by Ellen F. Davis and Richard B. Hays, 38–53. Grand Rapids: Eerdmans, 2003.

———. *The Theology of the Book of Revelation.* New Testament Theology. New York: Cambridge University Press, 1993.

Bavinck, Herman. *Reformed Dogmatics.* Edited by John Bolt. Translated by John Vriend. 4 vols. Grand Rapids: Baker Academic, 2003.

Bayer, Hans F. *Jesus' Predictions of Vindication and Resurrection.* WUNT 2/20. Tübingen: Mohr, 1986.

Beale, G. K. *The Book of Revelation: A Commentary on the Greek Text.* NIGTC. Grand Rapids: Eerdmans, 1999.

———. "The Descent of the Eschatological Temple in the Form of the Spirit at Pentecost, Part 2: Corroborating Evidence." *TynBul* 56, no. 2 (2005): 63–90.

———. "Eden, the Temple, and the Church's Mission in the New Creation." *JETS* 48, no. 1 (2005): 5–31.

———. *Handbook on the New Testament Use of the Old Testament: Exegesis and Interpretation.* Grand Rapids: Baker Academic, 2012.

———. *The Morality of God in the Old Testament.* Christian Answers to Hard Questions. Philadelphia: Westminster Seminary Press; Phillipsburg, N.J.: P&R Publishing, 2013.

———. *A New Testament Biblical Theology: The Unfolding of the Old Testament in the New.* Grand Rapids: Baker Academic, 2011.

———, ed. *The Right Doctrine from the Wrong Text? Essays on the Use of the Old Testament in the New.* Grand Rapids: Baker Academic, 1994.

———. *The Temple and the Church's Mission: A Biblical Theology of the Dwelling Place of God.* NSBT 17. Downers Grove, Ill.: InterVarsity Press, 2004.

———. *We Become What We Worship: A Biblical Theology of Idolatry.* Downers Grove, Ill.: InterVarsity Press, 2008.

Beale, G. K., and D. A. Carson, eds. *Commentary on the New Testament Use of the Old Testament.* Grand Rapids: Baker Academic, 2007.

Becker, Lawrence C., and Charlotte B. Becker, eds. *Encyclopedia of Ethics.* 2nd ed. 3 vols. New York: Routledge, 2001.

Becking, Bob, and Eric Peels, eds. *Psalms and Prayers: Papers Read at the Joint Meeting of the Society of Old Testament Study and Het Oudtestamentisch Werkgezelchap in Nederland en België, Apeldoorn August 2006.* OtSt 55. Leiden: Brill, 2007.

Beetham, Christopher A. *Echoes of Scripture in the Letter of Paul to the Colossians.* BIS 96. Boston: Brill, 2008.

Beisner, E. Calvin. *Psalms of Promise: Celebrating the Majesty and Faithfulness of God.* 2nd ed. Phillipsburg, N.J.: Presbyterian and Reformed, 1994.

Bell, John L., and Guillermo Cuellar. "O Great God and Lord of the Earth." In *Lift Up Your Hearts: Psalms, Hymns, and Spiritual Songs*, ed. John D. Witvliet, Joyce Borger, and Martin Tel, 293. Grand Rapids: Faith Alive Christian Resources, 2013.

Berkhof, Louis. *Systematic Theology*. Grand Rapids: Eerdmans, 1939.

Bernardino, Nomeriano C. "A Reconsideration of 'Imprecations' in the Psalms." ThM thesis, Calvin Theological Seminary, 1986.

Best, Ernest. *A Commentary on the First and Second Epistles to the Thessalonians*. BNTC. London: Adam & Charles Black, 1972.

Betz, Hans Dieter. *Galatians: A Commentary on Paul's Letter to the Churches in Galatia*. Hermeneia. Philadelphia: Fortress, 1979.

Biggar, Nigel. "Forgiveness in the Twentieth Century: A Review of the Literature, 1901–2001." In McFadyen and Sarot, *Forgiveness and Truth*, 181–217.

Billings, J. Todd. *Rejoicing in Lament: Wrestling with Incurable Cancer and Life in Christ*. Grand Rapids: Brazos, 2015.

———. *Union with Christ: Reframing Theology and Ministry for the Church*. Grand Rapids: Baker Academic, 2011.

Birch, Bruce C. *Let Justice Roll Down: The Old Testament, Ethics, and Christian Life*. Louisville: Westminster John Knox, 1991.

Bitrus, Ibrahim S. "God Who Curses Is Cursed: Recasting Imprecation in Africa." *JLRS* 6 (2018): 29–48.

Bliss, Philip P. "Hallelujah! What a Savior." Public Domain.

Block, Daniel I. *Deuteronomy*. NIVAC. Grand Rapids: Zondervan, 2012.

Blount, Brian K. *Revelation: A Commentary*. NTL. Louisville: Westminster John Knox, 2009.

Blumenthal, David R. "Liturgies of Anger." *Cross Curr.* 52, no. 2 (2002): 178–99.

Boase, Elizabeth, and Christopher G. Frechette, eds. *Bible through the Lens of Trauma*. Atlanta: SBL Press, 2016.

Bock, Darrell L. *Acts*. BECNT. Grand Rapids: Baker Academic, 2007.

———. *Luke*. 2 vols. BECNT. Grand Rapids: Baker Academic, 1994, 1996.

———. *Proclamation from Prophecy and Pattern: Lucan Old Testament Christology*. LNTS 12. Sheffield: Sheffield Academic Press, 1987.

Bonhoeffer, Dietrich. *Act and Being: Transcendental Philosophy and Ontology in Systematic Theology*. Edited by Wayne Whitson Floyd, Jr. Translated by H. Martin Rumscheidt. Vol. 2 of *Dietrich Bonhoeffer Works*. Minneapolis: Fortress, 1996.

———. *Creation and Fall: A Theological Exposition of Genesis 1–3*. Edited by John W. de Gruchy. Translated by Douglas Stephen Bax. Vol. 3 of *Dietrich Bonhoeffer Works*. Minneapolis: Fortress, 1997.

———. *Ethics*. Edited by Clifford J. Green. Translated by Reinhard Krauss, Charles C. West, and Douglas W. Stott. Vol. 6 of *Dietrich Bonhoeffer Works*. Minneapolis: Fortress, 2005.

———. *Life Together*. Translated by John W. Doberstein. New York: HarperOne, 1954.

———. *Prayerbook of the Bible: An Introduction to the Psalms*. Edited by Geffrey B. Kelly. Translated by James H. Burtness. Vol. 5 of *Dietrich Bonhoeffer Works*. Minneapolis: Fortress, 1996.

———. *Sanctorum Communio: A Theological Study of the Sociology of the Church.* Edited by Clifford J. Green. Translated by Reinhard Krauss and Nancy Lukens. Vol. 1 of *Dietrich Bonhoeffer Works.* Minneapolis: Fortress, 1998.

———. "Sermon on a Psalm of Vengeance—Psalm 58." In *Meditating on the Word,* translated and edited by David M. Gracie, 84–96. Cambridge, Mass.: Cowley, 1986.

Booij, Th. "Psalm 144: Hope of Davidic Welfare." *VT* 59 (2009): 173–80.

The Book of Common Prayer and Administration of the Sacraments and Other Rites and Ceremonies of the Church. New York: Oxford University Press, 1928.

Botterweck, G. Johannes, Helmer Ringgren, and Heinz-Josef Fabry, eds. *Theological Dictionary of the Old Testament.* 15 vols. Grand Rapids: Eerdmans, 1974–2006.

Bouma-Prediger, Steven. *For the Beauty of the Earth: A Christian Vision for Creation Care.* Grand Rapids: Baker Academic, 2010.

Bourque, Jeff. "Authority of Christ." From *Songs for the Book of Luke.* The Gospel Coalition, 2013, CD.

Bovon, François. *Luke 2: A Commentary on the Gospel of Luke 9:51–19:27.* Translated by Donald S. Deer. Edited by Helmut Koester. Hermeneia. Minneapolis: Fortress, 2013.

Boyd, Gregory A. *The Crucifixion of the Warrior God: Interpreting the Old Testament's Violent Portraits of God in Light of the Cross.* 2 vols. Minneapolis: Fortress, 2017.

Brettler, Marc. "Images of YHWH the Warrior in Psalms." *Semeia* 61 (1993): 135–65.

Briggs, Richard S. Review of *Imprecation as Divine Discourse,* by Kit Barker. *RBL* (2019), https://www.sblcentral.org/home/bookDetails/11582.

Bright, John. *The Kingdom of God: The Biblical Concept and Its Meaning for the Church.* New York: Abingdon, 1953.

Broadhurst, Jace. "Should Cursing Continue? An Argument for Imprecatory Psalms in Biblical Theology." *AJET* 23, no. 1 (2004): 61–89.

Brown, Derek R. "'The God of Peace Will Shortly Crush Satan Under Your Feet': Paul's Eschatological Reminder in Romans 16:20a." *Neot* 44, no. 1 (2010): 1–14.

Brown, William P. *Seeing the Psalms: A Theology of Metaphor.* Louisville: Westminster John Knox, 2002.

Bruce, F. F. *The Epistle to the Galatians.* NIGTC. Grand Rapids: Eerdmans, 1982.

Brueggemann, Walter. *Abiding Astonishment: Psalms, Modernity, and the Making of History.* Literary Currents in Biblical Interpretation. Edited by Danna Nolan Fewell and David M. Gunn. Louisville: Westminster John Knox, 1991.

———. "The Costly Loss of Lament." *JSOT* 36 (1986): 57–71.

———. *Deuteronomy.* AOTC. Nashville: Abingdon, 2001.

———. *From Whom No Secrets Are Hid: Introducing the Psalms.* Edited by Brent A. Strawn. Louisville: Westminster John Knox, 2014.

———. Introduction to *Old Testament Theology,* by Gerhard von Rad, 1:ix–xxi.

———. *Israel's Praise: Doxology against Idolatry and Ideology.* Philadelphia: Fortress, 1988.

———. *The Message of the Psalms: A Theological Commentary.* Augsburg Old Testament Studies. Minneapolis: Augsburg, 1984.

———. *Praying the Psalms: Engaging Scripture and the Life of the Spirit.* 2nd ed. Eugene, Ore.: Cascade, 2007.

———. "Psalm 109: Three Times, 'Steadfast Love.'" *WW* 5, no. 2 (1985): 144–54.

———. *The Psalms and the Life of Faith.* Edited by Patrick D. Miller. Minneapolis: Fortress, 1995.

———. *Spirituality of the Psalms.* Minneapolis: Fortress, 2002.

Brueggemann, Walter, and William H. Bellinger, Jr. *Psalms.* NCBC. New York: Cambridge University, 2014.

Bultmann, Rudolf. "Is Exegesis without Presuppositions Possible? (1957)." In *New Testament and Mythology and Other Basic Writings*, edited and translated by Schubert M. Ogden, 145–52. Philadelphia: Fortress, 1984.

Burton, Ernest De Witt. *A Critical and Exegetical Commentary on the Epistle to the Galatians.* ICC. New York: Charles Scribner's Sons, 1920.

Caird, G. B. *A Commentary on the Revelation of St John the Divine.* BNTC. London: Adam and Charles Black, 1966.

Calvin, John. *Commentary on the Book of Psalms.* Translated by James Anderson. 5 vols. Calvin's Commentaries 4–6. Reprint, Grand Rapids: Baker Books, 2005.

———. *Commentaries on the First Book of Moses Called Genesis.* Translated by John King. 2 vols. Calvin's Commentaries 1. Grand Rapids: Baker Books, 2005.

———. *Institutes of the Christian Religion.* Edited by John T. McNeill. Translated by Ford Lewis Battles. 2 vols. Louisville: Westminster John Knox, 1960.

Capes, David B. "Intertextual Echoes in the Matthean Baptismal Narrative." *BBR* 9 (1999): 37–49.

Carson, D. A. "Current Issues in Biblical Theology: A New Testament Perspective." *BBR* 5 (1995): 17–41.

———. *The Gagging of God: Christianity Confronts Pluralism.* Grand Rapids: Zondervan, 1996.

———. "Matthew." In vol. 8 of EBC, 1–599. Grand Rapids: Zondervan, 1984.

Carson, D. A., and H. G. M. Williamson, eds. *It Is Written: Scripture Citing Scripture, Essays in Honour of Barnabas Lindars.* Cambridge: Cambridge University Press, 1988.

Carter, Warren. "Love Your Enemies." *WW* 28, no. 1 (2008): 13–21.

Chapman, John Wilbur, and Rowland Prichard. "Jesus! What a Friend for Sinners." Public Domain.

Charney, Davida. "Maintaining Innocence Before a Divine Hearer: Deliberative Rhetoric in Psalm 22, Psalm 17, and Psalm 7." *BibInt* 21, no. 1 (2013): 33–63.

Childs, Brevard. *Biblical Theology of the Old and New Testaments: Theological Reflection on the Christian Bible.* Minneapolis: Fortress, 1992.

Ciampa, Roy E. "Scriptural Language and Ideas." In Porter and Stanley, *As It Is Written*, 41–57.

Clark, Gordon H. *The Word "Hesed" in the Hebrew Bible.* Bloomsbury Academic Collections Biblical Studies: Biblical Languages. London: Bloomsbury Academic, 2015.

Clements, Ronald E. *The Book of Deuteronomy.* In vol. 2 of *NIB*, 269–538. Nashville: Abingdon, 1998.

Clifford, Richard J. *Psalms 1–72*. AOTC. Edited by Patrick D. Miller. Nashville: Abingdon, 2002.

Collins, Adela Yarbro. *The Apocalypse*. NTM 22. Wilmington, Del.: Michael Glazier, 1979.

———. "The Appropriation of the Psalms of Individual Lament by Mark." In *The Scriptures in the Gospels*, edited by C. M. Tuckett, 223–41. BETL 131. Leuven: Leuven University Press, 1997.

———. "The Political Perspective of the Revelation to John." *JBL* 96, no. 2 (1977): 241–56.

Collins, Raymond F. *First Corinthians*. SP 7. Collegeville, Minn.: Liturgical Press, 1999.

Conzelmann, Hans. *1 Corinthians: A Commentary on the First Epistle to the Corinthians*. Translated by James W. Leitch. Edited by George W. MacRae. Hermeneia. Philadelphia: Fortress, 1975.

———. *Acts of the Apostles*. Edited by Eldon Jay Epp and Christopher R. Matthews. Translated by James Limburg, A. Thomas Krabel, and Donald H. Juel. Hermeneia. Philadelphia: Fortress, 1987.

Copan, Paul. *Is God a Moral Monster? Making Sense of the Old Testament God*. Grand Rapids: Baker Books, 2011.

Cosgrove, Charles H. *Appealing to Scripture in Moral Debate: Five Hermeneutical Rules*. Grand Rapids: Eerdmans, 2002.

Court, John M. *Myth and History in the Book of Revelation*. Atlanta: John Knox, 1979.

Craigie, Peter C., and Marvin E. Tate. *Psalms 1–50*. WBC 19. 2nd ed. Grand Rapids: Zondervan, 2004.

Cranfield, C. E. B. "The Cup Metaphor in Mark xiv. 36 and Parallels." *ExpTim* 59, no. 5 (1948): 137–38.

Creach, Jerome F. D. "The Destiny of the Righteous and the Theology of the Psalms." In Jacobson, *Soundings in the Theology of the Psalms*, 49–61.

———. "The Psalms and the Cult." In Johnston and Firth, *Interpreting the Psalms*, 119–37.

———. *Violence in Scripture*. Interpretation: Resources for the Use of Scripture in the Church. Louisville: Westminster John Knox, 2013.

Crites, Stephen. "The Narrative Quality of Experience." *JAAR* 39, no. 3 (1971): 291–311.

Curran, Charles E., and Richard A. McCormick, eds. *The Use of Scripture in Moral Theology*. Readings in Moral Theology 4. New York: Paulist Press, 1984.

Dahood, Mitchell. *Psalms I: 1–50*. AB. Garden City, N.Y.: Doubleday and Company, 1966.

———. *Psalms II: 51–100*. AB. Garden City, N.Y.: Doubleday and Company, 1968.

———. *Psalms III: 101–150*. AB. Garden City, N.Y.: Doubleday and Company, 1970.

Daly-Denton, Margaret. *David in the Fourth Gospel: The Johannine Reception of the Psalms*. AGJU 47. Leiden: Brill, 2000.

Date, Christopher M., Gregory G. Stump, and Joshua W. Anderson, eds. *Rethinking Hell: Readings in Evangelical Conditionalism*. Cambridge: Lutterworth Press, 2014.

Davids, Peter H. *The Epistle of James*. NIGTC. Grand Rapids: Eerdmans, 1982.

Davidson, Richard. "Earth's First Sanctuary: Genesis 1–3 and Parallel Creation Accounts." *AUSS* 53, no. 1 (2015): 65–89.

Davis, Ellen F. *Getting Involved with God: Rediscovering the Old Testament.* Lanham, Md.: Cowley, 2001.

Day, John. *God's Conflict with the Dragon and the Sea: Echoes of a Canaanite Myth in the Old Testament.* New York: Cambridge University Press, 1985.

Day, John N. "The Imprecatory Psalms and Christian Ethics." PhD diss., Dallas Theological Seminary, 2001.

de Boer, Martinus C. *Galatians: A Commentary.* NTL. Louisville: Westminster John Knox, 2011.

deClaissé-Walford, Nancy L. "The Theology of the Imprecatory Psalms." In Jacobson, *Soundings in the Theology of the Psalms*, 77–92.

deClaissé-Walford, Nancy L., Rolf A. Jacobson, and Beth LaNeel Tanner. *The Book of Psalms.* NICOT. Grand Rapids: Eerdmans, 2014.

Delitzsch, Franz. *Biblical Commentary on the Psalms.* Translated by Francis Bolton. 3 vols. Grand Rapids: Eerdmans, 1952–1955.

Delling, Gerhard. "ΒΑΠΤΙΣΜΑ ΒΑΠΤΙΣΘΗΝΑΙ." *NovT* 2, no. 2 (1957): 92–115.

Dempster, Stephen G. *Dominion and Dynasty: A Theology of the Hebrew Bible.* NSBT 15. Downers Grove, Ill.: InterVarsity Press, 2003.

Department of Defense Office of Inspector General. "Lead Inspector General for Operation Inherent Resolve Quarterly Report to the United States Congress | January 1, 2021–March 21, 2021." Accessed June 10, 2021. https://www .dodig.mil/Reports/Lead-Inspector-General-Reports/Article/2594393/lead -inspector-general-for-operation-inherent-resolve-quarterly-report-to-the-u.

deSilva, David A. *Seeing Things John's Way: The Rhetoric of the Book of Revelation.* Louisville: Westminster John Knox, 2009.

DeVries, Carl E. "Paul's 'Cutting' Remarks about a Race: Galatians 5:1–12." In *Current Issues in Biblical and Patristic Interpretation: Studies in Honor of Merrill C. Tenney Presented by His Former Students*, edited by Gerald F. Hawthorne, 115–20. Grand Rapids: Eerdmans, 1975.

Dibelius, Martin. *James: A Commentary on the Epistle of James.* Revised by Heinrich Greeven. Translated by Michael A. Williams. Edited by Helmut Koester. Hermeneia. Philadelphia: Fortress, 1976.

Disley, Emma. "Degrees of Glory: Protestant Doctrine and the Concept of Rewards Hereafter." *JTS* 42, no. 1 (1991): 77–105.

Doble, Peter. "The Psalms in Luke-Acts." In Moyise and Menken, *Psalms in the New Testament*, 83–117.

Dodd, C. H. *According to the Scriptures: The Sub-Structure of New Testament Theology.* New York: Charles Scribner's Sons, 1953.

Donne, John. *The Complete Poetry and Selected Prose of John Donne.* Edited by Charles M. Coffin. New York: Modern Library, 2001.

Doyle, Brian. "Psalm 58: Curse as Voiced Disorietation." *Bijdragen* 57, no. 2 (1996): 122–48.

Duck, Ruth C. "Come, Sing to God with All Your Heart." In *Psalms for All Seasons*, 50–51.

Dumbrell, William J. *The Faith of Israel: A Theological Survey of the Old Testament.* 2nd ed. Grand Rapids: Baker Academic, 2002.

Dunn, James D. G. *The Epistle to the Galatians.* BNTC. Peabody, Mass.: Hendrickson, 1993.

Eaton, John H. *Kingship in the Psalms.* SBT 32. London: SCM Press Ltd, 1976.

———. *Psalms: Introduction and Commentary.* TBC. London: SCM Press Ltd, 1967.

Edwards, James R. "Galatians 5:12: Circumcision, the Mother Goddess, and the Scandal of the Cross." *NovT* 53, no. 4 (2011): 319–37.

———. *The Gospel According to Mark.* PNTC. Grand Rapids: Eerdmans, 2002.

Edwards, Jonathan. "1033. Imprecations of the Old Testament." In *The "Miscellanies," 833–1152,* vol. 20 of *Works of Jonathan Edwards Online,* edited by Amy Plantinga Pauw. Jonathan Edwards Center at Yale University, 2002. Accessed October 1, 2019. http://edwards .yale.edu/archive?path=aHR0cDovL2Vkd2FyZHMueWFsZS51Z HUvY2dpLWJpbi9uZXdwaGlsby9nZXRRvYmplY3QucGw/Yy4xxOTozO jE5OC53amVv.

———. *A History of the Work of Redemption.* In vol. 1 of *The Works of Jonathan Edwards,* 532–619. Peabody, Mass.: Hendrickson, 2007.

———. "The Importance and Advantage of a Thorough Knowledge of Divine Truth." In *Sermons and Discourses, 1739–1742,* vol. 22 of *Works of Jonathan Edwards Online,* edited by Harry S. Stout. Jonathan Edwards Center at Yale University, 2003. Accessed November 30, 2017. http://edwards.yale.edu/archive ?path=aHR0cDovL2Vkd2FyZHMueWFsZS51ZHUvY2dpLWJpbi9uZXd waGlsby9nZXRRvYmplY3QucGw/Yy4yMToxMS53amVv.

———. *Religious Affections.* In vol. 2 of *Works of Jonathan Edwards,* edited by John E. Smith. New Haven: Yale University Press, 1959.

Ehorn, Seth M. "The Use of Psalm 68(67).19 in Ephesians 4.8: A History of Research." *CBR* 12, no. 1 (2012): 96–120.

Elliott, John H. *1 Peter: A New Translation with Introduction and Commentary.* AB 37B. New York: Doubleday, 2000.

Elliott, Susan M. "Who Is Addressed in Revelation 18:6–7?" *BR* 40 (1995): 98–113.

Ellis, E. Earle. *The Gospel of Luke.* Rev. ed. NCB. London: Oliphants, 1974.

Elwell, Walter A., ed. *Evangelical Dictionary of Theology.* 2nd ed. Baker Reference Library. Grand Rapids: Baker Academic, 2001.

Emadi, Matthew Habib. "The Royal Priest: Psalm 110 in Biblical-Theological Perspective." PhD diss., Southern Baptist Theological Seminary, 2016.

Eriksson, Anders. "Fear of Eternal Damnation: *Pathos* Appeal in 1 Corinthians 15 and 16." In *Paul and Pathos,* edited by Thomas H. Olbricht and Jerry L. Sumney, 115–26. Symposium. Atlanta: SBL Press, 2001.

Evangelical Theological Society. "ETS Constitution." The Evangelical Theological Society. Accessed December 1, 2016. http://www.etsjets.org/about/ constitution.

Evans, Ceri, Anke Ehlers, Gillian Mezey, and David M. Clark. "Intrusive Memories in Perpetrators of Violent Crime: Emotions and Cognition." *J. Consult. Clin. Psychol.* 75, no. 1 (2007): 134–44.

Fee, Gordon D. *The First and Second Letters to the Thessalonians*. NICNT. Grand Rapids: Eerdmans, 2009.

———. *The First Epistle to the Corinthians*. Rev. ed. NICNT. Grand Rapids: Eerdmans, 2014.

———. *Paul's Letter to the Philippians*. NICNT. Grand Rapids: Eerdmans, 1995.

Ferguson, Sinclair B. *The Holy Spirit*. Contours of Christian Theology. Downers Grove, Ill.: InterVarsity Press, 1996.

Ferguson, Sinclair B., David F. Wright, and J. I. Packer, eds. *New Dictionary of Theology*. Downers Grove, Ill.: InterVarsity Press, 1988.

Firth, David G. "Cries of the Oppressed." In *Wrestling with the Violence of God: Soundings in the Old Testament*, edited by M. Daniel Carroll R. and J. Blair Wilgus, 75–89. BBRSup 10. Winona Lake, Ind.: Eisenbrauns, 2015.

———. *Surrendering Retribution in the Psalms: Responses to Violence in Individual Complaints*. PBM. Eugene, Ore.: Wipf and Stock, 2005.

———. "The Teaching of the Psalms." In Johnston and Firth, *Interpreting the Psalms*, 159–74.

Fitzmyer, Joseph A. *The Acts of the Apostles*. AB 31. New York: Doubleday, 1998.

———. *The Gospel According to Luke (I–IX)*. AB 28. Garden City, N.Y.: Doubleday and Company, 1981.

———. *The Gospel According to Luke (X–XXIV)*. AB 28A. Garden City, N.Y.: Doubleday and Company, 1985.

Fodor, James. *Christian Hermeneutics: Paul Ricoeur and the Refiguring of Theology*. New York: Oxford University Press, 1995.

Foote, Billy J., and Charles Silvester Horne. "Sing to the King." sixsteps Music, worshiptogether.com, Songs. 2003. https://www.worshiptogether.com/songs/sing-to-the-king-phil-barfoot/.

Ford, David. *Barth and God's Story: Biblical Narrative and the Theological Method of Karl Barth in the Church Dogmatics*. StIKGCh 27. Bern: Lang, 1981.

Frame, John. *The Doctrine of the Christian Life*. A Theology of Lordship. Phillipsburg, N.J.: P&R Publishing, 2008.

France, R. T. *The Gospel of Mark*. NIGTC. Grand Rapids: Eerdmans, 2002.

———. *The Gospel of Matthew*. NICNT. Grand Rapids: Eerdmans, 2007.

Frechette, Christopher G. "Destroying the Internalized Perpetrator: A Healing Function of the Violent Language against Enemies in the Psalms." In *Trauma and Traumatization in Individual and Collective Dimensions: Insights from Biblical Studies and Beyond*, edited by Eve-Marie Becker, Jan Dochhorn, and Else K. Holt, 71–84. SAN 2. Göttingen: Vandenhoeck and Ruprecht, 2014.

———. "The Old Testament as Controlled Substance: How Insights from Trauma Studies Reveal Healing Capacities in Potentially Harmful Texts." *Int* 69, no. 1 (2015): 20–34.

Frechette, Christoper G., and Elizabeth Boase. "Defining 'Trauma' as a Useful Lens for Biblical Interpretation." In Boase and Frechette, *Bible through the Lens of Trauma*, 1–23.

Fretheim, Terence E. "God and Violence in the Old Testament." *WW* 24, no. 1 (2004): 18–28.

Fung, Ronald Y. K. *The Epistle to the Galatians*. NICNT. Grand Rapids: Eerdmans, 1988.

Furnish, Victor Paul. *II Corinthians*. AB 32A. Garden City, N.Y.: Doubleday and Company, 1984.

Gaffin, Richard B., Jr. "The Redemptive-Historical View." In *Biblical Hermeneutics: Five Views*, edited by Stanley E. Porter and Beth M. Stovell, 89–110. Downers Grove, Ill.: InterVarsity Press, 2012.

Garber, David G., Jr. "Trauma Theory and Biblical Studies." *CBR* 14, no. 1 (2015): 24–44.

Garland, David E. *1 Corinthians*. BECNT. Grand Rapids: Baker Academic, 2003.

Gauntlett, Henry J. "The Promise of Victory." In *The Psalter with Responsive Readings*, 349. Public Domain.

Gentry, Peter J., and Stephen J. Wellum. *Kingdom through Covenant: A Biblical-Theological Understanding of the Covenants*. Wheaton, Ill.: Crossway, 2012.

Gerstenberger, Erhard S. "Enemies and Evildoers in the Psalms: A Challenge to Christian Preaching." *HBT* 4, no. 1 (1982): 61–77.

———. *Psalms: Part 1, with an Introduction to Cultic Poetry*. FOTL 14. Grand Rapids: Eerdmans, 1988.

Giesen, Bernhard. "The Trauma of Perpetrators: The Holocaust as the Traumatic Reference of German National Identity." In *Cultural Trauma and Collective Identity*, ed. Jeffrey C. Alexander, Ron Eyerman, Bernhard Giesen, Neil J. Smelser, and Piotr Sztompka, 112–54. Berkeley: University of California Press, 2004.

Gillingham, Susan, ed. *Jewish and Christian Approaches to the Psalms*. Oxford: Oxford University Press, 2013.

———. *Psalms through the Centuries: Volume 1*. BBC. Malden, Mass.: Blackwell, 2008.

———. *Psalms through the Centuries: Volume 2, A Reception History Commentary on Psalms 1–72*. WBBC. Hoboken, N.J.: Wiley Blackwell, 2018.

———. "The Reception of Psalm 137 in Jewish and Christian Traditions." In Gillingham, *Jewish and Christian Approaches to the Psalms*, 64–82.

"Give Praise to Our God." In *Psalms for All Seasons*, 992.

Glueck, Nelson. *Ḥesed in the Bible*. Edited by Elias L. Epstein. Translated by Alfred Gottschalk. Cincinnati: Hebrew Union College Press, 1967.

Goheen, Michael W. "The Urgency of Reading the Bible as One Story." *ThTo* 64 (2008): 469–83.

Goldingay, John. *Psalms: Volume 1, Psalms 1–41*. BCOTWP. Grand Rapids: Baker Academic, 2006.

———. *Psalms: Volume 2, Psalms 42–89*. BCOTWP. Grand Rapids: Baker Academic, 2007.

———. *Psalms: Volume 3, Psalms 90–150*. BCOTWP. Grand Rapids: Baker Academic, 2008.

Goldsworthy, Graeme. *According to Plan: The Unfolding Revelation of God in the Bible*. Downers Grove, Ill.: InterVarsity Press, 1991.

———. *Christ-Centered Biblical Theology: Hermeneutical Foundations and Principles*. Downers Grove, Ill.: InterVarsity Press, 2012.

———. *Gospel-Centered Hermeneutics: Foundations and Principles of Evangelical Biblical Interpretation*. Downers Grove, Ill.: InterVarsity Press, 2006.

———. *Gospel and Kingdom*. In *The Goldsworthy Trilogy*. Eugene, Ore.: Wipf and Stock, 2000.

———. *The Son of God and the New Creation*. Short Studies in Biblical Theology. Wheaton, Ill.: Crossway, 2015.

Gombis, Timothy G. "Cosmic Lordship and Divine Gift-Giving: Psalm 68 in Ephesians 4:8." *NovT* 47, no. 4 (2005): 367–80.

González, Catherine Gunsalus, and Justo L. González. *Revelation*. Westminster Bible Companion. Louisville: Westminster John Knox, 1997.

Gorringe, Timothy. *God's Just Vengeance: Crime, Violence, and the Rhetoric of Salvation*. CSIR 9. New York: Cambridge University Press, 1996.

Govier, Trudy. *Forgiveness and Revenge*. New York: Routledge, 2002.

Grafius, Brandon R. "Text and Terror: Monster Theory and the Hebrew Bible." *CBR* 16, no. 1 (2017): 34–49.

Grant, Robert. "O Worship the King." Public Domain.

Green, Gene L. *The Letters to the Thessalonians*. PNTC. Grand Rapids: Eerdmans, 2002.

Green, Joel B., ed. *Dictionary of Scripture and Ethics*. Grand Rapids: Baker Academic, 2011.

———. *The Gospel of Luke*. NICNT. Grand Rapids: Eerdmans, 1997.

Griswold, Charles L. *Forgiveness: A Philosophical Exploration*. New York: Cambridge University Press, 2007.

Grogan, Geoffrey W. *Psalms*. THOTC. Grand Rapids: Eerdmans, 2008.

Gundry, Robert H. *Matthew: A Commentary on His Handbook for a Mixed Church under Persecution*. 2nd ed. Grand Rapids: Eerdmans, 1994.

Gunkel, Hermann. *Introduction to Psalms: The Genres of Religious Lyric in Israel*. Translated by James D. Nogalski. Macon, Ga.: Mercer University Press, 1998.

———. *The Psalms: A Form-Critical Introduction*. Biblical Series 19. Translated by Thomas M. Horner. Philadelphia: Fortress, 1967.

Guthrie, George H. *2 Corinthians*. BECNT. Grand Rapids: Baker Academic, 2015.

Habel, Norman C. "He Who Stretches Out the Heavens." *CBQ* 34, no. 4 (1972): 417–30.

Haenchen, Ernst. *John 2: A Commentary on the Gospel of John Chapters 7–21*. Translated by Robert W. Funk. Edited by Robert W. Funk with Ulrich Busse. Hermeneia. Philadelphia: Fortress, 1984.

Hafemann, Scott J. *Suffering and the Spirit: An Exegetical Study of II Corinthians 2:14–3:3 within the Context of the Corinthian Correspondence*. WUNT 2/19. Tübingen: Mohr, 1986.

Hagner, Donald A. *Matthew 1–13*. WBC 33A. Dallas: Word Books, 1993.

Hahn, Scott W. *The Kingdom of God as Liturgical Empire: A Theological Commentary on 1–2 Chronicles*. Grand Rapids: Baker Academic, 2012.

———. *Kinship by Covenant: A Canonical Approach to the Fulfillment of God's Saving Promises*. The Anchor Yale Bible Reference Library. New Haven: Yale University Press, 2009.

Hamilton, James M., Jr. *God's Glory in Salvation through Judgment: A Biblical Theology*. Wheaton, Ill.: Crossway, 2010.

———. *Psalms*. 2 vols. EBTC. Bellingham, Wash.: Lexham Academic, 2021.

———. "The Seed of the Woman and the Blessing of Abraham." *TynBul* 58, no. 2 (2007): 253–73.

————. "The Skull-Crushing Seed of the Woman: Inner-Biblical Interpretation of Genesis 3:15." *SBJT* 10, no. 2 (2006): 30–54.

Hankle, Dominick D. "The Therapeutic Implications of the Imprecatory Psalms in the Christian Counseling Setting." *JPT* 38, no. 4 (2010): 275–80.

Harman, Allan M. "The Continuity of the Covenant Curses in the Imprecations of the Psalter." *RTR* 54, no. 2 (1995): 65–72.

Harrington, Wilfrid J. *Revelation.* SP 16. Collegeville, Minn.: Liturgical Press, 1993.

Harris, Murray J. *The Second Epistle to the Corinthians: A Commentary on the Greek Text.* NIGTC. Grand Rapids: Eerdmans, 2005.

Harris, W. Hall, III. *The Descent of Christ: Ephesians 4:7–11 and Traditional Hebrew Imagery.* AGJU 32. Leiden: Brill, 1996.

Hauerwas, Stanley. *A Community of Character: Toward a Constructive Christian Social Ethic.* Notre Dame: University of Notre Dame Press, 1981.

————. *Matthew.* BTCB. Grand Rapids: Brazos, 2006.

————. *The Peaceable Kingdom: A Primer in Christian Ethics.* Notre Dame: University of Notre Dame Press, 1983.

————. "Story and Theology." In Hauerwas, Bondi, and Burrell, *Truthfulness and Tragedy,* 71–81.

————. "Vision, Stories, and Character." In *The Hauerwas Reader,* edited by John Berkman and Michael Cartwright, 165–70. Durham, N.C.: Duke University Press, 2001.

————. *With the Grain of the Universe: The Church's Witness and Natural Theology.* Grand Rapids: Brazos, 2001.

Hauerwas, Stanley, with Richard Bondi and David B. Burrell. *Truthfulness and Tragedy: Further Investigations in Christian Ethics.* Notre Dame: University of Notre Dame Press, 1977.

Hauerwas, Stanley, and David B. Burrell. "From System to Story: An Alternative Pattern for Rationality in Ethics." In Hauerwas, Bondi, and Burrell, *Truthfulness and Tragedy,* 15–39.

Hauerwas, Stanley, and L. Gregory Jones. "Introduction: Why Narrative?" In Hauerwas and Jones, *Why Narrative?* 1–18.

————. *Why Narrative? Readings in Narrative Theology.* Grand Rapids: Eerdmans, 1989.

Hauerwas, Stanley, and Samuel Wells, eds. *The Blackwell Companion to Christian Ethics.* Malden, Mass.: Blackwell, 2004.

————. "Why Christian Ethics Was Invented." In Hauerwas and Wells, *Blackwell Companion to Christian Ethics,* 28–38.

Hays, Christopher B. "How Shall We Sing? Psalm 137 in Historical and Canonical Context." *HBT* 27 (2005): 35–55.

Hays, Rebecca W. Poe. "Trauma, Remembrance, and Healing: The Meeting of Wisdom and History in Psalm 78." *JSOT* 41, no. 2 (2016): 183–204.

Hays, Richard B. "Can Narrative Criticism Recover the Theological Unity of Scripture?" *JTI* 2, no. 2 (2008): 193–211.

————. "Christ Prays the Psalms: Paul's Use of an Early Christian Exegetical Convention." In *The Future of Christology: Essays in Honor of Leander E. Keck,* edited by Abraham J. Mahlerbe and Wayne A. Meeks, 122–36. Minneapolis: Fortress, 1993.

——. *Echoes of Scripture in the Gospels*. Waco, Tex.: Baylor University Press, 2016.

——. *Echoes of Scripture in the Letters of Paul*. New Haven: Yale University Press, 1989.

——. *First Corinthians*. Interpretation. Louisville: John Knox Press, 1997.

——. *Reading Backwards: Figural Christology and the Fourfold Gospel Witness*. Waco, Tex.: Baylor University Press, 2014.

Hegel, G. W. F. *Philosophy of Right*. Translated by T. M. Knox. Oxford: Clarendon, 1952.

Hendrickx, Herman. *The Parables of Jesus: Studies in the Synoptic Gospels*. San Francisco: Harper and Row, 1986.

Henry, Matthew. *Matthew Henry's Commentary on the Whole Bible*. 6 vols. Peabody, Mass.: Hendrickson, 1991.

Herman, Judith Lewis. *Trauma and Recovery*. New York: BasicBooks, 1992.

Hicks, John Mark. "The Parable of the Persistent Widow (Luke 18:1–8)." *ResQ* 33, no. 4 (1991): 209–23.

——. "Preaching Community Laments: Responding to Disillusionment with God and Injustice in the World." In *Performing the Psalms*, edited by Dave Bland and David Fleer, 67–81. St. Louis: Chalice Press, 2005.

Hoehner, Harold W. *Ephesians: An Exegetical Commentary*. Grand Rapids: Baker Academic, 2002.

Hoekema, Anthony A. *The Bible and the Future*. Grand Rapids: Eerdmans, 1979.

Holladay, Carl R. *Acts: A Commentary*. NTL. Louisville: Westminster John Knox, 2016.

Holladay, William L. *Long Ago God Spoke: How Christians May Hear the Old Testament Today*. Minneapolis: Fortress, 1995.

Holmgren, Margaret R. *Forgiveness and Retribution: Responding to Wrongdoing*. New York: Cambridge University Press, 2012.

Hopkins, Denise Dombkowski. *Psalms: Books 2–3*. Edited by Linda M. Maloney. Wisdom Commentary 21. Collegeville, Minn.: Liturgical Press, 2016.

Hordern, Joshua. *Political Affections: Civic Participation and Moral Theology*. Oxford: Oxford University Press, 2013.

Horton, Michael. *The Christian Faith: A Systematic Theology for Pilgrims on the Way*. Grand Rapids: Zondervan, 2011.

Hossfeld, Frank-Lothar, and Erich Zenger. *Psalms 2: A Commentary on Psalms 51–100*. Edited by Klaus Baltzer. Translated by Linda M. Maloney. Hermeneia. Minneapolis: Fortress, 2005.

——. *Psalms 3: A Commentary on Psalms 101–150*. Edited by Klaus Baltzer. Translated by Linda M. Maloney. Hermeneia. Minneapolis: Fortress, 2011.

Irenaeus. *Against Heresies*. Vol. 1 of *ANF*, edited by Alexander Roberts, James Donaldson, and A. Cleveland Coxe. Buffalo: Christian Literature Publishing Company, 1885.

Jackson, Timothy P. "Christian Love and Political Violence." In *The Love Commandments: Essays in Christian Ethics and Moral Philosophy*, edited by Edmund N. Santurri and William Werpehowski, 182–220. Washington, D.C.: Georgetown University Press, 1992.

Jacobson, Rolf A., ed. *Soundings in the Theology of the Psalms: Perspectives and Methods in Contemporary Scholarship*. Minneapolis: Fortress, 2011.

Janowski, Bernd. *Arguing with God: A Theological Anthropology of the Psalms*. Translated by Armin Siedlecki. Louisville: Westminster John Knox, 2013.

Jeffrey, David Lyle. *Luke*. BTCB. Grand Rapids: Brazos, 2012.

Jenkins, Steffen G. *Imprecations in the Psalms: Love for Enemies in Hard Places*. Eugene, Ore.: Pickwick, forthcoming.

———. "Retribution in the Canonical Psalter." PhD diss., University of Bristol, 2015.

Jensen, Peter. *The Revelation of God*. Contours of Christian Theology. Downers Grove, Ill.: InterVarsity Press, 2002.

Jewett, Robert. *Romans: A Commentary*. Assisted by Roy D. Kotansky. Edited by Eldon Jay Epp. Hermeneia. Minneapolis: Fortress, 2007.

Jinkerson, Jeremy D. "Defining and Assessing Moral Injury: A Syndrome Perspective." *Traumatology* 22, no. 2 (2016): 122–30.

Jinkins, Michael. *In the House of the Lord: Inhabiting the Psalms of Lament*. Collegeville, Minn.: Liturgical Press, 1998.

Johnson, Alan. "Revelation." In vol. 12 of *EBC*, 397–603. Grand Rapids: Zondervan, 1981.

Johnson, Luke Timothy. *The Acts of the Apostles*. SP 5. Collegeville, Minn.: Liturgical Press, 1992.

———. *The Gospel of Luke*. SP 3. Collegeville, Minn.: Liturgical Press, 1991.

Johnston, Philip S., and David G. Firth, eds. *Interpreting the Psalms: Issues and Approaches*. Downers Grove, Ill.: InterVarsity Press, 2005.

Jones, L. Gregory. *Embodying Forgiveness: A Theological Analysis*. Grand Rapids: Eerdmans, 1995.

Jones, Serene. *Trauma and Grace: Theology in a Ruptured World*. Louisville: Westminster John Knox, 2009.

Juel, Donald. *Messianic Exegesis: Christological Interpretation of the Old Testament in Early Christianity*. Philadelphia: Fortress, 1988.

Kaiser, Walter C., Jr. "The People of Psalm 83." *BSac* 174 (2017): 259–66.

———. *Toward Old Testament Ethics*. Grand Rapids: Academie Books, 1983.

Kalland, Earl S. "Deuteronomy." In vol. 3 of *EBC*, 1–235. Grand Rapids: Zondervan, 1992.

Kameeta, Zephania. *Why, O Lord? Psalms and Sermons from Namibia*. Geneva: World Council of Churches, 1986.

Kaske, Carol V. "The Curse-Psalms in their Patristic, Renaissance, and Modern Reception." *Genre* 40, nos. 3–4 (2007): 129–42.

Kaveny, Cathleen. "Hauerwas and the Law: Framing a Productive Conversation." *Law & Contemp. Probs.* 75, no. 4 (2012): 135–60.

Keener, Craig S. *1–2 Corinthians*. NCBC. New York: Cambridge University Press, 2005.

———. *Galatians*. NCBC. New York: Cambridge University Press, 2018.

Keesmaat, Sylvia C. "The Psalms in Romans and Galatians." In Moyise and Menken, *Psalms in the New Testament*, 139–61.

Kelly, Geffrey B. Editor's introduction to *Prayerbook of the Bible*, by Bonhoeffer.

———. Introduction to *Life Together*, by Dietrich Bonhoeffer, edited by Geffrey B. Kelly, translated by Daniel W. Bloesch. Vol. 5 of *Dietrich Bonhoeffer Works*. Minneapolis: Fortress, 1996.

Kelly, Page H. "Prayers of Troubled Saints." *RevExp* 81, no. 3 (1984): 377–83.

Kelsay, John. "Prayer and Ethics: Reflections on Calvin and Barth." *HTR* 82, no. 2 (1989): 169–84.

Kenneson, Philip. "Gathering: Worship, Imagination, and Formation." In Hauerwas and Wells, *Blackwell Companion to Christian Ethics*, 53–67.

Kiddle, Martin. *The Revelation of St. John*. MNTC. New York: Harper and Brothers, 1940.

Kidner, Derek. *Psalms 1–72: An Introduction and Commentary*. TOTC 15. Downers Grove, Ill.: InterVarsity Press, 1973.

———. *Psalms 73–150: An Introduction and Commentary*. TOTC 16. Downers Grove, Ill.: InterVarsity Press, 1975.

Kimbrough, Wendell. "O God, Do Not Be Silent (Psalm 83)." Wendell Kimbrough (BMI), 2017.

Kinghorn, Warren. "Combat Trauma and Moral Fragmentation: A Theological Account of Moral Injury." *JSCE* 32, no. 2 (2012): 57–74.

Kistemaker, Simon J. *Exposition of the Acts of the Apostles*. NTC. Grand Rapids: Baker, 1990.

Klassen, William. *Love of Enemies: The Way to Peace*. Eugene, Ore.: Wipf and Stock, 2002.

———. "'Love Your Enemies': Some Reflections on the Current Status of Research." In *The Love of Enemy and Nonretaliation in the New Testament*, edited by Willard M. Swartley, 1–31. Louisville: Westminster John Knox, 1992.

Klebold, Sue. *A Mother's Reckoning: Living in the Aftermath of Tragedy*. New York: Crown Publishers, 2016.

Kline, Meredith G. *Kingdom Prologue: Genesis Foundations for a Covenantal Worldview*. Eugene, Ore.: Wipf and Stock, 2006.

———. *The Structure of Biblical Authority*. 2nd ed. Eugene, Ore.: Wipf & Stock, 1997.

———. *Treaty of the Great King: The Covenant Structure of Deuteronomy, Studies and Commentary*. Grand Rapids: Eerdmans, 1963.

Klingbeil, Martin. *Yahweh Fighting from Heaven: God as Warrior and as God of Heaven in the Hebrew Psalter and Ancient Near Eastern Iconography*. OBO 169. Fribourg, Switzerland: University Press Fribourg Switzerland, 1999.

Klink, Edward W., III, and Darian R. Lockett. *Understanding Biblical Theology: A Comparison of Theory and Practice*. Grand Rapids: Zondervan, 2012.

Knight, George W., III. *The Pastoral Epistles: A Commentary on the Greek Text*. NIGTC. Grand Rapids: Eerdmans, 1992.

Knox, Wilfred L. *The Acts of the Apostles*. Cambridge: Cambridge University Press, 1948.

Koester, Craig R. *Revelation: A New Translation with Introduction and Commentary*. AYB 38A. New Haven: Yale University Press, 2014.

Köhler, Ludwig, Walter Baumgartner, and Johann Jakob Stamm, eds. *The Hebrew and Aramaic Lexicon of the Old Testament*. Translated by M. E. J. Richardson. 5 vols. Leiden: Brill, 1994–2000.

Köstenberger, Andreas J. *John*. BECNT. Grand Rapids: Baker Academic, 2004.

———. "The Present and Future of Biblical Theology." *Them* 37, no. 3 (Nov 2012): 445–64.

Kraus, Hans-Joachim. *Psalms 1–59: A Commentary*. Translated by Hilton C. Oswald. Minneapolis: Augsburg, 1988.

———. *Theology of the Psalms*. Translated by Keith Crim. Minneapolis: Augsburg, 1986.

Krodel, Gerhard A. *Revelation*. ACNT. Minneapolis: Augsburg, 1989.

Kvanvig, Jonathan L. *The Problem of Hell*. New York: Oxford University Press, 1993.

Kwakkel, Gert. *According to My Righteousness: Upright Behavior as Grounds for Deliverance in Psalms 7, 17, 18, 26 and 44*. OtSt 46. Leiden: Brill, 2002.

Lacocque, André, and Paul Ricoeur. *Thinking Biblically: Exegetical and Hermeneutical Studies*. Translated by David Pellauer. Chicago: University of Chicago Press, 1998.

Ladd, George Eldon. *A Commentary on the Revelation of John*. Grand Rapids: Eerdmans, 1972.

———. *The Gospel of the Kingdom: Scriptural Studies in the Kingdom of God*. Grand Rapids: Eerdmans, 1959.

———. *The Presence of the Future: The Eschatology of Biblical Realism*. Grand Rapids: Eerdmans, 1974.

Lane, Tony. "The Wrath of God as an Aspect of the Love of God." In *Nothing Greater, Nothing Better: Theological Essays on the Love of God*, edited by Kevin J. Vanhoozer, 138–67. Grand Rapids: Eerdmans, 2001.

Laney, J. Carl. "A Fresh Look at the Imprecatory Psalms." *BSac* 138 (1981): 35–45.

Laniak, Timothy S. *Shame and Honor in the Book of Esther*. SBLDS 165. Atlanta: Scholars Press, 1998.

Larsson, Göran. *Bound for Freedom: The Book of Exodus in Jewish and Christian Traditions*. Peabody, Mass.: Hendrickson, 1999.

Laurence, Trevor. "Cursing with God: The Imprecatory Psalms and the Ethics of Christian Prayer." PhD diss., University of Exeter, 2020.

———. "Introduction: The Conditions of Interpretation and the Tools of the Trade." In Laurence and Paynter, *Violent Biblical Texts*.

———. "'Let Sinners Be Consumed': The Curious Conclusion of Psalm 104." In Laurence and Paynter, *Violent Biblical Texts*.

Laurence, Trevor, and Helen Paynter, eds. *Violent Biblical Texts: New Approaches*. Sheffield: Sheffield Phoenix Press, 2022.

Leithart, Peter J. *Deep Exegesis: The Mystery of Reading Scripture*. Waco, Tex.: Baylor University Press, 2009.

———. *Defending Constantine: The Twilight of an Empire and the Dawn of Christendom*. Downers Grove, Ill.: IVP Academic, 2010.

———. *Revelation 1–11*. ITC. New York: Bloomsbury T&T Clark, 2018.

———. *Revelation 12–22*. ITC. New York: Bloomsbury T&T Clark, 2018.

LeMon, Joel M. "Saying Amen to Violent Psalms: Patterns of Prayer, Belief, and Action in the Psalter." In Jacobson, *Soundings in the Theology of the Psalms*, 93–109.

Lenski, R. C. H. *The Interpretation of St. Luke's Gospel*. Minneapolis: Augsburg, 1946.

Lessing, Reed. "Broken Teeth, Bloody Baths, and Baby Bashing: Is There Any Place in the Church for Imprecatory Psalms?" *ConJ* 32, no. 4 (2006): 368–70.

Levenson, Jon D. *Sinai and Zion: An Entry into the Jewish Bible*. New York: HarperOne, 1985.

Lewis, C. S. *Reflections on the Psalms*. San Diego: Harcourt Brace Jovanovich, 1958.

Lewis, Jack P. "The Woman's Seed (Gen 3:15)." *JETS* 34, no. 3 (1991): 299–319.

Limburg, James. *Psalms*. Westminster Bible Companion. Edited by Patrick D. Miller and David L. Bartlett. Louisville: Westminster John Knox, 2000.

Lindars, Barnabas, ed. *The Gospel of John*. NCB. London: Oliphants, 1972.

———. *New Testament Apologetic: The Doctrinal Significance of the Old Testament Quotations*. Philadelphia: Westminster, 1961.

Lockyer, Herbert, Sr. *Psalms: A Devotional Commentary*. Grand Rapids: Kregel, 1993.

Longenecker, Richard N. *Galatians*. WBC 41. Dallas: Word Books, 1990.

Longman, Tremper, III. *How to Read Genesis*. Downers Grove, Ill.: IVP Academic, 2005.

———. *How to Read the Psalms*. Downers Grove, Ill.: InterVarsity Press, 1988.

Longman, Tremper, III, and Daniel G. Reid. *God Is a Warrior*. Studies in Old Testament Biblical Theology. Grand Rapids: Zondervan, 1995.

Luc, Alex. "Interpreting the Curses in the Psalms." *JETS* 42, no. 3 (1999): 395–410.

Lührmann, Dieter. *Galatians: A Continental Commentary*. Minneapolis: Fortress, 1992.

Lundbom, Jack R. *Deuteronomy: A Commentary*. Grand Rapids: Eerdmans, 2013.

Luther, Martin. "A Mighty Fortress Is Our God." Public Domain.

———. *What Luther Says: An Anthology*. Edited by Ewald M. Plass. St. Louis: Concordia, 1959.

Lysaught, M. Therese. "Eucharist as Basic Training: Liturgy, Ethics, and the Body." In *Theology and Lived Christianity*, edited by David M. Hammond, 257–86. Mystic, Conn.: Twenty-Third Publications, 2000.

———. "Love and Liturgy." In *Gathered for the Journey: Moral Theology in Catholic Perspective*, edited by David Matzko McCarthy and M. Therese Lysaught, 24–42. Grand Rapids: Eerdmans, 2007.

MacIntyre, Alasdair. *After Virtue: A Study in Moral Theory*. 3rd ed. Notre Dame: University of Notre Dame Press, 2007.

———. "Theology, Ethics, and the Ethics of Medicine and Health Care: Comments on Papers by Novak, Mouw, Roach, Cahill, and Hartt." *J. Med. Philos.* 4, no. 4 (1979): 435–43.

———. *Whose Justice? Which Rationality?* Notre Dame: University of Notre Dame Press, 1988.

Magonet, Jonathan. "Psalm 137: Unlikely Liturgy or Partisan Poem? A Response to Sue Gillingham." In Gillingham, *Jewish and Christian Approaches to the Psalms*, 83–88.

Marcus, Joel. *The Way of the Lord: Christological Exegesis of the Old Testament in the Gospel of Mark*. Louisville: Westminster John Knox, 1992.

Marshall, Christopher D. "Divine and Human Punishment in the New Testament." In In Date, Stump, and Anderson, *Rethinking Hell*, 207–27.

Marshall, I. Howard. *1 and 2 Thessalonians*. New Century Bible Commentary. Grand Rapids: Eerdmans, 1983.

———. *The Gospel of Luke*. NIGTC. Grand Rapids: Eerdmans, 1978.

Martin, Chalmers. "The Imprecations in the Psalms." *PTR* 1, no. 4 (1903): 537–53.

Martin, R. A. "The Earliest Messianic Interpretation of Genesis 3:15." *JBL* 84 (1965): 425–27.

Martyn, J. Louis. *Galatians*. AB 33A. New York: Doubleday, 1997.

Matera, Frank J. *Romans*. Paideia Commentaries on the New Testament. Grand Rapids: Baker Academic, 2010.

Mauro, Philip. *The Patmos Visions: A Study of the Apocalypse*. Boston: Hamilton Bros., 1925.

Mays, James Luther. *The Lord Reigns: A Theological Handbook to the Psalms*. Louisville: Westminster John Knox, 1994.

———. *Psalms*. Interpretation: A Bible Commentary for Teaching and Preaching. Louisville: John Knox Press, 1994.

———. "A Question of Identity: The Three-Fold Hermeneutic of Psalmody." Lecture delivered at Eden Theological Seminary, St. Louis, Mo., April 2, 1991.

McCann, J. Clinton, Jr. *Psalms*. In vol. 4 of *NIB*, 641–1280. Nashville: Abingdon, 1996.

———. *A Theological Introduction to the Book of Psalms: The Psalms as Torah*. Nashville: Abingdon, 1993.

McCartney, Dan G. *James*. BECNT. Grand Rapids: Baker Academic, 2009.

McConville, J. Gordon. "Law and Monarchy in the Old Testament." In Bartholomew et al., *Royal Priesthood?* 69–88.

McDowell, Catherine L. *The Image of God in the Garden of Eden: The Creation of Humankind in Genesis 2:5–3:24 in Light of the* mīs pî pīt pî *and* wpt-r *Rituals of Mesopotamia and Ancient Egypt*. Siphrut 15. Winona Lake, Ind.: Eisenbrauns, 2015.

McFadyen, Alistair, and Marcel Sarot, eds. *Forgiveness and Truth: Explorations in Contemporary Theology*. New York: T&T Clark, 2001.

McGraw, Ryan M. "'The Foundation of the Old Testament': John Owen on Genesis 3:15 as a Window into Reformed Orthodox Old Testament Exegesis." *JRT* 10 (2016): 3–28.

McKenzie, John L. "The Imprecations of the Psalter." *American Ecclesiastical Review* 111, no. 2 (1944): 81–96.

McKnight, Scot. *The Letter to the Colossians*. NICNT. Grand Rapids: Eerdmans, 2018.

———. *The Letter of James*. NICNT. Grand Rapids: Eerdmans, 2011.

McNicol, Allan J. *The Persistence of God's Endangered Promises: The Bible's Unified Story*. London: Bloomsbury T&T Clark, 2018.

Meilander, Gilbert. "Ethics and Exegesis: A Great Gulf?" In Bartholomew et al., *Royal Priesthood?* 259–64.

Menken, Maarten J. J. "Genesis in John's Gospel and 1 John." In *Genesis in the New Testament*, edited by Maarten J. J. Menken and Steve Moyise, 83–98. LNTS 466. New York: Bloomsbury T&T Clark, 2012.

Mennega, Harry. "The Ethical Problem of the Imprecatory Psalms." ThM thesis, Westminster Theological Seminary, 1959.

Michaels, J. Ramsey. *Revelation*. IVPNTC. Downers Grove, Ill.: InterVarsity Press, 1997.

Middleton, Paul. *The Violence of the Lamb: Martyrs as Agents of Divine Judgement in the Book of Revelation*. LNTS 586. New York: T&T Clark, 2018.

Miglio, Adam E. "Imagery and Analogy in Psalm 58:4–9." *VT* 65 (2015): 114–35.

Miller, Patrick D., Jr. *The Divine Warrior in Early Israel*. Harvard Semitic Monographs 5. Cambridge, Mass.: Harvard University Press, 1973.

———. "God the Warrior: A Problem in Biblical Interpretation and Apologetics." In *Israelite Religion and Biblical Theology: Collected Essays*, 356–64. JSOTSup 267. Sheffield: Sheffield Academic Press, 2000.

———. "The Hermeneutics of Imprecation." In *Theology in the Service of the Church: Essays in Honor of Thomas W. Gillespie*, edited by Wallace M. Alston, Jr., 153–63. Grand Rapids: Eerdmans, 2000.

———. *Interpreting the Psalms*. Philadelphia: Fortress, 1986.

———. *They Cried to the Lord: The Form and Theology of Biblical Prayer*. Minneapolis: Fortress, 1994.

Minear, Paul S. "Far as the Curse Is Found: The Point of Revelation 12:15–16." *NovT* 33, no. 1 (1991): 71–77.

Mitchell, David C. *The Message of the Psalter: An Eschatological Programme in the Book of Psalms*. Newton Mearns, Scotland: Campbell Publications, 2003.

Moberly, Elizabeth R. *Suffering, Innocent and Guilty*. London: SPCK, 1978.

Moberly, R. W. L. "The Use of Scripture in *The Desire of the Nations*." In Bartholomew et al., *Royal Priesthood?* 46–64.

Moberly, Walter. *The Ethics of Punishment*. Hamden, Conn.: Archon Books, 1968.

Moo, Douglas J. *The Epistle to the Romans*. NICNT. Grand Rapids: Eerdmans, 1996.

———. *Galatians*. BECNT. Grand Rapids: Baker Academic, 2013.

Morales, L. Michael. *Who Shall Ascend the Mountain of the Lord? A Biblical Theology of the Book of Leviticus*. NSBT 37. Downers Grove, Ill.: InterVarsity Press, 2015.

Morland, Kjell Arne. *The Rhetoric of Curse in Galatians: Paul Confronts Another Gospel*. Emory Studies in Early Christianity. Atlanta: Scholars Press, 1995.

Moule, C. F. D. "A Reconsideration of the Context of *Maranatha*." *NTS* 6, no. 4 (1960): 307–10.

Mounce, Robert H. *The Book of Revelation*. Rev. ed. NICOT. Grand Rapids: Eerdmans, 1997.

Mowinckel, Sigmund. *The Psalms in Israel's Worship*. Translated by D. R. Ap-Thomas. 2 vols. Oxford: Basil Blackwell, 1962.

Moyise, Steve. "Intertextuality and the Study of the Old Testament in the New Testament." In *The Old Testament in the New Testament: Essays in Honor of J. L. North*, edited by Steve Moyise, 14–41. JSNTSup 189. Sheffield: Sheffield Academic Press, 2000.

———. "The Psalms in the Book of Revelation." In Moyise and Menken, *Psalms in the New Testament*, 231–46.

———. "Quotations." In Porter and Stanley, *As It Is Written*, 15–28.

Moyise, Steve, and Maarten J. J. Menken. "Introduction." In Moyise and Menken, *Psalms in the New Testament*, 1–3.

———, eds. *The Psalms in the New Testament*. The New Testament and the Scriptures of Israel. London: T&T Clark International, 2004.

Murphy, Debra Dean. *Teaching That Transforms: Worship as the Heart of Christian Education*. Grand Rapids: Brazos, 2004.

Murphy, Roland E. *The Psalms, Job*. Proclamation Commentaries: The Old Testament Witnesses for Preaching. Philadelphia: Fortress, 1977.

Murray, David P. "Christian Cursing?" In *Sing a New Song: Recovering Psalm Singing for the Twenty-First Century*, edited by Joel R. Beeke and Anthony T. Selvaggio, 111–21. Grand Rapids: Reformation Heritage Books, 2010.

Mußner, Franz. *Der Galaterbrief*. HTKNT 9. Freiburg: Herder, 1974.

Neander, Joachim. "Praise to the Lord, the Almighty." Public Domain.

Nehrbass, Daniel Michael. "The Therapeutic and Preaching Value of the Imprecatory Psalms." PhD diss., Fuller Theological Seminary, 2012.

Nestle, Eberhard, Erwin Nestle, Barbara Aland, Kurt Aland, Johannes Karavidopoulos, Carlo M. Martini, and Bruce M. Metzger, eds. *Novum Testamentum Graece*. 27th ed. Stuttgart: Deutsche Bibelgesellschaft, 1993.

Neu, Jerome. "On Loving Our Enemies." In *The Ethics of Forgiveness: A Collection of Essays*, edited by Christel Fricke, 130–42. New York: Routledge, 2011.

Newton, John, and Laura Taylor. "Let Us Love and Sing and Wonder." Laura Taylor Music, 2001.

Nolland, John. *Luke 9:21–18:34*. WBC 35B. Dallas: Word Books, 1993.

Nordhoff, Krissy, and Michael Neale. "Your Great Name." Integrity's Praise! Music, TwoNords Music, 2008.

Nussbaum, Martha C. *Upheavals of Thought: The Intelligence of Emotions*. New York: Cambridge University Press, 2001.

O'Brien, Kelli S. *The Use of Scripture in the Markan Passion Narrative*. LNTS 384. New York: T&T Clark, 2010.

O'Brien, Peter T. *Colossians, Philemon*. WBC 44. Waco, Tex.: Word Books, 1982.

O'Donovan, Oliver M. T. "Deliberation, History and Reading: A Response to Schweiker and Wolterstorff." *SJT* 54, no. 1 (2001): 127–44.

———. *The Desire of the Nations: Rediscovering the Roots of Political Theology*. New York: Cambridge University, 1996.

———. "The Possibility of a Biblical Ethic." *TSF Bulletin* 67 (1973): 15–23.

———. *Resurrection and Moral Order: An Outline for Evangelical Ethics*. 2nd ed. Grand Rapids: Eerdmans, 1994.

———. *Self, World, and Time*. Vol. 1 of *Ethics as Theology*. Grand Rapids: Eerdmans, 2013.

Ojewole, Afolarin Olutunde. "The Seed in Genesis 3:15: An Exegetical and Intertextual Study." PhD diss., Andrews University Seventh-Day Adventist Theological Seminary, 2002.

Orr, William F., and James Arthur Walther. *I Corinthians: A New Translation*. AB 32. Garden City, N.Y.: Doubleday and Company, 1976.

Osborne, Grant R. *Revelation*. BECNT. Grand Rapids: Baker Academic, 2002.

Outka, Gene. *Agape: An Ethical Analysis*. Yale Publications in Religion 17. New Haven: Yale University Press, 1972.

Packer, J. I. Foreword to *Biblical Theology: The History of Theology from Adam to Christ*, by John Owen. Morgan, Pa.: Soli Deo Gloria Publications, 1994.

———. "Introductory Essay." In *The Doctrine of Justification*, by James Buchanan. London: Banner of Truth, 1961.

Parrett, Gary A. "Come, Lord Jesus, to Redeem Us." 2002.

Pattemore, Stephen. *The People of God in the Apocalypse: Discourse, Structure, and Exegesis*. SNTSMS 128. Cambridge: Cambridge University Press, 2004.

Peels, Eric. "'I Hate Them with Perfect Hatred' (Psalm 139:21–22)." *TynBul* 59, no. 1 (2008): 35–51.

———. *Shadow Sides: The Revelation of God in the Old Testament*. Carlisle, UK: Paternoster, 2003.

Peels, H. G. L. *The Vengeance of God: The Meaning of the Root NQM and the Function of the NQM-texts in the Context of Divine Revelation in the Old Testament*. OtSt 31. Leiden: Brill, 1995.

Penny, Donald. "Persistence in Prayer: Luke 18:1–8." *RevExp* 104 (2007): 737–44.

Peoples, Glenn A. "Introduction to Evangelical Conditionalism." In Date, Stump, and Anderson, *Rethinking Hell*, 10–24.

Perrin, Nicholas. *Jesus the Priest*. Grand Rapids: Baker Academic, 2018.

———. *Jesus the Temple*. Grand Rapids: Baker Academic, 2010.

Petrany, Catherine. *Pedagogy, Prayer and Praise: The Wisdom of the Psalms and Psalter*. FAT 2. Reihe 83. Mohr Siebeck: Tübingen, 2015.

Phillips, Elaine A. "Serpent Intertexts: Tantalizing Twists in the Tales." *BBR* 10, no. 2 (2000): 233–45.

Piper, John. "Do I Not Hate Those Who Hate You, O Lord?" October 3, 2000. Accessed March 20, 2017. http://www.desiringgod.org/articles/do-i-not-hate-those-who-hate-you-o-lord.

———. *'Love Your Enemies': Jesus' Love Command in the Synoptic Gospels and in the Early Christian Paraenesis*. SNTSMS 38. Cambridge: Cambridge University Press, 1979.

———. *The Pleasures of God: Meditations on God's Delight in Being God*. Portland, Ore.: Multnomah Press, 1991.

Plummer, Alfred. *A Critical and Exegetical Commentary on the Second Epistle of St Paul to the Corinthians*. ICC. Edinburgh: T&T Clark, 1915.

Pokrifka-Joe, Todd. "Probing the Relationship between Divine and Human Forgiveness in Matthew: Hearing a Neglected Voice in the Canon." In McFadyen and Sarot, *Forgiveness and Truth*, 165–72.

Porter, Stanley E. "Allusions and Echoes." In Porter and Stanley, *As It Is Written*, 29–40.

Porter, Stanley E., and Christopher D. Stanley, eds. *As It Is Written: Studying Paul's Use of Scripture*. SBLSymS 50. Atlanta: SBL Press, 2008.

Post, Marie J., and Timothy Hoekman. "Hear, O Lord, My Urgent Prayer." In *Psalms for All Seasons*, 26.

Poythress, Vern S. *Theophany: A Biblical Theology of God's Appearing*. Wheaton, Ill.: Crossway, 2018.

Pribbenow, Brad. "Prayerbook of Christ, Prayerbook of the Church: Dietrich Bonhoeffer's Christological Interpretation of the Psalms." PhD diss., Concordia Seminary, 2017.

Psalms for All Seasons: A Complete Psalter for Worship. Grand Rapids: Calvin Institute of Christian Worship, Faith Alive Christian Resources, Brazos, 2012.

The Psalter with Responsive Readings. Pittsburgh: United Presbyterian Board of Publication, 1912. Public Domain.

Rambo, Shelly. *Spirit and Trauma: A Theology of Remaining.* Louisville: Westminster John Knox, 2010.

Ramsey, Paul. "Liturgy and Ethics." *JRE* 7, no. 2 (1979): 139–71.

Rappaport, Roy A. *Ecology, Meaning, and Religion.* Berkeley: North Atlantic Books, 1979.

Reimer, A. James. "Jesus Christ, the Man for Others: The Suffering God in the Thought of Paul Tillich and Dietrich Bonhoeffer." *LTP* 62, no. 3 (2006): 499–509.

Ricoeur, Paul. "Lamentation as Prayer." In André LaCocque and Paul Ricoeur, *Thinking Biblically*, 211–32.

———. "Love and Justice." *Philos Soc Critic* 21, no. 5/6 (1995): 23–39.

———. "Naming God." *Union Seminary Quarterly Review* 34, no. 4 (1979): 215–27.

———. *The Symbolism of Evil.* Translated by Emerson Buchanan. New York: Beacon Press, 1967.

———. *Time and Narrative.* Vol. 1. Translated by Kathleen McLaughlin and David Pellauer. Chicago: University of Chicago Press, 1984.

———. "Toward a Hermeneutic of the Idea of Revelation." *Harvard Theological Review* 70, no. 1/2 (1977): 1–37.

Ridderbos, Herman N. *The Coming of the Kingdom.* Edited by Raymond O. Zorn. Translated by H. de Jongste. Philadelphia: Presbyterian and Reformed, 1962.

———. *The Epistle of Paul to the Churches of Galatia.* NICNT. Grand Rapids: Eerdmans, 1953.

Ringgren, Helmer. *The Faith of the Psalmists.* Philadelphia: Fortress, 1963.

Roemer, L., B. T. Litz, S. M. Orsillo, and A. W. Wagner. "A Preliminary Investigation of the Role of Strategic Withholding of Emotions in PTSD." *J. Trauma. Stress* 14, no. 1 (2001): 149–56.

Rogerson, J. W., and J. W. McKay. *Psalms 101–150.* The Cambridge Bible Commentary. Cambridge: Cambridge University Press, 1977.

Roloff, Jürgen. *The Revelation of John: A Continental Commentary.* Translated by John E. Alsup. Minneapolis: Fortress, 1993.

Rolston, Holmes, III. "Loving Nature: Christian Environmental Ethics." In *Love and Christian Ethics: Tradition, Theory, and Society*, edited by Frederick V. Simmons with Brian C. Sorrells, 313–31. Washington, D.C.: Georgetown University Press, 2016.

Rooke, Deborah W. "Kingship as Priesthood: The Relationship between the High Priesthood and the Monarchy." In *King and Messiah in Israel and the Ancient Near East: Proceedings of the Oxford Old Testament Seminar*, edited by John Day, 187–208. JSOTSup 270. Sheffield: Sheffield Academic Press, 1998.

Rosner, Brian S. *Paul, Scripture and Ethics: A Study of 1 Corinthians 5–7.* AGJU 22. Leiden: Brill, 1994.

Ross, Allen P. *A Commentary on the Psalms: Volume 1 (1–41).* KEL. Grand Rapids: Kregel Publications, 2011.

———. *A Commentary on the Psalms: Volume 2 (42–89).* KEL. Grand Rapids: Kregel Academic, 2013.

———. *A Commentary on the Psalms: Volume 3 (90–150)*. KEL. Grand Rapids: Kregel Academic, 2016.

Routledge, Robin. "Ḥesed as Obligation: A Re-Examination." *TynBul* 46, no. 1 (1995): 179–96.

Rowe, Robert D. *God's Kingdom and God's Son: The Background to Mark's Christology from Concepts of Kingship in the Psalms*. AGJU 50. Leiden: Brill, 2002.

Rowland, Christopher C. "The Book of Revelation: Introduction, Commentary, and Reflections." In vol. 12 of *NIB*, 503–743. Nashville: Abingdon, 1998.

Russell, Brian D. *The Song of the Sea: The Date of Composition and Influence of Exodus 15:1–21*. Studies in Biblical Literature 101. New York: Peter Lang, 2007.

Sailhamer, John H. "Creation, Genesis 1–11, and the Canon." *BBR* 10, no. 1 (2000): 89–106.

———. *The Meaning of the Pentateuch: Revelation, Composition and Interpretation*. Downers Grove, Ill.: InterVarsity Press, 2009.

———. *The Pentateuch as Narrative: A Biblical-Theological Commentary*. Library of Biblical Interpretation. Grand Rapids: Zondervan, 1992.

Sakenfeld, Katharine Doob. *Faithfulness in Action: Loyalty in Biblical Perspective*. Overtures to Biblical Theology. Philadelphia: Fortress, 1985.

———. *The Meaning of Hesed in the Hebrew Bible: A New Inquiry*. Eugene, Ore.: Wipf and Stock, 1978.

Saliers, D. E. "Liturgy and Ethics: Some New Beginnings." *JRE* 7, no. 2 (1979): 173–89.

Sanders, E. P. *Jesus and Judaism*. Philadelphia: Fortress, 1985.

———. *Paul and Palestinian Judaism: A Comparison of Patterns of Religion*. Philadelphia: Fortress, 1977.

Schaefer, Konrad. *Psalms*. Berit Olam: Studies in Hebrew Narrative and Poetry. Edited by David W. Cotter. Collegeville, Minn.: Liturgical Press, 2001.

Schnackenburg, Rudolf. *Ephesians: A Commentary*. Translated by Helen Heron. Edinburgh: T&T Clark, 1991.

Schreiner, Thomas R. *1, 2 Peter, Jude*. NAC 37. Nashville: Broadman and Holman, 2003.

———. "Editorial: Foundations for Faith." *SBJT* 5, no. 3 (2001): 2–3.

———. *Galatians*. ZECNT. Grand Rapids: Zondervan, 2010.

———. *The King in His Beauty: A Biblical Theology of the Old and New Testaments*. Grand Rapids: Baker Academic, 2013.

———. *Romans*. BECNT. Grand Rapids: Baker Academic, 1998.

Scott, J. M. "The Triumph of God in 2 Cor 2.14: Additional Evidence of Merkabah Mysticism in Paul." *NTS* 42 (1996): 260–81.

Scott, Matthew. *The Hermeneutics of Christological Psalmody in Paul: An Intertextual Enquiry*. SNTSMS 158. New York: Cambridge University Press, 2014.

Scroggie, W. Graham. *A Guide to the Psalms: A Comprehensive Analysis of the Psalms*. 1978; Reprint, Grand Rapids: Kregel, 1995.

Searle, John R. *Speech Acts: An Essay in the Philosophy of Language*. New York: Cambridge University Press, 1969.

Shay, Jonathan. "Moral Injury." *Psychoanalytic Psychology* 31, no. 2 (2014): 182–91.

Shepherd, John. "The Place of the Imprecatory Psalms in the Canon of Scripture." *Chu* 111, no. 1 (1997): 27–47.

———. "The Place of the Imprecatory Psalms in the Canon of Scripture." *Chu* 111, no. 2 (1997): 110–26.

Silber, Ursula. "'Whatever Is in Parenthesis We Do Not Include in Our Prayers'!? The Problematic Nature of the 'Enemy Psalms' in Christian Reception." *Eur. Judaism* 46, no. 2 (2013): 116–32.

Simango, Daniel. "An Exegetical Study of Imprecatory Psalms in the Old Testament." PhD diss., North-West University, 2011.

Sire, James. *Learning to Pray through the Psalms*. Downers Grove Ill.: InterVarsity Press, 2005.

———. *Praying the Psalms of Jesus*. Downers Grove, Ill.: InterVarsity Press, 2007.

Skinner, John. *Genesis*. ICC. New York: Charles Scribner's Sons, 1910.

Smith, Abraham. "The First Letter to the Thessalonians." In vol. 11 of *NIB*, 671–737. Nashville: Abingdon, 2000.

Smith, James K. A. *Desiring the Kingdom: Worship, Worldview, and Cultural Formation*. Vol. 1 of Cultural Liturgies. Grand Rapids: Baker Academic, 2009.

———. *Imagining the Kingdom: How Worship Works*. Vol. 2 of Cultural Liturgies. Grand Rapids: Baker Academic, 2013.

Smith, Robert S. "Songs of the Seer: The Purpose of Revelation's Hymns." *Them* 43, no. 2 (2018): 193–204.

Spaemann, Robert. *Persons: The Difference Between 'Someone' and 'Something.'* Translated by Oliver O'Donovan. Oxford Studies in Theological Ethics. Oxford: Oxford University Press, 2006.

Spohn, William C. "Christian Spirituality and Theological Ethics." In *The Blackwell Companion to Christian Spirituality*, edited by Arthur Holder, 269–85. Malden, Mass.: Wiley-Blackwell, 2011.

Spurgeon, Charles Haddon. *Psalms*. Grand Rapids: Kregel, 1976.

Stanley, Christopher D. *Arguing with Scripture: The Rhetoric of Quotations in the Letters of Paul*. New York: T&T Clark International, 2004.

Steussy, Marti J. "The Enemy in the Psalms." *WW* 28, no. 1 (2008): 5–12.

Strawn, Brent A. "Trauma, Psalmic Disclosure, and Authentic Happiness." In Boase and Frechette, *Bible through the Lens of Trauma*, 143–60.

Streett, Matthew. *Here Comes the Judge: Violent Pacifism in the Book of Revelation*. LNTS 462. New York: T&T Clark, 2012.

Stuhlmueller, Carroll. *Psalms 1 (Psalms 1–72)*. Old Testament Message 21. Wilmington, Del.: Michael Glazier, 1983.

Stumme, John R. "Inhabiting the Christian Narrative: An Example of the Relationship between Religion and the Moral Life." *Journal of Lutheran Ethics* 3, no. 1 (2003). https://www.elca.org/JLE/Articles/896.

Stump, Eleonore. "Dante's Hell, Aquinas's Moral Theory, and the Love of God." *CJP* 16, no. 2 (1986): 181–98.

Sumney, Jerry L. *Colossians: A Commentary*. NTL. Louisville: Westminster John Knox, 2008.

Sweet, J. P. M. *Revelation*. Westminster Pelican Commentaries. Philadelphia: Westminster, 1979.

Tanner, Beth LaNeel. *The Book of Psalms through the Lens of Intertextuality*. Studies in Biblical Literature 26. New York: Peter Lang, 2001.

Tate, Marvin E. *Psalms 51–100*. WBC 20. Waco, Tex.: Word Books, 1990.

Taylor, Charles. *A Secular Age*. Cambridge, Mass.: Harvard University Press, 2007.

Teigen, Ragnar C. "Can Anything Good Come from a Curse?" *Lutheran Quarterly* 26, no. 1 (1974): 44–51.

Terrien, Samuel. *The Psalms: Strophic Structure and Theological Commentary.* ECC. Grand Rapids: Eerdmans, 2003.

"Theology Takes Practice: *Fare Forward* Interviews James K. A. Smith." *Fare Forward.* December 4, 2013. Accessed May 17, 2022. http://farefwd.com/index .php/2020/12/16/theology-take-practice/.

Theron, P. F. "The 'God of War' and His 'Prince of Peace.'" *NGTT* 45, nos. 1–2 (2004): 118–26.

Thielman, Frank. *Ephesians.* BECNT. Grand Rapids: Baker Academic, 2010.

Thiselton, Anthony C. *The First Epistle to the Corinthians: A Commentary on the Greek Text.* NIGTC. Grand Rapids: Eerdmans, 2000.

———. *New Horizons in Hermeneutics: The Theory and Practice of Transforming Biblical Reading.* Grand Rapids: Zondervan, 1992.

Thomas, Heath Aaron. "Relating Prayer and Pain: Psychological Analysis and Lamentations Research." *TynBul* 61, no. 2 (2010): 183–208.

Thomas, Robert. *Revelation 1–7: An Exegetical Commentary.* Wycliffe Exegetical Commentary. Chicago: Moody, 1992.

Thompson, J. A. *Deuteronomy: An Introduction and Commentary.* Leicester: InterVarsity Press, 1974.

Thompson, John L. "Psalms and Curses: Anger Management, on Earth as It Is in Heaven." In *Reading the Bible with the Dead: What You Can Learn from the History of Exegesis That You Can't Learn from Exegesis Alone*, 49–70. Grand Rapids: Eerdmans, 2007.

Thompson, Leonard L. *Revelation.* ANTC. Nashville: Abingdon, 1998.

Thompson, Marianne Meye. *John: A Commentary.* NTL. Louisville: Westminster John Knox, 2015.

Tomlin, Chris, Jason Ingram, and Jess Cates. "Even So Come." S. D. G. Publishing, sixsteps Songs, Worship Together Music, Open Hands Music, So Essential Tunes, Chrissamsongs Inc., Go Mia Music, Vistaville Music, 2015.

Torretta, Gabriel. "Rediscovering the Imprecatory Psalms: A Thomistic Approach." *The Thomist: A Speculative Quarterly Review* 80, no. 1 (2016): 23–48.

Townend, Stuart, and Keith Getty. "O Church Arise." Thankyou Music, 2004.

Trinity Psalter. Pittsburgh: Crown and Covenant, 1994.

Tucker, W. Dennis, Jr. "Empires and Enemies in Book V of the Psalter." In *The Composition of the Book of Psalms*, edited by Erich Zenger, 723–31. BETL 238. Leuven, Belgium: Uitgeverij Peeters, 2010.

———. "The Role of the Foe in Book 5: Reflections on the Final Composition of the Psalter." In *The Shape and Shaping of the Book of Psalms: The Current State of Scholarship*, edited by Nancy L. deClaissé-Walford, 179–92. Ancient Israel and Its Literature 20. Atlanta: SBL Press, 2014.

Tucker, W. Dennis, Jr., and Jamie A. Grant. *Psalms, Volume 2.* NIVAC. Grand Rapids: Zondervan Academic, 2018.

Turner, David L. *Matthew.* BECNT. Grand Rapids: Baker Academic, 2008.

Urhan, Chrétien. "How Blest Is He Whose Trespass." In *Psalter with Responsive Readings*, 73. Public Domain.

Urhan, Chrétien, and Edward F. Rimbault. "How Blest Are They Whose Trespass." In *Psalms for All Seasons*, 207.

van der Kolk, Bessel A. *The Body Keeps the Score: Brain, Mind, and Body in the Healing of Trauma*. New York: Penguin Books, 2015.

van der Kolk, Bessel A., and Alexander C. McFarlane. "The Black Hole of Trauma." In van der Kolk, McFarlane, and Weisaeth, *Traumatic Stress*, 3–23.

van der Kolk, Bessel A., Alexander C. McFarlane, and Lars Weisaeth, eds. *Traumatic Stress: The Effects of Overwhelming Experience on Mind, Body, and Society*. New York: Guilford Press, 1996.

van der Kolk, Bessel A., and Onno van der Hart. "The Intrusive Past: The Flexibility of Memory and the Engraving of Trauma." In *Trauma: Explorations in Memory*, ed. Cathy Caruth, 158–82. Baltimore: Johns Hopkins University Press, 1995.

VanDrunen, David. *Living in God's Two Kingdoms: A Biblical Vision for Christianity and Culture*. Wheaton: Crossway, 2010.

———. *Natural Law and the Two Kingdoms: A Study in the Development of Reformed Social Thought*. EUSLR. Grand Rapids: Eerdmans, 2010.

Vanhoozer, Kevin J., ed. *Dictionary for Theological Interpretation of the Bible*. Grand Rapids: Baker Academic, 2005.

———. "From Speech Acts to Scripture Acts: The Covenant of Discourse and the Discourse of Covenant." In Bartholomew, Greene, and Möller, *After Pentecost*, 1–49.

———. *Is There a Meaning in This Text? The Bible, the Reader, and the Morality of Literary Knowledge*. Grand Rapids: Zondervan, 1998.

Vermeulen, Karolein. "Eeny Meeny Miny Moe Who Is the Craftiest to Go?" *JHS* 10 (2010): 2–13.

Versluis, Arie. *The Command to Exterminate the Canaanites: Deuteronomy 7*. OtSt 71. Leiden: Brill, 2017.

Volf, Miroslav. *Exclusion and Embrace: A Theological Exploration of Identity, Otherness, and Reconciliation*. Nashville: Abingdon, 1996.

———. *Work in the Spirit: Toward a Theology of Work*. New York: Oxford University Press, 1991.

von Rad, Gerhard. *Deuteronomy: A Commentary*. OTL. Philadelphia: Westminster, 1966.

———. *Old Testament Theology*. 2 vols. OTL. Louisville: Westminster John Knox, 1962.

de Vos, Christiane, and Gert Kwakkel. "Psalm 69: The Petitioner's Understanding of Himself, His God, and His Enemies." In Becking and Peels, *Psalms and Prayers*, 159–79.

Vos, Geerhardus. *Biblical Theology of the Old and New Testaments*. Grand Rapids: Eerdmans, 1948.

Vos, Johannes G. "The Ethical Problem of the Imprecatory Psalms." *WTJ* 4 (1942): 123–38.

Wallace, Howard N. "King and Community: Joining with David in Prayer." In Becking and Peels, *Psalms and Prayers*, 267–77.

Wallace, Ronald S. *Calvin's Doctrine of the Christian Life*. Edinburgh: Oliver and Boyd, 1959.

Waltke, Bruce K. "A Canonical Process Approach to the Psalms." In *Tradition and Testament: Essays in Honor of Charles Lee Feinberg*, edited by John S. Feinberg and Paul D. Feinberg, 3–18. Chicago: Moody, 1981.

Walton, John H. *Genesis*. NIVAC. Grand Rapids: Zondervan, 2001.

Walton, John H., and J. Harvey Walton. *The Lost World of the Israelite Conquest: Covenant, Retribution, and the Fate of the Canaanites*. Downers Grove, Ill.: IVP Academic, 2017.

Wanamaker, Charles A. *The Epistles to the Thessalonians*. NIGTC. Grand Rapids: Eerdmans, 1990.

Ward, Martin J. "Psalm 109: David's Poem of Vengeance." *Andrews University Seminary Studies* 18, no. 2 (1980): 163–68.

Warfield, Benjamin B. "The Importunate Widow and the Alleged Failure of Faith." *ExpTim* 25, no. 3 (1913): 69–72.

Watson, Francis. *Text and Truth: Redefining Biblical Theology*. Grand Rapids: Eerdmans, 1997.

Watts, Rikk. "The Psalms in Mark's Gospel." In Moyise and Menken, *Psalms in the New Testament*, 25–45.

Weaver, Dorothy Jean. "Luke 18:1–8." *Int* 56, no. 3 (2002): 317–19.

Webster, John. *Holy Scripture: A Dogmatic Sketch*. Current Issues in Theology. Cambridge: Cambridge University Press, 2003.

Weidmann, Frederick W. *Galatians*. Westminster Bible Companion. Louisville: Westminster John Knox, 2012.

———. *Philippians, 1 and 2 Thessalonians, and Philemon*. Westminster Bible Companion. Louisville: Westminster John Knox, 2013.

Weikart, Richard. "Scripture and Myth in Dietrich Bonhoeffer." *FH* 25, no. 1 (1993): 12–25.

Weima, Jeffrey A. D. *1–2 Thessalonians*. BECNT. Grand Rapids: Baker Academic, 2014.

Weinfeld, Moshe. "Sabbath, Temple, and the Enthronement of the Lord—The Problem of the Sitz im Leben of Genesis 1:1–2:3." In *Melanges biblique et orientaux en l'honneur de M. Henri Cazelles*, edited by André Caquot and Mathias Delcor, 501–12. AOAT 212. Kevelaer: Butzon and Bercker, 1981.

Weiser, Artur. *The Psalms: A Commentary*. Translated by Herbert Hartwell. OTL. Philadelphia: Westminster, 1962.

Wenham, Gordon J. *Genesis 1–15*. WBC 1. Nashville: Thomas Nelson, 1987.

———. "Prayer and Practice in the Psalms." In Becking and Peels, *Psalms and Prayers*, 279–95.

———. *Psalms as Torah: Reading Biblical Songs Ethically*. Studies in Theological Interpretation. Grand Rapids: Baker Academic, 2012.

———. *The Psalter Reclaimed: Praying and Praising with the Psalms*. Wheaton, Ill.: Crossway, 2013.

———. "Sanctuary Symbolism in the Garden of Eden Story." In *I Studied Inscriptions from before the Flood*, edited by R. S. Hess and D. T. Tsumara, 399–404. Winona Lake, Ind.: Eisenbrauns, 1994.

Wenham, J. W. *The Goodness of God*. London: InterVarsity Press, 1974.

Wenkel, David H. "Imprecatory Speech-Acts in the Book of Acts." *Asbury Journal* 63, no. 2 (2008): 81–93.

———. "Kingship and Thrones for All Christians: Paul's Inaugurated Eschatology in 1 Corinthians 4–6." *ExpTim* 128, no. 2 (2016): 63–71.

Wessel, Walter W., and Mark L. Strauss. "Mark." In vol. 9 of *EBC*, 601–793. Grand Rapids: Zondervan, 2010.

Westermann, Claus. *Praise and Lament in the Psalms.* Translated by Keith R. Crim and Richard N. Soulen. Atlanta: John Knox, 1981.

———. *The Psalms: Structure, Content, and Message.* Translated by Ralph D. Gehrke. Minneapolis: Augsburg, 1980.

———. *A Thousand Years and a Day.* Philadelphia: Fortress, 1962.

Wifall, Walter. "Gen 3:15—A Protevangelium?" *CBQ* 36, no. 3 (1974): 361–65.

Wilder, William N. "The Use (or Abuse) of Power in High Places: Gifts Given and Received in Isaiah, Psalm 68, and Ephesians 4:8." *BBR* 20, no. 2 (2010): 185–200.

Wiles, Gordon P. *Paul's Intercessory Prayers: The Significance of the Intercessory Prayer Passages in the Letters of St. Paul.* New York: Cambridge University Press, 1974.

Williams, William, and Jeremy Casella. "Guide Me O Thou Great Jehovah." 2037 Music (ASCAP), 2002.

Wilson, Gerald Henry. *The Editing of the Hebrew Psalter.* SBLDS 76. Chico, Calif.: Scholars Press, 1985.

———. "King, Messiah, and the Reign of God: Revisiting the Royal Psalms and the Shape of the Psalter." In *The Book of Psalms: Composition and Reception,* edited by Peter W. Flint and Patrick D. Miller, 391–406. Supplements to Vetus Testamentum 99. Boston: Brill, 2005.

Wirzba, Norman. *From Nature to Creation: A Christian Vision for Understanding and Loving Our World.* The Church and Postmodern Culture. Grand Rapids: Baker Academic, 2015.

Witvliet, John D. *The Biblical Psalms in Christian Worship: A Brief Introduction and Guide to Resources.* Calvin Institute of Christian Worship Liturgical Studies Series. Grand Rapids: Eerdmans, 2007.

———. "The Biblical Psalms in Christian Worship." Kavanagh Lecture delivered at Yale Institute of Sacred Music, New Haven, Conn., October 25, 2012. Accessed April 16, 2019. https://divinity.yale.edu/news-and-media/videos/biblical-psalms-christian-worship.

Wolterstorff, Nicholas. *Divine Discourse: Philosophical Reflections on the Claim That God Speaks.* New York: Cambridge University Press, 1995.

———. *Justice in Love.* EUSLR. Grand Rapids: Eerdmans, 2011.

———. "The Promise of Speech-act Theory for Biblical Interpretation." In Bartholomew, Greene, and Möller, *After Pentecost,* 73–90.

The Worship Sourcebook. Grand Rapids: Calvin Institute of Christian Worship, Faith Alive Christian Resources, Baker Books, 2004.

Woznicki, Christopher. "What Are We Doing When We Pray? Rekindling a Reformation Theology of Petitionary Prayer." *CTJ* 53, no. 2 (2018): 319–43.

Wright, Christopher J. H. *Living as the People of God: The Relevance of Old Testament Ethics.* Leicester: InterVarsity Press, 1983.

———. *Old Testament Ethics for the People of God.* Downers Grove, Ill.: InterVarsity Press, 2004.

Wright, Nigel G. "A Kinder, Gentler Damnation?" In Date, Stump, and Anderson, *Rethinking Hell*, 228–33.

Wright, N. T. *Jesus and the Victory of God*. Vol. 2 of *Christian Origins and the Question of God*. Minneapolis: Fortress, 1996.

———. *The New Testament and the People of God*. Vol. 1 of *Christian Origins and the Question of God*. Minneapolis: Fortress, 1992.

———. *The Resurrection of the Son of God*. Vol. 3 of *Christian Origins and the Question of God*. Minneapolis: Fortress, 2003.

———. "Romans." In vol. 10 of *NIB*, 393–770. Nashville: Abingdon, 2002.

Yarbrough, Robert W. *1–3 John*. BECNT. Grand Rapids: Baker Academic, 2008.

Youngblood, Kevin J. "Don't Get Even, Get Mad! Imprecatory Prayer as a Neglected Spiritual Discipline: (Psalm 69)." *Leaven* 19, no. 3 (2011): 153–57.

Zenger, Erich. "The Composition and Theology of the Fifth Book of Psalms, Psalms 107–145." *JSOT* 80 (1998): 77–102.

———. *A God of Vengeance? Understanding the Psalms of Divine Wrath*. Translated by Linda M. Maloney. Louisville: Westminster John Knox, 1996.

Zuck, Roy Ben. "The Problem of the Imprecatory Psalms." ThM thesis, Dallas Theological Seminary, 1957.

Index of Modern Authors

Index of Scripture

9 781481 316477